JULIAN M. STURTEVANT
1805-1886

JULIAN MONSON STURTEVANT
Instructor and Professor, 1829-1885
President, 1844-1876
Illinois College

JULIAN M. STURTEVANT
1805-1886

PRESIDENT OF ILLINOIS COLLEGE, ARDENT CHURCHMAN, REFLECTIVE AUTHOR

IVER F. YEAGER
Scarborough Professor Emeritus of Religion
and Philosophy, Illinois College

Foreword by
President Richard A. Pfau, Illinois College

THE TRUSTEES OF ILLINOIS COLLEGE
Jacksonville, Illinois 62650
1999

Sources of Illustrations and Maps

Julian Sturtevant (Frontispiece): *Autobiography.* Tallmadge Church, Ohio: Ohio Historical Society Photo, by W. T. Schultz. Yale's Old Brick Row: Hitchcock Chair Co.; painting by Mel Morgan. Map of College Lands (1829): Rammelkamp, *Centennial History,* 42. First College Building: (1829-30): *Alumni Quarterly,* Winter 1992, 10; painting by Donald Shirley. Four-Story Dormitory: from 1835 map of Illinois. Congregational Church (1835): from early map of Jacksonville. "The Old Homestead" (1852): *Autobiography,* facing 328. *Congregational Church* (1859): Congregational Church Archives. Handbill Announcing Sermon by Sturtevant: Photo in College Archives; also used by Rammelkamp, *Centennial History,* 212. Map of Campus Area, 1872: adapted from *Atlas Map of Morgan County, Illinois,* p. 80. Bust of Sturtevant: *Journal,* ISHS, Nov. 1977, 272; sculptor, R. C. Smith; courtesy Illinois State Museum. Memorial Tablet: photo by James T. Murphy. Photographs of the Sturtevant family and photo of Sturtevant Hall on jacket (and paperback): Illinois College Archives. Other sources identified in text.

Library of Congress Catalog Card Number 99-70909
ISBN: 0-9670361-0-0 (Hardcover)
ISBN: 0-9670361-1-9 (Paperback)

Order from Illinois College Bookstore,
Illinois College, 1101 W. College Ave., Jacksonville, IL 62650

This book is printed on French Opaque Vellum 70 lb. paper, which meets the minimum requirements of American National Standard for Information Sciences-Permanence of Paper for Printed Library Materials. The body of the book is set in Garamond 12pt.

Printed by Production Press, Inc.
Jacksonville, Illinois 62650

This book is dedicated to those
Presidents of Illinois College
whom I have come to know well during four decades:

Two Presidents, by their legacy to Illinois College and
their writings—

Julian M. Sturtevant, Second President, 1844-1876;
Charles Henry Rammelkamp, Sixth President, 1905-1932;

and
Three Presidents, whom I have known personally
while I served Illinois College in various capacities—

L. Vernon Caine, Tenth President, 1956-1973;
Donald C. Mundinger, Eleventh President, 1973-1993;
Richard A. Pfau, Twelfth President, 1993-.

With grateful appreciation for their intelligent, devoted service
to a Christian, independent, church-related, liberal arts college,

ILLINOIS COLLEGE.

Contents

Illustrations and Maps

Foreword

At first, were Julian M. Sturtevant to walk the campus of Illinois College in 1999, he would recognize very little of the campus he served more than a hundred years earlier.

Sturtevant would notice the changed physical landscape immediately. He would see new classroom buildings and residence halls, a splendid library and a well-outfitted fine arts center, a gymnasium and separate playing fields for soccer, football, baseball, and softball, and a modern track. The stately president's house in the southwest corner of the campus, and the handsome chapel in the northeast would catch his eye.

As he looked further, Sturtevant would find women students outnumbering men; there were no women in his day. Neither Greek nor Latin are studied regularly any more, and new subjects —microbiology, physical education, international relations, accounting—have entered the curriculum. Administrative personnel in offices unknown in his day—deans of students, residence life, food service, career planning, counseling, student activities—look after non-academic life.

Technology also has advanced, Sturtevant would discover. Telephones link the campus and the world. Microcomputers in open rooms, in faculty offices, in students' rooms, all linked to the electronic magic of the world wide web, open communications channels that operate at the speed of light. Science laboratories include equipment undeveloped in Sturtevant's time that offers students access to the latest advances in knowledge.

Yet, did Sturtevant look beyond these differences, he would see much about Illinois College that he would recognize as permanent. Liberal arts is the heart of the curriculum, the best preparation for life and work. Graduates of the College can think clearly, learn, communicate clearly, and make intelligent choices based on their personal values. Classes remain small, taught by faculty who bring the essential combination of academic preparation and concern for students. Literary societies offer students the opportunity to hone their abilities to think and speak. The Rambler, still written and published by students, discusses the news of the campus.

Sturtevant would be pleased to find that the College maintains its relationship with the founding denominations, now the United Church of Christ and the Presbyterian Church (U.S.A.). He would be glad that the disputes between the two churches have ceased, and that the College is able to preserve a Christian community in an increasingly secular age.

Dr. Iver Yeager's biography of Julian Sturtevant opens a window into the early history of the State of Illinois, into the workings of religion and education in the last century, and into the life of Illinois College in its formative period. Sturtevant served his College well and faithfully as its first professor and second president, and Yeager served his subject well and faithfully in presenting him herein.

Richard A. Pfau,
Twelfth President of Illinois College

Preface

The foundations of this book were established in my youth. Studying the Bible, and translating Caesar's *Commentaries on the Gallic War* in high school Latin, awakened my interest in the two major sources of our Western heritage, Christianity and classical culture. College majors in philosophy and history, along with courses in biblical literature, immersed me in historical studies. Graduate school likewise focused on those subjects—the field now widened, however, to embrace empirical theology, process philosophy, and the major religions of the world.

I taught at two other private, church-related, liberal arts colleges before accepting appointment, in 1958, as Dean of Illinois College. My interest was attracted to the school's connection with two denominations long-known for their promotion of higher education, the Presbyterians and the Congregationalists. I soon learned the story of Illinois College by reading President C. H. Rammelkamp's excellent *Centennial History*. After serving twelve years as Dean of the College, I continued at Illinois College as a faculty member.

In 1977 I became deeply engaged with the College's early history when President Donald C. Mundinger appointed me chairman of the College's sesquicentennial anniversary celebration. The historic role of Illinois College in the settlement of central Illinois and in the development of higher education in the Midwest alerted me to the significance of President Julian Monson Sturtevant. His leadership in higher education and religion was manifested locally in this particular College and in the Church to which I belong. I admit to having a strong affection for both Illinois College and the Congregational Church of Jacksonville. I also acknowledge having great respect and affection for Julian Sturtevant, even as I have become aware of the deep differences which distinguish my views from his. These differences result in large part from developments

in modern science and biblical studies, a more positive understanding of the role of women and minorities, and the pluralistic
character of our age requiring the reassessment of the role of
Christianity and the Christian Church.

I wrote my first paper on Julian Sturtevant in 1979 for fellow
members of The Club, a men's literary society which Sturtevant
helped to found more than a century earlier. A valued long-time
member of The Club, Professor Walter B. Hendrickson of
MacMurray College, suggested that I write a biography of Sturtevant.
At that time I was fully occupied with teaching and my committee
obligations. Only later did Walter's suggestion take root.

This biography is consciously sympathetic to Sturtevant and
the causes he espoused. It draws heavily upon his published and
unpublished writings and often utilizes his own words to tell his
story. Accounts of his conflicts with others, regarding College and
church affairs and theology, are told from his point of view. The
historical context of events in which Sturtevant figured is
described briefly to provide a broad framework.

The early records of Illinois College, the Congregational
Church of Jacksonville, and The Club abound with references to
Sturtevant. Yale University is also a rich resource, and a sabbatical
leave in 1981 permitted intensive collection of source material in
its libraries. Excursions to two other Connecticut sites important
in Sturtevant's life, Warren and New Canaan, provided both information and insight.

Mrs. Dorothy Hope (Tisdale) Eldridge, great granddaughter of
Julian Sturtevant, was the family custodian of much of the
Sturtevant family's correspondence and documents. She was most
gracious in sharing her knowledge and in giving to Illinois College
the letters Sturtevant had written on his trip to England. Her skill
in deciphering those letters—written in heavy ink on both sides of
thin sheets of paper—was invaluable. Some years after her death
her husband, the late DeWitt Eldridge, transferred additional
relevant material to Illinois College. The Eldridges' contributions
are very much appreciated.

My expressions of appreciation necessarily extend to a long list
of persons and institutions for a project having broad scope and
extending over nearly two decades. No one else has shared so fully

my "living" with Julian Sturtevant during these many years as my wife, Natalee. She has read nearly every page of every version of the text I have written. I am deeply grateful to her for her labors and for herself. Our son Kenneth and our daughter Ruth have been very helpful in acquiring the hardware and utilizing the software for word processing.

President Mundinger gave much encouragement at an early stage and provided tangible aid by establishing a fund to assist publication. He has read a draft of the text and notes faithfully and with much profit to the quality of the work. Other former colleagues at Illinois College have also read the text and have provided helpful comments. I am especially grateful to Dr. James E. Davis, Gardner Professor of History and Professor of Geography. His knowledge of 19th century American history, his zeal in discovering relevant sources, and his careful annotations, place me deeply in his debt. Other former colleagues have also helped by reading the text: President Emeritus L. Vernon Caine; Dean Emeritus Wallace N. Jamison; Dr. Frederik Ohles, Vice President for Academic Affairs, Dean of the College, and Professor of History; Dr. David H. Koss, Scarborough Professor of Religion; and Dr. Royce P. Jones, Professor of Philosophy. I thank them all; they have done much to ferret out mistakes and weaknesses. For errors invisible to those who have not seen the original sources, and for those which have thus far eluded me, I accept responsibility.

I thank Dr. Richard A. Pfau, President of Illinois College, for keeping this project alive in the College's budget and arranging for The Trustees of Illinois College to be the publisher. I am grateful to the Trustees for their sponsorship.

My brother, Anson A. Yeager, has generously provided much of the funding necessary for publication. In my early years on many occasions I benefited from the strength and wisdom of an older brother. His offer to help came at a time when I was discouraged, and his generosity heartened me to see this lengthy task through to the end. I am very grateful to him.

I received much help from the staffs of various libraries and organizations, and to them also I extend my gratitude: Schewe Library, Illinois College; the Illinois State Historical Library, Springfield; Hammond Library, Chicago Theological Seminary;

Sterling Library, Yale University; the Library of the Yale Divinity School; the Congregational Library, Boston; the American Antiquarian Society, Worcester, Massachusetts; the Library of Congress; the New Canaan (Connecticut) Historical Society; the Congregational Church (United Church of Christ) of Jacksonville; and the First Congregational Church, Tallmadge, Ohio. Other sources are acknowledged in the endnotes.

Three alumni have made helpful contributions. The late Dr. Harold E. Gibson '30 was indefatigable in pursuing facets of Illinois College's history and publishing his findings. He was also generous in sharing copies of documents, pictures, and maps. John Power '73, Publisher of the *Jacksonville Journal-Courier,* has promoted the writing and dissemination of local history through special features. Greg Olson '83 has compiled gleanings from the past in the newspaper's column, "Looking Back: 100 and 120 Years Ago."

Special thanks are due those who have made important collections in the College's Archives accessible. Travis Hedrick arranged the microfilming of the extant and extensive Sturtevant-Baldwin correspondence. Professor Emeritus Elizabeth R. Zeigler sorted, organized, and cataloged many boxes of Sturtevant's material and other early documents.

Iver F. Yeager
Scarborough Professor Emeritus
of Religion and Philosophy

Introduction

Julian Monson Sturtevant had the good fortune to be born to parents who valued both the Christian Church and good schools and who lived in communities which supported religion and education. At an unusually young age he committed his life to Christian service. In preparation for that, and despite very limited means, he graduated from Yale College. Subsequently he was ordained as a Congregational minister. Sturtevant spent his unexpectedly long life as an educator and churchman. Never robust, he survived the hardships of two frontier environments, enduring health problems which plagued him throughout much of his life. He withstood concerted and sustained opposition and personal criticism, most of it undeserved.

The story of Julian Sturtevant is the story of Illinois College and of the formative decades of higher education in the Midwest. It is also the story of extending Congregationalism from its New England base to the West, a story writ large in the founding of the Congregational Church of Jacksonville. More broadly, his story is the story of transplanting Christian civilization, as it was developed in New England, to the frontier. That entailed establishing and supporting appropriate institutions: the church, which was the foundation; the school and college; and participatory government. Those efforts presumed a society of responsible, educated individuals working together in voluntary associations, each organized for a specific purpose on which people of various theological positions and denominational affiliations could agree.

Illinois College originated with the Reverend John Ellis, who shared his dreams and labors with supporters in western Illinois. Their efforts came to fruition when they were joined by Sturtevant and his fellow theological students at Yale, organized as the "Illinois Association." Together they founded Illinois College on 18 December 1829. Even without the aid of the Easterners, Ellis would have established a "seminary" or academy in Jacksonville. But without their talent and resources, it would not have come into being as quickly and it would have been a very different institution. Without the dedicated service of Julian Monson Sturtevant, Illinois College would not have maintained its character as a non-sectarian Christian liberal arts college, and it may well have failed. Sturtevant was the first instructor and the second president. During fifty-six of his four-score years he was intimately involved in every crisis and triumph of that school. He managed to keep the College functioning and faithful to its purpose, despite financial disasters, strains arising from the slavery issue, and factional struggles within and between the Presbyterians and the Congregationalists, the two denominations to which its founders belonged. More than any other member of the Illinois Association, he fulfilled its dual purpose of founding a college and preaching the Gospel in western Illinois.

The nineteenth century witnessed the founding of a large number of similar colleges, and many of them likewise were blessed with capable leadership. The comparison of Sturtevant with four contemporary college presidents reveals remarkable similarities as well as significant differences. Sturtevant had at least an acquaintance with each of them: Alexander Campbell, Charles G. Finney, Aaron L. Chapin, and George F. Magoun.

All five men had for a time a Presbyterian connection, and all but one became Congregationalists. All were ordained ministers and in most instances powerful preachers, deeply concerned with conversion to faith in Christ. All were keenly interested in fostering education, often beginning with preparatory schools. All published articles, and several wrote books. All but one taught political economy, and two published a book on this subject. Significantly, the colleges which these men served have survived to the present.

Alexander Campbell was born into a Scottish Presbyterian family in Ireland. He followed his father in emigrating to America and together they established a movement which developed into a new denomination, the Disciples of Christ. His fervent preaching and rejection of creeds attracted many. Campbell's energy was devoted to education and in 1840 he started Bethany College in western Virginia. Named president, he served in that position for twenty years. Because of similar interests with Barton Stone and his Christian Church, Campbell visited Jacksonville and on one occasion, at least, was entertained in the Sturtevant home.

A historical sign in Warren, Connecticut, notes that the church in that community had produced two college presidents, Charles G. Finney and Julian M. Sturtevant. Finney was older than Sturtevant. His family had moved to New York State when he was two, but he had returned to Warren for later schooling. Unlike Sturtevant, Finney gained his advanced education by private study and in the same way acquired knowledge of the Bible and religion. Although he began his adult life as a lawyer he experienced a powerful conversion and was ordained as a Presbyterian minister. He conducted revivals in several eastern states and attracted many converts. Finney also attracted much attention because of his unusual theological views and his dramatic methods of evangelism, such as the anxious bench. He withdrew from Presbytery and became a Congregationalist. He was closely involved with Oberlin College in Ohio from its early years and was president from 1851-1866. Oberlin was the first college in America to become coeducational, and it admitted students without regard to color. Finney successfully established a theological department, a hope which Sturtevant shared but never realized.

Aaron L. Chapin and George F. Magoun were younger contemporaries. Chapin, a Connecticut native and a graduate of Yale College and Union Theological Seminary, came to Milwaukee to serve as pastor of a Presbyterian Church. He participated in the founding of Beloit College and was its first president, holding that office from 1850 to 1866. He joined the Congregationalists and served on the boards of other educational institutions and missionary organizations. He was active as an author and editor.

President of Iowa College from 1864 to 1884, George F. Magoun studied theology at Andover and Yale after graduating from Bowdoin College. Most of his adult career, as school principal, pastor, and college president, was spent in northwestern Illinois and in Iowa. He had strong convictions and was somewhat argumentative in discourse with others. He like Sturtevant met with the members of the Congregational Union of England and Wales, although Magoun's visit was made nearly twenty years after Sturtevant's

Civil War journey. Originally located at Davenport, Magoun's college moved in 1869 to Grinnell and assumed that name.

All these college presidents, including Sturtevant, were inspired by the religious enthusiasm generated by the Second Great Awakening. A widespread renewal of Christian faith, the movement began in the early years of the nineteenth century. It gave rise to evangelistic fervor and intense revivalism. It spawned numerous organizations to support a vast network of missions, domestic and foreign, and a host of voluntary organizations to distribute the Bible and promote Sunday Schools. It led to the founding of many schools and colleges. Almost coincidentally with the renewal of religion, the new nation launched the westward expansion which continued to the end of the century. Four of the college presidents named—Campbell was the exception—participated in carrying the religious and educational benefits of the Awakening to the ever-receding frontier. By 1884, when the last of the five presidents had retired from office, the "western frontier" was firmly incorporated in the nation's political structure and social-cultural heritage.

Julian Sturtevant consciously adopted certain principles which governed his lifework. He was convinced of the truth of the Christian faith and regarded the Scriptures, intelligently read and understood, as the foundation of religion and society. He believed that religion and education go hand in hand, and that the freedom of the individual and the well-being of society depend upon each other in fine balance.

The challenges which Sturtevant experienced as a youth, as a student at Yale, and as a pioneer missionary-educator in frontier Illinois, tested his remarkable abilities, restless energy, and dogged determination. He fulfilled at Illinois College the life contract into which he entered in New Haven in February 1829.

Sturtevant identified himself as a "Puritan" but more precisely as deriving from the "Pilgrim Puritans" of Plymouth Colony. Jacksonville became known as the Puritan stronghold in Illinois, boasting numerous Presbyterian and Congregational ministers who served as educators, pastors, or agents of various missionary and Bible societies. Both Presbyterians and Congregationalists asserted their orthodoxy in doctrine, although doctrine and especially church polity were frequently matters of contention among and between them.

Sturtevant espoused and practiced the obligation to establish a righteous society. He believed that God has given America the mission of Christianizing the world, a goal to be achieved, perhaps, by the year 2000. Sturtevant shared the post-millennialist view that God's faithful people can, with divine help, establish the good society; Christ will then come to begin his 1,000 year reign. These convictions placed an enormous obligation upon the people in the church; they also inspired a great vision and released tremendous energy not only for religious work but for the improvement of society and the well-being of humanity. Sturtevant did not share the pre-millennarians' expectation that Christ was coming very soon nor their passion to discover the precise date. Rather, Sturtevant was optimistic about the social order which regenerate, faithful Christians could achieve. However, he did not regard America's success as guaranteed; the future depended on the people's faithfulness to God and to their divinely given mission to establish Christianity even to the ends of the earth.

Abbreviations and Symbols

A   Sturtevant, *Autobiography*
AHMS   American Home Missionary Society
B   Baldwin, Theron (letters to Sturtevant, as B-S)
CCM   Congregational Church (Jacksonville) Minutes
CH   Rammelkamp, *Illinois College: A Centennial History*
EC   Eldridge Collection
EW   Elizur Wright Jr.
FM   Faculty Minutes, Illinois College
HRF   Hannah R. Fayerweather (before marriage)
HRS   Hannah R. Sturtevant (after marriage)
IA   Collection of Papers of JMS (Files 1-53)
IC   Illinois College
ICAQ   *Illinois College Alumni Quarterly*
ICCR   *Illinois College College Rambler*
ICQCC   Illinois College Quarter Century Celebration
ISHL   Illinois State Historical Library, Springfield
ISHS   Illinois State Historical Society
JC   *Jacksonville Illinois Courier*
JJ   *Jacksonville Illinois Journal* and *Jacksonville Journal-Courier.*
          (Information from "Looking Back" is designated JJ.)
JMS   Julian Monson Sturtevant
JMSJR   J. M. Sturtevant Jr.; or his "Autobiography."
JP   *Jacksonville Illinois Patriot*
LES   Ladies' Association for Educating Females
          (1833-53); Ladies Education Society (1853—)
S   J. M. Sturtevant (as in letters to Baldwin, S-B)
SH   *Springfield Illinois Herald*
SJ   *Springfield Illinois Journal*
SPC   Society for the Promotion of Collegiate and Theological
          Education at the West (or, College Society, College
          Education Society, Western College Society)
SR   *Springfield Illinois Register*
TB   Theron Baldwin
TM   Trustees' Minutes

THE WARREN STURTEVANT FAMILY
Warren (d. 1858) and Lucy (d. 1833) Tanner Sturtevant
Ephraim (1803-1881)
Warren D., Wheeler, Helen, Julia
Julian (1805-1886)
Huldah (Hinman)(1810-1860)
Christopher (1813-1892)

THE RICHARD FAYERWEATHER FAMILY
Richard (d. 1852) and Hannah (d. 1829) Fayerweather
Julia (Chamberlain) (1804?-1888)
Elizabeth (Sturtevant) (1805-1840)
Mary Jane (1808?-1887)
James (1810-1877)
Abraham (1812?-1850)
Silas (1814?-1850)
Hannah (Sturtevant) (1816-1886)

THE JULIAN M. STURTEVANT FAMILY
Julian Monson Sturtevant
m. *Elizabeth Maria Fayerweather,* 1829
Julian Monson (1830-1831)
Elizabeth Maria (1832-1840)
Julian Monson (1834-1921)
James Warren (1836-1873)
Hannah Augusta (1838-1891)
Edgar Lewis (1840-1840)
m. *Hannah Richards Fayerweather,* 1841
Elizabeth Fayerweather (1841-1922)
Caroline Wilder (1843-1845)
Lucy Ella (1846-1930)
Edgar Howard (1848-1855)
Alfred Henry (1850-1930)

Chapter 1: 1805-1829

Preparing for Christian Service

A Devout Family in Connecticut

Julian Monson Sturtevant, in the late years of his life, reflected on his commitment to the Christian faith and the educational ministry in which he engaged throughout his unexpectedly long life. On 15 November 1879 family and friends gathered at his home in Jacksonville, Illinois, to celebrate the fiftieth anniversary of his arrival in the frontier village. Then he had been the vanguard of a contingent of home missionaries bound for Illinois; now he was honored as one of the town's early settlers. The 18th of December that same year marked the semi-centennial of the founding of Illinois College, when he represented his Yale colleagues in that bold venture.

Four years later the Congregational Church of Jacksonville observed the golden anniversary of its establishment, an event in which Julian Sturtevant had a central role. Illinois College and the Congregational Church were the institutional embodiments of Sturtevant's dearest loves, and on the occasion of each celebration he delivered a long, carefully prepared address. His life had been dedicated to sustaining the Church of Christ generally and that one college in particular, and he was confident that both would far exceed his own span of years. Prospects were auspicious for a blessed future for these institutions, his family and friends, and his beloved nation, but that future was not guaranteed. He believed that faithfulness to God and the divine purpose was crucial to fulfilling all these great hopes. Grateful for reaching the Bible's extended limit of four-score years in 1885, Sturtevant recounted his first six decades in his *Autobiography*. He analyzed the influences which led him to become a Christian and to devote his life to the Christian ministry. He acknowledged the role of heredity in a person's life but gave greater credit to family upbringing and environment and especially the individual's will and industry.

Sturtevant's birthplace, Warren, was a farming area in Litchfield County in northwestern Connecticut. Like many New England communities it had a well-developed network of basic institutions: strong families embracing numerous adult siblings and spanning several generations; the church, to which everyone came on the Sabbath; the schools, provided at low cost to ensure that all children would be educated; and the annual Freeman's meeting to decide matters of local government. Because of the combination of individual responsibility and strong community spirit, these institutions were mutually supportive. The features of the Warren community together with the people's pride in being part of a new nation made a lasting impression upon young Julian Sturtevant. All these elements helped prepare him for the life-long mission he undertook when he committed himself, in his early twenties, to replicating New England's Christian civilization in Illinois, then the western frontier.

Western Connecticut was richer in human resources than in natural bounty. Four men who would be prominent in the early history of Illinois College lived within fifteen miles of each other: Sturtevant; Frederick Collins, later a trustee; Edward Beecher, Illinois College's first president; and Theron Baldwin, who became Sturtevant's lifetime friend and close colleague. Among the numerous clergymen who came from Warren were two who achieved prominence both as preachers and college presidents, Charles G. Finney of Oberlin and Julian M. Sturtevant of Illinois College. Deacons from Warren became active leaders in west central Illinois churches.

Regarding his own spiritual lineage, Sturtevant declared that "all my ancestors...were adherents of the religious faith and simple polity of the Pilgrim fathers." (A, 17) He wrote of the "ties of religious affection" which bound him to Warren. The pastor of the church was a good man but not outstanding. However, local ministers exchanged pulpits and consequently the Sturtevant family heard such preachers as the eloquent Lyman Beecher, and

Dan Huntington, and Samuel J. Mills. (All three would later be eclipsed in prominence by their own sons.) Julian as a boy was especially impressed by Beecher's "fervent enthusiasm" and "magnificent imagination." Overall the regular services of worship taught the youth "reverence for God, His Church and His holy Word." (A, 30) There were no other churches nearby and the church bore no denominational label; Sturtevant said that as a boy he would not have understood the term "Congregational." The church and the community were one, the people being united in a system of social order the foundations of which were deeply rooted in their religious faith.

Protesting that he was no aristocrat and that his ancestors were among the lowly, Julian Sturtevant was in the seventh generation of his family in America—and in fact his heritage was enviable. In 1642 Samuel Sturtevant had left Plymouth in England to come to Plymouth in Massachusetts. There he prospered and upon his death left a comfortable estate to his family. Other forebears had arrived even earlier on the Mayflower. Later generations served in the Revolution, grandfather Peleg Sturtevant achieving the rank of captain.

Julian's parents were Warren and Lucy Tanner Sturtevant who, like most of their neighbors, were farm people. Lucy's father was also a farmer but in addition had business interests as a tanner and a country merchant. Warren and Lucy had joined the church, known simply as the Church of Christ in Warren, a year before they were married by the pastor in 1801. Their first child died when only two days old. Their second child, Ephraim Tanner, was born in 1803, and Julian Monson two years later, on 27 July 1805. Sister Huldah Monson was born in 1810 and brother Christopher Cornelius in 1813.

Practical habits of industry and thrift were formed quite naturally in the Warren environment and were deeply embedded in Sturtevant's character. He declared that in his youth he was never idle. The same can be said about his entire life; only with his final retirement at eighty did he experience for the first time a sense of leisure. Economy likewise was an essential trait for survival in the harsh conditions of New England and even more so on the western frontier.

Important as the church was, the family had even greater influence in shaping the boy's religious development. His parents placed religion above all other interests. The family attended the Sabbath morning and afternoon church services regularly, and after dinner the father led family worship—an observance especially meaningful to Julian. The Westminster Shorter Catechism was recited, question by question for the younger children, and in its entirety for the older ones. Next the father read from Scripture and offered a short but heartfelt prayer to conclude the New England Sabbath. Much as they valued it, the parents did not regard the Catechism, commonly regarded as expressing "the Calvinistic faith of the New England fathers," as the absolute standard of faith. (A, 22) The object of faith was not the creed but God, and the standard of faith was not the Catechism but the Word of God. Moreover, the family believed that no church authority could dictate one's faith. Overall, Sturtevant's heritage enabled him to be "a bold and free, yet reverent, advocate" of reforms required to help the Church conform to the Word of God. (A, 36)

One Sabbath the family's worship profoundly affected young Julian. Their father had read the parable of the last judgment from Matthew 25. The realization that he would someday be judged for his life's actions nearly overwhelmed the boy, and for the rest of his days he was keenly aware of this solemn prospect. In later years he considered the literalness of the passage an unimportant issue, but he still believed that every man will be judged according to his deeds and assigned to an eternal destiny.

A few months later, when playing with Ephraim, Julian was greatly distressed by the realization that he was "a great sinner before God" and he deeply feared God's judgment. Ephraim empathized with Julian and shared both his conviction and his feelings. Their mother was away but upon her return she was sensitive to their anguish and assured them of God's mercy through Christ. Both sons changed markedly. Sturtevant later emphasized that his conversion was "honest and natural, the spontaneous outgrowth of my own nature and the religious influences around me." (A,33) He denied being motivated by fear, saying, at the end of his life, that he was Christian by a "hearty approbation and a deliberate choice."[1]

Before Julian was eleven years old, he and his older brother were received as members of the Church of Christ at Warren on 17 June 1816.[2] Few youngsters their age made confession of faith and participated in the Lord's Supper. The two boys had been examined by the pastor and lay officers of the church, although in consideration of their youth the questioning was brief. Congregational churches generally required new members to accept the locally adopted creed, a practice which Sturtevant later concluded was inappropriate. At the time of his reception into the church it was admission into fellowship which he valued and not the creed which was beyond his understanding.

Another very important factor in Julian's development was the family's concern for the education of the children. The father had little formal schooling but was a good reader and could write good English. The mother had somewhat more education and was fond of reading, especially fiction and poetry. Wanting the best available education for their children, the parents borrowed money to buy a farm nearer to the church and to the best school in the area. Julian started in the district school when five or six years old. Classes were held during both winter and summer, for terms of three or four months. The pastor of the church had a keen interest in the schools, visiting often and giving religious instruction. Julian learned reading, writing, spelling, and the Shorter Catechism, but little arithmetic. Reflecting in later years on his early education, he concluded that overall it was superior to modern schools with their multiple subjects, although rote memorization was overemphasized. The quality of teaching could have been greatly improved by the use of classical literature and poetry and even fiction.

Moving to Ohio's Frontier

Warren Sturtevant had secured a mortgage to meet the greater cost of the new farm. Although the land was poor even by New England standards, it might have been possible to pay the debt had it not been for the War of 1812. The markets for grain were restricted by the conflict and the resulting low prices brought financial ruin to many New England farmers. Peace was made in

1815, and later Warren Sturtevant and his brother Bradford walked to Ohio to seek new homes for their families.

Julian Sturtevant remembered all too well the reluctant departure the two families made in May 1817.[3] They were leaving relatives they likely would never see again. His mother felt deeply about another lack on the frontier; she cried as she walked behind the wagon, fearing her sons would not be able to get an education "out West." (JMSJR, 3) Traveling in two covered wagons filled with their bedding, clothing, and food supplies, the group crossed over the Hudson River to Newburg in New York and proceeded across Pennsylvania by way of Easton, Harrisburg, and Pittsburgh. The journey of five hundred miles took more than a month but the weather was moderate and usually the travelers found lodging at night. Julian, not yet twelve, was deeply impressed by "the magnitude of the world and particularly of our own country." (A, 42) Nearing their goal the travelers observed the Sabbath with Lucy Sturtevant's uncle in Canfield, Ohio. Their next stop was Tallmadge, where they spent several days visiting with friends who had left Warren before them.

Richfield, in northeastern Ohio, had been selected by the Sturtevant brothers for their new homes. However, no church or school had yet been established and there were no roads. A never-to-be-forgotten event occurred when the men of the family joined others to organize a church and share in communion. It was, Julian recalled years afterward, "a bright day in the record of my life." (A, 46) The event was also to have a profound influence which he could not have suspected at the time. The minister took note that among those eligible to receive communion were two young boys. He subsequently encouraged their families to arrange for their schooling and thus initiated Julian's formal preparation for the ministry.

Warren Sturtevant soon decided to sell his share of the Richfield property to his brother and to take his own family to Tallmadge, near present-day Akron. There he obtained some good land near the boundary of the heavily-forested area. The wild environment was vividly described by Julian in recalling his parents' experience of becoming lost. They had gone out to bring home their cows when, in the October darkness, they lost their way. A fierce storm arose, and the children endured a night of terror while they kept the lamps lighted and made loud noises in an effort to guide their parents to safety. The children were overjoyed when, at midnight, their parents finally returned.

During the fall the two older boys assisted their father in clearing the land and in constructing a log cabin. The new home was ready for occupancy by 29 November 1817—another memorable event. The cabin proved quite inadequate for keeping out the winter cold and the family suffered considerably. The older boys were able to attend school during the winter, seldom being absent despite the distance and frequently severe weather. Julian profited much from the instruction of the woman teacher, one of the best teachers he ever had; he especially valued her assistance with English grammar.

Happily Mrs. Sturtevant's fear that her sons would be deprived of both religious and educational opportunity had proved groundless. Tallmadge was actually a "New England community," and the sale of property was limited to such persons as the pastor approved. The founder was the Reverend David Bacon, whose son Leonard became a highly-respected churchman and a friend and adviser to Julian Sturtevant. Tallmadge was a purely Congregational community, although the church was known simply as "the Church of Christ." The fact that the familiar institutions and customs of New England could be established in frontier Ohio refuted Tocqueville's observation that Americans, so highly mobile, lacked a natural patriotism. Sturtevant countered that Americans do have a love for home, even when necessity forces them to emigrate to a new area. "Surely," he wrote, "those who transplant the home affections and all that is best in the institutions of their fathers, into the depths of the wilderness give the highest proof of natural patriotism." (A, 39)

The Tallmadge church[4] held regular services and in 1819 a Sunday School was established which the Sturtevant brothers attended. The minister who had presided at the summer service near Richfield now proposed that they should enter the academy to prepare for college. He recognized their religious earnestness and realized that such young men were the answer to the great need for educated ministers in the frontier regions. The principal of the academy offered free tuition but the boys felt that their father needed them at home. The parents wanted more than anything else for their sons to become Christian ministers and in the fall of 1817 both sons were enrolled. At the time Julian did not appreciate the emphasis on rote drill in Latin grammar and when classes ended in the spring he gladly returned home. He did what he could in helping to fell the forest giants and really did not want to return to school nor did he think his teacher would want him back. However, both boys resumed classes and soon Julian felt he was making real progress. The prospect of college was now more real and more appealing. By the winter of 1819-1820 Julian was doing well in Greek also, and at the close of the winter term in the following year he gave an oration in Greek.[5] He mastered Latin thoroughly and knew classical Latin poetry so well that years later, if someone read two consecutive lines to him, he could identify the source and describe the context. He and his brother spent their summers helping on the farm, although there was some opportunity for the boys to study on their own. They also were able to save some money which they earned from keeping bees and selling beeswax.

A religious revival occurred in Tallmadge in the fall of 1820. The interest was widespread and over the next several months special meetings were held for prayer two or three times a week. The Sturtevant boys rose early in order to complete their work before 5:00 P.M. so that they could attend. The religious faith of the community was deepened, there were no sectarian rivalries, and close friendships developed. Most of the young people united with the church, among them the Sturtevant brothers and Elizur Wright Jr., son of the academy's principal. The younger Wright was a faithful friend whom Julian deeply loved.

In the fall of 1820 the people of the church decided to erect a building and plans were drawn by a member who was an architect. In 1822 Julian was one of many who shared in the joyous labor of raising the building. Writing in 1885 he remarked, "It stands to-day in excellent order, a model of country church architecture." (A, 64) Another century has now passed and the edifice, still standing, has been designated by the Ohio Historical Society as "one of the finest examples of Connecticut

Tallmadge Church
Built 1822-1825

architecture in the Western Reserve."6

Elizur Wright Jr. planned to attend Yale and so the Sturtevants decided to go there also. The minister who had already given them so much encouragement provided them with an old horse and they purchased a small carriage. A fourth youth, interested simply in reaching the East coast, completed the travel party. The farewells were said on a morning in June 1822. After breakfast Warren Sturtevant gathered his family for prayers and chose the 27th Psalm for the parting Scripture lesson. He choked up when he came to the lines, "When my father and mother forsake me, then the Lord will take me up." A devout man from nearby Hudson, Owen Brown, came to the house just then, being accompanied by his son, John, later famous for the raid on Harper's Ferry. Mr. Brown quickly grasped the situation and, taking the Bible, he read the Psalm and offered a fervent prayer. Julian was deeply saddened at leaving his parents and their home, even though "far away in the future we discerned a region bright with hope." (A, 72) There was ample cause for Julian's sorrow; the future would provide few opportunities for seeing his parents and visiting their forest home.

Attending Yale College

From early childhood Julian Sturtevant had been directed toward the Christian ministry by his parents' desire. Their purpose had become his own intention when he experienced conversion. In the New England tradition the proper training for a minister was a liberal arts education, and it was to provide such training that the early colleges, notably Harvard and Yale, had been founded.

The Sturtevant brothers' choice of Yale was influenced by their friend's decision, yet it was a natural one. They had many relatives in Connecticut. Moreover, Yale fostered the kind of religious experience which distinguished it from Harvard. A prominent feature was the recognition that appropriate "means," such as heartfelt biblical preaching, were essential to conversion and thus the hoped-for salvation.[7]

Because their old wagon seated only two the boys used the "ride and tie" method of traveling. Two would ride for three or four miles, tie the horse at the side of the road, and start walking. When the other pair came to the vehicle they would climb aboard to overtake the two walkers and forge ahead. The boys conscientiously observed the Sabbath, spending their second one in Geneva, New York, with Cyrus Tanner, the Sturtevant boys' uncle. After a little more than three weeks they arrived in New Canaan, Connecticut, where they stayed with another uncle, Silas Beckley. Concerned that the three boys might not be well-prepared, the uncle arranged for them to be tutored by the local pastor, a Yale graduate. This intensive schooling was needed and it continued for about two months. The next stop was at Warren, where the old family home was now occupied by one of their Tanner uncles. Years later Julian recalled how deeply he was moved by seeing once again his grandparents' home across the road from the church and the familiar faces of many relatives.

In October the candidates for Yale's freshman class were ready to complete their journey. Transportation to New Haven was provided by Uncle Joseph Tanner, who preferred to take his own carriage instead of the one which had brought the youths so far. It was evening when they reached New Haven and drove past the college buildings. "Excitement rose to fever heat," Julian remembered. "That was our Mecca; our pilgrimage was ended." (A, 77) The uncle lodged the boys at an inn and called on President Jeremiah Day to inform him about the hopeful students. The next morning President Day met with the boys for about an hour and after examining them in Latin and Greek he determined that they were qualified for admission. The first experience of college life for Julian and his colleagues was the noon meal that day at the freshman tables in the College Commons; it was a bewildering contrast to their orderly meals. Because all the dormitory rooms had been taken before the boys arrived the three spent their first year as lodgers at Mrs. Atwater's. In subsequent years Julian and Ephraim roomed together in college facilities.

In a long and emotional letter Mrs. Sturtevant remarked about their "lonsum house" and assured her sons that their parents would never forget them. She urged them to be close to each other, to give help when needed, and to choose friends carefully. She hoped that they had not forsaken the way but if so, they must return like the prodigal son to God. She explained that she had been unable to get their winter coats in time to send them with a neighbor. The tailor required either cloth or money in advance for making clothing, and she had been obliged to sell a lot of her cloth previously. Meanwhile, she hoped to receive a letter from her sons by this week's mail. She concluded with a prayer that they might be useful in this life and then happy in death when they might all meet in the mansions of the blessed to part no more. She asked her sons to pray daily for their sister and younger brother, who "still remain thoughtless and unconcerned about their souls." The letter closed: "I remain your affectionate mother. Lucy Sturtevant."[8]

The education of Julian Sturtevant at Yale College extended beyond the classroom. The students represented broad cultural and economic diversity and he was now in the midst of "the most democratic portion of American society." (A, 80) Yale was the favorite college for southern families and numerous sons of wealthy planters were there. Present also were the sons of rich business men of the cities of the north, especially New York City. A third group included the sons of farmers from New England and the frontier, the latter readily identified by their dress and manners. Students like Julian, who had to work for a living, were disdained by those with greater means.

The 1822 *Catalogue* of Yale College listed the officers and faculty and then, by classes, the students. Julian and Ephraim Sturtevant and Elizur Wright of Tallmadge, Ohio, were among the eighty freshman students in the student body of about four hundred. The annual charges were approximately $120, including $33 for instruction, $9 for rent, about $70 for board, and additional amounts for wood and cleaning. Fees for books and laundry, stationery, and fuel for the classrooms brought the estimated total to $150 to $200, not including clothing, travel, and board during vacation periods. Students provided their own bed and bedding and furniture and their own candles. The organization, procedures, and rules of the College were printed in *The Laws of Yale College* (1822).

The teaching staff included the president, five professors, and six or seven tutors. The freshman class studied classical authors, English grammar, algebra, and geography. Sophomores continued these studies, completed Euclid's *Geometry*, and added Homer's *Iliad*. For the Juniors there were additional studies in the classics along with trigonometry, philosophy, history, and astronomy. Seniors read logic, Locke's *Essays*, and three works by Paley: *Natural Theology, Moral Philosophy*, and *Evidences of Christianity*. They also studied physics and chemistry. Arithmetic and mathematics were difficult subjects for Julian and he sometimes despaired. Only the generous assistance of the skillful Elizur Wright, who later achieved prominence as an insurance actuary, enabled him to succeed.

The decision to go to Yale had been a hard one for Julian but it was one he never regretted. A college such as Yale was essential to his plan to become a minister. Sturtevant concluded that the education it offered was doubtless the best that could be obtained anywhere at that time although he was quite conscious of its shortcomings. The curriculum was rigidly prescribed and the method of instruction was intensive recitation. During the first three years each of the three divisions of the class met three times daily with its tutor, who drilled each student individually. Only afterwards would tutors give explanations and answer questions; it was forbidden to ask for help beforehand. Beginning with the juniors the professors taught some of the classes, and in their senior year students benefited from additional instruction by the president. Classes were scheduled for five and a half days, with a half holiday on Saturday. Two hours were set aside in the evening for study. However, on the Sabbath—from sundown Saturday until that time on Sunday—there were no classes and no studying was allowed.

The diligent preparation required for classes combined with very limited resources forced Julian to practice strenuous self-discipline.

As he proved that he was equal to the task, he gained greater confidence in himself. An example of his achievement, in thought and
literary skill, is the ten-page oration which he delivered at the
Junior Exhibition in May 1825. The text, hand-written in a sewn
copybook, was entitled "The True Standard of Greatness." Julian
contemplated pursuits in which people seek distinction: "Martial
glory, literary distinction, and refined social feelings." These he
rejected. Voltaire, Hume, and Rousseau, three men of great literary
renown, had "assailed the fair fabric of Christianity, and employed
their mightiest efforts to undermine the very foundations of Society.
From them and their associates in this anti-christian conspiracy, has
flown a torrent of unpiety and licentiousness…." The young orator
declared that "Man must be looked upon not as insulated and
independent of those around him, but as a social and a moral
being." True greatness is achieved by contributing to the progress
of virtue and happiness in human life—brightening the prospects
of the unfortunate, kindling joy in the heart of the disconsolate,
and rescuing from their chains the victims of oppression.

Julian was one of fifteen in the junior class chosen for what he
called "the highest grade of honor," membership in Phi Beta
Kappa. (A, 102) The original records of Yale's *Alpha* chapter show
that Elizur Wright was also elected and subsequently Ephraim too.
The minutes of 19 July 1825 state that "the elected members were
initiated in due form & order…. Refreshments were then carried
around, and when a *quantum sufficit* had been eat & drank [*sic*]
the Society adjourned."[9] Long afterwards Sturtevant admitted
with some embarrassment that upon learning of his election to
Phi Beta Kappa he and his brother celebrated by "treating"
friends, in their room, to wine and brandy. This was the accepted
custom for such occasions and the liquor was obtained from a college
employee who had charge of such stores. (A, 102)

Julian was faithful in attending the Society's meetings, often
held twice in a given week. During his senior year he sometimes
participated in debates on issues which he confronted directly
in his mature years, such as the abolition of slavery, the removal
of the Indians across the Mississippi,[10] and the inclusion of
modern foreign languages in college curricula. The Society's
membership in the 1820s included several who would later be

Julian's colleagues in the Illinois mission. Edward Beecher, later to be president of Illinois College, was already a member and Theron Baldwin, Mason Grosvenor, and William Kirby were elected in 1826.

Now aware of his real strengths, Julian realized that he could "maintain a fair equality with the foremost competitors" in intellectual affairs and he no longer regarded himself as a "weakling." (A, 102) Devoting himself to his studies with even greater ardor, he ranked high in his graduating class and might have earned one of the three top honors except for a serious illness he suffered in his final term after a lengthy period of caring for a friend who had pneumonia. He was taken to a private home where he was given the utmost care by three maiden sisters, assisted by Elizur Wright. His illness was so severe that the doctor had warned that he could do nothing more for him. Theron Baldwin went to Goshen to bring Ephraim, who was teaching school there, to Julian's bedside. The roads were blocked by snow and when Theron and Ephraim finally arrived, they rejoiced to find that the patient had improved.[11] Julian was especially moved because friends collected funds to pay his expenses and because some of those who two years earlier had been quite unfriendly had come to wish him well.

The two brothers were keenly aware of the financial stringency of their circumstances. Fortunately at Yale those with limited funds were permitted to receive instruction, board and room. At the end of the term they would pay what they could and sign a note for the balance. From time to time anonymous credit entries were made in Julian's account with the college. Julian signed a note on 12 September 1826 at the time of his graduation, promising to pay $55.36 plus interest. He paid part of that amount in May 1828 and the balance in October 1830.

Julian's financial needs were supplied in part by the American Education Society, whose purpose was "to educate pious young men for the gospel ministry." Yearly certification of satisfactory progress and good moral habits was required as well as an annual declaration by the student that "it continues to be his serious purpose to devote his life to the gospel ministry." To guard against the waste of public charity the students were never given full support but "only sufficient to enable them to *live*, with the greatest economy as to their expenses, and the most strenuous exertions to assist themselves."[12]

The Society's aid had been crucial during Julian's first three years and part of the fourth. However, he decided early in his senior year to be independent, although at great personal sacrifice. About a year after he reached Illinois the Society sent Sturtevant a statement of his obligations; the grand total was $306 of which half was to be repaid. Any interest due as of 1830 would be canceled if he signed a new note for the principal and agreed to pay interest from that date. Sturtevant wryly commented in later years that although some believed Christian character was weakened by too much aid, no such mistake was made in his case. "I might have been quite willing to have dispensed with much of that discipline," he acknowledged, "but my heavenly Father understood the case better than I did." (A, 82)

Yale College had been founded in 1701 as "a counterweight against Harvard 'liberalism.'" (Smith, 200) Its "chief design was to furnish the churches with competent ministers of the Gospel" and there was never a time in its history, wrote George Fisher in 1857, that it did not have students who were preparing for the ministry.[13] All students were instructed in religion and required to attend the college's religious exercises. College officers conducted morning prayers before breakfast. The students stood when the president entered and the seniors bowed to him. The service was simple: an invocation, a reading from Scripture, and prayer. Julian was punctual in his attendance but acknowledged that it was impossible for him "to derive any benefit from [these exercises]. It was simply a matter of endurance." He later thought it amazing that "this monastic custom survived so long in our American Colleges." (A, 84) Evening prayers, held before dinner, benefited from a hymn sung by an excellent choir, the feature Sturtevant appreciated most.

The Sabbath worship in Yale's Chapel was much more meaningful. The College Preacher delivered a full course of lectures on Christian theology during the first service on the Sabbath. The content of lectures at the second service was more practical and gave effective aid to students in strengthening their religious and moral lives. Professor Nathaniel Taylor preached at occasional evening services during the week and although students were not required to attend, many did so, Julian among them. There was no "religious awakening" or revival during Sturtevant's student days, although many individuals had a conversion experience as a result of the various influences at Yale. Sturtevant estimated that about half the students were "professing Christians." (A, 91) The College Church at Yale was known simply as the Church of Christ; it was non-sectarian and all students who did not have other church connections were expected to join it. Recommended by the Tallmadge Church, Julian and his brother were received into membership on 5 January 1823, midway in their freshman year.[14]

The Friday evening prayer meeting, less formal, was "indispensable" to Julian's personal spiritual development. "In it we recorded each week our adhesion to Christ, and revived our consciousness of religious obligation and of the sacred fraternity which bound us together." (A, 93) His active participation continued throughout his college years. The records of the Society of Inquiry Concerning Missions for the period when Julian was a college student are not extant, and he did not mention participating in this organization during these years. The statements in his *Autobiography* about the "Society of Inquiry" clearly refer to its counterpart in the Theological Department where he enrolled later.

Sturtevant's very active participation in the Yale Moral Society is evident from its records.[15] Its constitution emphasized that morality is essential to happiness both in this life and the life to come and is necessary for the well-being of all human institutions. New members promised to live by the moral rules in the Bible. They would endeavor to suppress vice, to refrain from profanity, to never play any game involving property, and to never play cards. A first offense required the miscreant to prepare a written confession; a second offense led to expulsion.

Julian and his brother Ephraim joined this Society early in their first year. A subject which would later have direct personal significance for Julian was considered at the meeting of 2 January 1823: "Ought ministers of the Gospel read their sermons or deliver them from memory." Other topics were not only timely but of historical importance: will the aborigines ever become civilized? should discussion of slavery be encouraged in the northern states? Some subjects had far-reaching moral and political implications: should post offices be closed and stages prohibited on the Sabbath? ought religion to be supported by law? should there be a society for the suppression of intemperance? The vote of the members determined the winning side in the debates.

At the meeting of 24 August 1823 Julian was one of the disputants on the subject, "Ought a belief in the christian [*sic*] religion to be made a requisite for offices of state?" The minutes do not show which side Julian was on but in other societies it was usually seniors who took the negative position. In this instance, the negative won. Both Sturtevants, now seniors, participated in the discussion of 24 November 1825: "Do the principles of the gospel require the immediate emancipation of the slaves in the United States?" Again, the negative side triumphed but which side the brothers argued was not reported.

During the fall of 1823 some of the students engaged in unruly and even violent behavior. The governance of the college had become so lax that the situation approached what Julian later called a state of anarchy. Certain students who were quite dissipated caused great destruction of property and aroused fear among other students whom they bullied. The root cause, Sturtevant believed, was the lack of any bond between the faculty and the students. The student attitude that it was highly dishonorable to give information about the identity of culprits made it difficult for the authorities to take action. The most serious incident was a violent explosion in the College Chapel, only a short distance from the Sturtevants' room. The pulpit furniture was splintered and every window was shattered. Regardless, the students were summoned to morning prayers at the regular time. The president, taking no notice of the damage, entered and took his place and the service proceeded as usual.

The three students from Tallmadge, joined by a fourth, met immediately after prayers and pledged to report whatever information they could obtain about every violation. They knew that they would be labeled with the derogatory term, "Blue Skin," but they met that challenge by enlisting a hundred other students in the new "Blue Skin Club" and soon a majority of the students were participants. Three of the ruffians responsible for some of the disorders came to the Sturtevants' room to put a stop to their interference. The plan became known to the "Blue Skin" group and some of the members gathered in adjacent rooms. One of the intruders—Sturtevant referred to them as "the enemy"—raised a heavy cane to threaten harm only to have the weapon seized from behind. The attempt at intimidation was foiled and the invaders beat a hasty retreat. The threat was reported and the offenders were promptly dismissed. Violations continued for several weeks but in due time the Blue Skins could suspend their nightly watch.

Sturtevant believed that "the moral and Christian principle of the students saved the college." (A, 98) He would not forget the lesson regarding the vulnerability of an institution which tolerated student lawlessness. Although the terrorism on Yale's campus had stemmed in part from the conflict between southern and northern students, Sturtevant discerned underlying social-economic factors. Northern schools and businessmen eagerly sought southern patronage and discouraged any word or act which might diminish it. One remarkable aspect of the situation at Yale was that no student could speak against slavery in an essay without the risk of being the victim of insult or even physical attack. Later Sturtevant looked back upon these incidents as precursors of the Great Rebellion which erupted in 1861.

Although Yale had enormous influence on Sturtevant's intellectual and religious development, there is little information regarding its impact on his social and political thought. His student days provided experiences for subsequent reflection and he had numerous opportunities to listen to and engage in debates on important topics of the day. He had his first experience, and a vivid one, of living in a diversified social and cultural environment. Perhaps the political milieu of New Haven was so pervasive and so congenial that Sturtevant was not consciously aware of it. K. Alan Snyder has pointed out that under the influential Timothy Dwight, a long-term president just prior to Sturtevant's enrollment, Yale had become "a Federalist bastion." Dwight shared the dream of Jedidiah Morse, a Congregational minister, that America would become a Christian nation; in the context of the period, this meant a Calvinist-Protestant nation. Moreover, Snyder observed,

"Within the dominant Congregationalist-Federalist framework of the early national period, [Dwight and Morse] were, quite simply, champions of liberty."[16] Morse himself saw no distinction between Christianity and a republican form of government which promoted freedom. Sturtevant's views surely were influenced by his earlier years in New England and its Ohio colony and by his exposure to such ideas at Yale. He also was strongly convinced that the United States could and must be a Christian nation and he too was a champion of liberty. However, many years passed before he took an active role in political affairs.

The final months for seniors at Yale were rather flexible and frequently students were absent from the campus for the six weeks in June and early July prior to the senior exams. Another six weeks were set aside for students to prepare their orations for commencement. The two Sturtevants were among those who returned to the New Haven campus to receive the Bachelor of Arts degree at the commencement in September 1826. The baccalaureate sermon preached by the Reverend Eleazar Fitch further inspired Julian to fulfill his long-held determination to become a minister. Fitch declared that God's word sustains man in this life and promises the hope of a nobler existence in the life to come. His closing words were a benediction upon the graduating class: "And now, in view of the vicissitudes of this pilgrimage and the unchanging states of happiness and misery that lie beyond the grave, we commend you to God and the word of his grace, while we affectionately bid you, *Farewell.*"[17]

Achieving Independence at New Canaan

Before Julian Sturtevant reached his twenty-third birthday he came to love three places as "home." In later reflection he realized that the most precious link in each instance was the bond of religious affection. His first home was at Warren, and the second was the log cabin at Tallmadge in Ohio. He did not include New Haven although it was his residence for four years and he returned there many times. After college he found still another home in New Canaan, Connecticut, where he had been tutored before his admission to Yale. He lived there for nearly two years, becoming an active member of the community. Here he developed maturity, achieved financial independence, learned how to safeguard his health, gained experience as a teacher, and committed himself in marriage.

The immediate need confronting Julian and Ephraim when the difficult spring term ended was to recoup their finances. For various reasons, including Julian's illness, neither brother had obtained employment during the period when teaching positions were offered. Providentially a position at the New Canaan Academy became available. The quality of the school made it very desirable and under the circumstances the limited salary also was attractive. The very day when Julian learned of the opportunity he left by stagecoach for the five-hour journey to Norwalk. He stayed there overnight and the next morning walked five miles to New Canaan. His exuberant account of that last part of his journey expressed the joy he felt regarding this answer to his prayers. "The heart-ease and youthful joyousness of that morning walk in June [is] delightful even in the dim pictures of a far-off memory. It was not so much hope for the future as enjoyment of the present that brought happiness." (A, 107)

That happiness was sustained when Julian secured the position. The school admitted students from seven years of age to maturity and apparently without regard to ability or prior achievement. The basic subjects were taught: English grammar, geography, arithmetic, history, rhetoric, and logic. The normal enrollment from the town was swelled in the summer term by an influx of students from New York. In the summer of 1826 the enrollment was unexpectedly large and Sturtevant quickly realized that the task was too great for one teacher. He readily convinced the proprietors that another teacher must be engaged and was authorized to hire his brother. Ephraim, although shorter than Julian's five-feet-ten, was more robust and self-assured and already had some experience in teaching. He functioned as principal and the school was very successful.

Permission was given to Julian and Ephraim to close the school for two or three days near the end of July for their senior examinations. Hiring a carriage they drove to New Haven, completed the requirement, heard the reading of the list of approved candidates—their Latinized names among them—and enjoyed an elegant dinner at the College Commons with the officers and faculty. That evening they returned to New Canaan, the roadway illuminated by "the bewitching light of a full moon…. How buoyant we were in spirit they only can know who remember the joyousness of youth. Such was the summer that followed that dark and frowning spring." (A, 109)

Classes at the Academy were again suspended so that the Sturtevant brothers could be present for Yale's Commencement on the second Wednesday of September. Julian characterized the student orators—himself included—as "half-fledged." He modestly said that his subject was trite and the only merit of his contribution was "that of a directness and force that came from earnest thinking." The praise given him by the Commencement preacher was proof that others rated his performance more highly than he did. The preacher, the Reverend Samuel H. Cox, made a deep impression upon Julian. More important than Cox's eloquence were the keen thought and sincere conviction which he expressed. His sermon, "The Education of Young Men for the Christian Ministry," confirmed the young graduate's "faith in the Gospel as a means of renovating human character and winning back human society to its proper allegiance to God." (A, 111)

A contemporary account of the graduation was provided by Julian in a letter[18] to his friend, Elizur Wright, who could not attend the ceremony because of his teaching duties at Groton, Massachusetts. Describing the various activities, Julian reported the consensus that the exercises were unusually interesting. The only unpleasant episode was the demand by officials that the brothers pay the balance they owed immediately. The "greedy" men were persuaded to wait until the youths received their quarterly salaries. (5 Oct.)

In letters to Elizur, Julian described his experiences in New Canaan and disclosed his own religious concerns. With the usual decline in enrollment in the autumn term, Ephraim had resigned to permit the appointment of a less qualified teacher at a lower salary. The work now was still laborious for Julian but not so demanding as in the summer. He had 41 pupils and expected several more. He deplored the dull routine of hearing recitations: "hic, haec, hoc, [and] 'twice two are four.'" Occasionally he flogged a "rogue." (28 Dec.) Sometimes he regretted that College days were over. Earlier, Julian had struck a brighter note. He had moved to a new boarding place and now enjoyed "good old fashioned living: beef, pork, pumpkin pie and pudding, etc., etc." (9 Nov.)

Julian's health was good and he spent evenings studying Hebrew. For a time he suspended that endeavor when his room-mate and assistant, B. Y. Messenger, engaged him in singing; Julian was surprised at his own progress. He planned also to study Ecclesiastical History; he was intent on pursuing his long-held commitment to become a minister. However, he informed Elizur, some good friends had advised him to forsake that cause and prepare for medicine. "The reason, you will readily guess, [is] the impediment in my speech." He continued: "I have been too long, I trust, sincerely devoted to the object of preaching the gospel to relinquish it without an experiment.... I wish no greater honor than to be a successful minister of Jesus." (9 Nov.) Whatever the problem was, there is no indication that it persisted to cause difficulty in preaching or public speaking, in both of which he was engaged throughout his life.

Sturtevant's personal faith was fervent and he was convinced that unless one feels the Gospel truth deep in his own being, he cannot preach the message of salvation. "Do we not need the preparation of the heart more than anything else? If our hearts are deeply affected by the truths of the Gospel, we shall be likely to tell the story of a crucified Saviour so that it will be understood and felt, but if not we shall have at last to reflect that we have labored in vain...." Julian believed that the faculty at Yale had failed to exemplify this lesson. However, "[Edward] Beecher, young as he was, ...was really worth a score of such men as Mr. Fitch for usefulness." (28 Dec.) Three references to Beecher indicate that Sturtevant knew him and held him in high regard.

In New Canaan the Sturtevant brothers had quickly become active in the Congregational Church, the only church functioning in the village at the time. Nearly everyone attended the services, including the young people, although the official membership was mainly from the older generation. The pastor, though kindly and devout, was "quite destitute of fresh thought." What was needed, Sturtevant observed, was a minister "capable of interpreting the gospel in the language of the present" and making it relevant to the needs of the time. (A, 110-11) Julian and Ephraim took the lead in bringing people to Christ. The meetings aroused great fervor, and most of the younger people, both single and married, committed themselves to Christ and joined the church.

Julian had been more blunt in characterizing the minister in writing to Elizur than in his later recollection. He deplored the man's lack of leadership and his indifference to people with anxious souls. Because of the minister, this place was a "valley of dry bones." (28 Dec.) Julian's strenuous efforts to fill the spiritual vacuum in the new Canaan Church were the major focus of his sixth letter. He described the situation for his friend: "Sinners are perishing and who shall care for them and tell them their danger. I often wish that I were prepared to discharge the sacred office." (25 Jan.) Even so, Julian attempted to fulfill the people's two great needs. He was encouraging people to meet for prayer and had even conducted one meeting. Also, he was teaching a Bible class, with 15 to 20, each week. Such duties were the responsibility of the minister, but he refused to fulfill them. Sturtevant felt that he was over-reaching, but he believed that God wanted him to do this work. He was eager to learn about Elizur's role in the religious life of Groton.

Julian's evangelistic concern extended into the classroom. His school program included Bible reading, prayers, and his own remarks about religion—all intended to encourage the students to seek salvation. On this subject also he inquired about Elizur's opinion.

When Ephraim left New Canaan, Julian realized that for the first time he was on his own, and the separation caused real pain. Ephraim had been his constant companion and closest friend. With his aid and example, Julian had gained not only experience but self-confidence; and, because Ephraim was more adept socially, he had helped Julian to overcome his shyness. A further deprivation was Julian's separation from Elizur Wright, whom he dearly loved and respected, and who, he believed, was also being prepared by God for Christian service. Julian sought to compensate for his loss of his companions through correspondence with them and with his family. He eagerly welcomed news from Tallmadge, whether directly from home or indirectly through Elizur. The *Portage Journal* kept him informed about events in northeastern Ohio.

Julian expressed some anxiety about Elizur's spiritual well-being, hoping that Elizur, now in Massachusetts, had not succumbed to the golden calf of Unitarianism. Julian had read an ironic report in the *New York Observer* which purported to praise Rev. Dr. [William Ellery] Channing of Boston for discovering that the whole world could become Christian. Channing [the founder of American Unitarianism] blamed Paul for being so unaccommodating as to erect barriers to conversion. Sturtevant implied that the solution Channing offered was simply to accept the ways of the world.

Sturtevant recalled that at Yale the ministerial students felt that they must mingle with the world. They did not show their Christianity except in prayer meetings and in Chapel—and there only on the Sabbath. He lamented the reluctance of Divinity students to express their calling openly. Expressing agreement with Wright that there had been temptations at Yale, he confessed that his own besetting sin was ambition. This he regarded as "destructive to the religion of the heart." (28 Dec.) He feared that as a teacher he would still be subject to this danger and that it could affect him as a minister also.

Once again, as at Warren and at Tallmadge, Julian Sturtevant experienced the worship and fellowship of a unified religious population. He reported, years later, that at New Canaan the seeds of faith were permitted to grow without striving to force people's religious inclinations through excessive revival meetings. In that harmonious setting, revivals were properly spontaneous and natural because there was no occasion for the rivalry of competing groups. For the first time, he was able to take an active role in evangelism. Sturtevant also gave notable service to the New Canaan Sunday School, organized in May 1827. A plaque installed in the church on the occasion of its two-hundredth anniversary in 1933 lists Julian's name at the head of the long succession of superintendents from 1827 to 1933.[19]

The strain of conscientious attention to his teaching duties combined with his zeal in Christian work exacted a heavy toll on

Julian Sturtevant's rather frail health. Reaching the point of exhaustion at the end of each day's tasks he sought to improve his health by taking an hour's walk each morning before breakfast. The strenuous exercise simply brought on fatigue early in the day and he ceased the long walks, concluding that any form of exercise or indeed any activity (including religious meetings) before breakfast was unwise. He regained his strength during the spring but the heavy load of the summer term once again weakened him and he found it necessary to hire a substitute. This enabled him to spend several weeks of quiet at Rockaway on Long Island where he recovered his health.[20]

Sturtevant drew some important conclusions about educational practice from his two years of teaching at New Canaan. Although the school had a strong reputation and the boys from it excelled at Yale College, he was painfully aware of its limitations. The range of age and ability among its pupils was far too great to permit one or even two teachers to be effective. There were so many subjects for so many different groups that recitations were necessarily brief, and time did not allow Julian to inspire the students in the Latin class with an appreciation of the genius of Cicero. Often students were too young to do justice to the abstract subjects required of them.

"By far the most important event" of Julian Sturtevant's years at New Canaan occurred when he met and fell in love with Elizabeth Fayerweather. He remarked in his *Autobiography* that meeting her was "among the most kindly provisions of God's providence in my behalf." (A, 118, 119) Elizabeth Maria Fayerweather was the second child of Richard and Hannah (Richards) Fayerweather. Born in 1806, she had one older sister, two younger sisters, and three younger brothers.

Richard Fayerweather was one of the proprietors of the Academy. He had served as headmaster although he was not a teacher. Although Julian did not report it, he boarded with the Fayerweather family and thus had the opportunity to observe Elizabeth rather closely without revealing any personal interest. She was a merry girl who had several boy friends, any of whom seemed to Julian—still somewhat diffident—to be more likely to win her favor than he. He had more reasoned causes for his reticence. While still at Tallmadge he had read a book which depicted a lofty conception of marriage.[21] His very first impression of Elizabeth was that she fulfilled the highest ideal of womanhood, but he wanted to be sure. Most importantly, he needed time to assess Elizabeth's religious views because his life plan required marriage to a woman who was in complete sympathy with his own convictions.

When Julian was at last satisfied that Elizabeth fulfilled all his expectations, he spoke to her about his love—nearly a year after they had first met. Elizabeth had been aware of his reserve and his declaration of love quite surprised her. Happily for Julian, she accepted his proposal of marriage. He then recorded the terms of their engagement, mutually agreed upon that fifth day of April 1827. He had seriously pledged his heart and his hand to Elizabeth "with no other condition than that of receiving hers in return." The cause of Christ was his first object and he avowed that "next to this it is and shall be my object to promote the comfort and happiness of my dear Elizabeth." Julian's proposal had been preceded by prayer and supplication for the direction of Heaven. His statement ended with the earnest petition: "May heaven [sic] grant that I may never prove untrue to such engagements."

Sturtevant praised Elizabeth as being "much riper in character" than himself and as possessing "sound and cool judgment" and "first-rate common sense." Elizabeth had gained an excellent education in the Academy under the teachers who had preceded Julian. Her mother's brother was president of Auburn Theological Seminary in New York. Elizabeth had been a house guest for lengthy visits in the home of another uncle, a businessman in New York City. Thus she had acquired "the larger ideas and cultivated tastes and manners of the city" as well as having experienced the village life of New Canaan. What brought the greatest joy to Julian Sturtevant was that "her heart was an inexhaustible fountain of affection." (A, 118-20)

Although Julian wanted to return to Yale for theological studies in the fall of 1827, he continued teaching at the Academy until the next April in order to improve his finances. The additional months of waiting were made more pleasant by his nearness to

Elizabeth. Fortunately, the smaller enrollment of the winter term also enabled him to gain excellent health.

Theological Heritage and Final Preparation

The religious milieu into which Julian Sturtevant was born and within which he was nurtured and educated was quite homogeneous. New England churches were overwhelmingly Calvinistic in theology and congregational in polity, although Episcopalians, Baptists, Presbyterians, and Quakers were present. Congregationalism originated in the mid-sixteenth century English Reformation which required outward conformity with the newly-independent Church of England. Some devout people became convinced that the Bible and conscience required a much more thorough reform of religious practice. Most of these were "Puritans" who, remaining within the national church, sought to reduce ritualism, restrict the sacraments to biblical precedents, and improve the quality of the clergy. Still others, believing that the Church of England did not conform to Scripture, organized their own congregations and were known as "Separatists." They regarded the true church as a group of faithful Christians joined by their voluntary profession of faith in Christ. They believed that the congregation itself had full power to select its pastor, set forth its Christian beliefs, conduct worship, and celebrate the Lord's Supper and baptism.

The Separatists were not permitted to practice their faith in England and some went to Holland where religious freedom was practiced. Eventually a group known as the Pilgrims made the hazardous ocean voyage to America and founded Plymouth Colony in 1620; their church government was congregational. A decade later a much larger group of Puritans settled at Massachusetts Bay and subsequently many more immigrated to Massachusetts and Connecticut. Their connection with the Church of England was attenuated by their remoteness from English bishops and the result was virtual independence. The Pilgrims and the Puritans shared the same basic Calvinistic theology, and over the next two centuries retained that doctrine while adopting congregational government, sometimes with Presbyterian modifications. The practical need for unity in order to sustain a settlement in precarious circumstances had resulted in the acceptance in several colonies of the principle of religious uniformity. In accord with Calvin's precedent, the civil government supported the churches' authority and provided for their financial needs by taxation. These were "established" churches, an arrangement which continued after the Revolution and was in effect in Connecticut until 1818 and Massachusetts until 1833.

The cornerstone of Calvin's theology was the belief in God's absolute sovereignty, with corollary beliefs in predestination, the utter depravity of man, and obedience to God's will. Divine sovereignty involved some thorny issues regarding freedom of the will, the role of the individual in his regeneration, and God's justice. Jonathan Edwards (1703-1758), pastor of the church in Northampton, Massachusetts, was the great American theologian of Calvinism. He profoundly influenced its application to the practical life of the parish by drawing upon John Locke's view of the senses as the basis of knowledge. This provided the rationale for accepting the conversion experience as essential to the Christian life. Revivalism greatly increased in New England as a result of Edwards' preaching and within a few years swept throughout the colonies. Known as the Great Awakening, the movement aroused great fervor in churches which had become complacent.

The American Revolution contributed to the weakening of New England's churches because their pastors were so much involved in supporting the cause of independence. Moreover, the protracted conflict contributed to a decline in morality. The French Revolution with its accompanying great social upheaval was another potent influence. Americans took a keen interest in the events occurring in France and some, including a large number of students at Yale, shared in the popular European skepticism. In the 1790s only a minority of the students in that college were avowed Christians, while many were outright skeptics who enjoyed calling each other "Diderot" and "Voltaire." Timothy Dwight, Yale's president from 1795 to 1817, restored the college's religious purity and also strengthened its academic qualities.

The religious renewal at Yale was part of the Second Great Awakening, which began in the 1790s and continued for decades. The preachers of the 1740s who conducted revivals up and down the eastern seaboard were itinerants with no responsibility for the continuity of the converts' participation. Their impassioned preaching had encouraged excesses of emotionalism and peculiar behavior. The leaders of the later revivals were careful to keep them under the direction of local pastors and to foster enduring commitment. Coincidental with the rise of the new nation, this revivalism exerted great influence. "It followed always expanding western frontiers, created evangelists of endless variety, multiplied churches of all evangelical Protestant denominations, founded theological seminaries and colleges, created home and foreign missionary boards, and wrote dramatic chapters in the history of religion in America." (Atkins, 128)

One of the most prominent leaders in this period was Lyman Beecher, Yale—Class of 1797, formerly minister of a Presbyterian church in New York and from 1810 to 1816 the pastor of the Congregational Church of Litchfield, Connecticut. Beecher had remarkable energy and organizational skills and carried on a campaign to preserve the vigor of the Congregational churches of Connecticut. He encouraged preachers who were settled pastors to conduct the revivals, sometimes by exchanging pulpits; he himself occasionally preached in the church at nearby Warren which the Sturtevant family attended. Standards were raised and only committed Christians were accepted as church members. Beecher implemented the Calvinistic concern for a righteous society through the activities of voluntary associations, organizations devoted to Sabbath observance, restraining intemperance, and numerous causes. He also promoted the publication of tracts, small leaflets based on sermons, which were widely distributed as a means of spreading the Gospel.

A given voluntary association united individuals from various evangelical churches who cooperated to fulfill a specific need. Notable examples were the American Bible Society (1816), the American Tract Society (1823), the American Sunday School Union (1824), and the American Education Society (1826). Sturtevant was to be involved to some degree in the work of all these agencies and others. The cause of home missions was greatly furthered when New England Congregational efforts were combined in 1826 with those of the Presbyterian Church and the Dutch

Reformed Church to form the American Home Missionary Society. Under that Society's auspices Sturtevant would come to Illinois to serve briefly as a home missionary and his colleagues would engage in extended service.

A major challenge to Congregationalism developed primarily in Massachusetts but had wide repercussions. In the early nineteenth century many pastors and churches along the Massachusetts seaboard embraced a Unitarian theology, thus separating from the tradition of Trinitarianism. Another theological threat came from Arminianism, which rejected the Calvinistic doctrines of total depravity and limited atonement while asserting a larger role for the individual in the process of spiritual regeneration. Organizational competition arose with the rapid growth of popular denominations such as the Methodists, Baptists, and Campbellites, a phenomenon characterized by Sydney Ahlstrom as the "Sectarian Heyday."[22]

These developments and the continuing widespread and fervent interest in religion constituted an exciting time in theological education. On 1 April 1828 Julian Sturtevant began his formal studies in Yale College's Theological Department. Yale was not only a convenient location but the school which would best prepare him for the kind of ministry he contemplated. President Dwight had shaped Yale profoundly and much of his legacy survived. He had been very successful in reviving devout faith among the students and brought about many conversions. Although unable to add theology to the professional programs in law and medicine, he bequeathed to Yale one of his own students, Nathaniel W. Taylor, who in 1822 was named the Dwight Professor of Didactic Theology. This appointment made the proposed theological school a functional reality. Taylor was the most important member of that faculty and served for thirty-six years.

First year theological students heard Taylor lecture on "Mental Philosophy" and middlers took his classes on moral philosophy, theology, revelation, and the exegetical study of the Scriptures. These students and the third-year seniors were included in the weekly debates of the Rhetorical Society over which he presided.[23] Taylor combined rigorous logic in his thinking with a very emotional presentation. He believed that the essential truths of Christian faith could be expressed in words meaningful to the hearer. He moved beyond the traditional in substantive issues also. Although his system was based on Jonathan Edwards' theology, Taylor stressed freedom of the will to the point of limiting God's sovereignty.[24] Opponents regarded the view that a person could assist in his own regeneration by attending church, reading the Bible and praying, and avoiding the knowing commission of sin, as simply adding pride to the already heavy burden of sin. Denying that, Taylor emphasized that people engaging in such "means" are more likely to undergo conversion.

Taylor's reputation for theological liberalism and his great influence on Congregational clergy were important in the later controversies between the Presbyterians and Congregationalists. He himself was tolerant and believed that Christian union was possible if based on the substance of faith without requiring agreement on every statement; he was correspondingly contemptuous of sectarianism.[25] Although opposed to slavery, Taylor was an anti-abolitionist, believing in gradual change and Negro colonization. In most of these matters Sturtevant's views were in sympathy with Taylor's. The chapter in Sturtevant's *Autobiography* entitled "Theological Seminary" is devoted almost completely to Taylor's views, and he acknowledged that Taylor's influence on him was greater than that of any other person. He held fast to certain of Taylor's teachings throughout his life but in his later years he took pains to distinguish himself from his great teacher. Among the very positive and lasting influences were Taylor's approach to subjects and his classroom methods. Taylor insisted that his students were to think for themselves and emphasized their freedom to question what he said.

Returning to New Haven in April 1828 Sturtevant entered a course of study already underway. Professor Taylor was "in the midst of his celebrated course of lectures on moral government." (A, 121) Sturtevant presumably was also attending Taylor's lectures on "Mental Philosophy" and other topics. Some understanding of psychology was basic to moral philosophy and theology, and the subject was of lifelong interest to Sturtevant. For Taylor and for

Yale's Old Brick Row
About 1830

Sturtevant the ultimate basis of morality is the intuition of the greatest good of all. Both were convinced that truth can be known and shared and that knowledge of theological truths is grounded upon mental intuitions as surely as knowledge of mathematical and scientific truths. The reassurance of such knowledge in religion was important to students who likely were aware of Kant's religious agnosticism and of the attacks of Enlightenment "infidels." It was also basic to imparting religious truth through preaching.

Sturtevant stressed that he himself had acted upon Taylor's injunction to think for himself and consequently, he said, he remodeled his "theologic house" many times. However, Sturtevant agreed wholeheartedly with his mentor that all sin is voluntary, that is, an act of will by the person. The alternative was to believe that God condemns men for evil inclinations. Having been brought up to believe that human nature was not totally corrupted by the fall, Sturtevant could share Taylor's judgment. Agreeing that a moral governor would certainly punish the incorrigible offender eternally, Sturtevant added that it is equally certain that God is propitious to the penitent sinner. Any moral system must include the strenuous effort for reform, and the most effective means for inducing repentance is the atonement brought through the sacrifice of Christ on the cross. Christ's death on the cross showed that God is both just (righteous) and the justifier.

A *Catalogue* published by the theological students in 1838 listed Sturtevant with the Class of 1830. The records of the Moral Society included Sturtevant and his later colleagues as members during their college years and as theological students. The topics of meetings in 1828 and 1829, which Sturtevant presumably attended, were recorded. The students debated whether foreign or home missions had the greater claim on American churches and weighed the merits of the American Education Society, the primary source of support for many of them. They considered whether preaching should be rousing or temperate. In the minutes for 23 April 1829 Sturtevant was named as one of four middlers debating the question, "Did the Old Testament Christians believe the future punishment of the wicked to be eternal?"[26]

The members of the Moral Society provided several hundred books for their own use. Beginning 23 October 1828 Sturtevant borrowed eleven books, among them Towgood's *Dissent from the Church of England*, two volumes of Neil's *History of Puritans*, and volumes on American missions and the book of Revelation. The Theological Athenaeum subscribed to the *Foreign Quarterly*, *North American Review*, *Journal of Science*, the *Western Intelligencer*, and numerous religious newspapers and magazines. A list of members as of January 1829 included the names of Sturtevant and most of his later colleagues in the Illinois band.[27]

Sturtevant enjoyed the environment at Yale because he was surrounded by "cultivated minds whose tastes and aims were in harmony with my own." (A, 121) Yale's curriculum was centered upon the theology of New England Calvinism as reinterpreted by Taylor, and Sturtevant found Taylor's courses inspiring and demanding. He later deplored Yale's lack of biblical studies, realizing that the living language of Christ and the record of those who saw Jesus and heard him speak could convey enthusiasm and meaning which theological terms could not. His health now was excellent, and his only problem was the financial stringency which required him to teach one to two hours a day in a school for girls, a severe drain on his time. When Sturtevant left Yale to come to Illinois, he did not mind interrupting his theological studies because he wished to be a teacher, not a pastor. However, throughout his life he preached often—on the average once a week, and sometimes several times a week—and was in demand as a speaker for many ecclesiastical occasions. He acknowledged that had he known how much preaching he would do, he would have sought to complete his formal theological education.

Organizing the Illinois Association

The rapid settlement of the West was characterized by the virtual absence of civilizing forces. The hardships and crude living conditions on the frontier reduced many people to a state of near-barbarism and the schools were too few and too inadequate to overcome it. The lack of organized churches and preachers of the Gospel in the frontier areas meant that there was no effective check on the spread of infidelity. Many perceived another threat to the achievement of Christian civilization in the vast territories beyond the Ohio. People in New England and the Mid-Atlantic States had great fear that the Roman Catholic Church would take over the West. Rev. Lyman Beecher had warned of the danger from "Romanism and the great incoming emigration from the countries of the old world."[28] The Jesuits especially were considered dangerous because of their zeal, their foreign connections, and their sponsorship of schools in areas where there were no alternative opportunities for education. American Protestants were keenly aware of the excesses of the medieval Catholic Church and the forcible repression of the Reformers and their heirs. Rome's continuing links with authoritarian governments in many European countries engendered the fear that similar arrangements would be sought in America.

Those who lived in or emigrated from New England considered their way of life as the appropriate model for the West for the sake of both pure religion and true patriotism. They saw the fulfillment of the great national destiny and the propagation of evangelical faith as inextricably linked. Sturtevant remarked that at the time "No portion of our whole population was more intensely alive to the vastness of the destiny which was opening before us than the churches of New England." Their members believed that "the valley of the Mississippi must be filled with an enlightened Christianity...."[29] The perceived obstacles to the "civilizing" of the West were not overcome quickly. Horace Bushnell, a prominent Hartford minister, declared in 1847 that barbarism was still the "first danger." He regarded Roman Catholicism as the next most critical threat, all the more because of the rapid increases in immigration.[30]

The period of intense religious fervor aroused by the Second Great Awakening had brought to Yale's Theological Department young men who were committed to serving God by preaching and teaching. No doubt, as Don Doyle avers, there was an oversupply of ministers in New England. (Doyle, 24-25) Even so, the question was not whether to serve but where; certainly many would have to seek distant fields. These students had a very real conviction of the reality of God and that, coupled with the belief that the eternal destiny of the present generation was in jeopardy, motivated them to preach the Gospel of salvation. The great missions to foreign lands had already begun. Sturtevant declared that the need in America was so great that he could not consider a foreign field. The evangelization of the West was not only a religious obligation but a patriotic duty. The institutions of Christian civilization were to be extended throughout America and indeed would produce a blessing to the world. The urgency of the need was described in Sturtevant's recollections twenty-five years later: "there was a nation to be founded in a single generation, institutions to be planted which should become the vital organs of a mighty people, and exert a saving influence on millions yet unborn."[31]

At the time the most effective aid for theological students in determining where to serve was the Society of Inquiry Concerning (or, Respecting) Missions, an organization on many campuses. The chapter at the Theological Department of Yale College was founded in 1825 and named the "Society for Christian Research." Its object was "to acquire and diffuse information respecting the promotion and extension of Christianity."[32] The group met monthly for prayers, Scripture reading, and a dissertation by a member. Three committees reported on foreign missions, domestic missions, and people of color, and a fourth engaged in correspondence with mission societies in Europe and America. From this Society a smaller and more focused group would emerge and take as its name, the "Illinois Association."

In 1827 Mason Grosvenor, newly graduated from Yale College, was a member of the Society's Committee on Domestic Missions. He was responsible for reporting on the Western section—all the states on the east and west banks of the Mississippi River. Grosvenor was no doubt present at the meeting on 27 November to hear a presentation on "Missions to the Western Settlements."[33] The idea of organizing a group to go somewhere in the West may have been planted in his mind at this time.

When Sturtevant joined the Society he was placed on its Standing Committee. As chairman for the 25 November 1828 meeting he gave the opening prayer. Then Theron Baldwin, Grosvenor's classmate, spoke with great fervor and power on the theme, "What can *I*, as an *individual*, do?"[34] He gave examples of the kind of commitment he urged upon his fellow students: Martin Luther, David Brainerd, John Henry Howard, and Samuel J. Mills. Meanwhile Grosvenor had been seeking information to guide him in selecting which portion of that vast Western territory should be considered. He turned to the current issues of *The Home Missionary and American Pastor's Journal*, published monthly by the American Home Missionary Society. The Society promoted cooperative evangelistic efforts in the West and maintained a voluminous correspondence with its agents in the field. Excerpts from the agents' letters, along with timely articles, were printed in the *Home Missionary*.[35]

A letter from the Reverend John M. Ellis in the December 1828 issue of the *Journal* attracted Grosvenor's attention. Ellis glowingly reported that he had found the ideal site for a "A Seminary of Learning" on a hilltop near Diamond Grove not far from Jacksonville, Illinois. The letter appealed for assistance and Grosvenor eagerly prepared a rough draft of a three-page letter to Ellis. Grosvenor had not previously confided in anyone about his plan but now, inspired by Baldwin's address, he revealed it to him that very evening and soon after he informed Elisha Jenney and Julian Sturtevant. In the revised letter mailed to Ellis, dated 5 December 1828, he stated that the subject of going to aid the West had been discussed. Moreover, a group of students "thought of forming an association consisting of eight or ten.... One of their first objects would be to establish a Seminary of Learning...." Grosvenor directed searching questions to Ellis about Illinois and the plans Ellis's group had made.[36]

The next step for Grosvenor and his few confidants was to determine who should be engaged in the project. From the outset the plan was to undertake the mission as an organized group and not as lone individuals. Sturtevant referred later in his sketch[37] of the New Haven group to "the known power of combined effort among kindred spirits." ("Records," 1) Institutions were regarded as essential to the permanence of any work which might be done. Those who preached but did not organize churches, and those who distributed tracts without establishing schools, left no significant traces despite their zeal and the considerable financial support provided them. Christian responsibility encompassed the western people's salvation for eternity but also the establishment of Christian civilization in the present. Churches, schools, and government were essential to converting the people of America and to evangelizing foreign lands. The Yale students felt keenly that God was placing on them "the responsibility of planting the institutions of the Gospel over all these vast regions."[38]

The Minutes of Yale's Society for Christian Research reveal that in October 1828 Sturtevant had been placed on the Committee on Domestic Missions. On 30 December Sturtevant was the "dissertator" and discussed "'certain considerations which often influence a Theological Student in selecting his field of labour.'" He named three: climate, which he deemed worthy of regard; the "State of Society, in respect to refinement & fashion" [perhaps "comforts and conveniences"], deemed "unworthy"; and "the means of intellectual improvement"—a concern not to be "wholly neglected."[39] Surely this presentation by Sturtevant was inspired by the fact that, unknown to most of his listeners, he and some of the other members were actively engaged in selecting their field of labor. Grosvenor had revealed his plan to only a very few. The plan of going to Illinois to start a school was in fact rather wild. Indeed, after it was made public an established clergyman ridiculed the idea of founding a college in such a remote place.[40] Illinois had achieved statehood only a decade earlier and as yet was almost unknown.

The interest which Sturtevant previously had displayed likely influenced Grosvenor in his decision to approach him as a possible recruit. Two other factors were also in Sturtevant's favor. He had actually lived in a frontier situation in Ohio, and he was a fine scholar and already had experience as a teacher. The decision was made very early that Sturtevant would be designated as the teacher in the new school.

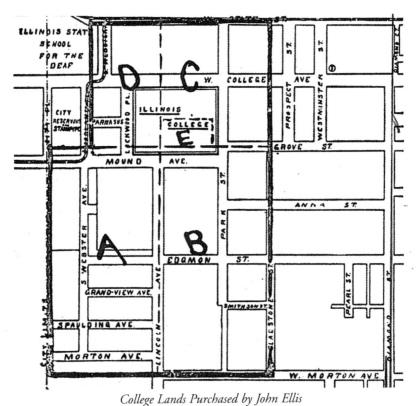

College Lands Purchased by John Ellis

Ellis purchased 227 acres even before he heard from the students at Yale. Five distinct parcels of land (designated by letters) were conveyed to the trustees by four deeds.

Baldwin, Jenney, and Sturtevant had responded with enthusiasm to Grosvenor's proposal. Correspondence was initiated with the officers of the American Home Missionary Society, which they hoped would provide direct financial assistance and, equally important, an endorsement which would facilitate raising money from church people in the East. Grosvenor went to New York during the January vacation to call on its officers and was given much encouragement. The four students then "began to think it was time to act. They held meetings, consulted together, and sought the direction of heaven." ("Records," 2) Soon "the association had taken form and personality," but no one had yet made a formal commitment. (A, 137)

Rev. John Ellis had previously organized stockholders in Jacksonville and the area to establish a seminary of learning. Some of the trustees arranged a day in early January 1829 to set the stakes for a building and as they rode by a house where Ellis was visiting he called out to them. He had just received Grosvenor's letter which he now read to the men on horseback. "You can't imagine how much it encouraged and animated us," Mr. Posey later told Mr. Lippincott. "It seemed to come to us from the Lord, in answer to prayer. We received it as such."[41] Relying on the judgment of the local men who could be consulted immediately, Ellis prepared an unofficial reply in response to Grosvenor's inquiries. The text of his first letter, dated 17 January 1829, survives in copied form in the "Records" (3) of the Yale group. Ellis began with the declaration: "Yours of Dec. 5 has been duly received and read with uncommon interest."

Responding to Grosvenor's questions, Ellis described the drastic need for schools in the West so that the people—many of them illiterate—would be able to read the Bible. He had selected Jacksonville as the location for his seminary because of the very favorable climate and the attractiveness of the site at Wilson's Grove. He emphasized that the aid of the New Haven group was most welcome, and he invited them to select Illinois as their western home. He gave assurance that it was by no means too late for them to have a major voice in the planning. Ellis promised to write the following week to provide information about the plans for the seminary.

The letters from Ellis were the only catalyst needed for the Yale men to form their association. Two other theological students accepted their invitation, John Brooks (a graduate of Hamilton College) and William Kirby (Yale, 1827). Grosvenor and Sturtevant drew up a constitution for their group, now called the "Howard Association."[42] A clue for explaining the selection of that name may be discerned in the man's career. An Englishman, John Howard (1726-1790) was motivated by his non-Conformist faith to devote his family wealth and his great energy toward social improvements, including elementary education, housing, and especially prison reform. Because they themselves were proposing to go far from their native New England, the Yale students were likely impressed by Howard's willingness to travel to several European countries in carrying out his Christian mission.

The stated object was "to promote the interests of Learning and Religion, by the preaching of the gospel and the establishment of a Seminary of Learning"—in a place to be determined. ("Records," 7) Certain conditions were set: that eight men be found to subscribe to this purpose, that the decision be made to establish the proposed seminary, and that adequate support be forthcoming. The Constitution was adopted in February 1829. Sturtevant summarized the need and the purpose. There was "a deep sense of the moral wants of the great Mississippi valley [and a desire] to extend to its inhabitants the blessings of education and a knowledge of the truth as it is in Jesus. The preaching of the gospel and the promotion of education were therefore at once selected as objects of prime importance...." Moreover, the students were convinced of "the importance of an immediate and extraordinary effort to save the souls of millions from eternal death, and our beloved country from overthrow and ruin...." Thus they would aim "a death blow at ignorance and sin, the twin foes of human improvement and happiness." ("Records," 1)

The students consulted with Professor Nathaniel Taylor and then held another meeting, on 21 February, for the six members to sign their Constitution and a Compact, formally agreeing to work together in Illinois. Julian Sturtevant had previously consulted with Elizabeth Fayerweather, who "cheerfully approved." His covenant with Elizabeth was intended to be lifelong, and similarly the Compact bound him for life to fulfilling its purpose. (A, 138) Such long-term commitment was standard for a Congregational minister who, upon being installed by a church as pastor, would serve until his death.

The text of the Compact, a paragraph-long sentence, is important because it was the theological rationale for the mission of the Howard Association. The initial phrase expressed belief "in the entire alienation of the natural heart from God" and "the necessity of the influences of the Holy Spirit for its renovation." Such influences were acknowledged to be aided by the use of "means," which were not stated but were understood to include Scripture reading, prayer, and especially preaching.[43] The destitute condition of the West was acknowledged as placing an urgent claim upon those in the East. The "fearful crisis evidently approaching" could only "be averted by speedy and energetic measures on the part of the friends of religion and literature in the older states." [The crisis included the threats of infidelity, barbarism, and Catholicism.] The signers expressed their conviction that "evangelical religion and education must go hand in hand in order to the successful accomplishment of this desirable object." They were therefore ready to go to Illinois to establish "a seminary of learning" and to preach in "important stations in the surrounding country." Their plan was subject to the requirements of practicality and to the permission of the Providence of God.[44]

Two days later Nathaniel Taylor and his colleague, Josiah Gibbs (Professor of Sacred Literature), added their endorsements. They certified that the plan had their "entire and cordial approbation." They declared that it was "of vital importance, to the best civil and religious interests of that portion of our country...." They further stated that the men undertaking this mission were highly qualified with respect to "ardent piety," "laborious perseverance," and "talents and literary acquisitions." President Jeremiah Day added his signature with the notation that he fully concurred in the faculty recommendations. He was "familiarly acquainted with a majority of the Gentlemen and [had] satisfactory information concerning the others." The plan, and the endorsement of these men and other theology professors, ministers, and prominent laymen, were printed in the East.[45]

The business of the Association was carried forward speedily. Mason Grosvenor was elected as secretary and John Brooks as treasurer, while Sturtevant was delegated to seek advice regarding the practicality of the plan. He was in New York by 28 February for a meeting with the Reverend Absalom Peters, executive of the American Home Missionary Society, and with clergy and lay leaders who supported that Society. These men were members of the Presbyterian and Dutch Reformed Churches; at the time no Congregational ministers were in public positions in the area. The plan received enthusiastic and unanimous approval, and promises were made that generous support would be forthcoming for such a cause. Sturtevant returned from his successful trip by 4 March. Reports of the various committees were received at a meeting held on that date and the members now regarded themselves as obligated to proceed. Grosvenor and Sturtevant were appointed to draft a proposal for the union of their Association with the trustees in Illinois and three days later the statement was adopted. An appropriate letter was sent to Ellis on 9 March, by which date the recruitment of an additional member, Asa Turner, had increased the number to seven.[46] The New Haven group declared its approval of the arrangements stated by Ellis, including the proposed location.

On the advice of their teachers, the Yale men set forth two general principles regarding the organization of the school in Illinois. A limited number of trustees would have complete control over the seminary, and that board would fill any vacancies by majority vote. The number of trustees should be limited to fifteen, although only ten would be named for the present. Of these, three were to be elected by the Illinois stockholders and the other seven would be the members of the Association. More detailed terms were also stated. The New Haven group would provide $10,000, $2,000 when the union should be effected and the balance within two years. The various testimonials of the Yale faculty were included with the letter, a copy of which was sent to Peters who was requested to write a supporting letter to Ellis. On 31 March the Howard Association met to authorize Baldwin, Sturtevant, and Turner to go to Illinois in the autumn, and in mid-April the three were commissioned as agents of the American Home Missionary Society.[47]

The arrangements between the two widely-separated parties proceeded smoothly and with amazing rapidity. All were convinced that the whole procedure was favored by the providence of God, and there was indeed a remarkable convergence of purpose and even of plan. The letter of 9 March from the Association at New Haven reached Jacksonville by 6 April and also a letter from Peters. A call was issued for those Illinois stockholders who could be summoned quickly and a message was prepared: "we cordially and fully approve of the principles and terms of the proposed union...." ("Records," 21) An official meeting of the Seminary stockholders was arranged for 18 April at which time the preliminary acceptance was affirmed by formal vote.[48] These men expressed their hope that the seminary in Jacksonville would serve well "all classes of American Patriots and Christians." ("Records," 22)

Ellis had written that during his forthcoming trip to the East he planned to visit the men in New Haven. He arrived there on 19 June, accompanied by Peters, and they and Professor Taylor met with the Association. Ellis presented the letters reporting the favorable response of the Illinois stockholders and the Yale men declared their "unwavering determination to cooperate." ("Records," 25) The Association had earlier directed Sturtevant to write the "sketch" of its history in their large bound "Records" book. Once both parties had formally approved the plan for union, the Yale men changed the name to reflect their destination. In half a dozen places in the "history" the name Howard was crossed out and "Illinois" was written above it. The first use of the new name was in the minutes for June 1829. ("Records," 24)

Ellis was asked to serve as their agent in the East, with the proviso that any funds raised were to be counted toward the promised $10,000. Several men met with him at Andover on 25 June to hear his report on the arrangements made in Illinois. A "Circular," dated 1 August 1829, and with an accompanying sub-scription list, was issued to publicize the proposed college in Illinois.[49] The importance of the Mississippi valley and its expected great population was stressed. The character of a people was said to be dependent chiefly on their institutions and therefore there was a compelling duty to establish those institutions which promote learning and religion. The school, to be known as "ILLINOIS COLLEGE," was carefully planned. A beautiful site had been selected near Jacksonville, "a flourishing town." Rev. Dr. Lyman Beecher was among those who cordially approved this project "to promote the interests of learning and religion, and give to these an early and decided influence on the rising institutions of the West." Further publicity was given by the *New York Statesman* (20 Oct. 1829) with a column headed "ILLINOIS COLLEGE." The account included the text of the Circular and a list of prominent men who endorsed the plan. Similar notices were no doubt print-ed by other newspapers in Boston and elsewhere.

Members of the Illinois Association, assisted by Ellis and Peters and others, visited many cities and churches in the East in quest of funds for their enterprise. The response was favorable, and sufficient funds were received by the end of August to enable Baldwin and Sturtevant to arrange their travel to the West. For reasons of health Turner did not accompany the others and delayed until 1830. The solicitation in the East was continued, Ellis having a major role because he could speak with the authority of one who knew the West first-hand. He addressed a meeting in New York City on 30 September which resulted in an additional two thousand dollars in subscriptions.[50] Ellis remained in the East almost until the end of the year. A significant consequence of the fund-raising appeals was that people in the East were informed about the opportunities in the West, and over the next few years thousands were encouraged to emigrate to that vast and still almost-unknown region.

Chapter 2: 1829-1833

The Early Years of Illinois College

Settling in Jacksonville, Illinois

Julian Sturtevant and Theron Baldwin were ordained on 28 August 1829 at Woodbury, Connecticut, in a joint service sponsored by the South [Congregational] Association of Litchfield County.[1] The charge to the candidates was given by a Presbyterian pastor representing the American Home Missionary Society. As an ordained minister Sturtevant was now authorized to fulfill all pastoral duties, and the very next Sabbath he preached in the New Canaan church. The congregation that day was large, his many friends listening with an attentiveness he modestly attributed to their great indulgence.

The wedding of Julian Sturtevant and Elizabeth Fayerweather took place before breakfast on 31 August 1829, in the parlor of the bride's home in New Canaan. As in other situations when momentous decisions were involved, Sturtevant experienced deep anxiety, this time because he had asked Elizabeth to enter upon an uncertain life in far-distant Illinois. The occasion was saddened by the absence of Elizabeth's mother, who had died some months before. Elizabeth's wedding garment was her traveling dress and after breakfast the newly married couple set out for a round of farewell visits. They went to Warren, where Julian's uncle, Joseph Tanner, was living. Julian attended the commencement at Yale and was awarded the Master's degree, customarily granted after three years in recognition of further study or professional activity.[2] After a final round of farewells at New Canaan the young couple set out.

The Sturtevants traveled by stage, canal boat, river steamer, and carriage, crossing New York State via the "Pioneer Line" because its schedule allowed passengers to observe the Sabbath. They enjoyed a view of Niagara Falls and a boat ride across the river below the Falls before proceeding to Buffalo for the Sabbath. Their next destination was Tallmadge, Ohio, to visit Julian's parents; he had returned to see them only once since leaving for Yale in 1822. Sturtevant treasured the visit and rejoiced that his parents now lived in a comfortable frame house, which he had helped them to purchase. They saw his brother Ephraim, who after a year of teaching at Western Reserve College had become principal of the Tallmadge Academy, and also his friend, Elizur Wright Jr. The newly-weds spent nearly a month at Tallmadge before resuming their travel.

River traffic in the late fall was hampered by low water and the next phase of the journey was made by stage to Wheeling. From there a steamboat on the Ohio River brought them first to Louisville, where they spent the Sabbath, and then to Cairo, Illinois. From that point their steamer plied its way to St. Louis against the current of the Mississippi. It is not clear from Julian's account when Theron Baldwin joined them, but according to Baldwin's notes he had been with them when they left New Haven in September.[3] At any rate they were together for the last part of the trip. On a Sabbath while they were en route the two young ministers conducted religious services, with Sturtevant preaching the sermon. A youthful passenger was surprised to discover that the preacher was the very man he had warned to be on good behavior because there was a minister on board.

Christian friends in St. Louis provided New Testament hospitality for the weary travelers. The lack of regular transportation to Jacksonville made it necessary to hire a driver and hack. In St. Louis they met James Edwards of Boston who, accompanied by his wife and her sister, was coming to Jacksonville to start a newspaper. The carriage had room for only four people and it was decided that the Sturtevants and the two women would travel in it. Edwards and Baldwin were to follow after obtaining horses and a wagon.

At mid-day on a Thursday in November the Sturtevant party was ferried across the Mississippi and that night they lodged in a house across the river from the mouth of the Missouri. Their accommodations were comfortable enough although, to the dismay of the ladies, only one room was available; however, the food was wholesome and ample in quantity. The next night a log house south of Carrollton provided neither good food nor comfortable beds. Even so the travelers were unprepared for the third night's unexpected stay. They had hoped to reach Jacksonville Saturday evening but their vehicle became stuck in a mudhole and they were forced to stay overnight with a large family in a cabin seven miles south of the village. Because Sturtevant was a minister the hostess insisted that he and his wife should have the only bed. Their host and a neighbor helped the driver and Sturtevant free the carriage, and early the next morning the travelers completed their journey.

Most of the details about the trip were recorded years later in Sturtevant's *Autobiography*. A contemporary report is in "Extracts from Letters from the West," copied by Asa Turner for colleagues at the East from letters written by Baldwin and Sturtevant. Dating his letter at Illinois College, 10 April 1830, Sturtevant addressed his "Dear Brethren of the Ill. Association." Despite the hardships of the trip he gave an encouraging report. "My rout [*sic*] here was to N. York, Albany, Niagara, Portage Co. Ohio, Wheeling Va., [the] Mouth of the Ohio, & St. Louis, making in all 2200 miles.... We always chose the best conveyances & best houses & consequently the highest prices, but not withstanding all this it cost us a little less than $75 each to perform the whole Journey." The sum of $150 was more than a third of a year's salary for a missionary in the West.

It was still early on Sunday morning, 15 November 1829, when the Sturtevants and their companions reached the village of Jacksonville. They were greeted warmly by Mrs. Ellis, whose husband, the Reverend John M. Ellis, was pastor of the Presbyterian Church. She informed Sturtevant that he was expected to conduct the morning service because her husband was away on an extended preaching mission. After a hearty breakfast and family worship Mrs. Ellis, carrying her year-old son, led the way across the muddy ground to the makeshift meeting house. The only place in Jacksonville for public worship was "a miserable log school house 20 ft. square, with no speaker's desk and floors and seats made of puncheons and generally occupied alternately by Methodists and Presbyterians, then the only churches in the place."[4] The people were attentive despite the new preacher's use of a manuscript and the discomfort of the crude seats. The Sturtevants were invited to dinner by Dr. and Mrs. Hector Taylor and subsequently made their home with that family for the winter.

The town of Jacksonville had been surveyed in 1825 and by the end of that year the first settlers and shopkeepers were established.[5] Writing a few weeks after his arrival, Sturtevant described Jacksonville and the surrounding area for his friend, Elizur Wright.[6] The village was in a county where the first white habitation had been built only ten years before. It had 500 to 600 inhabitants, living in 80 to 100 homes. More than half the houses were built of logs, the remainder—except for one brick house— were of frame construction with outside chimneys. The court house then being constructed in the public square was also of brick.

The area was "exceedingly beautiful," bordered by creeks and timber, and with a fine grove on the long ridge on which the College building was located. Indeed, Sturtevant was "highly gratified" with the situation. His early account was tempered in his late years by the memory that the village itself was very unattractive; any beauty in the area was the work of God, not man. In mid-November the prairie was clad "in the sombre brown of autumn, with scarce a tree or shrub to relieve the monotony." The land was flat in all directions except to the west, where there was "an elevation, which a New Englander might almost recognize as a hill." That hill was "crowned with a natural grove [and] against the front of the grove was already projected an edifice of brick, which…made an appearance of considerable dignity and magnificence." The "edifice" was the college building then under construction.[7]

Writing to Elisha Jenney, Sturtevant reported that "The soil is a rich black mould 2 feet deep on the top of Coll. hill, producing wheat, Indian corn, oats, flax, Irish and Carolina potatoes, and even cotton in its perfection and with little labour. The timber is Oak, Hickory, Butternut, Black Walnut, Sugar Maple, Cherry, Ash…." He continued: "Excellent land may be had in this part of the state and in any quantity," at prices from $1.25 per acre a few miles away to $6 to $10 in the vicinity, but only at very high prices in the village itself. Food was plentiful and cheap. ("Extracts," 24 Mar.)

Along with glowing descriptions of the abundance of good land and water, Sturtevant insisted, warnings must be given to prospective emigrants in the East of the rudeness of frontier life. They would have to endure poor housing, remoteness from friends and familiar scenes, and a population prejudiced and ignorant and jealous of Yankees. Most homes consisted of only a single room, and the schools were often but a mockery. Even so, he wrote, "there exists here no serious barrier to the enjoyment of life…." A mere forty acres would provide a livelihood with astonishingly little labor. "As to the prospects for supporting a family here nobody but Presbyterian Ministers need apprehend any difficulty…." ("Extracts," 10 Apr., 3 Apr.)

During the continued absence of Rev. Ellis, Sturtevant at the request of the Presbyterian Church served as pastor during his first seven weeks in Jacksonville. In a letter to Rev. Absalom Peters he emphasized the need for schools so that the people would respond to an educated ministry. There was no shortage of preachers—indeed, there were an estimated sixty or more in Morgan County. Virtually all of them were ignorant of the Bible and Christian doctrine. They engaged in "boisterous and a thousand times repeated exhortations." Sturtevant declared that "if we cannot elevate the intellectual character of this people we can never succeed in the great objects we would aim to accomplish in the West."[8]

Ellis returned to Jacksonville by New Year's Day, 1830, bringing the welcome news that the New Haven Association had reached its goal of $10,000 in subscriptions. (S-EW, 1 Jan. 1830) Sturtevant was relieved of the pastoral responsibilities at the Presbyterian Church in time to assume his teaching duties at the College in early January. However, he continued to preach, now at various neighborhoods in the area, including Jersey Prairie. He spoke warmly of the invitations from different denominations of Christians who were eager to hear the Gospel. Sturtevant had reminded Peters that he had received an advance of $100 toward his first year's salary of $400. He believed that the initial seven weeks of full-time missionary activity and the subsequent supply preaching amounted to somewhat more than one quarter's labor and he hoped that his "debt" might be canceled. His College duties, he wrote, would not permit him to engage in missionary labor on a regular basis.

The Sturtevant family worshipped with the Presbyterians. The New Canaan Church had issued a letter of dismissal for Mrs. Elizabeth Sturtevant to the Presbyterian Church in Jacksonville. She apparently maintained her membership there until her death in 1840. From their limited resources Sturtevant pledged several dollars toward the pastor's support; most of the other pledges were similarly modest in size. He also joined others in that Church in contributing to the cause of home missions, a proud achievement for a church which had just become self-supporting.

Founding Illinois College, 1829

The local trustees met twice with the two representatives of the New Haven Association, as those in the town often called it. The first time, Rev. J. M. Sturtevant opened the meeting with prayer, and the second time, Rev. Theron Baldwin. Arrangements were made for classes to begin on 4 January 1830, and the stockholders were notified to meet on December 18th. Baldwin returned to the Vandalia church but then made the long horseback ride to Jacksonville. He and Sturtevant and the local trustees convened on the appointed date in Seminary Hall (soon re-named the "College Building" and later called "Beecher Hall"). The men from New Haven read a letter authorizing them to represent the Illinois Association. They had brought $2,000 with them, and the terms of union previously agreed to were now formally adopted. For the present the Board would consist of the seven Yale men and three trustees chosen by the Jacksonville stockholders; Samuel Lockwood, John Wilkinson, and William Posey were elected. A motion was made to name the school "Illinois College" and without discussion or delay a unanimous vote of approval was taken. A prayer was offered by Sturtevant and the stockholders adjourned.

In his 1844 historical account Sturtevant reported the naming of the school without comment but he later emphasized that the resolution to designate it "Illinois College" was passed "certainly without any consultation with me." *(A, 165)* The tone of his statement suggests some dissatisfaction with the procedure if not the result. The name should not have been a surprise to Sturtevant. The Circular with the subscription list, used in the East, was dated 1 August 1829—-more than a month before his departure. That form stated that the school was "to be called the ILLINOIS COLLEGE."9

The earlier proposal of the Jacksonville trustees (Jan. 1828) was entitled "Outline of a Plan for the Institution of A Seminary of Learning in the State of Illinois." Subsequent references in the minutes of the Illinois stockholders designated the school as the "Institution" or the "seminary." "Seminary" implied a program of instruction beyond elementary schooling, including college preparation for some and practical studies for others; it was expected that college studies would be offered later.10

The naming of the new college was the final act of the stockholders of the "Jacksonville Seminary." The three newly elected trustees went with Baldwin and Sturtevant to a home for the first meeting of "The Trustees of Illinois College." The new Board elected Lockwood president and Wilkinson treasurer and appointed Sturtevant as secretary. Detailed plans were outlined for the classes and for appropriate public announcements about the opening of the school. Sturtevant was named Instructor *pro tempore*. In accord with views expressed both by Ellis's group and the Yale men, the College was to be open to all Christians.

From their arrival onward Sturtevant and Baldwin were the key members of the Illinois Association with regard to its educational purpose. Both also contributed significantly to its evangelistic aims, Baldwin serving as a home missionary for several years. The other members of the Association meanwhile completed their theological studies and by the end of 1833 all except one had reached Illinois to assist the College—some briefly, some at length; a few as professors or tutors, several as trustees; and most as pastors and home missionaries who were advocates for the school. Remarkably, the one whose arrival was long delayed was Mason Grosvenor, who had conceived the plan!

The plans and efforts of John Ellis and the local trustees were crucial to the success of the joint enterprise. Had it been necessary for the New Haven men to search for a site, cultivate an interest in a "foreign" proposal, and organize local support, their mission would have been seriously delayed. Ellis had persisted in his purpose to establish a school, and he had obtained the site in Morgan County. He carefully organized supporters in the area and issued a persuasive appeal for help. Not waiting for an answer, the Seminary trustees made plans for constructing a two-story brick building on almost the very day that Baldwin had delivered his stirring challenge.

Spanning a vast distance, the eastern and the western groups—when still unknown to each other—had shared a common faith and a common purpose. The entire proceedings which led to the establishment of Illinois College on December the 18th in 1829 were accomplished with deliberate speed and remarkable efficiency. Less than thirteen months elapsed between Baldwin's inspiring speech and the founding of Illinois College, and less than three weeks later the first classes were held. Grosvenor's vision had become a reality, and the Illinois mission had begun.

The establishment of the College was a matter of great interest, and indeed, "all sorts of interest," in the state. In a letter to Elizur Wright, Sturtevant reported that it was already obvious that the public was divided in its response. "Some look upon it with sneering contempt—some with bitter opposition, and we believe not a few hail it as the harbinger of better days to Illinois." Men in the community not only gave to the Presbyterian Church but also made subscriptions to the College. Sturtevant rejoiced in being engaged in this noble work. (S-EW, 1 Jan. 1830)

Instruction Commenced

Illinois College opened for instruction on 4 January 1830 in Seminary Hall. Erecting the stove and starting a fire were necessary preliminaries to the opening exercises, held in the presence of William Posey and nine students. After reading from the Bible Sturtevant briefly addressed the young men. Declaring, "we are here to-day to open a fountain where future generations may drink," he offered a prayer "committing the whole enterprise for the present and the long future to the care and protection of God." *(A, 166)*

College Building
(1829-1830)
(Note south entrance)

Decades later one of those first students published his remembrances in the student newspaper. Rev. C. B. Barton, Class of 1836, had become acquainted with Rev. Sturtevant upon his arrival in Jacksonville. The young boy had just lost his father and Sturtevant was his "comforter, counsellor, and friend." Moreover, Sturtevant aroused his "aspirations" for an education, and many other youths were likewise influenced to undertake "an independent course of investigation, decision and devotion...." (ICCR, 13 Mar. 1886, 6) Sturtevant, in the course of his pastoral work, had frequent opportunities to inform people about the new College. Five of the first students came from Morgan County (then much larger) and four from counties to the south, a region where John Ellis had ministered earlier.

Not one of the pupils who met with Sturtevant that cold January morning was prepared for college studies. There was no school system in Illinois and children received whatever education they had from their parents or from itinerant teachers in sessions of varying quality and length. A few of the nine boys had studied some Latin and perhaps half of them hoped to become ministers. For a year and a half the College served as a grammar school and academy; only in 1831 would any students be qualified for the

freshman class. Three among the original nine earned the baccalaureate degree in 1836 and a fourth in 1838; the others never
graduated. During the first year thirty to forty students enrolled
although many remained only a short while. Sturtevant evaluated
the boys' qualifications for admission and selected the textbooks
to be loaned to them. In class he provided students with examples
from English literature of fine writing and lofty thoughts. He
arranged (with Ellis) for their physical exercise. On duty at
Seminary Hall from nine to four, he then carried work to the
home, a mile distant, which he and his wife shared with the
Taylors. There he conducted the College's correspondence and
managed other business.

The boys had to find temporary quarters because the rooms on
the second floor of Seminary Hall were not yet ready. The distance
they had to travel from the village concerned Sturtevant, and he
deplored the high charges they paid to live with families in town.
By spring vacation the plastering was finished and four upstairs
apartments were available, each with a sitting room and bedroom.
One room was used for the library of one thousand volumes.
Science apparatus was also stored there but no space was available
for maps. The single large room on the first floor was for worship
and classes. Posey and Ellis determined what additional space was
needed and Sturtevant was authorized to confer with a builder. In
March a contract was approved for doubling the size of Seminary
Hall and for a frame building for boarding both students and
teachers.[11] The north addition was intended to house twenty-five
students or, in an emergency, thirty-five to forty. Sturtevant was
overseer of construction. The materials for the boarding house were
provided by the College and the work was done by students, some
of whom knew carpentry. A near-by log cabin was acquired to house
a family who provided meals for students at one dollar a week.

Money and workmen were scarce and the College adopted a
plan of manual labor in vogue in Europe.[12] Students could defray
their expenses by working two to three hours a day, either on
College farmland or in a College workshop. Seminary Hall was
surrounded by more than two hundred acres well-suited to cultivation. (The College's land encompassed most of the area presently
bounded by State and Morton and by City Place and Gladstone.)

In early April Sturtevant reported good progress in the system of student labor, although only five acres were under cultivation. Illinois soil required different farming methods; the hoe was almost useless and the plow was a necessity. During the April vacation Sturtevant rode eighty miles on horseback to spend a week at Vandalia consulting with Baldwin. The extended conference set the pattern for their long association in developing policy and making practical decisions.

Meanwhile the Sturtevants acquired a "home" of their own. Julian had taken Elizabeth to look at a rude log cabin which would be more convenient to his work and would relieve them from the crowded quarters they had in the Taylors' home. Upon seeing the cabin Elizabeth burst into tears. Recovering her composure, she agreed to the arrangement and by late March they were "keeping house in a little log house close by [the] college and college grove." ("Extracts," 24 Mar.) They were very happy despite the poor accommodation, and their happiness was increased when their son, to whom they gave Julian's name, was born on 7 June 1830. The spring weather was especially bad and Elizabeth, seriously ill, had to be nursed back to health by the patient care of Mrs. Edwards and Mrs. Lockwood. In October Sturtevant informed Baldwin that "Our little family are now in health. The 'young Prof.' is flourishing finely." (S-B, 4-7 Oct. 1830)

An earlier plan for Sturtevant to utilize an eight-week summer vacation for home missionary work was canceled in favor of continuing instruction at the College. Some help was provided by an able young lawyer who heard recitations, and with his help the first partial year of instruction was brought to an impressive close. The local *Western Observer* (21 Aug. 1830) announced the first annual examination for 25 August at 9:00 A.M. in the College's public hall, adding that "The friends of literature are cordially invited to attend." A visitor expressed amazement that such exercises could be carried out in a new country. Mr. Sturtevant, he said, conducted the examination "with life and animation…so that what is usually dull and tedious, was rendered attractive and interesting." The pupils were examined in basic subjects and in the classical languages, and then they presented original compositions and declamations. The writer commended the choral presentation of an anthem, "Strike the Cymbal," sung by the students—with some assistance.[13]

In early August arrangements were announced for the first full year of classes. Students could now obtain lodging in the College Building for twenty dollars per year for the combination sitting room (with fireplace) and bedroom; two to four occupants could divide the rental. A student association whose members furnished their own provisions employed a family to do their cooking and washing for 83 cents weekly. The College boarding house was to provide meals for $1 per week but the facility was not ready even by late November. The three terms of fourteen or fifteen weeks were to begin in September and end in August; vacations were at Christmas, in April, and after mid-August. The trustees emphasized their intention to make the school live up to its name as a *college*. The "English Course" included geography, history, mathematics, English grammar and rhetoric, and practical subjects such as surveying and bookkeeping. The "Collegiate Course" featured Latin, Greek, and higher mathematics. Frequent exercises in composition and declamation, and experimental lectures in chemistry and natural philosophy (physics), would be available to all students. "Globes and maps of the best kind, and a respectable library [were] already in the Institution."[14]

The curriculum instituted by Sturtevant and his colleagues was modeled after Yale's. Classes were held in each of the three major subject areas every day so that "the different powers of the mind will be cultivated in their due proportions, and a proper equilibrium secured."[15] The wording of the statement reflects familiarity with the *Yale Report of 1828*,[16] prepared as a reply to critics who argued for more practical studies. The *Report* acknowledged that improvements were needed and pointed out that the newer sciences and political economy were now taught. Yale's retention of the "dead languages" [Greek and Latin] was a deliberate decision in the interest of superior education. The central thesis was stated thus: "The ground work of a thorough education, must be broad, and deep, and solid.... The two great points to be gained in intellectual culture, are the *discipline* and the *furniture* of the mind; expanding its powers, and storing it with knowledge. The former of these is, perhaps, the more important of the two…. The habits of thinking are to be formed, by long continued and close application." (278) The classical program provided a common education for both professional and civic leaders, especially important for America's republican government. The ancient languages were deliberately retained as the best means to achieve a superior education. The *Report* resulted in the maintenance of the classics at Yale for the rest of the century. (Hofstadter, 1:278,276) Likewise preferring gradual change, Illinois College retained the classics until 1956.

Regular assistance with instruction was an obvious need by the fall of 1830 but the Association members in the East were unable to find a man to teach Greek and Latin. Some relief was provided for Sturtevant by the appointment of a steward to manage the farm, oversee the students' labor on the campus, and supervise the boarding establishment. The new College also needed a president and in May 1830 Sturtevant and Lockwood relayed the trustees' request to the men still in the East to choose the candidate. In August the Association elected Edward Beecher, a choice pleasing to Sturtevant because he knew Beecher well. Edward, the son of Lyman Beecher, graduated from Yale in 1822, the year Sturtevant enrolled as a freshman. He was a tutor at Yale and, after ordination, became pastor of the Park Street Church in Boston in 1826. Beecher's acceptance was dated 8 November 1830 and he arrived in Jacksonville in December. He proceeded to Vandalia to obtain a charter from the state legislature, but the petition was refused. Some legislators suspected a plot by land speculators and others believed the Presbyterians were seeking to gain control of the state. Sturtevant formally introduced Beecher to the Jacksonville trustees on 23 February 1831 and relinquished his own seat on the Board; there were to be only seven trustees from the Illinois Association. However, Sturtevant met regularly with the trustees as secretary for extended periods. Beecher went east with Baldwin in the spring in quest of additional funds and did not return until the next year. In his absence Sturtevant was acting president, a responsibility he would have more than once.

The enrollment grew considerably during the year of 1830-1831 and an estimated fifty to sixty students were present at one time or another. During the winter of 1831 Sturtevant was aided by Lucien (Lucian) Farnham, a graduate of Andover Seminary (Massachusetts). He became a member of the Illinois Association upon accepting its mission.[17] That spring William Kirby, one of the original seven, arrived and served as a tutor for two years. Failing health compelled him to resign and accept assignment as a home missionary. He was a faithful trustee until his death.

The first full year of instruction was celebrated by the "Annual Exhibition of Illinois College" on 17 August 1831, in conjunction with the trustees' meeting. The "Order of Exercises" began at ten o'clock with prayer and sacred music, followed by ten student declamations. Next were five original essays on such topics as "Dueling" and the "Character of the North American Indians." The three o'clock program included sacred music and seven student essays and concluded with more music and prayer. The prospect of having a few students qualified for freshman courses encouraged the trustees to appoint Sturtevant to the rank of Professor of Natural Philosophy and Mathematics in February 1831. He was allowed $500 for his services for the past year and $400 for the present year, plus boarding and house rent, and in addition, $100 for "extra & peculiar services rendered in behalf of the College." (TM, 24 Feb. 1831) Those services included supervising the completion of the south half of the College Building and the erection of the north half in 1830. He was on the committee which drew up the Code of Laws for governing the College. He helped to procure livestock and the necessary farm implements. Living quarters for Beecher and the Sturtevants were provided in the College Building; all were entitled to meals in the College dining room. Beecher's salary was set at $600.

In the spring of 1832 Edward Beecher returned to Jacksonville, bringing his family with him. The public was invited to his inauguration as president on 14 August. The guest speaker was John Russell, a pioneer in the region; a man of exceptional abilities, including fluency in several classical and modern languages, he delivered his address in Latin. Both Beecher, and Sturtevant who was inaugurated as professor, delivered speeches.[18] Both men pledged to discharge their duties faithfully and to uphold the Constitution of the United States and the laws of the State of

Dormitory
(1832-1833)
The Sturtevants lived in the South Wing (left), the Beechers in the North Wing. The
main building and North Wing burned in 1852. "Beecher" Hall is in background, right.

Illinois. The annual commencement was held the next day, when
"pieces original and selected" were presented. Fellow citizens were
respectfully invited to attend the examination of the students on
the following day.

A Four-Story Dormitory

Plans were now made for the construction of a large dormitory,
one hundred by forty feet and four stories high with a basement.
A wing on each end would provide homes for the Beecher and
Sturtevant families. A few months later plans were approved to
build a bakery, purchase a cart and yoke of oxen, and improve the
boarding house. Sturtevant and some trustees were delegated to
prepare the contract for the dormitory and superintend its erection. Much of the work was completed in 1832 and the two families were able to move into their homes late that year, although
the building was not ready for student occupancy until the following autumn. The trustees borrowed $7,000 to complete the
College's building program.

In August 1832 the trustees authorized the printing of the first
Catalogue of the Officers and Students in Illinois College, 1832–33.[19]
Printed in January 1833, the eight-page leaflet listed eleven
trustees, including Beecher and five of the original seven from
New Haven. The faculty included Beecher, as President; Rev.
Julian M. Sturtevant, Professor of Mathematics and Natural

Philosophy; and Rev. William Kirby, Instructor in the Latin and Greek languages. Erastus Colton was Instructor in the Preparatory Department and was assisted by the faculty. Eight students were classified in the Collegiate Department, four each in the sophomore and freshman classes, and eighty-eight were in the Preparatory Department. The *Catalogue* included the students who enrolled for the second term. About a third of the students were from Jacksonville and Morgan County and most of the others were from Illinois, but some came from Ohio, Missouri, Louisiana, the eastern states, and the Northwest Territory. Three pages of the *Catalogue* described the program and stated the expenses. Admission to the freshman class was determined by examination in Latin, Greek, English grammar, and arithmetic. The four year course listed the textbooks used for each class each term in Latin, Greek, mathematics, science, history, government, economics, and religion. "Experimental lectures" in physics and chemistry and exercises in speaking, composition, and debate, along with some recitations in Hebrew, rounded out the curriculum. The expenses for the year amounted to about seventy to ninety dollars. Students were to provide their own bed, bedding, furniture, fuel, candles, books, and stationery; plainness and economy in clothing were "warmly recommended."

In 1833 the faculty met Tuesday evenings at "6 1/2 o'clk." Beecher chaired the meetings, and after the opening prayer they discussed College business. Arrangements were made for preparing student declamations and compositions for commencement. Professor Sturtevant met with the debating society to urge the members to procure a library. Commentaries on the Scriptures were obtained for the College's library to aid in training students to be ministers. Mr. Colton was authorized to employ an assistant in his writing school, at the rate of 12 1/2 to 18 3/4 cents per hour. The faculty approved a subscription for the *Journal of Science* published by Yale's Professor Silliman.

The *Catalogue* announced that the Annual Commencement "will be holden on the third Wednesday in August in each year," but due to an epidemic it was postponed until 3 October. The day-long program began and ended with prayer and featured Sacred Music to begin and end the morning and afternoon sessions.

The subjects of the students' orations reflected awareness of major issues of the time: secession, abolition, nullification, African colonization, and the claims of the North American Indians. The patriotic theme was implicit in a speech on the "Character of George Washington," and two students—Richard Yates was one of them—spoke about education. A poignant note was sounded in a student's oration, "Imprisonment for Debt."[20]

The trustees, encouraged by contributors' pledges, added two very significant faculty men that fall, Truman Post and Jonathan Baldwin Turner. There were now four departments: Beecher was assigned to teach Mental, Moral and Social Philosophy; Post, Latin and Greek; Turner, Rhetoric and Oratory; and Sturtevant, Mathematics and Science. Kirby had resigned, but Colton continued in the Preparatory Department. Three students were now classified as juniors, four were sophomores, the freshman class numbered nine, and sixty-six pupils were in the Preparatory Department. The large dormitory was fully occupied, and the basement was now needed for the boarding establishment. In the eyes of the predominantly Southern residents of Jacksonville, the faculty members were all "Yankees." Sturtevant acknowledged that this was not expedient, but there was no alternative. Questions of College policy were brought before the trustees. Mr. Arthur Tappan of New York, a benefactor of various causes including Illinois College, inquired whether "colored youth" would be admitted. President Beecher was instructed to reply but regrettably the Minutes did not record the response. Years later Baldwin asked Sturtevant about this, and Sturtevant replied that the decision was affirmative; had it been otherwise he would have resigned. He also admitted that he did not think it would have been advisable under the circumstances because of the prevailing sentiment of the community.

Although Illinois College was established to provide education for boys and young men, its founders recognized the importance of education for women. Beecher and Sturtevant shared the common belief that the two sexes had different capabilities and functions and thus required different schooling beyond the elementary level. Women were to be prepared for domestic duties, including care for their families' physical welfare and the children's early education. By extension, they might also teach at the primary level in school. (However, most teachers at the time, even in elementary schools, were men.)

John Ellis conceived the plan for a seminary for boys and also for a school for girls. Mrs. Ellis had already started classes for girls, some of whom lived in her home. Sturtevant, proud of Elizabeth's fine education, was well aware of the influence of a mother's example and her tutelage. On 30 September 1830 interested citizens convened to plan a female academy. Judge Lockwood was called to the chair and Rev. J. M. Sturtevant was appointed clerk. They and John Ellis were assigned to prepare a report for the adjourned meeting two days later. Their recommendation for establishing a girls' seminary in Jacksonville was approved, and Sturtevant was among those elected as trustees. The Jacksonville Female Academy was scheduled to open for instruction in 1833.[21] Although there was no direct connection, the classes Mrs. Ellis had taught were recognized as the precursor of the school.

The Ladies' Association for Educating Females was organized on 4 October 1833 to provide financial and other assistance for girls seeking an education. The wives of Illinois College faculty members and trustees had prominent roles. The women themselves collected funds locally and solicited gifts from women's groups in the East. They disbursed the money and wrote and published their annual reports. It was not deemed proper for women to speak in public and so the anniversary meetings at which their reports were presented were conducted by their husbands. Elizabeth Sturtevant was involved in the Association and her husband sometimes participated in the public meetings.

It may have been when Sturtevant and others were in Vandalia for meetings of one of the various agencies that the Illinois State Lyceum was founded there. A member of the committee on the constitution, Sturtevant helped to define the Lyceum's objective: "to collect, preserve, and disseminate information" on education; on lyceums in various localities; on the history and inhabitants of Illinois from the earliest times to the present; and on the geography, population, commerce, government, etc., of the state.[22] The annual meetings were to be held henceforth in Jacksonville when people attended the College's commencement. The newspaper advertisement of Beecher's inauguration in 1832 included the notice that the Illinois State Lyceum would meet on the 16th. "Addresses may be expected from several members, on subjects relating to education and the general interests of Science." (SJ, 12 July 1832) Sturtevant served also on the correspondence committee and the committee which elected new members—among whom were his colleagues, Beecher, Brooks, and Baldwin. Because of the cholera epidemic in 1833 the members convened in October, when their discussion focused on the common schools. The 1835 session, probably held in the new Congregational Church, was apparently the last one.

Sturtevant's writing and publishing career had already begun, although on a modest scale. Soon after coming to Jacksonville he wrote a "Sketch of Illinois College" for Peck's *Guide for Emigrants*, published in 1831. Along with an account of its founding, Sturtevant described the College's buildings, its library, and its large farm, and its student body of about forty. This "Sketch" was apparently the first "history" of Illinois College[23] to be published and it was almost certainly the first writing by Sturtevant to appear in print, other than excerpts of his letters which were quoted in the *Home Missionary*.

The Evangelistic Mission

The men of the Illinois Association, in signing their solemn Compact, undertook a two-fold mission. They would provide aid and guidance to the proposed school, and they would preach at "important stations" in the area. Both school and church were essential because the two functions were mutually supportive. The preaching of the Gospel required that laity as well as clergy be educated because an ignorant populace would not accept the leadership of trained ministers. Moreover, the proper settlement of the region required citizens who were educated but also committed lay people in the churches. Only thus could the Christian civilization of New England be established in the West.

Instruction in religion was needed because many students had little if any experience either of church or Sunday School. Never intending to proselytize for sectarian purposes, said Sturtevant, "We earnestly desired to teach them the great universal truths of Christian faith and morality." (A, 192) All the faculty were "religious men," and following the practice at Yale, they conducted morning and evening prayers which featured Scripture readings and sacred music by a choir. The trustees decided that students should also attend public worship on the Sabbath. Distance from town and the quirks of weather made it all the more important to have religious services on the campus. Beginning in the winter of 1833 the College held one and usually two Sabbath services for those students who did not attend a parentally approved church in the village. Beecher and Sturtevant alternated in conducting the morning and evening Sabbath services, and Sturtevant reserved Saturdays for preparation. Over the course of years there were periodic revivals at the College and numerous students were "in the judgement of charity converted."[24] That cautious expression reflected the belief that only God could know the hearts of men.

Along with his responsibilities at the College Sturtevant also assumed evangelistic duties in the town and elsewhere. He became superintendent of the Sabbath School at the Presbyterian Church and preached when Ellis was absent. When not needed in Jacksonville he preached elsewhere. He attended many meetings and distributed tracts. He wrote (5 Feb. 1830) to the Home Missionary Society that he was doing all he could to spread the Gospel. However, he was still very sensitive to his limitations.

The hostility which characterized the attitude toward other Christian churches had come to Sturtevant's attention early and abruptly. Not only were there many churches in frontier Illinois but they often engaged in intense and sometimes bitter competition. About a month after his arrival the Presbyterian Church was supposed to have the use of the courthouse for worship while the schoolhouse was undergoing repairs. The Methodists had arranged a service that same Sunday and had already begun their service when Sturtevant arrived. He sat down and soon realized that he was the object of a strenuous attack by the Methodist preacher, Peter Cartwright, who emphasized that *he* had never been contaminated by going to college. Sturtevant was horrified by the attitude expressed there and by similar utterances by other denominational preachers. They assumed the validity of their own churches and denounced, often in strong language, other Christian groups. Sturtevant found this discord among Christians the most distressing aspect of life in Jacksonville.

The opportunity for preaching in area churches impressed Sturtevant with the need for a major change in his presentation. The theology which he had learned at Yale and its accompanying technical vocabulary were not suited to frontier audiences. Sturtevant determined to translate the formal concepts into "the popular language of everyday life" and he developed skill in using notes instead of a complete manuscript. (A, 186) He preached on Sabbath afternoons on the Scripture texts studied in the Sunday School lessons, and careful preparation enabled him to speak extemporaneously. Sturtevant officiated at numerous weddings recorded in Morgan County files and in Jacksonville and Springfield newspapers.

In early 1830 Sturtevant was elected treasurer of the Illinois Domestic Missionary Society.[25] (The national counterpart of that Society had been superseded by the American Home Missionary Society.) In August of that year he served on a committee to plan a State Sunday School Union. He frequently attended the December "anniversaries," the annual meetings of the societies responsible for distributing Bibles and promoting Sunday Schools; these sessions were sometimes held in Jacksonville and sometimes in Vandalia.

An announcement in the *Jacksonville Patriot* (15 June 1833) notified the public that a "protracted meeting," or series of revivals, would begin the following Thursday at 11:00 A.M. at the Presbyterian Meeting House. Sturtevant was named as one of the preachers, along with Baldwin, Beecher, Lucien Farnum (Farnham), and Albert Hale, all members of the Illinois Association and all serving as Presbyterians. Through the American Education Society, Sturtevant helped to recruit area young men to fulfill the great need for ministers. In the summer of 1830 he examined students at Illinois College to determine their qualifications for aid. That fall Sturtevant helped to organize the Illinois branch of the Society and was named secretary[26]. He published a notice of its anniversary meeting to "be holden at the Presbyterian meeting house in Jacksonville" on 3 October 1833. (SJ, 31 Aug. 1833)

Whenever his college duties permitted, Sturtevant attended the meetings of the Presbytery and Synod. He also subscribed to numerous publications for information about religious work elsewhere. In 1831 and 1832 the Jacksonville post office maintained records for collecting the postage on periodicals delivered to its patrons. During those years Sturtevant received eleven publications, including the monthly *Home Missionary,* several Sunday School papers, and a temperance journal. He received a newspaper published by John Mason Peck, a pioneer Baptist preacher, educator, and publisher in Illinois. The *Illinois Monthly Magazine,* the first literary journal in the state, was also on his list. Edward Beecher and John Ellis received eleven additional periodicals, and no doubt the men exchanged reading material with each other.[27]

The Jacksonville Temperance Society was one of numerous voluntary organizations in the community. Newspaper reports indicate that Baldwin and Beecher were much involved but that Sturtevant was not especially active.

Defending Freedom of Speech

So many dramatic events had previously occurred in Julian Sturtevant's life that it may seem pointless to designate a given year as exceptional. However, the momentous challenges of 1833 made that year remarkable. Prior events set the stage for an incident on New Year's Day. The settlers in Illinois had experienced much fear and some suffering because of the incursion of Chief Black Hawk and the Sauk tribe. A group of citizens met at the Court House in Jacksonville in June 1832 to consider the "distressed situation" of their "Fellow Citizens." Sturtevant proposed a resolution: "That the future extension of our population, and the prosperity of our country, require that relief should be promptly afforded to our suffering fellow citizens on the frontier of this State." (SJ, 14 June 1832) A sum of one hundred dollars was collected and the men agreed to publish the proceedings in the *Patriot* and other papers.

Some men issued a call for a meeting at the Court House, on 1 January 1833, to organize a "Peace Society" as a means of reducing the tension between the settlers and the Indians. Sturtevant was not present but was soon cast as a major figure in news accounts about the controversial event. Some who came favored the plan while others were committed to hostile opposition. A letter from an unidentified Jacksonville citizen, addressed to the *Springfield Illinois Herald* and printed in the 12 January issue, seemingly implicated Sturtevant—and in an unfavorable manner. The writer referred to some "amusement" in Jacksonville which occurred on New Year's Day when "one of the Professors from the hill" had spoken about the evils of war. The professor was said to have belittled the troops which were called to serve in the campaign against Black Hawk, declaring that the war had begun over a *"mere trifle —ONLY the massacreing a few women and children!"* The report added that a motion to tar and feather the speaker was greeted by loud cheers but "the bird had flown" and could not be found even after searching the College.[28]

Thereupon Sturtevant addressed a letter to the editor of the Springfield paper: "I observe with mingled emotions of indignation and regret, some statements fitted, and I fear designed, not only to bring unmerited odium upon individuals, but to throw contempt upon the institution in which I have the honor to be an instructor." He explained his reason for not letting the matter "pass by in merited neglect." Since he alone at the College had the title of Professor, he feared people might conclude that the accusations were aimed at him. For the sake of the College he could not "endure in silence the propagation of the most malignant slanders…." Sturtevant explained that Peace Societies were voluntary associations[29] of individuals for promoting peace by seeking through free discussion to inform the public of the evils of war. The movement, widespread in America and Great Britain, was in no way inconsistent with "the justice and necessity of defensive war."

Having consulted with people who were present at the meeting, Sturtevant now set forth the facts of the case. He reviewed the original report, enumerating its errors and refuting them. He pointed out that it was *not* a Presbyterian meeting. Indeed, the chairman was "one of the oldest settlers, and most respectable citizens [who] was never suspected of being a Presbyterian" and would not have felt flattered by such an allegation. The secretary of the meeting was a highly respected Methodist clergyman. Moreover, it was not a "Professor" but a teacher in the Preparatory Department who made the speech. The other three teachers at the College were not present, not because they considered the object evil or the proposal injurious to any one, but because "we considered the movement uncalled for, and likely to accomplish little or no good." The anonymous letter had alleged that the speaker referred to the massacre of women and children as a *mere trifle*. Sturtevant bristled at the very suggestion that anyone in Jacksonville would tolerate such a view. The speaker had observed that wars often begin over mere trifles but he had not said that the massacre was such. [Sturtevant did not identify the speaker; he was Erastus Colton, an instructor from 1832 to 1834.]

Sturtevant acknowledged, and he said he blushed to do so, that a motion to tar and feather the speaker and ride him out of town on a rail had indeed been made. But he denied that any meeting of citizens of Jacksonville had *approved* such a proposal. Moreover, the speaker had walked from the meeting in public view and could have been apprehended had anyone wished to do so. It was a matter of special shame, thought Sturtevant, that the reporter considered the incident to be a matter of amusement. Sturtevant emphasized the significance of the issue in a stirring defense of freedom of assembly and discussion.

Sir, is not this the boasted land of American liberty? Is not this the country and the age of free inquiry? Is it not the glory of our country that *opinion* is as free as the air or the water? And in this free and happy land, are the investigations of *any class* of men to be darkened by threats of "tar and feathers"? Is the standard of *persecution* to be reared? For what *is* persecution but *an attempt to arrest the progress of opinion by force, violence or false accusation?* Let it be distinctly remembered, that any attempt to put down even *false* opinion by such means, *is persecution.* What, then, shall we think of the sentiment of this writer? He calls it *"amusement"* to threaten "tar and feathers" against a fellow citizen, not for propagating false and dangerous doctrines, but for exercising the *unalienable right of freedom of opinion* in defence of a sentiment, which has long been a glory and a blessing to our nation. Sir, there is no mistaking this spirit; it is a spirit of bitter and relentless persecution, which has grossly mistaken its age and its country.[30]

During January and February the Springfield and Jacksonville newspapers devoted many columns to the incident.[31] The spirited exchanges and sometimes blunt editorial comments reflected the rivalry, typical of the times, between competing communities and their newspapers. An editorial in the *Patriot* (26 Jan. 1833) rebuked the Springfield paper for always seeking some excuse "for casting odium upon the literary institution at Jacksonville...." The *Patriot* strongly endorsed the College, declaring that "As a means of advancing the great cause of education and spreading intelligence thro' this region, we consider that Illinois College is a most valuable and beneficial institution."

Controversy with Wright over Abolitionism

In mid-February 1833 Julian was prompted—after three years of silence—to renew his correspondence with Elizur Wright.[32] He had sent his friend a copy of the first Illinois College *Catalogue* and had received in return a catalog for Western Reserve and a copy of the *Liberator*.[33] Julian expounded at length about the situation of Illinois College. Whereas Elizur was working among people who supported education and religious instruction, Julian noted that Illinois College was confronted by the most strenuous opposition.

[W]e have need of unbending purpose and iron muscles, for we are called to stem the current of popular opinion in all its foaming fury. The Devil has always given us to understand that he regarded us as no very welcome emigrants to these parts and always had an eye to all our operations, but recently he has come down upon us in great wrath, and he is sparing no pains to array his entire disposable force in one solid phalanx against us. Prejudices against Yankees, sectarian jealousies, anti-Presbyterian prejudices, Presbyterian "old schoolism," Campbellism, infidelity, atheism, Fanny-Wrightism,[34] are all wielded against us most dexterously; no mode of wielding popular ignorance & prejudice to our disadvantage is overlooked.

The Presbyterians, but a minority in the state, were weakened by their "wicked controversy."

Julian expressed his keen desire to renew his contacts with Elizur. He loved his old friend and was very fond of his letters. Also, he considered the two colleges as natural allies, and he and his colleagues in Illinois wished to form, with them, "a league, offensive and defensive." Julian could not have known how different the two men had become during the three-year interval, nor could he have foreseen that the initial good will and enthusiasm which each expressed would quickly give way to disagreement so profound that it would end their once close friendship.

In this letter, Sturtevant raised another issue, not mentioned explicitly in his list of problems. "You seem to have become burning hot abolitionists a[t] Hudson." However, he remarked, "we have too many vital questions at issue nearer home, even at our own door, to allow us much of time or feeling for that question...." Sturtevant acknowledged being dissatisfied with the American Colonization Society but, he declared, "I am not an abolitionist."

After sending greetings to Wright's father and others, Sturtevant concluded: "My dear friend we have a great work and little time to do it in. I feel that I must be about my father's business, or night will come before I have accomplished any thing. May God employ us for his glory, is the prayer of your affectionate friend, J. M. Sturtevant."

Elizur's response (9 March) was forceful and blunt. He confessed, with "gratitude to the Savior," that he was "an abolitionist, 'burning hot' enough to stand aloof from a church which... has sat down to the table of the Lord with the 'stealers & buyers & sellers' of the Souls & bodies of their fellow men." For Elizur, slavery —in a free country—was the issue and it could not be ignored. "How can one of our colleges exist for a moment as a Gospel institution while it shuns a Gospel question? Is a candle lighted to be put under a bushel?" Moreover, there was an important political issue. The union could not much longer be preserved without slavery being either abolished or accepted everywhere. Elizur mentioned that some of the trustees of Western Reserve might suppress the issue and cause his dismissal, along with two colleagues. He urged Julian to write promptly and express his opinions frankly, "along with the <u>facts</u> on which they are based." Ephraim, writing soon after Elizur, informed Julian that Elizur was now a "stranger," a hot abolitionist likely to lose his position.[35] Julian had already received that information, and from the man himself.[36]

The issue of slavery was now in the forefront. Julian, writing on 12 April, asserted that all good men agreed that slavery was an "intolerable evil" and further, that Christians were under obligation to remove it as soon as possible. The question, then, was to determine the best way to accomplish this end. The proposal to colonize the free colored men in Africa was based upon an appeal to the self-interest of the slaveholders, on the assumption that they wished to be rid of the problem. Julian argued against the plan because it did not appeal to the conscience, which he deemed the only effective impulse. For comparison he described a man "in the last stages of intemperance," suffering dreadfully, but unable to break "the simple habit of vicious indulgence." So, too, the slaveholders "will glide along down the current, regardless of [the danger] of national and individual ruin."

Turning to the abolitionists, Julian stated the position of the Garrison school as he understood it. "'Every slave must at once be made a freeman and every black man be raised to all the civil rights and privileges enjoyed by the whites.'" To make his point, Julian put this statement in the form of a syllogism: it is a terrible sin to deprive others of their rights; a black man, as well as a white man, has an absolute right to his liberty; and "Therefore, it is highly criminal in the sight of God to retain a single black man in bondage for a single hour...." This formulation of the argument revealed a fallacy—in the second proposition. Contradicting that point, Julian declared his personal conviction: "<u>no man either black or white has a right to his liberty when placed in Society any farther than he can enjoy it without injury to himself or the community</u>." To reinforce his argument, Julian noted that a man of 20, however well qualified to be independent, is nevertheless under the authority of his father until he is 21; this is derived from the law of God.

The same principle, Julian declared, is applicable to the slave population, which is "in such a state of intellectual and moral degradation that the interests of the community, as a whole, black or white, forbid their immediate emancipation." Julian was confident that Elizur would acknowledge that this conclusion was founded on "solid ground." However, he added an additional argument, from Scripture, noting that Paul did not speak about a slave and his master as Garrison does. Paul addressed them both as "Christians—as brethren in the Lord."

Julian divulged his own plan, first admitting that "the great problem [is] as yet to be solved." The slave should be "as speedily as possible elevated and qualified for the <u>duties</u> of a free man— and then let him enjoy a free man's privileges, if practicable in a colony, if not, among ourselves." Lest Elizur think that he lacked information about abolitionism, Julian added a note: "N.B. I generally see the Liberator—especially when it contains anything from you or your colleagues."

Elizur's response of 3 July was delayed because of a trip to the East.[37] Upon returning to a large amount of correspondence, he assured Julian that the letter to him was the first to be written. It provided little comfort to Julian. Elizur quoted the long sentence which Julian had underlined and declared that "the statement [is] much too large to be swallowed whole." No one can foresee an injury which might be committed by a person in the future; to keep a slave in bondage for that reason would be to punish him in advance for an unknown crime. Elizur agreed that the basis of parental authority is the law of nature, that is, of God. However, Julian's comparison is not valid; at 21, the son would be free, whether wise or foolish, learned or ignorant. Elizur questioned Julian's reference to Scripture, also, indicating that important infor- mation is lacking about the nature of the relationship between the master and slave who are mentioned. Surely the New Testament does not justify holding slaves as property. Finally, Elizur insisted that government must support the right of every man to his liber- ty until he commits some crime which injures the community.

Elizur's refutation of Julian's arguments must have rankled, especially the statement that Julian's "usually excellent discrimina- tion seems...to have been at fault in this matter." Elizur's closing note of triumph in his cause could hardly have been pleasing. "I long to number you & your worthy confreres in this little band of <u>devoted</u> abolitionists. I know I shall soon. The cause moves onward. The Lord is surely on our side."

That expectation was premature. It was many years before Julian, always anti-slavery in his convictions, joined the ranks of the abolitionists. Elizur's convictions resulted in his dismissal from Western Reserve College; even that College was threatened by association with abolitionism—how much more Illinois College in its hostile environment! Julian and Elizur ended their friendship. Although the last extant letter[38] was written by Elizur, Julian (in his *Autobiography*) explained that he had freely criticized certain positions taken by Elizur which he deemed untenable, and that Elizur soon ended their correspondence. Their serious disagreement over abolition is itself an adequate explanation. In later years Elizur became an atheist, perhaps because he regarded Christianity as guilty of supporting the slave system for so long. Samuel Willard in his "Memorial" to Sturtevant explained that Wright had turned toward a "skeptical radicalism" and consequently "these two strong, earnest, honest men met to disagree, and to part without regret...." (XCVII) Whatever the circumstances, Julian considered the loss of friendship with Elizur, whom he credited with saving his life during his grave illness at Yale, as one of the most painful experiences of his entire life. *(A, 219-22)*

Student Unrest . . . A Cholera Epidemic

The College's staff was afflicted by still other problems. A student who read a composition at a College exercise in the Chapel on 6 February 1833 was highly disrespectful to the faculty and was dismissed the same day. The student requested a meeting with the faculty to explain his performance and three days later, upon presenting an apology, he was readmitted to the College. About the same time some students left due to "groundless disaffection." Among those who withdrew was Stephen Hempstead and near the end of the term, his brother Samuel also left. Frontier youth did not quietly accept the decisions of College officers. The *Springfield Illinois Herald* freely offered its columns to those with complaints against Illinois College and published "opprobrious" letters by the Hempstead brothers.[39] In a lengthy protest Stephen acknowledged that he had been dismissed "for a non-attendance on prayers" but asserted that this action was unjust. He incorporated the text of a petition signed by students at the College and citizens of Jacksonville who argued that the dismissal was an act of oppression; Hempstead was said to be justified because the house where he stayed was far from the campus. Hempstead, a native of Connecticut, was over twenty at the time and had served in the Black Hawk War. He later moved to Iowa and in 1850 became the second governor of that state.

Also crowded onto the front page of the *Herald* were statements by another student, Henry A. Cyrus of Morgan County, and by J. M. Sturtevant, Secretary of the Illinois Branch of the American Education Society. Cyrus protested that he had not been granted funds needed for his education even though Sturtevant had given him statements which certified his moral character and his seriousness as a student. Earlier reports indicated that he had not attended church on the Sabbath. The student's name was not listed in the *1833—34 Catalogue*, so presumably the controversy was not resolved in his favor.

An unusual protest occurred when students petitioned the faculty to schedule morning prayers at 4:30 instead of 5:00 and to have breakfast at 6:00 instead of 6:30. The reason for the desired change was "so that after two hours of labor subsequent to breakfast they might have a 1/2 hour to themselves" before classes began at 9:00. The request was denied on the ground of the "many inconveniences" to the faculty. (FM, 12 June 1833)

A problem of a very different sort had arisen in mid-summer with the worst outbreak of cholera in Jacksonville's history. The *Patriot* warned in its issue of 22 June that although the disease had not yet afflicted the population, it was important to clear the streets of vegetable matter and dead animals and to require leper vaults for the burial of the dead. The first death from cholera occurred within a week. Somewhat later, Professor and Mrs. Sturtevant took a carriage ride out of town and upon returning learned that Mrs. John Ellis had died. Within forty-eight hours her two children and her niece also died, and Sturtevant assisted with the burial arrangements for the family. At the time Ellis was in Indiana making arrangements to move there. Sturtevant said that Ellis was notified regarding the tragedy, although the news was slow in reaching him. (A, 201)

The instructors at the College were requested to shorten the lessons so as not to endanger students' health, and those students who wished to go home were given permission. Finally, classes were suspended and commencement was rescheduled for 3 October. Similarly, meetings of the Illinois Lyceum and the American Education Association were delayed until that time.

The scourge lasted for six weeks and, according to Sturtevant, more than ten per cent of the people died. One of the fatalities was Mrs. Lucien Farnham. Both Mrs. Edward Beecher and Mrs. Sturtevant became very ill but recovered quickly. Newspaper reports indicated that by late August the epidemic had virtually ceased, having claimed forty-one victims. The population of Jacksonville as of 1 June was reckoned at 1300, so the toll was much less than Sturtevant's estimate.[40]

After the disease had spent its course, Beecher and Sturtevant went to a teachers' convention at Cincinnati. They traveled most of the way by stage, traveling night and day to Louisville and then boarding a river steamer. Sturtevant was pleased with the great improvements in transportation which had occurred since his journey to Illinois four years earlier. However, travel was still expensive and he could not afford to visit his parents in Tallmadge. While in Cincinnati the two men stayed for a week in the home of Lyman Beecher, Edward Beecher's father, and enjoyed "a wonderful rest." There Sturtevant first met Harriet Beecher, whose sparkling conversation impressed him greatly.

On Trial for Heresy

Warren, Tallmadge, and New Haven were essentially homogeneous religious communities and Sturtevant maintained that he had not been aware of "Congregationalism," although that was the form of church organization in all three places. Professor Taylor had delivered lectures on church government, but Sturtevant paid no attention to them or to the subject. He learned the significance of church polity soon after arriving in Illinois when he was personally affected by an arrangement made before his birth. Early in the nineteenth century both Presbyterians and Congregationalists had perceived the great challenge to evangelize new territories. Many in both denominations regarded Presbyterianism as better suited to frontier conditions, and some Congregationalists deemed the sacrifice of their form of government to be justified. In Connecticut the organization of local churches had developed a semi-presbyterian character which obscured the distinction 'from Presbyterianism.

In 1801 a Plan of Union was adopted by the Presbyterian General Assembly, a national body, and the Connecticut General Association, representing the Congregational churches of that State. Its purpose was to promote cooperation between the two denominations in evangelizing western New York and the region beyond. A church of either denomination would serve members of both and could call as its pastor a minister of either persuasion. Limited resources of both men and money could thus be utilized more efficiently because there would be only one such church in a given community. An appeals process dealt with disputes between a church and a minister having different affiliations. The Connecticut General Association was so prominent that other New England Congregationalists followed its lead.

Doctrinally the two denominations shared a common ancestry in Puritanism and the theology of John Calvin. Their divergence with regard to church government had actually been made explicit in the first statement on Congregationalism published in America, *The Cambridge Platform of 1648*. In it the churches of Massachusetts declared their acceptance of the substance of the Westminster Confession, recently adopted in England during a period of Presbyterian rule. However, they excepted from their approval "those things which have respect to church government & discipline"—an exclusion of major proportions and profound import. (7) They strongly preferred congregational government rather than presbyterian order which placed local churches under the jurisdiction of Presbytery, Synod, and General Assembly.

Sturtevant acknowledged that by adopting the Plan of Union the Congregationalists in effect restricted their polity to New England and assigned the West and the South to the Presbyterians. He denied, however, that there was any formal action ratifying the division of territory.[41] In Illinois the Plan of Union resulted in the organization of Presbyterian churches only, although large numbers of ministers and lay people were New England Congregationalists. Almost all the members of the Illinois Association were Congregationalists but took it for granted that they would affiliate with the Presbyterian Church when they reached Illinois.[42] These men had acknowledged that it was highly desirable that the proposed seminary at Jacksonville should "be as it is Presbyterian in its character." (Records, 18)

In 1830 the Presbyterian churches and ministers of Illinois, organized as the Presbytery of Illinois, were part of the Synod of Missouri. The Presbytery was scheduled to meet in Springfield in March, and Sturtevant realized that he should arrange for acceptance as a member. His College duties did not permit his absence so, following John Ellis's advice, he sent a letter. He had learned only recently that Presbyterian procedure required ministers to affirm the Westminster Confession as embodying scriptural truth and to accept Presbyterian polity. For him this involved "grave and unexpected questions" which he could not have answered affirmatively. (A, 169-70)

The Sturtevant children had been drilled on the Presbyterian Shorter Catechism, but the parents regarded it as subordinate to Scripture and as subject to the right of "private judgment." Now, studying the Westminster Confession for the first time, Sturtevant realized that he could not consent to it nor could he accept Presbyterianism as the biblically mandated form of church government. Some important Scriptural truths were omitted from the Confession, notably the assurance that God forgives the repentant sinner. Although assured that assent would not imply acceptance of every provision, Sturtevant could not in good conscience give the appearance of doing so. Fortunately, his application was approved even in his absence, and so without ever agreeing to the "constitutional questions" he was admitted to Presbytery.[43] In May 1830 the Presbyterian General Assembly ruled that all Congregational ministers accepted thereafter must answer the questions. Sturtevant's comment was pointed: "So quickly was the door closed by which I had entered." (A, 173)

The men of the Illinois Association, by receiving the assistance of the American Home Missionary Society, implicitly agreed to the Plan of Union as it operated in Illinois. Sturtevant later wished that they had not accepted its aid although he admitted that without it they could never have undertaken their western mission. He entered upon his service with the Presbyterians in Illinois in good faith, regarding his relationship as fraternal and for the sake of the greater welfare of the Church of Christ. He sought to avoid involvement in strictly Presbyterian issues.

Edward Beecher and Theron Baldwin did not share Sturtevant's reservations about accepting Presbyterianism. They counseled patience, believing the Presbyterian Church would surely be divided over issues such as evangelistic methods, interdenominational cooperation, and slavery. However, instead of eventual relief due to distant changes, a local charge of heresy was preferred against Beecher, Sturtevant, and William Kirby in March 1833. The accuser was a nearby Presbyterian minister, Rev. William Frazer. When the Presbytery's ecclesiastical tribunal met (on 23 April) at Jacksonville, Beecher was the first to be brought to trial and pleaded not guilty. (Spinka, 44)

Sturtevant, arraigned the following day, denied that any such court had the right to try him for his religious convictions. It was charged that his views were contrary to Presbyterian doctrine and contrary to the Scriptures. He made no plea regarding the former, declaring that he had never assented to the Presbyterian standards. Regarding the latter he pleaded "Not guilty" and stated his case. In doing so he made "a pointed criticism" of Frazer's theological views and the man responded "in a storm of angry passion." (A, 200) The accuser's behavior made any lengthy defense unnecessary. The trial of Kirby was brief.[44]

The Illinois College men were acquitted by a large majority and Frazer was deposed for making a libelous attack in the newspaper. However, Frazer appealed the decisions and the Synod reinstated him. Sturtevant and Beecher were not present at the session because their return from the Cincinnati meeting was delayed when Sturtevant became ill. For some reason the charges of heresy were not prosecuted. Sturtevant, who had anticipated an unfavorable decision, was greatly relieved. Three students had left the College because of the supposed heresies of the instructors. Sturtevant noted that they had been influenced by Rev. Frazer, then living a few miles from the campus. Probably Frazer had encouraged these students in annoying the College—an effort, Sturtevant wrote, "not entirely without effect."[45] He was grateful that Frazer had lost his power to cause further trouble for Illinois College.[46]

A Congregational Church: A Challenge to the Plan of Union

When Julian Sturtevant arrived in 1829 no Congregational church existed within five hundred miles of Jacksonville. Yet many Congregational ministers in the West were now Presbyterian pastors, and many Congregational lay people were members of Presbyterian churches, including the one in Jacksonville. John Ellis was pastor of that church, founded in 1827. Ordained as a Congregationalist in Massachusetts, he had come to southern Illinois in 1825 and had worked diligently as a Presbyterian. As early as 1832 some New England lay members in Ellis's church expressed dissatisfaction with the situation, a feeling greatly intensified by the heresy trial of the Illinois College faculty. During the fall of 1833 two men met with Beecher and Sturtevant to inform them that thirty or more lay people wished to form a Congregational church. The two ministers were invited to assist. In the conversation Sturtevant expressed his "growing attachment to the principles of Congregationalism," but Beecher had no sympathy with the plan. (A, 195) Both discouraged the proposal because a second church would only divide the small numbers; Sturtevant thought that in a few years there would be enough people to organize a new church. The laymen informed Beecher and Sturtevant that they had not come for advice but for assistance and if refused they would turn elsewhere.

Both national and local factors were involved. Much controversy had arisen in the East because of the widespread influence among Congregational ministers of the "New Haven theology." Sometimes referred to as Taylorism, it was objectionable to conservative Presbyterians. The Presbyterians were divided, some very strict in maintaining their polity, doctrine, and traditional worship, while others were willing to work with the Congregationalists and to accept revivalism as an appropriate means. These issues were much more divisive in the West than in the East, although within a few years they led to a national division between the "Old School" and the "New School." The latter group were more congenial with Congregationalism but came to regard its extension as inimical to their interests; they wanted New England emigrants to augment their own numbers. Locally the immediate problem was the difficulty in raising sufficient funds for a much-needed building.

Congregationalism had already made its debut in Illinois. In 1831 a group organized a church in Massachusetts for the purpose of moving as a congregation to Illinois and establishing the town of Princeton. In February 1833 the first Congregational church organized *within* Illinois was founded at Fairfield, later re-named Mendon. The Presbyterian church at Quincy, established in 1830 by Asa Turner, was reorganized as a Congregational church in 1833. A Congregational church formed at Timewell became Presbyterian within a year.

The proposed church at Jacksonville would thus be the fifth Congregational church in Illinois.[47] However, the Jacksonville situation was unique; it would be the only town in the state which would have both a Presbyterian and a Congregational church, and thus it presented a direct challenge to the Plan of Union. The erstwhile Congregationalists were eager to return to their familiar ways. They believed that the only scriptural and practical basis of church membership was credible evidence of Christian character, not affirmation of Christian beliefs in words which were "not from God." (A, 205) A congregation should prepare its own confession of faith; that practice was consistent with the declaration of John Robinson, one of the earliest Pilgrim "fathers," that there was yet more light and truth to break forth from God's Holy Word. Another principle was also fundamental. A person must assent fully and freely to a declaration of faith, rejecting mental reservations which some advocated for the sake of "unity" with the Presbyterians. The heresy trial confirmed the view that much of the strife among Presbyterians resulted from their form of government.

The lay people in Jacksonville proceeded without Beecher and Sturtevant. In early November a committee drafted a constitution, a statement of faith, and a covenant. The documents were modeled upon similar statements used in New England churches and likely upon the statements of the Yale College Church. Sturtevant was not named as having a part in their preparation, but he expressed pleasure that in later years the constitution still retained the original provisions: that Christian character was the only basis for membership, that baptism could be administered either to infants or adults, and that adults could choose immersion if they wished.

Rev. Asa Turner of Quincy had agreed to officiate at the organizational meeting of the new church but sent word at almost the last minute that he could not come. William Carter, the last of the New Haven Association to reach Illinois except for Mason Grosvenor, consented to preach. An alumnus of Yale College and newly graduated from the Theological Department, he was licensed to preach but was not yet ordained and so was not authorized to receive new members. Two days before the service, when Beecher and Sturtevant were again asked to assist, Beecher reluctantly agreed. Sturtevant, after twenty-four hours of prayerful consideration, also consented. That Saturday evening, with Carter present, he reviewed the credentials of the thirty-two men and women who were to be the charter members.

The formal organization of the Congregational Church of Jacksonville took place at an afternoon service on Sunday, 15 December 1833, in the Methodist Episcopal Church. The minister of that church took part, Beecher and Sturtevant offered prayers, and Carter preached the sermon. Sturtevant received the new members and presided at the Communion service. In his address he explained why he, a member of another denomination, was involved in the proceedings of the Congregationalists. First, he customarily joined with any Christian group in appropriate worship; and second, he "cordially approved of the principles of church government" which were the basis of the new church. (A, 207) This was his first opportunity to make a public declaration of his convictions. He was pleased that members of other denominations who were present shared in the Lord's Supper, which he believed should be open to all Christians. The new congregation called itself the "Independent Church," a name suggesting that it had no fellowship with other churches; the next year it became the "Congregational Church."

The founding of the Congregational Church in Jacksonville

was the beginning of direct resistance to Presbyterian domination of the West and thus a major step in extending Congregationalism beyond New England. Sturtevant's espousal of Congregational principles made him unpopular with many Presbyterians, who were pleased that Beecher did not share Sturtevant's views. Sturtevant was happy that the differences with Beecher in no way affected their friendship. He was greatly dismayed subsequently when he was severely rebuked by Dr. Absalom Peters of the American Home Missionary Society. Sturtevant was heart-broken and considered resigning, but he believed he had acted in good conscience and in accordance with God's providence.

Because one church in Jacksonville was already receiving aid from the Missionary Society, the Congregational Church could not expect any assistance. Elihu Wolcott, a charter member, went East in early 1834 to seek funds. Sturtevant, writing to introduce him to Eastern friends, described the situation.

"There is in all this section of country...an increasing disposition to adopt the more simple & more scriptural forms of the venerable Fathers of New England—Several such churches have already been formed among us.... [A] Church has been recently organized in this village on Congregational principles." He observed that the Church had procured a suitable pastor and needed a house for worship. "[W]hether it will be practicable to obtain [aid] or expedient to ask for it you gentlemen can judge much better than I."[48]

Apparently little or no help was received.

Relatives Come to Illinois

The first winter which the Sturtevants experienced in their new environment had been mild and was no gauge of what they were to endure the following year, the winter of the "deep snow." The frigid siege of 1830-1831 began during the Christmas holidays. Sturtevant's language conveys a vivid impression of the severity of that storm. "Snow covered the entire country to the depth of at least three feet on the level.... When the storm ceased and the bright sun beamed down upon the landscape a fierce northwest wind arose, and for weeks swept over the prairies.... The newness of the country greatly increased the hardships of that winter. Our fuel was yet in the forest, and even much of our food supply remained still in the fields covered by the deep snow.... No morning dawned upon us for many days when the thermometer registered less than twelve degrees below zero." (A, 179-80)

The severe weather forced the Sturtevants to leave their crude cabin and to take refuge in the College Building. Their hardships that year were brought to a tragic climax by the death of their first-born. In May 1831, when only eleven months old, "the little Prof." developed a sudden illness and died within a few hours. Far from their family homes they buried their infant son in a prairie grave, surrounded by a wooden fence. Sturtevant said that Elizabeth's heart was almost broken and that "She never recovered the full buoyancy of her spirits," although their marriage continued to be happy. "Nothing remained for us but to... go on with our work." (A, 181-82) The next year, on 24 February 1832, their second child was born, a daughter who was given her mother's name, Elizabeth Maria. She grew to be a beautiful child who had her mother's merry nature.

Encouraging New England families to emigrate to the West was a stated purpose of the Illinois Association of New Haven. New England farmers needed the good land of the Mississippi Valley, and that region needed "active, intelligent, and pious laymen" as settlers.[49] The many visits to eastern churches to seek funds for Illinois College, both before and after Baldwin and Sturtevant came to Illinois, provided occasions when the needs of the West and the opportunities it offered could be set before people in the East. Within a decade many relatives and friends of both Julian and Elizabeth Fayerweather Sturtevant would be among the eager emigrants to Illinois.

However, New England was not the first or the major source of settlers for central Illinois. Richard Power has noted that as of 1840 the Southerners had a forty-year head start in the state. The "Yankee invasion" introduced a population with a very different culture, much more dynamic and with strong economic and political views based upon religious faith. Their movement from the eastern regions was much more rapid than that of the Southerners, and unlike the latter group they kept in close touch with their families and friends in their states of origin. This greatly strengthened their sense of obligation to replicate New England culture and thus sustain their sense of destiny. These people were, Power declared, very industrious in character and were determined in their efforts to transform both the culture and the landscape of Illinois. They were quick to introduce educational and religious organizations and to plant fruit and shade trees. Their keen sense of order was reflected both in their attention to the public welfare and in the maintenance of their farms. The differences between the two population groups which converged in Illinois were the source of much of the tension and conflict which developed and which so often directly affected Illinois College. It took a long time for the diverse populations to blend into a new strain which Power labeled as "neither Yankee nor Southern, but 'Western.'"[50]

Ephraim, Julian's older brother, reported on the problems in the church at Tallmadge and about family difficulties. Brother Christopher, now nineteen, was extravagant in his dress, refused to help on the family farm, and was abusive to his parents and his sister. Ephraim asked if there were not some place at Jacksonville where Christopher could come so that those evils could be removed. Later he acknowledged receiving the newspaper with Julian's letter about the Peace Society meeting. He advised Julian that their parents were failing rapidly and that he himself had suffered because his wife and baby had died and he had lost his property. Happily, there was also some good news. Christopher was now employed at a store in Akron and doing well. Huldah was at home and probably would teach during the summer. In his *Autobiography* Sturtevant reported that his mother died in November 1833. He regretted deeply that financial stringency had prevented him from visiting his parents a few weeks earlier when he and Beecher were in Cincinnati.

At the beginning of 1829 the Richard and Hannah Fayerweather family was still complete and both parents and all their children were living in their New Canaan home.[51] Richard Fayerweather was industrious, producing wheat and corn and livestock on his farm and engaging in business enterprises. He was a founder and part owner of the New Canaan Academy. The three oldest children were daughters: Julia, Elizabeth, and Mary Jane. James was next, and after him were Abraham and Silas; the youngest was Hannah. The birth-years of the children ranged from 1804 to 1816.

Mrs. Fayerweather died in February 1829 and a few months later the sons and daughters began going their separate ways. In August Elizabeth married Julian Sturtevant and accompanied him to Illinois. The two younger brothers went to sea and arrived in the Sandwich Islands (Hawaii) on a whaling vessel in May 1831. James graduated from Yale in 1831 and was in Illinois later that year; in the fall of 1832 he was temporarily an instructor in Illinois College's Preparatory Department. Fewer members of the family remained to care for the boarding pupils and Julia complained that there was not enough help. She said that "Hannah has no faculty of taking care of the children nor bearing their noise." Julia was characterized by her brother Abraham as the "housewife" among his sisters, while Mary Jane was the seamstress who made new clothing for the family and repaired pupils' garments when necessary. She also shopped in New York City for hats and dresses for herself and her sisters and purchased clothing and furniture for shipment to Elizabeth in Illinois.[52] Abraham remained in Hawaii the rest of his life except for a voyage to the northwest coast of North America in late 1833. He maintained a considerable correspondence with his family, despite the fact that letters did not reach their destination for a year or more and sometimes were lost. Silas continued his career on the sea in Atlantic shipping for a time but never fulfilled Abraham's hope that he would make at least one more voyage to Hawaii to see him.

For Julian Sturtevant, the most significant member of his wife's family to follow them to Illinois was Hannah Richards Fayerweather. In his *Autobiography* he referred only briefly to Hannah's arrival in Jacksonville, saying simply that she had been "a constant member of my family from a period prior to the birth of my eldest surviving child." (A, 251) The reference was to his second son, born 1 February 1834; he, like the first son who had died in infancy, was given his father's name.

Hannah was born 19 December 1816 and was only twelve

years old when her sister married Julian Sturtevant. Her desire to come to the West was awakened early, and she reminded Elizabeth of that in a letter of 3 October 1831. Mr. Jenney, a member of the Illinois Association, had preached in the New Canaan Church the day before. Hannah protested that Mr. Jenney had "cheated me about going to the West with him." Apparently he had not honored a promise to take her with him and that, she said, was not fair. She feared that now she would have to wait until Mr. Sturtevant himself came for her. Informing her sister that they had received no mail from her for two months, she added that nine or ten were "subjects" of a revival but she was not among them; her older sisters thought she should wait for a while. Meanwhile Hannah attended the academy, studying Latin and Greek and perhaps mastering composition which earlier had caused her to complain.[53] Brother James wrote to Abraham in 1832 that Hannah had now grown quite tall and lady-like.[54]

Hannah's opportunity finally came. On 30 September 1833 she wrote to tell a friend about leaving very soon for Illinois.[55] She traveled in the company of three couples, the men all ministers —one of them Rev. William Carter of New Canaan. The party's route was via New York City, Baltimore, and Wheeling, and presumably from there via the Ohio and Mississippi Rivers to St. Louis and by stage to Jacksonville. On 20 October Hannah wrote a long letter from Wheeling to Jane and subsequently, in a letter dated 6 November, she reported her arrival in her "new home."

The time of Hannah's journey is corroborated by her entries in a small bound notebook which she had labeled "Text Book." The title was meant quite literally; in it she recorded the Scripture texts used by preachers in their sermons. For example, Mr. Jenney had preached twice on 2 October 1831, taking texts from Job 24:13 and Acts 2:37. Hannah's last entry for a New Canaan church service was dated 29 September. The next entry, on the following line, was dated "3rd November 1833."[56] On that Sabbath the morning preacher was Mr. Sturtevant and the afternoon preacher was Mr. Beecher. Obviously Hannah had reached her destination and was now worshipping with her sister's family in the Presbyterian Church. Subsequently in Hannah's notebook Mr. Sturtevant is listed several times as the preacher in the Presbyterian Church.

There is a brief but significant entry for "December 15th 1833 P.M.": "At the formation of the Congregational church of Jacksonville. Mr. Carter, from Ephesians 5th Chap. 1st V." (Text Book, 20) Hannah was present at the founding of that church which was to be so important not only in the lives of the Sturtevants but also in the development of Congregationalism in the West.

Within a decade Sturtevant's younger brother, his sister, and other relatives were residing in Illinois, some of them to remain there for the rest of their lives. During the same period Elizabeth's father, two of her brothers, and her three sisters also emigrated to central Illinois.

Although Julian Sturtevant was meticulous in meeting his many obligations, financial and otherwise, he apparently did not keep a record of the family's finances. Salary payments and reimbursements for expenditures on behalf of the College were recorded in the College's own "leger" books. Sturtevant retained receipts for the payment of his taxes and legal documents for his own property. The office of the Morgan County Clerk and Recorder of Deeds recorded many real estate transactions in which Sturtevant was engaged personally and on behalf of Illinois College. He also was the agent for relatives and others in the East in purchasing land and paying taxes.

Sturtevant's ownership of real estate was in part unavoidable; the College more than once granted lots to him and other members of the faculty in lieu of cash salary. But in part it was simply an activity which was a central feature of the settlement of "the West." Julian probably enjoyed such transactions, although compared with many he was restrained and seems to have avoided unwise speculation.

Sturtevant was generous to a fault in contributing to the College and to the churches he loved so much. When the Presbyterians sought funds for a building he pledged twenty dollars, half of which he paid in August 1830; he received a request the following May for the balance. In later years he contributed to the Congregational Church and throughout he gave much to Illinois College and even provided loans when funds were not forthcoming from other sources. The pattern of financial responsibility was set early. He was the "principal" for the note which six men of the Association signed at Yale on 6 September 1829. Sturtevant's papers include receipts for purchases made on behalf of Illinois College in 1829 and 1830: $30 for a pair of globes, $5 for partial payment of a lathe, and $9.58 for more than four hundred feet of black walnut and cherry for which the charge was two cents per foot.

Some compensation was given for Sturtevant's ministerial services at the Presbyterian Church in Jacksonville and at other churches, although most churches had very little money. He likely received some small fees for marriages he performed.

Chapter 3: 1834-1844

Achievement and Disappointment; Family Joy and Family Sorrow

The First Graduation, 1835

By 1834 Jacksonville's population had increased to 1800 and continued to grow. The village boasted sixteen stores, several taverns and boarding houses, a court house in the square, a market house, two saddlers, three cabinet makers, six tailors, eleven lawyers, and ten physicians. Mills for flour, lumber, and carding wool were in operation, and also three brickyards. Two newspapers were published weekly, the *Patriot* and the *Gazette*. The Presbyterians, Methodists, and Episcopalians each had a substantial building by 1832.[1] Jacksonville was the largest and in many respects the most important town in the state and it was claimed by some that it was the "intellectual and cultural center."[2] Morgan County, estimated to have 25,000 people, had several Bible Societies, more than three score Sunday Schools, and an equal number of common schools in session at some time during the year. The progress of Illinois College was to a considerable degree related to the local community. Many of its difficulties resulted from the collision in Jacksonville of "two antagonistic civilizations" and the impact of the national financial crisis in 1837.[3]

In the early months of 1834 Sturtevant engaged in numerous routine duties. One evening in early February, at "6 1/2 o'clock," he lectured to the students in the Chapel on "Habits of Application to Study." On another occasion and at the behest of the faculty he addressed the students on the subject of deportment. As secretary of the trustees he informed J. B. Turner of his promotion to "Professor of Rhetoric & Belles Lettres." At the same time Truman Post was named Professor of Latin and Greek. Sturtevant prepared a report on behalf of his faculty colleagues and presented it to the trustees.

At their meeting on 20 March 1834 the trustees assigned Lockwood and Sturtevant to draft the plans for raising $10,000 in Illinois. They also instructed Sturtevant to proceed to the East to obtain funds for the College and authorized him "to expend whatever he may deem expedient for the purchase of books & Philosophical apparatus." (TM, 20 Mar. 1834) The mission was important for the College and provided an opportunity for Sturtevant's professional development. It also allowed his wife a welcome visit to "the home of her youth." (A, 209) She, their daughter Maria (now two years old), and a very young Julian M. Sturtevant Jr., born 2 February, were in the traveling party. So, too, was Elizabeth's sister, Hannah, who had arrived in Jacksonville only a few months earlier.

In a preliminary report in September 1834, Sturtevant recommended a general fund drive, and arrangements were made for Baldwin to join him in the East. Sturtevant went to Amherst to inspect new scientific apparatus at a college and while there participated in discussion with "cultivated minds." (A, 209-10) He especially enjoyed a literary circle which included "a remarkable woman," Mary Lyon, then engaged in establishing Holyoke Seminary. Sturtevant had one fault to find in her—the same one he had found in another woman he also greatly admired, Catharine Beecher. These women were so capable that Sturtevant had difficulty remembering in the spirited discussions to extend "that courtesy ever due to the sex." (A, 212)

Sturtevant hired a couple to look after the dormitory and was authorized to hire an agent for the College. In a letter he prepared for his colleagues, he emphasized their unique responsibility for establishing a respectable literary institution and improving the system of education in Illinois. They also were responsible for *persuading* men to become Christian not only in word but in deed and truth. It was not enough to check open vice "or to keep a certain complicated set of moral machinery in motion or perhaps to increase its velocity a little from year to year."[4] Such actions alone would not aid much in the world's conversion. Sturtevant had discussed these themes in an address at the annual meeting of the American Home Missionary Society soon after he arrived in the East. He had also stressed the need for ministers who were both pious *and educated*, and sought to redirect to the colleges of the West some of the extensive financial support being given to the Bible, Tract, and Sunday School Societies. Such societies, he was convinced, could not fulfill the essential mission the Yale men had undertaken.

After a year's absence Sturtevant, and his family, returned to Jacksonville and he was appointed president pro tempore because Beecher was absent. The prolonged visit in the East had renewed Sturtevant's spirit: "Words cannot express the pleasure I experienced that season in the natural scenery of New England. Its hills and valleys, its clear brooks running over their pebbly bottoms, its bays and rivers, the magnificent prospect revealed on every hand by the inequalities of its surface, its villages lovely in their neatness even when architectural adornment was wanting, were in striking contrast with the monotonous levels, the turbid rivers, the muddy brooks and the unfinished towns of the region where I had spent the previous five years." (A, 212-13) Sturtevant intended someday to return to New England and spend his retirement years there. Realizing that landscape gardening and trees can beautify any country, he eventually came to appreciate his "Western home." The soil of the Illinois prairie was in his judgment unequaled for the growth of trees, and he encouraged planting them on the campus.

Finally, in February 1835, the State Legislature granted the long-sought charter to Illinois College.[5] Lingering fears of the potential economic and political power of those associated with the College resulted in two prohibitions. The College was not permitted to establish a theological department nor own more than 640 acres; both restrictions were removed a few years later. The Charter also imposed an admissions requirement which coincided with the announced policy: the College must be "open to all denominations of Christians, and the profession of any particular religious faith shall not be required of those who become students...." (Sec. 11) In 1837 the trustees published a code of laws which prescribed in detail the governance of the College. It included the text of the Charter and prescribed the duties of the trustees, the president, and the faculty. The course of study was listed and specific subjects were assigned to the various professors. The required religious exercises and the arrangements for students' room and board were stated.

In 1834-1835, two-fifths of the 26 College students and one-third of the 67 preparatory students were from other states, including thirteen in the East, South, and Midwest; "Washington City, D.C.," was also represented. The wide age-range of the students compounded the problems of instruction and the trustees limited admission to boys of fourteen and over. Two years later the College enrollment reached 42, while the preparatory students numbered only 22. The number of good preparatory schools was increasing rapidly, and because the professors had been required to assist in supervising the younger students, the Preparatory Department was eliminated in 1837. The faculty could now devote full attention to the collegiate program, with a consequent elevation of scholarship. Moreover, the expense of the salary for an instructor was eliminated. Due to the Panic of 1837 "the college and the community together were to be hurled from what seemed to be the pinnacle of their prosperity into the deepest disappointment and embarrassment."[6] From that point on the College experienced a series of disasters, relieved fortunately by some notable achievements.

The first graduation ceremony for Illinois College, and the very first such college exercise in the state, was held in September 1835. Starting in 1830, the College had conducted a "commencement" at the beginning of the new academic year.[7] This, however, was the first occasion when degrees were conferred. Because Beecher was in the East Sturtevant as acting president presented the first college diplomas granted in Illinois. The recipients were Richard Yates— later the Civil War Governor of the state, and Jonathan Spillman— lawyer, Presbyterian clergyman, and composer of several popular tunes, including the music often coupled with Robert Burns' "Flow Gently, Sweet Afton." The ceremony was "holden" in the new Congregational Church building on the east side of the public square; it was the largest auditorium in the village and there was a big audience, including many persons from distant parts of the state.

The need for adequate instruction in the sciences received early attention. Arrangements were made in 1833 for lectures in chemistry and for suitable apparatus. The duties of "Lecturer in Chemistry" were added to Sturtevant's portfolio in 1836. In 1837 Dr. Samuel Adams, who held A.B., A.M., and M.D. degrees, was appointed Professor of Chemistry, Mineralogy, and Geology. In 1839 the teaching of

Congregational Church
(1835)
East side of Square

astronomy was assigned to Sturtevant along with mathematics and natural philosophy (physics). He loved to teach and his enthusiasm inspired the students. Along with instructing classes he assisted in raising money and recruiting students. As secretary of the trustees he was present when official actions were taken. He took his turn as secretary of the faculty in 1841-1842 and for a time he was librarian.

After an interval of three years financial necessity led to the restoration of the Preparatory Department, with enrollment limited to students preparing for college entrance. Instruction in French was provided for the upperclassmen. Student competence in Latin had reached a level worthy of public recognition and in 1840 the salutatory address was in that language. By 1841 instruction was offered in botany, zoology, and animal physiology. The enrollment in the College reached a high of 54 in 1842-1843 and the senior class of 12 was the largest yet.

The trustees wished to record the history of the College and directed Rev. Thomas Lippincott to write about the developments leading to its founding. The ten years beginning with the opening of classes were described by Sturtevant in four long letters he addressed to Lippincott in 1844. He did not include the last four years because they were "a season of much toil and conflict and privation; [and] I should not know where to begin or end in writing its history. The past loses itself in the present and the future God only knows where or when it will end."[8]

Student energies were concentrated, to the extent that the faculty could direct them, on the academic and religious programs supplemented by occasional lectures and periodic revivals. A Rhetorical Society was functioning as early as 1836 and sponsored an address in 1843 by Henry Ward Beecher, then a pastor in Indianapolis. A counterpart of Yale's Society for Inquiry Regarding Religion was organized. Some short-lived literary societies may have been established as early as 1836.[9] The two societies which survived and generally have flourished to the present day are Sigma Pi, dating from 1843, and Phi Alpha, founded in 1845. The alumni held their first meeting in September 1839, thus ranking the Illinois College Alumni Association as one of the oldest in the United States.

Life for students was often difficult and especially so for those with limited funds. Samuel Willard, Class of 1843, reported on his studies and his living conditions in letters home. He had to economize severely and for a time lived on five and a fraction cents weekly; his menu three times a day was "bread, melasses & water." Despite a hectic schedule he somehow arranged time for music, adding a request in one letter for his father to bring an A string for his bass viol.[10]

Student misdeeds were common and the faculty's disciplinary actions were duly recorded. The regulations for conduct, spread over three pages of the *Laws of Illinois College*, prohibited fire arms, intoxication, assault upon fellow students, Sabbath violations, gambling, "impure conversation," "corrupt books," and other forms of misbehavior. In 1841 the amended *Laws* required pledges of total abstinence from alcoholic beverages except for sacramental and medicinal purposes. Any student carrying deadly weapons was subject to dismission or expulsion; the latter penalty recommended that he not be admitted elsewhere.

Often the disciplinary problems were related to attendance at College Chapel. A series of such cases involved Thomas Beecher, charged with disturbing the worship of God. Despite reproof by Sturtevant, he showed no signs of reforming and was suspended indefinitely. The faculty asked President Beecher to send appropriate notice to the student, who was his brother, and to their father. A few months later Thomas requested readmission, which was granted conditionally. Father Lyman approved the arrangement but said that if his son fell "under the influence of the opposition line or the anti-government Party" or engaged in supper parties in his room, Sturtevant was to inform him and he would "interpose parental influence."[11] Thomas's conduct was sufficiently good to allow him the A.B. degree in 1843. A few years later he was invited to teach mathematics at Illinois College but, having a better position in Hartford, he declined.

The Minutes of the trustees and faculty refer frequently to the twice-daily prayers and other religious observances at the College. The purpose was not to augment any given denomination but only to encourage the conversion of the students for the sake of their eternal salvation. Revivals sometimes began on the campus and sometimes in the churches; often the "interest" extended to both. In the winter of 1834 about eight to ten young men were regarded as "hopefully converted." "It seemed to be God's blessing poured out upon the regular religious instruction of the college."[12] Attention was given to guiding suitable candidates into the ministry. Like other institutions, Illinois College observed an annual "day of fasting and prayer for the outpouring of the Divine Spirit on the colleges of our land." (FM, 21 Feb. 1842) The faculty appointed Sturtevant to conduct a Bible class on campus. After Beecher's departure Sturtevant assumed the full burden of the Sabbath morning services and other faculty conducted the afternoon service by turns.

In November 1841 forty students petitioned the faculty to change the time of morning prayers from half-past seven to half-past five. The faculty denied the petition and asked Sturtevant to address the students on the subject. Student choral music was instituted very early as part of evening prayers but was not appreciated. In January 1843 a large number of students, noting the feeble and undisciplined state of the choir, requested that the singing be discontinued. Professor Adams was directed to confer with the petitioners and to arrange for improvement.

Aid from the College Society

President Beecher devoted most of his time to fund-raising and was assisted periodically by faculty members and trustees. Earlier the prospect of unlimited prosperity seemed a certainty and the trustees had expanded the faculty and constructed a large dormitory. A series of problems confronting the College reached climactic levels in 1837. Foremost was the severe economic depression. Men who had made subscriptions to the College were bankrupt and could not pay. Gifts of land aggravated the situation because taxes had to be paid on property not used for instruction. In 1839 the trustees issued "An Appeal on Behalf of Illinois College." Previously its primary financial support was from "foreign aid," that is, assistance from the East. Now, only half of the needed $6,000 could be derived from that source. In 1840 a strenuous effort was made to obtain community support for the College and public meetings for that purpose were well attended. One group, attributing the prejudice against the College chiefly to the issue of slavery and abolition, then adopted a proposal favorable to the College. Sturtevant declared that "For a time College was decidedly popular. I hardly ever saw such a change upon Society in my life; for many months Jacksonville seemed at peace."[13]

Unfortunately the response was inadequate and the crisis worsened. In July 1840 the property of the College had been valued at $232,910 and the debt was $18,000. In three years the valuation had decreased by half while the debt had increased to $29,427. The loss to the College due to unpaid subscriptions was over $100,000. In 1841 Sturtevant was directed to visit all parts of Illinois and sections of Iowa and Wisconsin to seek aid. The next year Beecher again went East, taking his family with him; he believed he could be more effective in fund-raising while residing in the East instead of making those long journeys.

The faculty bore the brunt of the College's penury. In 1839 the professors' salaries were $1,000 but were reduced to $700 in 1842 and to $600 the next year. However, Sturtevant was to have an additional $200 as acting-president and for supplying the College pulpit. The establishment of a medical school in 1843 made matters worse; Sturtevant complained bitterly because the trustees had spent $2,000 to repair buildings, including $300 to remodel the workshop into a medical hall. In response to a protest submitted by Sturtevant on behalf of the faculty, the Board remitted the unpaid balance of pledges the professors had made. The faculty's salary payments were not only low but often in arrears, causing faculty families to suffer real want. On one occasion when Sturtevant had to be away for a lengthy period he was able to leave only five dollars with his family. He expected the College's treasurer to provide for them but the family received only ten dollars.[14] That may have been the time recalled by Julian Sturtevant Jr. when the children were fed bread crumbs and water flavored with molasses.

The nation began to recover from its economic distress in about five years but the College's woes continued essentially until the next depression, which occurred in 1847. The founding of Knox College in 1837 generated serious competition for both students and money because Knox appealed to the same constituency. Sturtevant observed years later that "this was the darkest period in the history of Illinois College" and that for a full decade progress was hardly perceptible. (A, 234)

Eastern churches chafed under the added burden of supporting numerous colleges in the West in addition to the established eastern schools and the numerous missionary societies. Theron Baldwin conceived a plan for an association which would raise funds in the East for a limited number of western institutions. In March 1843 representatives of four colleges and Lane Theological Seminary met at the Seminary in Cincinnati. The colleges were Western Reserve and Marietta in Ohio, Wabash in Indiana, and Illinois College, represented by Sturtevant. Baldwin's proposal met with approval and the organization was christened with a name as clear in stating its purpose as it was unwieldy: "The Society for the Promotion of Collegiate and Theological Education at the West." Usage shortened the name to the "Collegiate Education Society," or the "Western College Society," or simply, the "College Society." Baldwin was chosen secretary and a New York office was arranged. Sturtevant attended the anniversary meetings and submitted Illinois College's annual reports and requests for funds.

The responsibility for mundane College business was routinely assigned to the faculty: obtaining chairs and candle-sticks, shovels and tongs, tables for the recitation rooms, and a hod and pokes for the Chapel. Sturtevant and Adams were designated to consider protection of the buildings from lightning. The faculty ruled that the College grounds were not to be used as cow pasture. An unusual enterprise was the provision of a cemetery, a facility too often needed by the faculty. In 1838 the trustees arranged for an area south of the campus to be enclosed and lots were offered for sale. Several interments in the area, perhaps including the Sturtevants' first-born son, had already been made.

Denominational Tensions . . . Another Investigation

Illinois College was founded by the cooperative effort of area laymen and Presbyterian (formerly Congregational) ministers who were supported by the American Home Missionary Society. It was a "Plan of Union" institution, one of several, with the potential support of two denominations noteworthy in their advancement of education. Differences between the denominations and increasing tensions within Presbyterianism subjected Plan of Union colleges to great stress. The cleavage between the Old School and New School Presbyterians deepened, triggering a schism in 1837-1838. There were now two General Assemblies and in many communities (including Jacksonville) a second Presbyterian church was established. The New School party, sympathetic to the Plan of Union, opposed the spread of Congregationalism as hindering the increase of its own numbers and strength. Sturtevant characterized its opposition to Congregationalism as "intense hostility" arising from the conviction that "the whole region west...was consecrated to Presbyterianism." (A, 198) Members of this branch of Presbyterianism sought repeatedly to gain control of Illinois College and, failing to do so, withheld support. Congregationalists became less enthusiastic about supporting the Plan of Union and began to develop a strong sense of denominational identity.

Sturtevant concluded quite early that hierarchical church government was not suited for the West. Although increasingly vocal in advocating Congregationalism, he was not a "sectarian" Congregationalist. Both Sturtevant and Leonard Bacon, a leading churchman, favored the old New England style which brought into common fellowship all the Christians of a community. "Sectarian Congregationalists" were those who formed an exclusive fellowship on the basis of doctrinal tests or an anti-slavery position or some other issue.[15] Sturtevant remarked many times that the original purpose had been to establish Illinois College under the control of "patriotic, religious men" and not under any sect or political group. The aim was "to qualify young men for the intelligent and efficient service of God both in the Church and in the State." The College was never intended "to be a Presbyterian or a Congregational institution, but a Christian institution sacredly devoted to the interests of the Christian faith, universal freedom and social order." (A, 237) Others held quite a different view, among them Rev. A. T. Norton, a Presbyterian, who deplored what he regarded as a shift in the College's affiliation from Presbyterian, to Presbyterian and Congregational, and then Congregational only.[16] The issue proved to be an enduring one and representatives of the two denominations would vie for control of Illinois College for more than a century, with now one and now the other being in the ascendancy. The denominational conflict was costly to Illinois College, depriving it to a large extent of Presbyterian support and diminishing Congregational aid.

Sturtevant had been present at the founding of the Congregational Church of Jacksonville and continued to be involved with it in a variety of ways. He preached at the dedication of its building, completed just in time for the College's first graduation exercises. At the service he reiterated his support of Congregationalism. The Sturtevant household had direct representation in the church when young Hannah Fayerweather became a member late in 1835. The church expressed its support of Sturtevant when it asserted the right of an accused person to a trial by a body responsible to the local congregation. When the Congregationalists found themselves in financial difficulties, Sturtevant and Beecher sought more than once to reunite them with the Presbyterians and even wrote a constitution; their efforts were futile. Nevertheless the Congregationalists declared their desire for fellowship with all evangelical Christians. They invited other churches to join in a day of public Thanksgiving on 29 November 1838.

Representatives of five Congregational churches in the area met at Jacksonville in October 1835 to organize the Congregational Association of Illinois.[17] Sturtevant was not a member of the

Association because of his Presbyterian affiliation, although occasionally he served as a representative of the local church. He likely would have opposed the extreme anti-slavery position which the Association adopted.

In 1836 Sturtevant presided at the organization of the Church of Christ (Congregational) at Waverly in a meeting in the home of his uncle, Deacon Joseph Tanner, the first permanent settler in the village. The Tanners and many early residents of the community had come from Connecticut. Sturtevant was instrumental in encouraging relatives and friends to emigrate to Illinois, and he had recommended the location for the town. In 1837 the church called its first pastor, Rev. Elisha Jenney, one of the original seven in the Illinois Association. In the ensuing years Sturtevant often preached there when it lacked a regular pastor. The town had no Presbyterian church and so the new church did not directly challenge the Plan of Union.

In the early 1840s "the general feeling of antagonism which existed between the Congregationalists and Presbyterians" (CH, 120) manifested itself in a conflict which threatened the very existence of Illinois College. Sturtevant naturally felt dismay and sought zealously to preserve the College if it were within human power to do so. "If it fails because the Providence of God is against it I can bear it," he wrote to Baldwin, but he said he could not tolerate failure resulting from blunders he and his colleagues might make.[18] The seeds of conflict were embedded in the contradictory statements made when the two founding groups arranged their merger. In their letter of 9 March 1829 to Rev. John Ellis, the men at Yale (all but one having Congregational origins) had agreed that the College should be Presbyterian. They failed to grasp the implications of the Plan of Union as it was being applied in Illinois. The Illinois stockholders, however, had agreed to the two conditions set by the Yale men: the Board of Trustees should have entire control of the school, and the Board itself would have sole power to fill any vacancies. Those principles were inimical to control by Presbyterian bodies.

Sturtevant stated his position in letters exchanged with Baldwin in 1843 and 1844. He expressed his view of the controversy and argued the case for himself and his colleagues. He assured Baldwin that he did not intend to conceal his views nor would he think that Baldwin was guilty of interference for "'straightening' us here at the College." (S-B, 12 May 1843) One complaint was that Professor Adams, a layman, had fulfilled the role of a minister in preaching and giving a benediction. Sturtevant agreed that perhaps Adams had not acted wisely, but declared that he had acted within his rights as a free man.

Another issue was fundamental: the charge that the faculty was guilty of holding opinions which were not approved. Allegedly the faculty met privately to express questionable ideas. Sturtevant insisted on reasonable freedom for such discussion. He argued not only for the right to "a latitude of opinion" essential to self-respect and the respect of others but insisted that the trustees must support that right. (S-B, 12 May 1843) Baldwin replied that the critics regarded the faculty as Congregational in their sympathies. Sturtevant declared that the denominational affiliation of faculty members, whether Presbyterian or Congregational, should not be a concern; the only question was whether they were good men and capable teachers.

Sturtevant steadfastly defended his own views which, he insisted, were thoroughly scriptural. For him it was the Bible and not any creed or confession of faith which provided the standard of Christian belief. He believed that even the Old School people would vouch for his orthodoxy. The views of Professors Post and Adams would have been acceptable to the Presbyterians, apart from the matter of church order. Nevertheless critics could find cause for sounding the alarm. Beecher, still affiliated with the College although now absent from the campus, was not altogether conventional in his religious views. J. B. Turner was the most dubious and also the most public in expressing his beliefs. He printed his own creed in a newspaper he published in 1843-1844. Part of Turner's statement may have been acceptable but conservatives objected to many of his affirmations. His assertion that the Sermon on the Mount contained all that is essential to salvation seemed to construe Christianity as merely a moral code. Emphasizing that churches are voluntary organizations, Turner asserted that they have no control over baptism and the Lord's Supper, and both should be available to "all sincere believers."[19]

Rev. Robert W. Patterson, an alumnus of the Class of 1837 and now pastor of a Presbyterian church in Chicago, was especially concerned about the orthodoxy of the College's faculty. Exceptionally able, he was the tutor at the College in 1839-1840. He had attended private discussions in which the faculty expressed ideas very freely and talked about unconventional views without necessarily espousing them. Later Patterson reported to others the comments he had heard, an action the faculty regarded as a breach of confidence. He challenged Sturtevant to disprove his charges and expressed disapproval of Sturtevant's view of creeds. Patterson emphasized that he was "not an enemy of the College, but a would-be friend," and he grieved that he could not have confidence in his Alma Mater.[20] Some critics thought that the faculty would be even more extreme if it were not for the constraint of the Presbyterians. They suspected that the faculty was harboring transcendentalism and thus fostering skepticism and moral relativism; such teachings of course were considered to be highly improper in a Christian college. The term, "transcendentalism," was derived from Immanuel Kant's philosophy but there were other and divergent elements in the American movement known by that name. A basic view was the conviction that *Reason* provided an understanding of man, nature, and God as a harmonious whole, the All. The movement was popular among some of the country's leading literary and religious thinkers, including Ralph Waldo Emerson. Some exponents drew heavily upon Oriental religions, especially Hinduism. Many interpreted the Bible to minimize the importance of miracles in authenticating scriptural authority. To orthodox Christians transcendentalism was equivalent to infidelity.[21]

Sturtevant did not deny the presence of "transcendental skepticism" among the students in 1843 but said the claim that the faculty had taught the "heresy" was absurd. Some students had indeed found it not only interesting but compelling.[22] Samuel Willard and other students had shared with each other their doubts about the church and creeds.[23] Opinions such as they expressed about the Bible and biblical interpretation were then regarded as grave errors. Some say that the Sigma Pi Literary Society was founded to enable students to consider such subjects without hindrance. The records do not explain how the students came to know about transcendentalist thought. Sturtevant later quoted a poem written by Professor Adams which told of a visit by "A sage of transcendental fame" who sought to enlighten the people of "this benighted region." The visitor, not identified, was Emerson.[24]

The situation for Sturtevant and his colleagues became grave when the Presbyterian Synod appointed a committee to investigate charges of heresy against the faculty. Sturtevant told Baldwin that "if Synod had wished to kill the College at a blow, they would have found it difficult to devise a step more directly tending to the result." (CH, 125) He considered resigning but declared that now the trustees must uphold the faculty; if they failed to do so, his usefulness would be minimal although he would stay despite the obloquy if it appeared to be his duty. He did not believe he deserved such treatment from the Synod.

A member of the Synod committee in a letter to the Board of Trustees made broad accusations against the faculty. The faculty protested that they were unfounded and so broad as to make refutation impossible. With the Synod committee present, the trustees questioned the four professors closely, as they themselves requested. Acting as Sturtevant had predicted, the Board the next day declared its satisfaction with the orthodoxy of the faculty and their instruction.[25] He told the faculty that he did not regard the trustees as Presbyterians (which most of them were) but as "in general sound minded honest liberal men" who would not make the College sectarian. Sturtevant was very dissatisfied with the failure of the Synod's committee to recommend either vindication or condemnation of the faculty. He took part in a lengthy discussion at the next Synod meeting and at last the Synod voted to dismiss the subject, neither preferring charges nor rejecting rumors adverse to the College. The Synod did express the wish that the College would continue its "great work of literary and Christian education." (A, 258)

The issues involved in the controversy spread beyond the College and the Synod. Baldwin forwarded the statements by the faculty to some of New England's leading thinkers in New England, including Leonard Bacon, and these authorities sustained the professors' views. Baldwin sent some of Sturtevant's letters to Bacon, leading Sturtevant to write directly to him, saying that he would have phrased them with greater care had he written to someone other than a lifelong friend. He acknowledged his conviction that the church has no right to exclude anyone from the Lord's Supper nor even from baptism, although a local church has the right to decide who can become a member.[26] Sturtevant assured Bacon that he and his associates did not introduce the subject of Congregational polity in their public statements nor did they proselytize for that denomination. Sturtevant denied that they had assailed Presbyterianism and declared bluntly that it was the Presbyterians who were engaged in warfare against him and his colleagues. The real cause for the whole controversy was the Presbyterians' objection to the growth of Congregationalism in Illinois and Iowa.

Sturtevant admitted that he was both in theory and "fervent attachment" a Congregationalist. That system he believed was most likely to preserve the purity of the church and the evangelical character of the ministry. He informed Bacon that a majority of the trustees were good conservative New School Presbyterian ministers and ruling elders. The College men agreed that the conflict between the two denominations "at the West" could not continue. "The only true issue [between them]," said Sturtevant, "is between Hierarchy and Independency...."[27]

The Slavery Controversy

Slavery was an issue when the United States Constitution was adopted and even before. The westward expansion of the nation led to the admission of additional states, and conflict ensued over the balance between slave and free states because that factor determined the control of the Senate. Illinois was a free state but many of its early settlers came from Missouri and Kentucky, where slavery was legal. The local situation was characterized by Sturtevant as "quite peculiar." (A, 215) The majority of the area's people were Southern in their sympathies, although many had left the slave-states to avoid the competition from slave labor. Tension quickly developed between them and the New Englanders at Illinois College. A fair proportion of the first students came from Southern states, and some persons believed that the College sought to persuade them to adopt the abolitionist cause. The nearness to St. Louis further aggravated the problem because its newspapers were outspoken in their hostility to abolition and therefore to Illinois College.

Supporters of slavery ranged from those who upheld its legality to some who believed it sanctioned by morality and the Bible. Opponents also exhibited great variety. Sturtevant had learned in childhood to oppose slavery. He agreed with William Lloyd Garrison that slavery was sinful and he felt that the nation was subject to God's judgment for permitting it to exist. He disagreed with Garrison who advocated in extreme language immediate and absolute abolition. That remedy was impossible because the Constitution itself recognized the system but, contrary to those who denounced the Constitution for that reason, Sturtevant emphasized that the provision for amendment offered a political solution. He supported those who aided fugitive slaves, saying that "there are times when good citizenship has no higher expression than the loyal acceptance of a penalty for breaking a law which conscience forbids one to obey." (A, 218)

Sturtevant's position did not satisfy anyone. He "went too far against slavery to win the favor of its advocates, and not far enough to gain the approbation of its assailants." (A, 223) In early November 1837, while attending the Presbyterian Synod of Illinois, Sturtevant was engaged in discussing whether Elijah Lovejoy should continue his newspaper in Alton. Sturtevant alone argued that the attempt to install another press would result in disaster. Sturtevant knew Lovejoy well, having often entertained him in his home,[28] and he contrasted Lovejoy's "mild, temperate, and gentlemanly language" with Garrison's violent rhetoric. Lovejoy, he said, was "bold and fearless, [but] nevertheless an amiable, affectionate, and lovable man." (A, 222)

President Beecher was a close friend of Elijah Lovejoy and entertained him as a guest for the College's 1837 commencement. Beecher went to Alton in early November for a convention called by Lovejoy to consolidate the opposition to slavery. Despite great antagonism the Illinois State Anti-Slavery Society was formed. Other members of the Illinois Association who had prominent roles in the movement were Asa Turner, William Kirby, Albert

Hale, and Flavel Bascom. All the professors at the College were unanimous in their opposition to slavery, although Sturtevant (and his close friend Baldwin) were moderates.[29] Because it would not have been wise for Sturtevant to leave when President Beecher was absent, he did not go to Alton. Also, he was committed to performing a marriage at that time.

Beecher remained in Alton to help Lovejoy guard a new press and, thinking that the danger had subsided, he set out to return to Jacksonville. That very night, 7 November 1837, Lovejoy was martyred. Because intense feelings had been aroused on both sides there was fear that a mob might be stirred up against Beecher and the College. The faculty, including Sturtevant, prepared to resist any such action. The threat did not prevent students from gathering at their dormitory to hold a meeting in protest against the Alton mob[30] and fortunately there was no overt action against the College. Enrollment at the College had declined but it was largely the result of closing the Preparatory Department and not, as the St. Louis newspapers and other "enemies" charged, due to the faculty's abolitionism.

An incident in Jacksonville was instrumental in changing local opinion. A male slave, brought to the town in 1834 by a Southern family, had exercised his right to freedom in the free state of Illinois. In 1838 the man was seized by armed men and forcibly taken to the South on a river steamer. The gang leader, indicted for kidnapping, was acquitted. The miscarriage of justice shocked the community, at first paralyzing and then rallying the anti-slavery forces. From then on opposition to slavery steadily increased, although there were few days when the faculty was not "rendered more or less unquiet" because of the controversy. For a time the churches of the community feared to let their buildings be used for the exhibitions where students delivered their essays because most of them were vocal in expressing anti-slavery sentiments.[31]

Sturtevant acknowledged the need to assume a more active personal role against slavery and apologized for having delayed so long. He assessed the criticism against the College's role as "the most unavoidable, the most violent, and the most protracted" assault it ever endured. Indeed, "the force of the storm beat upon us just in proportion to the conspicuousness of our position and the weight which men attached to our influence." (A, 214) He attributed the College's slow growth primarily to this problem. His extensive discussion of this issue in his *Autobiography* testifies to its importance.

The Morgan County Colonization Society was a branch of the national society, organized in 1817 to raise money for purchasing slaves and returning them to Africa. Sturtevant addressed the group in Jacksonville on 8 June 1841,[32] but it is doubtful that he had an active role in the Society; overall the organization had little success. Sturtevant did not believe that the men at the College should be involved in controversial organizations, but neither his colleagues nor the students heeded his example.

Once again slavery became the focal point of controversy in early 1843 when some students, among them Samuel Willard, aided a Negro woman's escape. The woman, a slave in Missouri, was brought to Jacksonville when her mistress came on a visit. The students' action aroused some in the community against the College. Thirty-six citizens signed a notice, published as a broadside, expressing displeasure at "the late outrage committed upon the property of a widow lady visiting our town…." The Prudential Committee of the Board was called to take protective action and the faculty again accepted partial responsibility for helping to defend College property. The protesters decided not to take any direct action against the students and left it to the College to defend her own reputation.[33]

The Congregational Church of Jacksonville was known as the  "Abolition Church" and was the only church in the area which supported that position. Among the members of the congregation prominent in the movement was Elihu Wolcott, the first president of the Illinois State Anti-Slavery Society. Wolcott aided Emily Logan, the sister of the man who had been kidnapped, in gaining legal status as a free woman; money collected at a communion service was given to defray part of the expenses. She was one of three members identified in church records as "colored." Each Sunday a church member taught "a class of colored children" but did so in her own home because even some Congregationalists "were not free from a disposition to look with disfavor on negro *[sic]* children being admitted to the Sabbath School."34

Neither Sturtevant's writings nor the church's records report any specific role for him in the church's opposition to slavery. In his *Autobiography* he acknowledged that the Congregational Church deserved credit for much of the increased sympathy for anti-slavery attitudes in the community. "In it the negro *[sic]*...was recognized and treated as a brother. From its very organization it was known as the 'Abolition Church,' and those not willing to extend Christian fellowship to all of God's children, whether white or black, rich or poor, would not seek membership there. It has always stood forth in bold relief as the representative of freedom, intellectual, personal and ecclesiastical." The church gained neither wealth nor a large membership but, Sturtevant declared, it has been "a power for good wherever its influence has been felt." (A, 229-30)

Community Service . . . Addresses and Articles

As an ordained minister Julian Sturtevant not only preached the Gospel and administered the Lord's Supper, he also performed baptisms, conducted funerals, and officiated at weddings. The "Marriage Record" books of Morgan County list eighteen couples for whom Sturtevant performed the marriage rite during this period. He served the local Congregational Church in various capacities, preaching for extended periods when there was no regular pastor. The Church's Minutes noted when he was paid for conducting the worship services, and he was often called to "take the chair" to preside at a meeting. He sometimes preached for several weeks at a time at the Congregational Church of Christ at Waverly. He rode horseback and avoided violation of the Sabbath by traveling Saturday and returning early on Monday morning for his classes.

Meanwhile Sturtevant held standing in the Presbytery but considered himself as a co-worker with the Presbyterians. Often called to fill Presbyterian pulpits, he delivered two "excellent sermons" at Naples on the Illinois River in the autumn of 1835.35 In 1836 he went to the home of Dr. Charles Chandler, some twenty-five miles north of Jacksonville, having been appointed by the Presbytery to assist in organizing a Presbyterian Church. Later, serving as moderator for that church, Sturtevant was present to administer the Lord's Supper.[36] He attended meetings of the Presbytery and Synod, as at Canton in the fall of 1840.

Joseph Duncan was Governor of Illinois from 1834 to 1838. He built a large family home in Jacksonville, about a quarter-mile north of the Sturtevants' campus residence. Duncan had been elected a trustee of Illinois College in 1835. There were some social visits between the two families. Mrs. Elizabeth Duncan recorded in her Diary several instances when Sturtevant preached in the local Presbyterian Church. On the Sabbath before Christmas (1841) he had chosen his text from Ecclesiastes [9:10], which Mrs. Duncan paraphrased thus: "Whatever thine hands find to do, do it with all thy might." Another time Mr. Sturtevant preached both in the morning and again in the afternoon; the latter service was the installation of Rev. William H. Williams as pastor. ("Diary," 30, 59, 60, 67) Sturtevant's growing reputation led to invitations to give the prayer for the Illinois Senate in February 1843 and for the House that December.

When Governor Duncan died, Rev. Julian Sturtevant conducted the "solemn and impressive" funeral on 16 January 1844 at the Presbyterian Church.[37] Drawing from the book of Psalms, Sturtevant began his lengthy sermon with reminders of the mortality of human beings, witnessed by everyone not only in the passing of the older generation but also in the deaths of their peers and even children. After outlining Duncan's military and political career and his ardent support of education, both collegiate and public, Sturtevant described Duncan's religious life as much stronger than the public knew. He appealed in emotional language for his listeners to heed the dying man's injunction to make their peace with God, asking, "Whose turn shall come next?" (14) The sermon concluded with expressions of sympathy for the mourning family and with biblical quotations expressing the need for trust in God.[38]

That the Duncan family held Sturtevant in high regard was shown in his appointment as trustee of land which Governor Duncan had set aside in his wife's name to preserve a trust her father had established.[39] Its purpose was to provide for her support and the children's education.

From the very time of his arrival in Illinois Sturtevant lamented the divisions and hostility between Christian groups. He fully sympathized with a pertinent statement in the Minutes of the Congregational Church—and likely he inspired it. The church declared it had the purpose "to promote the unity and brotherhood of the Church of Christ at large." (CCM, 16 Sept. 1841) The specific occasion was an invitation to the Methodist Conference to occupy the Congregational house of worship on the Sabbath.

Sturtevant eagerly preached the Gospel to any group, although he was careful to distinguish himself from beliefs and practices which he regarded as unsound or wrong on the basis of Scripture. On one occasion in 1840 he preached to some Campbellites (Disciples) at their church near Jacksonville. During the service he realized that they would follow their custom of celebrating communion every Sabbath. Believing that it would be a breach of Christian hospitality to do otherwise, he joined with them "in breaking bread in the name of the Lord." Sturtevant's meeting with the Disciples quickly became known, provoking a storm of criticism. Soon, however, people began to acknowledge the propriety of his action and Sturtevant was pleased that he had aided in breaking down "unchristian barriers" around the Lord's Supper. He was careful to explain that he rejected utterances by some Disciples which he considered almost blasphemous. Sturtevant's own orthodoxy was demonstrated when he publicly criticized the gravely erroneous and "shocking doctrines" of a Disciples preacher. Sturtevant spoke outdoors for two and a half hours to "a great multitude consisting mostly of Disciples, Methodists and regular Baptists" and in the presence of that preacher. (A, 246-48) The man's influence rapidly declined and happily there was no permanent damage to Sturtevant's friendly relationship with the Disciples.

Jacksonville was not alone in experiencing religious strife. After a visit to "Sangamon bottom" in the summer of 1843, Sturtevant spoke of the religious turmoil there. He described another town in the area as "a moral landscape which beggars all description." "Presbyterianism, Congregationalism, Unionism, abolitionism, Women's rights-ism, and all other new isms" wrought not only confusion but destruction. Yet Sturtevant dared to hope that the iron chains of immemorial prejudice would disintegrate and permit the masses to enter into new and better combinations.[40]

Along with his manifold duties at the College and his family responsibilities, Sturtevant continued his active role in community affairs. He was a trustee of the Jacksonville Female Academy and participated in the annual public meetings of the Ladies' Association for Educating Females. (At that time Mrs. Elizabeth Sturtevant was a member of the Executive Committee of the Ladies' Association.) In an address at its 1839 meeting Sturtevant declared that just as young men are educated by the government at West Point for service to their country, so children should be educated by the community for service to the public. Sturtevant was a leader in the Illinois Teachers' Association, founded in Jacksonville at the time of the 1836 Commencement. Heading that organization was his associate, John Brooks, who had established a "Teachers Seminary" in Waverly. In 1845 the Teachers' Convention was held in Jacksonville at Commencement time. The following year Sturtevant wrote an essay for the Convention's Chicago meeting.[41]

In 1837 E. T. and C. Goudy, publishers in Jacksonville, established a monthly periodical, *The Common School Advocate*. It was the first educational journal in the West and continued publication for one year. The paper was edited by Illinois College faculty and associates. The September issue noted that Sturtevant was chairman of the study on "the best modes of country organization for the promotion of common schools." (69) It also reported his address to the annual meeting of the Teachers' Association on the subject of manual labor seminaries. Sturtevant declared that the system of manual labor for schools did not deserve the degree of public approval it received. Other forms of exercise were better adapted to individual needs and interfered less with studies than a rigid schedule of labor. Moreover, it was neither practical nor possible to rely on manual labor to defray educational expenses. The public should be willing to pay for education because it is a great blessing to the people. Students should not be ashamed to labor but they should keep in mind "the main end of all—the cultivation of their minds, that they may serve with the full-grown fruit of all their talents the cause of GOD and HUMANITY."[42]

When Illinois College ceased its preparatory classes in 1837, there was still need for such schooling. The *Advocate* announced the opening of the "Jacksonville Academy" in "a large and commodious room in the basement story of the Congregational church." The advertisement appeared over the names of the trustees, among them Post, Turner, and Sturtevant. Later the public was informed that room and board could be obtained at Illinois College for Academy students who were fourteen or over.

Sturtevant
(Artist unknown; undated)

As a member of the committee issuing a call for a convention to establish common (public) schools in Illinois, Sturtevant addressed the assembly when it met in Springfield in mid-December 1840. In 1843 he gave a series of lectures in Springfield presenting the need for a state superintendent of schools; however, no action was taken for a year or more.

The trustees and faculty of Illinois College encouraged the State of Illinois to found specialized educational institutions. In 1839 approval was given for an "Asylum for the Education of the Deaf and Dumb in Illinois," to be located in Jacksonville. The Governor appointed a Board of Trustees which included ten men from Morgan County, among them Julian Sturtevant and others associated with Illinois College.[43]

The men from Yale were deeply patriotic and on at least one occasion recitations at the College were dispensed with so that all could attend "a public celebration of the father of his country." (FM, 21 Feb. 1842) In 1841 Sturtevant addressed the Jacksonville Mechanics' Union, which skilled workmen had organized to provide relief for needy members and their families and also for "the promotion of literature, science and the mechanic arts."[44] Sturtevant's discourse on democracy was scholarly with many references to classical and historical sources; the text was published by the Union in 1842. He defined democracy as government in which the people rule and declared that America was not less democratic because its democracy was representative in form. The fundamental qualities of the citizens of a democracy are knowledge, skill, and virtue, which elevate them "to the condition of intellectual, social and immortal beings." (5) Sturtevant disagreed with Tocqueville's assertion that equality of condition is the essence of a democracy; it is rather freedom of access to knowledge, power, and wealth for all classes and individuals.

The emergence of the democratic movement world-wide and its culmination in America were the consequence of "the decree of heaven…that knowledge and power shall be imparted to the people." (8) Behind this movement was an omnipotent "unseen hand"— Sturtevant borrowed the phrase from Adam Smith. Four significant factors contributed to the rise of democracy: the compass, improving navigation; labor-saving machinery, relieving the masses from dependence on the land; the printing press, making knowledge available to all; and the equalizing influence of Christianity, which places both "the king and the cottager…on the same platform before the tribunal of divine justice." (12) Maintaining the power of the people requires intensive effort in the formation of individual character and thus necessitates a system of education both effi-cient and universal. Virtue is essential in the exercise of power in a democracy, and national virtue can be achieved only through the Christian religion. Finally, power must always be exercised through duly constituted laws and offices, not by individuals taking justice into their own hands. Sturtevant's closing sentences conveyed both optimism and sober warning. The principle of democracy is God-given and therefore safe forever, but "this country is yet an experiment" and may fail. (17) "Let us then feel each and all of us our responsibility as put in trust with the safe keeping of the sacred principle of democracy—responsibility to our country, to the human race, to our posterity, and to God." (18)

In articles published in 1843 and 1844 Sturtevant discussed the sacred task of evangelism. All Christians agree, he said, that "*the whole world is to be converted to the Christian faith.*" Each denom-ination thinks this can best be achieved by bringing everyone into its own fold. But something is lacking. Every Christian group must measure every aspect of its doctrine, especially, and also of its organization, against "the acknowledged infallible standard," the Bible. Free investigation of the Bible must be continued because it is the common fountain of religious truth and only it must be required by Christians; no aspect of the church is to be protected from "the progressive advancement of biblical knowledge."[45]

Two organizations, said Sturtevant, accomplish much good work but do not merit the extensive support and financing provided by church people.[46] The American Education Society had assisted him and many other poor youth to gain an education and prepare for the ministry. Often, however, recipients were too young to pledge their lives to the ministry with the result that many men unsuited to that calling felt obliged to undertake it. The Society should raise funds but allow the colleges to select and watch over the beneficiaries of its aid. Even more searching criticism was focused on the tract societies. Their evangelism in the West was highly inefficient because a large percentage of the population was illiterate. Frontier people can and will hear living speakers and there is a vital need for an educated ministry who can *speak* the Gospel; of course, preparing such men requires permanent institutions. Moreover two such men can be placed in the field for what the tract society pays to support one itinerant distributing tracts. Some of these arguments had been previewed ten years earlier in an address Sturtevant had delivered before the American Home Missionary Society. That Society, he had said, had undertaken a great enterprise, "to give to the entire population of this land the stated labours of an *educated* and *pious* ministry," and achieving that goal depends upon "institutions of learning and religion."[47]

Sturtevant published a review of J. B. Turner's *Mormonism in All Ages*. The Mormons were currently headquartered in Illinois and were the subject of great interest as an example of what some regarded as widespread fanaticism. Turner had done a great service, Sturtevant wrote, by analyzing the types of persons attracted to such a phenomenon and by demonstrating its similarity to the religious fallacies of earlier history. Sturtevant bluntly condemned Mormonism as the "shameless imposture of Joe Smith and his associates" and declared that "Its details are loathsome and disgusting...." (109) He regarded Joseph Smith's claims as based on mere human testimony, whereas the Bible is attested by miracles (acknowledged even by hostile witnesses) and by the prophecies of hundreds of years which were fulfilled in Jesus. The fruits of any claim to inspiration must be tested for consistency with Scripture and reason, and in Sturtevant's view the Mormon claim failed on both counts.

Letters about Family Life

Little information is extant about the Sturtevants' sojourn in the East in 1834-1835.[48] The entire family returned to their home on the Illinois College campus in April 1835. The birth of another son gladdened them when James Warren was born on 27 February 1836. Elizabeth Maria was now four years old, and Julian Monson Jr. was two. Hannah Augusta was born on 12 May 1838 and Edgar Lewis on 29 January 1840. The Sturtevants' home, adjacent to the College's huge dormitory, was adequate for the growing family. Relatives and friends were often guests, sometimes for lengthy stays; the gracious hospitality afforded by Elizabeth and Julian was much preferred to the inns of Jacksonville.

Letters written in January 1838 by Elizabeth and Hannah to their Connecticut cousins provide intimate glimpses of family life.[49] Elizabeth's letter will be quoted at length.

> We have had such a warm pleasant winter, that nobody has been shut up at all.... We have had but a few cold days & none sufficiently so to freeze in the house.... We received duly some letters & a little bundle from you by Mr. Enoch Mead. He did not come here, but sent them immediately from Alton. We are very much obliged to you for the patterns as well as the letters.... I did my part towards making up a little package of letters to go East at our Commencement time, & sent them by Mr. Gaylord....
>
> Miss Mary Coffin is kind enough to come in every day & with three other children Maria & Julian form a little school for her, for two hours in the morning. They occupy our front basement room, which we use for a dining room.... Hannah has made [Julian Jr.] two suits of clothes, out of his Father's, & a white collar, & a cloak out of his Uncle James' "wrapper." Maria wears the same little green cloth cloak which Caroline gave her.... James Warren has to take whatever descends to him from being outgrown....

I believe we told you that Mr. S[turtevant] was preaching in the Pres[byterian] Church for a short time…In consequence of Mr. S. preaching in town, I suppose, the good people have made us some little presents. H[annah] has had a handsome calico dress & a pair of black silk stockings; Maria a white fur cape & black beaver bonnet trimmed with blue; Julian a black beaver hat & three silk kerchiefs.… My present was a pair of black silk stockings & a double worked collar. Mr. S. had two silk kerchiefs.

We are taking clear comfort this winter in living without boarders. We eat & drink what we please, & nobody to criticize —or suggest improvements, in the manner of cooking. We cannot help saying to each other, even now, how comfortable to be by ourselves. We learn by experience. We used to buy our milk at six cents per Quart, take all the cream for tea & coffee. But last summer Mr. S. put up a little barn…& now we keep a cow. I keep the cream for butter, & so far we have made half a dollar's worth every week since we commenced. This would be a small matter to some people, but it is rather an important item to us.…

How did you pass Thanksgiving day? I hope you thought of us a little for we thought much of you. I wished we could celebrate the day too but we did nothing remarkable on that day. Christmas we treated ourselves to a turkey—the only one that we shall probably have this winter. It is a day quite celebrated here; most every one expects to give or receive a Christmas gift. As we could not give, we did not receive.…

[Jany. 3rd.] Will you not some day come out here & see us all? I hope to visit you all again some time. Mr. Sturtevant loves New England better & better every year. Sometimes I think that he is almost an <u>enthusiast</u> with reference to his native land.…

I fear the late Alton affair will diminish your favorable impression of the West somewhat, but I think the spirit of mobs will not be tolerated.… [F]or some time I could not help feeling that mob law would meet with more approbation in <u>this</u> State than in any other. But there has been such expression of feeling that I now feel that mobs will hereafter be quelled here as they have been at the East…. Mr. Sturtevant thinks that everybody has a right to his own private opinion but that the college officers ought not to take any part in the public matters of so exciting a question. An anti-slavery leader or any other leader ought to be disconnected with any other interest….

Elizabeth said she had no adventures to relate because she stayed home almost as much as her mother did. She added, "I mend almost as much too…. Do, dear Laura, write to me soon…. [Y]our affectionate cousin. Elizabeth."

Writing crosswise at the top of the first page, Elizabeth added: "Mr. Sturtevant intended writing something about some business matters, but he has such a violent pain in his face that he cannot write, or talk enough to make it intelligible enough for me to write. He will write about it before long. I will just say we have never said a word about it to any one—my brothers do not know anything about it. I believe they know that Mr. S. hired[?] some money of Caroline but they know nothing definite." The reference to "business" matters is puzzling; possibly Sturtevant had borrowed some money at interest. In later years he sometimes sought to borrow money from a friend.

Hannah wrote an almost equally long letter, to another cousin, on the third and fourth pages of the very large folded sheet which Elizabeth had used for hers. She described some social activities and fashions and told of knitting mittens for the children. Just before Christmas she and other young women were invited by Mrs. Duncan to assist in making dresses for wax dolls the Governor had brought from New York for their two young daughters. None of the dresses was finished on that occasion. Hannah did not wish to take hers to finish at home because, she wrote, "I had three babies to work for all the time."

Both Elizabeth and Hannah had mentioned with keen interest the recent marriage of Virginia Nash and John Todd Stuart.[50] Mrs. Stuart was the niece and ward of Judge Lockwood, president of the Board of Trustees. Her husband was a first cousin of Mary Todd Lincoln and later examined Lincoln for the bar and took him into his law practice. Julian Sturtevant had officiated at the wedding on 25 October 1837. Hannah was a bridesmaid and wore a dress—given to her by Mrs. Stuart, silk stockings—from

Mrs. Lockwood, and a silver flower for her hair—from Mrs. Clay. Hannah continued, describing their evenings together.

> E[lizabeth] and myself are reading together Travels in Egypt, Arabia Petrea[sp.?], & the Holy Land, by Stephens.... We wait till the children get to bed, then E. takes her work & I the book till some interruption occurs to compel me to lay it aside. It is the only way & time we can read anything.... You know what a systematic body E. is—her household is almost as systematic as it can be. I have my particular work, Emily hers, & E. superintends the whole, doing a little here & there. James Warren sleeps with me. I get up to breakfast at 1/2 past seven (the baby wakes when I get up). After breakfast I sweep & dust the parlor, the two entries, & two pairs of stairs & trim the lamps, make my bed, & clear up my own room. Some days [I] sweep E.'s room & make her bed. I used to make almost all the pies & cake we used but somehow E. has taken the pie making into her own hands, & as for cake we don't have any. Mr. Sturtevant is more fond of warm bread & milk than anything else we can set before him, [so] that we sometimes think it is hardly worth our while to make any-thing but good bread & butter. E. has learned by practice & experience to make most excellent bread. I assure you we live very happily this winter.

The third part of the final fold of the letter was tucked in and provided space for additional comment. "I attend our sewing Soc[iety] nearly every week. We meet Tuesday evenings. Miss Coffin & myself are a committee to select reading. We are now reading 'An Irish Heart,' No. eleven of Sargeant's Temperance Tales. Have you read that? It is one of the most affecting tales I ever read.... The Society are working for the Female Academy this year; they require a Library & Philosophical Apparatus—and an additional building. [What] our funds shall go towards purchas-ing...has not been certainly [deter]mined."

The main source of income for the Sturtevant family was the salary from Illinois College. Had the payments been timely and in cash, the family might have fared well enough but neither of those conditions was regularly met. The faculty contributed to the

College, in effect reducing their salaries. Sturtevant had some additional income from preaching, weddings, and funerals although he sometimes reduced his College salary accordingly.

Very soon after returning from the East in the spring of 1835, Sturtevant made two purchases of Federal land, perhaps for some of the relatives and friends he had visited. One tract was a quarter-section (160 acres), the other about 42 acres; both were in Madison County, and the price was the standard $1.25 per acre. Receipts on file show that later that year he purchased two plots (totaling about 144 acres) in Sangamon Country, just east of Waverly. In one case Sturtevant used Military Land Scrip, but there is no explanation of how he obtained that. In 1836 he purchased 240 acres, in LaSalle and Logan counties.[51] Although Sturtevant surely did not have funds to make such purchases for himself, he may well have enjoyed engaging in such ventures for others.

Sturtevant bought land close to Jacksonville for farming and pasture, and to obtain firewood. In September 1835 Sturtevant arranged to buy an eighty acre plot on the east side of present Lincoln Avenue between Morton and Superior and an additional forty acres on the west side of Lincoln, between Michigan and Diamond Grove Cemetery. Sturtevant signed a mortgage in the amount of $3475, due in 1837; interest was payable at the rate of twelve per cent. In 1838 Sturtevant sold eleven acres of woodland from the parcel west of Lincoln for $200 and a large supply of wood for fuel. The buyer was to deliver twenty cords of oak and hickory before March 1839 and fifty-six and a quarter cords of wood before November. Apparently the buyer relinquished the land and in 1839 Sturtevant and his wife mortgaged the two parcels with one hundred twenty acres to Judge Lockwood for $800, which they were to pay within two years. In 1845 the parcels were sold to Richard Fayerweather for $3600.

In 1836 Illinois College prepared a plan of the lots the trustees wished to sell in the area north, east, and south of the campus, to be known as the College Hill Addition. In 1840 several lots north of College Avenue, somewhat west of Park, were transferred to Sturtevant for services rendered and an additional $175. Subsequently additional lots in College Hill east of the campus were turned over to Sturtevant, although the transfer was not recorded until 1847 when the area was plotted again.[52] The value of the Sturtevant property and the taxes varied considerably from year to year. In 1838 he paid real estate taxes of $3.96 and a tax of sixty-five cents on personal property. The real estate valuation ranged from $130 in 1841 to $478 the following year; his personal property was assessed at $245 to $300 and his taxes ranged about three dollars.

The Sturtevants purchased two lots in Waverly in the mid-1830s. Julian served as an agent for Elizabeth's aunt, Diana C. Richards of New Canaan, Connecticut, in obtaining three lots in that town which she owned for about thirty years. In the early years the valuation of the land ranged from $10 to $30 per lot and the tax bill varied from eighteen to thirty-five cents.

Supplemented by other records, the extant correspondence provides sketches of Julian's and Elizabeth's relatives, many of whom followed them to Illinois. Two of Elizabeth's brothers, James (with his family) and Silas, lived at nearby Rushville. The father, Richard Fayerweather, was encouraged by his children to join his sons in the summer of 1837; he was accompanied by two daughters, Julia and Mary Jane.[53] About two years later, Richard and the daughters settled near Jacksonville, and James and his family moved to Burlington, Iowa.

Julian was likely instrumental in arranging for his sister, Huldah, to obtain a position (1839-1840) at the Monticello Female Seminary which had recently opened under Theron Baldwin's supervision.[54] Brother Christopher brought his family to Jacksonville in 1839 and became an active member of the Congregational Church. Mrs. Duncan noted in her Diary (April 1841) that they had been invited to Julian Sturtevant's home to meet C. Sturtevant's family. Brother Ephraim, still in Ohio, wrote to urge Julian to sign a deed when their father sent it.

In 1838 Silas Fayerweather went to New Orleans, where he was to remain the rest of his life. He wrote to express gratitude to Julian, for whom he had great respect, and observed that their father had received far better treatment from his son-in-law than from his own sons. Abraham Fayerweather had remained in the Sandwich Islands, and in March 1839 he married Mary Beckly, the daughter of an Englishman and his wife, a Hawaiian chiefess.

Elizabeth's Death . . . Marriage to Hannah

Overall, Julian Sturtevant declared, his health had been better than he would have expected and his endurance for the kind of work he was engaged in was great although physically he could not match most men. However, he periodically suffered ailments which sometimes incapacitated him for weeks or months. Summer weather was oppressive and during the hot months of 1835 he became gravely ill. J. B. Turner, writing to his fiancee, reported that in addition to managing the College in the absence of both Beecher and Post, he had to give "frequent attention during the day and night to Mr. S. who was then dangerously sick...."[55] By September Sturtevant had recovered and was able to preside at the College's graduation ceremony. In 1844 a different affliction hindered Sturtevant when he was preparing the history of the College; his eyes were so sore that he had to rely on Hannah as his amanuensis. Explaining this to Lippincott, he said that his friend would not regret the substitution.

Julian experienced his most serious illness in 1839—a sharp attack of malarial fever, a disease uncommon in Jacksonville. Apparently he did not suffer any lasting effects from it, but his wife was not so fortunate. In August Elizabeth became very sick with the same disease and made a very slow recovery, eventually being able to resume her household duties. Julian went to Springfield on College business right after Christmas, but a week later was notified that his wife had suffered a relapse. Hurrying home, he found that she was seriously ill, her condition being complicated by pregnancy. On 29 January 1840 Elizabeth bore their sixth child, Edgar Lewis. Two weeks later, on 12 February, she succumbed. Elizabeth was buried next to the grave of their first son, the first Julian Monson Sturtevant Jr.

Julian was devastated by the death of his beloved wife. He often saw her in his dreams and more than forty years after she died he had an especially vivid dream. Elizabeth, in "unearthly" beauty, stood before him. She said "I never loved you so much before" and then she embraced him. In his intense effort to respond, Julian awakened. The dream left a deep impression upon him although he remarked that he made no effort to interpret it. He was convinced, however, that after his own death he would meet her again "in like angelic brightness, and with like assurances of undying affection." The only fitting tribute he could render her was to declare that she was "perfected womanhood." He decried the notion that heroism was dead, recalling the bravery that Elizabeth and other women had exhibited in coming to a "new home in the wild West." (A, 146, 240-42)

Even the comfort of his friends, who assured him that Elizabeth had gone to a happier place, could not overcome Julian's "unutterable sorrow." At the time the only thought which could assuage his grief was "the assurance of the unfailing kindness, wisdom and love of a Heavenly Father. I opened not my mouth because God had done it." (A, 241) There were many expressions of sympathy for the grieving husband, from those nearby and from relatives in the East and from Silas and Abraham. Silas sent $200 to help with burial and other expenses.

The death of the infant son, Edgar Lewis, in July—only a few months after his mother's death—was probably not unexpected. An even greater blow was the sudden illness which after a few days resulted in the death of Elizabeth Maria on 20 November.[56] Eight years old when her mother died, she was seemingly in good health. Once again bereavement brought great pain to Julian Sturtevant, but in time he could express his gratitude to God for his daughter's loveliness and for having loved her and for having been loved by her. He was convinced that "such loveliness cannot die. It is only transplanted to the garden of God." (A, 242)

When Elizabeth died there were five children to be cared for, the oldest a little less than eight years old; fortunately Elizabeth's sister Hannah was there to help. She was also present to share the sad watch over the illness and death of the youngest and then the oldest of her sister's children. The remaining three children ranged in age from six to two years. Cousin Laura had written (12 Mar. 1840) that Hannah would "feel like a Mother" to the children because she had been with them for so many years. Sisters Julia and Mary Jane and father Richard were not far away and gave Hannah support.

For his own sake and for his children Sturtevant resolved to marry again. Referring to Elizabeth's death, he wrote: "I did not then, and still less do I now, subscribe to the doctrine that a man thus painfully bereaved at the age of thirty-four best honors the memory of the departed by remaining unmarried. The sweet remembrance of years of conjugal happiness is not a preparation for a life of loneliness." He continued with a brief account of his second marriage. "Hannah Richards Fayerweather, the youngest sister of the departed one, had been a constant member of my family from a period prior to the birth of my eldest surviving child. She had shared with her older sister the cares and burdens of rearing them all, and from the time of their mother's death had taken, as far as might be, the mother's place. It seemed that nothing could be so well for me and my children as that she should become the wife and the mother. Accordingly on the third of March, 1841, we were married, and experience has abundantly justified the wisdom of the step." (A, 251)

Hannah certainly knew well not only the children but also their father when she consented to become the second Mrs. Sturtevant. The wedding took place in the Sturtevant home with their close friend and neighbor, Edward Beecher, officiating. Julian Jr., little more than seven years old at the time, remembered the occasion very well. "[O]ne morning…father called his children into a quiet room and told us that in a few minutes he and our dear Aunt Hannah were to be married by Doctor Beecher and were then to depart immediately for Burlington, Iowa, where they were to make a visit at the home of mother's brother James. When we reached our front porch where we were to witness the beginning of their wedding journey, we were startled by a flapping sound over our heads and, looking up, were astonished to see every one of the fifty-six windows in the front of the four-story dormitory decorated with a white sheet." (JMSJR, 14)

A visitor to Jacksonville twenty-five years later recalled participating in the students' celebration of the Sturtevants' marriage after the couple returned from their wedding journey. He and the other boys had stood on the woodshed behind the home and in the dead hours of the night had made "hideous music upon tin pans and such like inelegant instruments, in honor of the Professor's wedding…."[57]

There was potentially a problem with Sturtevant's second

marriage. The Presbyterian Church had a rule, regarded as biblically-based, which was understood by many to prohibit marriage to the sister of a deceased wife. Sturtevant had assured Beecher that he did not consider this interpretation of Scripture to be correct and that his own conscience was clear.[58]

Beecher then "cheerfully consented" to officiate. (A, 252) Both families gave their endorsement to the marriage. Letters of congratulation came from Hannah's brother Silas and in due time from her brother Abraham in Hawaii. Ephraim had written, "You need have no fear of our being displeased at your choice, whatever others may be."[59] The marriage was a happy one and a great blessing for both Julian and Hannah and for the children.

A few months after this marriage a Presbyterian minister was deposed by the denomination's General Assembly (Old School) because he had made a similar marriage. Sturtevant believed the Assembly's action to be "a great and cruel wrong" because such church law was not based upon Scripture. (A, 252) The continuing controversy led Sturtevant to publish an article entitled "The Levitical Law of Incest." It received wide attention and Sturtevant credited the response as the major inspiration for embarking upon a life-time of writing. He demonstrated that marriage to the sister of a deceased wife was not included in the biblical catalog of prohibited relationships in Leviticus 18. He deplored the church laws which were based on gratuitous explications of Scripture and led to the exclusion of loved Christian brethren, with accompanying pain to their wives and "their innocent and unoffending offspring." (436) He appealed to "the enlightened and benevolent general morality of the gospel" as the basis for Christian conduct rather than specific divine enactments clearly intended for a people of the past. His plea to the churches was to modify their laws on these subjects so that "no more victims may be immolated to this system of intolerance and oppression." (444)

Hannah's family responsibilities increased when their first child, Elizabeth Fayerweather, was born on 2 December 1841. Another daughter, born on 23 September 1843, was named "Caroline Wilder" for Mrs. Theron Baldwin; sadly, the little girl died when less than two years of age. The older children not only did not feel neglected but thought that their new mother even favored them, and Julian Jr. had happy memories of the home and its many interesting visitors. The young sons were early assigned regular chores in caring for the livestock. Their reward was the pleasure of riding horseback; they had no saddles so rode bareback or with a blanket. A second element of childhood training which the father deemed essential was early instruction in language. Realizing that even young children can learn language with ease, the parents taught them Latin and arranged for Professor Adams of the College to teach German to Julian and his brother Warren. They learned some German poetry by heart.

Sometimes Julian Jr. went to the First Presbyterian Church with one or more of his aunts. There was worship both morning and afternoon and so the family took luncheon between the services at the home of "Father" John Adams, who was in charge of the Jacksonville Female Academy. Julian and his brother also attended the Presbyterian Sunday School, joining a class with the sons of other ministers who lived in Jacksonville while engaging in various home mission assignments.

Hannah's long presence in the household made it easier for her to fulfill the expected role of a professor's wife in church, community, and social obligation. Just two weeks before her wedding, Hannah (in the company of Miss Wolcott and others) had spent an afternoon with Mrs. Duncan in her home not far from the College campus. Mrs. Duncan recorded in her Diary that the visit was "quite pleasant." (19 Feb. 1841) Hannah was elected president of the Ladies' Association for Educating Females and served two years in that office; thereafter she was vice president for a number of years. Hannah even in the early years when the children were still small sometimes traveled with her husband. One such trip was in the summer of 1843, when Julian was seeking funds for the College in the towns of Lewiston and Farmington, north of Jacksonville. Later there were longer trips, including a journey to the East in 1844; the help of her sisters made it possible for Hannah to be away.

Busy as he was Julian Sturtevant was often called upon by other members of the two families for assistance. Clearly they regarded him as competent and honest and they assumed his willingness; he did not disappoint them. Christopher engaged in some farming ventures, leasing fifteen acres near Jacksonville owned by his sister Huldah. In June 1841 he moved his family to Rushville, leasing a farm which Huldah had purchased from Richard Fayerweather. Christopher had accumulated heavy debts and filed a petition for bankruptcy. He asked Julian to place a notice of this in the *Jacksonville Illinoian* and promised to repay him. Christopher needed help in regaining possession of a cow, the family's only source of milk. The cow, which had been taken by creditors, was actually Huldah's because she owned the Illinois College draft used for payment.[60] Christopher and Ann Sturtevant transferred their membership to the Presbyterian Church at Rushville in 1843.

Huldah visited in Jacksonville in April 1841 and she and a colleague from Monticello were invited to dine with Mrs. Duncan, wife of the former Governor. On 11 April 1842 Huldah married Col. John Jay Hinman, a lawyer and business man in Rushville. Warren Sturtevant, father of Huldah, Christopher, and Julian, had been a widower since his wife Lucy died; he married again in 1843.[61]

Richard Fayerweather joined the Congregational Church in Jacksonville in June 1840 on profession of faith. Silas in New Orleans ceased writing after 1840. Abraham, however, continued his letters although at long intervals. He reported the birth of three daughters and of a son who died at an early age. In a letter of 3 September 1844, he said that he had recently received letters dated in July 1843 and remarked, "I notice by your letters that Mr. Sturtevant has quite a family...." Julian officiated at the wedding of Hannah's older sister, Julia, on 22 July 1844. Julia's husband was Timothy Chamberlain, a charter member of the Congregational Church. Julia soon transferred her membership there.

Sturtevant's family responsibilities were enlarged in a different manner when he was appointed guardian of his young cousin, Edward Allen Tanner, in January 1841. Edward's parents, who had settled in Waverly, both died and Edward lived with older siblings until he was about fourteen. He came to the Sturtevant home in Jacksonville to obtain a good education. Julian was responsible for overseeing the legacy of $250 which the boy's father had left for his care.

Chapter 4: 1844-1850

The Early Years of Sturtevant's Presidency

Sturtevant Elected President, 1844

The flow of immigrants had increasingly shifted to the northern part of the state, and yet Jacksonville's population reached 2700 by 1850. The effects of the financial collapse of 1837 had cast a deep shadow over Illinois College, and even when prosperity returned it did not share equitably in the region's new wealth. Other problems were chronic: the conflicts with the Presbyterians, the festering quarrel over slavery, and the need to define the nature of the College in its frontier environment.

Upon Edward Beecher's departure in 1842 Sturtevant served as acting-president and presided at the meetings of the Board and at the commencement exercises. In February 1844 President Beecher resigned his office so that he could devote more time to his philosophical and theological studies. Sturtevant, because of the desperate financial situation, proposed to resign from the College when a new president was elected. Baldwin and Sturtevant were both considered as candidates and each was willing to defer to the other. Sturtevant said that if he were to remain at the College, he preferred his present position so that he could speak freely regarding church relations and religious issues. In the autumn Baldwin, as a trustee, wrote to the noted Congregational scholar in New Haven, Dr. Leonard Bacon, to ask whether Sturtevant's theological views should disqualify him from the presidency; he sent him Sturtevant's 1843 letters on church government. Bacon replied that there was no hindrance to his election.[1]

Sturtevant was in the East in quest of funds for four months during the late summer and fall of 1844. He found the trip refreshing and his health was improved. He was pleased to learn that many people had read his articles and he was gratified that, in contrast to the criticism he so often received in Illinois, others shared his views. He also enjoyed the opportunity to obtain books and the leisure to read them. The end of that welcome diversion was noted briefly in the Faculty Minutes for 4 November 1844: "Prof. Sturtevant, having returned from the East, took the chair as 'acting President.'" In that capacity Sturtevant joined the trustees in their meeting on 27 November and reported on his fund-raising efforts. The Board had learned about statements discrediting the College which had circulated at the recent Synod meeting, and the faculty, including Sturtevant, were asked to meet with the trustees. In their session the next day the Board members declared they were "perfectly satisfied with the orthodoxy of the Professors of this College & wisdom of their Instructions." (TM, 28 Nov. 1844) They then proceeded to elect Sturtevant as president; with one abstention, the vote was unanimous. Baldwin's affirmative vote was sent by letter. Sturtevant acknowledged the Board's action and requested time to consider.

Writing to Baldwin, Sturtevant declared that "The one <u>great question</u> now before my mind is—Shall I take upon myself the toils and cares and fearful responsibilities (doubly fearful from the solemn crisis to which we have come) of the Presidency of Illinois College." He cautiously expressed his opinion that he could serve "the cause of the College, of my country and of God better in the Presidency than in my present station." He believed that with the exception of the New School Presbyterians, men of other churches and of no church approved of his appointment. He enumerated solemn duties which would be his: to be wise, firm, and humble, and "to shed over this College the holy influence of piety and to lead the successive generations of students to Christ." Then he asked his good friend, "How can <u>I</u> ever be sufficient for these things? ...And then can I ever overcome the opposition which is now arrayed against me?" Paraphrasing Moses' protest against proceeding to the Promised Land without God's presence, he declared, "Truly I can say if the Lord go not up with me, carry me not up hence." (Cf. Exod. 33:15) Sturtevant concluded with a plea to Baldwin: "<u>Pray for me and write to me as soon as you can</u>."[2]

Already under instructions from the trustees to undertake another "agency" in the East, Sturtevant—after a delay of two weeks—accepted the appointment. The students, however, had not waited for Sturtevant's formal acceptance before demonstrating their enthusiasm. Years afterward he recalled vividly their response when the trustees announced their decision.

> Soon after dark that evening the college bell rang merrily and I was summoned to the front of the building, to find every window brilliantly illuminated. The lights in the fourth story had been ingeniously arranged to spell my name, the fourteen windows giving just room for a window to each letter and the two periods after the initial letters J. and M. The slope between the college and the town and the very wide prairie beyond was then almost devoid of trees and the illumination could thus be seen for a great distance. I was greeted with a great burst of applause and returned to my house astonished, bewildered and humbled. I felt myself utterly unworthy of such demonstrations. (A, 258-59)

Sturtevant's son Julian later recalled that the windows "had many small panes, [and] had a lighted candle for every pane except in the fourth story, where each of the fourteen windows had either a letter or a period, made also with candles, so that the top story read, 'J. M. S T U R T E V A N T.'" (JMSJR, 15) Sturtevant acknowledged the students' compliment: "No one fact could be more grateful to my feelings at this moment than that the appointment made yesterday is acceptable to the students of this college. But for this fact I should not feel that I could accept the honor tendered me by the Trustees.... I respond to it by expressing the hope that not only the name, but the whole history of the college whoever may preside over it may be written in light—not the light which is addressed to the eye, but that truth which is the light of the soul."3

The community, especially the churches, demonstrated strong support for the trustees' choice. From the day of Beecher's departure, for more than thirty-four years, Sturtevant served as the president of Illinois College in fact and for thirty-two of those years in name as well. Along with his administrative duties Sturtevant enthusiastically accepted a new teaching assignment as

Professor of Mental and Moral Science; he had, he said, "a growing interest in the new department." (A, 259)

Julian M. Sturtevant was inaugurated President of Illinois College on Wednesday, 25 June 1845. The event was an added attraction for the many who came to Jacksonville for the commencements at the several schools and for special events. The State Teachers' Meeting was announced for Monday of that week, with Sturtevant as the featured speaker. The Society of Alumni would meet at the Methodist Church in the evening after commencement, and the next evening the Ladies' Association for Educating Females would meet at the Congregational Church.

The commencement exercises, scheduled for 9:00 A.M., were in the College Grove at the northwest corner of Mound Avenue and Woodland. A natural amphitheater had been prepared by erecting a stage and a large awning. Between fifteen hundred and two thousand people were present. Accounts in local newspapers called attention to the presence of women and the fact that the multitude had seats.[4] Sturtevant described the setting for Baldwin: "[A]round and above hung the luxuriant foliage of the venerable primeval forest where only a few years ago the savage roamed unmolested and where [we] heard the howl of the wolf. Never was College Grove so beautiful.... I am sorry we did not Daguerreotype it." (S-B, 2 July 1845)

The "Order of Exercises" was printed as a one-page program. Prayer was the first item on the agenda and the very last. Sacred music was presented at the beginning and conclusion of the forenoon and afternoon sessions. A reporter described the occasion: "The music was beautiful, and in listening to the anthem as the sounds rose and fell, with the earth beneath, and the green boughs and the broad heavens above a softer and holier emotion rested within the heart." (JJ, 27 June 1845) Students delivered orations both morning and afternoon. The A.B. degree was awarded to eleven, the largest class to date. The M.D. degree was granted to five men and the A.M. to two alumni; five honorary M.D. degrees were also conferred.

Although not noted on the program, the ceremony inaugurating Sturtevant as the College's second president was held just before noon and was similar to that held for Edward Beecher in 1832. The president of the Board of Trustees, Judge Samuel D. Lockwood of the Superior Court of Illinois, was in charge. Sturtevant's inaugural address came at the end of a full day of speeches and ceremonies; nevertheless the people were "a most attentive and apparently interested audience." (S-B, 2 July 1845).

After introductory remarks President Sturtevant presented his address on "AMERICAN COLLEGES." He declared that the people of America have been from "their very cradle a *College building people*" (5) and thus the collegiate system is a product of American society. The great central idea of that society and therefore of its education is a religious concept, "the right of every man to worship God according to the dictates of his own conscience." (11) Devotion to truth acknowledges no authority but God and rejects every human institution which would stand between the person and God. Planting "institutions of education over all the mighty west" would fulfill "all our hopes as Protestants, Republicans, and Americans." (17) The new president continued. A free society requires a system of common education because free people demand "knowledge as the very life of society." (23) That system in turn requires religious teachers with high intellectual qualifications. When such teachers investigate and communicate truth regarding religion, the very basis of society, their spirit of inquiry is extended to every other field. Sturtevant noted that the men of Illinois College had been instrumental in developing a system of public education in the state and declared that its "ultimate success is certain." (18)

Sturtevant emphasized that collegiate education was appropriate not only for the clergy but also for other professions and for public leaders generally. Early education for all youth was essential and therefore the responsibility of government, while higher education was properly sponsored by voluntary associations and privately financed. Sturtevant denied that liberal education was elitist. It was absurd to think that "Democracy can only find its complete realization…by reducing all men to the same intellectual level, and giving to all individuals (themselves always excepted) an exact equality of condition and of influence." (8) Leaders were essential and must have appropriate education. The colleges were "charitable institutions" making education available to anyone willing to persevere in acquiring learning; probably there was no place more democratic than the benches of a lecture room where only one's ability and effort determined what one could learn.

Truly American colleges had three essential traits. They were *liberal*, "successfully directing one's mental powers to the investigation of truth and the acquisition of knowledge…." (25) When the members of all professions engaged in a common course of education they would "together exult in the limitless capacity of the mind of man for knowledge." (26) American colleges were to be *free*, dedicated to "that great fundamental idea of American society—*the right of private judgement*…. (27) Reasoning power, not traditional authority, distinguishes the true from the false. Sturtevant objected to Romish education which limited access to learning and restricted it within narrow confines; he also criticized Protestant colleges which defended "a prescribed and prejudged system." (29)

Finally, Sturtevant declared, *"Our Colleges must be religious."* Intellectual freedom was an opportunity for "the true spirit of Christianity," not for irreligion and infidelity. "There is such a thing as religious truth, fixed, settled, eternal, religious truth…." (31) Sturtevant decried the timid believer who fears intellectual freedom and commended "the free, reasonable and healthful action of the human mind." With such colleges, the church and the nation were safe. Let then those who would aid this cause with their influence, their prayers, and their property come forward and "cheerfully bear the burden." (32)

In a letter to Baldwin, Sturtevant remarked that this commencement presented "increasing evidence that this College is the center of a great movement in this vast growing community in favor of the extension of a republican and a Christian system of education and the rapid increase of the knowledge of God." (S-B, 2 July 1845) However, enthusiasm was tempered in the local newspaper which praised the occasion but issued a caution to the College. Sturtevant's address was described briefly, as "replete with sound sense and logical reasoning." (JJ, 27 June 1845) Several paragraphs were required, however, to express dissatisfaction with student orators who "lugged anti-slavery sentiments into their speeches." The editor's advice was blunt: the College was just beginning to recover from the years of prejudiced opinion due to abolitionism, and continued expression of such views might renew that prejudice with ten-fold force.[5]

The Medical School . . . Student Life

The frontier College had assembled a remarkable group of well-trained, dedicated, and hard-working men for its faculty but in 1847 two of them resigned. Sturtevant deeply regretted the loss of Truman M. Post who, unable to support his family on the uncertain College salary, had accepted the pastorate of a St. Louis church. In the case of J. B. Turner the departure was not only welcomed by the president but had been urged by him for two years. Turner's unconventional ideas about religion aroused deep suspicions among the Presbyterians. Their fears were aggravated by Turner's article in the *New Englander* proclaiming the superiority of Congregationalism to Presbyterianism. Sturtevant told Baldwin that the man must be tougher than a salamander to endure so long! The trustees could not dismiss him because the College owed him a substantial amount of salary and also they feared a public outcry. All were relieved when Turner presented his resignation. Arrangements were made to pay the salary due him, there was good feeling on both sides, and Sturtevant and Turner maintained a cordial relationship throughout their lives.

The founders believed that Illinois College, like Yale, should offer professional studies in law, medicine, and theology. In 1839 the trustees considered the appointment of a professor of law but lacked the necessary funds. In 1843 while Sturtevant was acting-president a medical school, the first one in the state, was established. The faculty of four included the College's highly-talented Samuel Adams, himself a medical doctor. Space in the Chapel building, including the north attic, was leased for the purpose and the next year the former workshop was utilized. The first class of five were awarded the M.D. degree in 1845. In 1846-1847 there were thirty-nine students—one more than the total in the four College classes. The school ceased abruptly at the end of 1847-1848. Samuel Willard, a member of the last class to graduate, believed the chief cause was the low remuneration compared with doctors' earnings in private practice. (CH, 100)

The dream of establishing a theological professorship seemed within reach in 1845 when the trustees of the Blackburn Seminary Fund transferred its lands to Illinois College. Seeking to fulfill the stated purpose of that Fund, the Illinois College trustees established the Blackburn Theological Professorship in 1849 and named Sturtevant as the temporary incumbent.

There was some hope, in 1847, that Illinois College would be recognized as the state university and thus able to draw upon the educational funds accumulated by the state. Sturtevant confided in Baldwin that some wanted a board which, like Yale's, would include government officers although a majority would be from Illinois College. The most serious obstacles were rooted in sectarian jealousies, and by 1849 the plan was dead. Sturtevant concluded that the introduction of political influence would have been injurious to the College's moral and religious character.

The senior class of fourteen in 1844-1845 was the largest ever and instructing that class was Sturtevant's responsibility. The senior subjects included philosophy, logic, ethics, theology, government, and political economy. The name of Tocqueville, and the title of his great work, *Democracy in America*, first appeared in the College's catalogs for 1845-1846 and 1847-1848, respectively.[6] Sturtevant long continued using Tocqueville's work which he regarded with appreciation and a critical eye. The freshman class numbering twenty-four was also the largest yet, and the total enrollment of fifty-four matched the previous record. Only ten were in the Preparatory Department due to stricter admission policies, and nineteen were enrolled in the medical department. Increases and declines in enrollment were matched by corresponding changes in Sturtevant's mood.

The faculty directed the president to send thanks to the ladies of the Jacksonville Female Academy for the *Koran* given to the College's Library. The trustees granted permission for the faculty to admit students from the female academies or other institutions in the town to certain courses of lectures.

Serious disciplinary problems continued and students were subjected to fines, suspension, and expulsion for making loud halloos in the dormitory, causing physical damage to the buildings, attacking each other with sticks and stones, and insolence toward the faculty. Intoxication was a common offense. A student, inadequately disguised by his blackened face, caused a disturbance which resulted in his suspension. Another was expelled for "firing of crackers in and about the College buildings." (FM, 11 July 1848) Still another was dismissed after he polluted the Presbyterian Church with a discharge of *Aqua fortis*. One incident was reminiscent of Sturtevant's experience while a student at Yale. Twice on successive nights heavy logs were rolled down a flight of stairs in the dormitory, causing damage, and a student who refused to give information was dismissed. Sturtevant explained in Chapel that the principles of governance require testimony in the case of flagrant disorders which are prejudicial to the common interest. The Bylaws were further revised by Sturtevant and two trustees in 1848. The regulations prohibited students from having guns or gunpowder on the campus, forbade playing cards, and restricted students from borrowing from the Library a translation of a classical book used in the classes. Students were assessed a fee of $1.00 annually for using the Library, which was open two days a week.

The students who organized the Phi Alpha Literary Society in 1845 acknowledged that they might not be as pious or intellectual as others. Phi Alpha was more democratic in its membership and meetings and embraced a greater diversity of opinion. The two societies represented broad political differences: Sigma Pi men found the Whig party congenial. Phi Alpha favored the Democrats and included students from Kentucky and Missouri; its membership represented both sides of the slavery issue. Among the members of Phi Alpha there was considerable opposition and even hostility toward the faculty and especially Sturtevant. A small manuscript booklet entitled "Biography of The Members of the Phi Alpha Society" includes brief paragraphs by two dozen men who were students at various times from about 1845 to the 1870s. Several expressed good wishes to Phi Alpha that it might triumph over rival Sigma Pi. A former student claimed that he was expelled because he refused to drink with the rascals of the faculty and was leaving to find a more moral atmosphere. The most notable person recording his feelings was G. M. McConnell, who enrolled in 1848 and soon after joined Phi Alpha. He wrote (in part):

"During the July of /51 I was very unexpectedly advised by that d___d old Hypocrite Sputz that I would do just as well at home as at College. The reason of this atrocious deed was that I refused to attend Examination to be tried and that I preferred to tell his majesty Sputz that he was a d____d fool, which everybody knows is true. To the Soc. I give the following 'Excelsior.' Sub hoc Signe vince."[7] Inspiring the Society with the motto, "Higher," McConnell urged its members to conquer its foes.

Financial Strains . . . The Blackburn Lands

The greatest direct threat to the College's very existence during the early years of Sturtevant's presidency was its chronic financial plight. His quest for funds often involved personal hardship, which he likened to marine travel. He told Baldwin that he was hesitant to undertake so "long and hazardous a voyage" to New York as he planned in January (1845) and would carefully check his "spars and rigging before setting sail." (S-B, 3 Jan. 1845) His journey, of course, was by land but not less arduous for that.

[I]t was a stage ride pursued night and day from Springfield, Illinois to Cumberland, Maryland. Before we reached Terre Haute the mud had become so deep that the stage coach was exchanged for a mud wagon, that is, a common lumber wagon with a canvas cover stretched over bows of oak, and no springs except the small ones attached to the seats. The short seats, intended for two, frequently held three, and brought heads and bows so near together as to threaten us every moment with concussion of the brain as the vehicle lurched from side to side.... [W]e did not make more than sixty-five or seventy miles in twenty-four hours. One look at the hovels opened for the entertainment of travelers reconciled me to ride on in discomfort rather than to try to rest in such places. (A, 262-63)

Sturtevant would not travel on the Sabbath and found a good place to spend that day in Richmond, Indiana. On Monday he resumed his journey, now in a fine coach which made "seven or eight miles an hour over the macadamized national road." (A, 263) The trip continued to Dayton, Columbus, and Wheeling and then through the magnificent mountain scenery to

Cumberland. From there Sturtevant took the train and reached New York before the next Sabbath.

Significant aid was provided by the new College Society, which in its first year appropriated $3,774 to Illinois College and thereafter varying amounts. Sturtevant was obligated to solicit funds on behalf of the Society and visited pastors and churches in Connecticut and Massachusetts, where the Congregationalists were predominant, and in New York and other middle states, where there were more Presbyterians. In New Haven the paid subscriptions totaled some $600, some of which he retained, saying "I have felt compelled by my last information from my wife to send her $25. While I leave her alone with that family on her hands I cannot leave her penniless too." (S-B, New Haven, 13 Mar. 1845) He also paid a debt of $50 and kept about $40 for his expenses. At some places he found an utter lack of enthusiasm to contribute to any cause. When reporting to Baldwin that a given church had contributed $7.78 he added sarcastically, "Enormous!!!" (S-B, Boston, 21 Apr. 1845) Returning home after two months in the East, Sturtevant and the trustees conducted a drive which obtained more than $3,000—helpful, but not sufficient. Sturtevant was convinced that there was ample wealth in Illinois if only people would share it, and he concluded that if God wanted the College to have money, it would be forthcoming.

In late 1845 Sturtevant wrote to Baldwin saying that the College had passed through "'seven years of famine.' ...[O]ur case was never so desperate as now." (S-B, 26 Nov. 1845) His personal funds were exhausted and somehow he must obtain $100 to $150 for the winter ahead. Sturtevant insisted that the treasurer should not defer payment of faculty salaries in favor of creditors; the burden of debt should be borne by the trustees and not the faculty. In March 1846 Sturtevant told Baldwin that he must obtain $50 by 1 April but, he declared, "I know not where I am to obtain a dollar." (S-B, 12 Mar. 1846) He did receive $50, and in time, but very little more by August when he was again near despair for his family's well-being. His lament was plaintive: "Perhaps we have so sinned against [God] that he will never make this College the instrument of his praise." (S-B, 3 Aug. 1846)

The College was in grave financial difficulty when it received a windfall in 1845. The trustees of the Blackburn Seminary Fund concluded that its resources were insufficient to start a new college and, with court approval, transferred more than fourteen thousand acres to Illinois College. Nathaniel Coffin, the College treasurer, proposed that these lands and all the other College land not directly used for instruction should be sold. The plan was to sell three hundred shares of stock at one hundred dollars to pay the debt of thirty thousand dollars. Sturtevant opposed this plan because he had already secured pledges of several thousand dollars and he believed land values would recover. He proposed to exchange the lands at normal prices for State of Illinois bonds at face value; the bonds at the time were selling at about sixteen per cent of face value. Interest paid by the state would yield current income and later, when the state redeemed the bonds, the College would obtain fair value for the lands it had given up. The business men on the Board believed that the state would never be able to pay off the bonds and rejected Sturtevant's proposal. This was the only occasion when he seriously disagreed with the Board. His wisdom was proven a few years later when the bonds were redeemed.

The trustees voted to proceed with the stock plan and thus with the sale of the lands. Sturtevant was one of four who subscribed to ten shares for one thousand dollars; he said he was willing to add another thousand. He realized that if the plan failed there would be no alternative but "to suspend instruction and sell the buildings."[8] Happily, by the spring of 1847 most of the salaries due the faculty were paid. For the first time in years Sturtevant was free from anxiety and he could now spend fifty cents without apprehension. Moreover, the Presbyterian Synod and the Congregational Association both encouraged contributions to the College. The local Congregational Church arranged for collecting funds to assist the trustees in "meeting their engagements to [the] Instructors." (CCM, 31 June 1847)

Sturtevant made an extended trip on behalf of the College Society, visiting major cities in Connecticut and Massachusetts, and he was so encouraged that he planned to buy some books for the College. Stopping in New York in mid-September, he continued on to Detroit, Chicago, and Jacksonville. He returned to a joyful welcome at home and was happy to find his family in good health.

About half the land owned by the College was sold at a series of auctions in 1848. Coffin assumed responsibility for paying all the debts within a year in return for the remaining 135 shares of stock. He then resigned, as he had agreed to do. The full amount was eventually obtained from the sale. The College had survived its financial crisis, and Sturtevant was relieved that Coffin was no longer the College's treasurer.

The "prosperity" of the College continued and by April of 1848 the salaries of the faculty were paid fully and even a bit in advance. The budget for 1848-1849 seemed modest enough: $3,300 for salaries for four instructors, $1,000 for repairs, $90 for insurance, and $210 for library, apparatus, and other expenses. The estimated income, however, was only $2,000, and Sturtevant hoped the College Society would meet the deficit.

For a time Sturtevant was preaching four times a week and he saved enough from his Sabbath labors to accumulate over $500 for refurbishing the Chapel with a pulpit, a raised stage, and seating for two hundred—including a special section for ladies and visitors. The treasurer had opposed the plan and would neither provide funds for the project nor superintend the work. That task also fell to Sturtevant who said the outcome would be great "if I live it through." (S-B, 4 May 1848) When the repairs were completed he declared the room equal to any in New England.

Before long there was a serious financial reversal and in January 1849 Sturtevant declared, "The crisis of this College has come." It would not do to talk about saving the College the next year, he said, "we must save it this year." (S-B, 15 Jan. 1849) The College was again in arrears in paying faculty salaries but this time Sturtevant escaped hardship. The College owed him $200 but some debts due him had been repaid and he was able to pay most of his bills. He managed to donate $400 to the College.

The trustees determined in July 1849 to seek an endowment fund of $50,000 to support five professorships. Again Sturtevant was among the first to make a pledge and was one of only two on the Board to subscribe $1,000; his generosity was near to being a fault. By April (1850) the subscriptions amounted to more than half the goal. Certain Presbyterians among the trustees and the faculty refused to contribute or otherwise assist. Quoting Matthew 10:36,

Sturtevant wrote that "a man's foes shall be they of his own household," but he maintained that the College would be saved despite them. Presbyterians elsewhere, as in Quincy, rallied to support the endowment effort. Beardstown yielded a thousand dollars, which led Sturtevant to boast that this time he had done "Pretty well for a place where ten years ago I spent a Sabbath and preached and had to pay a heavy tavern bill and buy candles with my own money and light the school-house for evening services with my own hands!" (S-B, 16 Apr. 1850) Income from tuition and the rental of houses and lands would produce about $4,800, which would provide for the salaries; the amount of $760 was still needed for other expenses.

Sturtevant warned against the attempt by President Blanchard of Knox College to secure aid from the College Society. Nevertheless the Society granted assistance to Knox in 1846 on the ground that it really was not in competition with the college in Jacksonville because it was a hundred miles distant. Also it had a different clientele, New Englanders who settled in northern Illinois and supported it, in contrast to the Southerners of the central part of the state—who so often opposed Illinois College.

There were occasional quarrels, by mail, between Sturtevant and Baldwin about the allocation of funds made by the Society and once whether the Society had actually paid the amount it claimed. After clarifying their different interpretations each apologized to the other. When in 1849 a better-paying position was tendered to Baldwin, Sturtevant pleaded with him to remain with the Society until "The great Pioneer work to which in our youth we devoted ourselves will have been accomplished." (S-B, 25 Apr. 1849) Baldwin reassured his friend of his own strong commitment and added that he did not consider himself on a bed of down!

Between the time he was elected president and his inauguration Sturtevant spent about five months in the East as an agent for the Society. Two years later he was absent from home for more than two months for the same purpose. He was able to make side trips (July 1847) to Tallmadge and Hudson to visit his father and brother. In the late summer of 1849 he resumed the Eastern solicitation after delaying some weeks because of an outbreak of cholera in the communities south of Jacksonville; he did not wish to leave his family with the threat of an epidemic in his community.

Once Sturtevant had arrived Baldwin urged him to remain and to address the Society at its Anniversary meeting. The Society, he added, would want his speech for publication.

Sturtevant's appeals on behalf of the Society were often made in sermons and addresses and later printed in the Society's annual reports and in various periodicals. He argued in the *New Englander* [9] that the diffusion of civil and religious freedom requires two institutions: education devoted to the search for truth, and a church which knows no authority but the Bible, no head but Christ. Education founded on these principles of Puritanism is essential to government which recognizes the equality of all citizens. The right of private judgment when acknowledged in religion is extended to other realms, such as scholarship and government. The people's assent can then be gained through conviction based on truth and reason. Christians thus have a major responsibility to help finance the colleges.

At the College Society's fourth annual meeting (1847) Sturtevant characterized colleges as "the great organic power of society" and emphasized the need to establish the western colleges on a permanent basis. (SPC-4, 46) At the sixth anniversary Sturtevant affirmed the great mission given to Puritanism, to Christianize America and the world. All English-speaking people should join "to accomplish the noble destiny which God has assigned us, of conquering the world with the Bible and the schoolmaster." (SPC-6, 47) To fulfill its mission American society has three functions—religion, education, and government. Three institutions correspond: "The free church, with its 'learned and pious ministry'—the State strong for the protection of individual right, but powerless for oppression—the College—the Schoolhouse. These are the monuments of the Pilgrims...."[10] Sturtevant concluded: "We are called to take possession of a continent for Jesus Christ.... What distant wilds of the earth shall not swarm with Anglo-American immigrants in the next one hundred and fifty years? ...Brethren, let us respond to these calls with joyous and thankful hearts." (48, 51)

Religion—Basic, but Divisive

The fundamental concern of the men of the Illinois Association was to aid in the eternal salvation of the people in the West, including of course the students in Illinois College. Sturtevant described the most likely perils for youths. Some Protestant students in their eagerness for an education became entrapped in a Jesuit school, falling prey to Romish superstition and Papal despotism.[11] Some, enrolling in other schools to escape the slough of ignorance, turned from Christianity to rationalism and skepticism, succumbing to godless infidelity. Even more seductive was the Transcendentalism which had spread from eastern schools to Illinois College. Sturtevant refuted the intruding philosophy in his baccalaureate sermon for the Class of 1845. He told Baldwin that he "showed up" Orestes A. Brownson, a leader in the movement, and later he expressed the fervent hope that with the graduation of that class "the leaven of Transcendental scepticism seems nearly to have worked itself out [and that] the time is near when it will exist only in the memory of the past and in the fears of Mr. Eddy and Mrs. Ayers." (S-B, 2 July, 6 Oct. 1845). Rev. Chauncey Eddy was the pastor and Mrs. David Ayers a member of the First Presbyterian Church. Her husband, a College trustee, led the pro-Presbyterian faction in the Board.

The College encouraged revivals and provided worship and instruction to aid students in making their personal decisions for Christ. In the winter of 1847 sixty to one hundred were attending the Sabbath evening lecture, and the weekly prayer meetings were well attended even though religion in Jacksonville was at a very low state. In 1848 Sturtevant reported to the College Society that Illinois College had been blessed with "six marked seasons of religious revival," in 1832, 1834, 1838, 1840, 1842, and 1848. (SPC-5, 35) At least four of these coincided with revivals in the churches of Jacksonville. The most powerful and permanent of the earlier efforts was the one in 1834, when the College's three large dining rooms were the site of solemn religious gatherings. In 1848 no less than fifty and perhaps as many as one hundred students were converted, many of them having had no religious upbringing to prepare them for salvation. Sturtevant was then preaching at the Congregational Church, where meetings were held every night of the week. He preached two or three sermons on the Sabbath and sometimes an additional one during the week. The great interest in religion throughout Jacksonville extended over more than three months.

The faculty's commitment to evangelism was contagious among many of the students. Forty-one of the eighty-seven graduates prior to 1848 were in the ministry or preparing for it. Several alumni became foreign missionaries, among them Samuel B. Fairbank '42 who, after attending seminary in Massachusetts, returned to Jacksonville for ordination. Sturtevant conducted his examination in theology, preached the sermon, and gave the charge to the candidate. Fairbank spent fifty years as a missionary in India. Among other alumni who went to foreign lands were Thomas Laurie '38 (to Persia, in 1842) and William Ireland '45 (to Zululand, in 1845).[12]

Formal instruction in religion was provided through the customary Senior courses in "Evidences of Christianity" and "Paley's Natural Theology." In June 1845 the trustees recommended the introduction of a course in "the Historical and Philological Study of the Bible." Although this proposal was not adopted, it reflected awareness of scholarly developments in biblical studies, especially in German universities.

Scarcely a week after his inauguration President Sturtevant advised Baldwin that he expected trouble soon from the New School Presbyterians and that Turner was a prime target. A few weeks later he reported that the minutes of the recent Synod were unjust and unchristian. The orthodoxy of all those at the College was assailed and some claimed that students were exposed to unorthodox views of Gospel truth and church government. The Synod's publication of such statements gave sanction to them. In reply Baldwin observed that some fault lay with the staff. Sturtevant in his response repeated Baldwin's statement: "we have 'all made mistakes which have created unnecessary irritation.'" Sturtevant inquired what these mistakes were and whether he was wrong in his opinion of the peculiar organization of the Presbyterian Church. If his "views" were in error, he was guilty of "a great mistake." He denied being hostile to the Presbyterian Church and said he was still willing to submit to it. However, he opposed control over local institutions by supposedly superior organizations because Scripture did not authorize it. Sturtevant asserted that his doctrinal views were biblically-based and orthodox. Ecclesiastical opinions were a different matter, and on that subject

Sturtevant claimed religious freedom for himself and for others. But he was also opposed to the evil of sectarianism, and he recalled that between 1833 and 1840 his two sermons against sectarianism had led to the unsuccessful efforts by himself and Baldwin to unite the local Presbyterian and Congregational Churches.

The Synod delegated a committee to report on Illinois College at the fall meeting in 1845. Rev. A. T. Norton as chairman had written a statement attacking the trustees and faculty but had not shown it to the other committee members. Sturtevant called the proceedings disgraceful. A full year had been allowed for the committee's work, and now by leaving the issue unsettled the Synod seemed to confirm the doubts previously expressed about the College. Sturtevant, invited to address the Synod, spoke for more than two hours and succeeded in lessening the prejudice. He informed the Synod of the trustees' unanimous satisfaction with the orthodoxy of the faculty except for Turner. Subsequent statements by the Synod were generally favorable.

Previously Sturtevant had sent personal letters to Baldwin stating his views on church government. Writing now to Baldwin, Sturtevant expressed astonishment that copies of these had fallen into the hands of Mr. Norton by way of a Mr. Carey to whom Baldwin had given them. Sturtevant reaffirmed the views he had expressed earlier; they were his "<u>deliberate</u> and <u>solemn</u> <u>protest</u> 'vs.' the <u>despotic</u> and <u>therefore</u> <u>factious</u> <u>organization</u> of <u>Protestant</u> <u>Christendom</u>." However, he acknowledged that he had said some things "unguardedly" in "the freedom of confidential friendship." Such things, he said, should not fall into the hands of a heresy-hunting person like Norton.[13]

In the spring of 1845, when charges were circulating about unsound teaching at the College, someone reported to Baldwin that Sturtevant's "modes of speech" indicated a disturbed state of mind. Baldwin had taken these statements seriously and conveyed his concern to Sturtevant, who asked his friend to reverse his judgment. Sturtevant reviewed the records both of the Association and the Synod and insisted that they provided no evidence of disturbance. He believed Baldwin had failed to bring his "usual calm, cool, deliberate judgement" to bear on this matter, and he told him so. (S-B, 31 July 1845)

Rev. Chauncey Eddy continued his severe criticism of Illinois College. Many members of his church disagreed with his views and manner and were attending the Congregational Church. At the insistence of his congregation Eddy was compelled to invite Sturtevant to preach in his church for the first time in nearly a year [presumably at an evening service]. A truce in the "war" was declared, and Rev. Eddy now said that he would support the cause of the College and Rev. Norton said that he would cease his opposition. The suspension of hostilities was only temporary because two months later Sturtevant received "a very calumnious letter" from Rev. Ansel D. Eddy, the brother of Chauncey Eddy. Sturtevant told Baldwin that the source of these charges could be deduced from "the little footprints of Mrs. Ayers." Her husband, he added, was not innocent either, and the two could harm the College greatly. Sturtevant wrote a lengthy reply, requesting Eddy to send copies of his own letter and of Sturtevant's reply to both Baldwin and Leonard Bacon. If he did not, Sturtevant himself would. He was convinced that the two Eddys were waging a campaign against him. (S-B, 19 May, 11 July, 3 Aug. 1846)

Sturtevant reported at the end of October that the 1846 Synod meeting was very favorable. However, in May 1847 Rev. Eddy preached a very sectarian sermon when his church dedicated a new building. He claimed that true Congregationalists were identical with Presbyterians and would uphold Presbyterian teachings because they were what the Bible taught. The majority of the church members were mortified. Sturtevant had already made plans for a fund-raising trip to the East. Now he had an additional purpose, to counter the influence of Chauncey Eddy who was going East and would "doubtless report all along his track on the orthodoxy of Illinois College." (S-B, 17 June 1847)

Yet another investigation of Illinois College was conducted when the College Society in 1846 sent two eastern clergymen, Rev. Ansel D. Eddy and Rev. Joseph Towne. Sturtevant's reservations about Eddy were understandable. Towne, a Congregational pastor in Boston, was afterwards characterized by Sturtevant as magnanimous because of his willingness to hear both sides. Fortunately Towne wrote the report and on the whole it was very favorable. The rumors about the faculty had been investigated and the only credible suspicion centered on Turner. President Sturtevant and Professors Post and Adams were declared to be men of sound piety. They were described as superior men having unquestioned intellectual ability and "great independence of mind" and as being "honestly & enthusiastically devoted to the cause of education," even at great personal sacrifice.[14] Eddy urged that Illinois College receive effective aid from the East and pleaded for an end to the denominational controversy.

The report declared that none of the causes for the agitation about the College should be attributed to it. The limited local support resulted from numerous causes, among them the fact that college education was not prerequisite to a professional career and the moderate position of the faculty on slavery. The College Library was deemed most inadequate. The College Building looked fine from a distance but showed signs of poor construction. On the plus side the College had fine philosophical (scientific) apparatus, imported from Paris at great expense and regarded as among the best in the United States. The report concluded with a hearty recommendation for continued support for Illinois College, emphasizing that "It must not fail." (B-S, 5 Oct. 1846, 19 Mar. 1847)

In the fall of 1847, Sturtevant preached at a Sabbath evening service in Rev. R. W. Patterson's Presbyterian Church in Chicago. Afterward Sturtevant felt exhausted and because he had to rise early, he went to his hotel. Patterson followed him and discussed the College's situation for an hour, informing Sturtevant that Presbyterians like himself were dissatisfied with the Board of Trustees. Patterson's effort was just another example of the "unsleeping vigilance of the Presbyterian guardians." (S-B, 4 Oct. 1847)

Meeting in Jacksonville in 1847, the Synod recommended without dissent that the churches aid the College Society and the colleges. Norton advised Sturtevant that a motion to reconsider would be submitted. Sturtevant was told that the Presbyterians lacked confidence in the College's trustees because those who were Presbyterian in name were not so in fact. Sturtevant and Adams were regarded as undermining Presbyterianism to the advantage of Congregationalism. Sturtevant welcomed Norton's proposal that Presbyterians be added to the faculty and urged him to cooperate in finding suitable candidates. The renewed debate lasted for eight hours and ended without any action. Sturtevant noted that Post and Turner had now left the College and so "Dr. Adams and I only are left of the obnoxious Faculty." (S-B, 10 Nov. 1847) Baldwin replied that if a burlesque of the Diet of Worms had been intended, no better way could have been found than to call the president of Illinois College before the assembly.[15] However, he urged the friends of the College to declare "a general amnesty as to the offenses of their Presbyterian foes." (B-S, 30 Aug. 1848)

The local conflict was partially resolved when Rev. Eddy was dismissed by his church. (S-B, 4 May 1848) Sturtevant's election as Synod moderator in 1848 certified his acceptability to most Presbyterians. A plan was announced to merge the Old and New School churches in the area, but Sturtevant vowed he would not be a part of it, declaring "I am an Independent...." (S-B, 25 Apr. 1849) Tension at the national level was evident when the "Congregationalized Presbyterianism" of such men as Dr. Lyman Beecher was criticized at the 1849 Presbyterian General Assembly.

The continuing conflict between the Presbyterians and the Congregationalists inspired Sturtevant to write two articles for the *Independent* in 1849. [He used his pen-name, although readers likely knew the identity of "Robinson."] He defended the right of Congregationalists to establish their own churches in a community where other churches were present. He rejected the proposal that the majority in a community should have their own church and that others should unite with it until their own numbers increased. In practice Old School Presbyterians and Methodists insisted on having their churches, expecting the Congregationalists to concede. Congregationalists are willing to cooperate, but not at the expense of their principles. Moreover, it is difficult to start a church after others are well established. Congregationalists have a duty to support evangelical preaching, but they also have a duty to establish their own church as early as possible. Despite Presbyterian prejudices, Congregationalists have doctrinal standards, and they are scriptural. Presbyterians err in assuming that all churches organized congregationally, such as the Unitarians and Campbellites, are part of Congregationalism. Sturtevant refuted a second Presbyterian assumption with his declaration that the Congregational order was in fact capable of maintaining the faith both in spirit and in form.

In his second article, Sturtevant challenged the Presbyterian claim that their government had superior ability to protect the purity of the faith. He cited reports from Presbyterian authors in several periodicals on the laxity of Presbyterianism in Scotland, England, and various European countries. These churches—even in Switzerland, the homeland of Calvin's church—were infected with Unitarianism and Rationalism. Many clergy and laity were not pious, although some Presbyterians had now adopted the Congregational system of examining new members. The alleged "looseness" of Congregationalism was far more effective in maintaining the faith than Presbyterian "bolts and bars." "Centralization tends to corruption, independence, to purity." In New England those Congregational churches and members which became Unitarian had been cast out. People in the West should not abandon the system which worked so well in both Old and New England.[16]

Sturtevant concluded that the New School Presbyterians would not be satisfied until they had a college under their exclusive control; their numbers were few, he said, but they were influential. He was convinced that the survival of Illinois College would depend mainly on those who were in sympathy with the *Boston Congregationalist* and the *New York Independent*, two prominent Congregational newspapers. Sturtevant was agreeably surprised when the Quincy Presbyterian churches were opened to him to speak on behalf of the College. Baldwin advised Sturtevant that he believed the New School Presbyterians and the Congregationalists would soon be united with respect to the various boards and institutions. His expectation seemed to be fulfilled when Sturtevant was appointed to a Synod committee regarding the establishment of a union theological seminary. The Presbyterian Synod of Illinois met at Collinsville in late September of 1850 and Sturtevant wrote a long dispatch for the *Independent*.[17] He reported that the longest discussion centered upon the proposal to found a "Theological Seminary" in Illinois for "the great Northwest." It seemed possible that the two denominations might jointly found a "union" institution. He believed that most people in the two churches agreed on "the great fundamental principles of the evangelical system" and would "give and take entire freedom in non-essentials." He was confident they would cooperate in great Christian enterprises. Sturtevant and Baldwin shared an optimism which proved to be unrealistic. Within a few years the denominations established separate institutions in Chicago, the Presbyterian (McCormick) Theological Seminary and the Congregationalist Chicago Theological Seminary.[18]

In 1845 Rev. Reuben S. Kendall ('39), a promising scholar, was appointed to teach the classical languages. Sturtevant's initial satisfaction was dimmed by the man's divisive influence. Although a Congregationalist, Kendall was associating with the Presbyterians and sympathized with them because of his own conservative views. It would be better, Sturtevant thought, if Kendall were affiliated with the Presbyterians. Mr. Ayers vehemently opposed the appointment in 1849 of William Coffin, Class of 1841, to the chair of mathematics and science because he was not Presbyterian. He also objected to the election of Rev. Albert Hale, pastor of a Presbyterian Church in Springfield and a member of the Illinois Association, as a trustee. Ayers insisted that Hale was really not a Presbyterian but a Congregationalist.

Despite evidence of religious fervor the cloud of Transcendentalism was still hanging over Illinois College in 1850. A news item under the pseudonym, "Delta," reported the "painful fact…that more infidelity is found among [the College's] members than in times past." Sturtevant responded vigorously, declaring that the report was mischievous and contained much misinformation about both the town and the College. He called attention to the six hundred students in Jacksonville in the schools under religious auspices. The College's reputation in the community was demonstrated by the contribution of $10,000 in the past year, most of it from people in orthodox Congregational and Presbyterian churches. At times when the threats of "the powers of darkness" were severe, "a band of young disciples…stood up firmly beside their instructors for the honor of Christ." (*Independent*, 15 Aug., 12 Sept. 1850)

The Larger Community

Writing to Baldwin, Sturtevant described the civic responsibility of the man who heads a college: "The President of a College should take an active part in the whole moral and social conflict of his age." (S-B, 7 Feb. 1849) Sturtevant heeded his own dictum. As a college president and a minister, he traveled a great deal and attended innumerable meetings. He was intensely interested in public affairs, insatiably curious about human society, and fascinated by the rapid progress in communication and transportation. The prospect in 1848 that the telegraph would soon link Jacksonville to Springfield and Chicago in one direction and to Quincy and western Missouri in the other was exhilarating. "Maybe we will sometimes talk a little," he told Baldwin. (S-B, 20 June 1848) In October the lines were in operation and what happened in New York was often printed and circulated in Jacksonville before bedtime. Soon he received from Baldwin a telegraphic dispatch, sent one day and delivered at eight the next morning. Rapid improvements were made in transportation also; the Illinois and Michigan Canal had now been completed, and any day the first train of cars was expected to arrive from Naples on the Illinois River. Travel to the East had improved so much that in August 1849 Sturtevant required less than a week to go from Jacksonville to Connecticut—and only 72 hours from Chicago to New York. "What times!" he exclaimed.

In February 1844 Sturtevant attended a gala affair, a "Citizen Supper," at the Mansion House in honor of a man who had pursued a felon for seven hundred miles. The hunted man had fraudulently taken property and his capture was celebrated as a victory for justice. Sturtevant was among those citizens who spoke at the supper and offered a toast: "Liberty, Law and Order—without the last two, the first cannot exist."[19]

Unwilling to identify himself with any political party, Sturtevant nevertheless had closer sympathies with the Whigs than with the Democrats. The Whig party was gaining strength in central Illinois and the local district was the only one in the state to send a Whig to Congress in 1844. That same year a Whig newspaper, the *Morgan Journal*, began publication in Jacksonville; in subsequent years it became a strong supporter of Illinois College and its president. In 1846 Abraham Lincoln, a Whig, was victor in the Congressional race over the famous Methodist circuit rider, Peter Cartwright, who campaigned as a Democrat.

A poem written by a student was "a downright good for nothing affair, a glorification of the Mexican War," Sturtevant complained to Baldwin in 1847. (S-B, 26 June 1847) The comment indicates that Sturtevant was opposed to that war and likely because he feared acquiring Mexican land would expand slave territory. Sturtevant strenuously opposed the evil system and argued in an essay that the College Society could not expand into the South because of the irreconcilable contradiction between the Puritan college and abominable slavery. He was most displeased because in the printed article his forthright statements had been softened, a change for which he blamed the editor.[20]

By 1848 Sturtevant was convinced that slavery was the foremost national issue and was persuaded that year to cast his first vote[21] in a presidential election. He had not been eligible to vote in 1828 because of a change of residence and he refrained from voting in subsequent elections because he could not conscientiously support either party. His vote for Martin Van Buren in 1848 represented support for the party and not enthusiasm for the man. The Free Soil party had adopted as its slogan "Free Soil, Free Speech, Free Labor, and Free Men,"[22] and Sturtevant regarded it as the only hope for ending slavery. In 1849 Sturtevant and others, with the assistance of Congressman Abraham Lincoln, petitioned for the abolition of the slave trade in the District of Columbia.[23] The Illinois House passed a strong resolution supporting the Wilmot Proviso to keep slavery out of territory obtained from Mexico. Commenting on that and on the report that another Pope had fled Italy, Sturtevant observed, "Verily these are stirring times." (S-B, 15 Jan. 1849)

Along with the church and liberal education, public education was a cause dear to the Illinois Association.[24] Sturtevant had reaffirmed his commitment in his inaugural address, and he delivered lectures in Chicago and Springfield on the need for public education. The Jacksonville and Springfield newspapers published notices, signed by J. M. Sturtevant as chairman of the committee, of the 1845 teachers' convention to be held in Jacksonville. Nine questions, including the following, were listed for discussion:

whether education should be the same for males and females; whether communicating knowledge or disciplining the mind should be primary; and whether education should be extended to all classes. Sturtevant addressed the convention and was an officer of the teachers' organization.

A prolonged campaign for state legislation to permit taxation for free schools succeeded in 1845. School meetings in Jacksonville, drawing big crowds, were like Yankee town meetings "and such debates as we do have." (S-B, 22 Dec. 1847) Telling Baldwin a secret, Sturtevant reported that he had become a popular leader and had led the people to vote for a public school. Casting aside his usual modesty, he boasted that "My whole plan has carried triumphantly" and the district would soon build a school with tax money. (S-B, 13 Mar. 1848) The West Jacksonville School District, with Sturtevant as chairman, was organized in 1848. Apparently he was treasurer and retained the minutes for 1849, when a tax of thirty-five cents per hundred was levied. He was one of two hundred thirty-one named on the District list. His home on the campus was not taxable but his several lots were. It has been said that Jacksonville had the first free school in the state. The building constructed in 1850 by the District was later used as the Second Ward School; it was located at the corner of State Street and Fayette.[25]

When the trustees of the Jacksonville Female Academy proposed in 1846 to pay its debts by selling the school to the Methodists, the townspeople rallied and raised enough money to pay half the amount. The financial problems persisted and two years later Sturtevant with others signed a note to cover the obligation. At the 1848 meeting of the Ladies' Association for Educating Females, Sturtevant praised the women for their perseverance. Citing the great need in the western states for qualified teachers of both sexes, he predicted that the proportion of female teachers would be increasing. He maintained that a free society cannot allow any young person to be debarred from educational opportunity by poverty. He pleaded for universal education, declaring that the idea of perfect civilization requires that "each and every individual intellect shall receive that cultivation of which it is susceptible, and be applied to the uses for which God has created and fitted it…. God creates <u>no</u> superfluous mind, and to suffer the precious gems of intellect to lie unquarried in the deep beds of popular ignorance, while the world is perishing for lack of knowledge, is a shameful prodigality of the noblest gifts of God." Sturtevant's case for the Academy was described as "ably and eloquently presented." (LES-15, 16, 4)

Correspondence with Miss Catharine Beecher in 1849 pertained to a woman's school which she wanted to establish in Illinois, probably in Quincy. Baldwin had written a letter to her which she found troubling—possibly the College Society had denied her request for aid. She showed the letter to Sturtevant, who perused it and concluded in his own mind that Baldwin could not in justice have done otherwise. Sturtevant reassured Baldwin, saying, "As Antisthenes in derision advised the Athenians, she is trying to make asses horses by calling them so." Sturtevant informed Baldwin that Miss Beecher had totally alienated Governor Slade, who had written to Sturtevant hoping he could counteract her influence. Miss Beecher had asked Sturtevant to be a trustee for some educational apparatus, worth about $3000 to $4000, which she wished to place in his hands for the College's use; he explained to Baldwin that he could not refuse her request.[26]

The concern of leaders in Jacksonville for the public welfare extended to persons with special needs. The Asylum for the Deaf and Dumb[27] was authorized in 1839 although instruction did not begin until 1845; Sturtevant was one of the original Directors. When Dorothea Dix brought her crusade for proper treatment of the insane to Jacksonville she was welcomed as a guest in the Sturtevant home. Sturtevant encouraged her to present her proposal before the State Legislature, which she did, and the hospital was established in 1847. He remarked that "This movement is the result of the labors of that prodigy of Female heroism Miss D. L. Dix." (S-B, 4 Mar. 1847) Jacksonville was chosen as the site instead of Peoria because its population was superior in its ability to provide care at a benevolent institution. Miss Dix wrote a very warm letter to Sturtevant expressing appreciation for his support and sent "friendly regards" to Mrs. Sturtevant and others in their "pleasant town."[28] That summer Sturtevant planned to request

"Miss Dix the philanthropist" to assist in obtaining help for the College "from the nabobs of [Boston]." (S-B, 17 June 1847)

In 1847, at a public meeting at the Methodist Church, Sturtevant gave an address in support of a resolution on behalf of the founding of a school for the blind. He also pledged $30 toward a fund of $350 for supporting such an institution for the first two years. The expectation was that the privately-funded school would show the feasibility of the program.[29] In 1849 the legislature appropriated the needed funds—"another overflowing of the liberality of our Legislature upon Jacksonville," Sturtevant told Baldwin. (S-B, 15 Jan. 1849)

A claim on behalf of Jacksonville as "the Athens of the West" was stronger than that of most towns with similar ambitions. In the fall of 1848 there were about four hundred pupils above the grade of common school. By 1849 seven important educational and care institutions had been established in Jacksonville, the College being the first and the "nucleus." (S-B, 15 Jan. 1849) The College had its own preparatory school, the Presbyterians had Jacksonville Female Academy, the State had institutions for the deaf and the blind, and citizens had organized the West Jacksonville Public School. The Methodists founded their Illinois Conference Female Academy in 1846, with instruction commencing two years later.[30]

Several hundred Portuguese Protestants on Madeira fled to Trinidad to escape persecution for converting from Catholicism. A commercial enterprise brought them to New York but then abandoned its plan to locate and employ them. A Jacksonville man learned of their plight and a committee was organized to bring the people to central Illinois. Sturtevant, Rev. Albert Hale of Springfield, and the Governor of Illinois were designated to arrange their relocation. Sturtevant wrote letters on behalf of five churches regarding travel arrangements. The Portuguese were urged to delay the trip for some weeks because of an outbreak of cholera in the area. Sturtevant encouraged them with the hope that "our thoroughfares will be safe for the journey in a few weeks from this time."[31] In November 1849 three hundred fifty refugees reached Jacksonville and established a strong community.

Leadership in Ideas and Institutions

Sturtevant's leadership in supporting numerous good causes was significant because of the quality of his thinking. His candid assessment in late years was that his life had been "one of more than ordinary thoughtfulness. I have not only thought much, but I have thought independently." (A, 10) He was conscientious in adhering to basic principles, establishing the facts, applying the canons of logic, and finally stating his conclusions in lucid English. He fiercely defended his right to speak freely and guarded the same right for others. A strong element of Yankee practicality pervaded his actions.

In his travels to the East, with sometimes lengthy stays, Sturtevant frequently saw old friends, chief among them Theron Baldwin. He expressed the hope that the two of them and Mason Grosvenor could get together to talk about the College "as we used to twenty years ago." (S-B, 25 Apr. 1849) Sturtevant met new friends—and sometimes acquired new antagonists. His arduous journeys actually improved his health, rejuvenating his spirit by contact with the intellectual and cultural life of the East.

Sturtevant expressed his opinions very freely in writing to Baldwin, and he employed vivid and colorful language. Indeed, Baldwin was the one person in whom Sturtevant confided College problems that he could not share even with his wife. He used his friend as a sounding board for some of his ideas and plans. Baldwin often edited Sturtevant's writings and sometimes suggested topics for his articles. He was frequently a messenger for Sturtevant, taking his contributions to various publishers, arranging for the printing of examination questions or diplomas for the College's graduating classes, paying bills, and collecting money owed to Sturtevant for his articles. Sturtevant regretted that he could not reciprocate Baldwin's favors and gladly assisted Baldwin in selling his house in Jacksonville.

Sturtevant nourished his broad interests in a variety of subjects by his avid reading of a variety of newspapers, journals, and books. Some information about his reading habits can be gleaned from his correspondence with Baldwin, who sometimes purchased books for him. In one instance a shipment arrived but one volume was missing, "Augustinianism and Pelagianism," by a Professor

Emerson. (S-B, 22 Dec. 1847) Sturtevant mentioned to Baldwin in 1845 that he was subscribing to the *Christian Observer* and the *Christian Messenger*. In 1848 he acknowledged receiving two copies of the *Journal of Commerce*. Probably the periodicals which Sturtevant read during these years included those which published his articles.

Appropriately Sturtevant took care to maintain his spiritual life. Family worship was customary in the household and although he did not mention it, he surely must have prayed regularly by himself and with Hannah. He observed an annual fast day whether at home or while traveling; in writing to Baldwin from Boston he mentioned that he had just returned to the city that morning and had been keeping the fast day.

In 1847 Sturtevant was engaged by the local Congregational Church as its supply minister. He continued for two years although, he told Baldwin, neither he nor the College could really afford for him to do this extra work. During the last two months of 1847 he was to be paid $6.00 per Sabbath. Often the fees for preaching did not represent additional income for Sturtevant because he deducted such receipts from his College salary or used them to fund special projects at the College.

Sturtevant performed the other duties expected of a minister, in addition to being moderator and preaching at the Sunday services. He presided at the communion services, performed marriages, and conducted funerals. When requested he baptized adults by immersion, leading to the rumor he reported to Baldwin that he was now a Baptist.[32] The Congregational Church paid the Baptist Church one dollar for filling its pool.

In one of his frequent complaints about the pastor of the Presbyterian Church, Sturtevant declared to Baldwin that he himself had done far more in preaching about human sinfulness in a single sermon than Rev. Eddy had accomplished in many sermons. His own achievement, he asserted, had been "to produce conviction of the deep thorough depravity of mankind—depravity as fact not theory." (S-B, 4 May 1848) This was one of the principles of Reformed theology emphasized by Calvin and Edwards and others to convince people that they must rely on the grace of

God through Jesus Christ for salvation. Sturtevant believed that no orthodox man, hearing him preach, would doubt his orthodoxy. ·

At various times Sturtevant preached at churches elsewhere, such as the Presbyterian Church in Beardstown. When that church became Congregational in 1850 Sturtevant gave the dedicatory address. He continued to preach occasionally at the Congregational Church in Waverly. In February 1847 he gave the Pilgrim Day oration for the New England Society in St. Louis. Sturtevant also preached at Truman Post's church in St. Louis when Post was at Illinois College to give his lectures on history. In 1848 for the first time he was invited to preach in the Presbyterian Church and two Congregational churches in Quincy. A Springfield newspaper reported that "President Sturtevant, of Illinois College, Jacksonville, is expected to occupy the pulpit of the Third Presbyterian Church (court-house) to-morrow, 12th inst."(SJ, 11 May 1850)

As chairman of the business committee of the Lord's Day Convention of the Sabbath, "Rev. Mr. Sturdevant" made a report which resulted in the adoption of several resolutions. (SJ, 15 July 1847) Sturtevant also attended meetings of the area Congregational Associations and the state-wide General Association of Illinois. He participated in the ordination of several Congregational ministers and frequently was assigned to question the candidates about natural theology or doctrine. He sometimes preached the ordination sermon, especially when the candidate was an Illinois College alumnus.

There were important pulpits in Boston and in New York (at Pilgrim Church and Broadway Tabernacle) and in other eastern cities which Sturtevant was invited to fill from time to time. Often the specific message was the College Society's needs and the arrangements were made by Theron Baldwin. Baldwin wrote while traveling in Connecticut that he had seen Dr. [Horace] Bushnell in Hartford and that Bushnell wanted Sturtevant to preach for him, but there is no information about an actual invitation. Bushnell was a fellow-student with Sturtevant at Yale and now was one of the most prominent preachers in the East.

In 1844 Sturtevant first attended a meeting of the American Board of Commissioners for Foreign Missions, now an essentially Congregational organization. In gratitude for his service to the

Jacksonville Congregational Church its people subscribed funds to make Sturtevant a Life Member of the American Board. He attended the anniversaries in the East whenever he could. He came to realize that the Gospel is for the whole world and he sought to overcome all human barriers to true Christian fellowship. Such work he believed calls forth "the mightiest energies of our Nation" and not simply the churches. He informed Baldwin in 1849 that he had been preaching much that spring about "our country" and that he would continue that theme if he came East during the summer. He said that he saw more clearly than ever that "Anglo Americans are to people the world." (S-B, 25 Apr. 1849)

As an alumnus Sturtevant was invited to preach in the Yale Chapel in early March 1845. He wanted to attend the twentieth reunion of his class at Yale the following year but lack of money made it impossible. For the same reasons he abandoned his hope of attending the world Congregational convention in London.[33]

Sometimes, in reporting to Baldwin his poor success at fund-raising for the College Society in certain eastern cities, Sturtevant expressed his reactions in blunt language. In one eastern city he collected $124.50, a relatively large contribution but, he declared, that city was "the coldest place I have been in." He continued, alluding to a prominent preacher of the Great Awakening: "The remains of [George] Whitefield repose beneath one of the pulpits in which I preached, but I fear his spirit has fled from this con-gregation as well as from his mouldering bones. Things bear to my notion the appearance of dead orthodoxy." (S-B, Newburyport [Mass.], 16 Apr. 1845) Sturtevant thought it would be well to find some way of reaching some of the rich men of Boston who were outside the circle of Congregational orthodoxy, presumably refer-ring to people in the Unitarian churches of that city.

In early 1845 Sturtevant engaged in an evening's discussion in a club at New Haven with Dr. Leonard Bacon, an old friend, and Dr. Joseph Thompson, who became a good friend, and others. Sturtevant was asked to state his views on the Lord's Supper in relation to church government and discipline. After the formality of a protest he agreed to answer questions and in response he declared that the Lord's Supper is an "ordinance" which belongs to the church universal. The "power of the keys" by which the organized church has claimed authority over the Lord's Supper has caused much grief and conflict. On this point, Sturtevant believed, John Calvin and John Knox as well as Pope Gregory VII were in error. He advocated returning to the simpler teaching that the ordinances belong to the universal church, which he believed would open the way for full fellowship. (Later, Sturtevant recalled that no one in the group had thought his views to be alarming.) He believed that the multitude of Christians could then unite around "the Christ of the New Testament, the Christ of the immaculate conception, the crucifixion, the resurrection and the ascension." (A, 266)

The first of two significant meetings which Sturtevant did <u>not</u> attend in 1846 was convened in Michigan City, Indiana, in mid-summer. The purpose was to bring about changes in the operation of the Plan of Union in Illinois to provide more freedom for Congregationalism. Only two men of the forty-eight in attendance were associated directly with Illinois College. Both were trustees: William Carter, pastor of the Pittsfield Congregational Church, and William Kirby, now Illinois agent for the Home Missionary Society. Jonathan Blanchard used the occasion to secure an endorsement of Knox College and to advocate a strong abolitionist stand. Both these efforts were deemed detrimental to Illinois College. Sturtevant earlier had expressed his dismay over the prospect of a contest with Knox over funds and criticized the curriculum at Knox as superficial, an imitation of Oberlin's. (S-B, 6 Oct. 1845)

In the late summer a meeting at Albany, New York, established the American Missionary Association, which advocated strict separation from churches with slave-holding members. Both meetings threatened the cooperative efforts with the Presbyterians, including the American Home Missionary Society which sought to serve all churches. Sturtevant, Baldwin, and their associates regarded the more extreme positions as hindering the overall mission of the church. A concrete result of Blanchard's efforts was the inclusion of Knox College as one of the beneficiaries of the College Society.[34]

An article in the *New York Observer* (22 Nov. 1845) prompted a strong protest from Sturtevant, who charged that it was a shameful attack on Western Congregationalism. The author was identified only as a Jacksonville man but Sturtevant was certain he knew his identity, although he did not disclose it. (It probably was Rev. Chauncey Eddy.) A lesser aggravation was the slow mail delivery of the papers; he received the 13 February issue at the end of the month. "So you see," he said, "we are living out of this world." (S-B, 30 Mar. 1847) In February 1849 Sturtevant asked Baldwin to pay his bill of $6.00 at the *Observer*, deducting that sum from the next draft sent to the College, and to direct the paper to stop at the end of the year.

Soon after the Towne-Eddy report on Illinois College was published by the College Society, Sturtevant planned to reply to an article about it in the January (1846) *Repository*. He believed that the author had betrayed the very citadel of Protestantism. Both Towne and Baldwin recommended that he not respond and apparently he accepted their advice. Sturtevant wrote for the *New Englander* a review of Baldwin's First and Second Reports of the Western College Society[35] and forwarded his article to Baldwin, who replied that he liked it very much. Baldwin mentioned that Sturtevant was behind the times in projecting the extension of the United States to the Rio Grande. To fulfill its "manifest destiny" the country must push north at least to 54° 40' if not, with Mr. Douglas, to the Arctic Ocean.

Several years later Sturtevant wrote to Baldwin saying that although they had failed to include a proviso against slavery when the College Society was founded, they must not fail now to have a proviso against ignorance and for the preaching of the word of God. He declared that Minnesota, Oregon, California—and perhaps New Mexico, and Utah—all were demanding or would be demanding aid. The Society must have full access to the churches to seek their support for the Colleges. Sturtevant disdained the notion some had that it was not proper to discuss aid for colleges in the pulpit on the Sabbath.

In their letters Sturtevant and Baldwin often commented on articles they had read in various periodicals.[36] Sturtevant subscribed to or had access to the *Christian Messenger* and the *Watchman of the Valley*, whose editor, he was pleased to note, vindicated the rights of Congregationalism.[37] He was asked to be the state correspondent for the *New-York Evangelist* and was willing to try although uncertain about his ability.[38] Another opportunity for Sturtevant to become involved in publishing was an invitation in 1849 to join three others in editing *The Herald of the Prairies*,[39] a Congregational newspaper established in Chicago three years earlier. Baldwin pointed out that it would be impractical because the four men lived far apart. Moreover, he warned, one of the others— President Blanchard of Knox—would cause more problems in a week than Sturtevant could resolve in a month. Apparently nothing came of the proposal.

When Sturtevant wrote his 1850 letter refuting "Delta's" charge of infidelity at Illinois College, he signed his own name.[40] However, he used his pseudonym, "Robinson," when he published two other items in the *Independent* that same year. His "Letter from Illinois" reported on the recent Synod meeting. His article on "The Pilgrim Fathers" was intended to exonerate the Pilgrims of Plymouth Rock from the common indictment of cruel persecution, especially the Salem witchcraft executions. Sturtevant emphasized that it was the Presbyterians in England who, during their brief reign, passed legislation enforcing the death penalty for a series of offenses, including any committed in the colonies, against orthodox Christian doctrines. The Plymouth Pilgrims had nothing to do with those actions nor were they responsible for the persecutions in the Massachusetts Bay Colony or the witchcraft trials at Salem. Those who settled that Colony were of "original Presbyterian origin and sympathy." The Pilgrim fathers of Plymouth were exemplary in their adherence to the two basic doctrines of Protestantism: "the right of conscience" and "the Bible and the Bible alone." When any man or church in America can match their record, "let that man, or church, step forward, not to *vindicate*, but to take a proud and solitary stand by the side of the followers of JOHN ROBINSON."[41]

The *Springfield Sangamo Journal* announced in January 1845 that a series of lectures on scientific subjects, by Sturtevant and others, would be delivered before the Mechanics' Union. In 1848 the same newspaper announced that the Union Musical Association would meet on 4 October at Pisgah, in Morgan County. "An address on the subject of music may be expected from President Sturtevant of Jacksonville." In 1847 Sturtevant spoke before Quincy's Library Association on the "causes of poverty of dense population." (S-B, 19 Feb. 1847) In late 1849 he again lectured before the Association and was highly praised. Adding to its brief report of that event a Springfield paper commented that "it would be a great treat to our citizens, were some of the literary gentlemen, connected with the Illinois College, disposed to favor us with lectures in the winter season." Perhaps in delayed fulfillment of that request Sturtevant spoke on two successive evenings in May 1850 "on the spread and general prevalence of the English language, and its influence in Christianizing the world." (SJ, 5 Jan., 13 May 1850)

The honorary Doctor of Divinity degree was awarded to Sturtevant by the University of Missouri at its commencement on 24 August 1848. He belittled the honor in writing about it to Baldwin, saying, "What ought to be done with such a toy by such a one as I?"[42] Nevertheless he added the "D.D." to his name and was henceforth addressed as "Dr. Sturtevant." His wife was sometimes referred to as "Mrs. Dr. Sturtevant."

A Large and Expensive Family

The marriage of Julian Sturtevant and Hannah Fayerweather was happy both for them and for the children of both his marriages. Three more children were born to the couple, Lucy Ella in 1846, Edgar Howard in 1848, and Alfred Henry in 1850. These were difficult years because of financial constraints. The College's situation was bleak and in August 1846 Sturtevant admitted to his friend in New York that "I've never suffered for want of money so much as during the last year." His family too was filled with gloom and he felt they could not long endure. Nevertheless Sturtevant was generous in making loans to indigent students; the money was transferred from the College salary credited to his account but not always paid regularly. The College connection affected the family's welfare in another way. Some merchants paid their obligations to the College by providing goods for which Sturtevant often had to pay exorbitant prices.

There were occasions when the family came first. Baldwin

requested Sturtevant to come East in the summer of 1848 to assist in fund raising. Hannah's fourth child was due in August and Sturtevant replied, "The condition of my family answers imperatively No!" (S-B, 20 June 1848) A year later, when he acknowledged that his family had become "large and expensive," his financial situation was much improved. (S-B, 26 June 1849) His family was indeed large. The 1850 census listed the parents, Elizabeth's

The Sturtevant's Home, 1832-1852
The "South Wing." The side was adjacent to the 4-story dormitory; the windows and door were added after the 1852 fire. Later it was the "Club House," where students boarded.

three children, and the three surviving children of Hannah. The household was in fact much larger than the family of eight! Hannah's father, Richard (69), and her sister, Mary Jane ("37," but probably 42), were now living with the Sturtevants. Also present were D. Hale and R. Hale, ages 25 and 2, both female, both born in Alabama, and both designated "B" for "Black." Presumably the mother was a cook. Also included were a couple from Madeira, A. and R. Nuns (Nunes?); A. Nuns, 41, was a laborer. In 1850 arrangements were made for Edward Fayerweather, James' six-year old son, to live with the Sturtevants and attend Jacksonville's good schools. Hannah's fifth child, Alfred, was born in December 1850, too late for the census.

In September 1846 Sturtevant remarked that his health had not been very good that summer although he was not presently ill; fortunately, the family was well. In July 1849 he was sick in bed for nine days and remained very weak for some time. An alarming amount of cholera was reported in St. Louis and the towns along the rivers although not in Jacksonville.

In 1844 the College sold Sturtevant several lots on the east side of Park Street, just across from the campus. The purchase included the lot at the northeast corner of Park and Grove, later the site of Sturtevant's home. Also included were some lots to the north on Park, and several to the east on Grove. For some reason the transfer was not recorded until 1847. Hannah's name often appeared on real estate transactions, along with Julian's. In January 1845 Julian and Hannah sold two sizable parcels to her father; at the same time they obtained from him six acres west of Lincoln and a quarter mile south of Morton. Samuel Adams paid Sturtevant $250 for two lots across from the campus for building a family home; the house, still standing, has long been known by the name of Adams' son-in-law, Lippincott. Sturtevant purchased an expensive lot in the original plot of Jacksonville; it was on the east side of North Main and just north of Railroad Street and cost $1,000. The taxes paid by Sturtevant in 1845 amounted to $1.88, with $1.31 due on real estate valued at $217 and fifty-seven cents on personal property valued at $95. In 1849 he paid $9.68 in real estate taxes on a valuation of $845.

The memories of family life which the eldest son recorded in his unpublished autobiography were chiefly from the years 1845 to 1854; most events and situations were not dated precisely. Sturtevant gave his sons their first lesson in farming in the spring of 1845 when Julian Jr. was eleven and James Warren was nine. He had bought an old wagon and harness and the boys were to drive the team and wagon to the blacksmith shop to get a plow. Realizing that they were ashamed to be seen with the old wagon, he drove it himself—the boys following on foot. Loading the plow, the three drove to the family's twenty-acre field, half a mile south of the College. The team was hitched to the plow and father "plowed as if he had never done anything else." After showing how it was done, he left them to work until noon when they returned for dinner, each riding one of the horses.[43]

The boys' father quoted his father's saying that no idle bread was to be eaten in his house, and the same rule was applied in Jacksonville. The boys awakened early and took care of the stables and milked two or three cows. They joined the family for prayers, a service short but unhurried. A shelf near the table held a Bible for each member and each in turn read a verse from a selected chapter. Breakfast was at seven and then the boys began their work in the field or meadow or woodlot. Except in the busy season the boys would come home by eleven o'clock to prepare lessons to be recited after dinner to one of their parents.

Julian Jr. expressed his regret that he and Warren had not been allowed to attend public school and mingle with boys their own age. They were taught by their parents but also attended a sort of "dame school" with the children of Governor and Mrs. Duncan. Their formal schooling began when they enrolled in the College's Preparatory Department. The boys had some time for recreation but overall their lives were much too sober, Julian Jr. thought. From about 1844 to 1847 the boys attended a Sabbath School class at the Presbyterian Church.

Mother Hannah had the primary responsibility for managing the household. She and her sisters made much of their own and the children's clothing. Most of their food was obtained from the family's garden, orchard, and livestock.

Mother made lye by filling a barrel with wood ashes and then letting water seep through; the lye was combined with grease from the kitchen to make soap. She made her own starch from wheat or potatoes and the family made straw hats from strips of braided oat straw. Before the family acquired a mold their candles were made by dipping strings into melted wax. Their beautiful whale-oil lamps were used only on special occasions because both lamps and oil were so expensive. The children were expected to be at the table with their parents' frequent guests, and the older children assisted with the serving. Julian Jr. especially remembered such guests as Catharine Beecher and Alexander Campbell. He had proudly driven the family carriage (a "Dearborn") to take Miss Dorothea Dix to call upon prominent citizens in the community. Miss Dix was the Sturtevants' house guest for some time.

"Mother"—Hannah—was remembered with great affection.

She had great patience and never lost her temper even under the greatest pressure. Father was a sad man, often wearing "a very sorrowful expression of countenance" and frequently the look of pain. He spoke with a sad voice about "the wife of his youth." And yet he "enjoyed a hearty laugh and he and his second wife lived bravely and happily together...." (23) The younger Julian did not wish to be regarded as finding fault with father who was most loving to his family. "The worst that could be said was that he did not love his family less but Illinois College more." (29)

When Grandfather Fayerweather and his unmarried daughters first moved to the Jacksonville area they lived on his farm. When he was no longer able to manage his affairs he and his remaining maiden daughter, Mary Jane, lived with the Sturtevants. Julian Jr. remembered that Grandfather had many folk-beliefs which led to arguments with father. He thought that the moon influenced the crops and determined the proper time to slaughter animals. Father tried to convince him otherwise by explaining the teachings of modern astronomy, but his effort was futile.

After his second marriage, Warren, Julian's father, continued to live in Tallmadge. In early 1847 he wrote to Julian to acknowledged Julian's letter of 5 January which enclosed a little more than twenty-one dollars—money which Julian had collected for him. A second letter was an urgent plea for financial help, motivated by "imperious necessity." He expressed the wish to see Julian that spring but supposed he should not expect it. Fortunately Julian was able to visit his father and step-mother in mid-July on his way East. The next year Julian advised Baldwin that he had made a draft on the College Society for $158.47 in favor of his father. That amount would be deducted from money due Illinois College and subsequently from Julian's salary.

Julian's sister Huldah, with her husband John Hinman and their children, moved to Ottawa, Illinois, about 1845. The oldest child, a daughter, died in 1846. The other four children and their father died in 1849, some because of scarlet fever, others because of cholera. Huldah, now a childless widow, visited Julian's family in April 1850 and then made her home in Beardstown.[44]

Brother Christopher and his family continued to live in or near

Beardstown. Christopher had tried farming but gave that up and entered business. The adults joined the Congregational Church in Beardstown in 1850, probably when it transferred its affiliation from the Presbyterian Church or soon after; possibly their presence influenced that change.

Julia Fayerweather[45] Chamberlain and her husband Timothy were parents of one daughter, Hannah, born 8 July 1846. Mary Jane Fayerweather transferred her membership from the Presbyterian Church to the Congregational Church in April 1848 and now the three living sisters of the family, as well as their father, were all members of that church. The date of Mary Jane's membership may indicate the approximate time when she and her father came to live with her sister Hannah's family. James Fayerweather and his family were living in Burlington, Iowa. Abraham, in Hawaii, wrote in April 1849 about his desire to send his daughters to Illinois "to enjoy the advantages of my native country and at the same time to make good Yankees of them." Unhappily both he and his wife Mary died in 1850. Hannah's inquiry about her brother's death was answered by a missionary who said he could not give her the comfort of knowing that her brother had attained "the pearl of greatest price," salvation.[46]

Silas apparently did not communicate with his family during the decade prior to his death on 8 September 1850—just two months before Abraham died. The father was in ill health and could not travel to New Orleans to settle his son's estate. Consequently Julian Sturtevant boarded a steamboat departing from St. Louis on 30 September. Writing to Baldwin on 2 October while en route, Sturtevant declared that his friend would doubt the writer's sanity when he noted the address, "Steamer Amaranth, near New Madrid" [Missouri]. Sturtevant would mail this letter from Memphis, admitting that this was "a strange latitude for my epistle to emanate from." He was already in a new world although "they say" it is a part of his country. He explained the circumstances and said he did not expect to miss more than two to three weeks of the College term. After Silas's large debt was paid and bequests were honored, about $1,100 remained for Hannah Sturtevant. Silas had owned some slaves and the Fayerweather-Sturtevant family paid the necessary fees to provide their freedom.[47] In Jacksonville's Diamond Grove Cemetery a large stone tablet marks the grave of Richard Fayerweather and memorializes Abraham and Silas, neither of whom is buried there. The grave and marker were moved from the Illinois College Cemetery in 1873.

Chapter 5: 1851-1855

Celebrating the Quarter-Century Mark

Additions to Curriculum and Faculty

Illinois College made important additions to its curriculum during the early 1850s. Modern foreign languages became a regular offering when Professor Adams was authorized in 1850 to teach German that fall and French the following year. Sturtevant, as the temporary Blackburn Professor of Theology, planned a theological class in the fall of 1851 with instruction to be provided by himself, other faculty, and pastors of the Presbyterian and Congregational churches. The trustees affirmed the criteria for the Master of Arts degree. Awarded usually to alumni, it could be granted three years after the A.B. to men of good moral character who gave evidence of appropriate progress in literary and scientific attainments.

The trustees adopted several measures to strengthen science instruction. A Bachelor of Science curriculum was instituted in the fall of 1852, only a year after Harvard granted the first such degree in the United States. The course was shorter than the A.B. program because the classical languages were omitted. The *Independent* reported in 1854 that the Bachelor of Science degree was awarded for the first time; two of the twelve graduates received that degree. Professor Adams was allowed $100 for expenses to improve science instruction by visits to eastern colleges. As soon as the College's books could be moved to a room in the dormitory, a cabinet of minerals would be installed in the attic story of the Chapel. The College was now more attractive to students, enrollment spurting from seventy-one in 1851-1852 to nearly one hundred two years later.

The trustees in 1851 revised the *Laws of Illinois College*, incorporating new policies. The faculty were to reside near the campus during term time to be easily accessible to students. Any outside activity which might interfere with College duties required approval by the trustees. The president could veto faculty decisions, but a two-thirds vote could override his veto. The faculty were authorized to enter student rooms and to require students' testimony on matters "pertaining to the publick interests." The faculty were to make semi-annual reports to parents regarding their sons' progress and deportment. Students were to be disciplined in a mild and parental manner and penalties were to be chiefly moral. Students could appeal adverse faculty decisions to the president and even to the trustees.

The faculty granted a day of vacation for Thanksgiving. In mid-December 1851 the students successfully petitioned for one week of vacation beginning 25 December. Rewarding superior performance, the trustees established prizes in the amount of twenty dollars annually for excellence in declamation and debate.

Edward Beecher wished to join the faculty but Baldwin advised that his well-known theological views made him unsuitable, a conclusion Sturtevant had already reached. Beecher visited Jacksonville in the summer of 1851 and Sturtevant then took him in his carriage to Beardstown. The two men discussed the College fully and freely. In writing to Baldwin, Sturtevant spoke warmly of Beecher's purity of heart and his sincere attachment to Christ. However, he perceived that Beecher had far "less practical insight and wisdom" than he previously thought.[1] (S-B, 17 July 1851) Professors Reuben Kendall (Classics) and William Coffin (Mathematics and Astronomy) resigned in 1852. Kendall's departure was a relief to Sturtevant but he and Adams had to add Coffin's classes to their own already-heavy teaching loads. Mason Grosvenor left his position with the College Society about 1 December 1852 "to engage temporarily in the business of instruction at Illinois College." (SPC-10, 20) Baldwin discouraged appointing him to teach theology, saying that their friend was not suitable for the position. It is not clear whether Grosvenor came to Jacksonville at that time, but he did teach mathematics at the College in 1853-1854. Julian Sturtevant Jr. was appointed as tutor in 1855.

Successful fund-raising efforts begun in 1849 made possible

new and permanent appointments. In 1852 Rufus Nutting accepted the position in classical languages and the following year Rufus Crampton was appointed to teach mathematics and natural philosophy. In 1854 William D. Sanders joined the faculty as Professor of Rhetoric. Both Nutting and Sanders were Presbyterians, which pleased certain trustees and others of the College's Presbyterian constituency. Sturtevant judged these men to be able and was relieved that "the religious divisions of the college seemed to be past...." (A, 273)

Improved rail transportation facilitated attendance at commencement week exercises by visitors from a wide area. The Sangamon & Morgan Rail Road advertised excursion rates at half the usual fare in mid-week in 1851. Except for that year, when disease discouraged attendance, the festivities continued to attract large numbers. The *New York Independent* in 1853, quoting from the *Chicago Congregational Herald*, noted that the College's annual income had exceeded expenditures by five hundred dollars.

The literary societies supplemented the academic resources of the College. Sigma Pi incorporated its Library Association in 1851, Sturtevant serving as a trustee. To raise money for its library, it arranged public lectures, given sometimes by faculty, sometimes by famous visitors. These were held in various churches, including the Congregational Church. Sigma Pi was favored by the faculty and by President Sturtevant, who was elected an honorary member in its early years. His two oldest sons were members, as were other faculty sons; not until the 1880s did a faculty son join rival Phi Alpha.

Whether a faculty member or a trustee was Presbyterian or Congregational did not matter to Sturtevant. He simply wanted the person to be Christian and competent. However, some trustees who were New School Presbyterians insisted on having more Presbyterians sympathetic to their views. In 1851 David A. Smith, a prominent local lawyer, urged the election of Rev. Livingston Glover, pastor of the First Presbyterian Church (New School) in Jacksonville. Rev. Glover strongly opposed agencies linked to the Plan of Union, such as the American Home Missionary Society, and Sturtevant characterized him as being "most obnoxious" to the College's warmest Congregational friends. Sturtevant wanted only candidates who had the unanimous support of the present trustees. Because he himself opposed Glover, Smith's effort failed. Smith then voted against all other candidates and thus none was elected that year. Sturtevant assured Baldwin that he would welcome Presbyterians like Lippincott and Brooks; the more of them, the better. Smith continued to support Glover and he was elected in 1852. Also elected were Rev. Edwin Johnson, the new pastor of the Congregational Church, and J. W. Lathrop, a lay member of his church. Glover and Smith twice proposed Rev. A. T. Norton of Alton as a trustee but Sturtevant's strong opposition prevailed. Instead Richard Yates, the College's first graduate and "an exceedingly influential man, ...one of the staunchest friends the College ever had," was chosen. (S-B, 30 July 1853)

Financial Difficulties . . . A Great Fire

In July 1851 Sturtevant reported to the trustees that the College's indebtedness was $1,794.62, chiefly salary due the faculty. The endowment was earning ten per cent and the interest and other income could produce almost enough to pay the debts. Sturtevant then embarked on the hard task of raising the funds needed to complete the fifty-thousand-dollar endowment. The situation of the College improved markedly and Sturtevant informed Baldwin that the College was prospering, largely because of the scientific course. Indeed, he said, "Dr. Adams and I regard it as the dawn of a new day." (S-B, 16 Nov. 1852) However, he insisted that the new program was not a replacement for the classics, which he stoutly advocated.

In 1853 the trustees authorized the sale of the west part of the College lawn, the area bounded by College and Grove (Mound), City Place and Asylum (Woodland), at not less than $300 per acre. Rev. Leonard Bacon visited the College and urged that still more land be sold; Sturtevant however wished to delay until land values increased. The Medical Hall and the west half of the College barn were put up for auction. It was imperative now to increase the endowment funds and Sturtevant in 1853 circulated a leaflet which respectfully solicited contributions. An appeal in 1854 sought scholarships for students.[2] That year the salaries for the president and the faculty were increased by $100, bringing the former to $1100 and the latter to $850. Nearly all the income was drawn more or less equally from four sources: tuition, interest on subscription notes, investments, and the College Society. Library fees, the sale of catalogs, and rents produced more than $400.

In the arduous process of raising money Sturtevant had an unusual experience. Rev. William Carter in Pittsfield urged Sturtevant to make amends with a man who some years before offered a horse to the College. Carter chided Sturtevant for examining the animal as if he were a jockey, "and all this about a gift horse!!"[3] Sturtevant had not told the donor that he was thinking of buying the horse from the College and unintentionally insulted him.

In 1850 Gideon Blackburn's heirs charged that the original purpose of the trust, to found a school in Carlinville, had not been fulfilled. They claimed that the lands should revert to them. The court decree approving the transfer of the land to Illinois College was reversed on a technicality and a long series of legal proceedings ensued. David A. Smith[4] and Abraham Lincoln represented Illinois College, and when one of their motions was approved by the court, Sturtevant expressed some optimism. Unfortunately the circuit court's judgment in 1854 was that the lands, now valued at $100,000, must be returned to the original Blackburn trustees. The case was appealed to the Illinois Supreme Court and on 2 February 1855 Justice Walter Scates affirmed the decision. Illinois College was deemed to have no title to the lands because the donor had established a specific trust to be fulfilled at Carlinville. The Blackburn trustees were ordered to compensate Illinois College for the taxes paid on the lands and appropriate interest. Sturtevant believed that fairness would lead them to do more than that, perhaps even sharing equally, because if Illinois College had not accepted the land it would likely all have been lost.

The Blackburn "gift" continued to generate problems although Illinois College was relieved of guaranteeing the warranties for the sale of those lands. Sturtevant concluded that the final arrangement would not cost Illinois College one dime, but he was mistaken. Coffin's lawsuits to gain recognition of his title to the lands failed and he then sought remuneration from the College for his alleged losses. Sturtevant did not think the College owed him anything, but an arbitrated settlement awarded him somewhat over three thousand dollars. Sturtevant declared that at last "we have reached the bottom of the pit which was dug for our College by the Blackburn land donation." (S-B, 16 Mar. 1857)

The untimely passing of William Kirby was the first toll exacted by death upon the seven original members of the Illinois Association. Kirby died on 20 December 1851 after contracting pneumonia while returning home from the church at Naples during wintry weather. Sturtevant delivered the sermon[5] at the memorial service for his close friend and associate. Kirby was the instructor from 1831 to 1833, during which time he also shared the burden of the heresy trial. He was extremely faithful in attending meetings of the College's Board, sometimes traveling two hundred miles on horseback. Sturtevant lauded Kirby as an example of serving God rather than seeking worldly success. He passionately urged young men present to resist the worldly baits of the tempter and to devote their lives to founding institutions of religion and learning in the regions still further west, even to the thousand islands which stud the Pacific. Sturtevant's account was published in pamphlet form and abridged in periodicals. "Robinson" explained in the *Independent* that Kirby was censured [in 1833] because he had organized Congregational as well as Presbyterian churches. In the *Home Missionary*, Sturtevant acknowledged his puzzlement over Kirby's early death but declared his acceptance of God's sovereign will.

Disaster struck on the evening of 30 December 1852 when fire consumed the four-story dormitory building. The faculty and the few students who were in town were attending a church meeting. The alarm was sounded but by the time Sturtevant reached the scene half the roof was in flames. J. B. Turner rallied help to save the south wing. Some furniture was removed and the College's books were saved, though much damaged. Sigma Pi's library, recently moved to the third floor of the building, was totally lost. The periodicals and pamphlets which Sturtevant had collected over the past twenty-five years were destroyed. Unfortunately an insurance policy for $4,000—over half the coverage—had lapsed.

For forty-eight hours Sturtevant was despondent and then he began to recover. The plight of the College was presented at a public meeting and drew a gratifying response from the community. Two weeks after the fire Sturtevant concluded that the problems facing the College had never before seemed so easy to solve. His account of the destruction is vivid.

> Those lurid flames that lit up the night for thirty miles around have thrown some light upon our work. If so God be thanked. It surely seemed otherwise while those flames were moving slowly but incredibly from story to story and from room to room consuming as it seemed to me our cherished hopes and the labors of our lives. It was an aweful [*sic*] night never <u>never</u> to be forgotten. When the morning dawned the walls were all standing in desolate aweful loneliness. While we were at breakfast the middle partition wall…gave way and drew along with it the side walls in one huge indiscriminate ruin, leaving three of the tall chimney stacks (one of them having fallen during the fire) standing like monuments of desolation projected upon the beautiful grove in the rear…. [I]t is now one of the most hideous ruins you ever looked upon. It makes my heart ache yet every time I look upon it. (S-B, 13 Jan. 1853)

Reports of the fire were printed in local and Springfield newspapers and in the *Cleveland Plain Dealer*, from which it was reprinted in the *New York Times*, where Baldwin read it. The *New York Independent* (20 Jan.) carried a report by "Hesperian," who was at the scene. The town, he said, had a good fire engine but unfortunately there was no organized company to man it. The account was sympathetic and attributed the lapse of the insurance policy to the company's failure to send a notice and a recent personnel change in the treasurer's office.[6]

The *Alton Daily Morning Courier* rendered much less sympathy and expressed surprise that the College planned to continue. Acknowledging that the professors were generally good scholars, it declared that Jacksonville was no proper place for educating young men. The *Morgan Journal* of Jacksonville attributed the College's general difficulties to its exclusive emphasis on classical instruction. At the same time, however, the writer stated that its curriculum was the very foundation of the College's excellent reputation! He also praised the College for being in accord both with America's political institutions and with "true and liberal Christianity." (JJ, 15 Jan. 1853)

President Sturtevant dropped a "bombshell" before an audience in Jacksonville by announcing that the College might move to another location, to a place making the highest bid. His listeners, he informed Baldwin, were astounded. Baldwin, alarmed, telegraphed a warning which he repeated in a letter: "Ten thousand in Jacksonville worth twenty or thirty thousand elsewhere." (B-S, 24 Jan. 1853) He pointed to the history of the College, its unrivaled site, and the other institutions it had attracted to Jacksonville. His letter could not have reached the trustees before they decided on 26 January that if the people of the area failed to support the College, "it must and shall be removed." Sturtevant reminded Baldwin of the lack of adequate support and the serious privation so often suffered by the faculty and their families. Also he recalled that when wealthy citizens were approached they often dismissed the agents of the College as beggars. For years, Sturtevant said, he had considered Quincy a better location.

Sturtevant considered resigning from the College and again Baldwin issued a warning: "I should think a long time before I should tempt the Devil to stir up opposition or cool off zeal—by pledging myself to quit unless public good will came up to a definite mark." (B-S, 15 Feb. 1853) Apparently few took seriously the thought of removing the College, and nearly all the "disaffected" men in the Presbyterian Church now gave something toward a new building. Rev. Glover made a strong appeal at a public meeting, and David A. Smith subscribed five hundred dollars, the largest pledge thus far. Much of the promised support was due to the work of a committee consisting of one Campbellite, two Methodists, and one "non-professor" of religion. Others warned that moving the College to Quincy would generate greater competition with Iowa College at Davenport (later, Grinnell) and with Knox.[7]

Fortunately the Chapel was not destroyed and fortunately too the science apparatus was in that building. Some students lost everything they owned in the blaze but friends of the College, including John Ellis, provided assistance. College buildings would be adapted for students who could not obtain rooms in town and for a boarding facility. Remarkably the loss of the dormitory had little effect upon the College's enrollment.

A New Academic Building

Sturtevant wished to erect "a substantial and handsome building" for academic purposes and to replace for public use the "meager and unsightly" Chapel building.[8] He was determined to have no student accommodations on campus. When President Julius Reed of Iowa College inquired, Sturtevant explained the advantages. Because the students were living with families, they are "more regular, more studious, and much more moral. College tricks are unknown. College discipline in the old sense of it, obsolete. Our Faculty are Instructors; under the old system they were police officers. A far more kindly feeling exists between instructors and pupils." The students "were never so happy and content as now." Morning prayers were at 8:45 because the students had to walk a mile from town; classes ended at noon so the students could return to their rooms.[9]

Within weeks plans were developed for the erection of "a college edifice worthy of the wealth and civilisation of the county." (S-B, 13 Jan. 1853) Sturtevant thought that twenty thousand dollars would be needed to provide a chapel, a library, rooms for a minerals cabinet and philosophical apparatus, lecture rooms, and five recitation rooms. The Board authorized a contract and the plan drawn by Mr. Rumbold of St. Louis was chosen. The front elevation showed two towers, the taller one to the north having a stairway and thus an additional entrance to the second floor. Rumbold's sketch depicted a smaller connecting building to the north for the chapel.

The trustees voted in January 1854 to proceed with building to the extent that funds permitted. Work progressed sufficiently for the cornerstone ceremony to be held on 7 October. The "Order of Exercises" began with a speech by Rev. T. M. Post, after which "Pres't. Sturtevant" offered prayer and laid the cornerstone. Rev. L. M. Glover, who with Sturtevant constituted the committee on arrangements, also spoke. The assembled group then sang a hymn which had been composed for the occasion; the tune was a familiar one, "America."[10] Further work on the new edifice, contingent upon available funds, proceeded slowly.

The revised *Laws* adopted by the trustees in 1851 explained that the "Religious Exercises" were intended only to produce in the students a sense of God's presence and of accountability to him. The president was to conduct the evening prayers every day except Sunday. That fall the faculty arranged for Sturtevant to teach a Bible class every Sunday morning. The campus Society for Missionary Inquiry, having become inactive, was reestablished. Among the members listed in the record book were Sturtevant and faculty colleagues, along with numerous students.

The Commencement exercises for 1852 were reported in glowing terms in the *Independent* (22 July) under the pseudonym "Hesperian." Sturtevant's sermon on the Sabbath afternoon of July 4th was characterized as vigorous and expansive in thought, and graphic and inspiring in expression. His text was Revelation 21:1 and his theme was "*the bright prospects of human destiny.*" Hesperian considered it remarkable that a man who had suffered so many trials at the hands of calumnious detractors should speak so grandly of hope and good cheer. He complimented Sturtevant profusely: "Age and care have begun to silver his locks, but they have not touched with their frost his intellect nor his heart. The fire of genius burns as brightly as ever in the one, and the flame of piety and philanthropy in the other."[11]

A revival late in 1852 was described by Sturtevant. "The present is a time of refreshing religious interest.... From twelve to fifteen [students] have *seemed* to have come out on the Lord's side.... Besides the conversion of sinners, the work has brought cold back-slidden Christians to confession and renewed consecration;... This has not come upon us without an evident previous preparation of the way of the Lord. Our weekly prayer-meeting has... been attended by nearly half of our whole number of students—thirty to forty present in the evening."[12]

Although the revival was cut short by the Christmas vacation and the great fire, another outpouring of God's spirit occurred soon after. "Prayer was offered continually; places of religious assembly were thronged with eager and earnest worshippers; back-sliders were reclaimed, and with humble confession began to do their first works; it was evidently a work of conviction of sin...and we are permitted to hope that not less than ten or twelve hopeful young men were brought out of darkness into light." (SPC-10, 30)

A general revival blessed the College in 1854, this one aided by the preaching of a missionary who had served in India under the auspices of the American Board. Sturtevant was pleased that the claims of the ministry and of missions were presented and he enthused that "if we can only send enough such Missionaries I believe God will convert all India." The campus revival had begun about a week before the fast day for colleges and continued for weeks afterward. It spread to the Congregational and New School Presbyterian churches and also to the Jacksonville Female Academy. A prayer meeting with nearly fifty present most days was conducted for forty-five minutes before morning prayers. "One after another of our young men there come out and declare themselves on the Lord's side." (SPC-11, 29)

An editorial in the local *Weekly Constitutionist* praised Sturtevant's baccalaureate address of 9 July 1854. Referring to Nehemiah's strong interest in his country, he had cited him as a noble example of Christian [*sic*] patriotism. The students were enjoined to foster that love for country which comes from the memories of old familiar scenes and embraces a proper "Conservatism"—a due regard for the laws, manners, and customs of one's country. True patriotism does not condone aggression; the nation has no more right to engage in war for conquest and plunder than a man has to rob and cheat. Most importantly, patriotism means devotion to religious and political freedom.

The debate over skepticism at the College was renewed in 1855 in exchanges between Rev. R. W. Patterson and Rev. Theron Baldwin in the pages of the *New-York Evangelist.* Patterson charged that nine young students had come to the College as "professors" of religion and had become skeptical, rejecting evangelical Christianity. Baldwin refuted Patterson's charge, declaring that there were only three; moreover there was a big gap between being skeptical and rejecting Christianity. When Baldwin inquired whether J. B. Turner might have been a factor, Sturtevant replied that Turner had not taught any Bible class at the college "since he developed his present skepticism." When students asked Sturtevant to permit such a class, he had responded with an unqualified prohibition. Also, he had strenuously resisted any plan for Turner to teach a Bible class in any church in town.[13]

Essays for the College Society

At Baldwin's request Sturtevant presented the cause of the College Society in a series of six articles in the *Independent* in 1851. Using his pseudonym, "Robinson," Sturtevant discussed the Society's achievements, its needs, and the great challenge it faced. Its aim was "to secure to each of the New States in its very infancy a thorough and efficient system of collegiate and theological education...." (22 May) Once the needs of present colleges are satisfied, there will be calls for help in the new states added to the Union. "God is giving this great continent to one free and Christian people. And the tide of emigration rests not for an hour. Industry and art, commerce and capital are all in motion, and great secular enterprises are daily springing up which are fitted to excite the admiration of the world. Shall then the spirit of our fathers, which founded the halls of learning in the forests of New England, slumber?" (26 June)

The College Society was dedicated to *Christian* education, said Sturtevant, in contrast to sectarianism which threatened civil liberty because it preempted the very basis of freedom, religious liberty. Drawing a metaphor from physics, Sturtevant declared that if ecclesiastical bodies gain control of education and thus of religion, "We shall never look directly upon the uncolored and unrefracted light of God's truth as it comes to us from the divine word and Spirit, but always more or less bent from its course and discolored by our ecclesiastical media." (3 July) The proper operation of a college requires that it be controlled by an independent board of committed Christians.

In 1851 Rev. Joseph P. Thompson came to the campus as a representative of the College Society. Beginning his formal report with the now-customary praise of the site, he lodged serious criticisms. He described the Chapel Building as very inadequate and as inferior to other public buildings in the town. His warning about the hazardous location of the Library, on the third floor of the dormitory, was prophetic. In a letter about his travels Thompson was even more generous in his praise of the site and even more critical of the facilities. The Chapel Building, he said, was low and cramped; "the recitation rooms are poorly finished, and the whole structure looks old and crazy. It was built with poor brick and in dear times. The *people of Jacksonville* should replace… such an eye-sore…."[14]

Baldwin invited Sturtevant to address the Society's tenth anniversary held in the new Music Hall in Boston in May 1853. The Society had accomplished much during its first decade. More than two hundred thousand dollars had been raised in the East to aid eleven institutions. Three of the original beneficiaries, including Illinois College, were still receiving assistance along with six additional institutions, among them Knox, Beloit, Iowa, and the German Evangelical Seminary near St. Louis. In his speech Sturtevant emphasized that the institutions of Christian society, the church and the college, must be coextensive with the entire population. The Society's policies avoided two dangers, sectarian control of colleges and reckless proliferation.[15] Sturtevant's speech was a powerful endorsement of the Society:

> There is in modern times but one race of men which has yet shown any power of transplanting civilization to the wilderness. That one is the race which builds the church and the schoolhouse simultaneously with the emigrant's cabin, and founds its halls of learning within hearing of the woodman's axe, and the huntsman's rifle. This is the central idea of our national history. [The College Society is] adapted to the great and peculiar ends of our national existence…. For as certainly as Rome was called to conquer the world by her arms, so certainly we are called to conquer it by knowledge, and the religion of Christ. ("Address," 1853, 28)

Sturtevant was in New York for several days prior to delivering the address and wrote to his wife that because the occasion was immensely important he planned to closet himself for most of a week to prepare for it. Afterwards he assured Baldwin that he would have copy ready for the printer by the deadline. He was dismayed in reading the proofs to find many errors, omissions, and word substitutions which distorted his meaning. He asked Baldwin to look to it thoroughly and later reported that there were no errors of importance in the printed text.[16]

Following a pattern already established, the Society's Board granted permission for Illinois College to complete its endowment—and thus end its dependence on the Society. Traveling to New York in August 1853 for that purpose, Sturtevant observed the contrast of the difficult mission of the churches with material progress.[17] It was now possible to travel continuously by rail from Bloomington [Ill.] to Albany [N.Y.] and in only forty-seven hours! "Would that our enterprises for Christ were prosecuted with equal energy: but Alas! the children of this world are in their generation wiser than the children of light." (S-B, 15 Aug. 1853) However, a year later those children of light rallied to the support of Illinois College and were praised by Sturtevant, who declared that the Society had saved the College "*from extinction.*" (SPC-11, 19)

While still in the East, Sturtevant preached two sermons in Springfield, Massachusetts, on an exceptionally hot Sabbath in August 1853. Expecting to start home soon, he planned to spend a week in Ohio to prepare a sermon for an ordination in Peoria. Later when at home and planning another trip, Sturtevant urged Baldwin to reply by telegraph because the mails which ought to come through in three days often required eight. The "outrageous" service was due to the fact that "all our Post Masters are Democrats and that is the all-important matter!" (S-B, 8 Nov. 1853)

An Ardent Congregationalist

When the Jacksonville Congregational Church called Rev. Edwin Johnson as pastor, Sturtevant was instrumental in the arrangements and subsequently participated in his ordination in March 1851. Although Johnson was only twenty-four Sturtevant considered him to have rare talent for the ministry because of his piety. The new pastor's zeal was contagious and in June the church voted to have not only the morning service on the Sabbath but also a prayer meeting in the afternoon and preaching in the evening. A prayer meeting was conducted regularly on Wednesdays.

Oddly, Julian was the last of the Jacksonville Sturtevants to affiliate with the Congregational Church. In 1851, "At a Meeting for Prayer Bros. J. M. Sturtevant & Wm. Kirby signified their desire to become members of this Church, and both being well Known by the Church for several years to have been acceptable Preachers of the Gospel in good standing in the Ministry, it was moved & seconded that they be received by this Church as members thereof, which motion was unanimously adopted." (CCM, 3 Mar. 1851) He was "gradually and almost imperceptibly gliding into Congregational connexions," Sturtevant advised Baldwin, who replied that he would do nothing to check his friend.[18]

In 1854 Dr. Samuel Adams presented a motion for the church to construct more appropriate accommodations for public worship. Anticipating the need for a good site Sturtevant and two other men purchased lots which were later sold to the church. When the congregation held its annual meeting in December 1855, Sturtevant moved to sell the old church property.[19] A building committee was chosen, with Sturtevant, Adams, and the pastor as members; Sturtevant functioned as chairman. Thus at the same time that a new College building was under construction Sturtevant was engaged in a similar project on College Avenue. He also served as a trustee, and he arranged for raising money by subscription, rather than by "selling" seats. When the pastor was absent he administered the Lord's Supper at the Sabbath evening service.

A major controversy arose in 1855 when Dr. Adams brought charges against another member, Dr. David Prince, a prominent physician who had taught in the Medical School. He had been absent from Jacksonville and the church for more than two years; moreover, Adams claimed, the man was no longer in sympathy with the church's statement of faith. In a lengthy rebuttal Prince acknowledged that he would rejoice to see a wider latitude of doctrine allowed. The congregation voted to dismiss him but sixteen members protested. No mention is made of any role by Sturtevant, but it is unlikely that Adams would have acted without consulting him.

Long active in the local Congregational Church, Sturtevant increased his participation in the area, state, and national Congregational organizations. In February 1851 he preached the sermon when the Waverly congregation dedicated its new building.[20] He and Kirby took the lead in organizing the Morgan Congregational Conference, including the churches and ministers of the area. He participated in 1852 in the organization of the First Trinitarian Congregational Church of St. Louis, the congregation which as the Third Presbyterian Church had called Rev. Truman Post in 1847 as its pastor.[21]

By 1852 the General Congregational Association of Illinois included one hundred ten churches, nearly that many ministers, and some six thousand members. In reporting on its annual meeting in Peoria, Sturtevant told Baldwin that it exceeded "in numbers, talents, & piety" any other meeting he had attended in Illinois. He expressed reservations, however, because some were tinged with the fanaticism of Dr. Blanchard. He commented ruefully that the brethren thus afflicted were engaged in fighting "windmills with all the courage of a hero." But, he added, these brethren love Christ and they will learn that a windmill is a windmill. (S-B, 27 May 1852) Sturtevant was designated to represent the General Association at Eastern associations.

Sturtevant and S. G. Wright prepared a "Narrative" of the state of religion in the General Association. (*Independent,* 10 June 1852) More than half the churches had experienced revivals with the conversion of many sinners, probably one thousand. New churches were formed and Sabbath School attendance had increased. Little progress could be reported in the cause of temperance but attitudes regarding slavery were changing. "There is in our churches a growing and it is believed imperishable conviction that the system of slavery which still exists in our beloved country is in conflict with the benevolent principles of the Gospel, and a deepening purpose to seek its utter removal from all our borders by such means as shall be honorable to God and just to man." Ministers and churches clearly had a deep attachment to "that fundamental principle of civil and religious freedom," that the law of God must be obeyed when the law of man [the Fugitive Slave Law] conflicts with it. Progress was reported for both Illinois and Knox Colleges and gratitude was expressed for the revivals among their students. The Illinois Congregationalists strongly supported public elementary and secondary education.

Sturtevant was increasingly active in several voluntary associations affiliated with the Congregational churches. In 1851 he became a corporate member of the American Board of Commissioners for Foreign Missions and attended the 1854 anniversary at Hartford, Connecticut. The Board directed the missions to American Indians, and at Hartford Sturtevant reviewed the report on the Choctaws, Cherokees, and Dakotas. He also attended the 1855 meeting at New York City.

The Jacksonville church elected Sturtevant in his absence as a delegate to an Albany Convention to be held in October 1852. Hannah, learning of this, pointed out that it was essential for her husband to be present at the opening of the fall term. Sturtevant had notified Rev. Leonard Bacon, the chairman, that he did not expect to attend, and at Bacon's suggestion he wrote a letter for publication in the *Independent*. He explained that *Western Congregationalism* had sprung up from the circumstances of Western society without any plan. Congregationalists in the East should support the spread of Christian truth by founding churches and other permanent institutions, cooperating with union efforts to preach Christ. Congregationalists should also be forthright in acknowledging their own heritage. New churches should determine their denominational affiliation by majority vote, and Congregational churches should be organized wherever they would not undermine support for existing churches. "The form of the 'plan of union' of 1801 may have become in a degree inoperative and obsolete," he remarked, "but its spirit still lives...."

The Convention delegates, noting that the Presbyterians had in effect repudiated the Plan of Union even before 1837, declared that it was indeed abrogated. Congregational churches connected with presbyteries should vigorously uphold the privileges guaranteed them under the Plan. Moreover, any colleges founded and sustained by the two denominations should have the continued support of both. The Convention approved withholding funds from those churches in the slave-holding states which would not permit preaching the full Gospel for the awakening of conscience to the wrong of slavery.[22] [These were Presbyterian churches; few Congregational churches were established in the South.]

The Presbyterians and Congregationalists disputed at length over the composition of the faculty and the Board of Trustees and about the general orientation of Illinois College. Dr. Lyman Beecher's concern about the soundness of the College's staff was allayed by the Presbyterian Synod's positive evaluation: "Illinois College is now in a more healthy and vigorous condition than at any former period, and is evidently deserving as it receives the confidence of the Church. We express our gratitude to God that a greater number than usual of pious young men are now in its halls." (SPC-7, 26) The issue was revived, however, when Professor Kendall voiced a complaint. He was part of a little clique in the local Presbyterian church who charged that Sturtevant's preaching departed from the great cardinal doctrines of Christianity and failed to bring men to Christ. Reports reached Baldwin that Sturtevant was philosophizing in his sermons. Sturtevant vigorously denied that charge, declaring that his sermons were practical and were devoid of the speculative. "My mind strongly reacted against the philosophizing spirit of our common teacher in theology [Nathaniel Taylor]. From much of his philosophy I have seceded, to rest only in the simple testimony of scripture." (S-B, 16 Nov. 1852) Sturtevant thought Baldwin had given too much credence to the reports. Sturtevant's views on church government again aroused concern and the rumor spread that he was erratic in his thinking. Baldwin, fearing that the College might be damaged, shared Sturtevant's private statement with friends in Illinois and in the East. All were reassured and Sturtevant expressed the relief he felt: "My intimate friendship with Mr. Baldwin was placed upon a sure foundation for the rest of our lives." (A, 244-45)

Sturtevant was elected moderator of the Presbytery for a second time, even though he had now joined a Congregational church.[23] He said he was known as a "Congregational Presbyterian" because his standing in the Presbytery was derived from the old Plan of Union, and he expected "to claim and exercise those rights till the last. (S-B, 27 May 1852) He usually avoided involvement in strictly Presbyterian issues and may have been intentionally left uninformed about a controversial proposal in 1853. All New School ministers were urged to remain silent regarding slavery at the forthcoming General Assembly. The purpose was to avert a threatened secession by some of the Southern churches and their sympathizers. Brother Hale in Springfield received the document but, Sturtevant noted, "I have not been thought worthy." (S-B, 30 July 1853)

The Convention of Congregational Churches of the Northwest was organized in 1853 when Congregationalists realized that the Presbyterians would not join in founding a union seminary. Sturtevant deplored plans to found a "Northwestern Congregational Seminary" because it was based on "those very sectarian principles which in Presbyterianism he had "honestly and earnestly censured and deprecated." He regretted that no college officers were on the planning committee. He no doubt felt that such a seminary would end any hope for a theological department at Illinois College; he still believed a liberal education was best for preparing ministers. , (S-B, 17 June 1854)

Sturtevant delivered a brief but eloquent address at the 1853 meeting of the American Home Missionary Society.[24] He praised the heroism of those who had served as four-hundred-dollar-a-year home missionaries, living in cabins in the wilderness and gathering congregations in log school-houses without choir, organ, or pulpit. Such men and their families are the true heroes, not the Roman legionnaires. The people at Plymouth Rock planted a germ which "is now about to take possession of this whole globe...." Sturtevant remarked that although he would not tell of "the trials of that wife [Elizabeth]," he would emphasize that it is in "the cabins of the missionary in the far West [that one will] often find one of the noblest spectacles on earth—female heroism." He continued his paean to the pioneer missionary home: "I may find coarse fare; I may find hard toil, and, for this world, poor pay; but I shall find a cheerful, joyous, gladsome family...." Away with that false Christianity which seeks to reach Heaven by avoiding the sacrifice of comfort and wealth—"[I]t will get hypocrites into the Church, but never get souls to Heaven." Sturtevant uttered a solemn warning to young theological students: if they think themselves too good to serve in the wilderness, their Lord will tell them they are not good enough for him. "That great law of cross-bearing has not been repealed...."

Congregationalism as Anti-Sectarian

The American Congregational Union was formed in 1853 to express and increase the unity of the Congregational churches and to promote "the extension of the kingdom of Christ." The Union published the *Congregational Year-Book* with information about the churches, ministers, organizations, and colleges. The first volume listed Sturtevant as president of Illinois College and included him in the alphabetical list of ministers. The 1854 *Year-Book* named him as one of the vice-presidents of the Union, an office he held for many years. He was designated as representing the Union to the General Association of Illinois.

An invitation to address the Union's annual meeting in May 1855 came as a surprise to Sturtevant; it was also a great compliment to him—the other discourse was to be given by President Woolsey of Yale. Through his writings Sturtevant was attracting attention as a vigorous spokesman for Congregationalism. Despite his anxiety he delivered his speech with confidence because his views were based solidly upon Scripture. He may also have taken heart from the advance notice in the leading Congregational newspaper: "Dr. Sturtevant is a clear, bold, vigorous and original thinker, a profound and accurate reasoner, a writer of much force and beauty, and an earnest and even impassioned speaker.... His well-known liberal and Catholic [sic] spirit, and [his study of this subject] for twenty-five years, lead us to expect from him a discourse of no ordinary interest and value." (*Independent*, 3 May 1855)

Entitled "The Anti-Sectarian Character of Congregational Church Polity," the speech lasted for an hour and three-fourths. It was delivered first at the Union's meeting in Brooklyn and a second time, by popular request, at the Broadway Tabernacle in New York City. After years of defending his views of the church in seeming isolation in Illinois, Sturtevant was overjoyed at the warm reception given by "those great assemblies of intelligent Christians." (A, 274) The address was so powerful that it induced Rev. Absalom Peters, a Presbyterian all his life, to declare that he was now a Congregationalist.

It was not necessary, Sturtevant began, to prove once again the right and duty of Congregationalists to carry their New England polity wherever they went. He denied any desire to add one more sect to the myriad swarming over the West; he "would as soon engage in an effort to increase the supply of granite rocks in New Hampshire, or of mosquitoes along the banks of the Mississippi." (8) Sturtevant explained that "*The* church is the whole glorious company of the redeemed in Christ Jesus on earth and in heaven. *The visible* church is the whole number of those on earth." (12-13) Although the diversity among denominations is often innocent and admissible, serious divisions arise among Christians from doctrine, ceremonies, and government. A basic criterion separates evangelical and latitudinarian sects, but when the Bible is foremost sincere Christian creeds are not a problem. Modes of worship cause division but unless church government is used to enforce ceremonies, they cannot be divisive.

Centralized authority exercised through one or several humans is divisive when physical force is used to implement decisions. In contrast, congregational polity cannot be divisive because it is purely local. Its assemblies for "provincial, national and even oecumenical fellowship, correspondence and cooperation...exercise no governmental function. They leave the government of the local church complete within itself." (29) Sturtevant assured the audience that the American Congregational Union was not an assembly with authority over the local churches. When division does take place, it is accomplished with much less conflict than in any centralized system. The only schism within *orthodox* Congregationalism resulted from the belief that the local church can require a given mode for the baptism of a candidate [i.e., immersion] and can exclude from the Lord's Supper those who were not baptized in that manner.

A Federalist Paper argued that the multiplicity of sects is the only safeguard against established religion. In refutation Sturtevant cited the ease with which the Congregational churches of New England separated themselves from the state, in contrast to the situation in Scotland and England. A national church government tends toward alliance with government; local church government does not, relying instead on the voluntary principle.

The Plan of Union was premised upon willingness to cooperate with other Christians, and as a result "The church of Christ was planted in the wilderness, and for that good men will thank God forever." (44) Because the New England fathers did not seek to extend their form of church government to the West, "Presbyterian churches composed of Congregational materials[25] were organized by hundreds." (44) Congregationalists ask only for the right to their polity even as they acknowledge the right of others to theirs. The divisive tendency in Presbyterian polity and the unifying tendency in Congregationalism have been made evident. It must be admitted, said Sturtevant, that Congregationalism has "no monopoly of saving gifts and graces," and that God does not call us to propagate our polity by any feverish zeal. (48) If God brings about its broad acceptance,[26] the whole church of God "shall enjoy through the long cycles of the millennium, the peaceful reign of truth, freedom and charity." (50)

A Festival of Congregational Union was held in conjunction with the formal sessions. At the dinner Sturtevant responded to a toast: "The pioneers of learning in the West. The ages meet where they labor; the Puritan age in its self denial; the future age in its promise of glory." Sturtevant disclaimed any qualifications for speaking but evoked laughter when he added, "My gift to perform the more material duties of the supper-table was never particularly questioned." Laughter erupted again when he reported that his first sermon in Jacksonville was "in a log-cabin in which no sensible swallows would make their nests." Sturtevant declared that the ages were united in the founding of institutions of learning in the primitive conditions of the West.

He invoked the vision that Puritan principles would yet be planted over the entire region: "let all those vast and fertile prairies be studded over with all the appliances of the noble Christian civilization of the Pilgrim Puritans...." Applause accompanied his final comment, that only one race, the Anglo-American race, has "founded a college within the sound of the woodman's axe...." Only if that effort is carried on will they succeed in reclaiming "that vast domain and make it the home of a Christian civilization. (*Independent*, 17 May 1855) The *Year-Book* included excerpts from Sturtevant's address. The *Congregational Quarterly* reported the proceedings of the Union in its first volume and noted that this address was "a valuable contribution to the religious literature of the denomination."[27]

In May 1855 the General Association of Illinois held a four-day meeting in Jacksonville. Sturtevant was a delegate and an active participant. He helped arrange the religious exercises, reported on the American Tract Society, and discussed the aims and plans of the American Congregational Union. He probably assisted in arranging the delegates' visits to the state institutions for the Insane, the Deaf and Dumb, and the Blind.

Sturtevant and Baldwin shared confidences regarding Edward

Beecher's theological views and his efforts to present them in a book. Beecher sought to mediate in a controversy between Professor Edwards Amasa Park of Andover and Professor Charles Hodge of Princeton. Although moderate as an expositor of the New England theology, Park was unacceptable to conservative Presbyterians who regarded Hodge as the authority on sound Protestant thinking. Sturtevant himself believed that Park's system would be accepted and, concluding that Beecher was far from ready to publish his book, felt no concern about him.

Rev. R. W. Patterson continued opposing Sturtevant and the course of affairs at Illinois College. Patterson claimed to know the details of the College's business, Baldwin commented, even though he lived two hundred fifty miles from the campus. Using the initial "P" to signify his authorship, Patterson published a statement in the *New-York Evangelist* in 1855 implying that New School Presbyterians had no practical participation in the existing colleges in Illinois. He alleged that Presbyterian young men at Illinois College were mostly drawn away to Congregationalism. Baldwin, as "B," responded that thirty-five alumni had entered the ministry and of these fifteen to eighteen were Presbyterians; there would be more such students if men like "P" ceased turning them away by creating public distrust of the College. Two of the present professors at the College were New School Presbyterian ministers and of the sixteen trustees, eight were New School Presbyterians— six ministers and two laymen.[28] However, Patterson wanted more Presbyterians on the faculty and, urged by Baldwin, Sturtevant relaxed his insistence that denominational affiliation should have no part in selection. As a consequence Sanders, a Presbyterian minister, had been appointed. Before accepting he had consulted with Patterson regarding the stability of Presbyterian support for the College. Sturtevant had become convinced years before that so long as he remained president Patterson would never be a friend of the College. It was, he knew, his good fortune to have Baldwin as his staunch ally in the controversy with the Presbyterians.

An unsigned criticism ridiculing Sturtevant's views on Congregationalism appeared in the *New-York Evangelist* (26 July 1855) under the title, "A Great Discovery." The first paragraph, lauding the marvelous progress "of the great car of material improvement," might have intrigued Sturtevant. When the writer declared that none of the new inventions could match a recent discovery "achieved mainly by one of our contemporaries," Sturtevant could have justifiably reacted in anger. The *Evangelist* declared that now "our sagacious neighbor the *Independent*" has devised "the grand panacea" for sectarianism, "*that all the world become Congregational.*" The writer mockingly rhapsodized about the wonder of this discovery, then chided the *Independent* for implying that "President Sturtevant had a hand in the matter" by referring to his Brooklyn address. The anonymous writer admitted that he had not read the address but was absolutely certain that it could not have been, as some alleged, an assault on Presbyterianism. The writer declared that "President Sturtevant is an honorable man. President Sturtevant is not Janus-faced. President Sturtevant is himself a Presbyterian, a member 'in good and regular standing' of the Presbytery of Illinois." He has answered the constitutional questions, affirming the government and discipline of the Presbyterian Church, and therefore he could not be guilty of the alleged treachery. Surely, said the anonymous writer, the claims for Congregationalism must be attributed to the *Independent.*

The mail moved quickly in the opposite direction and Sturtevant sent his spirited rejoinder in a letter published in the 23 August *Evangelist.* He referred to the article as "ironical" but it was in fact sheer sarcasm. The writer may have been deliberately baiting Sturtevant, knowing that he was admitted to Presbytery just prior to the 1830 requirement for Congregational ministers in the West to accept Presbyterianism. Sturtevant emphasized that he was indeed a member "in good and regular standing" of the Presbytery of Illinois and denied with equal emphasis that he had ever been asked to affirm "the questions" or had ever done so. He explained to those who should have known that "there was once, 'a Plan of Union.' It was an honest, fraternal, catholic effort, not to make over all Congregationalists into Presbyterians" but to enable them to co-operate so that the people of the two denominations could have fellowship with each other, "in the same churches…each enjoying his own preferences, in respect to church government." So far as ministers were concerned, the Plan of

Union was abrogated by the action of the General Assembly in May 1830.[29]

Although Sturtevant had suffered numerous attacks, the ministers and churches of the Presbytery of Illinois had given him "proofs of confidence and Christian affection" and he in turn loved them. People understood that his "connection with them [was] religious rather than ecclesiastical. These brethren knew that his preference regarding church polity was Congregational and that for years he had been "connected as a private member, with a Congregational Church, and with the 'Morgan Association,' since its organization." "In other words," Sturtevant remarked, "I have had, in common with many of my brethren, both East and West, both a Congregational and Presbyterian connection." Sturtevant noted that his Presbyterian colleagues had not expressed any desire to change their relationship. He concluded: "I may not, however, in the times of intense partizanship…much longer consider a double connection expedient."[30] That double connection soon ended. After twenty-five years (Roy, 36) Sturtevant separated from the Presbyterian Church because his connection with it "no longer seemed to promote harmony and facilitate cooperation." (A, 275) Happily the change did not sour his good personal relationships with many Presbyterians.

The Slavery Issue Intensifies

During the 1850s the issue of slavery became increasingly controversial. The Compromise of 1850 made it easier for masters to claim fugitive slaves. It authorized any new territory to enter the Union as a slave state if its constitution permitted. Actually, there were no such admissions, and California was admitted as a free state. Sturtevant was now convinced that the proslavery people, not content with maintaining the existing system, were striving zealously to extend it—an effort he described as a madness which courted divine intervention. Political action to end slavery seemed impossible and Sturtevant was almost tempted to echo what Cassy, on Legree's plantation, had observed about God: "He is not here." (A, 280) In central Illinois a person could not speak out against slavery even in most churches because the Southern prejudice was so strong; the Congregational churches of Jacksonville and Mendon were notable exceptions.[31] Sturtevant became increasingly open in his support of abolition and he, Turner, and others attracted wide attention in attempting to organize a "Free Democracy" movement in Jacksonville.[32] The College had gained a vigorous new spokesman in Professor Sanders, who became "the outstanding faculty champion of the anti-slavery cause in these later years." (CH, 196, 198)

The New Englanders in Jacksonville were not politically inclined but left such leadership to others who came to central Illinois about the same time, notably Abraham Lincoln and Richard Yates, the College's first graduate. Yates was bold in his anti- slavery pronouncements while serving in the Illinois legislature. Elected to Congress in 1850 and 1852 he voted against slavery, as in 1854 when Senator Stephen Douglas led the victory for the Kansas-Nebraska bill. Yates attributed the loss of his seat in Congress to his strenuous opposition to that act, and in 1858 Douglas defeated Lincoln for the Senate. Sturtevant had long discussions with Yates and assured him of strong support if he would assume leadership. Yates "promised to do what he could." (A, 283) For the present he did not espouse abolition but sought to prevent the expansion of slavery; any other position, Sturtevant acknowledged, would have made it impossible to organize the Republican Party in central Illinois. Northern Illinois did not share the strong sympathy with the South.

Sturtevant devoted an entire chapter of his *Autobiography* to the overthrow of slavery, an achievement which he regarded as revolutionary. Although he believed that more attention should be given to the effect of the Spirit of God upon people's thinking, he acknowledged two influences in the 1850s as the primary human contributions to that outcome. In 1852 Harriet Beecher Stowe published *Uncle Tom's Cabin*, which sold rapidly and achieved wide circulation; a play, based on the book, amplified Stowe's message. A Jacksonville committee which included Elihu Wolcott and J. B. Turner bought and distributed five hundred copies of the book; Sturtevant's role, if any, was not reported. However, Sturtevant's admiration for Mrs. Stowe and for her book was very great, and he declared that he had "never witnessed any other such revolution in public sentiment" as she had accomplished. The book fulfilled a holy purpose by painting "a great national crime in all its enormity" with the aim of eliminating it. (A, 278) The second great influence had its origin when the Republican Party developed its organization in central Illinois, achieved with much help from Jacksonville people. That new party became the vehicle for Lincoln to emerge as the nation's leader and eventually to become the Great Emancipator.

The local community had experienced much turmoil, but after a county election in November 1853, Sturtevant reported that "Temperance and good order have carried all before them. We no longer feel ourselves to be in a meager minority in Morgan County. The progress of the county in intelligence [education?] and morality has been wonderful. I am of the opinion it has no equal in the State." (S-B, 10 Nov. 1853) The prospects for religion and education were very bright because every town was seeking to provide churches and schools.

On the state level, too, there were encouraging developments in the field of education, and Illinois College faculty and alumni were leading the way. President Sturtevant spoke on behalf of popular common school education at a meeting in the Hall of the House of Representatives. (SJ, 13 Jan. 1851) In 1855 legislation facilitated the establishment of public schools. Soon afterward Newton Bateman, Class of 1843, became the state superintendent of public instruction; his assistant was his classmate, Samuel Willard.

In his report to the College Society in 1855, Sturtevant called attention to the excellent opportunities in Jacksonville for education at all levels. These institutions were the result of "distinct and persevering efforts." Similar efforts were made to establish preparatory schools throughout the state, so that Illinois College could concentrate on *college* studies. (25-26)

Sturtevant was in demand in Springfield as a speaker. On 20 December 1851 he addressed the guests at the New England Supper at the City Hotel; the theme of "the Puritan fathers" was a favorite of his. On 27 February 1854 he addressed the Young Men's Christian Association, meeting in the Second Presbyterian Church, and a few weeks later he preached at the church's morning service.[33] In December 1855 he addressed the Illinois State

Teachers' Association, in which he held membership, on "the utility of the study of the classics." An animated discussion followed the speech, with J. B. Turner and the Hon. N. W. Edwards participating; John Brooks and Newton Bateman were also present. The report noted that Mrs. Sturtevant was in attendance.

Despite his participation in several major events in 1855, Sturtevant found time to write an extended commentary on a novel published some years before by Charles Kingsley. The book, *Alton Locke: Tailor and Poet.—An Autobiography*, was written as if told in the first person by a tailor. Locke was portrayed as doubly oppressed, first by a severe and punishing mother who did not believe her children could be in God's grace, and then by an economic system which subjected him to such competition that he lived in abject poverty. Sturtevant scoffed at the notion that competition was the real problem and could be eliminated. Kingsley proposed for labor to be organized, a solution the reviewer deemed ineffective because "Both capital and labor must be free...." (176) For Sturtevant the real causes of poverty and suffering were personal immorality, which could be ameliorated by overcoming ignorance and vice, and unwise national policies such as wars of mad ambition. Kingsley offered as another remedy for the tailor's woes "a religion of the imagination," a corruption of Christian doctrine quite astounding, thought Sturtevant, for an English cleric. (174) The tailor's supposed conversion was brought about by looking at pictures and hearing readings from the Bible and English poets. Sturtevant called this mystical transcendentalism, not Christianity. It was a conversion without confession of sin and repentance and without acknowledging that our sins are forgiven by the death of Christ.

Another fault in the story was the tailor's rejection of biblical miracles in the usual sense. Sturtevant asserted that the term "law" simply refers to the uniform methods in which God usually acts. Nothing prevents God from deviating from his custom, and there should be nothing shocking when God manifests his power and presence in some different manner. Metaphysics cannot assail miracle, thus understood. However mistaken the author's interpretation of the Christian faith, wrote Sturtevant, he has called "earnest attention to the sufferings of the neglected and famishing laborer.… To impart the blessings of Christian civilization to the laborer is the great problem of this age, and must be solved, or all our hopes are doomed to a bitter disappointment." (183) Sturtevant was aware of the hopeless poverty in the cities of Europe and Britain and the "sweating" work done for low wages in homes. He condemned the "heartless and cruel policy of the British government which neglects the education of the laborer." (172) Sturtevant was cognizant of such social-economic theorists as Charles Fourier.

Sturtevant continued to be an avid reader of the religious and secular press. His subscriptions to New York's *Daily Times* and *Independent* were arranged by Baldwin who, when requested, paid Sturtevant's bill of two dollars for the latter newspaper.

The Quarter-Century Celebration

President Sturtevant in March 1851 invited the members of the Illinois Association and their western counterparts to meet at commencement in July. Among others who replied that this was not a good time, Baldwin explained that he was the only agent at the present for the College Society. However, Edward Beecher came and Sturtevant had a good visit with him. After hearing him preach Sturtevant concluded that he had been tamed by Boston audiences and had little of "that fiery fervor for which he used to be distinguished." (S-B, 17 July 1851)

Subsequently it was agreed that the 1855 commencement should be the occasion for a reunion and celebration. The trustees "requested [Sturtevant] to prepare and deliver a Discourse on the occasion" and he and others were appointed to make arrangements. (TM, 11 July 1854) The College now was decidedly prosperous and enrollment was increasing. When Baldwin received the current *Catalogue* of officers and students, with the accompanying course of study and list of regulations, he complimented Sturtevant. "Your last catalogue tells a better story than any before published," he wrote, and he asked for copies to be sent to the College Society's agents. (B-S, 31 Mar. 1855)

The trustees met on 10 July 1855 at Sturtevant's home, and the following day six of the original seven Yale men were present at the

First Presbyterian Church for the somewhat-delayed twenty- fifth anniversary celebration. After prayer by Theron Baldwin, the choir and congregation sang a hymn written for the occasion. The tune was "Scots wha ha" and the opening words were joyful: "Welcome, welcome, happy day! / Bidding hopes and memories play, / Brightly o'er our pilgrim way, / Like the bow of heaven." President Sturtevant delivered his discourse and Thomas Lippincott offered prayer. The closing song, also prepared for the occasion, was sung to the tune of "Auld Lang Syne." The words recalled the toils and tears of the early struggle and gave thanks to God even as exultant hope, born of memory, gave assurance that "Faith e'en now can see the morn / Fast brightening into day." (ICQCC, 3, 4)

That evening the guests "assembled in the parlors of the Mansion House, in Jacksonville" for the "Social Re-union of the Founders, Patrons, Alumni, and Friends of Illinois College." (ICQCC, 38) Some of the men's wives were in attendance. The blessing was asked by Asa Turner and the guests then "discussed" the bountiful viands set before them. A series of toasts was offered. John Ellis, who arrived too late for the morning session, was called upon first. Truman Post spoke eloquently about the first faculty, giving special praise to one "whose enthusiasm and energy have been the nerve and the heart-beat of this enterprise for a quarter of a century...." Any doubt about that person's identity was dispelled by added references to his "clear and rapid logic" and his "practical instinct." He is the one, said Post, who "still rallies all the forces of the enterprise" and cries out in "the thick of the fight, 'Ho, comrades, stand fast! Never give up the ship!'" (ICQCC, 39-40) The wives and the children, many of whom now reposed "in yonder beautiful sleeping-place of the dead," were also remembered. Mason Grosvenor recalled the "sacred seven" members of the New Haven Band [one of the earliest uses of "band"], and Theron Baldwin spoke of the College Society. Richard Yates, protesting that he had not been warned that a speech was expected, expounded at length about his classmate Jonathan Spillman, about Jacksonville as "the Athens of the West," and about Sturtevant and the College generally. Other toasts and responses concluded the program. "It was now about eleven o'clock, and after having sung

'Auld Lang Syne,' the company separated, all regarding it as one of the most delightful social seasons ever witnessed in Jacksonville." (52)

The trustees, meeting the following day, adopted a resolution of thanks to Sturtevant for his address. Baldwin moved that they prepare for the Semi-Centennial Anniversary by entering upon "a course of efforts" which would enable the College to fulfill its mission and "maintain its advanced position among the colleges of the West." (TM, 12 July 1855)

President Sturtevant's "Historical Discourse" of 1855 is the authoritative account of the early history of Illinois College. In addition to his own writings and his excellent memory he had many resources to draw upon.[34] He often talked with Baldwin when he was in the East and met with members of the Illinois Association who were trustees and with others at various ecclesiastical meetings. Grosvenor had recently taught at the College and perhaps at that time brought with him some letters and possibly the original "Records" book of the Association. Sturtevant could refer to the Minutes of the trustees and faculty and the College Society's annual reports.

In his address Sturtevant asserted that Illinois College had but one source, "that unfailing, unflagging purpose...to disseminate, by means of *Institutions*, the influence of the Gospel, coextensively with our ever-expanding population." (6) It was manifested in two separate streams of causation, the dedicated effort led by John M. Ellis in Illinois, and a small group of young men in New Haven. These streams coalesced in November 1829 when Sturtevant and Baldwin arrived in Illinois to join with the local stockholders in founding Illinois College. Individual men in both groups were recognized for their roles in the College's founding. Sturtevant also acknowledged the vital support given to the cause of education by his wife, Elizabeth, and by Mrs. Ellis. "They were lovely and noble spirits both." (23)

It was obvious to all that the whole enterprise had been guided by Providence in developing the plan for an independent board and securing the needed subscriptions. The College was intended to be Christian but not sectarian; every effort would be made to bring the students to a saving knowledge of Christ but no attempt would be made to proselytize them for a given church. The specific purpose was to provide liberal education to prepare young men for the Christian ministry and the professions. The College became the parent of other private institutions for preparatory schooling and female education. Its people strongly supported public education and the several state institutions in Jacksonville. People in New England who were asked to pledge subscriptions for the College were thus informed about Illinois, and thousands were encouraged to emigrate.

The College had achieved marked success in both its educational and evangelistic purposes. The A.B. degree had been awarded to 130 men, and more than a thousand other youth had received instruction. Revivals brought about the hopeful conversion of many youth, a goodly number of whom became preachers of the Gospel. Two problems marred the College during its first years, the erection of the large dormitory and the manual labor plan. The great financial crisis of 1837 nearly closed the College, but since 1849 it had been steadily recovering. Sturtevant gave much credit to the College Society for averting financial disaster. The current condition of the College was favorable, some thirty-five thousand dollars having been subscribed toward the 1849 goal of $50,000. Construction was underway on a new building for academic uses.

Dry humor lightened the serious tone of the discourse. Mentioning the crude log cabin where he preached his first sermons in Jacksonville, he observed (24) that "There was a state of democratic equality in the congregation, which would have done good to the heart of a thorough-going leveller."[35] Concluding on a serious note, Sturtevant remarked that there may be another such gathering when the half-century mark is reached. "Who of us will be here on that day? The curtain falls—darkness covers the landscape. Brethren, there is another meeting where we shall all be present! O, may we all hear the sentence, 'Well done, good and faithful servant!'" (37)

The "Historical Discourse" was used by the editor of the *American Journal of Education* in preparing the first of a series of sketches of American colleges.[36] The editor planned similar articles in later issues on earlier colleges such as Harvard. The lead admirable and readily usable source.

A New Home, A Growing Family

The 1850 census reported fourteen persons in the Sturtevant
household in the south wing of the old dormitory. That number
was increased when Alfred was born in December and when
Edward Tanner came, probably in 1851. The need for a larger
home was obvious. Sturtevant owned several lots on Park Street
across from the campus and he mortgaged the land to the College
in January 1852 for $1,000, an amount subsequently increased.
(The debt was satisfied in 1853.) Sturtevant thought Baldwin
would be astonished at the size of the new house on the corner lot
but, he assured his friend, "it is not too large for my great family."
(S-B, 6 Apr. 1852) However, the project was taking longer and
proving more expensive than he had hoped.

The value of the family's property increased rapidly in these
years because of the new home. The valuations for the state, county,
and school district in 1854 amounted to $4,365 and for the city,
$3,000. The corresponding figures for personal property were
identical, $710, and the total tax bill was $53.89. The Sturtevants
by themselves made no additional land purchases in these years
but were parties with Hannah's relatives in the sale of Richard
Fayerweather's lands.

Hannah's letters to her husband are the major source of family
information during these years. Her letters were well-written regarding content, grammar, and penmanship. An especially poignant
example of her frequent expressions of devotion is in her letter of 20
July 1852: "My dear <u>husband</u>, if we ever live to meet again I do think
I will try to love you more & make you more happy than I have ever
done before." A month later she wrote, "I begin to count the weeks
before your return; how painful these absences are, but there is a
home for us where we shall not be separated. May we all be prepared
for that eternal home of rest." (20 Aug. 1852) Julian's letters, fewer
in number, were usually marked "private" although Hannah read
excerpts to the family. The children were very pleased when they
received a letter addressed to them, and three of them replied.

The summer of 1852 was difficult for many families, including the Sturtevants. Nearly every one in their household was sick. Warren, Edward (Tanner), Libbie (Elizabeth), Ricarda Nunes, and Mrs. Minard (a house guest reluctant to leave) had all been stricken by diarrhea. "Baby" (little Freddie), one and a half years old, was severely afflicted by dysentery and his mother had given him up as hopeless. Little Eddy became quite sick and was given brandy two or three times a day. Hannah herself had a slight attack of dysentery and took turpentine to relieve it. Later in the day she had a chill and, fearing an attack of typhoid, she took a footbath and "a fiery dose of brandy & pepper" which sweated the chill away. (15, 24 July) Most of the family recovered fairly quickly but Eddy's sickness lingered. Freddie was very weak and needed much care; Warren took him for rides in the carriage in the mornings and evenings. Hannah promised to telegraph in the future if serious illness occurred. Dr. Samuel Adams had been attending the family but would be leaving town so Hannah chose Dr. Reed.

The Old Homestead, Built in 1852
Three generations of the family lived here, from 1852 to the turn of the century. Now known as Fayerweather House.

The move to the new house was planned for May 1852 but apparently was delayed. Late in August Hannah reported that "our new house proves to [be] all that we anticipated, airy & convenient." She expected to complete arranging her husband's study soon. The carpenters and masons had not finished their work and though the cistern was serviceable, the well could not be used until a pump and pipe were obtained. The shade trees and bushes were flourishing despite dry weather, and Jane's oleander had many blossoms. Warren, sixteen, was both manly and kind and looked after affairs at home and at the College buildings. The family was enjoying the fruit of Mr. Sturtevant's labor in the garden, which was producing a plentiful supply of tomatoes, cucumbers, onions, corn, and other vegetables. They had not had a ripe watermelon because some boys, probably the same ones who had broken into the barn, had raided the patch.

Hannah managed some College business during her husband's absences. She had written to three young men one afternoon and Jane remarked that Hannah had a new office, deputy president. Jane said that if Mr. Sturtevant did not come home quickly he would find that his wife was wearing the breeches. "Are you alarmed?" asked Hannah. (4 Sept. 1852) She reported that only seven rooms at the College remained vacant and so a good enrollment could be anticipated. However, only two teachers were certain and rumors hinted that President Sturtevant was having difficulty filling the vacancies.

Hannah complained strongly because the College had taken up her husband's vacation and because so many College affairs were her responsibility. When her husband suggested that he would take her east with him on some future trip, she had a firm response. "How can both of us leave our family—if I find it such a burden to bear in your absence—what will become of them if both of us are absent. No. I cannot think of it till Hannah [Augusta] is grown & the little ones are sufficiently under authority to be controlled by her." Moreover, Hannah explained, "I have lived so long at the West that except to see two or three relatives I do not care at all for the East."

The risks of travel were another cause of worry for Hannah. She mentioned a railroad accident and the collision of a Lake Erie boat and feared for her husband who soon would be traveling on that lake. She discovered that her husband had left his life preserver in his study and she hoped that he had obtained another one. "I wish you were safely over those lakes," she told him. (25 Aug., 7 Sept.

1852) In virtually every letter Hannah reported some person's death or expected demise. Nannie Duncan, near death, spoke of how much she appreciated the comfort given her by President Sturtevant. She lamented, "Oh to think I shall never see that good man again, & he has done me so much good." Three young men and three young women had died, and Hannah interpreted the frequency of such events as God giving "warning upon warning... that our life is a vapor that appeareth for a little time & then vanisheth away." In her next letter she wrote that "as a parent I should take heed to do all I can to secure the preparation of our children for a like summons.... If our children give evidence of possessing the pearl of great price we can then be satisfied with whatever allotment of Providence God sends." She exclaimed that more than half her own family "lie beneath the clods of the valley." (15 July, 25, 29 Aug.)

Hannah had taken an hour to help the two older girls with a difficult arithmetic problem about interest. Lucy was expecting to receive a Bible and was learning a lesson nearly every day. Warren had a "place" at the free school but probably would not be continuing there. Warren himself wrote to his father about the work of two men, apparently tenant farmers on College-owned lands. Although they had many expenses, Hannah hoped they could get a piano because Hannah Augusta was talented musically. Young Julian was very thin; the long days of teaching at a country school were taking their toll of his strength.

The family followed the course of Mr. Sturtevant's travels in the East and noted his attendance at Yale's commencement and various anniversaries. Warren wanted father to get some good new music for the girls, whose singing he loved to hear; he mentioned a piece set to "Eva" in Uncle Tom's Cabin. Hannah was much relieved when at last she learned that her husband was homeward bound. She advised him to come by way of Terre Haute to avoid the crowded stage from LaSalle to Springfield. She was greatly pleased to hear that he had secured the needed faculty.

The year 1853 was in some respects much better, although it was again necessary for the president to be absent for extended periods. Despite her earlier protestation Hannah accompanied her husband to the East in April. Although Julian was ill when they arrived, he called on a "noble man" who had pledged to be one of twenty contributors toward a $20,000 goal. Now, afflicted with chills and fever, Julian returned to their hotel, unable to fulfill his preaching appointments at two churches that Sunday. He admitted to Baldwin that he was only "an apology" for a man. After recovering he resumed his solicitations and Hannah visited relatives. Julian wrote to arrange their meeting when she came to New York in

Hannah F. Sturtevant
From a Daguerrotype made in 1853.

early May; from there they would go to New Haven. He asked Hannah to bring his razor strop—he needed it—and he ended with the words: "Hannah, you do not doubt the love of Your affectionate husband," and signed his name in his customary fashion, "J. M. Sturtevant." (JMS to HRS, New York, 4 May 1853) One time, when both parents were away, Rev. Johnson wrote about College business and added a personal note: "The people at the Presidential mansion are quite well." (30 May 1853) The Sturtevants returned before the end of July.

Hannah remained at home when Julian left in August for a strenuous six-weeks' effort to complete the Fifty Thousand Dollar Endowment Fund. She encouraged him in his "abundant labors," and she prayed for such prosperity for the College that they could enjoy peaceful vacations with him at home. She feared that the work might terminate his life prematurely. Hannah, feeling lonely, realized that he must feel more lonely too on this trip after having had her company on the previous journey. Although he did think she was particular at times, it would be a relief to him if she were near to brush his coat or hair or hat and to pack the trunk. Their separation was aggravated by the irregular mails which delayed Julian's letters for two weeks or more. Eager to hear from him, she adopted "patience" as her motto—and was rewarded with five letters within less than a week.

That summer was very hot and again as in 1852 the ice man ran out of his precious commodity. Evening carriage rides were about the only relief. Busy as she was, Hannah found some time for reading. Among other books she read "Scarlet Letter" by Hawthorne and said she did not like it; she did not think the book was bad but it did not have any purpose. Charles Kingsley's "Yeast" was her next selection but she found it somewhat transcendental in its principles and that was disgusting to her; she might not even finish it. She had recommended "Michelet" to Warren and thought he would read it. Their sons and daughters did not understand the papacy. They had been brought up as Protestants to know that the Catholics are wrong, but they needed to read some history of that church and its doctrines and practices so that they would have a clear understanding.

The family enjoyed their very pleasant house, and their illnesses were not as severe as the previous summer. The piano tuner gave assurance that theirs was an excellent instrument which would give long service. Ricarda was helpful in the house and was now preparing tea instead of coffee for their breakfast.

Present for the opening of the College term in September, Sturtevant arranged a third trip to the East in late November. Hannah wrote that Thanksgiving in Jacksonville was rather dull and instead of gathering the family it had scattered them. They had thought of father in Greenwich with Hannah's aunts and cousins. Hannah had gone to church on Thanksgiving Day for the first time in years and heard an excellent sermon by Mr. Johnson.

The mild weather continued into early December and made it pleasant for Hannah Augusta and Elizabeth "to walk to town & back" for public school. (8 Dec. 1853) Hannah had been boarding Mr. Grosvenor but when he mentioned that Mrs. Grosvenor would be coming to Jacksonville, the wife who ordinarily was so long-suffering declared enough! "I positively will not board them after she comes." (8, 12 Dec. 1853) During one of Julian's absences her brother James' family had stayed for six weeks. James had bought a barrel of flour, $5.00; and two turkeys, fifty cents a piece; also, he gave Hannah a gold dollar. Two attempts to ease Hannah's work by hiring girls had failed; both had to be dismissed because they could not be trusted.

Hannah planned to direct her next letter to her husband at Tallmadge. She concluded with a typical expression of love. "All send much love to their dear Father. You are constantly remembered by us when we assemble around the altar of family prayer. Ever yours most affectionately." (15 Dec. 1853) Julian expected to start for home on 21 or 22 December, and probably all the family were at home for Christmas.

In the late summer of 1854 the usual Illinois heat was made even more intense by a serious drouth. The water in the well at the barn was low although the cistern and the house well were still satisfactory. The ice man warned that there would be no more ice. Julian wrote that he missed his usual diet of milk and vegetables, and Hannah responded that if he were at home he would not have it either. They had only a few beans and tomatoes, and the cows were giving but little milk because the pasture was so poor. Hannah supposed that the drouth was just as much a judgment upon the people as the cholera.

Enduring four weeks of her husband's absence Hannah declared that she wanted this to be his last begging trip to the East. She asked him to give "a great deal of love" to the dear friends and relatives and hoped he would bring some daguerreotypes of the cousins for the children. Having received Julian's letter from Tallmadge, she replied that it was very strange that two brothers and a sister, all of whom boasted of being better off than he, "should be willing to allow you to bear the burden of the support of your Father. Amidst all the injustice & selfishness of the world, it is comforting to recollect that there is an impartial Judge, omniscient & over all. If we have a clear conscience we shall not fear to stand at that judgement bar." (5 Sept. 1854) Hannah enclosed a letter to Abraham's children so that Mr. Pierson could take it to Hawaii when he went.[37]

Julian Jr. described his father as naturally very intense in every way, in his convictions, his affections, and his emotions; his family prayers were "fitted to thrill." The son remembered "the tones, tremulous with emotion, the flash of his wonderful blue eyes, [yet it] was not the emotion of terror but an expression of solemn responsibility and the fullness of solemn joy." (JMSJR, 42) The father prayed earnestly that his children would never fight against God but would have a place in God's service. "

In his early teen years Julian Jr. had been conscientious to an extreme degree. When he was about sixteen both he and Warren, who was very close to him, underwent "a rather violent revolt against the religious attitude of our home." They were not rebelling against severe discipline; the sons were seldom punished and never harshly or unjustly. Nor was it a protest against too much hell-fire in the parents' teaching. Father had told of the pain he himself experienced from teachings given in his childhood, and he had not wished to teach his own children "a religion of terror." (JMSJR, 42) Father expressed his dismay that his elder son's conscience seemed to have vanished. Regardless of his father's admonitions, Julian Jr. had determined to be a wild college boy even before he entered college in the fall of 1850. "Wild boys drank whiskey, played cards, smoked, swore, and stole chickens, which were eaten at night. I did all those things and threw my troublesome conscience into the rubbish heap." (44) Warren did not participate in his brother's wild behavior, but at the time he hated being good.

Some experiences during the summer after his sophomore year led Julian Jr. to take a new view of religion and the eventual outcome was his conversion. At about the same time his sisters Hannah Augusta and Elizabeth were also converted. It was with great joy that Julian Sturtevant informed Baldwin in late 1852 about what the Lord had done for his family in "the hopeful conversion" of three of his children.[38] Subsequently they were admitted to membership in the Congregational Church.

Julian Jr. was awarded the A.B. degree by Illinois College in 1854. Both sons were members of Sigma Pi and aided in replacing the Society's library lost in the great fire. In his mature years Julian Jr. looked back upon Jacksonville with pride; it was, he said, a good place to grow up. It was where free public schools had first been established in one of the great western states. And the Jacksonville liquor ordinance had been passed long before the more-famous Maine prohibition law of 1846.

The family's faith sustained them in 1855 when Edgar Howard, seven years old, died on 11 October 1855. The parents were in the

East when he was stricken by dysentery. Julian Jr. and Hannah's sister were in charge of the household and shared the vigil. "Dear Aunt Jane, who always did much for us children, had hardly closed her eyes for a week...." The telegraph was not in general use and Mother Hannah, unaware of the boy's condition, arrived home only in time to see him die.[39] There were no undertakers then to care for the dead, and after getting the rest of the family off to bed, the older brother carried the body downstairs and prepared it, "as fittingly as love without experience could, for the grave...." (JMSJR, 77-78)

Warren Sturtevant relied more for emotional support and financial assistance on his second son, Julian, than on his other children. Huldah Hinman, a widow and bereft of all her children, moved to Beardstown, probably in 1850. That was where Christopher and his family were living, as well as several other families who had come from Warren, Connecticut. Huldah, Christopher, and his wife Ann all joined the Congregational Church in Beardstown in 1851. In 1852 Huldah wrote about living with Christopher's family while a new addition to the home was being built. She and Julian met in New York that summer. Christopher, now a merchant, achieved the success which had eluded him in his attempts at farming.

The younger Julian remembered both his Grandfather Fayerweather and Aunt Jane as "kindly and helpful members of the household" in Jacksonville. (JMSJR, 16) Richard Fayerweather died on 2 January 1852 at the age of seventy-four. In his will, made in 1845, he named Julian Sturtevant as his executor. At that time Richard's estate must have been fairly substantial; however, when Sturtevant filed the petition for probate, the estimated value was not more than $300. The oldest of the Fayerweather children, Julia, lived near Jacksonville with her husband, Timothy Chamberlain, and their daughter. The various Sturtevant and Fayerweather families in Jacksonville and Beardstown visited each other quite frequently.

James Fayerweather continued as a U.S. Mail Agent although in 1851 his territory was reduced to include only Iowa. The *Springfield Illinois Daily Journal* commended him as "a most indefatigable officer. His exertions in ferreting out mail robbers and securing their conviction, has [*sic*] been most untiring and successful." (4 July 1851) Later James was employed in the railroad business in Burlington.

The Sturtevants enjoyed a visit from Caroline, daughter of Theron and Caroline Baldwin in the summer of 1851. She had been enrolled in the Monticello Seminary for the preceding year. In 1855 the adult Baldwins were guests of the Sturtevants during the Quarter Century Celebration. Expressing his thanks, Baldwin said that they had very pleasant memories of their western visit and especially "the time that we spent under your friendly & hospitable roof." (B-S, 1 Aug. 1855)

Chapter 6: 1856-1860

Gathering Strength Before the Storm

A New Academic Building

Returning to the East after the grand Quarter-Century Celebration, Theron Baldwin re-read the letters he and Sturtevant had exchanged since 1843. He told his friend that they formed "quite a complete history of your 'times' in Illinois." (B-S, 24 Mar. 1857) He regarded every attack upon the president as an attack also on the trustees and therefore they should defend him. Expressing himself frankly, Baldwin said there were points on which he had not sympathized with Sturtevant in some of the controversies of the past—but none of these differences was fundamental. Certainly, Baldwin remarked, they and all their colleagues could be justly proud of Illinois College.

President Rammelkamp observed that "There is little doubt that Illinois College was at that time…the most important institution of higher learning in the state." (CH, 194) A less positive aspect of the New Englanders in Jacksonville has been noted by Don Doyle. Doyle remarked that the Yankees, only seven per cent of the town's diverse population, could not tolerate "foreign ways" and sought to impose their own social order by promoting temperance and Sabbath observance.[1]

The College's instructional program was described in newspaper advertisements for the fall term in 1857. The classical course of four years was "substantially the course required in the most thorough American Colleges." (SJ, 13 Aug. 1857) The Bachelor of Science course, omitting Greek and Latin, could be completed in three years; French and German were optional.[2] The large and beautiful new classroom building, with commodious rooms and modern improvements for heat, light, and ventilation, would be ready for use in September. Tuition and fees amounted to thirty-six dollars per year and board in private homes cost two to three dollars per week. The old South Wing and the Grove house were rented to the students for their Boarding Club for $150 and $130, respectively. The reorganized Preparatory Department was now managed by Professors Nutting and Crampton, assisted by Professor Sanders. It provided the two years of Greek, Latin, and mathematics prerequisite to the classical course. The scientific course required only one year of prior study in mathematics, grammar, and geography.

The faculty determined the use of the new "College Building" [Sturtevant Hall] well before its completion. On the first floor the southeast room was assigned for Greek and Latin recitations, the northeast room for rhetoric, and the southwest room for mathematics. The northwest room was the Library. On the second floor, the Chapel occupied the east room and the natural philosophy department the southwest room. The president would use the northwest room for his recitations. The south half of the old building [Beecher Hall] was assigned to the literary societies, who paid for furnishings but were not charged rent. The north part was a reading room and housed the Preparatory Department.

Completion of the new building was delayed by lack of funds and the scarcity of workmen, despite high wages at the time. Carpenters were earning two dollars a day and masons as high as two dollars and fifty cents, but even at those rates it was hard to retain laborers, most of whom preferred to obtain land and be their own bosses. Finally the project was finished and the new structure was opened on 10 September 1857; the Chapel on the second floor was dedicated one week later. Sturtevant wrote a glowing account of the building for the College Society's annual report: "It proves all we hoped or expected. It is, indeed, a new era in our history…. Our machinery is moving on with a power quite unequaled hitherto." The College had been "sobered by long and heavy strokes of adversity" but was now "standing on a foundation upon which the rains have descended and the floods come without being able to shake it." (SPC-14, 22) In the fall term of 1858 the enrollment reached 160: 49 in the A.B. program, 39 in the B.S. program, and 72 preparatory students.

The New College Building
(1864-65 *Catalogue*)
Dedicated September 1857.
Named Sturtevant Hall, 1888.

The praise of the new facility by a visitor from the College Society was most welcome. The "second College Edifice" was described as "a new and beautiful structure, affording ample and pleasant accommodations for recitations and lectures, and a large hall for Chapel Exercises." (SPC-16, 53) Sturtevant was proud of the large trees on the campus, many of which he had planted.

In the spring of 1860 Sturtevant described his heavy schedule, intensified periodically by doubling up senior class meetings when he prepared to be absent. Routinely he needed six hours a day to prepare for and hear recitations. He wrote one sermon each week and handled the correspondence and general College business. Delayed salary payments necessitated greater attention to "personal affairs"—presumably earning money by additional preaching or writing for publication, or perhaps aiding the family larder by spending more time in his garden now that the older sons were away. Sturtevant remarked that the situation was neither to his taste nor his usefulness.

The College's commencements, held on Thursdays during the week of such activities in Jacksonville, featured music and student orations and the awarding of degrees. Sturtevant preached the baccalaureate sermon on the prior Sabbath afternoon, at the College Chapel or one of the churches. The literary societies sponsored reunions at the Mansion House or other dining places. In 1860 Sturtevant and Sanders were delegated to arrange an Alumni Festival in the new College Building.

Student misbehavior required much faculty attention. Professor Adams addressed the students regarding their rudeness to ladies attending lectures at the College. Some students at a concert in town were rowdy. The president of the student boarding club was informed that no "conviviality" was allowed in the buildings they occupied. A particularly grave offense was the distribution of bogus printed programs caricaturing those the College prepared for exercises and commencements. They contained jokes and cartoons which lampooned both students and faculty. Even the police could not stop the practice which continued for a decade. (CH, 286-87)

The case of William Springer in 1857 was one of the most difficult. A junior, he prepared a brief for his speech and presented it to Professor Sanders as required. Sanders deleted a part he regarded as an attack on the Republican Party and thus political rather than literary. Springer countered that some speeches the preceding year had been critical of the Democratic Party. He finally agreed to remove the designated parts except for his praise of Democrat James Buchanan's election as president. The entire junior class petitioned Sturtevant on behalf of Springer and was informed that the matter was entirely in Professor Sanders' hands. Springer arranged for a printed broadside to publicize his cause. The local *Morgan Journal* upheld the College, while the *Jacksonville Sentinel* (a Democratic paper) sided with Springer. The *Springfield Register* attacked the *Journal* as the lackey of the College and called upon the professors ("abolition preachers") to act like men and Christians.[3] Sturtevant and Sanders were charged with having devoted themselves to abolitionism and treason to the Constitution, and the College was described as "the fountain and hot-bed of ultra abolitionism."[4] Missouri newspapers also joined the fray and Eastern newspapers picked up the story. Sturtevant called the affair unpleasant and said that both Sanders and he had been called villains. Springer, who was expelled, was causing some mischief among the students. Sturtevant, believing the community supported the College, maintained utter silence.[5]

Just between them, Sturtevant told Baldwin, Sanders was imprudent and when feelings were aroused he was apt "to throw oil into the fire." (S-B, 10 Apr. 1857) The broad political differences in the area's population were reflected in the two student literary societies. Sigma Pi was Republican and Phi Alpha, to which Springer belonged, had Democratic sympathies. Springer had borrowed some ideas from a recent sermon by the pastor of the First Presbyterian Church, and Sanders' involvement in a controversy at the church may have influenced his feelings toward the student. In later years Springer was elected to the United States Congress. Peace was eventually made between him and the College, and he was awarded an honorary LL.D. degree in 1890.

Other events also had a negative effect on the College's enrollment. Disciplinary action was taken against some youths who had played a very mean trick, and several others asked to be separated from the College. Sturtevant characterized the transfer of an outstanding student to Yale as the kind of action which always harmed the College. The competition from distant colleges, especially the University of Michigan with free tuition, was becoming keener. The sophomore class was weak but the freshman class had 35 students and things looked cheerful.

Although the College maintained its scheduled religious exercises and there was no recurrence of skepticism, religious fervor was at a low ebb in the College and in the town. In 1857 Sturtevant and Sanders were directed to make arrangements for the annual day of fasting and prayer for colleges in mid-March; usually that observance aroused some degree of religious interest among the students. In the spring of 1858 during the final drive to complete the Fifty Thousand Dollar Fund, Sabbath services were suspended because the faculty were compelled to reduce their work load. That autumn the only discouraging note was the low state of morals and religion among the students. Only about a third of the students professed religion and many of the others were very heedless—the result, Sturtevant thought, of the area's heterogeneous population and diverse morality.

Julian Sturtevant Jr. reported a conversion of particular interest which occurred while he was an instructor in the Preparatory Department. An older pupil asked him for a private interview. The student was troubled because his efforts to act as a Christian mortified him; for example, he had knelt in the street to pray. His counselor told him that all that God wants is good intentions and good common sense and that a person should seek to do what is useful and sensible. The identity of the student, who was not named, is obvious from Julian Jr.'s comment that some years afterwards [1889] Illinois College conferred upon him an honorary degree for his scientific attainments in the exploration of the Far West. The student was John Wesley Powell, a freshman in the scientific program during 1855-1856 and enrolled the following year in the Preparatory Department.[6]

A New Congregational Church Building

Receiving $10 for each service, Sturtevant preached often in the Congregational Church when the minister was away or in the interim between ministers. The church elected him to a second term as trustee. While he was chairman of the music committee the new hymnal he recommended, the *Sabbath Hymn and Tune Book*, was adopted for use. The congregation sold its building on the public square in 1857 and the plans for the new church, prepared by William Backus and Co. of Chicago, were approved. The goal was to construct an appropriate building equipped with up-to-date "warming apparatus" and newly-available gas lights. The College Chapel was used for evening prayer meetings and communion.

In the fall of 1859 Sturtevant, as chairman of the building committee, reported that the new structure was now almost ready for use although the spire at the southwest corner was not yet completed. Also unfinished were the lecture room at the rear of the church and, above it, the pastor's study and two rooms for Sabbath School classes and social purposes. The new building was dedicated on Sunday, 4 December 1859. Rev. Truman M. Post of St. Louis, a former professor at the College and formerly pastor of the church, preached at the morning and evening services. Sturtevant proposed that as soon as lights could be installed in the lecture room the congregation should hold "a concert of prayer for the conversion of the world on the [first] sabbath evening of each month." (CCM, 25 Dec. 1858)

Congregational Church
Dedicated December 1859.
(520 West College)

The Congregational Church was identified very early as the "Abolition Church" because among its members were several very active leaders in that movement. In 1859 Sturtevant was eulogist at the service for one of its most prominent lay members, Elihu Wolcott, who had been elected president of the Illinois State Anti-Slavery Association when it was organized at Alton in 1837. Sturtevant praised the man's character and "his unbounding adhesion to his convictions." Whether people agreed with Wolcott or not, he said, they should unite in honoring him.

When the General Association of Illinois met in Ottawa in May 1856, Sturtevant was chosen moderator. The Association named him a delegate to the corresponding bodies in Massachusetts, Vermont, and Maine. Conveniently, the General Association met at Jacksonville two years later, and the clerical and lay delegates visited the College's campus. The 1860 meeting was exhilarating, Sturtevant said; it was characterized by vigorous debates and unanimous decisions, thus demonstrating the power of persuasion and also vindicating Congregational church order.

The newly organized Congregational Association of Southern Illinois was described in a news account over Sturtevant's initials.

He observed that the session was characterized by confidence "in the gradual but sure prevalence of the principles upon which our churches are founded."[7] He now held membership in the new Association instead of the Morgan Conference. In 1857 Sturtevant assisted in organizing a Congregational church in Indianapolis. He later rejoiced that "Congregational churches are multiplying without hands or efforts." (S-B, 6 Dec. 1859)

In October 1858 nearly four hundred Congregational ministers and lay delegates representing more than six hundred churches in seven states met in Chicago for the Triennial Convention. The meeting "was dignified, harmonious, and devotional." (S-B, 25 Oct. 1858) Although the financial prospects of the new Chicago Theological Seminary were splendid, Sturtevant expressed reservations about a newly inaugurated professor. The man's elocution was excellent but he seemed a "Dr. Woodsman." He had even said that theology cannot give a certain answer to the question of what is sin; how then could the man teach theology?

In a lengthy review of *Protestantism in America*,[8] Sturtevant praised the author, Philip Schaff, as "a learned, pious and accomplished foreigner" (537) who had made America his adopted home. He noted that Schaff disagreed with the distinctively American view that republican government and separation of church and state were suitable for other countries. Schaff thought that the majority of Americans wanted to save the Union whatever compromises with slavery that might require. Sturtevant believed that the 1856 election refuted that opinion by checking the territorial expansion of slavery. This proved that the great majority were "unalterably resolved on protecting both the Union and freedom." (539)

The present denominational system is but a transitional stage, Sturtevant observed; the independence of local churches is the goal toward which the Reformation principles are tending. Ultimately the moral unity of Christendom will triumph, but the immediate imperative is for "cooperation with our brethren in planting the Church in this and all lands." (552) Schaff was credited for recognizing "that the future of the world's destiny is to be decided on American soil." (538) At the heart of that belief, Sturtevant wrote, is "the ultimate destiny of Protestantism, especially in this country, as it stands related to denominationalism." (540) The review was unsigned but the identity of the author soon became known. Sturtevant did not have to wait long for strong reactions. The *New-York Evangelist* made a personal "onslaught" on him, and only Baldwin's advice prevented an impassioned reply. A Presbyterian member of the College's Board lodged a vigorous protest.

Fifty-Eight Thousand—in Subscriptions

Two-thirds of the Fifty Thousand Dollar Fund was subscribed within two years, but receipts amounted to only $3,600. The income had to be augmented and tuition was increased from twenty to thirty dollars. After years of delay hope dwindled that the College would qualify for the Joseph Spring estate of $2,300. Alluding to the Blackburn case, Baldwin warned against repeating "the experiment of paying back money." (B-S, 3 Apr., 2 May 1856) Fortunately, in October 1856 the legacy was paid by order of the Massachusetts Supreme Court.

Henry Ward Beecher had promised $10,000 to endow a professorship in his name, but getting the money proved difficult, especially after Beecher asked his church members to send rifles to Kansas. Sturtevant had called on him so many times that he was ashamed to go again. Baldwin went to Brooklyn determined to stay "till I had run him down." (B-S, 21 June 1858) Finally Beecher told him to telegraph Brother Sturtevant that he could count on the money. The amount paid now totaled over sixteen hundred dollars.[9]

Money was sought from a number of sources. Plans were made in 1856 to extend the street which passed directly in front of the "Deaf & Dumb Asylum" southward, cutting off seven acres of College land. A purchaser contracted for two acres of the tract west of the Asylum for $2,000, a sum which would help pay the College's debt to the faculty but was not sufficient to pay Sturtevant's salary. Selling more of those lots and the Medical Hall lot should produce, Sturtevant believed, at least $4,500 for completing the new building and for the endowment. He also hoped to obtain funds in northeastern Ohio where his family had lived but found the towns there destitute, like a "stranded, dismantled, mastless vessel abandoned to rot on the land."[10] Theron Baldwin borrowed from a friend so that he could pay his personal pledge of $200. John Ellis in his will designated $500 for scholarships for promising ministerial candidates.

A major effort was needed and in March 1856 Sturtevant arranged a meeting of some trustees with the faculty to hear his proposal for a new Fifty Thousand Dollar Fund with a deadline of 1 June 1858. Ten thousand dollars would be allocated for buildings, library, apparatus, and aid for indigent students; the remainder would be added to the endowment. David A. Smith subscribed $2,000 and Professors Sanders and Nutting $500 each. Although Sturtevant believed that most of the fund should be—and could be—raised in the West, he also realized that it would be necessary to obtain $20,000 in the East. Reporting the Society's approval of that plan, Baldwin declared "this is evidently the last time for Ill[inois] College, but I trust in God that we shall somehow reach a successful end." (B-S, 28 Apr. 1857) People in the East believed that the West now had ample wealth of its own. Sturtevant countered with an article, "The West [Is] Still Needy," emphasizing the importance of protecting the population from many enemies, chief among them Romanism, Infidelity, and Mammonism. The East had responded to the need of the West in 1829 and the need was even greater now. Another means of encouraging contributions for colleges was the Society's new periodical, the *Western College Intelligencer.*

The Panic of 1857 initiated a prolonged depression which was especially severe in the northeast, the source of much of the funding received by Illinois College. Consequently, the prospect for completing the Fifty Thousand Dollar Fund was gloomy. "If we fail," Sturtevant wrote Baldwin, "our condition will be a very disastrous one." (S-B, 19 Nov. 1857) By 1 December the situation had reached a critical stage and the faculty turned to Sturtevant and Sanders. Sanders, however, was needed by his family and Sturtevant feared to undertake the work in winter; he had suffered alarmingly the previous year from colds and coughs. Sturtevant appealed to Baldwin to help "through this pinch" (S-B, 1 Dec. 1857) and Baldwin replied that perhaps he could come in the spring. Sturtevant was freed from campus duties to give full attention to the campaign. The ministers of the local Congregational and Presbyterian Churches heard the seniors' recitations and assisted with daily prayers, while Sanders took charge of Sunday Chapel.

Writing to Hannah in late January 1858 from Princeton (Illinois), Sturtevant acknowledged his difficulties. Because the roads were awful few people had come to church that Sunday and he had to call on prospective donors. He walked ten miles to obtain one subscription of one hundred dollars. He lamented that it did the College's reputation no good for people to see its president going about, alone and on foot, seeking money. Later in the spring, while at Quincy, Sturtevant became ill from something he had eaten but managed to keep on working.

Writing next from St. Louis, Sturtevant informed his wife that he expected to be home by Friday evening because that was as long as his clean linen would hold out and rather too long for his patience. He would spend the Sabbath at home and then go to Chicago for his last trip. He used a rather strange analogy to express his weariness. "I have heard it said that a married woman who is rebellious about the matter of an increasing family may expect the series to be uninterrupted till she becomes perfectly reconciled and willing. If the same law applies to soliciting money for public objects I fear that there is a great deal of it in store for me yet, for I am far from being willing and acquiescent in that kind of employment." (21 Apr. 1858) Two letters from Chicago in early May were generally more positive. He was determined "to get the College out of the woods this time." He spoke of the great wealth in a church he visited which likely would give the College less than a little New England church. "Shame! Shame!!"

With only a few weeks remaining Sturtevant advised Baldwin that "What we do must be done quickly." (S-B, St. Louis, 19 Apr. 1858) And amazingly, it was done. At noon on 31 May Sturtevant telegraphed Baldwin, "Fifty-eight thousand," adding a reference to Psalm 126, a Psalm of rejoicing. Fearing that Baldwin would think there was some mistake about the large amount, he sent a letter with the details. Since 3 April when he and Sanders had commenced their intense effort, they had been "on the flood tide of success." More than $7,000 had been obtained at Quincy, $2,700 in St. Louis, nearly $5,000 in Chicago, and more than

$6,000 in Alton. Even Pisgah, a small village some miles from Jacksonville, had yielded $2,000. (S-B, 1 June 1858)

Sturtevant praised Sanders as "an earnest and very efficient man" and noted with pleasure that denominational differences had virtually disappeared. (A, 274) The two men had presented the cause in their local churches on a recent Sabbath, and the following day "it began to rain money." The week's work in Jacksonville and the vicinity produced more than $14,000 and an overall figure for the area of more than $21,000. Adding the Beecher professorship and the indigent fund brought the total to more than $76,000. Their success was all the more remarkable because only months earlier the College had raised $10,000 for the new building. "We have certainly no occasion to say hereafter that the College has no friends at home," he wrote. "Illinois College dwells among its own people. It is at home." (S-B, 1 June 1858) Happily there was cooperation among the "Presbyterians and Congregationalists and patriotic public spirited men who were connected with neither denomination." (A, 276) Moreover, the freedom of the faculty had been maintained. The goal was attained without the aid of Baldwin, who had been unable to join them. However, the Society and Baldwin felt responsible for the full collection of the $20,000 approved for solicitation in the East.

The arduous task of obtaining subscriptions did not end the College's financial plight. The pledges due on 1 June amounted to $8,000 but only $5,000 was received and the College lacked sufficient cash to pay salaries in full. The amount due to Sturtevant was $1,400, "every dollar of which I am in urgent want of." (S-B, 18 Oct. 1858) The following year his situation was even worse, the College owing him $2,000. Indirectly asking Baldwin for help, he inquired whether his friend knew of anyone from whom he could borrow $500. His security was ample for the loan; his house was worth $10,000 and free of encumbrance, and the College could assure payment in two to three years. Sturtevant would pay ten per cent interest if necessary. Meanwhile, he wrote, "I do not know how to get along." (S-B, 6 Dec. 1859) The financial stress led the faculty to require students to pay their bills before obtaining a certificate of standing or receiving a degree. Despite Sturtevant's hard work the goal of financial stability was still beyond his grasp.

Protesting Denominational Control

Sturtevant remarked in 1856 that there was but one cloud over Illinois College, the problem of its relationship to the two denominations—an issue raised once again by Rev. A. T. Norton. The College proposed to issue a circular to inform the public about its plans. Some Presbyterians wanted a pledge of equality between the two denominations with regard to trustees and faculty. Sturtevant believed that would be a breach of the very principles of union upon which the College had been founded. He confessed to Baldwin that "The repeated coming up of this Ghost or rather living demon disheartens me more than any thing else ever did and makes me sick of trying to co-operate." (S-B, 9 Apr. 1856) Nevertheless, Sturtevant yielded to suggestions from friends and spent a Sabbath at Alton with Mr. Norton. Together the men drew up a statement of principles acceptable to both.

A day later Norton addressed a letter to Sturtevant requesting a definite arrangement for dividing the assets of the College if in fact one denomination should gain control of it. Norton added two postscripts: such a statement would guarantee the success of the current fund drive, and besides "Pres. Sturtevant should not suffer his own views of church polity too greatly & manifestly to dictate & shape the language of that circular." (S-B, 23 Apr. 1856) Sturtevant was now convinced that Norton would not cooperate with the College until he had succeeded in molding it according to the Presbyterian system of ecclesiastical boards. He asked Baldwin, if Norton were elected to the Board, would not the president have to consult with "the oracle of Alton" regarding every matter? Did not Baldwin agree that the original principles on which the College was founded were sufficient and should be maintained?

Baldwin, although Norton's cousin, essentially agreed with Sturtevant. He declared that Illinois College was not bound by charter to any denomination. Moreover, any requirement for a certain number of Presbyterians would raise a most vexing question, deciding who was a Presbyterian. Old School Presbyterians did not consider all New School men to be real Presbyterians. The Illinois College situation had wide implications because the College Society dealt with nine other colleges with similar foundations. The circular as published acknowledged that the two denominations had mutual rights and interests in the College but made no mention of a possible division of resources. Baldwin assured Sturtevant that support for the union position was substantial both in the East and in the West.

At the very time when the College hoped to conclude the Fifty-Thousand Dollar drive, David A. Smith asked to meet privately with Sturtevant.[11] He expressed his strong disapproval of Sturtevant's publication of his views extolling Congregationalism at the expense of Presbyterianism. The review of Schaff's book had aroused much anger among the Presbyterians, even more than Sturtevant's 1855 address. Smith said that success would be possible if Sturtevant would cease talking about church government. Sturtevant replied that if the trustees regarded his writings as inappropriate they could request his resignation at any time, but he would remain as president "only as a free man, at perfect liberty to speak and publish at my own discretion." (A, 275) Moreover, Sturtevant said, if the *New-York Evangelist* were correct in reporting that he sought to keep students out of the Presbyterian Church, the trustees should remove him at once. Sturtevant denied the charge and said that those who read his articles understood his "intense zeal for the visible unity of all Christ's disciples." Smith responded that Sturtevant should not even think of resigning and thus, Sturtevant wrote, "the tragedy ended in a comedy." "God forbid that I should sell the smallest portion of my freedom of utterance, even in such a crisis, either for place or money. I have not done it." (S-B, 1 June 1858) Other Presbyterians were not so forgiving; he was excluded from speaking for the College in Rev. R. W. Patterson's church in Chicago.

Far from being silenced by David A. Smith's warning, President Sturtevant published several articles in 1859 on church government, Christian unity, and sectarianism. He argued that the earnest seeker can decide which among the many claimants is the true church by applying these criteria: proclamation of the Divine Word, genuine Christian devotion and behavior, and the kind but firm rejection of those who deny Christ. However, the true people of God are found in all evangelical denominations, and apart from explicit commandments from Christ a group may adopt various practices, such as baptism by immersion. Christ has left certain matters to the good sense of his people, and if in a given church there are allowable elements one dislikes he should withdraw from it peacefully. The real culprit in fomenting sectarianism is the belief that a human organization with a human head can be identified with God's kingdom; Sturtevant proposed to designate this fundamental error as "Jesuitism." Christ founded the Kingdom of heaven as a moral and spiritual kingdom, "the empire of truth and love." He did not found any polity whatsoever, either civil or ecclesiastical; indeed, the Lord's kingdom "is not of this world."

In a series of articles in the *Independent* in 1859 Sturtevant examined recent Presbyterian proposals for funding Presbyterian churches which were denied aid by the Home Missionary Society. Analyzing each plan, he explained that such denials occurred when churches were in violation of the Plan of Union or anti-slavery principles. He concluded that if the Presbyterians adopted their proposed church extension program it would mean the end of cooperation with the Congregationalists.

The prolonged controversy led Sturtevant to set forth his views on "Denominational Colleges" in the *New Englander*. He argued his case with the force of logic and the evidence of experience. He apologized for using the word "denominational," then a relatively new term attractive to those who wished to extol a particular religious body without incurring the negative implications of "sect." He also explained the combination of "denominational" with "colleges," noting that until recently the great collegiate institutions of America had never been regarded as belonging to any particular group but as suitable for educating all youth. The most effective method of denominational control is direct and exclusive, but this subordinates the school to the denomination's interests. Also, because denominations are by nature susceptible to division, colleges as permanent institutions should be separated from such conflicts. Sturtevant observed that sound colleges must be founded upon the basis of "a broad and comprehensive platform of Evangelic Faith." (87) They must be governed by enlightened individuals who are Christians but not Sectarians. This was the only escape from the proliferation of colleges now spawned by the joint motives of sect and local interest. Congregationalists themselves must forego the denominational "mania" and willingly cooperate in sustaining colleges which are true to Christian principles regardless of denominational affiliation.

Sturtevant had regarded the *New Englander* as the best journal for his views on "Denominational Colleges" but thought he could expect no pay. Baldwin spoke to the editor who assured him that there would be some compensation. Learning this, Sturtevant forwarded the essay to the journal. He described his article for Baldwin: "It is at least thorough, earnest and outspoken. It is full of the utterances of deep convictions and life experiences." (S-B, 2 Jan. 1860) He anticipated severe treatment by the *Chicago Congregational Herald* and the *New-York Evangelist.* He wanted copies sent to every Congregational and Presbyterian minister in Illinois. Baldwin ordered two hundred fifty reprints but dared not risk more because if friends did not help, the expense would come out of his own pocket.[12]

The article led to correspondence from Rev. H. L. Hammond, editor of the *Congregational Herald.* Hammond informed Sturtevant that his essay had dropped like a bombshell in the *Herald's* office. The staff of the Congregational newspaper apparently felt that union constitutions of colleges conceded too much to the Presbyterians. Sturtevant resolved to challenge the assumptions made by the *Herald* that a college could not survive without sectarian control. However, he would not send his views to that periodical because, he explained to Baldwin, "That would be only to make myself an ass to carry any 'riders' which [the editor] might choose to put on." (S-B, 20 Mar. 1860) The *Herald* also charged that Sturtevant was incorrect in stating that the New England colleges were not "Congregational" colleges.

In the late 1850s the tensions which had been mounting *within* New School Presbyterianism found expression in Jacksonville's First Presbyterian Church. Although the Synod of Illinois was on record as opposing slavery, the majority of the Jacksonville Presbyterians did not agree; the members who held anti-slavery convictions were steadfast but only a minority.[13] Moreover, Rev. Glover, Pastor of First Church and a trustee of Illinois College, had placed himself squarely against cooperation with the Congregationalists and thus in opposition to the principle so important to Sturtevant, that the College should not be under denominational control.

The quarreling which developed within the First Church was described by Sturtevant as "the worst I have ever been acquainted with." (S-B, 23 Nov. 1859) Charges were brought against Rev. Glover by dissenting members, and a commission of the Illinois Presbytery met for six weeks taking testimony. A large majority of the members of the church supported Glover but about twenty others were attending the Congregational Church. Sturtevant said it appeared that "the anti-Glover war" would last "as long as the siege of Troy." (JMS to son Warren, 2 Feb. 1860) Glover was acquitted by a single vote and his supporters cheered him and "groaned" Sanders, who was in the opposition. Sanders and Nutting had been involved in the quarrel and at some harm to the College, thought Sturtevant. The resolution of the Glover case brought an end to the agitation which had plagued that church for a year and a half, and by June a new church building was under construction.

The minority group now planned a separate church, a gloomy prospect in Sturtevant's view because the growth of the new church would come from the same social and moral elements in the population as the Congregational Church. With authorization from the Presbytery, forty-five members organized in May 1860 as the Westminster Presbyterian Church; the meeting was held in the Congregational Church. The designated speaker was ill and Rev. A. T. Norton, long antagonistic toward Sturtevant and the College, took his place. Sturtevant told Baldwin that Norton preached one of his church extension discourses "with the horns knocked off." (S-B, 11 May 1860) Norton was narrowly sectarian, claiming that Presbyterianism is thoroughly in accord with the Scriptures and that the more fully a man conforms to Presbyterian standards the better Christian he is.

Sturtevant declared that in the days of their fathers or even in the days of their own youth, denominationalism had not been so intense. Baldwin reflected about their own denominational connections in the past. He recalled that "All the original seven of our Ill[inois] Association except Br. Brooks were Congregationalists, unless possibly Br. Sturtevant was a member of a Pres. Church in Tallmadge, but soon we were all merged in the great Pres[byterian] System. Then a stampede commenced. Did we act at these different period[s] as Congregationalists or Presbyterians or as <u>Christians</u>?"14

The prolonged controversy led the two friends to further reminiscence. Sturtevant recalled the first time he attended prayers at Yale College. On that occasion, for the last time, an officer of the college was inducted with the requirement that he give public assent to the Saybrook Platform. That statement of Calvinist doctrine and semi-Presbyterian church order had been adopted by the Congregational churches in Connecticut in 1708 and was accepted as the standard in that state. The young student from Tallmadge had then "just caught a glimpse of the retiring goblin" at the Yale Chapel. Sturtevant did not suppose that the presence of a freshman, seated in the upper gallery of the old Chapel and half dead with fright, had anything to do with scaring away the beast. But he believed that had that beast continued his visits into that same student's mature years at Yale, the student would have shown him fight. Sturtevant would not now tolerate the beast's presence "amid the classic shades of our College hill." (S-B, 25 Sept. 1860) Baldwin, to be certain regarding Yale as an example of a nonsectarian college, made an inquiry. President Woolsey replied that he knew of no principle requiring Yale's officers to be Congregationalists; at present one Episcopalian tutor and one Baptist were serving the College.

From his consideration of the issue Sturtevant had forged two significant principles for higher education. First, colleges should not be subverted to the interests of other institutions, including churches, and second, a person in academic life should have complete freedom to express his views. Rammelkamp commented that "Undoubtedly President Sturtevant was doing a great service for the cause of higher education not only in Illinois College but throughout the West by his vigorous protest against denominational control of colleges." (CH, 188)

Lecturer, Preacher, Author

In February 1856 Sturtevant was asked to write an article for the College Society's *Western College Intelligencer*.15 A year later he prepared a lecture on the destiny of the "colored" race in the United States. He believed his views were of great importance to the resolution of the slavery controversy and asked whether Baldwin could arrange with some of their friends for him to speak in New York. Apparently no opportunity was presented.

In late March Sturtevant received a letter asking him to be a candidate for an endowed professorship in didactic theology at the Congregational seminary in Chicago; the salary would be two thousand dollars. He expressed doubt to Baldwin that he would be elected but stated that his departure would not be an escape from a sinking ship; the College was in the best condition for a decade. Sturtevant wrote again on 3 April to explain that the invitation to an interview had given the date as 15 April when it should have been 1 April. The error was Providential—he missed the meeting without being responsible for doing so. Meanwhile Baldwin advised him that placing his name on the market for a position would be a grave mistake unless assured that he would be elected; moreover, his resignation would be detrimental to the College. Sturtevant was a special lecturer on "Modern Sects" at the Chicago Theological Seminary from 1859 through 1862. He was also one of the "gentlemen appointed as Lecturers" in 1860 in the Oberlin College Theological Department, where his topic was the "Relation of Sects to the Church."[16]

During these years Sturtevant performed only two marriages of record in Morgan County. An early alumnus, Rev. Rollin Mears, died—or as Sturtevant put it, God took him—and Sturtevant conducted the funeral service for his former student. Mears had been pastor of the Congregational Church of Waverly in 1846-1847 when the church forthrightly denounced slavery. Sturtevant's most frequent ministerial function was preaching, which he took very seriously.[17] His own pulpit style was likely mirrored in his description of an English minister who preached in the Congregational Church and, with his wife, visited the Sturtevants during commencement week in 1856. Sturtevant praised him, saying that he could not be distinguished from the best class of American preachers accustomed to the West. "His style is simple, direct, and free from technical language—his manner energetic, his gesticulations abundant and forcible, and his doctrine that of New England. It was a treat to us all." (S-B, 20 June 1856)

In April 1858 Sturtevant reported to Hannah that he had preached three times at three churches in Quincy on the Sabbath. He gave a sermon on Monday evening and was scheduled for another on Wednesday evening. The following Sabbath he did "the usual amount of preaching" in St. Louis. Other out-of-town engagements included services at churches in Jerseyville and again in St. Louis, where he received fifty dollars. Once, after arriving in New York, he was invited to preach and arranged for Warren to send his sermon notes, which helped him out "quite wonderfully."

In 1858 while on a visit to his father in northern Ohio Sturtevant attended the commencement at Western Reserve College and also heard the Phi Beta Kappa address. The occasion featured a speech by the governor of Ohio at a dinner party where Sturtevant also spoke. Among the many friends he saw was Thomas Beecher, who addressed one of the literary societies. Sturtevant reported that "our Tom Beecher" had delivered "a good-natured, startling, brilliant, false, good for nothing address… to a vast and really brilliant audience, who were delighted."[18] Sturtevant himself was invited to deliver the Phi Beta Kappa lecture at Western Reserve College in 1860.

Sturtevant often expressed his longing for conversation with people in the East. Among those he respected most was Dr. Leonard Bacon of New Haven. He also appreciated Joseph Thompson, who had visited Illinois College and was now an editor of the *New York Independent.* The editor of the *New Englander,* William L. Kingsley of New Haven, was another valued friend. Sturtevant acquired a reputation in his own family for becoming excited about meeting old friends. While traveling to Tallmadge he was seated on the omnibus next to Governor Chase of Ohio, whom he had met twenty years previously. Describing this happy circumstance, he surmised that Libbie would say, "father is in ecstasies, as usual."[19]

Americans to Christianize the World

An invitation Sturtevant could not refuse designated him as the preacher for the anniversary meeting of the American Home

Missionary Society in May 1857. Milton Badger added a personal note: "You have been in the midst of our Home Missionary field, almost from the Commencement of the Society's labors, ...and you can speak on this subject as no other man can." The letter included the welcome news that the Society would pay his expenses to New York. Choosing the title, "American Emigration," Sturtevant preached the sermon twice, in New York and Brooklyn. He declared that although Jesus instructed his disciples (Matt. 10:5,6) to go only to the people of Israel, his purpose was to establish the Christian Church wherever the Jews lived, not to restrict the true faith to them. Just as God committed to those ancient Jews the propagation of the Gospel in the Roman Empire, God now has committed to the American people the task of converting the world to Christ. It is the function of the American Home Missionary Society to "*follow the American emigrant, in all his migrations, and to plant the permanent institutions of the Christian faith wherever he builds his cabin.*" (8) Thus, the people of New England were to fulfill the role of missionaries in the present age. God had led them "to this good land of ours, to lay the foundations of a free religious republic, which, though it had no model in the past, was to be the hope of the future." (7) Here they constructed their homes and established church and state as the foundation of American society.

Utilizing statistical projections, Sturtevant demonstrated that there would be sufficient numbers of this Pilgrim people to accomplish the universal mission. A population of "*one thousand millions*" could be reached by the year 2000, although three hundred million would be adequate. Those who can now carry forward the great work are the white population of the sixteen Free States. The Southern states will bear their part "in fulfilling our great religious destiny [only] after that system of oppression, so fatally in conflict with our origin, our history, and our religion, shall have been completely swept away. Such a day, I trust, is coming. The Lord hasten it in his time!" (12)

Foreign immigration will continue to augment the population of the United States. God's design evidently is to use more than the people physically descended from Puritan stock to build up "a great free religious nation." (28) The foreign elements were already being assimilated into America's social structure, largely through the English language, and they were not materially changing the basic religious character of our country. Thus the population Sturtevant extolled had "certain religious and social characteristics, and [bore] the moral lineage of the Pilgrims of the Mayflower." (14) These people would be motivated by "one single moral force—*the characteristic religious system of the English dissenters of the seventeenth century.*" (20)

Sturtevant attributed the remarkable success of the early immigrants to three specific factors. First was the dignity they accorded Christian marriage and the family, leading them to go forth as settlers, not celibate explorers. Second, such people were not only educated but willing to work. Third, American emigrants to the western states and territories have been characterized by their "peculiar public spirit," their "social constructiveness." They have brought with them "all the institutions of a ripe christian [*sic*] civilization, [namely] The schoolhouse, the college, the church, the teaching ministry...." (24, 25) All these features must characterize the continuing westward expansion of America to the coast of the Pacific and beyond.

There are vast unoccupied areas into which American emigrants can expand. North and South America can provide a magnificent home for a billion people, and there are great regions of Africa and Asia with abundant resources but few people. Sturtevant declared that without doubt the migration of the English Puritan stock, and specifically the moral successors of the Mayflower Pilgrims, is intended by God to be the means for planting "the gospel of Jesus Christ in every land, before the year of our Lord, 2000." (30) He was confident that one great obstacle, slavery, would surely be removed. "I can not believe, that God has doomed one half the soil of this home of the free to perpetual slavery." (27) But an even greater obstacle might yet arise, the deterioration of the religious character of the American people. Sturtevant insisted he was not declaring a "doctrine of manifest destiny." The hoped-for future of America was not guaranteed; worldliness might invade the churches, and the religious element might be entirely absent from our migrations. "Our frontier may thus be inhabited by a people knowing no God but money, and no freedom but that of licentiousness." (31) "We can [not] subdue a continent by an emigrant population without religion, without the Church, the school, the ministry…." (31-32) Sturtevant defined the task now facing the American Home Missionary Society: to spread "the religious faith and the religious institutions of English Puritanism over the world." (33) With faithfulness to God in that mission the biblical promise would be fulfilled, and the present and future generations in America will possess "this good land which the Lord gave unto our fathers…. " (34; Deut. 26:1-2)

Although his opposition to the great amounts spent on the distribution of tracts was well-known, Sturtevant was asked to address the meeting of the American Tract Society in Boston in 1859. He boasted in a letter to Baldwin that he had exercised severe self-denial in refusing the invitation; actually it was the severe shortage of faculty which kept him on the campus.

In mid-September 1859 Sturtevant requested Baldwin to obtain money due him from the *Independent* for nine unsigned articles. Dr. Thompson had arranged for him to receive five dollars per column, and Sturtevant supposed that the associate would take care of it. An apologetic note asked Baldwin to "excuse the trouble I make you," but he did need the money. (S-B, 11 Oct. 1859) Baldwin's letter with the check for $37.67 crossed Sturtevant's plea in the mail.

In 1857 Sturtevant had considered writing about women's education but perhaps did not do so until invited to address the commencement at Rockford Female Seminary on 14 July 1859. On his way he stopped at Beloit College in Wisconsin to attend the commencement. Sturtevant's speech, "Rights of Women," was summarized in the *Rockford Register*,[20] which described it as "an exceedingly able address" characterized by "great felicity of language and illustration." Sturtevant explicitly denied the equality of the sexes, as usually understood. Nature has provided for contrasts in this as in other instances, and just as the two sexes wear different garments so too do they have different duties. The mingling of the sexes in the common schools is suitable but in the higher seminaries of learning they should be separated and engage in different studies. Experiments in coeducation have shown that the tension was too severe for one sex and too little for the other. Girls between the ages of fourteen and twenty-one should have rest and not labor.

Outlining the appropriate education for a woman, Sturtevant said that the first requisite is a thorough knowledge of the common language. A woman has a right to a home and the blessings of family life, and she should acquire the skills needed for her duties as wife and mother. Sturtevant had no sympathy with nunneries and cited Luther's marriage to a nun as his noblest action. He emphasized the importance of religious training in schools like Rockford and expressed the hope that Rockford Seminary would never try to be a college.

An especially important sermon was the one Sturtevant preached when his elder son, Julian Jr., was ordained on 5 July 1860 at the recently organized Congregational Church in Hannibal, Missouri. He also preached at the installation of Rev. C. C. Salter as minister of the Congregational Church in Kewanee. The new pastor was the son of C. J. Salter, a highly-respected deacon in the Waverly Congregational Church. The father had been a prominent lay religious leader in New Haven when Sturtevant was a student at Yale and the two men had become friends. Sturtevant no doubt had encouraged Salter to bring his family to Waverly.

Political Activity; Support for Lincoln

The population of Morgan County reached a little more than twenty-two thousand by 1860 and of that number one-fourth were residents of Jacksonville. By that year important segments of two railroads had been completed, connecting Jacksonville with Petersburg to the northeast and Manchester to the south. Sturtevant eagerly welcomed such improvements in transportation,[21] believing that they would provide "unprecedented" opportunities for growth which would result in higher land values. The College might yet become rich, he thought, from its real estate. However, that was predicated upon selling all the grounds except the immediate campus.

Jacksonville generally lived up to its reputation as a healthful place; it was spared the severe cholera epidemic which claimed thirty lives in Waverly in 1857—proportionately greater than the devastation in Jacksonville in 1833. The *St. Louis Intelligencer* paid the community high praise in 1857 when it commented editorially, "no city in the West has as great, if any an equal distinction with Jacksonville, Illinois, for her institutions of Charity and Learning. Among the latter, 'Illinois College,' stands eminent. It has a wide reputation and an organization now greatly extending that reputation." (SJ, 3 Aug. 1857) The College's continuing influence on education and government was extended by its many alumni who became teachers and public officials. When Newton Bateman, Class of 1843, proposed a local high school, Sturtevant and Sanders were instructed by the faculty to offer the College's assistance. The free public school law of 1855 added the power of state law and the public purse to the efforts to provide public education.

The faculty of the College was invited to St. Louis for the opening of Washington University in 1857. In August of 1858 Sturtevant went to Springfield to attend the Convention of American Instructors of the Deaf and Dumb. A senator expected to chair the meeting could not come and Sturtevant substituted for him. "He [filled] the post, as he does every other to which he is called, with ability. His remarks to the Convention, on taking the chair, were impressive and appropriate." (SJ, 14 Aug. 1858) Representatives from ten states were in attendance.

Two warmly-contested elections occurred in Jacksonville in 1857. One was an effort to abolish the anti-liquor ordinance, the other was to elect town trustees. Sturtevant insisted that he had nothing to do with either except to cast his own ballot. However, "the defeated clique said openly before the first of the two elections that I had governed Jacksonville long enough and declared their purpose to put me down." (S-B, 10 Apr. 1857) The opposition was soundly defeated in both elections and, Sturtevant declared, the corrupt faction had largely lost its power.

Jacksonville quite early gained the reputation as the home of the "abolitionist church" and the "abolitionist college." Several men prominent in that church, and most of the College faculty—some of them leaders in the church—were outspoken abolitionists. Added to these were several who as students had been derisively referred to as "abolitionist pups"; not surprisingly, the College was blamed for corrupting youth. Some of these same persons and ideas were instrumental in the formation of the Republican Party in Illinois. Paul Selby, Class of 1853 and editor of the *Morgan Journal,* issued a call in 1856 for editors to meet and join in opposition to the Nebraska policy. At this meeting Lincoln first publicly declared his support of the principles later adopted by the Republican Party. The same group of editors called for the Bloomington Convention in May 1856, the first Republican State Convention in Illinois. Among those attending that or a similar meeting in Springfield were several men who had previous or current connections with Illinois College or the Congregational Church or both.[22]

The formation of the Republican Party revived Sturtevant's hope, and he regarded it as significant in central and southern Illinois not only as a great political force but also as "a great moral upheaval."[23] Sturtevant was now emboldened to take a more active role in politics, and he wrote to Lincoln to encourage him to be a candidate for Congress in 1856. He said that, because of the country's great need for such a leader <u>now</u>, he was making no apology for "meddling with politics." He acknowledged that Lincoln did not need "the place—it can add nothing to your honors." He believed that Lincoln could be elected, although this was not a certainty. He assured Lincoln that, whether he were victorious or not, the effort would not damage his "political prospects." Indeed, "The friends of freedom in the State will none the less remember you...."

Admitting that he had "no political weight," Sturtevant declared that the convictions he expressed were those "of one who loves his country only too ardently for his own peace at the present crisis; of one who reposes full confidence in your integrity, your principles and your wisdom; one who regards you as providentially raised up for a time like this; and one who feels that should we even be beaten in this contest for the right, it would be some consolation that we had Hector for a leader."[24]

In his reply, Lincoln thanked Sturtevant for his "good opinion of me personally, and still more for the deep interest you take in the cause of our common country." He rebuked Sturtevant for thinking it necessary to suggest that such a move would further his own political career. That was assuming that he was "merely calculating the chances of personal advancement." Lincoln had decided not to run for office because he thought that it would "hurt, & not help the cause." He declared his willingness to make any personal sacrifice, but he was not willing to sacrifice the cause itself.[25]

In 1856 Sturtevant sought to make up for previous inaction on the political level and even campaigned for John C. Fremont. Reading a biography of the man disappointed Sturtevant's hope for an inspiring leader. However, he believed the party platform was based on righteous principles. (It had a strong anti-slavery plank, stronger even than the 1860 platform.) The *Illinois State Register* claimed that Sturtevant had given Fremont speeches all over the area and had told great lies about bleeding Kansas. The news account was certainly wrong regarding the latter point and likely had exaggerated the former statement. Democrat James Buchanan won the presidency "by the skin of his teeth." Sturtevant cited reports that he had pretended to adopt Republican principles, and he feared that Buchanan would likely favor the slavery party once he assumed office. He also believed that Buchanan's victory in Illinois was gained fraudulently. However, the state offices had been wrested "from the corrupt hands that have controlled [them] for twenty years" and that, he confided in Baldwin, was "almost glory enough." (S-B, 26 Nov. 1856) Later Sturtevant was concerned about Buchanan's administration because the Democrats did not seem to know whether Buchanan or Stephen Douglas was their master.

Extra-legal efforts to further the cause of emancipation troubled Sturtevant. Writing to his son, Warren, he promised to forward news accounts of "that infamous outbreak of folly and fanaticism at Harper's Ferry." He likely had read about that incident in the *Independent* for 20 October 1859. He feared that "the Slave power is in a fair way to have its revenge on a few misguided fanatics soon." Noting that [Senator] Palmer[26] was opposed to the provisions of the Kansas-Nebraska bill, Sturtevant believed his work was hindered by the Harper's Ferry incident.

Abraham Lincoln, about four years younger than Sturtevant, came to central Illinois with his family not long after the Connecticut Yankee began his life's work at Illinois College. Both grew up in frontier environments but otherwise were very different.

Lincoln was essentially self-taught, Sturtevant had two degrees from Yale. Lincoln's ability to overcome the limitations of his background was especially remarkable to Sturtevant. Significantly, both men were highly principled, and both had the determination and skill to achieve a chosen goal.

His friendship with Lincoln was a source of pride for Sturtevant. He may have had some influence upon Lincoln's thinking through some of the young men from the New Salem area who attended Illinois College. In any case Sturtevant could say, "I knew him intimately," long before Lincoln sought national office. He described Lincoln as "in the foremost rank among the most truth-loving men I have ever known.... His constant aim was to express truth.... He was a true and righteous man. This was the Moses whom God had raised up to lead his people out of Egyptian bondage, and yet he never had the advantage of the arts of civilization taught in the palace of Pharaoh. To have known Lincoln I esteem one of the greatest blessings of my early settlement on what was then the frontier of our civilization." (A, 286)

Sturtevant attributed Lincoln's power to persuade and lead people to his great candor, his deep sense of moral obligation, and his ability to grasp the great principles which underlie a free society. Lincoln's southern background, his origins among poor whites, and his ability to move southern people through his eloquence were providentially-determined factors which were basic to his greatness. Sturtevant noted the utter contrast between Lincoln and Stephen Douglas, who had come to Morgan County just a few years after Sturtevant. Douglas used his speaking ability to arouse people's emotions and prejudices with the intention of winning their support regardless of truth.

Writing in his *Autobiography* (287) decades later, Sturtevant recalled "as though it were but yesterday" the first speech he had heard from Lincoln on slavery. Lincoln addressed some two thousand people from Morgan and surrounding counties. He spoke guardedly, calling slavery a great evil but proposing simply to prevent its extension; in this manner he won support without offending people. Lincoln used an argument from what Sturtevant called "natural theology." The reason the Creator gave every man one mouth and two hands was that each was to live by his own labor and not that of others. "That day," Sturtevant emphasized, "I first learned that Abraham Lincoln was a great man."

On another occasion Sturtevant was at the railway station in Jacksonville when Lincoln, on his way to Winchester, got off the train. The two men walked together to the hotel a quarter of a mile away. Sturtevant remarked that Lincoln must be weary and Lincoln acknowledged that he was. He then expressed his determination to continue his efforts because he believed that if Douglas's position were accepted, Illinois would be a slave state in fifteen years. This thought anticipated the famous speech which Sturtevant heard Lincoln deliver in Springfield on 16 June 1858 in a room "filled to its utmost capacity with grave and thoughtful men." Sturtevant wrote, "I shall never forget my emotions as the tall form of our leader rose before us and he gave utterance to the memorable words: 'A house divided against itself can not stand.'" (A, 291; Mark 3:25) Lincoln declared that the government cannot endure half-slave and half-free. He did not expect the Union to be dissolved nor did he expect the house to fall. He did expect that it would cease to be divided; it would be all free or all slave. The Nebraska doctrine and the Dred Scott decision had set machinery in motion which if it continued would make slavery lawful everywhere.[27]

Lincoln was elected an honorary member of Phi Alpha Literary Society in January 1859 and of Sigma Pi a few months later. On 4 February of that year he lectured for Phi Alpha in Union Hall, the former Congregational Church building. Lincoln's topic was "Discoveries, Inventions, and Improvements." Realizing that the Society's hope for raising funds for its library were dashed by the small attendance, Lincoln offered to settle for his railroad fare from Springfield and fifty cents for his supper.[28]

Sturtevant had good news to report to Baldwin regarding the state ticket in 1860. Two graduates of Illinois College were candidates, Richard Yates ('35) for Governor and Newton Bateman ('43) for Superintendent of Public Instruction, and both were elected. Yates governed during the major part of the Civil War and thus could direct the great resources of Illinois to the support of Lincoln, the Union, and ultimately, emancipation. Sturtevant was attentive to developments in Washington also and told his son Warren the exciting news about the election of a Whig Republican as Speaker of the House of Representatives.

During the campaign of 1860 Sturtevant gave full support to Lincoln. Writing to Baldwin he declared, "We are all awake for Lincoln in these parts.... Lincoln is a true man, an honest man, and a great man, I do believe the very best representative of Republican principles whose name is before the American people." (S-B, 1 June 1860) Contrary to Herndon's claim that Lincoln was an unbeliever, Sturtevant regarded Lincoln as a Christian. He appreciated Lincoln's great honesty in refusing to avow creedal teachings of a church when he did not accept them and therefore never joined a church. Sturtevant explained this action as the result of failure to distinguish between being Christian in one's life and wrongly thinking that to be a Christian one must accept the theological doctrines espoused by a church. Sturtevant believed that although Lincoln never joined the Church, he gained in later years a better understanding of "the real meaning of faith in Christ" and "did very openly declare himself a Christian." Sturtevant stated the essence of being a Christian: "Christianity is not a system of metaphysical philosophy. It is 'repentance towards God and faith in our Lord Jesus Christ.'" It is "a just, practical, concrete conception" of character and life, not the theology of Calvin or the Episcopal Church. The church might learn from Lincoln what religion really is for the multitude. (A, 294,295)

Hardly anyone who was in the Republican Party expected that Lincoln's election to the presidency in 1860 would result in war.[29] On the other hand, most of those who advocated slavery or supported the South did expect it, and the people of Great Britain likewise believed that conflict would ensue. Sturtevant recalled that a large church conference was in session in Jacksonville when Lincoln's election was reported. A prominent churchman who supported Douglas wept openly, saying there would be war.

Endorsing the Abolitionist Cause

Sturtevant admittedly was behind others in becoming an abolitionist, partly because he desired to avoid involving the College in public controversies. Slavery was a horrible system and he had always hated it and wanted to end it; meanwhile he hoped it could be prevented from spreading. He long believed that the remedy was education, persuasion, and political action, not force. Only when he realized that a concerted effort to legalize slavery in all the states and territories was likely to succeed, did he openly support abolitionism. By the middle of the 1850s the need for direct action impelled Sturtevant to participate in the political process.

The *Independent* in November 1856 published a fairly long article, "Consistency," without attribution. Sturtevant admitted to Baldwin that he sustained "a parental relation" to it and this time had sent the article directly to the editor. (S-B, 26 Nov. 1856) Sturtevant was chagrined because there were so many mistakes but the fault was his own because the printer had been unable to read his "wretched hand writing." Despite such problems the item was significant because in it Sturtevant spoke out against a feature of slavery which perhaps was not obvious to many abolitionists, and he displayed a sensitivity to slaves as persons. He had read a recent article deploring the possibility that Utah might become a state despite its "fanatical and filthy" practice of polygamy. He sympathized with that writer's concern but, quoting the proverb that "consistency is a jewel," he spoke of a much greater evil, the fact that fifteen states denied the right to marry to a large proportion of their population. There was a grave prospect that the horrid system of slavery might be extended, perhaps on the ground that it was a domestic matter for each state to settle.

Christians must reject the claim that the pulpit and religious press should refrain from political issues. It was likely that polygamy would also soon be regarded as a forbidden topic. The fear of dissolving the Union must not be allowed to silence good men and leave either crime unrebuked. Once it is granted that Congress cannot legislate regarding "domestic institutions" there would be no way to eliminate either polygamy or slavery. "We are deciding this and all kindred questions *now* for ourselves and for posterity." Pulpit and press must speak out vigorously against that system in Utah and elsewhere which denies marriage to a large population.

In February 1857 the *Independent* published an essay under Sturtevant's name which also expressed his views about slavery although in a somewhat oblique manner. The opening paragraph demonstrated his skill in using language sharpened by wit and sarcasm to argue a case. An article in the *Edinburgh Review* had aroused the ire of U.S. Senators because it dealt with "that darkest of American questions, Negro Slavery." The reaction of the Senators was like that of hornets stirred up by frolicsome boys, said Sturtevant, but with added humiliation—the Senators could not sting those who annoyed them. Sturtevant advised them to keep cool because outside the slave-holding states, free speech and free printing could not be suppressed. "The discipline of the bludgeon and the bowie-knife is certainly admirable, most effectual where it can be applied. But the civilized world, outside of these fifteen American states, is so stupid as not to discern its beauty and moral fitness, and so unreasonable as not to submit to it, nor even to recognize the authority of Judge Lynch." Indeed, the literature of the world is against the "peculiar institution" of the Southern states.

Sturtevant's purpose was to respond to the attack in the *Review* on Mrs. Stowe's book, *Dred*. She was criticized for representing Southern society in one or two extreme characterizations. Sturtevant observed that similar objections had been made previously to the depiction of Simon Legree in *Uncle Tom's Cabin*. He insisted that in both books Mrs. Stowe had shown the great variety of persons involved in the slave system and did not seek to convince the reader that all were equally and extremely evil. He also defended Mrs. Stowe's peculiar inclusion in both works of a person who became almost angelic under the influence of the Gospel.

The reviewer said that Mrs. Stowe had grown up in a society produced by extreme Puritanism and that "professing Christians" of the northern cities were set apart from the rest of their society. Because the reviewer was himself an American Sturtevant believed his ignorance of American religion and society was inexcusable. Any American should know that the people of New England and New York were very familiar with Southerners. Many of the latter sent their sons to New England colleges, and "every watering-place in all the North swarms with Southern travelers and pleasure-seekers." Sturtevant himself could testify to knowing several Southerners who might have been the inspiration for some of Mrs. Stowe's characters. "New England religious people are not too Puritanical" to observe and report upon their more fashionable if less pious neighbors, declared Sturtevant. The reviewer would do well to note that Mrs. Stowe herself gave brilliance to the society in which she lived. Sturtevant said there may be greater intellectual breadth and more sympathy with universal humanity outside than inside the New York society praised by the reviewer.

Personal and Family Life

The Sturtevant household did not gain any new members during the years 1856-1860 and happily there were no losses by death. Significant changes occurred, however, as the two older sons matured and left the close family life of the home on Park Street. Numerous letters, exchanged between the parents and between them and the two sons, provide considerable information.

Almost every year Julian suffered from at least one bout of illness compelling him to lay aside all but the most pressing duties and occasionally even those; sometimes he was unable even to write to Baldwin. In the winter months of 1857 he experienced colds and coughs so severe as to be alarming. In the spring of 1859 Sturtevant felt run down; this time it was not illness but simply that he had been doing double or even treble duty. The stimulus of conversation with eastern men would help restore his vitality and he asked Baldwin for help in locating a summer vacancy in some pulpit so that he could pay travel expenses. His preference was for Boston because it was further north. However, he went to New York to supply the pulpit of Broadway Tabernacle when his friend, J. P. Thompson, took his vacation. In 1860 the summer heat persisted for weeks and Sturtevant was too debilitated to do anything of importance. By mid-September the weather was cooler and he expected to resume work.

Hannah expressed her concern for his well-being to her husband even more bluntly than before. She wrote, "These continued drains of thought & time towards the pecuniary interests of the Institution are more than you can endure much longer, I am sure. To me it seems wrong to waste the energies of your best days in this manner any longer. I will not say wrong but a matter greatly to be regretted." (1 May 1857) Hannah's own responsibilities were made heavier by Julian's extended absences. The children suffered the usual childhood diseases, such as the measles which they contracted in the spring of 1857. Hannah herself nearly died from an illness in May 1859.

While in Quincy in April 1858 Julian had written urging Hannah to

employ such help as she needed for the spring work. "When the College
pays me I surely can use money more freely for our family expenses than
I have been." A week later, in a letter from St. Louis, he pleaded with her.
"I suppose you are cleaning house and bring yourself quite to exhaustion
every day. I beg you will not do it. I would rather the house should be
dirty." And yet he followed immediately with a proposal which could
only have increased her duties. Sturtevant suggested a plan for improving the family's finances by taking in student roomers. If he would put a
furnace in the cellar and gas in all the rooms, he and Hannah could take
his study for their room and he would use the downstairs room for a
study. The other front room downstairs could be used for their parlor.
They could rent the two garrets, the boys' room, and their room, to students. They would furnish fuel and lights and charge the students about
$1.00 per week each. The students would use the back stairs and the
south door so they would not interfere with the family. "We can add in
that way some three hundred dollars to our income. What do you say?"
There is no record of Hannah's response but surely she said no.

During Sturtevant's absences his wife occasionally had to deal
with College affairs and always had to supervise the household, garden, livestock, and farm. The cost of feeding the family had been
increased by inflation. On a Saturday in late April 1857 flour was
$7 a barrel but by Monday the price had risen to $8.50; beef was 12
1/2 cents. Hannah did not think they could continue to board their
nephew, Edward Fayerweather, for $3 per week. Hannah reported
that Warren and Antonio had made two attempts to drive cattle
they had for sale but both times Mr. Strawn was not at home and
they could not obtain payment. In early May Hannah described
their many chores. "We are getting on with our affairs, farming, gardening, housecleaning, etc., much after our usual way. Don't you
feel it a relief not to be here at this important season of the year? Our
peach trees are now in bloom & the pear trees are coming out very
full. I can't tell how the apple or plum trees will be." Hannah added
that the strawberries had not been doing well but that the raspberries gave promise of an abundant yield. The asparagus was nearly
dead but Mr. Turner had given her some young roots to replace it.
The ground had been very dry and the pasture was so poor it could
not be used, with the result that they were getting low on feed.

Whenever father departed on a trip he gave James Warren a series of assignments and added to the list by mail. Writing from Providence, Rhode Island, in April 1857 Sturtevant instructed his son to plant the Chinese sugar cane seeds; when he came home he would bring a new variety of beans. Warren was to save room in the garden for fifty hills of beans and squash. In April 1858 Sturtevant sent instructions from Chicago for Antonio to plow when the weather permitted and then plant grain right away. Antonio was to cover the corn heap so it would not spoil; the price of corn had gone up and it was now worth money.

When Warren was away his father wrote to him about the family, the church, and especially the farm and livestock. In the early summer of 1858 he reported that the Hungarian grass had been sown and the potatoes planted, the corn was up, the wheat looked fine, and the pasture was well-fenced. Because of the rain the prospects for the garden were excellent. Only one problem, the perennial one, plagued them—Antonio's inefficiency. The family missed Warren very much and not only because of his worthiness as a worker.

When absent in early August 1859 the elder Sturtevant sent instructions to his son to sell any corn that could be spared right away because the price was bound to fall. He advised him to return a lame horse to the seller, and a few weeks later he directed Warren to buy three or four small hogs. After returning home, and when Warren was again away, Sturtevant wrote in the fall to ask how much of the wheat they were to receive from their tenant farmer. He reported finding a shorter road to obtain their firewood on the south side of the Willow branch and they now had fourteen loads. Antonio was at work digging the potatoes. Alfred, nearly nine years old, could ride any of the horses and drove the cows to and from the pasture every day.

The next winter was severe and all the wheat was killed. Anticipating the crop failure Sturtevant at first expected to rent out the land. My mid-March 1860 he decided he had enough of managing a farm in addition to his other duties, and he told Warren he had no time for it any more; was it safe, he asked, to wait to dispose of the land until Warren came home?

Some carpentry work was needed on the Park Street house in 1859. The itemized bill included 17 hours of joiner's work at $1.75, 370 feet of lumber at 3 1/2 cents per foot, and hardware and painting, $14.50, for a total $57.20. The valuations and taxes on the Sturtevants' real estate continued to soar, especially with regard to state, county, and school taxes. For those governmental units the Sturtevants' real estate was valued at $7,920 and their tax bill (paid in 1859) amounted to $101.08. The corporation tax for that year added about $20. The Federal Census for 1860 reported the value of Sturtevant's real property as $11,000 and his personal property at $800.

Julian Monson Sturtevant Jr. was the only son to follow in the path of the father although not his very footsteps. After graduation from the College in 1854 he was assistant to Newton Bateman in the West Jacksonville Public School, and the following year he instructed in the Preparatory Department of the College. In the fall of 1856 he enrolled in Andover Theological Seminary in Massachusetts, one of the first such seminaries to be established separately from a college. It was a "rigorously orthodox" school, its faculty creed representing the "quintessence of New England Calvinism."[30] There were additional reasons for selecting Andover. Professor Calvin Stowe was married to Harriet Beecher, who of course was well known to the family; students were warmly welcomed to their home. Many relatives of Julian Sr. and Hannah lived in Connecticut and New York, and some of them provided not only hospitality during vacation periods but valuable assistance in obtaining preaching assignments and other employment. Julian Jr. shared a seminary room with the son of Romulus Barnes, a member of the New Haven Band. They were visited by Theron Baldwin and his son, a student at Phillips Academy. Baldwin remarked to Sturtevant, "so there were together three sons of members of the Illinois Association—verily we get along in the world." (B-S, 6 Jan. 1857)

During the spring vacation of his first year Julian Jr. spent several weeks working for the Hartford City Mission. After his father visited him there he wrote to his mother, "I enjoyed, you cannot tell how much, a visit from father." Julian Jr. called on Dr. Horace Bushnell, pastor of an important church in Hartford, and was "very much interested in a long theological discussion" into which Bushnell drew him.[31] In the winter and spring of 1858 Julian Sr. was engaged in the intensive effort to complete the Fifty-Thousand Dollar Fund. Writing to his mother, the son expressed anxiety about his father's "trying and laborious life and his recent affliction (Oh how I should feel to loose [*sic*] my father.) & wanted to write to him my love & my sympathy but have not found time or felt that I knew how." (17 May 1858) Receiving word that the Fund drive had been completed successfully, he wrote to his father to express his great joy.

The son responded to his father's request for detailed information regarding the senior professors at the seminary, and the father complied with the son's request for help in preparing a book list for a course. Julian Jr. informed his father about publications of interest to both. When a "mean little" article appeared in the *Boston Recorder* about father's essay on American Protestantism he had commented, "That article of Father's seems to stick in the throats of all the conservatives wonderfully." (21 June 1858) In his letters the son agreed with his father that revivals are a manifestation of God's saving grace. Also, he was inclined to agree that all who loved Jesus Christ in sincerity and truth should be invited to the Lord's table.

Considering the high standard which his father set by example as well as by word, Julian Jr. sometimes felt woefully inadequate. In an undated letter to his father he confessed, "I am so weak & wicked that it seems as if I never should be fitted as you say you desire for the work of the Christian ministry. Do pray for me." He made no secret of his keen desire to visit his family before completing his seminary studies. He wrote to his mother that he had tried and would continue to try to "keep the chain tight that binds me to [father]." (17 May 1858) When he received the very welcome news that father advised him to come home, he replied that nothing would make him happier than to see his family again. It would be so nice to sing with the girls and to see the familiar places. His visit home awakened interest in his father's early years and he regretted that he never had enough time to talk with father. He asked for copies of his father's discourse about the founding of the College to give to friends who had requested them.

In a private letter the father advised his son to undertake the "study of woman." A few months later the son reported that he had now seen and studied a good many young women, but "all of them were either persons whom my judgment condemned or else persons whom I could not love." His conclusion was, "I don't think any of them will do."

Dependent on his father for most of his funds, Julian Jr. worked part-time as a chaplain at Phillips Academy and at a state prison and occasionally did some preaching. Near the end of his third and final year he assisted Baldwin, sometimes speaking in two churches on the Sabbath in presenting the case for aiding the western colleges. Baldwin wrote, "I was greatly pleased with him—with his views—his spirit—his intelligence & his wide awake appearance." (5 May 1859) Sturtevant responded, "You speak kindly of my boy. We hope good of him." (13 May 1859)

Julian Jr. anticipated his father's presence at his graduation exercises and was pleased to learn that his sister Hannah would also be present. The proud father said that of four student speakers, only one was first-rate—Julian Jr. Indeed, his piece was the best the father had heard anywhere and he had recently been at Beloit and Yale. Julian, he said, was profound in thought and just in his reasoning; he had manifested "a far-reaching perception of principles and [was] very forcible in delivery." The other speeches were "dull-dull." (3 Aug. 1859)

About the end of September 1859 Julian Jr. set out for Illinois, apparently accompanied by sister Hannah. He had been corresponding with the Congregational Church in Jacksonville about filling the vacant pulpit there for one year but, aware of opposition, he declined. He accepted an invitation to supply the church for a limited time and served it for about six months. Julian Sr. told Warren that the women of the family felt keenly the ill-natured things some people in the church were saying about Julian Jr. and so he thought it best for him to leave. Julian Jr. agreed and preached as a candidate at the new Congregational Church in Hannibal, Missouri. Julian Jr. received assurances that his anti-slavery position was known and accepted by the Hannibal congregation and he became their pastor; most of the congregation were Northerners or sympathetic to such views.[32]

In later years Julian Jr. compared himself with his father. He regarded himself as more understanding and more pastorally oriented; he was less strict, less ordered, and more compassionate. He was quite sensitive about his father's limitations in dealing with the family, limitations which arose from overwhelming devotion to the cause of Illinois College. However, the son was restrained and respectful in his comments and did not want anyone to think ill of his father.

James Warren was in the Class of 1856 at Illinois College and was appointed tutor in the Preparatory Department for the following year at a salary of $450. He taught in the school at Rushville for the year 1857-1858 and complained much about its problems. His cousin Warren DeForest Sturtevant, teaching at a different school, became involved in a quarrel at the boarding house where both men took their meals. The Jacksonville Sturtevants cautioned their son not to let his cousin draw him into the controversy and recommended that he not remain at Rushville. He was urged above all to take a stand as a religious man, an injunction indicating that he was not yet converted. In the fall James Warren accepted a warm invitation from the school at Danville but felt somewhat overwhelmed. His father assured him of the family's confidence and reminded him that he was prone to being gloomy and overly sensitive to his inadequacies.

The Sturtevants wanted Hannah Augusta to have a year away from home, and there was some thought that she might prepare for teaching music. That had to be accomplished economically because for three years expenses had exceeded income. An exchange with the Baldwins was proposed; Hannah Augusta would live with them in New Jersey, and the Baldwins' son would come to Illinois College. Apparently the plan was not feasible.

Lucy became a member of the Congregational Church by profession of faith. In early February 1860 Alfred, replying to a letter from his brother Warren, told him about the livestock and his studies and said he was reading the Life of B. Franklin. The tableaux party was at the Academy the next evening and Alfred would be in two scenes, Ichabod Crane's school and Rip Van Winkle. He also had news about a wedding; when Pa married a couple in the church after the prayer meeting only Ma and Lucy saw it, and the couple's folks only knew about it afterward.[33]

Edward Tanner, the much younger cousin of Julian Sr., had been a part of the Sturtevant family for some years. In 1857 he graduated from Illinois College, the salutatorian of his class. The following year he had a teaching position at Mud Prairie, near his birthplace, Waverly.

Julian's father wrote to him in October 1857 to acknowledge receiving two recent letters and the sum of $6.28. He felt his life was coming to an end and he did not expect to see any of his children many times more. "I want, if I cannot see you, you should let me hear from you often." He had read Julian's missionary sermon three times and judged it to be "a very important discourse." Warren rejoiced that his grandson was doing so well in his preparation "for the great work of the gospel ministry." Sturtevant's father died on 29 April 1858 at the age of 78 and was buried in Tallmadge beside his first wife.

Julian's older brother, Ephraim, continued to live on a farm in East Cleveland, Ohio. A widower twice, he had two sons and a daughter, the children of his second wife. The daughter, Helen Louisa, may have been the Helen Sturtevant who joined the Congregational Church in Beardstown in 1855 and died there the following year.[34] The older son, Warren DeForest, arrived uninvited at the Jacksonville Sturtevants' home in October 1858. He came "to tarry," having sent a very heavy trunk by stage. The family was not pleased.

Julian's sister, Huldah Hinman, and his brother Christopher, with his family, were both living in Beardstown. Christopher in 1857 became secretary of the new Springfield, Keokuk and Warsaw Railroad. In June 1858 Christopher and other citizens of Cass County gathered to protest Federal policies regarding slavery. He was a delegate to the State Republican Convention that year. In March 1860 Christopher's wife, Ann, died of consumption after an illness of several months. Julian described the funeral service and said it was a most melancholy day. His daughters went to Meredosia the next day, to be met there by Christopher's carriage and taken to Beardstown to spend a week or two with the family. About the same time sister Huldah, the last survivor of her own family, also died at Beardstown, from typhoid pneumonia.

Hannah Sturtevant's sister, Julia Chamberlain, and her family continued to reside near Jacksonville, and brother James and his family were still in Iowa. Abraham Fayerweather's eldest daughter in Hawaii, Julia H. Fayerweather Afong, wrote to her aunts in Jacksonville in February 1860. She informed them that she had been married for three years and had one daughter and one son. Mrs. Afong said they had not had a letter from any of their dear aunts in a long time and hoped to hear from them.[35]

Chapter 7: 1861-1865

The Civil War Years:
Involvement in National Issues

Troubled Times

In early 1861 Julian Sturtevant was apprehensive that the North would make concessions which would strengthen slavery. He was especially fearful that a national convention might tinker with the Constitution, and he hoped that God would enable Lincoln to stand firmly on his principles. Echoing Lincoln, he told Baldwin he was "most deeply impressed with the belief that we cannot have a country half slave and half free...." Writing late in the afternoon on 4 March he noted that there was still no report by telegraph about the inauguration at Washington. He admitted to having an "apprehensive foreboding of evil," although the Union flag was flying all over Jacksonville and gave it a festive appearance. The *Springfield State Journal* had published its strongest anti-slavery article yet with the declaration that slavery will be ended in civil strife and blood. (S-B, 4, 12 Feb., 4 Mar. 1861) Sturtevant prayed that God might spare his dear country.

The outbreak of armed conflict between the North and South brought into sharp focus the cultural tensions which had been present in Jacksonville for decades. Paradoxically, in Illinois Stephen Douglas from Vermont became the spokesman for the South, while Lincoln from Kentucky was encouraged in his support of freedom by the New Englanders in Jacksonville and northern Illinois. That both major presidential candidates in 1860 had lived in central Illinois testified to the importance the state had achieved.

The people of central Illinois were now even more heterogeneous because of immigrants from Germany, Ireland, and elsewhere. The

New England population no longer dominated local politics and in 1861 the town voted to permit the sale of liquor. By the next year there were twenty licensed grog-shops and in addition billiard parlors, bowling alleys, and brothels—all deemed unfortunate consequences of the relaxation of temperance.

The sharp division between the Northern and Southern sympathizers was expressed in their different political parties and in the newspapers which served as their media. The Republican party was the political organ of New Englanders who were anti-slavery if not outright abolitionist in their convictions, while the Democratic party included some "copperheads" who opposed the War. A local Democratic newspaper gave sarcastic praise to "loyal" citizens who were encouraged to prove that loyalty by volunteering in response to Lincoln's call for three hundred thousand more men in the fall of 1863. It also castigated the "abolition jollification" held at Strawn's Hall, where J. B. Turner allegedly confused democrats with the copperheads and declared that Lincoln should have shot half the copperheads of Morgan County and hung the rest. "Such is Lincoln abolition." (JC, 3 Nov. 1984)

With the beginning of hostilities most of the people of Jacksonville, whatever their origin, were united in their support of the Union effort. The town always met its quota of soldiers without resorting to the draft. Volunteers were encouraged by public enthusiasm and pride and by bounties (from both private and public funds) which rose from $50 to $500 for each man who signed up. Yet there were expressions of harsh feelings and occasionally threats of violence. After a full-scale Fourth of July celebration in 1861, the tensions were so great that no public observance was held for the next three years. Harassment of Southern sympathizers and warnings against Copperheads were not uncommon, while the office of the Republican newspaper was twice the object of arson attacks. Not until 1865 was it possible to organize a community celebration on Independence Day. That year fifteen to twenty thousand people from Jacksonville and the surrounding area came to the fairgrounds for a gala celebration of the founding and preservation of the Union. (Doyle, 232-41)

The College's Struggle for Survival

The dual effort of preserving the Union and abolishing slavery required much of loyal citizens. More than two hundred alumni and students of Illinois College answered the call for military service. Richard Yates, the first graduate, was Governor throughout most of the Civil War years and guided the state in supplying the manpower and resources so desperately needed for victory.

The War inevitably had a serious impact on enrollment. In 1860-1861 the total enrollment was 119 students, nearly a hundred of them College men. The faculty met on 12 April 1861, the day Fort Sumter was attacked, and asked the president to notify students that "College exercises are not and will not be suspended in consequence of excitement attending military operations." Soon afterwards twenty-six College and preparatory students enlisted. By the fall of 1862 over fifty students had entered military service and Sturtevant confided wearily to Baldwin that the College had been called "to bear a heavy part in the calamities of our country...." (S-B, 18 July 1862) In 1863 Sturtevant found it necessary to deny rumors in the East that the State of Illinois would forsake the Union cause. His ironic explanation to Baldwin was forceful: it was "the hotheads proclaiming reason at Springfield" who made that prediction. Sturtevant insisted that they were not representative. (S-B, 12 Jan. 1863)

In February 1863 Sturtevant told Baldwin that if the War continued and new calls were made for men to join the army, there might be so few students that the College could not operate. He suggested suspending operations and adding the income of four to five thousand dollars to the endowment. He cautioned Baldwin that this was strictly between the two of them, adding "I have never breathed it here, not even in my own bed chamber." (S-B, 23 Feb. 1863) Baldwin responded with the warning not to mention the idea to anyone; the College should continue even if it were reduced to the number of students with which Sturtevant began thirty-three years before. He often passed on information about victories and comments on the political aspects of the conflict. He remarked that "we little thought when we entered Illinois in 1829 that in 1861 a President-elect would leave it for the nation's capital to inaugurate governmental changes not inferior in importance to our Revolution itself." (B-S, 11 Jan. 1861)

The Class of 1861, numbering sixteen men, was the largest to that date and was not exceeded until 1880. At the exercises in June 1862 diplomas were awarded to ten seniors, one of them absent because of military service. Several orations were directly related to the Civil War, among them, "Can this Government Exist Permanently Half Slave and Half Free?" and—the valedictory address—"The Conditions of National Peace." The alumni were addressed by Rev. J. M. Sturtevant Jr. of Hannibal, Missouri, in a meeting at the Congregational Church. His subject was "Equality in Relation to Democracy." (JJ, 26 June 1862) Despite the circumstances, the commencement was described as idyllic. The exercise was held in Strawn's Hall (Opera House), a large auditorium used for concerts, lectures, and public meetings.[1] The doors were opened to admit only the ladies at a quarter after eight and already a large number had gathered. At nine the procession formed at the Congregational Church and the faculty, trustees, friends of the graduates, and the graduates proceeded to Strawn's Hall; by half-past nine the hall was filled. The students' orations were described as "first rank," not only in presentation but in content. The ladies, well supplied with flowers, cast bouquets and wreaths upon each speaker as he left the stage.

That Class could have numbered fourteen. Before conferring the ten diplomas Sturtevant explained that four other young men of acknowledged scholarship and good character were supposed to deliver orations and graduate. Professor Sanders had accepted the orations submitted by three of them, but they refused to participate unless he also approved the fourth oration. He had judged that one to be "political" and unsuitable to the occasion. (CH, 198-99) The faculty had a copy of it, the president said, and any one who wished "could examine it himself and judge of the correctness of the Professor's estimate of it." (JJ, 26 June 1862)

For the second time students had raised the issue of free speech on the Illinois College campus. Their effort is of special interest because of Sturtevant's consistent and vigorous defense of freedom of speech for himself and the faculty. The records are virtually silent in this matter, partly because the Faculty Minutes for a period during and after the War have long been missing. Also there is a six-months' gap in the correspondence between Baldwin and Sturtevant in the first half of 1862 and there are only ten letters for the remainder of the year. Writing to Baldwin on 18 July 1862, Sturtevant gave a surprising explanation of why he had not written; it was because he had nothing of interest to write. Contradicting himself, he declared that the year had been "one of more than ordinary difficulty, and perplexity." Moreover, "the pressures of every day's cares and burden and sometimes sorrows, have been as much as I could bear." He cited several examples: the country's plight, the reduced enrollment, and the difficult situation at the local Congregational Church. Also, his family was in financial straits due to unpaid salary, now $2,500 in arrears. He did not mention the protest regarding free speech.

The *Jacksonville Sentinel*, however, provided ample coverage. The editor, remarking that this was the same issue as the Springer case, said that the faculty encouraged "republican" sentiments while suppressing "democratic" views. Springer and the four students in the 1862 controversy were all members of Phi Alpha. According to the Society's 1890 *Catalogue*, "During the War there was a strong Democratic element in the society, and although the debates and decisions were not disloyal, they did not always uphold President Lincoln." (CH, 209) The *Sentinel* reported that the four students, at the request of prominent men in the city, hired the same hall and delivered their speeches at 3:00 P.M., after the regular commencement was over. The lengthy statement which the students had distributed as a handbill was also printed in the newspaper. The *Sentinel* continued to publish stories about the incident for the next several weeks and newspapers in the area also publicized it.[2] All four students were eventually awarded diplomas, the last one not until 1891.

President Sturtevant upheld the freedom of the College from ecclesiastical control as well as the right of the faculty to discuss, discretely, any theological topic. President Rammelkamp in his *Centennial History* explained the restrictions on student expressions as necessarily and justifiably stronger in 1862 because of the Civil War. For Sturtevant and his colleagues slavery was more than a political issue. It was a *moral* issue and indeed a *religious* issue, because slavery was contrary to Christian principles of brotherhood and equality. In 1862 the nation was embroiled in war because of slavery and the situation called for firm resolve. It was a moral necessity to distinguish the College from the "democratic" stance which was strong in the area.

In 1861 the College's financial situation was so desperate that the western part of the College grounds was rented for hog pasturage. Sturtevant and Baldwin continued sparring with Henry Ward Beecher to get him to fulfill his pledge, and over the next few years payments of several hundred dollars were sent. In 1869 Sturtevant bluntly inquired of Baldwin, "Can Plymouth Church be made to fork over?" (S-B, 7 June 1869) The eventual answer was negative; the Beecher professorship was never established.

A few months before the Civil War erupted, Sturtevant advised Baldwin that "our College was never half so truly prosperous as now. There is only one draw-back. Our subscriptions are not paid." (S-B, 4 Feb. 1861) His ironic tone hinted at the hardship the faculty endured because their salaries were in arrears. The gratifying success of the "$58,000" subscription in 1858 was dimmed by the slow receipt of *cash;* as of November 1863 little more than $30,000, had been collected. There was temporary relief both for the College and the faculty in the midst of the War. Hannah sent the good news to her husband in England: "Your salary for the year has been entirely paid, [Judge Berdan] having just sent to me a check for $200 & something more, and the other professors also, to within $20.... Dr. Whipple has been more successful than usual in collecting the endowment fund, & Judge Berdan thinks the College will hereafter be able to pay the back salaries...." (22 June 1863)

Subscribers not only were slow to pay but sometimes voided their pledges because of lack of funds. There were other problems. In May 1864 the College had $5,000 to be invested but it was very difficult to loan money at any rate of interest; that fall, when lending was possible, interest was a mere two per cent. Major gifts were made even less likely because of the rapid decline in the price of gold. The College had to undertake a determined campaign or surrender the cause. The faculty agreed they would not "give up the ghost" without another effort.

A long-continued quest for a large donation involved the inventor, Azel Lyman, a graduate of the Class of 1842. Lyman, a member of Beecher's church, had previously mentioned giving stock in railroad cars and then in 1857 suggested stock in an experimental gun he was developing. The beginning of the Civil War and the use of iron-clad ships gave promise that Lyman's "accelerating gun" would be very valuable because the projectiles could penetrate heavy armor. Periodically Baldwin informed Sturtevant of Lyman's work and the prospects for obtaining funds for Illinois College. At Lyman's request Sturtevant wrote a letter introducing him to Lincoln, and Lincoln personally authorized a test of Lyman's gun in the Washington Navy Yard. The invention was recognized as a serious threat to investors who had put millions into the new ships and someone sabotaged a crucial trial. The hope for a substantial gift was never fulfilled.[3] Lyman's career as a scientist and inventor was reported in the *Scientific American* when he died in 1885.

In 1862 the editor of the *New Englander* requested Sturtevant to write a major article presenting the case for the moral claim of the western colleges on the "Wealthy." Sturtevant distinguished between two kinds of objects for charitable giving and the funding appropriate for each. The societies for distributing Bibles and religious tracts are well-served by annual donations, but colleges must have the assurance of permanent endowment which requires large donations. Alluding to Tocqueville, Sturtevant noted that some believe that democracy tends toward an equality which not only lifts up the lowly but depresses the superior, resulting in "the dull monotonous level of mediocrity." (84) A true university must include all the departments of learning—literature, science, and art—because "the republic of letters" is a unity having one aim, "to cultivate, adorn, and enrich the mind." (92)

The question was whether a democratic society, having the best system of universal education at the basic levels, could match the university standards achieved even by the poorest European monarchies. The government which sustains popular education cannot be expected to pay for the college education which only the few will receive. And yet such an education should be within "the reach of any gifted and enterprising mind, though born and reared in poverty and toil." (91) The only recourse is to seek "the liberal contributions of the wealthy" for the endowment of first-rate colleges. (86) The man with great wealth will want to provide adequately but not abundantly for his family because inherited wealth is dissipated by later generations. The best cause to which a large legacy can be devoted is a college and such a gift is "the noblest monument which any man can rear to his own memory." (96) Unfortunately, Sturtevant's logic and persuasion did not produce a large gift for Illinois College.

The Faculty Minutes for February 1861 recorded additional suggestions for improving the singing in the Chapel. The annual observance of the fast day for colleges was planned and Sturtevant consulted with the pastors of the town churches regarding their participation. In February 1863 the College experienced a heightened religious interest which continued for two weeks, with some "hopeful conversions." Baldwin included in the College Society's 1863 *Report* excerpts of Sturtevant's letter of 23 February. Most students were involved to some degree in the daily prayer meetings. "You will join with us," Sturtevant urged, "in thanking God, that in a time of so much darkness and gloom, He has cheered us by such a boon...." (SPC-20, 71)

One last attempt was made to establish a chair in theology. Sturtevant was named Professor of Didactic Theology in May 1865 and was directed to arrange and deliver appropriate lectures. He waived any increase in salary for the extra duties but would receive the interest from the Spring Legacy Fund. That sum was far short of an endowed professorship, and there was some question whether the arrangement met the terms of the Legacy. A year later the trustees rescinded the action and also Sturtevant's appointment to that professorship.

An Advocate for Freedom

Sturtevant addressed the Alumni Association at Yale a few months after the War began. He interpreted the national conflict as the means God chose to impress some lessons upon the

American people. Four vices had been growing rapidly and he believed Providence intended to eradicate them through the present adversity. First was the view that Christians must never resort to the use of force to resist evil. The Old Testament provided examples of the righteous use of force not only in war but also in punishing criminals. History teaches that "To refuse to bear arms in defence [*sic*] of a free and just government, to neglect to exert force for the defense of the innocent [and] the punishment of crime, is for society to abdicate its highest function, and give over this world to the rule of anarchists and despots." The divinely promised "long reign of peace on earth [will come] by effecting such changes in the social, political and moral condition of the world, through the dissemination of freedom, instruction, and a pure Christian faith, as shall render a long reign of peace and justice possible." (7)

Even more harmful was the prevalence of self-indulgence. Men, and especially women, regarded everything they could imagine as utter necessities and consequently charity was dried up. The present war would surely develop habits of self-discipline and self-sacrifice. "A third vicious tendency" (11) was the lack of respect for a strong national government, illustrated in the disgraceful situation requiring Lincoln to slip into the nation's capital "unattended and unknown, under the cover of the friendly darkness of the night...." (12) Tocqueville had discerned the unique quality of American government as both national and federal. However, Sturtevant said, he did not realize that once such a federation establishes a national government the individual states are no longer free to withdraw at will. America's government is in some respects national, the government having limited powers over individuals, and in some respects a federation, with the states having certain other powers—also limited—over individuals.

The fourth vice in which America had indulged was perhaps the most dangerous. It was the lack of "loyalty to right, to changeless eternal justice." (18) Justice and God's laws are superior to the will of the people and "as truly limit the power of popular majorities however numerous, as of crowned despots." (19) Any nation contravening God's principles of right and justice for all creatures, including the red man and the black man and even animals, will meet God as their avenger. "[A] free nation is not one in which the majority rules and may do what it pleases, and all it pleases, but one in which justice is done to every man, and if possible to every brute and every insect.... Our freedom must rest on the everlasting foundations of justice—justice to men of all colors and conditions," the rich and the poor, the weak and the strong. (20-21)

This vision of the future did not portray a domineering North nor a subjugated South. It was the prospect of blessedness in which "the relation of the white man, the heaven appointed lord of our soil, to the African, hewer of our wood and drawer of our water, [will be] adjusted on principles of equity and mercy to both...." People will again behold the flag of the Union as symbolic of freedom. Sturtevant could see "a regenerated nation moving on in sublime majesty to take possession of a continent in the name of freedom, of justice, and of God." (21)

Writing in the *Independent* in June 1862 Sturtevant warned of the danger of intervention on behalf of the South by the two greatest nations on earth, France and England. Despite the risk of involving them, the North could not compromise with the slave interests. Reconciling the opposing forces would be like mixing oil and water, right and wrong, God and Satan. The hoped-for restoration of the peaceful enjoyment of Constitutional freedom made "the destruction of slavery [a] military necessity."[4]

A meeting which President Lincoln held in early 1862 with members of Congress from the slave-holding border states led Sturtevant to reflect that there was no significant difference between Southerners avowing states' rights and those protesting interference with property rights. He believed both groups sought to shield the system of slavery from the freedom of thought and speech which the Constitution secures. Slavery had reduced one-third of the population from the status of persons to that of chattels. The iniquitous system had been safe so long as Northern men wore padlocks on their lips, but now those men were speaking out. The success of the Republican party in the 1860 election made it clear to the South that the Union would be preserved and the principles of the Constitution upheld.[5]

Sturtevant was invited to address "the great war meeting of Christians, representing all denominations," in Chicago's Bryan

Hall on 7 September 1862. The purpose was to endorse a "memo-rial" calling upon President Lincoln to emancipate the slaves. Speaking to a large audience, Sturtevant declared: "The most fundamental and essential thing in our glorious free government is its sacred guarantee of the moral freedom of the human soul, the right of every human being to think, to believe, to utter all truth, to vindicate all righteousness and protest against all wrong under Heaven." The early acceptance of slavery had unfortunately con-tradicted that promise, and thus "The rebellion commenced the day the Constitution was adopted." Sturtevant had become aware of that contradiction during his student days at Yale when utter silence regarding slavery was enforced by the threats of personal violence from Southern youths. There was no use seeking to conciliate slavery, and the argument that slavery was in the best interest of the Negro must be rejected. "Do we hesitate to break his yoke lest we should harm him? He asks of us no such croco-dile tears in this hour. God is telling us [that] we cannot hold him in bondage any longer…. [N]ow is the accepted time; …this is the day of our national salvation."[6]

The audience was immense and there were "oft repeated out-bursts of applause, which not even the sanctity of a Sabbath evening could repress." The memorial to Lincoln was adopted by a unanimous rising vote, and the assembly concurred that putting down the rebellion was "as obvious a Christian duty as prayer, preaching, charity to the poor, or missions to the heathen."

President Sturtevant was more willing to participate in political affairs when the candidates and office-holders were men he knew and trusted. Governor Richard Yates had sent him an urgent request in mid-September 1862. He was going to attend a governors' conference in Pennsylvania and he wanted his mentor's views on the present terrible crisis. Sturtevant responded promptly, expressing his ardent conviction that the slaves must be emancipated. He declared that the war was "*inevitable, a logical necessity of our history.*" He extended the provisions of the Constitution; he interpreted it as intending "to guarantee and perpetuate freedom—freedom of thought, utterance and action—the individual moral freedom of every man." Yet wherever the forces of slavery held power or undue influence, these constitutional provisions had been nulli-

fied. The Union had but one enemy and it was not the South nor
Jefferson Davis but slavery. The news must be conveyed to both
masters and slaves throughout the South that the Federal
Government was committed to the cause of universal freedom.
Loyal masters should be compensated, so far as possible.
Sturtevant prayed to "the God of our Fathers" to give the nation
wisdom, holy energy, and courage "to direct all the storm and fury
of war . . . till freedom triumphs, and a peace is established on the
durable foundations of justice to all men."7

In an essay on the African Race in America Sturtevant looked
beyond the current struggle to consider the consequences of
emancipation for those who would be freed.8 He analyzed the
ambivalence of Northerners regarding the African Americans.
People who in conscience favored emancipation shrank from
advocating it publicly because they opposed equality on the social
level. For example, marriage should be possible among all citizens,
and any man should be able to rise to the highest office. The people
of African descent were separated not only by slavery but by
color,9 a trait so marked "that a small taint of the blood of the
servile class can be detected with unerring certainty." (601)
Sturtevant concluded that "the masses of the people never will consent to a political and social equality with the negro [sic] race." (603)

The public must acknowledge emancipation as essential to
restoring and perpetuating the Union. But how can people be
reassured that emancipation will not lead to the fusion of the two
races—or a war of the races on our own soil? Colonization was an
acceptable solution, but it was inadequate to the urgency of the
present crisis. Fortunately the laws of nature established by the
Creator make possible a different outcome. When two unequal
groups come together, the result will be either amalgamation—which
is detrimental to the stronger group, or absorption—causing the
lesser group to disappear. Resorting to purple prose, Sturtevant
asserted that the rare occurrence of intermarriage with Negroes or
Indians is regarded as monstrous; moreover, the progeny are
regarded as part of the inferior group. It is evident from American
history that "even the Indian perishes, for the most part, not
by the sword or the rifle of the white man, but by the simple

competition of civilization with the Indian's means of subsistence."
(605) The Negroes' inability to compete economically will result
in their virtual disappearance from the American scene.[10]

The census tables demonstrated that free Negroes actually
reproduce at a lower rate than their counterparts in slavery; slaves
reproduce rapidly because of the wicked commercial interests of
their owners. Once Negroes were emancipated they would have to
compete with more highly skilled whites and as a result they
would be compelled to work at low-paying jobs. Most Negro men
would realize they could not afford to marry and have families;
those who did would find that many of their children died, a fact
borne out by their higher mortality rates in the census tables. The
result of emancipation would be that "Like his brother, the Indian
of the forest, [the Negro] must melt away and disappear forever
from the midst of us." (609) It was not a matter of race alone;
large numbers of other people living in the cities had the same
hard lot and their children perished in great numbers. Despite the
claim that it was a kindness to the Negroes to keep them in
bondage, slavery is not justified. It is "an unmitigated curse" (610)
for them and indeed such a great curse to the whites that it should
never have been allowed to exist.

Sturtevant reassured his readers that "The negro [sic] does not
aspire to political or social equality with the white man. He has
evidently no such destiny, no such hope, no such possibility. He is
. . . constantly becoming weaker; …He asks not to rule us: he only
craves of us leave to toil; to hew our wood and draw our water, for
such miserable pittance of compensation as the competition of
free labor will award him—a grave." If America would grant him
this humble boon throughout the entire nation, "we may expect
the speedy return of peace, and such prosperity as no nation ever
before enjoyed." (610)

Sturtevant's Mission to Great Britain

Sturtevant returned from Chicago on 10 January to discover "a
new and unexpected order of things." In the fall eight seniors had
been enrolled, including a Kentucky secessionist who was dismissed for neglect of his studies. That led his classmates to withdraw

and so, Sturtevant informed Baldwin, "the Class of 1863 will be a blank on our catalogue." He did not regret the loss because awarding diplomas to any of the men would have disgraced the College. (S-B, 12 Jan. 1863)

Sturtevant desperately sought to find employment for the second term because the seniors were his entire class and all of them had withdrawn. After weeks of anxiety, a solution to his problem came most unexpectedly. On 20 March 1863 he received a letter with the startling proposal that he should go to England as an emissary for the Union cause. That very day he wrote about it to Baldwin. He said that friends in Chicago would pay all his expenses, and yet he was hesitant. Baldwin wired his answer: "By all means go to England." The trustees urged Sturtevant to accept, assuring him that his regular salary would continue. The "friend" who made the proposal was alumnus Eliphalet Blatchford, Class of 1845, whose Chicago business firm had prospered greatly.[11]

From childhood Julian Sturtevant had been taught to venerate England. He knew well her history and her literature and he greatly respected the heritage of liberty which England had passed on to America. "I love her," he wrote, "and her scenery and many of her institutions still seem to me as parts of my dear native land." (A, 308-9) Those scenes were so well known to him from his reading that he felt quite at home when he visited them in person. He was also keenly aware of England's role in America's Civil War. A Cabinet Minister asserted that America could end its Civil War only by amicably separating North and South. Sturtevant declared it was an outrage to presume that the North should acquiesce to slavery. Papal despotism at its worst had never proposed so horrible a teaching as the premise of slavery, that "capital ought to own labor," a principle which denies the humanity of three-fourths of mankind. Slavery "annihilates for all these toiling, suffering millions the rights of the husband, the wife, the parent, the child; it makes female beauty or loveliness an article of merchandise, and sells the infant at its mother's breast to the highest bidder."[12]

The schedule for his journey allowed Sturtevant little time to arrange personal and College affairs. He left a list of more than a dozen personal debts for Hannah to pay when funds were available. Livingston Glover, the Secretary of the Board, prepared a letter properly embossed with the official seal of the College which authorized Sturtevant to receive any contributions which might be offered. Arriving in Chicago on the evening of 30 March Sturtevant went to Blatchford's office to obtain additional letters of introduction. He boarded the train for New York the next day, and there and in New Haven and Washington, D.C., he obtained still more letters from prominent men in business, education, the church, and government. One very important letter remained to be secured. Sturtevant had written to President Lincoln informing him that at the request of friends he was going to England to present "the cause of our dear country and of universal liberty." Lincoln sent a note on 3 April to the Hon. Charles F. Adams, the United States Minister to England, to introduce Sturtevant as President of Illinois College. "He visits Europe in no official character. He is a worthy and capable gentleman; and also is one of my most highly valued personal friends. I shall be much obliged for any kind attentions you may find it convenient to show him." (Basler, 6:160-61)

Blatchford sent final instructions to Sturtevant in care of Baldwin. Travel funds were provided through an order for one hundred pounds in gold and four hundred pounds in English currency. Blatchford suggested a writing kit and loaned his own "yacht-glass." He urged Sturtevant to order the *New York Evening Post* and the *Independent* for delivery in England; the *Post* could be sent two or three times a week. Sturtevant boarded the *City of Washington*, a steamer equipped with sails, and departed for Liverpool on 11 April. He had great misgivings about leaving the College for so long and "a most unreasonable dread" of being so far from his homeland. And yet the trip was the fulfillment of "a bright dream of [his] childhood." (A, 303, 305)

Hannah was instructed to write on Fridays and again on Tuesdays so that her letters would reach New York just in time to be placed on board a steamer. Sturtevant wrote frequently, usually addressing his letters to his wife. Often letters reached their destination only after three or four weeks. Daughter Hannah Augusta expressed the hope that "Jeff Davis' privateers" would not get hold of any more of Uncle Sam's vessels until father and his letters were beyond their reach.[13] Fortunately Sturtevant made the journey in safety and virtually all the letters to his family were received and subsequently preserved. However, none of the voluminous letters he wrote to Blatchford from England have been located, and only one of Blatchford's is extant.

The first part of the voyage was sheer misery for Sturtevant and the account of his seasickness is graphic, but he recovered in time to enjoy his last days on the ship. In Liverpool he set about to become acquainted with his surroundings. He attended church in the city and was invited to dine at the home of a prominent merchant who himself was strongly pro-Union; others in that family were equally fervent in their support of the South. Many British families were likewise divided in their sympathies.

Sturtevant was frustrated because invitations to speak were accompanied by the instruction to say nothing about the American conflict. The *London Patriot* was quoted in the *Independent* (4 June) as reporting that he "very prudently refrained from expressing any political opinions and sympathies, and limited himself to the single point [on which all are agreed], a hearty reprobation of slavery." As a delegate from the American Congregational Union Sturtevant attended a meeting of the Congregational Union of England and Wales and made a speech at the dinner. He had been assured that the Congregationalists in England hated slavery but he was keenly disappointed to discover that most prominent church leaders lent no support to the Northern cause. Finally, on 11 May at a Baptist Chapel Sturtevant gave his first lecture on American affairs.[14] He exulted in a letter, written that very night, because it was "a most decided success."

Often while traveling in England and Scotland Sturtevant was invited to stay in the homes of business men and church men, sometimes remaining several days. In family settings and sometimes with invited guests he held spirited conversations. He was invited to a discussion at a Congregational College in London. He seized whatever opportunities he could to present the Union cause; when that was not possible, he had to speak and preach on other topics. Every situation required a new speech, which was necessarily extemporaneous. "No other part of my life," he wrote later, "has surpassed those months in mental activity." (A, 322-23)

Handbill Announcing Sermon by Sturtevant
The small print states that Sturtevant would give "an account of the Present State of American Affairs" at the 4:30 Tea Meeting.

But not all of his days were occupied with his mission. He much enjoyed a visit to Windsor Castle in early July and delighted in scenes in Scotland which were dear to readers of Walter Scott's novels. An unexpected pleasure was a meeting in London with an alumnus of the Class of 1845, William Ireland, on furlough from his missionary station in Africa.

The twenty-four letters which Sturtevant sent his family from Great Britain and Europe are delightful to read despite his wretched handwriting because of the broad scope of his observations, his keen insights, his direct language, and his excellent powers of description.[15] Sturtevant was very favorably impressed by England's environment, both natural and man-made. He was unprepared for the beautiful parks, the vast estates, the magnificent mansions, and the manifestations of wealth he witnessed in England; he was also unprepared for the squalor of Liverpool and Glasgow. After spending most of May near London he went to Bristol, where his hosts escorted him along the banks of the Avon to the Bristol Channel. The river ran in a chasm between two majestic masses of rock. At low tide it was like the "Mauvais-Terre," a small creek flowing through Jacksonville, yet at high tide it could float any vessel of the British Navy. Sturtevant described the "large tracts of land…laid out in lawns and ornamented with trees and shrubbery and walks and drives. Here the athletic play at cricket, the military parade and the men and women of leisure ride."[16] Acknowledging that many would think that the landless millions ought to have this land to provide for their necessities, Sturtevant admitted that there were two sides to this question. He remarked, atypically, "For my part I am inclined, with all my reforming tendencies, [to] let things remain as they are in this respect." (Bristol, 2 [June]) The problem of the landless could be resolved only by opening all the cultivated lands of England to free sale.

The magic spell of England's beautiful parks could not wholly suppress Sturtevant's native American egalitarianism. Describing the beautiful home and grounds of David Stuart, Esq., of Liverpool, he remarked that the only regret is that "so small a portion of mankind are able to enjoy that abundant gratification of our love of the beautiful, which art is able to provide." His Calvinistic view of God's benevolence and man's sinfulness could not be suppressed either, and he added that such lack "is not owing to any niggardliness by God's provision but to human indolence, profligacy, passion and vice. If every human being would faithfully perform his part all men might enjoy all these beauties." Sturtevant anticipated Julian Jr.'s response: "But you will say, 'Tell about England, and moralize—as father always must—at another time.'" (Liverpool, 28 Apr.)

Writing to Hannah from Hawick, Scotland, Julian reflected

that "The stillness which reigns all over the landscape makes one feel that nature is keeping a Sabbath. The forests, the lawn and the distant hillsides...seem to be resting in tranquil joy under the smile of heaven. From the impression of this scene one might hope that man is at length at peace with man and earth reconciled to heaven." (5 July) In England once again Sturtevant rhapsodized in a letter to his daughter, Hannah Augusta: "I passed a night in a little valley as beautiful and tranquil, as rich cultivation, a most peaceful lake and majestic mountains on every side could make it.... The evening was clear, and for England wonderously [*sic*] bright.... I felt how great is God, how little am I and all that pertains to me." (Oxford, 13 July)

Oxford was characterized as "a city of Colleges," twenty of them, with three thousand students. Sturtevant described the old buildings as "blackened with smoke and dust or grown with moss." New College was exceptional. "Do not suppose from its name that it is of recent origin; it is 600 years old. The chapel is more exquisitely charming than any other architecture I have seen." He rejoiced in the excellent music and the sermon, which was "full of all depth and tenderness of Christian feeling and the rarest felicity of language and sincerity and an inimitable tranquil earnestness [which] made it the rarest treat I have had in England.... For once, Oxford had my full sympathy." Nevertheless, in America "we can have...all the elegant and varied culture of Oxford with none of its narrowness [or] sectarian bigotry." Dissenters had recently been allowed to enroll as students at Oxford, but they still could not receive her "emoluments"—her salaries. (Oxford, 1 June)

Following his visit to the Palace of Holy Rood in Edinburgh, the Yankee from Illinois deplored the luxury and corruption of the royalty of the past. Observing the ruins of Kenilworth and the still intact castle at Warwick, he remarked that "Magnificence is the aim, however costly. And I pray God that [in our country] the hard earnings of honest industry [may never be used by] Princes and Nobles for such costly display of their own greatness as is here.... The cost of either of these castles would found and endow all the colleges in the U.S.A. and leave an ample fund besides. I do not wonder [that] Oliver Cromwell leveled his canon [*sic*] at Kenilworth." (Oxford, 13 July)

The rich architecture and the excellent music of England's great cathedrals impressed Sturtevant deeply. Although he considered York Minster to be the finest, it was an evening service at Westminster Abbey which evoked a meditative response. "As the day light faded, the gas light which was all a glow of brightness over the audience reached that lofty ceiling but dimly, and into the remote parts of that vast edifice it scarcely penetrated at all. Of course it invested those solemn aisles, and quaint old carvings, in deeper mystery, and the spirits of the men of departed ages might well be supposed to be hovering around those tombs of the buried great." He realized that he had expressed an uncharacteristic mood of respect for such things and he hastened to forestall any false conclusions which Hannah might draw. "Well, well, you will say—that will do! my husband will die a conservative worshiper of the past after all." "Think you so?" retorted Sturtevant in this imaginary conversation: "I tell you the Church of England is a dead thing. Westminster Abbey is a splendid tomb; the religion which is taught and exercised there is as dead as the men that moulder beneath its foot-worn pavements.... I wonder not that such a man as Thomas Carlyle has filled the world with the cry of sham! sham!" Sturtevant continued in this vein, asserting that England would sooner overturn freedom of speech than allow "a vigorous attack upon the establishment [which would] shake its foundations...." He demanded: "Do you think your husband is growing old fogy now?" (York, 15 June) And yet he had acknowledged to his son Warren a powerful conflict within himself, because "I, American, Republican, Independent, Antiprelatist" nevertheless had exulted in the grandeur of the Abbey. (2 May)

Sturtevant was equally blunt in commenting about the dissenting churches—the "chapels," as they were required to call themselves. They too fail to live up to their heritage and "chatter and gibber" in feeble imitation of the harlot step-mother. (15 June) He was annoyed by the attention given to garb and liturgy by their ministers, who seemed to him to be "miserably aping Westminster Abbey at an infinite distance." The omnipresent Gothic architecture evoked a comment about the appropriate style for college and church in America. "If with money enough I would plan a Library building for Illinois College it should certainly be Gothic and nothing else;

but if I were going to build a place for Christian teaching and worship there should be nothing Gothic about it. In general style and impression our church[17] is almost a model, grave and sober yet light and cheerful." (4 May)

Charles A. Spurgeon was a Baptist preacher and a visit to his Chapel prompted a rare positive judgment about religion in Britain. [Baptists and Independents (Congregationalists) were not allowed to call their buildings "churches."] Sturtevant described the huge tabernacle as "a perfect gem of church architecture for the 19th century." When Sturtevant was there, some six or seven thousand were in the audience, and the singing was "entirely Congregational, like the roaring of a forest, or the voice of many waters…. [There was] no ritual, no liturgy, no robes and such like solemn triflery, no shadow of the perished superstitions of the past…." Moreover Spurgeon was a champion of the masses and the poor and although he seemed indifferent to theological issues, Sturtevant admired him as an honest simple-hearted preacher, sincerely intending to declare God's truth. He added: "I can feel all the awe of Westminster Abbey; but as an instrument of power on the living present give me Spurgeon's Chapel. Give [me] the house of the living rather than the grave of the dead." (8 May)

Analyzing Britain's Hostility

Sturtevant reflected on issues relating to his primary mission. Here, in the cradle of liberty and among a people who had no like for slavery, there was much hostility toward the North and much sympathy toward the South. Many Englishmen expected and even hoped that the Union would founder. "The bubble has burst," was the verdict pronounced on the floor of Parliament by an aristocrat. (*Three Months*, 14) After a few weeks in England, Sturtevant declared that "there is not one man in a thousand in England who does not believe that the restoration of the [American] Union is absurd and impossible and regard us Americans as fools for expecting it." (Oxford, 1 June)

The nature of the social system became clear to Sturtevant when he realized that one word furnishes the key to all the social problems of England. "That word is 'rank.' We talk of caste in

India, say rather caste in England; the power of it is wonderful and pervades the whole nation from the Queen to the beggar." How can such an artificial state be maintained? The answer, surprisingly, was in his own explanation to a British audience of the reason why "the slaveless whites of the South…are made to give their votes for its continuance. It is lest by emancipation, the Negro should become their equal." (14 May)

Everyone in England wanted to preserve the system. "Each one of those Bishops," Sturtevant noted, "is the recipient for life of revenues by comparison with which our President's salary is a trifle." (8 May) "Each grade above the lowest favors the perpetuity of [the] system of rank, lest those below…should be exalted to his level…. Verily human nature is everywhere the same. English Aristocracy and American slavery are sustained by the same forces. In neither case are men willing to be equalized before the law, and let every one's standing in society be decided entirely by his merits." (14 May) Westminster Abbey was a powerful symbol of how all the features of life were knitted together in England. "And with her religion, and her church Architecture and her hierarchy, she has closely united her monarchy, her Aristocracy, her history, her glorious literature and even her freedom. The monument of her great Commoner occupies a most conspicuous place among her illustrious dead here congregated and canonized. All the elements of English society are here seen bound up in one bundle, as comprising one whole." This closely-knit system embraced the contradictory elements of English society: "its pure Christianity and its superstitious formalism; its freedom and its despotism, its rights of man and its privileges of the few…." (2 May)

Recognizing Aristocracy and Establishment as the twin pillars supporting this whole structure, Sturtevant could then understand why England regarded "the prosperity and the happiness of our country with dislike and dread" and wanted America to be divided. They were even willing to give slavery "a long lease of its life for the sake of accomplishing a thing which they very much desire." (York, 15 June) The United States has neither aristocracy nor an established church; it is equalitarian and free. A successful, prosperous America will seriously threaten England's traditional social system. Some Englishmen candidly admitted that it would be much easier for them to dominate and exploit America in commercial matters if its people were divided into two nations. Sturtevant resolved his ambivalence: "Any man who lands in England with my opinions and tastes cannot thoroughly like England, without renouncing all his previous thinking." (14 May)

Sustaining Family Ties

Five members of the family were present at the depot when Julian boarded the train for Chicago to begin his journey to England; only Libbie, Lucy, and Fred were still at home with Hannah and Jane. Julian Jr. was pastor of the Congregational Church in Hannibal, Missouri, and James Warren and Hannah Augusta were teaching school in the same city. The diminished household some-times included a hired girl, paid $1.50 weekly plus washing. Part of the time a hired boy assisted with the outdoor work.

Some of Julian's letters from abroad gave instructions about the orchard and garden. He asked Hannah to plant "a fine lot of sweet corn the last of June. And I hope to get a little of it with you. How I shall miss it here!" (Bristol, 2 [June]) Hannah duly reported on the expected yield from their garden and orchard. The early part of the growing season was very dry and unusually cool; a fire was needed in the parlor every morning in early June. The fruit trees and bushes promised an abundance of cherries, currants, apples, grapes, pears, raspberries, and quinces, and a fair supply of peaches and strawberries. The potatoes were small and Hannah gave the surplus to the poor who were in great need. Fortunately late rains saved the crops from ruin.

Fred could harness the two horses, Dick and Meg, to the carriage and knew how to drive them handsomely. Often neither Fred nor Warren was available to take letters to the post office and so Hannah and Libbie sometimes drove the smaller buggy with Dick. Emergency repairs were required when their own or other people's livestock broke through the fences. When Warren returned home for the summer, Hannah no longer had such worries.

Hannah wrote that for several weeks there were no services at their own church so they went elsewhere. On 30 April she and Lucy had gone to Westminster Church to observe the National

Fast Day. Sometimes Dr. William Milburn, a former student and now chaplain of the U. S. Senate, was the guest preacher. Hannah wondered if Julian would acquire the same European habits Dr. Milburn had; as their house guest he wanted his coffee served to him in bed at nine, and he did not dress until noon.

The war news was reported to "Mr. Sturtevant" very briefly because he probably read the details in the American papers which reached England before their letters. Warren, writing after the Union loss at Chancellorsville, noted that the army in the East seemed "doomed to defeat and disorder." (22 June) Libbie, referring to the invasion of Pennsylvania, wrote that "something is almost always going wrong." (28 July) Actually, the Union had recently won important battles at Gettysburg and Vicksburg—victories which later were recognized as the turning points of the War.

Strong tensions in the community sometimes flared into open antagonism. Whenever the Federal troops suffered a defeat, Hannah wrote, "The Copperheads fairly hiss," and they were even bolder now. Much excitement was aroused when secessionism was openly expressed at the Jacksonville Female Academy. The girls were shouting "hurra" for Jeff Davis and singing songs expressing Southern sympathies. The principal said the girls were doing it just for fun, but Hannah thought it wrong to treat so serious a subject as a mere trifle. (10 May) When the report came that Vicksburg was taken and the entire Mississippi River was now open for Federal ships, the Union supporters shouted in the streets and fired guns and some of them made an immense bonfire in the public square.[18] Knots of people joined in singing the "Star-Spangled Banner." Warren had not yet returned and the family stayed home because there was no one bigger than Fred to protect them. There was *good* news when Lee was defeated at Gettysburg. The whole country was jubilant and, declared Hannah, "John Bull & Napoleon may as well keep still." (12 July) The family mentioned General Grierson of Jacksonville and his success in reaching Louisiana. They reported about Governor Yates' fine Fourth of July speech at Chicago. There was *bad* news, also, about the riots in New York City.

The Congregational Church had observed the National Fast Day in April 1863 by holding a prayer meeting. Now such meetings were held daily in the late afternoon in the lecture room. Two men from the Christian Commission, which provided spiritual encouragement to the soldiers, had inspired the services. Daughters Hannah and Libbie attended and when Mrs. Sturtevant went in mid-July over one hundred were present; the prayer meeting was about the only thing people were going to any more.[19] Writing on 31 July Hannah declared that she was not satisfied even though the Mississippi was now open. A public day of thanksgiving was set for 6 August but Hannah was not ready for it yet: "When Charleston is taken & burned up, then I am ready."

While in Great Britain Sturtevant became sick and his hostess, a Mrs. Warne, cared for him. His family was concerned about his well-being and prayed for his safe return. They were also fascinated by his travels and his visits to places they all knew from reading English history and literature. The visit to Scotland was especially appealing to the two Hannahs, both hinting to be present on a subsequent journey. Sturtevant's letters to his wife and children expressed his affection for them. An almost constant theme was the loneliness that sometimes was overwhelming. His letter of 17 May was so gloomy that he did not mail it. In a letter to be read only by his wife he told of dreaming that she was in bed with him. He often wished that she could be with him to enjoy the beautiful sights and pleasant company of his visits. Indeed, he was tempted to envy richer friends who could take their families with them, but he then prayed that God would help him resist that evil. He counted the days of absence and in his last letter from England he noted that he had been away for 108 days—and it would be 57 more days until they would be reunited. Yet outwardly he remained cheerful and busied himself with his mission and with sight-seeing. The many friends he made in England helped to ease the pain of loneliness.

Occasionally both husband and wife were light-hearted. Hannah wrote on 3 May, admitting that at first she had grave doubts about her ability to attend to the outdoor responsibilities. Now she flattered herself that after just five weeks she had "become quite a manager indoors and out." She continued: "Maybe shant be willing to give it up when the 'lords of creation' return." Her husband replied that he too now had control of certain affairs which previously were not in his domain—such as packing his trunk. However, the things he would not need until his return were on top and the items he needed daily were on the bottom. Having pressed levity far enough he offered a truce. "Ah my dear wife, I think we shall both be very glad to return, as the diplomatists say, to the 'status in quo ante bellum.' I am sure I shall and I think I shall not find your reluctance unconquerable." (Bristol, 2 [June])

Sturtevant frequently asked his wife to tell him whether she had enough money. Actually she was relieved of that anxiety because the College paid faculty salaries when due. She assured him that she was heeding his injunction to be provident. She informed him that she wished to sell some of the stock. "Sell any of it that you think best," he advised. But "I prefer you should not sell the children. I should rather they would not sell you, but you may sell anything else you like." A serious note ended the long-distance repartee: "And may God preserve you all in health till I return." (Edinburgh, 23 June) In the letter Sturtevant did not mail to Hannah he had said, "I hope too that God will spare your life and health that I may not return to find that room a house of affliction, or more lonely and desolate than this I am now occupying in a land of strangers." (London, 17 May)

Hannah had been ill the summer before and her husband had urged her to write to Dr. Chandler for the same prescription, if the sickness recurred. Wistfully she expressed the desire to be with her husband, and she hoped for God's continuing preservation of him. She also wondered how he managed to get along without her to care for him and his clothes—to remind him to wash his neck, to lay out his clean clothes, to brush his coat. The family had a "frolic," she told him, over his comment about the inconveniences of single life. Yes, Hannah wrote, she does think she is of some consequence to him, and *he* has made her think so, too. (3 May 1863)

Sturtevant's fifty-eighth birthday (26 July) was a special occasion for letter writing and everyone at home wrote to send good wishes. By now he had concluded his mission in Great Britain and was making a brief tour of Europe. Writing that day from Zurich, Sturtevant declared he was indeed "a solitary stranger in a strange land." When his family's letters reached him they conveyed the family love which Hannah explicitly noted: "How universally confidence & affection [have] prevailed in our family circle." (17 April)

The schedule for Hannah's letters was reduced to one letter weekly for a designated sailing from New York. Postage was twenty-four cents for the family's letters; his letters were written on thin paper and when sent collect the postage was thirty or thirty-one cents; when paid in advance, the rate was higher and had to be paid in gold. Sturtevant's failure to receive any family messages during his first two weeks in England made him almost petulant and he repeatedly implored his wife and children to write. When he received five letters at one time, he rejoiced that famine had turned to feast. He then advised his children not to take his somewhat caustic complaints too much to heart; after all, he wrote to daughter Hannah, "I had no thought of cutting any of you off from a share of my vast estate, or of ever being very angry with you…." (Oxford, 13 July)

Often Sturtevant mentioned the food he was served. As a guest at the home of Rev. Mr. Binney in a suburb of London, Sturtevant dined upon "a very nice dinner of fresh Mackerel, excellent beef steak, and a rice pudding made without eggs (which you know I like), with stewed pie plant." (London, 8 May) He added: "My appetite is for some reason twice what it is at home at this season," and later he marveled that he had not gained weight from eating so much during his trip. However, the menu was frequently plain and Sturtevant missed his wife's cooking. He reported, "I eat roast beef and mutton and have ham and sausage as I never did before. One must eat them here, or not eat at all. John Bull don't [*sic*] eat roast beef after all because he is so fond of it but because he has nothing else to eat. No pies, no baked potatoes, no warm cakes of any kind, no mush, or corn bread, no brown bread except the graham. At this season no vegetables except potatoes and cabbages…." (Bristol, 21 May)

It had been necessary for Sturtevant to procure a new wardrobe in London and he described it for his wife.

> There walks the streets of London, and sometimes he rides in omnibuses and sometimes in Cabs, a man wearing a stovepipe hat, quite new and sleek. A *white* neck tie going once

around the neck and tied in a double bow, a sort of corded silk vest, a fine broadcloth-frock coat and doeskin Pantaloons, and an overcoat of tweed cloth…. If you should meet him I think he would know you, but I have some doubt whether you would recognize him as the same man who has so long worn the felt hat and…long heavy overcoat. I got the doz[en] collars in Chicago as required by high authority, and my supply is most ample for changing every day if I become an exquisite…. My overcoat, coat, vest and pants, the last three quite rich and beautiful, cost me 7 pounds sterling, less than $35." (London, 8 May)

Later, Sturtevant sent a daguerreotype of himself, made in Edinburgh at nine in the evening, which brought special delight; his family pronounced the "Carte visite" an excellent likeness. He had taken pictures with him to give to people he met.

Observing that the younger English women were generally less beautiful than their counterparts in America, Sturtevant also noted that the older women were usually more attractive, excepting of course "a lady in whom we are all a good deal interested." (London, 2 May) He was impressed by the very pleasant manners of the people. He saw Princess Alexandra, seated in the gallery of the House of Parliament, chatting with her companion in much the same way that American girls would do. Sturtevant enjoyed the company of a young lady on two different excursions and felt compelled to "confess." Miss Stoddard, daughter of his host at Glasgow, accompanied him on a trip on the River Clyde. She was a very bright girl of 20. Later his escort was Miss Katie Sykes, "a very sprightly little lady of 18," a house guest of his hosts at Oxford. She went with him to Blenheim Castle, the estate given by Parliament to the Duke of Marlboro. Sturtevant now gave a full account of his day with Miss Stoddard. "I may as well confess all my sins, now that I am on the penitent stool. At Glasgow I was attended by a bright-faced young girl of twenty in my trip down the Clyde to Arran. She is a girl that is a girl. She talks French, reads Latin, plays and sings finely, reads all the poetry going, and rides sixty miles in a day on horseback." He feared that she might have a breakdown but if not, he should advise her never to marry, lest "the race of the Amazons should be renewed. I am sure that no ordinary man will be able to manage her." (London, 16 July)

Sturtevant worried about the College and about their church. Before his departure he had hoped that in England he might find "a mine of resources for the College, from which may yet be derived the means of its growth, its power, its true greatness." (Chicago, 31 March) He wrote to Mr. Blatchford about obtaining the support of wealthy men so that the College could better "meet the necessities of a great free people." His plan, he said, was based upon what he had learned at Oxford. (16 July)

Hannah reported on affairs at the College during her husband's absence. Professors Adams and Crampton were especially helpful, and of course the payment of salaries was welcome news. Sturtevant missed the June Commencement exercises and Hannah was glad he was not present to witness the unusual event—in 1863 there were no graduating seniors. Hannah missed some of the proceedings because of illness but relayed a full account.

Wednesday morning was occupied by the prize speakers, of whom Henry Barnes received the first prize and [Truman O.] Douglass the second.... The afternoon was given to a lecture before the Sigma [Pi] Soc. by Dr. Nelson. It was very fine: The influence of the Mathematics upon the mental & moral developments....

The customary reunion was held in the evening at the Mansion House; sixty-five were present—Warren said more than he expected.... Thursday, 1st was conferred eight degrees, Masters; the Oration failed; then the Alumni meeting followed immediately....

In the evening was an exhibition of the subs; tickets sold at 25 cts to pay the expenses & anything over was to be handed to the Soldiers Aid Soc. The house was full & they have passed over to the Soc. $122. The exhibition consisted of declamations & two Colloquies, the Merchant of Venice & the Elixir of Life. On Friday Eve. I invited Mr. & Mrs. Glover & Dr. Curtis, Prof. & Mrs. Nutting, & Prof. & Mrs. Crampton to tea. We had a very pleasant time.... We had no service at our church on the Sab[bath] so we heard Dr. Curtis in the morning at Westminster & in the evening at Strawn's Hall. He preaches very well. We all liked him. (HRS to JMS, 22 June 1863)

Under unusual circumstances, the trustees had approved one

baccalaureate degree. It was awarded to Calvin Goudy, originally of the Class of 1839 and henceforth listed with that class. Unavoidable circumstances had prevented him from completing the course in Greek during his senior year. Probably the diploma was presented to Goudy in private. The A.M. degree was awarded to eight men of the Class of 1860 and also to Goudy.

Probably the most anticipated letter from the traveler had been the report, received on 10 May, of his safe arrival in Liverpool. Hannah had not heard from her husband for three weeks, the longest period without some communication since their marriage. Later she was pleased that her letter of 31 July was "our last letter to be sent across the Ocean." For Sturtevant, the reunion with his family seemed a long way off, and "God only knows what may happen before it is accomplished, but let us trust in God and look forward with cheerfulness and hope.... I pray God to spare the lives and the health of us all to meet again joyful in God's goodness, content with our lot and grateful for all his long-continued kindness." (London, 16 July) Sometimes Sturtevant admitted, he had been tempted to seek a life of tranquillity, letting "this great sinful, suffering world go on as it will without troubling myself much about it...." (To Lucy, London, 4 May) Rebuking himself, he continued: "God never meant I should lead such a life.... Jesus Christ did not come to this world in any such spirit. And his people have no right to desire to live on any such principle." Nevertheless Sturtevant sometimes admitted his weariness even though "I am not an old man." (Bristol, 2 [June]) When writing about the lake country, he admitted that "No spot on earth that I have ever seen is so inviting to one weary with life's fierce conflict and longing for rest." (Oxford, 13 July)

His family's letters and the American papers provided Sturtevant with accurate news about the War and dispelled the gloom spread by the *London Times*. In his last letter from London, dated 16 July, Julian wrote, "We have received to-day the News of the Repulse of the Confederates up to the 3rd inst. at Gettysburgh. And Southern sympathy is not nearly so smiling as usual." He explained that he had not sent accounts of his journey to the *Independent* because at present the publication of his views would do more harm than good.

Having managed so thriftily in Great Britain, much aided by the generous hospitality of new friends, Sturtevant was able to make a brief tour of the continent. It was the support of England which the North so sorely wanted and there was no need for Sturtevant to extend his mission to Europe; the language barrier would have made that difficult. In France, Germany, and Switzerland he followed the usual itinerary for tourists.

Reporting to the Public on His Mission

At first there were few invitations for Sturtevant to speak to the public about the role of England in the Civil War. Soon, however, there were opportunities to lecture in Illinois and in adjacent states on British opinion. In writing to Baldwin on 5 November, he reported that he had already lectured three times, had accepted four more engagements, and had others under consideration. In an article prepared for the *Independent* Sturtevant reviewed a speech by England's Attorney-General which was reported in the *London Times*. The speaker praised the South for its bravery and endurance. He failed to realize that the North had exhibited those same qualities and seemingly he was unaware that slavery was the prime cause of the war in America. Sturtevant counseled understanding of "such utterances from eminent Englishmen" because they arose from ignorance and the powerful forces of self-interest which influenced the governing class. Sturtevant denied wishing "to excite the war spirit against England."

In early 1864 President and Mrs. Sturtevant were in Galesburg where he delivered his lecture and while there they had seen Edward Beecher and Elisha Jenney. The public did not seem receptive to Sturtevant's views. Sturtevant submitted articles to the *Independent* but they were not published. That newspaper had given much coverage to Henry Ward Beecher's visit to England and Europe, which took place at about the same time as Sturtevant's.[20] In writing to Baldwin earlier Sturtevant had remarked that he believed his observations on England were more important than Beecher's. Beecher had been warmly applauded by his large audiences in England, but they consisted of people with little influence on the government. Possibly Sturtevant included such comments in the articles he had submitted; if so, that would explain how Beecher's people learned about his opinions and then lodged a protest. Sturtevant once again called upon Baldwin to smooth over an offense: "Please my dear brother try and do as well as you can for me as in many previous similar scrapes." (S-B, 2 Mar. 1864) Sturtevant sent in care of Baldwin a letter addressed to the editor of the *Independent*, asking his friend to review the text before delivering it. Baldwin read it to the editor but omitted the complaint Sturtevant had made about being "shut out" of the paper.[21] The editor told Baldwin that he regarded Sturtevant's thinking as exceedingly sound and that he himself thought Beecher's views were rose-colored.

Meanwhile the *New-York Evangelist* (18 Feb. 1864) printed a strong attack, written under the pen-name, "Ambrose," on Sturtevant's Galesburg lecture. The inaccurate and disparaging report drew a sharp response, with Sturtevant asserting that justice required the newspaper to print it; the editor complied. Several factual errors were in need of correction, and furthermore, Sturtevant maintained, the personal attacks were unwarranted. Ambrose claimed that the lecture had belittled Henry Ward Beecher's efforts in England, a charge which Sturtevant rejected. He borrowed Samuel Butler's witty words in *Hudibras* to express his sarcastic denial: Ambrose had remarkable vision indeed to be able to see what was not there to be seen. He also had convincing evidence to support his denial that he had offended Dr. Edward Beecher. He said he did not know "what griefs 'Ambrose' may have to avenge, that he should drag my name before the public in the way he has." Subsequently Sturtevant received numerous comments from those who deplored Ambrose's bad grace and congratulated Sturtevant for taking him to task.[22]

The editor of the *Evangelist*, Rev. Henry M. Field, gave further offense in proposing to omit those statements in Sturtevant's protest which he deemed "not in the best taste or temper." The text of Sturtevant's reply to Ambrose is available only as it was printed in the *Evangelist*; if the editor had toned it down, the original must have been very strong. The timing of Field's notice required a response the very evening Sturtevant received the letter. Sturtevant wrote a furious complaint and sent it directly to Field, objecting not only to the very short time allowed for a reply but also to the editor's willingness to exercise charity on behalf of Ambrose when he had been utterly oblivious to that man's "malignant onslaught" on Sturtevant. Sturtevant told Baldwin that he had reviewed his letter to Field with the faculty but this time he did not send his protest to Baldwin to have "the Devil taken out it." (S-B, 2 Mar. 1864)

Later Sturtevant took pains to assure Baldwin of his gratitude for the assistance he had given on so many occasions. He owed much of his reputation to Baldwin's kind suggestions and wise counsel. Their intimate relationship now extended over thirty-five years. Sturtevant regretted that the kindness had been so one-sided; Baldwin had done so much more for him. He said that neither had ever sought the other's aggrandizement but wished only to promote the Kingdom of Christ. Reciprocating, Baldwin expressed his own thanks to Sturtevant and acknowledged their "long and intimate friendship which to me was ever a source of great profit & pleasure…. We have lived in a stirring age [and we] have lived to see…the grand accomplishment of that upon which our youthful hearts were set." (B-S, 7 Apr. 1864)

At least Sturtevant had honor in his own territory. He delivered an address in the Home Lecture series sponsored by Sigma Pi; his topic—"First Impressions of Foreign Lands." And finally the long-hoped-for invitation to speak at a public meeting in Chicago arrived, enclosed with a warm letter from Blatchford. Addressing the ladies and gentlemen present, Sturtevant reported his observations of the present attitude of the British toward America. He denied having any hatred toward England and said he wished only to "speak the truth with freedom and fairness." (2) He had been shocked by the prevailing attitude of sympathy for the South and found it hard to believe until he realized the causes for it. The root cause was an "organic disease in the English body politic": "The government of England is the government of the many by the privileged few." (12, 13) The aristocracy which limited the monarchy and gave a measure of freedom to the middle class had then taken to itself great privileges and wealth. The inheritance system favored the elder sons but the established church and the military provided handsome situations for the younger sons and therefore the clergy and the military officers supported it.

All the people of England seemed to agree that there must be a monarch and that aristocracy and church establishment were essential to sustain it.[23] The British saw the continuing success of America with its system of equality as a great threat to their own society and hence wished to see it fail lest the English people be tempted to emulate it. British listeners could not conceive of schools intended for all children but Sturtevant had assured them that his son and his daughter attended such a school.

The English newspapers, chiefly the *London Times* and the *Saturday Review,* were responsible, Sturtevant believed, for much of the misinformation about America and the consequent prejudice against the North. Indeed, the press was satanic but the real problem was with the aristocracy and its sympathizers; the papers only told them what they wished to hear. The British people and their government wanted a divided America which would not threaten English commerce and the English class system by its power and wealth. England had not learned the lesson of the American Revolution, that it could not ultimately succeed in policies toward colonies or former colonies based simply on profit. Three times in his address Sturtevant labeled the British attitude toward America as criminal, and he declared that the whole population was responsible. He reported as almost unbelievable the action of the Congregational Union. At the very meeting where he was instructed to say nothing about the American conflict, the Union passed a resolution expressing hostility to slavery.[24] Declaring that he loved England still as the mother of freedom, Sturtevant hoped that she would come to share the great inheritance of freedom being wrought in America. America must reject Britain's pessimism regarding the outcome of the War.

With Blatchford's assistance, the Chicago address was published in 1864 in pamphlet form. It bore the primary title, *Three Months in Great Britain*—and a lengthy subtitle. Friends in England also printed the address but reduced its length by one-third. Four lines from Robert Burns, beginning "Oh wad some power the giftie gie us," were printed on the cover. The introduction stressed that Sturtevant's remarks were directed to that class of society which he met during his visit and did not apply to the large portion of the middle class and the great majority of the working class who throughout the conflict had been true to the Union cause. Sturtevant was said to have underestimated the force of public opinion in influencing the government. An Edinburgh daily, the *Caledonian Mercury*, printed "a flattering editorial" on Sturtevant's lecture and four columns of lengthy extracts and very favorable comments. He had at last reached British opinion on the great questions. This would not have happened, he thought, if "that hornet J. Ambrose Wight had not stung me" or if he had followed the advice of timid friends who urged him not to reply to the attack. (S-B, 9 May 1865)

Changes at the College

In the spring of 1864 President Lincoln issued a call for men to give One Hundred Days' Service. Professor Crampton put aside his teaching duties and raised a company of a score or more of student recruits, who named him captain. All the seniors had volunteered and Sturtevant advised Baldwin that the College would not even attempt to have a commencement. However, in June the trustees approved seven candidates for the Bachelor's degree. An honorary D.D. was approved for the Rev. Enoch Mellor of England.[25] In an unusual action in July, the trustees acceded to a request from St. Paul College. The school, in Palmyra, Missouri, had disbanded due to rebellion in that state and asked that honorary Master's degrees be awarded to four men who had completed their baccalaureate studies and had exhibited exemplary loyalty to the Union. In late September Crampton's company, having had no combat duty, was mustered out.

Baldwin wished to cite the contribution made to the Union cause by the institutions which had been aided by the College Society. Sturtevant was too busy to search the records but he estimated that probably over one hundred had been in military service. A full accounting was not made until long after the War, when President Rammelkamp listed some 240 men in the Union forces and 12 in the Confederate service. Among Illinois College volunteers ten were killed in battle or died from wounds. Over one hundred men of Sigma Pi served in the Union forces—and none on the Confederate side, while ten of those in Confederate service were from Phi Alpha. The Sigs debated topics relating to the War, such as whether a state has the right to secede. After the surrender of the Southern forces, they considered whether the leaders of the rebellion should face the death penalty.[26]

Considering the stresses which the Civil War imposed upon Illinois College, it was fortunate that its faculty was both capable and loyal. Sturtevant issued a two-page circular in 1864 stating that "The friends of *Illinois College* will be glad to learn that, notwithstanding the sacrifices which patriotism has demanded from its students and patrons, the institution is still doing its accustomed work." Some adaptations were made to suit "the wants and conveniences of the agricultural community, [and the] exigencies of individual students." The College year was now divided into two terms extending from mid-September until early April, followed by an optional term of two months. The revised calendar enabled the sons of farmers to be at home when their labor was most needed. Sons of Union soldiers who had been killed or disabled were to be admitted without charge.

The new system was more flexible without "lowering the standard of the accepted American College curriculum." Each student could proceed at his own pace and could be examined on any part of the course when he wished. Thus he could master a subject in one term or in five if necessary and graduate in less than four years or as long as five or six. For four years students were not cataloged in the traditional classes.[27]

The *1864-65 Catalogue* announced changes in curricular organization which remained in effect for several years. Courses were grouped in ten departments and the topics of each course were listed in detail. Probably Sturtevant taught all four courses in each of two departments. The first department, "Moral Philosophy," included "Logic," the traditional study of syllogisms, and "Mental Philosophy" which comprehended sensation, perception, emotions, instincts, appetites, and freedom of the will. "Ethics, Theoretical" dealt with conscience, the moral commandments of God, natural religion, and revelation. In "Practical Ethics" students learned duties to God, prayer and Sabbath observance, and duties to man: justice, veracity, the relation of civil society and individual duties and rights, and relations between the sexes, including marriage.

"Evidences of Religion—Natural Religion" was the first listing in the Department of "Social and Religious Philosophy." It dealt with the future life and rewards and punishment. In "Revealed Religion" the students learned about miracles, prophecy, and divine revelation as evidence of the validity of Christianity. "Political Economy" examined cost and value, competition, labor, capital, banking, exchange, and wealth. In "Philosophy of American Democracy" the class studied the origin of the American Republic; local, state, and federal government; freedom of the press; universal suffrage; and "the durability of the Union." Authors of texts included [Richard] Whately, [Joseph] Butler, and [Alexis] de Tocqueville.

In 1865 Edward Tanner, Class of 1857, returned to his Alma Mater as Professor of Latin. His appointment was significant, but it was not sufficient to meet the increased needs of the College. Sturtevant explained to Baldwin that the College must be "greatly enlarged" or it could not compete. He wanted to separate physics from chemistry and add a second science teacher. Modern languages had been taught somewhat sporadically; now a regular department should be established. More classrooms were needed as well as better scientific apparatus and improved collections of specimens; the library was inadequate; and at least two tutors were essential. The projected cost was $50,000. Competition with other institutions became an ever greater problem, partly because rapid improvements in rail service made it easier for students to travel further from home. Knox College competed both for students and financial support from the same two denominations. When President Blanchard left Knox in 1857 and founded Wheaton, the competition was intensified although the new college never succeeded, as Knox had, in gaining support from the College Society. Blanchard continued to cast doubt on Illinois College and its loyalty to Congregationalism.

The founders and early faculty of Illinois College, J. B. Turner among them, were strong supporters of common schools for youth. Turner concluded that the region also needed advanced

education—different from the liberal arts—and he sought unsuccessfully to direct the development of Illinois College toward
agriculture. As early as 1850 he began to give public addresses in
support of state universities for the industrial classes, and for more
than a decade he advocated that cause. Turner deserved much of
the credit for stimulating wide interest in the concept, and in
1860 two candidates for the presidency, Abraham Lincoln and
Stephen Douglas, both agreed to sign appropriate legislation. In
1862 Congress passed, and Lincoln signed, the Morrill Act. This
bill set aside vast tracts for "land grant" universities to provide
instruction in agriculture and the industrial arts.

In 1864 Governor Yates appointed Sturtevant to a commission
for recommending the allocation of money for an agricultural
college. Some advocated dividing the funds among many colleges
but Sturtevant and others main-
tained that they should be kept
intact—an arrangement favoring Illinois College as the
administrator. J. B. Turner, on
the committee to draft the legislation, regarded Illinois College
as best able to fulfill the intended function. However, strong
protests to the Governor killed
this hope. In 1865 the legislature approved the establishment
of a state university; deciding
where to locate it required two
more years.

The prospect of a state university was both a problem and an
opportunity. Sturtevant worked

Portrait of Julian Sturtevant
G. P. A. Healy
(Sigma Pi Literary Society)

hard to bring it to Jacksonville. He envisioned Illinois College as
the central institution, providing traditional higher education,
while other schools would teach the practical subjects; his overall
plan was inspired by England's example. He hoped also that other
denominations would establish colleges in Jacksonville, sharing
academic resources and responsibilities. If church bodies could

agree to found "a great Christian university" that would be even better. By January 1865 Sturtevant realized that Champaign was likely to be chosen as the site of the state university. He regarded such decisions as influenced more by corruption than by merit.[28]

There were other challenges also. The founding of Chicago Theological Seminary had signaled that the colleges in the West could not maintain a monopoly in the preparation of young men for the ministry. Professor Sanders in 1864 established The Young Ladies' Athenaeum—hardly a threat to the enrollment of young men, although the diversion of Sanders from his College duties caused difficulty. Moreover, Sanders' advertisements for his school seemed to deprecate the College's traditional curriculum.

Sturtevant suggested to Baldwin that they should now review their own roles, in preparing to fulfill the plans they had entered upon "with the ardor of youth." (S-B, 15 Sept. 1864) He welcomed Baldwin's suggestion for an association of colleges, meeting annually to consider mutual concerns. This would enhance planning already under way at Illinois College regarding its future. Sturtevant planned to correspond with the new president of Knox but conflicts developed within that college and between it and the Presbyterians in Galesburg; Sturtevant concluded that not much good would result.

In late 1865 Sturtevant proposed to Baldwin that any person giving $250,000 to the endowment could name the College as he wished. No such gift was ever in prospect. Sturtevant also considered obtaining support from other denominations for Illinois College as a Christian but "non-sectarian" institution. He acknowledged the difficulty of the plan by alluding to the biblical account of the Philistines' capture of the ark, the chest containing the sacred symbols of God's presence. (1 Sam. 4-7) Sturtevant asked Baldwin whether "these 'milch kine' that never bore the yoke [could] be harnessed to the cart and made to carry back the ark of God into the land of Israel." (8 Dec. 1865) Thus he likened Christian sectarians who had never established colleges to milk cows which were not only untrained but had new-born calves confined in a pen. In the biblical story the "kine," despite the odds, left their young behind and carried the ark back to Israelite soil, thus demonstrating God's power. Unfortunately Sturtevant's idea had no happy outcome.

Soon after the Civil War ended, enrollment in the College made a quick recovery, reaching one hundred twenty-five students. The income from tuition and fees would be more than twice the previous year's. Despite the good prospects Sturtevant reflected on the College's financial woes and recalled the instances of misman-agement: the huge dormitory, "that manual labor business," and the unfitness of Mr. Coffin, the College's treasurer, 1836-1848. The sale of the College's lands still rankled in Sturtevant's memory. At least, "since the College freed itself from its great debt by the ruinous and ever to be deplored sacrifice of its property," its financial practices had been free from censure. (S-B, 21 Aug. 1865)

The need for more adequate financing was obvious. The faculty could not live on their present salaries. The immediate need was for $4,000 beyond the anticipated income of $10,000, and the long-term need was far greater. The College must have $150,000: one-third for additional staff and curricular improvements, one-third for additions to buildings, and one-third for books and scientific equipment. With such improvements, the College would double its enrollment. The means for attaining this ambitious goal had been proposed earlier by the faculty, when Sturtevant was asked to direct a bold question to Theron Baldwin: "Can you spend the rest of your days to better purpose, than by adding a quarter of a million Dollars to the funds of Illinois College?" (15 Sept. 1864) Baldwin could not accept the challenge at that time. A year later Sturtevant wrote, "My brother, I cannot feel content to die or to resign my place in Illinois College till it is in some such manner provided for its great mission. Shall we not resolve that to the best of our ability, we will endeavor to achieve for it such an endowment? I cannot rest without making a serious trial." (S-B, 7 Nov. 1865) Two months later Baldwin was on the scene.

Honoring Lovejoy, Yates, Lincoln

Sturtevant gave public honor to three men prominent in the cause of freedom, men whom he had known personally. Owen Lovejoy, the brother of Elijah Lovejoy, had been encouraged by Beecher to become a Congregational pastor, and he served the Congregational Church in Princeton, Illinois, for seventeen years.

Lovejoy was elected to the U. S. Congress and died while in office. Sturtevant was requested to speak at Princeton at the dedication of a monument to his memory. The ceremony was held on 1 June 1864 and Sturtevant's address was printed in the Princeton newspaper. Sturtevant declared that permanent monuments such as those he had seen in England are significant because they commemorate great men and great events. The monuments in England heralded the struggles and achievements of aristocracy. If America is to endure as a nation it must represent in its monuments the great principle of freedom, the rights of mankind. (Loud cheers) There was no promise that all men would have the same condition of life, but that did not violate the principle of equal opportunity. Every American wants a national constitution and government which will prevent the repression of any man. "No power shall come in to interfere with the right of any man to be rich or learned, or to achieve anything else which he may legitimately aspire to achieve."

Both Owen Lovejoy and his martyred brother were true to the "great and grand principle underlying the best hopes of the world—the principle of freedom and equality, the universal rights and brotherhood of man." Sturtevant recalled the incident in 1838 when Owen Lovejoy was denied ordination to the Episcopalian priesthood because he would not promise to remain silent on slavery. Despite disappointment, he was cheerful and hopeful. Yes, Lovejoy had been intolerant but his was the righteous intolerance of sin and wrong. He had continued steadfastly in the cause of freedom and almost witnessed the consummation of that struggle. The news account concluded: "Mr. Sturtevant's speech was listened to throughout with profound interest, and at the close was followed with loud and prolonged applause."

When Governor Richard Yates completed his term of office he returned to Jacksonville, his former home. At a formal reception on 17 January 1865 at Strawn's Hall, Sturtevant welcomed him on behalf of the community and congratulated him on his distinguished service during the great conflict. In his public life Yates had been "eminently true to those principles of liberty, equality and justice on which the foundations of [his Alma Mater] are laid…." The Governor's courage and wisdom had placed Illinois "among the foremost of the sisterhood of States in defending national unity and liberty." Therefore, Sturtevant said, "in the name of our country, and of humanity, we thank you." An important task which lay ahead for the Congress which Senator Yates would soon join was to amend the Constitution so as to forever vanquish slavery.

Abraham Lincoln had the strong support of Sturtevant even before his election to the Presidency. Along with other Congregationalists, Sturtevant had urged Lincoln to issue a proclamation of emancipation months before he did so. A year and a half later Sturtevant forwarded to Lincoln resolutions adopted by the Triennial Congregational Convention which urged the President to set a day for national fasting and prayer on behalf of the struggle for freedom. The Convention protested the atrocities committed against the colored troops by the Southern armies and the government was urged to take measures to protect them. Lincoln replied to Sturtevant, thanking him for sending the resolutions and for his kind note. Lincoln's brief letter, a fine example of his penmanship, is in the Illinois College Archives.[29]

Sturtevant's admiration for Lincoln was expressed in the strongest terms in a letter to his daughter, Elizabeth. His great joy when the Civil War ended was abruptly changed into deep sorrow when Lincoln was assassinated. He declared that this act was not the killing of a tyrant but of "the truest friend of liberty that ever sat in the seat of authority." He predicted that this awful tragedy would bring to a climax "our hatred of the rebellion and of the cause of the rebellion," but he also prayed that God will "tranquilize our spirits and give us faith in Him in this dark hour." (A, 329)

Nationalizing Congregationalism

The local Congregational Church ranked very high among the numerous claims for Sturtevant's attention and devotion. He was frequently moderator of official meetings, examined candidates for membership, and encouraged the church to observe the day of fasting and prayer on behalf of colleges. Sturtevant must have concurred in the decision (in 1863) to add to the tower so that the bell from the 1835 building could be hung. His pledge of $700 toward the church's debt of $5,000 was completely paid in March

1864. He rejoiced that now the edifice could be furnished and a superior organ installed.

In 1860 Sturtevant made the motion to call Rev. Charles Marshall to serve for one year, as pastor, at a salary of $1,000. Later a serious conflict arose regarding the doctrinal fidelity of the man's preaching and the congregation voted by a slim majority to continue him. His pastorate ended in 1862. Sturtevant referred to this problem in his comment that the church had passed "through a fiery trial." (S-B, 18 July 1862; CCM, 9 July 1862) Echoes of earlier theological turmoil lingered, and Sturtevant regarded J. B. Turner as the leader of those who sought to make a "broad church."[30] "God be praised, the plot is defeated," Sturtevant wrote to Baldwin. (S-B, 15 Mar. 1864)

During the Civil War Sturtevant became increasingly active in the national affairs of the Congregational churches, and not by mere coincidence. Awareness of the their powerful and expanding nation aroused many churchmen to the opportunities facing the denomination. New organizational forces were needed to meet challenges such as the opening of vast areas in the West and South. Sturtevant's reputation as a vigorous spokesman for the denomination was enhanced when, at the request of the *Independent* in 1863, he contributed an article on Congregationalism as the first in a series on various Protestant churches. Noting that the Congregational churches had neither a written creed nor a centralized government, Sturtevant maintained that their organizational rules were simply the "principles of common law, founded on natural equity and the precepts of Christ."

Congregationalists are unanimous, Sturtevant asserted, in regarding Christianity as divinely given through "a supernatural and miraculous revelation," embodied in the Old and New Testaments as interpreted by standard methods applied to languages. The fundamental teachings of the Bible begin with the acknowledgment of God as Creator and as governing the universe with wisdom and justice. The Godhead consists of three distinct persons: God as Creator; Christ as the Redeemer who dwelt in human flesh and through his death atoned for our sins; and the Holy Spirit, who acts to make men aware of their sins and of the means of redemption. Men are free agents, responsible for their own actions. Men are also sinners and deserving of severe punishment; those who repent and have faith and live a new life shall enjoy God's salvation. On the day of judgment Christ will settle the eternal destiny of all, the righteous entering into life eternal and the wicked going away to everlasting punishment.

Sturtevant emphasized that the word "church" applies with equal truth to the local group, the faithful in all churches, and the redeemed in heaven. Christ is the only superior authority over the local church, yet fellowship with other Christians is cherished. The Congregational order is eminently practical as the best means of avoiding the divisions which inevitably result when centralized authority seeks to require conformity.

Jonathan Blanchard, one of Sturtevant's most vociferous antagonists, voiced sarcastic praise for such views—considering that Illinois College itself was guilty of "that fierce and savage sectarianism." Sturtevant protested in a letter to the editor of the *Independent* that there was no such conflict between the trustees and himself as Blanchard implied. (*Independent*, 19 Feb. 1863) He told his wife that publication of Blanchard's comments was a horrid blunder and must have been instigated by the Devil. He sent a private note to the editor exposing Blanchard's purpose to undermine Congregational support of Illinois College and Beloit in order to divert it to Wheaton College.

Congregational churches were consistently opposed to slavery and thus were virtually excluded from the South. Unlike other major Protestant churches, they avoided schism when North and South began to divide. At War's end the Congregationalists enjoyed the triumph of their cause. The slave system had been abolished. Not only was the Union preserved but it was more unified and had a much stronger federal government. Correspondingly, Congregationalists recognized the need for a national organization even while preserving local control of churches. And they welcomed the opportunity of establishing churches, schools, and colleges in the South, especially among the freedmen.[31] Several of the colleges still flourish more than a century later.

It was only at long intervals that Congregationalists met to consider comprehensive issues. The impetus for a national council came from the West and specifically from Illinois which was still in the forefront of home missionary and educational efforts. The Triennial Convention, meeting in April 1864 at Chicago, adopted resolutions outlining their churches' duty regarding freedom for the remaining slaves and the opening of a vast region for missions. The representatives affirmed the right to extend their order to all regions of the country and to all people, regardless of race. They asserted that "more of general and national concert and co-operation" should be secured to accomplish the appropriate missionary action. (*Debates*, 2)

These decisions were the basis of resolutions adopted the following month by the General Association of Illinois which met at Quincy on 27 May 1864. President Sturtevant was chairman of the committee to which the matter had been referred. The report he presented called for a national convention to assemble at an appropriate time to carry out the Chicago resolutions. Each orthodox Congregational church would send its pastor and one other representative. Comparable bodies in other states responded favorably to the proposal and the delegates assembled in Boston on 14 June 1865 for ten days. The Council began "a new epoch for Congregationalism." (Atkins, 379)

Sturtevant was one of the five men acknowledged by Atkins as most influential in planning the Council. (200) The other four were all from the East—among them his friends, Leonard Bacon of New Haven and Joseph Thompson of New York City. Sturtevant served on numerous advance committees: arrangements, preparation of the call, nomination of persons to present the topics, and evangelization of the West and South. At Boston he was also a member of the committees on church polity, the Rules of Order, and the response to foreign delegates (Canada, France, and England and Wales). He was co-author of some reports.[32]

Keynote Sermon at the Boston Council

The opening session of the Boston Council was held in the Mount Vernon Church with more than five hundred delegates from twenty-four states in attendance. Several of Sturtevant's colleagues from the Illinois Association were present: Elisha Jenney, Asa Turner, Flavel Bascom, Edward Beecher, and William Carter.

Truman Post had a prominent role, as did both Bascom and Beecher. Also present was Rev. Julian M. Sturtevant Jr., a delegate from Missouri. The delegates were seated on the main floor and spectators crowded the galleries. The Council was called to order by its president, Governor W. A. Buckingham of Connecticut, and "six hundred powerful voices," with gallery accompaniment, sang the 78th Psalm. A visitor from England read the Scripture and offered prayer. After another hymn Sturtevant delivered the sermon.

Atkins remarked that "Any denomination assigns its most distinguished clergymen to stellar roles in its stellar meetings." (382) Sturtevant was selected to preach the keynote sermon because he was the spokesman of the denomination regarding the explicit business of the Boston meeting: how best to organize Congregationalism for the mission now opening before the churches. He had previously addressed the issue in sermons and articles; now he had the concentrated attention of the whole denomination. A Boston newspaper reported that "the pioneer missionary, college founder, and State organizer, preached a memorable sermon two hours in length."[33] The *Independent* (22 June) described the sermon as "an able and fearless exposition of the influence of the congregational church order in originating and forming our national character and institutions, and of the obstacles which prevented its prevalence west and south of New England. It was listened to with profound attention for two full hours, and your readers will have the satisfaction of perusing it in the columns of *The Independent* next week."[34] The "Sermon" was also published in the *Debates and Proceedings* of the Council.

The Scripture text which Sturtevant chose for this sermon, the most important one he ever preached, was Jeremiah 6:16—the prophet's injunction to the faithful to seek the old paths as the good way in which to walk. Sturtevant reminded his hearers that "the past is ever the parent of the present." (*Debates*, 31) He did not advocate servile imitation of the fathers; the task now was to determine those seminal principles of national life which would develop strength and beauty and productiveness.

Acknowledging Tocqueville's example in delineating basic principles, Sturtevant declared that the principle underlying all social arrangements is that individual human beings are the direct subjects of the government of God. This foundational concept makes possible the greatest amount of liberty for the individual consistent with the provision of social wants. So far as government is concerned, the smallest unit competent to act is to be preferred. In religion, men of earnest faith will always be drawn into religious societies; consistent with the example of the Pilgrim Fathers, these societies will be locally governed and independent of all authority—save that of Christ—in doctrine, worship, and discipline. In New England the local church was responsible for the moral, religious, intellectual, and physical well-being of all the people within its boundaries, including the sick and the poor. It provided both religious instruction and secular education. That model could be extended so that every township, six miles square, would have a local society to provide for the inhabitants. A network of such religious organizations was essential as the foundation of social and political freedom. Responding to an earlier demurrer, that "Mr. S." could not make New England in the West, Sturtevant admitted that was true but said he would not cease trying. He traced the failure to establish the New England system elsewhere to four causes.

The heterogeneity of the population, with its resulting multiplicity of competing religious sects, was a prominent factor. Slavery was a fatal hindrance, denying Negroes a "place in society as independent and personally responsible human beings." (41) A third obstacle was the diversion of large sums of benevolence monies to the distribution of tracts and Bibles; directed to the establishment of permanent institutions (churches and colleges), the funds would have produced far greater results. The fourth deterrent to the establishment of Christian civilization in the West was the Congregationalists' own failure to adhere to their principles. As a result of their cooperation with others who were tenacious of their conflicting polity, great numbers of both ministers and lay people were channeled into Presbyterian churches.

Sturtevant enjoined his audience to remain steadfast in devotion to that great religious principle which was crucial to the success of "this grandest social experiment of the age." (46) The equality of all disciples was taught by Jesus himself. The congregational polity was the only system consistent with the democratic principle governing national life. At the risk of seeming to violate "established inter-denominational law" and "criminally" disturbing the peace

(49-50), Sturtevant urged his hearers to speak forthrightly in avowing the scriptural and practical truth of congregationalism. He implored them to be earnest in fulfilling the God-given task of planting the gospel under the "sunlight of civil and religious freedom, from the Atlantic to the Pacific, and from the eternal snows of the Arctic to the eternal verdure of the Tropic." With undue optimism Sturtevant declared that the nation's population "very soon" must surpass that of China; he was nearer the mark in predicting that America would soon exceed "in wealth and ubiquitous influence the empire of Britain." The immediate task was "to found and nurture the institutions of learning, freedom, and religion, for a mighty nation...." (52) And then "the Lord will at last appear,[35] and lead his people over Jordan into the promised land of freedom and blessed fellowship." (50) Should not God's people therefore pour out their wealth like water and give their wealth, and their sons and daughters, and themselves, freely and fully to the great cause?

During the Council's deliberations Sturtevant commented on major issues. In support of the report of the Committee on Evangelization in the West and South, he declared that the recent war had been waged for the sake of the basic political principle, "the equal rights of man." Now a mighty spiritual conflict is at hand, to preserve and strengthen the very foundation of civil and political freedom. Local churches must be established all over the West and South because the church is basic to the popular education which is essential to democracy. This effort need not and should not compete with existing Presbyterian and Methodist churches, whom he wished God-speed in their work. (This remark drew the applause of the delegates.) The achievement of the churches' task will require of all laymen the degree of self-denial always expected of the clergy. There is sufficient wealth among the members of the churches, if only they will give.

Four prominent debaters, Sturtevant among them, responded to a "Declaration of Faith" proposed as representing the fundamental doctrines of Christianity common to all evangelical [Protestant] churches.[36] The draft proposal stated that Congregationalists accepted the confessions of faith written in seventeenth-century England, along with the Calvinistic system. Denying that such statements embodied the "substance" of Christian doctrine,

Sturtevant wanted a confession of faith expressed "in original living words of our own." (*Debates*, 355-56) When the statement of faith was finally adopted explicit references to the earlier confessions and Calvinism were omitted. A rising vote of the assembled hundreds approved the revised form; Sturtevant had won at least a partial victory. The new Declaration of Faith included virtually all the points which Sturtevant had expressed in his 1863 article on Congregationalism; in that essay he had succeeded remarkably in stating the essence of Congregationalism.

When Julian Sturtevant delivered his sermon in Boston the audience gave rapt attention and frequently applauded. He had not anticipated that he would soon be engaged in a prolonged "debate" on the nature of the church with a prominent divine from another denomination. A brief summary of his "Sermon" was included in a report about the Council in the *Boston Daily Evening Traveller.* (15 June) The *Traveller,* a secular newspaper with a readership of thirty thousand, published as a weekly feature a column entitled "Episcopal Church." The author, originating from Puritan stock, was Frederic Dan Huntington. For some years he served as minister of an important Unitarian church in Boston and later as preacher at Harvard's Chapel. In 1860 he gained standing as an Episcopal priest and was appointed rector of a Boston church. Having read the reporter's summary of Sturtevant's address, Huntington launched a severe criticism of his depiction of the Christian Church. This led to a sharp response by Sturtevant and a series of exchanges which filled more than thirty columns of print over the next several months.

Sturtevant argued that the New Testament churches were strictly congregational. Each local church was governed by elders under a presiding officer and the whole group made basic decisions. The functions of teaching, preaching, and praying were shared by all. They had fellowship with other such churches but there was no centralized authority over them. Huntington insisted that the biblical church was a visible, organic body with Creed, Ministry, and Sacraments. The church founded by Jesus Christ was perpetuated through the succession of bishops, and the Episcopal Church is in that succession; hence it is truly the Christian

Church. Huntington did agree that there is no single visible head of the church on earth and he also denounced the Romish usurpation. He added that everyone knew what he thought of the Congregational system: all the evidence was against it, Scripture, history, and human nature.

The two men engaged in charges and countercharges, each citing authorities to support his own case and undermine his opponent's. Huntington said that the Pilgrim way was less than three hundred years old. Sturtevant emphasized that Huntington had all the zeal of a new convert. Congregationalists, he declared, had aroused the national conscience against slavery while the Episcopal Church was inert. Huntington took pleasure in noting that many fine ministers had left Congregationalism to become Episcopal priests, and Sturtevant retorted that Episcopalian traffic was heavy on the path to Rome. Huntington stood for the ancient creeds, while Sturtevant believed that each congregation should produce its own statement of faith in contemporary and meaningful language. Sturtevant decried the emphasis on elaborate raiment; Huntington spoke of sensitivity to beauty and the richness of tradition. Sturtevant responded that he did not always wear black in the pulpit but on warm days he would wear white linen. Huntington recognized the validity of tradition along with Scripture and history, while Sturtevant echoed Luther when he noted that the only adequate authorities were Scripture and reason. Huntington believed that the Episcopalian sense of order supported civil government, while Sturtevant maintained that Congregationalism was the ally of both religious and civil liberty. Sturtevant, attacking Huntington's admission that the Episcopal Church teaches her own children humble deference to her wisdom, declared Congregationalism to be in wholehearted accord with the right of private judgment.

Each man urged more than once that their discussion be conducted with a spirit of charity but each also used powerful adjectives and sarcasm. The heading for some early columns, "The Theological Controversy," was replaced by a more irenic phrase, "The Theological Discussion." Despite the gentler title the warmth of the debate increased in the final months of 1865. Sturtevant referred to certain of Huntington's arguments as ludicrous, his language as pompous and grandiloquent, and his manner as arrogant. Huntington, more sophisticated, was also condescending; he did not sign his own name but sometimes used "Churchman" as his signature. Sturtevant, he said, made assertions while he himself had the facts. Each man sought to embarrass his antagonist by citing a scholarly authority from the other's church in support of an argument. Huntington, a New Englander himself, knew some of the less exemplary aspects of the Puritan tradition. Sturtevant cited damaging observations he had made when attending services in English churches.

Both Sturtevant and Huntington sought to prove too much and too decisively. Huntington won a point in the discussion of biblical authorship, referring to a dimension of continental scholarship which perhaps was not familiar to Sturtevant (or possibly not welcomed by him). Sturtevant scored in showing that Huntington's stress upon the organic unity of the Episcopal Church as the truly Christian Church was negated by the obvious separation of the American church from the Church of England and by the existence of other claimants to such an elevated position. Although the controversy occupied space in the *Traveller* for six months neither disputant could claim victory and neither would admit defeat. Support for Sturtevant's position was expressed in an unidentified news clipping: "The descendant of the Puritan accepts the challenge, and replies to his reviewer in a way which completely unhorses the knight of Episcopacy." (EC, 21)

In December Sturtevant sent a final article to close the long controversy and reported to Baldwin (23 Dec.) that Huntington's connection with the newspaper would terminate on 1 January. He added, "The Lord used my poor agency" to break up an arrangement which threatened freedom and religion. Handicapped by the utterly inadequate library at Illinois College, Sturtevant had to request research assistance from prominent eastern friends, such as Noah Porter and Leonard Bacon.[37] He said that he had felt like a fortress commander, beleaguered and out of ammunition. He wished heartily that some rich man of Boston would endow the College.

Sturtevant's son discounted the rancorous spirit of the exchange. He declared that "the controversy with Bishop

Huntington which grew out of that discourse was on both sides a fine illustration of the candor and courtesy which ought always to characterize theological discussions." (A, 329-30) Shortly after Sturtevant's death Huntington, elected a Bishop in New York State in 1869, gave generous praise to Sturtevant and his achievements in a memorial statement.[38]

Essays and Sermons . . . The Club

Sturtevant's active mind thrived on stimulating discussion and on books and the religious and secular press. He was eager for opportunities to express his views in person and through the printed word. In December 1861 Sturtevant spoke at the eighth annual meeting of the Illinois State Teachers' Association at Bloomington on the subject of "Female Education." In January 1863 he spent two days lecturing on sects at the Chicago Theological Seminary. When in Chicago he frequently called on the Blatchfords and sometimes was a guest in their home; Hannah accompanied him on at least one occasion. Sturtevant had many opportunities to preach in local churches and at national gatherings. Baldwin in February 1861 hoped he could arrange for him to supply Henry Ward Beecher's pulpit in the Brooklyn Church during August. Receiving a special invitation in 1861 from the Old School Presbyterian Church in "Petersburgh" Sturtevant took the "Rail Road" on a Saturday and spent the Sabbath there. Mrs. Duncan heard him preach at the First Presbyterian Church in Jacksonville on the Sunday before he left for England, and he preached there also in the winter of 1865.

In two brief articles in 1861, Sturtevant shared his reflections on the proper character of preaching. Decrying the emotional appeal of many professional lecturers whose only purpose was entertainment, he contrasted the pulpit actor and the pulpit orator. With the former, religion languishes and unwarned sinners go to perdition. The will is "the citadel of the soul" and the preacher of the Gospel must persuade men to be reconciled to God through Jesus Christ and to do that which is good. Like Paul, the true pulpit orator of today will use every weapon to turn men to God: "instruction, argument, rebuke, the justice and severity of God, the dying love of Jesus, gratitude for his unequaled compassion, the fear of perdition, the hope of the life everlasting." "That man who can win souls to Christ has…the noblest gift that God ever bestowed on a mortal." ("Pulpit Drama" and "Pulpit Eloquence")

Sturtevant applied some of his criteria for distinguishing entertainers from orators in his 1864 review of a book by Bayard Taylor, *Hannah Thurston.* Taylor, one of the stream of professionals on the lecture circuit, spoke in Jacksonville in Strawn's Hall on "Life in the Arctic Regions" and "The American People." (JC, 31 Jan. 1982) There is no direct evidence that Sturtevant was in attendance, but he was familiar with the man's style and the content of some of his speeches. In his judgment, Taylor was an "actor" who could please an audience but who could not compete with Thackeray, Dickens, and Bulwer in writing fiction. Taylor had invited readers to evaluate his portrayal of certain features of American society: women's rights, total abstinence, revivals, spirit-rappings, and socialism. Unfortunately, Sturtevant commented, Taylor conceived of religion as ceremony and ritual. He lacked the basic qualification for undertaking his announced task because he was not in sympathy with "that profound religious earnestness, which has been a most striking American characteristic from the landing of the Pilgrims to the present time.…" (497) Taylor was contemptuous of important virtues, such as total abstinence. To him revivals were simply the means by which sects scrambled to recruit more members, often from each other. Moreover, Taylor overlooked the unique character of religion in America: the seriousness with which people practice their religion, the exceptional freedom allowed, and the fact that most sects originated in other countries. America's great advantages are freedom of inquiry and a free Bible, and consequently the wrongs and follies which long plagued Europe are seen to be erroneous.

More satisfactory was Bayard Taylor's presentation of female characters. Women are indeed earnest and sincere in their love for others, in aiding the victim and upholding the oppressed. But, said Sturtevant, in actuality women are not content to fulfill their natural role and accept their inevitable dependence on men. He denied that the doctrine of equal rights necessarily implies that women should vote, or hold office, or engage in public discourse.

"Let us understand the doctrine of equal rights to be the right of every man to be a man, and every woman to be a woman, and let woman be content with her natural and peaceful dominion over domestic and social life...." (509)

People abroad were intensely interested in the ultimate result of the great American experiment in freedom and equal rights. Unfortunately, said Sturtevant, "Anything which seems to afford evidence that American character is degraded and depraved, is seized on with more avidity by the London Times and the Saturday Review, than a story of a 'Confederate' victory, or a Federal defeat." (514) An example in Taylor's book was the leading male, who lacked education and moral and religious culture. The author's "portrait of 'American life' [was] "false and slanderous." (516)

During the Civil War when travel was more difficult, Sturtevant found a replacement for Eastern dialogue in Jacksonville. Sixteen men met on 17 September 1861 at the home of Professor William Sanders to found "The Club." President Sturtevant was called to the chair. Others who had some association with Illinois College were Samuel Adams, R. C. Crampton, David A. Smith, Rufus Nutting, E. P. Kirby, and J. B. Turner. Andrew McFarland and David Prince were also present. The purpose of The Club was "mutual entertainment and instruction by conversation & discussion, written or oral, on all [subjects] of interest and intelligence." The group met on the second and fourth Mondays of each month to have "conversational discussion" of a topic chosen at the previous meeting or to discuss an essay or oral presentation from a member or other person. The group usually met in the homes of members. An elected secretary kept a record of questions proposed and discussed and notified members of the meetings; often the names of those present were listed. Often little if any detail was provided about the leader's presentation.

Ten topics suggested at that first meeting were directly or indirectly related to the Civil War. The remainder of that session was devoted to discussing whether Major General Fremont ought to resign. Sturtevant was appointed to lead the next discussion: "What should be the immediate policy of the Government in respect to the slave population?" The fourth meeting was held at his home. In April 1862 Sturtevant "read a long and interesting paper on the subject of 'Christian Union.'" Subsequently he proposed a discussion on temperance reform and he was the leader at his home. In the fall "Prest. Sturtevant presented the question, 'Are there good reasons to be found in the past history & present condition of the world, for anticipating a long future of universal peace?'" Most of the widely-varied comments were negative. Whether the political equality declared in the Constitution could be applied to the Negro population was suggested by Sturtevant in March 1863. A subsequent meeting focused on "Compensated Emancipation."

Upon his return from England in 1863, Sturtevant shared his observations with his friends. The meetings he led in 1864 covered a wide range of interests: "Citizenship-Sovereignty," "Freedom of the Will," and "a great and noble university" in Jacksonville. Although hosting The Club only once in 1865, Sturtevant was the leader four times. He presented some thoughts on the relationship of democracy and the laboring classes; that meeting was at the home of David A. Smith—across the street from his own home. Another session, in May, dealt with punishment in civil government, perhaps with reflections on appropriate treatment of the defeated Southerners. Later on Sturtevant's topics were "The Moral Law of Giving" and "The Credibility of History."

Family, Relatives, Friends

The Federal Government imposed an income tax to pay the expenses of the War. The first such tax in America, it applied to those earning $800 or more. For 1863 Sturtevant's tax was $23.40; the tax rate was five per cent, indicating a taxable income of $468. The following year his tax was $14.70 on taxable income of $294. No receipt is available for 1865. Sturtevant's real estate and personal taxes increased from $104.21 in 1861 to $169.44 in 1864. Only one land transaction was recorded under his name in the county office, the sale of two lots on Grove Street to Edward Tanner; the price of $1,044 reflected the increase in property values.

Pastor Julian Sturtevant Jr. lived at the home of Col. and Mrs.

J. T. K. Hayward in Hannibal, Missouri. His father's desire for him to find a wife was fulfilled when he married Katherine, the Haywards' daughter, on 26 November 1861. Father officiated and, Julian Jr. recalled, he did not forget to include the word "obey." In 1863 a daughter was born and named Elizabeth for her grandmother; sadly the baby died in infancy. In June 1865 both Julians were at the Boston meeting and made the return trip together. When Baldwin inquired in August 1865 whether Julian Sr. thought his son might serve as an agent for the College Society. Sturtevant replied that he did not know.

Sturtevant was anxious for his second son, James Warren, to be settled in a suitable occupation. Warren considered going East to attend law school and his father asked Baldwin's recommendation among Yale, Cambridge, and Albany. However, Warren accepted a teaching position at Hannibal. The parents' anxiety about their son's salvation was relieved when Warren joined his brother's church at Hannibal in 1863.

Daughter Hannah Augusta was appointed vice-principal of the Young Ladies' Athenaeum which Professor Sanders founded in Jacksonville in 1864. The Board of Instructors included President Sturtevant and other members of the College faculty. Libbie, the oldest of Hannah's and Julian's children, wanted very much to teach and her father expressed his regret that, regardless of how much he had done for education, he could do nothing to help her secure a position. He admitted that he did not want all the family to leave Jacksonville.

The frequent letters Hannah and the children wrote to Sturtevant while he was in England provide the most sustained and detailed record of the family available. Lucy especially was mentioned often. She was attending the free school in Jacksonville and started Virgil and geometry but found them hard-going; however, her mother said, Lucy was a determined student. Hannah queried, what was to be done with her next year, when she had finished the free school; should they consider the female seminary at Rockford? Julian believed that the school would be too strenuous. After he mentioned visiting Walter Scott's home at Abbotsford, Lucy wrote to tell him that she had just finished reading *Quentin Durward* and had already started *The Heart of*

Midlothian. For some weeks she taught a class of six girls in the Colored Baptist Sunday School. Men and women in that church who were turning gray were just now learning to read. Lucy declared that when father returned from distant England she would have two Thanksgivings, the national day in early August and their family celebration upon his return in early September.

Alfred, only twelve, did much of the hard outdoor work. Enrolled in the free school for the morning classes, he missed about half the time when the work demanded it. While hauling hay he suffered a severe strain, but he was still able to go to school and to church and to attend the boys' prayer meeting. Despite his injuries he went outdoors to supervise the hired boy, John. By mid-July he was quite well again. Alfred was admitted as a member of the Congregational Church in October 1864, and now all the Sturtevant children were among the "hopefully converted."

During the Civil War Julian's younger brother, Christopher, served on the examining board in Cass County for drafting men for military service.[39] He married a second time in April 1865, at Mount Sterling; his new wife was Priscilla Birdsall.[40] Several of the children born to Christopher's first wife, Ann Eliza, were still in the home. No children were born of the second marriage.

Hannah E. Chamberlain, the daughter of Julia and Timothy, married James Dunavan in January 1863 in a ceremony performed by Sturtevant. James Fayerweather visited at least twice while Julian was overseas, and on one occasion he brought some of his family for an extended stay. In 1864 Hannah's aunt, Diana Richards, died; Hannah was to receive household goods, and the Sturtevant daughters were to receive some residual income.

Theron Baldwin and his wife visited for a day in the early summer of 1863 and Hannah told them about her husband's experiences in England. When they discussed the College's financial situation, Hannah said she feared the prospect of yielding control to the Presbyterians in order to secure money. She dreaded the possibility that all of her husband's hard work in collecting funds should result in the aggrandizement of Presbyterianism as had happened at Knox College.

In her last letter to her husband while he was in Europe,

Hannah called his attention to a report in the *New York Post* about the heresy trial of Charles Beecher. She asked, "Is it not a sign of the times? Is it not also one of the fruits of Edward's pre-existent system?" (31 July) Charles was greatly influenced by his older brother's views about the suffering of God and the preexistence of the soul. Many orthodox Congregationalists like Hannah and Julian looked askance at some of Edward's theological speculations. Despite the strong support of Edward and other Beechers, Charles was convicted of heresy. although some years later that verict was rescinded.[41]

The letters exchanged between Sturtevant and Baldwin were seldom sharp in tone. An exception occurred in March 1865 when Baldwin proposed showing some of his friend's letters to "a distinguished person." Sturtevant replied that he certainly would object to Baldwin's permitting anyone else to see his letters, which, he said, were written not only hastily but in confidence. He had often poured out his inmost anxieties and hopes to Baldwin as the one person other than Hannah in whom he placed utter confidence regarding certain matters. Sturtevant added an explanation of why Hannah could not accompany him to the Boston meeting: it was too expensive. "Living on $1250 a year when a dollar is worth but 50 cts is not easy." (S-B, 9 May 1865)

Chapter 8: 1866-1870

Adjusting to a New Age

Aiding the College's Recovery

The effect of the Civil War on the colleges in the Mississippi Valley was "very disastrous," according to President Sturtevant. (A, 302) Few students were left on college campuses and after the War many young men were eager to take advantage of new opportunities in business, industry, and the lands of the West. Inflation reduced the value of money by one-half and brought increased hardship for faculty. Some colleges which had closed never reopened, others merged to pool limited resources. Illinois College shared in the distress caused by the War but also in its triumph. The participation of alumni and students in the victorious Union struggle was cause for congratulations. The trustees expressed pride in "the sons of the college" who obeyed the call to arms; they also conveyed sympathy to the families of those who had perished. (TM, 6 June 1866)

Along with the vast social, political, and economic changes resulting from the War, other important developments also affected the College. The population of Morgan County surpassed 28,000 by 1870, and Jacksonville likewise grew, nearly doubling to more than 9,000. The graded school system was inaugurated, with an elementary school in each of the four wards, a "colored" school, and Washington High School which opened in 1867. Civic improvements included the construction of an imposing court house on a new site on West State Street. The Jacksonville Street Railway began operations with horse cars in 1870. Both public and private funds were needed for these purposes, thus limiting the resources available to Illinois College.

In January 1867 the College had fewer than a hundred students, and Sturtevant anticipated that income would fall $1,500 below the previous year's. Baldwin urged Sturtevant to drop all preparatory work, and Sturtevant agreed that there was "a <u>stern necessity</u>" to limit the College to collegiate studies. (S-B, 16 Feb. 1867) They had not foreseen that free public education might be extended to the university level, constituting an unexpected source of competition for students. In the fall of 1867 classes opened with only fifty in the College programs and the next year there were barely thirty; Sturtevant called the situation "a merry farce." (S-B, 26 Sept. 1868) In 1869 the College again undertook preparatory education but with an important change. To encourage attendance by younger boys living in town a site was obtained at Kosciusko and Morgan, across from the Congregational Church. Dr. Samuel Whipple's gift of $10,000 financed a suitable building. The new arrangement obviously fulfilled a need because in its first year more than a hundred pupils enrolled. It was, however, inconvenient for the teachers to divide their time between two buildings three-fourths of a mile apart.

Major problems confronted the College and its president. Large sums were needed for the operation and endowment of the College. Strong opposition from minorities, both faculty and trustees, obstructed basic policies. The Illinois Industrial University, founded in 1867, had the potential of destroying Illinois College. These problems and others were discussed in the letters exchanged with Theron Baldwin during these years. Sturtevant urged Baldwin to regard his letters "as a sort of photographic series of pictures setting forth the successive aspects of the College question as they present themselves to my mind." (S-B, 14 Mar. 1867) Baldwin said that the possible failure of the College would be a calamity signaling that "our New Haven movement [had] failed in its grandest feature." (B-S, 25 July 1867) Other achievements would survive—the numerous Presbyterian and Congregational churches they had founded and "the noble public school system of Illinois," which was planned and established by the men at the College. (SPC-25, 59) Leonard Bacon credited the Illinois Association with having "saved the West" by their efforts and the stimulus they gave to similar missions to other states.[1]

The graduating classes for a decade beginning in 1864 ranged from four to eleven. In 1868 the traditional classification of students was resumed and the *Catalogue* again listed the studies for each class each semester rather than by departments. Plans were made to teach French and German in alternate years. Special courses were open to both College and Academy students and also, for a fee of $5, to the public. Sturtevant wanted to have the regular courses taught by a few permanent professors "to give body and character to the institution." Short courses and special lectures would be staffed by faculty or by distinguished visitors, such as Dr. Hiram K. Jones and Dr. Andrew McFarland. Some short courses were taught in the lecture room of the Congregational Church for the convenience of townspeople.

The problem of competitive schools was partially resolved when a plan was adopted for "a first rate Classical, Scientific, and Commercial School" in the new building. (S-B, 12 Mar. 1869) In 1869 Illinois College acquired the Business College which Crampton started in 1866. Now, its students—along with those in the Whipple Academy—were counted in the total enrollment. In 1869-1870 the College itself had a faculty of five and enrolled 40 students, while the downtown branch had 218 students, including some females in the commercial program.[2] There were 10,000 books in the College Library and the budget was $8,000; the assets totaled $250,000.

The commencement in 1870 was on 2 June, and that afternoon Phi Alpha celebrated its twenty-fifth anniversary. In the evening the Sturtevants hosted the Alumni Reception. A special feature was an address by a former student, Major J. W. Powell, on "The Canons [*sic*] of the Colorado." Despite losing an arm during the Battle of Shiloh in 1862, Powell in 1869 was the leader of the first expedition to complete the hazardous journey through the Grand Canyon.

Staff changes included Professor Nutting's resignation in 1866. In 1870 Mason Grosvenor, at long last given a regular faculty appointment, came to teach Moral Philosophy. Sturtevant, relinquishing that post, was made Professor of Mental Science and Science of Government. He was listed as Instructor in those subjects and others at Whipple Academy and as Instructor in Political

Economy in the Business College. The staff was augmented in the fall of 1870 by Alfred Sturtevant, appointed to teach both at the College and the Academy.

In the aftermath of the Civil War few of the students were church members but, said Sturtevant, the Holy Spirit was present on the campus in January 1866. Attendance at the weekly prayer meeting increased from five to sixty and frequently the sessions were held daily. Indeed, a "very unusual religious interest [was manifested] in all the churches of the town, and in most of the schools,…in which the town remarkably abounds; and the work in [the] college was greatly aided by the Sabbath services and the numerous praying circles of the several churches." Some forty to fifty students experienced conversion and the Day of Prayer was well attended. (*Congregationalist*, 1 June 1866)

A comprehensive report was prepared for the College Society's Twenty-fifth Anniversary meeting at Marietta College in 1868. Acknowledging that young men tend to be wayward, Sturtevant said the likelihood is greater that a youth will be converted while in a college setting than elsewhere, provided there are proper religious influences. [At Illinois College, "Revivals have been of frequent occurrence, and often of such power and prevalence as to exert a strong and decisive influence on…a large portion of the students." The history of the College showed that seasons of revival often occurred because the teachers had a sincere faith and were earnest in their desire to bring pupils to Christ. Two elements were essential: "all teaching in whatever department of knowledge should be given from a Christian stand-point, [and the faculty must bring] Christian truth before the minds of the students, clearly, earnestly and argumentatively…." (SPC-25, 6) The most effective program at Illinois College for accomplishing this was the Sabbath afternoon lectures on religious subjects.]

The baccalaureate address in 1868 was perhaps the first occasion when Sturtevant declared publicly that the College was in effect a Congregational institution. Many ministers and laymen from numerous Congregational churches in the state were in town for the meeting of the General Association and attended the service. It is essential, Sturtevant said, for families to teach true religion to their children. Christian schools and seminaries and colleges supplement such teaching, and when that training is gained for the whole church and throughout the world, the millennium will come. Sturtevant rejoiced that as the frontier moved westward so had the church and with it the school. The highest level of Christian cooperation was exemplified in the churches so well represented in the audience. A true example of the kind of college which such churches should support was Illinois College, based on broad evangelical principles. It was not necessary to make that College "Congregational" because the very nature of its service to Christ, the church universal, and the state constituted it that way.

The final words were addressed to the eleven graduates, among them Sturtevant's nephew, William Fayerweather. "Do not live for yourselves but for your country, your fellow-men, your God. There are great works of humanity, of patriotism, of piety, which will ever demand your heads, your hearts, and your hands.... Love your country, love the church of Christ,...love God.... Love yourselves last." On behalf of the faculty and himself, the president bade them farewell. (JJ, 2,3 June)

A Strenuous Financial Campaign

Theron Baldwin heeded Sturtevant's plea for help and was granted a leave of absence for two months from the College Society, with pay. He joined Sturtevant on 18 January 1866 in presenting a plan to the trustees, and two days later Sturtevant was relieved of his College duties so that the two men could concentrate upon raising funds. A leaflet dated 22 January 1866 and addressed "To the Friends of Illinois College" introduced the campaign with the statement that "It is well-known that this Institution is the oldest College in the State." The founders were motivated by patriotic and Christian aims and through their efforts they had contributed to the educational and moral development of thousands of young men. It seemed likely that "the original purpose of the Yale College band to make Jacksonville, as to educational influences, the New Haven of Illinois," would be largely fulfilled. Moreover the new academic program was judged by distinguished educators to be "a most important advance on

the College system of this country as well as of Europe." The statement characterizing the College was concise: "Christian without
being sectarian, conservative without being bigoted, progressive
without being radical, and aiming at no ephemeral popularity, it
has been from the begining [*sic*] a power in the State."

The College's financial need was graphically portrayed. The
faculty was very inadequately paid (especially during the War), the
science equipment and library were very limited, and the buildings
were insufficient. The amount of $50,000 was urgently needed,
with additional sums required for future progress. Rev. Theron
Baldwin, D.D., was introduced as Secretary of the Western
College Society, and he and Sturtevant were authorized to undertake
the endowment campaign. The appeal was made for sufficient
resources to enable the College to achieve a position worthy of "its
founders, of its past history, of the magnificent State [of Illinois],
and of the present age...."

The campaign got off to a slow start in Jacksonville. Sturtevant
then solicited funds in Springfield and Princeton. He had some
initial success in Chicago and wrote to tell Hannah that he would
stay there until sickness or death warranted his leaving; actually it
was the lack of further results which brought him home. By early
April Sturtevant reported that the total subscriptions amounted to
less than $10,000; with Commencement approaching he felt
under great pressure. The more modest goal of $25,000 was set. At
Baldwin's suggestion a very important plan was adopted to circum-
vent the denominational prejudice against the College: the fund
would be designated as an endowment for the presidency.
Contributions of $2,500 each were made by two good friends of
Sturtevant and of the College, E. W. Blatchford and Col. Charles
G. Hammond, both prominent Congregationalists of Chicago.

Meanwhile Baldwin had returned to New York City, and
Sturtevant wrote to advise him of impending failure. "The nearer
the time approaches the more solemn and dangerous the crisis
appears, and the more ruinous the consequences of failure
appear." (S-B, 26 Apr. 1866) Sturtevant proposed to seek funds in
the East as the only remaining hope for success. Baldwin's
response was direct, "I think you had better come," and he recommended May as the best time. Sturtevant's efforts in the East

were worthwhile, and although he came home for Commencement he returned to the East soon after. He obtained subscriptions in Boston, New Haven, Providence, and elsewhere, and by early August the total was just over $23,000. He rejoiced that Governor Buckingham of Connecticut sent $100 without even being asked. Now very tired, he was still determined. The final gap was closed when two donors offered to share the amount still due at the end of the campaign.

The new President's Fund benefited the faculty because the president's salary was no longer included in the budget. The trustees, seeking to relieve the instructors from the need to take outside employment, approved salary increases—subject to the availability of funds. That fall the balance sheet was again disappointing; the number of students was smaller and tuition income was nearly a thousand dollars less than the previous year.

There was a heartening response from Lemuel Foster, one of the later members of the Illinois Association, who offered $500 with an additional $500 if necessity required. Sturtevant told Baldwin that he would have to "nail" Foster for the full amount, and he wrote to Foster to explain the circumstances. He quoted from Foster's reply: "in an extra mid-day approach to God in prayer daily for special objects, I have for more than 30 years made Illinois College one of these objects. And I have often, when… riding alone, got down from my horse & knelt on our broad prairies to observe that occasion. Indeed I have regarded the College from the first as vitally connected with Christ's cause in our State." (S-B, 2 Oct. 1866)

Sturtevant was determined to increase the professors' salaries to $1,500 for 1867-1868. At least $100,000 was needed for endowment, and by August a new campaign was underway. Sturtevant complained that the College could expect no help from Glover's church while Sanders was on the faculty. Sanders' Athenaeum was a rival of the Jacksonville Female Academy, which was sponsored by the First Presbyterian Church of which Glover was pastor. Added grief was caused by people who stirred up the students with false reports that the College must soon close.

When Sturtevant appealed in 1867 for more help from the College Society he received a terse refusal from Baldwin: "You have the full amount." (B-S, 5 Jan. 1867) The Society had its own difficulties; Baldwin could not send his payment of $125 for the Sturtevant Foundation on time because his salary had not been paid when due and so he sent a partial payment on the interest.

The trustees appointed a committee of community leaders to recommend improvements to the campus grounds. Among the members were J. B. Turner, Dr. Andrew McFarland of the State Hospital, and Dr. Joshua Rhoads of the institution for the blind. Funds were provided for needed repairs to the Library Building. Despite these efforts unwelcome publicity regarding the College's facilities was published in a report about the General Association's meeting in Jacksonville:

> Illinois College, over which Dr. Sturtevant presides, has a spacious campus on a swell of ground commanding a fine outlook, and ornamented by numerous noble trees. We were disappointed in the number and size of the buildings, expecting something more spacious and imposing. One, well-built, impressive structure, showing from far, contains the public rooms for the professors, while an unpretending edifice in the rear holds the library and cabinet. Students board in families. There is much need of a little taste and labor in improving the really beautiful grounds with suitable paths and shrubbery. (*Advance*, 4 June 1868)

Sturtevant admitted that the grounds were not in the highest style of the gardener's art but argued that they were at least decent. He confessed to Baldwin that anxiety over the College's financial distress pressed on him night and day and, echoing Paul, he declared he was "cast down but not quite in despair."[3]

The trustees took drastic steps to obtain funds in 1868 by selling a large part of the campus. The College Grove Addition was plotted by the County Surveyor and consisted of thirty-nine lots, all but one of appropriate size for homes. A street was planned immediately in front of the new College Building [Sturtevant Hall] and two rows of lots were charted between that street and Park, from College to Mound. Similarly two rows of lots were laid out between Lockwood Place and Asylum Street [Woodland], the prices ranging from $800 to $1,000.

At the Twenty-fifth Anniversary of the College Society in 1868 Sturtevant, who had been present at the Society's founding, was given the honor of moving the adoption of the annual report. In his speech he illustrated the significant work of the Society by describing its role in sustaining Illinois College. That College had trained hundreds of men for public service and had certainly done much "to plant and quicken into healthful growth the germs of a truly Christian civilization…." (SPC-25, 60) Sturtevant paid warm tribute to Theron Baldwin, saying that his departure from Illinois in 1843 to assume the Secretaryship of the Society was a great loss to Illinois College and to him personally. "This Report shows to our full satisfaction that this sacrifice was not in vain…. [H]is name cannot fail to be held in loving and grateful remembrance." (SPC-25, 113)

The Denominational Issue, Again

The consolidation of Illinois College and Knox College was mentioned in 1866 as one of several possible solutions to the financial crisis. Another possibility was the removal of the College to Quincy or its relocation to the site of the proposed state university if it were not established in Jacksonville. Rev. R. W. Patterson claimed that Illinois College had only a Presbyterian constituency; Sturtevant responded by calling attention to the increasing number of Congregational churches in Illinois. However, because there were more of them in the northern part of the state, Knox's Galesburg location had merit. That, coupled with Sturtevant's commitment to having one strong collegiate institution in Illinois, added to the arguments in favor of merger. Meanwhile Knox College became more definitely Congregational; Baldwin thought the Presbyterians had yielded at Knox in order to make Jacksonville their battleground.

The effort to improve the College's finances had inevitably brought the issue of denominational relationship to the forefront. When the Prudential Committee of the Board met with the faculty before the fund drive began in 1866, Professors Sanders and Nutting urged that all future faculty appointments should be divided equally between the Presbyterians and the Congregationalists; moreover, the presidency should alternate between them. The proposal was contrary to the agreement made at the College's founding and moreover would require amending the College's charter. Sturtevant addressed a memorandum to the Prudential Committee outlining the historic understanding that the College was to be Christian but not denominational. The assumption some held that from the beginning the two denominations had a joint interest in the College's property was false. As of 1829 there were no Congregational churches within five hundred miles, and New School Presbyterianism did not emerge until eight years later. The College, declared Sturtevant, does not exist for the sake of the denominations but "for learning, for our country, for the whole Church of God."

At the June 1866 meeting Sturtevant addressed the trustees at length. Strongly opposing the revolutionary proposal made by Sanders and Nutting, Sturtevant said that was "not the boat in which I embarked in my youth, and I do not feel disposed to go aboard in my old age." He urged the Board to adopt certain principles summarized in these words: "Our conception of the College...was that it should be controlled by sound evangelical men, who could be trusted to administer it for Christ and his church, and that in administering it they were bound to appoint to the various posts of instruction, some trustworthy, evangelical men, of the highest qualifications for their respective departments, and that beyond this they were not to be held responsible for the denominational relations of the candidates."

Sturtevant acknowledged that the great majority of the trustees had been Presbyterians and most of the faculty had been Congregationalists but that was due to circumstances, not intent.[4] He urged approval of the plan to raise $25,000 for the endowment of the presidency and to accept the substantial subscriptions made on the understanding that the College would continue to be non-sectarian. The trustees considered the issue at length and unanimously adopted the basic points advocated by Sturtevant. Sturtevant was pleased that at last E. W. Blatchford of Chicago had been elected to the Board because increasingly that city would be a major source of funding.

The outside activities of Crampton and Sanders were a problem not only internally but with regard to the public. Crampton agreed to cease active involvement in the Business College although he continued as owner for a time; Sanders, however, was adamant. Baldwin urged Sturtevant to have the Board declare that an outside connection by a professor was inconsistent with the good of the College. Efforts by some trustees to rein in Sanders were stymied by his assertion that the Presbyterians would protest strongly against any interference with his school. "This is humiliating and disheartening," complained Sturtevant. (S-B, 8 July 1867) The tension was even worse the next year, leading Baldwin to comment that Sturtevant was "over a volcano" which would soon erupt. (B-S, 8 Jan. 1868) At the 1868 meeting some longtime Board members supportive of Sturtevant were absent. Among those present who rallied to his side were three members of the Illinois Association: Brooks and Hale, who were Presbyterians, and Carter, the lone Congregationalist. Fortunately Glover, the pastor of the First Presbyterian Church, also assisted. Although he had not always been a friend he now "did noble service." (S-B, 9 June 1868)

At a meeting in July the Board granted Sanders' request to be heard. He presented a lengthy explanation of his connection with the Athenaeum and claimed that the issue was simply a pretext for ousting him from the College because he was a Presbyterian. The Board granted him permission to remain for further discussion and to be present at the afternoon session when it would be Sturtevant's turn. Speaking at length, Sturtevant declared that if Sanders' charges were true, he himself should be removed at once; if not, Sanders was to be censured. No action was taken.

The Board voted, at the request of one of its members, to hear three non-members who supported Sanders and his plan for the College. One of the visitors asserted that it was Sturtevant's duty to resign and the trustees' duty "to put [him] out" because of actions he had taken against Presbyterian nominees. The ensuing discussion proved these charges to be false, and the man admitted that the rumors had caused great conflict between the two denominations. "The agony was over," Sturtevant told Baldwin. (S-B, 10 July 1868)

Unhappily, the controversy had not ended. Sanders circulated the report that that due to Sturtevant's inept administration the

College was dead or dying. He also claimed that he had been vindicated at the recent Board meeting. Sturtevant wished to publish a notice of the trustees' action and arranged for a prominent citizen to make a public request for this information. This appeared in the local *Journal* (20 Aug. 1868) under the name of "Civis." Sturtevant prepared a brief statement to accompany a summary of the trustees' action but at the urging of two trustees, he asked the newspaper to withhold the items. Upon returning from a weekend trip to St. Louis, he discovered that they had been published and with them "Civis No. 2." (JJ, 24 Aug. 1868) This called for the publication of the statement made by the three non-members. Sturtevant responded with a public notice that no copy of that material had been submitted to the secretary and that it was up to the party involved to publish it. Sturtevant considered the affair to be "the mortifying ordeal of my life." (S-B, 25, 26 Sept. 1868)

A plan announced by Sturtevant was a possible remedy for the College's plight. He invited any Evangelical Christian denomination, such as the Lutherans, to endow a professorship and name the professor. Illinois College would thus be the nucleus of a university; no offers were forthcoming. In early 1869 Sturtevant was cast into despair by the "Presbyterian hostility" of local trustees, some of whom advocated closing the College for a time. Sturtevant corresponded with President Gulliver of Knox College regarding a possible merger and confessed to Baldwin that "the thought of the surrender of this beautiful site with all its cherished hopes and sacred memories, and this home of my life, is as painful as can well be imagined." (S-B, 4 Feb. 1869) Such a merger was proposed by Crampton and Tanner, unaware that their president had considered it. An undated news account quoted Gulliver as denying rumors that Illinois College was to be absorbed by Knox and that a professorship would be offered to Sturtevant. Sturtevant also denied that any such arrangement had been made.

Baldwin advised caution in suggesting such a change; before a minister threatens to leave a church unless his salary is raised, he should be quite sure they will not take him at his word. The report prepared for the trustees showed that the College had much worth right where it was, the assets amounting to more than $235,000. The invested funds totaled nearly $82,000, including the remnant of the $50,000 fund of 1858 ($1,500) and the President's Fund ($6,000). [It is not clear why these amounts were so low.] Even in the darkest hour Sturtevant thought "the vessel may yet right herself and have a successful voyage," and by spring the outlook for the College was indeed more hopeful. (S-B, 16 Feb. 1869)

Sturtevant felt that his opponents on the Board were determined to oust him. His situation was made even more difficult by the continuing opposition of Sanders, whom he regarded as vigorous, bold, and unscrupulous. He believed that the low enrollment in the College, a mere thirty students, was a direct consequence of Sanders' attacks. Baldwin advised that Sturtevant should not even think of resigning but should be patient. To Sturtevant's continuing dismay not a single local trustee gave him any support. Was it any wonder, he asked Baldwin, that he sometimes thought of retreating, either with or without carrying the College along? It was time for the trustees to stand squarely on the 1866 declaration that the College should be independent.

When the Board met in June 1869 a communication from Sanders was presented which attacked Sturtevant "with unprecedented malignity." (S-B, 7 June 1869) At the same time, Sanders submitted his unconditional resignation and the Board accepted it unanimously. The turmoil caused by Sanders was at last ended. However, the College's financial difficulties were not resolved. Presbyterians such as Glover were "blocking the wheels" by refusing to provide funds and at the same time making it impossible to obtain money from Congregationalists who feared the Presbyterians would gain control.

In 1869 the denominational control of the College was still a live issue. However, in 1870 the Congregationalists achieved greater representation on the Board. Rev. W. H. Savage, a "Congregational Presbyterian," was elected as a trustee and so too was the minister of the new Congregational Church in Springfield, Rev. John K. McLean. Rev. Glover concluded his pastorate that year and retired from the Board. Often Sturtevant had expressed his exasperation with the man's narrow views but in two crisis situations he had stood firmly behind the President. Rev. Jenney also resigned. Other than Sturtevant the only remaining trustee of the original ten was John Brooks. Meanwhile, except for two or three, the men of the New Haven Association without consulting each other had withdrawn from the Presbyterian Church to become Congregationalists.

The State University Decided

In 1850, after his efforts to make Illinois College an agricultural and industrial school failed, J. B. Turner had begun a public campaign for state universities funded by the government. In 1860 two of the presidential nominees, Douglas and Lincoln, agreed to approve such legislation; subsequently, on 2 July 1862 President Lincoln signed the Land Grant University Act. In 1865 the Illinois legislature passed a resolution to found a university, thus spurring keen competition among several communities. Sturtevant hoped that Jacksonville would be the successful contender and that Illinois College would be the liberal arts component.

Sturtevant much preferred to have higher education conducted under auspices which were Christian *and nonsectarian*, but in the West such an institution could not gain the support a denominational school could rally.[5] His commitment to excellence was so strong that he was willing to close the colleges, even his own, if their existence made it impossible to have a unified state university. ("Remarks," 1866) Sturtevant expended much effort to bring the university to Jacksonville, and he considered various ways in which Illinois College would be related to it as the liberal arts component.

The community also had keen interest in the location of the university. Morgan County's bid of $491,000 was the highest of the four submitted. The considerable resources of Illinois College, valued at $176,000, were a major element. In addition, the town voted 889 to 35 to levy taxes to raise $50,000, and the county expected to raise $200,000. Well-to-do citizens added substantial pledges. By early 1867 the outlook was gloomy even though Sturtevant believed that the Champaign "swindle" had been exposed and that Jacksonville was a strong candidate. Despite Turner's considerable influence and despite Champaign's offer of the lowest bid, that city won the prize. The only means by which Jacksonville could have secured the university, Sturtevant said, would have required paying the entire local bid in greenbacks as bribes to the legislators.

Still intent on a positive outcome, Sturtevant declared that all the western colleges must develop a strong relationship with the public systems. He proposed strong ties between Illinois College and the schools in Jacksonville and Morgan County. He also believed the existing colleges could be brought "into harmonious and efficient co-operation with the state university. I mean mine shall be." ("Remarks," 1866) One positive result of the whole affair was that the people of the area were more aware of the importance of Illinois College.

The Death of Theron Baldwin

The long and remarkable friendship between Theron Baldwin and Julian Sturtevant ended abruptly when Baldwin died at his home in New Jersey on 10 April 1870. These friends for life had

Theron Baldwin

shared a profound commitment to Christ and to the particular form of the church they believed to be in accord with Scripture. Baldwin, far more than other members of the Illinois Association, shared with Sturtevant the joy and anguish of Illinois College, and until his death he served as trusted adviser and personal confidant. Sturtevant was called on once again to preach at the funeral of a colleague; the Society paid his travel expenses. In his sermon Sturtevant emphasized the vital commitment his friend had made to two closely-related causes, education and religion. Baldwin was a key figure in the formation of the New Haven Association and accompanied Sturtevant in 1829 on the journey to found Illinois College. In 1843 he conceived of the College Society for coordinated fund-raising on behalf of selected Western colleges. As its Secretary he significantly influenced Christian higher education from Ohio to the Pacific Coast.

Baldwin's articles and addresses on higher education were another vehicle for his influence. His concern for Illinois College was unfailing, and only a person of his great integrity and skill could be evenhanded in the treatment of all the institutions while maintaining a special relationship with one. Sturtevant noted the significance of Christian colleges in establishing democracy in America and remarked that despite his keen analysis the great French philosopher, Tocqueville, had failed to observe this.

Sturtevant characterized Baldwin as selfless and extraordinary in the goodness of his character. As he had lived so he died, strong in his faith in God; his example should inspire those who knew him to continue his work. Sturtevant expressed sympathy to Mrs. Baldwin and extended thanks for the help she had given her husband in his noble work. The sermon and other brief articles about Baldwin were published. In 1875 Sturtevant published a "Sketch" describing Baldwin's New England background and his conversion during a revival in his home church when he was about sixteen. From that time on Baldwin had sought to win souls to Christ as a college student, as a home missionary in Illinois, and by fostering Christian higher education. The second half of the Sketch was devoted largely to the founding of Illinois College and its history through four decades, with due reference to Baldwin's prominent role. Sturtevant explained that Baldwin and he shared a common conception of liberal education and agreed in opposing the multiplication of sects and colleges. Both believed that "the union between pure religion, learning, and freedom is not only natural but vital and inseparable...." (48)

Evangelism, in Action and Essays

Sturtevant took seriously his church responsibilities, both locally and in the larger fellowship. He was a regular and generous contributor to the local Congregational Church and insisted that its bills be paid promptly. The church called Sturtevant to its pulpit on occasion, as when Pastor Roberts went to St. Louis to seek funding for the College in the spring of 1866. Sturtevant's family was also active in the church. Hannah, while her husband was in Chicago, relayed a request from her sister Jane. He was to ask Mrs. Blatchford about the cost of a sofa, table, and pulpit chairs so that the women's society of the church would know how much money to raise.[6]

In 1866 Sturtevant preached at the General Conference of Congregational Churches in Missouri. He was present at the ordination of five graduates of Chicago Theological Seminary for the foreign mission field; one of the five was an alumnus of Illinois College. He assisted in the installation of a new pastor at Beardstown. He preached the dedication sermon at the organization of the Congregational Church of Webster Groves near St. Louis. When the First Congregational Church of Springfield was organized in 1867, Sturtevant was a member of the council and in the evening he addressed the assembled congregation and representatives. He participated in a council at the Monticello church; Baldwin, who had assisted in organizing that church many years before, was present also.

In the fall of 1867 Sturtevant called attention to the resolution approved by the Southern Association of Illinois urging a more active missionary presence in southern Illinois. When the Congregationalists of the state met in Jacksonville in 1868, Sturtevant advised the group that a more aggressive policy was needed to establish new churches in the region. He was keenly interested in the national effort to establish a three-million dollar Memorial Fund for assisting financially distressed churches, aiding theological seminaries, and building a headquarters (the "Congregational House") in Boston.

Although his involvement with Presbyterianism was now much diminished, Sturtevant preached on a Sunday evening in November 1868 at the First Presbyterian Church, reporting on the College Society's Twenty-fifth Anniversary meeting. The following spring Sturtevant supplied the pulpit of the First Presbyterian Church in St. Louis for a time. When a minister was ordained at Chandlerville Sturtevant preached the sermon. In September 1869 Sturtevant attended the council convened by the Hannibal church when his son Julian resigned his pastorate. Hannah relayed to her husband invitations to preach two Sabbaths in two St. Louis churches in September 1870; she suggested they might want to hear his Pilgrim sermon. That same year while in Connecticut he preached in the New Canaan Congregational Church.

Basic convictions about Christian doctrine, the church, and sectarianism were the subjects of a dozen articles published by Sturtevant during 1867-1870. Borrowing a title, Sturtevant explained "The Enthusiasm of Humanity" as the infusion into humans of the divine spirit of philanthropy, the love of mankind, through Jesus Christ. It was not the wise men of Greece or Babylon who inspired selfless activity on behalf of others but a "Galilean peasant" who, though he lacked formal education, grasped the profound idea and lived it. Jesus devoted himself to relieving the suffering of the lowly classes. He was king of that kingdom which is not of this world, yet the society which he founded is the most vital force in modern civilization.

This essay incorporated an example of Sturtevant's biblical interpretation. He suggested that the phrase in the book of Daniel about the stone cut out of the mountain may refer to the church which Jesus was to establish in the midst of the Roman Empire. If Daniel did indeed foresee the rise of the church, Sturtevant remarked, it could have been only because God revealed that to him. Jesus did foresee the rise and growth of the Christian Church; therefore, the appropriate response to that vision is for us to "reverently receive him in his supernatural and divine character."[7]

In a sequel Sturtevant analyzed the origin of the "philanthropic spirit" which, not indigenous to human nature, is traceable to Jesus and subsequently to the Christian Scripture and the church. Jesus' amazing achievement can be explained only by his miraculous and supernatural character: his birth with God as his father, his power over nature, his miracles which brought healing to the suffering, his death on the cross, his resurrection, his ascension into heaven, and his founding of the universal church. Rejection of the supernatural and divine nature of Jesus will arrest that philanthropic impulse which began at Bethlehem and Calvary.

Writing about "Faith and the Church," Sturtevant acknowledged that the great truths about Christ and his mission are essential but insisted that the beginning of Christian faith is "a living, loving person," Jesus. In an article on "Religion and Theology," he argued that speculative theology is not important but that practical theology is essential to understanding Christian doctrines and moral teachings. The writings of [Nathaniel] Taylor and [Lyman]

Beecher of the recent past, and of [Edwards] Park and H. B. Smith of the present, are very helpful. Practical theology demonstrates that God is "A person of will and affections," not "an impersonal, unconscious abstraction." It considers the nature of sin and deals with the Son of God and his work of redemption. The unique morality of the Gospel lies in its doctrine of "self-sacrifice for the good of others." To know God truly is essential to teaching and observing the two great commandments of love for God and neighbor. Christian theology teaches who the neighbor is, that God has made of one blood all the nations of mankind.

Some time after Sturtevant's defense of theology, the editor of the *Independent* made a very brief visit to Jacksonville. He talked to several men who supposedly told him that Sturtevant had departed from evangelical truth. The editor then published an account of this "village scandal" so that he could enter "A Plea for [His] Friend." Sturtevant's response was perhaps the most furious statement he ever published. With dripping sarcasm he thanked the editor for defending him from a peril he did not know existed and from assailants who had not revealed themselves to him. Surely the editor believed that the falsity of the charges was so obvious that he did not need to say so and yet he had repeated the accusations in detail. One of the chief points of "upbraiding" related to the connection of religion and theology. Any readers who had seen Sturtevant's recent article on that subject, in the editor's own paper, would know at once that the supposed accusations were not justified.

In a commentary on an address by Dr. Joseph Thompson, Sturtevant praised him for stating "the true philosophy" not only for missions to the heathen but for all Christian self-sacrifice. History demonstrates that human communities, no matter how good to begin with, degenerate and perish if they rely only upon their own efforts. The depravity of human nature must be acknowledged, and rationalism and naturalism must be repudiated. Only God can bring salvation and therefore the single aim of the Christian church is to proclaim, at home and in foreign lands, that God is manifest in Christ. Christians should cooperate in spreading the gospel over all the world just "as earnestly as the friends of freedom united in suppressing the great rebellion."

Asking "The Trial Question," Sturtevant sought to determine the one indispensable teaching which distinguishes Christianity from other religions. He concluded that it can best be expressed in the words of Jesus in Luke (19:10), that he had come to seek and to save the lost. The church in America has the divinely appointed duty to bring the gospel to the superstitious and pagan people of Africa and Asia and elsewhere. The import of this mission relates to the very destiny of the American nation. The liberty of the people of this vast land can be preserved only by imbuing them and the government itself with the spirit of Christianity. Our government and our people must be filled with the spirit of helpfulness to the needy. Thus the "trial" [test] question for the American churches and the American people is whether they will seek to save the lost millions. They must attend to "The spreading pestilence that devastates the wretched hovels of the poor" and likewise the "moral pestilence," the ignorance and superstition, rampant in the land of our own abode.

An article prepared for the *Nation* by its London correspondent prompted Sturtevant to analyze "The Morality of Skepticism." Saying that the *Nation* too frequently tended toward unbelief, he noted that the reporter had described the prevalence of skepticism not only in England's intellectual class but even in its church. The history of unbelief, Sturtevant said, can be traced to the philosophers of antiquity, but whatever the age, "Negation is not the stuff to make martyrs of." Even Voltaire on his deathbed wanted the sacraments of the church. And why not? asked Sturtevant. Religion lifts humanity above earthly desires by inspiring "an assured faith in a future state of rewards and punishments, when all the wrongs of this world shall be redressed, and all its virtues duly honored and rewarded."

From his arrival in Illinois Sturtevant was disturbed by the evil of sectarianism in Protestant Christianity. In an article (1867) on the subject, he proclaimed that Christians should be one in Christ. The multiplication of sects had progressed in America far more than in Europe and in the American West far more than in the seaboard states. Combined, the churches in Illinois could sustain one outstanding college, but each sect wants its own college and the result is that not one of them is strong. Moreover, because of the fear of sectarianism religion has almost been excluded from the whole system of public education despite the fact that the people are Christian. The end result of this is that "we shall be a Christian people no longer." (10) Another evil consequence of sectarianism is that Christians cannot bring Christ to the world. And yet there is reason for optimism. Ten years before no one expected that slavery could be remedied, but God heard the prayers of the people and brought deliverance. If the faithful earnestly entreat God, there may yet be deliverance.

Asked to serve on behalf of the American Tract Society, Sturtevant declined because the Society had to ignore doctrinal and organizational differences among the denominations which gave it support, lest it give offense to any of them.[8] Silence regarding denominational differences was absurd and mischievous, Sturtevant wrote. He deplored the multiplicity of denominations but believed the only means by which the Christian Church could find its way out of the wilderness of sectarianism was through freedom for "bold, free utterance." (6) Congregationalists believe that God is still making his truth known among all evangelical denominations. The very "life of Congregationalism lies in an effort to realize universal Christian cooperation in freedom…in an endeavor to bind together the whole church of God under heaven by the law of love, and not by Ecclesiastical Power." (10)

The Urgency of Christian Mission

The Theological Department of Yale College invited Julian Sturtevant to deliver the oration at its Anniversary on 20 May 1868. The thesis of his address was that the Christian ministry, truly understood, is congregational and is not the exclusive function of ordained individuals and hierarchies. His views, he asserted, were based on the Scripture, accepted as the revelation of God. The minister is not a mediator but "a teacher of God's revealed truth" (701) and he does not possess any special power. Regrettably, at the time of the Reformation when the Protestant forefathers "came out from Babylon," they brought a lot of Babylon with them. (703) The view has persisted that only ordained men can preach, baptize, conduct the Lord's Supper, pronounce the benediction, and console the sick. Many Congregational churches in the West, lacking an ordained minister, have been without baptisms and the Lord's Supper, when actually any member of the congregation could have fulfilled those functions. Sturtevant favored allowing laymen to expound the word of God and having the officiant, minister or layman, ask the blessing of God upon "us" instead of "you."

None can be saved but those who have become Christ-like, and only those who share the spirit of self-sacrifice can teach Christianity. That spirit has been exemplified in the missionaries who have carried the Gospel to the West and have established the institutions of Christian civilization. Yale deserved great credit for sending forth her sons to accomplish those tasks in greater numbers than any other college.

The Christian minister needs the fullest education available to enable him to apply the Christian religion to the varied circumstances of individual, social, and political life. Therefore, schools and colleges are utterly essential to prepare a teaching ministry which can be effective among the powerful intellectual elements of contemporary civilization. Sturtevant pitied those who scorned the fundamental doctrines of the faith, such as the divinity of Christ, his atonement, and his resurrection—and yet claimed to be Christians. If the gospels are myths and the supernatural is delusory, no wise man would want to be a Christian. Sturtevant warned his hearers never to give Yale over to "a science which knows no God but nature, and no soul but force.... But let that evangelical spirit which laid her first foundations inspire her still...." (720)

In 1846 a small group of Congregationalists had organized the American Missionary Association in order to bypass the constraints laid upon the American Home Missionary Society by those hesitant to condemn slavery. In 1865 the National Council gave the Association the special duty of ministering to the needs of the freed slaves in the South. In 1869 President Sturtevant, of "Jacksonville College in Illinois," was invited to deliver the "annual discourse" for the Association. His theme, "The Crisis of the Hour," was derived from the urgent message of repentance preached by John the Baptist. His text was John's warning that the ax is now laid to the root of the tree and every tree which does not bring forth good fruit will be hewn down and cast into the fire. (Matt. 3:10) The dramatic power of these words was reinforced by their repetition throughout the address.

When the New Haven band was planning its mission to Illinois, the members were greatly concerned about the growing numbers of Catholics and the potential threat presented by their church. Sturtevant now stressed the urgency of the God-given mission to preach the Gospel of salvation in America and to the world. He first demonstrated the implications for that part of the population descended from the Protestant stock of England and western Europe and then turned his attention to those "fellow-citizens of African, Chinese, and Papal origin." (4)

The Jews of the first century failed to accept the Gospel and consequently did not carry it to the Roman world. God has given the free church in America "all the advantages of free thought, a free Bible, and free worship." (6) He has now placed that church in a position to "arise and conquer the world for the kingdom of Christ." Such freedom and such power as Christians enjoy in America had never before been given to any people. Moreover, the present situation was peculiar in that the descendants of those who fled religious persecution under popery and monarchy were now providing a hospitable refuge to the adherents of spiritual despotism. More could be done for these new immigrants: "They are our neighbors, our fellow-citizens. We can preach Christ to them...." (6-7) The Protestants of America should not expect that the two can coexist; as Lincoln said, a divided house cannot stand. "We must convert them, or they will convert us." (7) The little leaven of the Reformers had proven to be sufficient in their time. Will the same development occur in the land of the Pilgrims? "It all depends on the quantity and the activity of the leaven." (8)

In addition to facing the old Roman paganism in Catholicism and the still older paganism of the Chinese immigrants, the church must acknowledge responsibility to the four million people "whose ancestors were violently torn away from the still deeper and darker paganism of Africa...." (8) These people were imploring the help of the churches to find the way of life. Giving the ballot to the former slaves is not sufficient; the Gospel must be diffused throughout the South, among both former slaves and former masters. That such an effort can succeed was evident in the success of the missions to the Sandwich Islands.

The urgent task was hindered by the unwillingness of various Christian churches to give up their centralized and humanly administered governments. Among other obstacles are the desire for wealth and ease and the unwillingness of Christian women to devote their lives to family duties and bear sons and daughters for the cause of Christ. Sturtevant parodied their complaints: "What a drag! What a confinement! What a hard lot!" "[T]he failure of Protestant American women to perform the maternal function" was cause for exultation in the camp of the enemy. (11)

If Protestant men and women prove faithful to the Christian religion, the future of America is bright. The question is whether the colored man will share in it. "Will he become a thoroughly enlightened, civilized, cultivated man, self-governed, industrious, temperate, frugal?" Will he have a strong family life and train his children in faithfulness to country, church, and God? Will he educate his children? "Will he, in short, apply Christian principle to a life of self-denying industry and active enterprise? If he will,...[w]ealth, influence, power will be his...." (13) But if not, he will continue in the condition of poverty he knew in slavery, and because of the hard lot of the poor his children will perish. What "we" must do for him, and what he must do for himself, must be done quickly. (13)

The pagan Asian people and the millions coming from papal Europe face much the same situation. The Roman Catholic Church has trained its masses in ignorance and superstition, and this condition has been the intent of their priests who fear nothing so much as America's free schools. If the Catholic people adhere to the pope and priesthood, they will soon find that the ax is at their root. Twelve centuries earlier the triumphant "Mohammedan" armies proclaimed, "'The Koran or death.' There is something terribly analogous to this in the present great aggressive movement of Christianity. It marshals no armies.... And yet it does present the alternative of submission or death. It does form the only style of character before which nothing else can stand in equal competition." (14-15)

The warning of John was directed by Sturtevant to the

American [Protestant] churches. They must undertake the great missionary work at home and abroad which God has set for them. Otherwise spiritual devotion will lapse, morality and family life will decline, and intelligence, industry, frugality, and wealth will decay. "[L]iberty can not live in this country without Christian morality; Christian morality can not live without Christian faith; and our prosperity can not outlive liberty." The only means for continuing liberty and prosperity is to imbue "the masses with a fervent, enlightened Christian faith." (15) Will the people in the American churches meet the challenge of this crisis? "The ax lieth at the root of the trees." (16)

Women's Employment . . . Suffrage

During the years 1866-1870 Sturtevant was present at more than half of the sixty-six meetings of The Club when attendance was recorded. The sessions were suspended during the heat of summer and occasionally canceled in favor of "religious meetings" [revivals], or the concert by Norwegian violinist Ole Bull, or the address by Frederick Douglass on "Reconstruction." Some of Sturtevant's presentations were on the subjects of his articles, such as whether male and female education should be the same. His talk on "the improvement of the condition of women" was followed by animated discussion. He considered the possible locations for the Illinois Industrial University and read a paper (April 1870) proposing "an extension of our public education in Jacksonville to include a High School, and a University attached to or rather to co-operate with Illinois College." At another time he read "a long & well-digested paper on the position of Spain and other Catholic countries in regard to the circulation of the Bible, during 300 years past."

Other members of The Club led discussions on a wide variety of subjects: the Pope, divorce, the Bible in the public schools, Comte's Positive Philosophy, social and political issues, the railroads, and such men as Grant and Lincoln. Profound inquiry was not, however, the members' only interest; the secretary noted that the supper, with unusual profusion and richness of food, was becoming more and more *the* prominent feature of the meetings.

When speaking to businessmen in Springfield about "A Truly American System of Education," Sturtevant returned to the theme of his inaugural address. He emphasized the significance of education for a democratic society, saying that "the American merchant should have the...most enlightened views of all the social problems which claim the attention of a free, self-governing people." The right of a producer of wealth to possess it is a natural and universal law. Beyond that the owner of wealth is "the treasurer of society and of mankind" and must be taught how to use it wisely for the benefit of his country and the human race. Such education should be informed by "absolute truth, justice and human right." It should be universal because American society assumes the right of every human being not only to the fruits of his labor but also to cultural and personal development. Negative behavior such as tobacco spitting and profanity should be overcome and more attention given to the correct and elegant use of language. Finally, American education must inculcate "pure morality derived from the Christian faith."

A Convention of College Presidents was called by several men, among them Rev. Jonathan Blanchard of Wheaton College. Sturtevant replied that because of the very short notice it would be difficult for him to attend. He asserted that denominationalism had generated too many colleges in Illinois. Also, he opposed a suggestion to divert the College and Seminary Fund of the State of Illinois, or its Federal Land Grant funds, to denominational colleges. On other issues and at other times, Sturtevant said, he would be very willing to meet with his colleagues. The group met without Sturtevant and their subsequent report in the *Chicago Tribune* included comments about Sturtevant's letter which he found objectionable. He requested the newspaper to print his letter in full so that readers could judge it for themselves.[9] Sturtevant told Baldwin that Blanchard was as usual mean and malignant; Illinois College and its people must be on the alert because their enemies never seemed so various nor active as now.

While in Chicago in quest of funds Sturtevant attended the anniversary observance at Chicago Theological Seminary in 1866. Numerous Congregational pastors and prominent Congregational laymen, many of whom he knew, were present. In mid-June 1868 both Sturtevant and his wife were invited as guests of Monticello Female Seminary at its Twenty-fifth Anniversary observance.

The Catholic threat to democracy and religious liberty continued to be a matter of concern for Sturtevant. In an essay on "Freedom of Speech" he commented on a report that police had quelled an attempt by Catholics to punish a Protestant minister who had spoken against their church. He deplored the attitude of intolerance shown by the very group which expected others to tolerate it. He declared that for three and a half centuries thousands of Christians have regarded the Catholic Church as "the irreconcilable enemy of human liberty and human progress."

An excellent vehicle for Sturtevant to address a wide church readership was provided in 1867 when some Congregationalists in Chicago established a family newspaper, *The Advance.* Illinois and the Midwest now had now enough Congregationalists to sustain a religious newspaper, although it was intended as a national publication to counter "the unsound doctrines and irreverent spirit" which had lately been espoused by the *New York Independent.*[10] Sturtevant boasted in a letter to Baldwin: "You see the 'Advance' is in the flood tide. I am at present high in favor with its controlling power. My articles are eagerly sought." (1 Oct. 1867) Sturtevant's first article in the new periodical had appeared in its second issue, and over the next several years there were more than a dozen others.

A recent poem by Whittier which Sturtevant enjoyed told about a cultured city woman who came one summer to New Hampshire where she and a rough-hewn farmer fell in love; they married and had a happy home "among the hills." Sturtevant asserted that the character of New England farm people had been "formed by the Bible, by public worship and the preaching of the Gospel from an intelligent and thoughtful ministry," along with the spirit of love and self-sacrifice so central to Christianity. Modern-day improvements in the schools were welcome but could not substitute for the old virtues of religious faith, common sense, industry, and frugality. It is of utmost importance, Sturtevant concluded, that the values of New England's rural civilization be perpetuated.

The beginning of "The New Year" (1868) was the occasion for reminding people to consider the major tasks which lay ahead. As individuals and as a people, Sturtevant wrote, we "have a work to do, battles to fight.... What is the work before us? what are the conflicts which await us, in the year now beginning?" With regard to the national political leadership, a choice must be made between those who led the Union's struggle for freedom and those who sought to continue slavery.[11] In the sphere of religion there were two fundamental issues, the manifestation of unity among Christians and the proclamation of the Gospel to the masses in this and other lands. Such tasks can be accomplished only by "restoring to the church the spirit of primitive Christianity," the spirit of loving self-giving like that of Christ himself.

The examination of economic laws as the basis for understanding social life was of increasing interest to Sturtevant. In a brief article, "Hard Times," he observed that acquiring the necessities and wants of life takes up a large part of the lives of most men. He analyzed the factors which currently were hampering that effort and noted that the inflation caused by the recent "great and terrible war" was a principal cause. The course of action which Sturtevant advocated had several elements: all taxes should be reduced to the lowest level; the nation's credit must be maintained; and extravagance and corruption, rampant even at the highest levels, must be rebuked and rooted out. There might perhaps be a silver lining; financial adversity may teach the old virtues of frugality and justice and thus prove to be a much-needed national discipline.

Along with defining the proper kind of education for women, Sturtevant discussed their relationship to men. It is essential, he believed, for all to acknowledge the God-given nature of women and for women to accept their intended place in society as wife and mother. He prepared a series of articles in 1867 and 1868 regarding women's employment. Why, he asked, are women compensated at a rate so much lower than men even if they do the same work as men and do it as well? He denied that it was due to the selfishness of those who are the "lords" of society. Rather it results from a fundamental law, the law of supply and demand. A man can engage in many different occupations and thus has various opportunities for earning adequate or good wages.

The only way women could command wages equal to those of men would be for them to compete with men in all occupations. However, they cannot compete with men in farming, horse-shoeing, digging canals, and constructing railroads because of the "inevitable laws which regulate the growth and development of human muscle." Women can do as well as men in teaching, retailing, typesetting, and clerical work, but too many women seek jobs in the few occupations in which they can compete with men, resulting in wages below the level of subsistence. The employment problems of women and the inequality of their wages are the consequence of a law of God and nature which man can neither repeal nor counteract. God has provided for women to be the "loved and cherished companions of strong and vigorous men" and to share the wealth of men as their wives. ("Women's Wages")

A few women of genius, such as Mrs. Harriet Beecher Stowe, have been free to earn wealth and fame by their gifts. But there are few geniuses of either sex and the "inevitable law of wages" prevents most women from achieving independence. Women scorn domestic life because it places them in dependence upon men. Actually, marriage is a relationship of mutual dependence; men depend upon women for the homes which provide beauty and comfort and nobility and the very cement of social life. Without woman, man "is but a solitary wild beast, retiring to his lonely den to devour his prey." ("Woman's Independence")

Zealous advocates were declaring that women as well as men should so far as possible pursue that vocation for which they are best suited. Sturtevant not only conceded the point, he insisted upon it. The Creator designed "truly feminine employment's" for which women are perfectly suited both mentally and physically. Moreover civilization is utterly dependent upon women for the fulfillment of these duties. All men and women who are healthy in body and mind should marry, and theoretically every woman could expect to rule over a household. But society is not perfect and many men are unsuited for marriage; it is better for a woman to be unmarried than to live with a brutal man, and therefore many women must find employment. The most satisfactory situation for an unmarried woman is domestic service in a family, thus providing for herself and also relieving a wife and mother of the often overwhelming duties of the household and family. Yet because of a morbid attitude toward such service many women prefer to be ill-paid in other work. ("Woman's Employments")

Sturtevant had read about women who attempt to earn their

living by purchasing a sewing machine to do piece work. Too often the rate of pay was so low that they could neither support themselves nor make the payments on the machine. "Shylocks" who thus exploited the women were condemned. But, queried Sturtevant, "Who Are the Shylocks?" The actual cause of the suffering was the law of wages which is no more subject to the employers' control than the orbit of the planets. So many women sought such work that the rate per piece was inevitably driven to a ruinously low level. The relief of these suffering people would have to be provided by charity, supported both by employers and "those humane theorizers who denounce those employers as 'Shylocks.'" Domestic service was the solution, Sturtevant believed.

"Ruined Young Men" are the consequence when women, failing in the vain effort to earn their own living, become fallen women. Young men are vulnerable when parents are lax in their religious observance and are preoccupied with wealth and prominence. Men and women who themselves have indulged in vices should not be surprised that their children are ruined by youthful vices. Also causing ruin are circumstances which prevent great numbers of young men from even hoping to enjoy "the virtuous pleasures of married life" or at least not for a long time. "The consequence is terrible to contemplate. Driven to desperation by the cravings of the most imperious of the appetites with which our Creator has endowed us, they seek in the company of the most fallen and abandoned of the female sex those indulgences which they think their hard lot forbids them to enjoy in ways which virtue and religion approve.... [T]his vice is nearest of all the train[s] to the gate of perdition.... Over every door of the strange woman should be written— *This is the Gate of Hell*."

Because so many thousands of young men descend into ruin in "vicious celibacy" there are equal numbers of women who are likewise compelled to remain unmarried. Thousands of parents ask what they can do to save their boys; the answer is to train their children for Christ. The fundamental solution for society is to heed God's intention, that men and women share life in a home. In brief, "marriage is the hope and celibacy the ruin of woman." Sturtevant reiterated his view that inequalities in the wages paid to men and women are the result of laws of nature and are not subject to legislative remedy. ("Wages of Men and Women")

In a lengthy essay in 1870 Sturtevant dealt with the current movement to broaden suffrage. Long ago, he remarked, patriarchy led to
monarchy, and the excesses of monarchy led men to demand some
form of popular government to guarantee their rights of property,
liberty, and life. Sturtevant denied that there is any natural right to
choose one's own rulers. [He thus rejected Locke's theory that government arises from a social compact.] If a government is good, it
should have one's consent; if not, it is to be rejected on that ground
alone. The Declaration of Independence does not recognize voting as
one of the inalienable rights. "We are not born voters...." (142)

The basic criterion for determining eligibility for voting is not
the rights of the individual but the well-being of the country. The
voter's true allegiance must be to that country and to no other
authority, such as the Roman Pope. He must have a certain degree
of intelligence and education and a certain level of moral integrity.
The voter must also have a measure of personal independence.
The relationship of husband and wife is not a matter of equal part-
nership because the husband assumes responsibility for his wife
and the wife trusts her husband for support and protection. A wife
presumably would vote as the head of the family dictated. The
fundamental and governing principle, Sturtevant declared, "is that
great, God-made, permanent reality, SEX...." (152) Finally, the
ballot should be withheld whenever it would interfere with duties
at a higher level than voting, such as a wife's duty to her husband.

The fundamental principle at stake in the current social revolution, according to Sturtevant, was the existence of the family.
Serious differences between husband and wife regarding political
issues would injure that delicacy of spirit appropriate to the
woman in the home. To bring woman out of her seclusion and
dependence would make family life impossible. Political conflicts
must be left to men because a woman drawn or driven from the
sacred shelter is quite capable of falling. Women's suffrage would
be "a dark day for American liberty." (156)

A Buffalo Hunt; The Destiny of the West

Unlike earlier conquerors, Sturtevant observed, "the Christian
people of this country" seek to supply every area reclaimed from

the wilderness with "all the institutions and instruments of the highest civilization." (SPC-25, 114) He published further reflections about this process after an excursion to Kansas for a buffalo hunt in June 1869.[12] The small party, hosted by a railroad executive, departed from St. Louis and arrived that evening in Kansas City. The next morning their train left that booming terminus of half a dozen railroads at an early hour. "After passing the beautiful and already gloriously historic cities of Lawrence and Topeka, [they soon left behind] the traces of civilization." Stopping for supper at Salina, they continued across a landscape rarely "enlivened by a single tree."

Interrupting their travel "in the dead of night," the party was met at Hays City by messengers from "Gen. Custar" [sic] who was to be their host for the hunt on their return trip. Continuing westward they observed, in the morning, small herds of buffalo and numerous carcasses of that animal. The land was parched, the grass was thin, and the cactus plentiful; the area was aptly named the "Great American Desert." Before noon they reached Sheridan, the end of the rail line, just fifteen miles from the Colorado border. Fifteen to twenty wagons, drawn by teams of four to eight mules each, were loaded at that place every day to transport freight to points as far southwest as Santa Fe and even northern Mexico. "There are trustworthy indications," Sturtevant wrote, "of a gigantic opening commerce, which will justify and reward the constructing of this great natural highway, even through a region so desolate and sterile." He was of course referring to the railroad, not to Interstate 70 which somewhat parallels the party's route.

Returning to Hays City the men and women spent a quiet night in their car, left upon a side track. About noon they were greeted by Custer, described by Sturtevant as young and having "the energy and dash of a brave officer...[and] most admirably fitted to command obedience and win affection." Horses were provided for the men who wished to engage in the hunt, while the ladies rode in the General's carriage or in the four ambulances. "For myself," wrote Sturtevant, "I took the position of a non-combatant, and rode in an ambulance, for the protection of the ladies.... Gen. Custar did the same." Sturtevant was provided with a beautiful rifle but admitted that he was no Nimrod and did not know how to shoot it.

About forty officers and soldiers from Fort Hays served as an escort for protection against hostile Indians. The party traveled across the rolling prairie for about fifteen miles before sighting a small herd of buffalo. Five animals were killed, one of them given its mortal wound by a Congregational pastor from Kansas City. Sturtevant did not share the broad enthusiasm. An invitation to dine with the General at the Fort was declined, and the party spent the night in their railroad car before returning to St. Louis.

The sight of so many buffalo carcasses led to questioning whether the creature should be killed in such great numbers. However, there was clear justification for driving the animals away from the tracks of "our great continental railways" in order to remove the Indians who hunted them. "It is now a necessity of civilization…that there should be free and unobstructed transit by rail from the Atlantic to the Pacific." The Indian "sees in the Railways his mortal enemies bringing the only remaining resource of his barbarous life into immediate peril. He is right; the Railways do threaten his only remaining support in savage life with annihilation." Sturtevant expressed the inevitable conclusion in rhetorical questions. "What then? Has the Indian a right to the soil where the buffalo ranges?" "Have a few thousand savages a right to build an everlasting barrier across the great highway of civilization, …that they may live by chasing these herds of buffalo over it?"13

Reasoning from principles derived from classic economic theory and the Protestant work ethic, Sturtevant responded with an emphatic negative. He accepted John Locke's thesis that it is human labor which bestows value upon the resources of nature. Therefore, "Man does not in any age or land acquire a right to the soil of this earth by roaming over it in indolence, and gathering its spontaneous productions, but by tilling it." The "great original wrong of our policy towards the Indians" was recognizing them as tribal nations with a right to the soil. The Indians should have been regarded as individuals, with rights as such and as subject "to the law of a just and righteous government." Americans should abandon the practice of offering the Indians firearms and whisky and instead offer them "the implements of husbandry, soil to till and full protection in tilling it, and over and above all these the gospel of salvation." Moreover, "The principle so forcibly expressed by the Apostle, 'if any man will not work neither shall he eat,' is fully applicable to the Indian." No one has a right to live in "idleness and barbarism." If the Indian refuses the life of civilized industry, the whites must "see to it that he interrupts the progress of civilization as little as possible...." In an earlier address Sturtevant had asserted that both the Negroes and the Indians would be unable to compete with the white man in the labor market and both would eventually die out in North America. The Negroes could survive by colonizing a tropical climate, but that alternative was not available to the Indians.

Sturtevant and His Family

The biographical sketch of Julian Sturtevant, compiled for the fortieth anniversary of Yale's Class of 1826, described his career in three sentences. His major addresses were listed and his overseas trip was emphasized. There was praise for his outstanding service to the cause of education in the West. His two marriages were noted and the surviving children were named.[14]

Periodic illness afflicted Sturtevant. While he was in Springfield in late January 1866, the fever he suffered earlier returned to plague him. Hannah wrote urging him to be careful about his diet and to warm his feet before he went to bed. He was seriously ill in 1867 and for three months he was too feeble at times even to fulfill the cares of the day. He told Baldwin that he was like Sisyphus ceaselessly trying to roll a rock up a steep hill. By late September his health was "tolerable." At commencement time in 1869 he explained to Baldwin that he had not written earlier because he had been too unwell or had company. He was ill again in the summer of 1870.

Fortunately there were better times. During a long stay in the East in the summer of 1866, Julian had the comfort of Hannah's intermittent company; presumably she stayed with relatives in Connecticut and New York while he went from city to city. Having secured nearly $20,000 in subscriptions, Sturtevant wrote to Baldwin in late July saying, "I hope the Lord will so strengthen me that my hopefulness, endurance, and active energy will hold out till this work is accomplished." In late August both the

Sturtevants met Baldwin at his office in New York and accompanied him to his family home in Orange, New Jersey. By the time they reached home in mid-September, Sturtevant could pronounce the prolonged effort in the East as quite successful.

Hannah frequently reminisced about events of the past in her letters to her husband. Writing on 30 January 1866 she asked whether he had remembered that yesterday's date was the day when Edgar Lewis was born twenty-six years ago. "How much you have passed through since that time both of joy and sorrow! And your cares and labors for the College have been a large part of them." Years later Hannah recalled their happy visit to Andover during the summer of 1869 when they stood on the shady bank and threw stones into the water of Pomp's pond. In July 1870 Julian was away and Hannah wrote to tell him that his family remembered him on his birthday. She reminded him that a year earlier they were enjoying themselves at Martha's Vineyard. Together the couple went to Beloit, and after they had returned to Chicago Hannah continued on to Jacksonville where Fred met her at the depot. That summer the Sturtevants were house guests in Vermont of a family Sturtevant had met the previous year on the Kansas trip.

Julian's remembrances were indeed a combination of the happy and the sorrowful. In his remarks at the College Society in 1868, he noted that it was almost exactly thirty-nine years before when Theron Baldwin and he and his wife Elizabeth made their memorable journey to Illinois. He spoke of Elizabeth as "the wife of my youth, one of the noblest and loveliest of her sex, whose Christian heroism is worthy to be held in everlasting remembrance, and it will be, for she has long been a saint in glory...." (SPC-25, 113) Sturtevant remembered Elizabeth with great fondness and yet without diminished love for Hannah.

The 1870 Federal census listed Julian's occupation as "Minister of the Gospel" and Hannah's as "Keep House," while Elizabeth (28), Lucy (23), and Alfred (19) were simply "At Home." Other members of the household were Mary "Fairweather," 62; Caroline Stonebridge, 52, Domestic Servant, born in Prussia; and George Henderson, 25, "Ostler" [Hostler], native of Illinois. Sturtevant's real estate was valued at $14,000 and his personal property at $12,000; even allowing for inflation the increase in the latter category from $800 in 1860 is impressive. Jane Fayerweather's personal property was valued at $4,000.

Receipts for payment of the Federal Income Tax provide some information about family finances. Sturtevant's taxes (beginning with 1866 and omitting 1869) were: $22.90, $40.85, $78.06, and $32.80. Based on the rate of five per cent (and half that for 1870) on income in excess of $800, Sturtevant's taxable income was respectively $358, $797, $1,541, and $1,312. The 1866 tax included $2 on the piano, $2 on the carriage, and $1 on Sturtevant's gold watch. The $1 tax applied also in 1867 and 1868. For 1869 and 1870 real estate taxes were about $200.

After the War the Sturtevants and their Fayerweather relatives resumed their activity in land transactions. There were about a dozen sales of plots ranging in size from two and a half to forty acres. Several of these tracts were located south of Morton on both sides of the county road (Lincoln) and had once been owned by Richard Fayerweather. Two forty-acre plots which were sold by the Sturtevants and Mary Jane Fayerweather were located northwest of Jacksonville. An 1868 sale of ten acres south of Morton and east of Lincoln brought $2,000, and some plots brought an even higher price.

Julian Sturtevant Jr. continued as pastor of the Congregational Church in Hannibal until 1869. The cycle of family joy and grief was repeated when their second child, Caroline, was born in 1867 and died two years later. In 1870 Julian Jr. accepted a call to the Congregational Church in Ottawa, Illinois. James Warren, still in Hannibal, accepted employment with a railroad. Daughter Hannah Augusta became assistant principal at Professor Sanders' Young Ladies' Athenaeum in 1866 and lived at home. She married James H. Palmer of Springfield on 27 May 1869; the wedding took place in Jacksonville, with the bride's father officiating. The Palmers moved to Springfield and welcomed the birth of their first child, James Allerton, on 30 June 1870; at the time he was the only living grandchild of Julian and Hannah.

Libbie went to Hannibal in June 1867 to stay with her sister-in-law, Katie, while Julian Jr. attended the Commencement activities in Jacksonville. She expected to play in a concert and was practicing for it, presumably on a piano. It was hot and she amused herself by reading German literature, playing backgammon, and collecting riddles to puzzle Lucy with. She wondered if brother Julian would learn to play croquet while in Jacksonville. Reporting her plan for returning home, Libbie added: "D.V. [God willing] as Julian says." Lucy apparently remained at home during these years. Alfred, the youngest child, enrolled in 1866 in Illinois College and the Jacksonville Business College. He graduated from Illinois College in 1870 with the A.B. degree; his Valedictory address was entitled, "The Intellectual and Moral Inequalities of Men."

Ephraim's son, Warren DeForest, graduated in 1866 from the medical department at Western Reserve College. His younger brother, Wheeler, had been in the Union cavalry during the war of rebellion and later was engaged in business in St. Louis. Ephraim's daughter Julia was married and she and her husband had a son and a daughter.[15] Christopher, the youngest of the Sturtevant brothers, and his wife moved to Galena in 1866 and transferred their church membership to the Presbyterian Church. About two years later they moved again, this time to St. Joseph, Missouri, where he engaged in newspaper work.

Sister Julia Fayerweather and her husband, Timothy Chamberlain, continued to reside on their farm southeast of Jacksonville. Sister Mary Jane in the summer of 1870 made an extended visit in the East with their Connecticut cousins, the Meads, having accompanied them when they returned home after a visit in Illinois and Iowa. James Fayerweather, employed by the Chicago, Burlington, and Quincy Railroad, maintained his family home in Burlington, Iowa. William, the only one of his sons to graduate from Illinois College, was in the Class of 1868.[16] James corresponded with the children of their brother Abraham, in Hawaii, and relayed news about them to his sisters. Hannah was pleased by the report that they were all worshipers of the true God and not idol-worshipers. The Jacksonville family also received two newspapers featuring the Jubilee celebration of the landing of the first missionaries in Hawaii in 1820.

In the spring of 1866 Sturtevant, in a letter, told the Baldwins that he would be glad to meet their daughter Mary "at the cars" [the train] and that they would enjoy her company. Presumably Mary had completed her studies at Monticello Female Seminary and would accompany Sturtevant to the East. The close friendship and frequent correspondence between Sturtevant and Baldwin continued until the latter's death in 1870.

Hannah informed her husband by letter about the card Mrs. Warne had sent announcing the death of the Warnes' son. It was Mrs. Warne who had cared for Julian when he was ill while in England, and Hannah suggested that her husband should write to her.

Chapter 9: 1871-1876

The Last Years of Sturtevant's Presidency

Sustaining the College's Purpose

Evidence of America's maturity was widespread in the period culminating in the centennial year of 1876. The State of Illinois had observed its semi-centennial in 1868, and in 1870 it achieved fourth-place among all the states with its population of two and one-half million. In 1875 the City of Jacksonville marked half a century of growth from a lone settler's cabin. Civic organizations provided support for a public library and encouraged art. A site was acquired for a new school on the southeast side of town and the city waterworks were completed. The United States celebrated one hundred years of independence in 1876 with a spectacular exposition in Philadelphia.

These same years provided the final opportunities for Julian Sturtevant to direct Illinois College toward the long-sought goals of non-sectarian Christian liberal learning, academic excellence, and financial stability. His retirement from the presidency in 1876 marked nearly fifty years of Illinois College's service to youth and of his service to the school. The early history of the College is to a large extent his biography.

A leaflet assured the alumni in 1871 that Illinois College was prominent among the forces which guided "the wonderful development of this country." The influence of its alumni and former students "has everywhere been felt...in giving strength to our free institutions. In politics and in law, in the pulpit and the teacher's desk, as physicians and as business men, [they] are conspicuous for...their influence in public affairs. The College has borne a part in the history of this State and country which should be a source of gratification to all...."[1] A few years later Sturtevant reviewed for the trustees the role of the College in the overall educational scheme. In its early history it encompassed the whole range of education but now, providentially, its function was the proper one of liberal higher education. Every effort must be made to attract the youth of the area; they, Sturtevant declared, are the most valuable students any college can enroll. Although a goodly number is important, the policy must be "to educate scholars rather than to have many students." (TM, 26 May 1874)

Usually half or more of the men in the graduating classes earned the A.B. degree. However, the scientific program was popular and all agreed that it had been wise to establish the B.S. curriculum twenty years earlier. It was of even greater importance now because "scientific research and discovery are engaging the acutest intellects of this 19th century." The three-year program caused some problems. Many students were seduced from the classical studies and even the best among them failed to acquire "culture and polish." The obvious remedy was to extend the scientific course to four years, which was done in 1873. Instruction in the sciences was greatly strengthened by the establishment of the Hitchcock professorships in mathematics and natural science. Lectures on geology and meteorology were added and the library subscribed to scientific journals. The faculty had recently approved a program for post-graduate degrees, and in 1872 Sturtevant informed John McClintock, Class of 1869, that the Ph.D. degree would be conferred upon him after "a satisfactory examination in one or two branches of science or philosophy." There is no record that the doctorate was awarded.

Preparatory instruction was resumed in 1869 with the establishment of Whipple Academy in a new building near downtown, at Kosciusko and Morgan. Alfred Sturtevant was employed in 1870 as tutor in the College and assistant in Whipple Academy, and a few years later he became principal of the Academy. Preparatory education was a matter of considerable interest to many, and in 1875 the state Congregational Association named Sturtevant as chairman of a special committee for organizing a Congregational preparatory school in Illinois. (*Advance*, 21 Oct. 1875) Church and academic leaders had discussed the need for some years and action was now deemed appropriate because of "the too successful attempt to exclude Christian culture from the public schools." The Illinois College faculty agreed that such schools were important feeders for the colleges but deemed it unwise to found new institutions in competition with Whipple and the department at Knox. They voted to continue the discussion after the "Sociable Supper" at the Congregational Church but left no record of any decisions.

The staff determined that it would be "a good influence upon the students and the community to have a lecture by some member of the Faculty, now and then." (FM, 28 Jan. 1875) Sturtevant was among the participants. On one occasion there was no business before the faculty and "a social gathering of the families of the Faculty took the place of the usual meeting." (FM, 19 Jan. 1872) Sturtevant entertained the seniors at tea and sometimes took dinner with the Boarding Club.

Keenly aware of America's significance in the plan of Providence, Sturtevant must have been fascinated by the Centennial Exposition in Philadelphia. He prepared a history of Illinois College for display as part of the exhibit for the State of Illinois. He was in the East that summer and most likely attended the Exposition, although no record has yet been found nor is there a copy of the history in the College's Archives.[2]

The faculty adopted the policy that "Colored students [are] to be admitted as others, if they apply." (FM, 19 Sept. 1872) The Minutes do not indicate whether any did so. Arrangements were made in 1873 for Portuguese young men to attend classes under the sponsorship of the Presbytery, which provided tuition for at least one of them. A student dismissed from Blackburn University applied for admission in 1875. He had refused to give information about the author of a newspaper article censuring the president. Sturtevant examined the student and granted him admission; however, he is not listed in the catalog of alumni.

The faculty encouraged certain student activities and sought to restrain others. All students were required to participate in the Wednesday afternoon exercises in declamation. Phi Alpha and Sigma Pi wanted the same selection and the faculty decided in favor of the Phis. Sigma Pi then sent a somewhat discourteous note to the faculty. Sturtevant sometimes reviewed the students' compositions and prepared notices about the exhibitions for *Advance* and the *Quincy Whig*. In the spring of 1875 the President could not preside at the Freshman Exhibition and Dr. Adams filled his place. Student participation was encouraged by the establishment of endowed prizes in oratory (by Henry Hall, 1871) and in speech (by Thomas Smith, 1872).

In 1870 the faculty granted a holiday for the day after Thanksgiving. In mid-December school closed on Wednesday afternoon to allow for two weeks of vacation at Christmas. In 1873 the faculty decided to allow only Thanksgiving Day but relented when nearly all the students petitioned for the Friday holiday. The minute recording this change was introduced with the phrase, "Thinking it unwise to refuse...." (FM, 13 Nov. 1873) The faculty in October 1873 permitted students to place a swing on campus; that tradition has continued with some interruptions— duly protested—into the late twentieth century.

Not all student activities were benign. Prior to commencement in 1871 Professor Crampton was instructed to confer with the police to prevent a repetition of earlier episodes when some students circulated bogus programs crudely satirizing both students and faculty. (CH, 286-87) The police were not successful and the prank continued for several years. Ball playing on the campus caused unspecified difficulties and Sturtevant was requested to make appropriate comments when the students met for prayers. Students obtained keys and locked the doors one evening while alumni were meeting. New locks were installed to prevent access to buildings but they did not hinder someone from locking Professor Clapp out of the Chapel. The accused students were summoned before the faculty, who had to interrupt the proceedings to stop other students who were blowing horns outside.

Commencement exercises were held in various auditoriums, including the College Chapel and Strawn Opera House. The number of graduates ranged from a low of four in 1875 to nine in 1873 and 1876. The *1887-88 Catalogue of Alumni* shows that twelve of the forty-three who graduated from 1871 through 1876 subsequently earned advanced degrees in medicine, theology, and law at various universities, including Yale, Chicago, and Michigan. The literary societies held their anniversary exercises on the Wednesday of commencement week. Sometimes the Alumni Association met in the forenoon of commencement day; occasionally the President hosted a reception for alumni in his home. In 1871 the Alumni were authorized to nominate three trustees and also, once the Alumni Endowment Fund was fully subscribed, to nominate a professor, subject to Board approval. In 1872 Rev. Thomas Beecher, Class of 1843, was invited to be the speaker.

An old graduate told a reporter as they drove through the "most classic and beautiful city" that "this is the Athens of the West." The evidence to justify the claim was the large number of educational institutions in addition to the common schools and the high school: the Jacksonville Female Academy, the Illinois Female College, the Athenaeum and Conservatory of Music, the Jacksonville Business College, and "most conspicuous of all, the grand old Illinois College, of which our denomination is justly proud." As a result the town had "the evidences of highest culture, refinement and happiness on every side." The city was described as charming with "its broad, shaded streets, its groves, gardens and splendid residences...." Two railroads provided access from every direction, and the state institutions brought wealth and importance. There were twenty churches. Overall the city was characterized as quiet, without the noise of a commercial metropolis or the pollution of a manufacturing center. To sum it up, the city was "by nature, art and association, a student's paradise." (*Advance*, 8 June 1871)

Illinois College continued to face competition from other institutions for students and funds. Sturtevant protested against those who disparaged the College by comparing it with schools conducted on very different principles. Oberlin claimed an enrollment of twelve hundred but hardly more than ten per cent were in the collegiate program. Sturtevant wrote a lengthy essay analyzing the relationship of the "Colleges and State Universities." The state system was firmly established but was not a perfect solution for the people's needs. Moreover, state institutions could hardly be genuine universities because the exclusion of religion contradicted the very name. "To exclude that subject is to descend from the universal to the partial...." (463) American society and the emphasis on education, Sturtevant noted, were the outgrowth of New England civilization. From its common schools a great public school system developed, public because only the state had sufficient resources to provide free elementary education for all. Because the church is distinct from the state, there is a tendency to separate religion from education. The schools were not hostile to religion but left it to the church, the family, and the individual. Academies and colleges under appropriate religious direction could fulfill the whole range of expectations for liberal learning. These institutions were sustained by voluntary contributions and in them religion still had a very important place.

A combination of public elementary education for all and privately supported higher education for the few would have been very satisfactory. Unfortunately the Christian people of America lost that great opportunity. Despite the efforts of the Western College Society, the denominations founded too many schools—most of them inadequately funded. The demand for state-supported universities was the inevitable consequence of that folly, and if the present trend of sectarian rivalry continued people might even accept a state religion to escape the anarchy in the churches. A few privately-funded colleges with sufficient endowment and spread throughout the country could fulfill the nation's spiritual need.

View of Illinois College in 1874-75
(1874-75 *Catalogue*)
Club House   Chapel   Library Hall   Dormitory
The fence separated the small campus from the lots on the west side of Park Street. The same view was pictured on the front page of early issues of the *College Rambler*.

A New Dormitory

The enrollment in the College in 1870-1871 was 55, reached 62 the following year, and then decreased for three successive years to 44. Students were paying about $6 weekly to board with families —twice the amount at competing colleges. The only way to reduce the cost was to provide good housing and board on the campus. The need for a new dormitory was apparent, and Sturtevant presented that cause to the trustees and faculty. Such a facility would develop "that college *sprit du corps* [*sic*]; those strong personal friendships, and class associations which so endear the students to each other and to the Alma Mater." In December 1871 Professors Crampton and Storrs were instructed to prepare plans for a dormitory, completing them within two months. Construction proceeded slowly as funds became available. The faculty requested Sturtevant and Storrs to obtain a suitable box for documents to be placed under the cornerstone. In May 1873 Crampton reported that $15,000 had been subscribed thus far. The walls, principal partitions, and the slate roof were completed by October but nothing more was done until the following May. The need to complete the building was now urgent and the trustees let the final contracts. Sturtevant loaned the College $1,000 and Crampton was directed to "find his recreation during

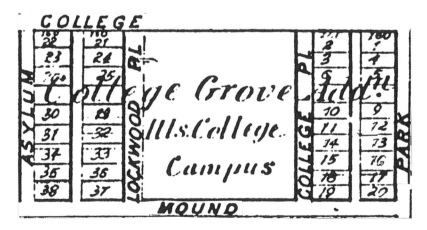

Map of Campus Area, 1872
The lots on the west side of Park Street were re-purchased by the College soon after President Tanner took office in 1882.

the vacation in raising $6000." (TM, 26 May 1874) The new "Dormitory Hall" was ready for occupancy in the fall of 1874. Professor Crampton's plan for a boarding house in the old South Wing was approved.[3]

Enrollment jumped to 60 in 1875-1876, Sturtevant's last year as president. In that year 78 preparatory students and 221 in the Business College brought the total figure to 359. A brief news item datelined "Illinois College" stated that "the new dormitory is full, with the exception of two or three rooms. The boarding club numbers about fifty. Board averages $2.35 a week, a great reduction on old rates. There is a strong and growing spirit of loyalty to the institution, among the students." (*Christian News*, Jan. 1876)

Although Illinois College had been removed from the list of beneficiaries of the College Society, the sum of $700 was paid during 1870-1871, presumably a pledge made previously. The College made a good case in 1872 for raising $10,000 for endowment and the request was granted. The Society's contributions, first arranged when Sturtevant was acting president, continued throughout much of his presidency. The total provided by the Society was $61,178.17, more than double the amount raised for either Wabash College or Beloit College.[4]

President Sturtevant invited the College Society to hold its Twenty-eighth Annual Meeting in Jacksonville in November 1872. The number who came was disappointingly small and indeed insufficient for a quorum. Those present gathered at the Congregational Church and constituted an "Educational Convention" in lieu of an official meeting. By 1873 the College Society had become "the organ of the Congregationalists" and "responsible only for the colleges they plant."[5] In its *Thirty-first Report* the College Society announced its union with the American Education Society, thus forming the American College and Education Society. (May 1874, 8-9) The College Society had served the institutions and the Education Society had provided funds for needy students. The two organizations competed for donations to the detriment of both but especially the colleges, and Baldwin and Sturtevant had strongly advocated such a merger years before. Many donors preferred giving aid for students rather than institutions but, as Sturtevant wryly argued, a good college is necessary if a student is to utilize scholarship funds for an education.

As of June 1871 about $20,000 had been added to the funds of the College and income increased to $16,000, double the amount at the end of the Civil War. The trustees continued to "sell" lots to the faculty, usually in lieu of cash salary. Sturtevant obtained part of a very large lot bordered by City Place, Mound, and Asylum (Woodland). He paid $1,500 in cash, the balance of the price ($2,941.91) covered by salary due him. Sturtevant recommended in 1871 that a house be built on the campus for a caretaker in order to attract a qualified person and to allow a corresponding reduction in cash salary. The "Janitor's Cottage" was built, southwest of Sturtevant Hall, and remained in use for about a century. Some additional income was obtained, perhaps to offset the cost of printing, by offering advertising in the *1872-'73 Catalogue*. Eames' Book Store, Harper & Brothers, and the Jacksonville Female Academy placed ads. So too did a Jacksonville clothier and J. B. Turner, who listed "Fruit, Shade, Ornamental Trees, and Hedge Plants." Turner offered silver maple trees, 8-16 feet, for 10 to 20 cents and hedge plants for $2 to $3 per thousand.

The Trustees' Minutes for 1873 (4 June) reported the amounts in various funds. The Fund of 1858 was nearly $25,000, and the Presidency Fund, $20,000. That year the professors' salaries were set at $2,000 and Alfred Sturtevant as an instructor was to receive $1,050. Unfortunately, inflation had eroded purchasing power. Professor Crampton, now the College's financial agent, arranged with Samuel Hitchcock of Massachusetts for $50,000 in railroad bonds to endow two professorships. Crampton was appointed as the Hitchcock Professor of Mathematics and Henry E. Storrs was made Hitchcock Professor of the Natural Sciences. The College's insurance in 1873 indicated the value of the College's property as amounting to more than $39,000 for the buildings, library, and apparatus; some additional coverage was recommended. Even in those years the College had problems with "parking" and the faculty called attention to the prohibition against hitching horses to the College fence. The janitor was instructed to move any horses found there to some other place.

When Sturtevant resigned the presidency on 31 May 1876, the

College's endowment funds totaled approximately $112,000. Over half was in the General Fund, about one-fourth in the Hitchcock Fund, and somewhat more than $22,000 in the Presidency Fund. The endowment produced more than $7,600 in interest, and tuition income (about three-fourths of it from the Business College) was about the same amount. The year's expenditures, $15,676.08, were about two hundred dollars less than the total income. Although the balance looked good, the accumulated salaries owed to the faculty amounted to nearly $7,000 by 1875. An urgent plea from the faculty impelled the trustees to take action. The decision was made to pay the faculty from the money on hand, on a pro rata basis, and to borrow enough (at a rate not exceeding ten per cent) to cover the balance due. Sturtevant's salary was exempt from the budget stress because it was derived from the Presidency Fund; in 1875 the amount was $2,237.

The death of Rev. William Carter, on 9 February 1871, was a great loss to Julian Sturtevant. Carter was a native of New Canaan, the town Sturtevant came to love when he taught there, and the two men had been friends since their college days. Carter was a member of the "second division" of the Illinois Association and was a trustee of the College from 1844 until he died. Both men participated in the founding service of the Congregational Church in Jacksonville and Carter was its first pastor. For many years he was pastor of the Congregational Church at Pittsfield. Carter had arranged for Sturtevant to preach at his funeral, which was in the Pittsfield church.

The tribute to Carter began with a review of the religious background of the New England stock from which both men had sprung. Rooted in elements of England's own experiments in religious freedom, the colonists and their descendants were zealous in spreading their language, freedom, and religion to the North American continent. Both men had sought active roles in fulfilling that destiny, and they shared a common commitment and a common cause in Illinois College. Both also promoted the growth of Congregationalism in the West; Carter was a founder in 1844 of the General Association of Illinois. The two men shared moderate positions regarding temperance and slavery, both actively supported revivals, and both had a deep love of music. In personal habits both were frugal and yet liberally supported the Christian mission. An aspect of Carter's theology which Sturtevant did not share as deeply was the study of prophecy for proving the inspiration of the Scriptures.

The College Now Congregational

A significant change in 1871 brought Congregationalists into majority status on the Board of Trustees. Three new members of the Board were chosen, Edward P. Kirby of Jacksonville, C. G. Hammond of Chicago, and Lorenzo Bull of Quincy. Sturtevant exulted that all three were elected unanimously and all were well-known Congregationalists. "The fight is over; there is nothing now opening before the College but a future of peaceful growth." The College was now independent of external control. Newton Bateman, Class of 1843 and a trustee, had said he would vote only for a Congregationalist because "it is indispensable to the success of the College that the public understand that Congregationalists control it and are responsible for it." Sturtevant added, "This is exactly my position." (JMS to Warren, 2 June 1871) Other additions to the Board in Sturtevant's final years as president were three local men, Rev. Martin K. Whittlesey (a Congregational minister), Dr. Hiram Jones (Class of 1844), and Julius E. Strawn. The College meanwhile lost the services of several prominent men. Theron Baldwin had died in 1870 and Rev. William Carter in 1871. Richard Yates, the College's first graduate and a trustee before his election as Governor, died in 1873. E. W. Blatchford and C. G. Hammond, good friends of Sturtevant, resigned in 1875.

In the 1870s Illinois College continued its observance of the annual Day of Prayer for Colleges, the actual date often arranged by Sturtevant to coordinate campus and church services. Sturtevant's Sabbath afternoon lectures were scheduled for "2 and 1/2 o'clock" and daily prayers were at the last hour of the afternoon. The faculty conducted the prayers in rotation; President Sturtevant was in charge on Fridays and Mr. [Alfred] Sturtevant on alternate Wednesdays. A faculty committee on music arranged to borrow a hymnal, *Songs of Zion*, from the` Congregational Church. Apparently those books were not satisfactory because the committee recommended the adoption of *Chapel Songs* and the purchase of fifty copies was authorized. The Sunday afternoon service began with the singing of the "long meter doxology." A vote of thanks was extended to students in 1875 for their efforts in procuring an organ for the Chapel.

Sturtevant's 1871 baccalaureate address was "pronounced to have been one of his very best efforts." (*Advance*, 8 June 1871) In 1872 his sermon was on "Wisdom" and his text was from Proverbs 4:7. Responding to the popular demand for "practical education," Sturtevant reasoned that the truly practical education teaches the arts of living and the skills for success. A knowledge of human nature is essential, and that can be learned by studying language, literature, and history. The moral laws of the Kingdom of God are learned from the word of God. "The only practical method of reforming and improving society is to conform our lives to this standard and to persuade other men to do so." (*Advance*, 4 July 1872) In 1874 Sturtevant preached from Acts 9:6, urging the graduates to consider high aims in choosing their lifework. Overall, "the past year [had] been a season of spiritual blessing to the College and Academy, many hearts having received new impulses to a better life." (*Advance*, 11 June 1874)

Dr. Sturtevant remained seated while he preached the baccalaureate sermon in the College Chapel in 1875. About six weeks earlier his ankle had been broken when he was thrown from a buggy. Nevertheless his sermon was said to be "one of the most scholarly and powerful which the President ever delivered." His text was "The field is the World," from Matt. 13:38, and his theme was the "Missionary Spirit." Though seventy years of age Sturtevant "looked the picture of health and vigor. His mind is as keen as ever, and he is thoroughly alive to all the issues of the day." After the service, when the reporter engaged him in conversation about the College, Sturtevant's enthusiasm was kindled. "It was plain that its success and prosperity lie nearest his heart. He believes, and rightly we think, that a grand destiny is before it in the near future." (*Advance*, 17 June 1875) The baccalaureate services were held in the Congregational Church in 1874 and again in 1876.

The faculty received an offer of any writings by Emanuel Swedenborg which the College did not already possess. Swedenborg had combined religion and science in mystical and speculative terms and regarded his New Church as superseding orthodox Christian churches. Moreover, he repudiated the orthodox doctrines of the Atonement and of the Trinity.[6] In view of the strong insistence on orthodoxy by Sturtevant and others it is remarkable that works by Swedenborg were accepted.

The Yale Divinity School, formerly the Theological Department of Yale College, celebrated its Semi-Centennial Anniversary in 1872. Sturtevant was invited to speak but was unable to attend, and his address was read on his behalf. His speech began with a review of the rapid development of home missions in the 1820s. A clearer vision had burst forth that the great Mississippi valley should be settled "by an English speaking Anglo-American population" and speedily annexed "to the great American Republic." (65) Without the Gospel the flood of settlers "would be incapable of American liberty" because they would fall prey either to "infidelity or the superstitions of Popery." (66) The American Home Missionary Society was founded in 1826 to avert this crisis. Among those enlisting to save the country and the world were the members of the New Haven Association. For them the compelling question was, "[H]ow can we conquer and hold the great Mississippi valley for Christ?" (67) Their answer was a dual mission embracing liberal learning and evangelization, and the result was the founding of Illinois College and many churches in the surrounding area.

Yale's influence was not denominational and upon coming to Illinois the young men affiliated with the Presbyterians. They discovered that Presbyterianism in the West was quite different from what they had earlier understood and they realized that it was not the church of their fathers. Within four years after the first men from Yale had arrived in Illinois, the first Congregational churches were organized in the state, two of them assisted by members of the New Haven Association. The beginning of the resistance to Presbyterian hegemony was certainly made in central Illinois, declared Sturtevant, and it was led by the men of that Association.

Thus they were a part of "the great Congregational revolution... west of the Alleghanies." (70)

Illinois College has been "a radiating center of civilization" for the region's heterogeneous elements through its support for "intellectual and moral culture, freedom of thought, and a pure and enlightened religious faith." (71) Among its three hundred graduates it counted more than sixty ministers of the gospel and many eminent statesmen and educators. Additional thousands had passed through its classrooms and hundreds were converted in the revivals of religion on the campus. The New Haven Association was Yale's "earliest and much its largest single investment...." (72) Sturtevant's address concluded with the devout hope that the students of Yale's Divinity School would continue to regard the world as their field.

The annual meetings of the Jacksonville Congregational Church were held when possible on 15 December, the anniversary of its founding. When the members met in the lecture room on that date in 1874, Sturtevant offered the prayer and was elected moderator. When Rev. William Savage resigned in 1875, Sturtevant was on the committee which arranged for Rev. Eli Corwin to accept the pastorate. Five years later Sturtevant had a part, apparently as chairman, in calling Rev. H. E. Butler as pastor. In another role, Sturtevant contacted one of his St. Louis companions on the Kansas buffalo hunt to obtain a supply of St. Clair Port for communion.[7] The sacramental use of wine was acknowledged as appropriate by the *Laws* of the College.

Various activities of the local church were consistent with Sturtevant's views, although they may not have involved him directly. Collections for the poor were approved for Communion Sabbaths. Aid was given to the Bible Society, a cause recommended by the Sunday School. Forty-four men were engaged in the study of various mission fields, including the Sandwich Islands. When the First Presbyterian Church closed its building for repairs, its people were invited to join the Congregationalists for worship. Special arrangements were made for seating the young ladies of the Jacksonville Female Academy during this period, and the Congregational Church was offered for the Academy's anniversary exercises. In 1874 invitations were sent to Grace Methodist Episcopal Church and Westminster

Presbyterian Church to attend a mass temperance meeting. Sturtevant on occasion preached at other local churches, such as Westminster and the Brooklyn Methodist Episcopal Church.

Through the years Sturtevant participated in Congregational church councils in the area at Springfield, Bloomington, and Pekin as well as at the Jacksonville church. In 1872 he attended the semi-annual meeting of the Southern Association at Sandoval and represented the College at the meeting of the Quincy Association. A council of particular interest to Sturtevant was convened at Chapin on 4 October 1873 for examining the credentials of his cousin and colleague, Professor E. A. Tanner. On the following day Tanner was ordained; although the record is not explicit, Sturtevant likely preached the sermon.

In 1873 Sturtevant represented the local church at the General Association meeting in Elgin. In 1875 he presented a report on behalf of the committee on preparatory education, noting that several very desirable offers of sites and buildings had been received from various towns around the state. No funds were yet available and a new committee was authorized to continue the project. (*Advance*, 1 June 1875) At the General Association meeting at Quincy in 1876, President Sturtevant "read one of his clear and forcible essays, on the relation of a sound theology to church organizations." He showed Christianity's antagonism to ritualism and centralized power and demonstrated its affinity with freedom and with purity of doctrine and life. Professor C. A. Clapp gave an address on "The Christian Woman," described as an "argument against the socalled [*sic*] Woman's Rights' movement." Sturtevant was one of three who endorsed the speaker's views, and his friend Flavel Bascom was one of eight inclined against the more extreme statements expressed by Clapp. Much lively discussion ensued and the time allotted for it was extended to an hour and a half. (*Advance*, 1 June 1876, 743)

In 1873 when the sixth Triennial Convention was held in Chicago, with two hundred representatives present, Sturtevant was a member of the Board of Visitors appointed to examine the Chicago Theological Seminary. He reported for the Board that the results for each department of study were gratifying and exhibited clear improvement over previous years.

Triennial national councils were held beginning with the Oberlin meeting of 1871. Sturtevant, representing the Southern Association, chaired a committee on procedures for bringing together churches in need of ministers and ministers who were without pulpits. By custom the delegates preached at local churches of various denominations, and on Sunday evening Sturtevant delivered the sermon at the Baptist Church. At the Council's Monday evening session he offered the prayer, after which—and probably by his arrangement—his favorite hymn was sung: "I Love Thy Kingdom, Lord." The next triennial meeting was at New Haven in 1874 and again Sturtevant represented the Southern Association. He was named as the delegate to a corresponding body, the General Convention of Baptist Churches.

The anniversaries of the American Board of Commissioners for Foreign Missions, in which Sturtevant held a life membership as a director, were additional opportunities for him to share in the mission of the larger church. The faculty granted him a leave of absence so that he could attend the 1875 meeting.

"President Sturtevant, having been invited to attend the Brooklyn Council for the trial of H. W. Beecher, was encouraged to go." This brief entry in the Faculty Minutes (3 Feb. 1876) is the only notice in the College's official records of Sturtevant's participation in the most unusual meeting he ever attended. In addition to his concern for the well-being of the denomination, Sturtevant had personal reasons for being present. The Sturtevant and Beecher families had been acquainted since the early years of the century, and Edward Beecher, the older brother, had been Sturtevant's colleague at Illinois College. Sturtevant sometimes preached in Henry Ward Beecher's pulpit in the Plymouth Church in Brooklyn, appealing directly or indirectly for funds for the College.

Rumors had circulated about Beecher's alleged adultery with the wife of a prominent member of his church. The church called for a council to convene in mid-February to advise it regarding procedures.[8] Sturtevant wrote to Leonard Bacon, stating that if some of the men from Yale were going he also would go; he added that if they were not present he himself would rather be almost anywhere else.[9] Two hundred fifty ministers were present and more than one hundred thirty churches were represented. Among ministers without pastorates were Dr. Bacon, the moderator, and Sturtevant. Sturtevant was on the committee to advise Plymouth Church how to deal with members who had charged gross immorality but now refused to affirm or deny such statements. Four brief addresses were printed in the published *Proceedings* of the Advisory Council, among them the remarks of Dr. Bacon, President Porter of Yale, and President Sturtevant. In his address Sturtevant rejected the claim some had made that the Council's purpose was "to whitewash Brother Beecher and his church." He wanted something done "to put an end to this great scandal." He favored the plan for a committee of five respected men who would investigate the matter fully and render their judgment. Meanwhile, Sturtevant declared, Beecher was to be regarded as innocent until proven guilty of clearly defined charges substantiated by named witnesses.

In discussing "The Advisory Council" Sturtevant noted that twenty-five hundred members of Plymouth Church were united in their faith in Beecher. He acknowledged also that even the wisest and best men were divided in their opinion regarding Beecher's innocence. He believed that a large council of pastors and delegates could not be convened for the lengthy period required to try the case and so he favored a small commission. Later Sturtevant considered the obstacles placed in the way of establishing "The Commission of Five." He repeated his determination to regard Beecher as innocent until proven guilty. If the scandal continued without resolution, he said, it would be due to those who exerted so much effort to defeat the plan which had been devised. Several men wrote to Sturtevant to express agreement with his views. No church commission ever settled the issue but the public's verdict was "guilty." That judgment was influenced by a civil suit in which Beecher answered nine hundred times that he did not know or could not remember. The *New York Times* in 1878 repeated its earlier determination of Beecher's guilt and said this conclusion was supported by broad evidence.[10]

Religion Essential to Education, Society

It was now abundantly clear, Sturtevant declared in an essay in 1871, that *Christian* colleges are essential for the Northwest (the upper Mississippi Valley) to attain "the full growth and development of a Christian civilization...." (1) Religion cannot be excluded from higher education because people are passionately involved with it, whether in support or in opposition. If Christian believers control a college they will seek to make the curriculum and the faculty Christian in their influence on students. Conversely, unbelievers will have the contrary effect. A man without religious convictions can teach a subject well but that duty is far less than a teacher's full responsibility, which is "to form character, to develop manhood." (5) An effective Christian influence is essential for nourishing the positive virtues of morality, the love of truth, patriotism, and the ideal of self-sacrifice. Local circumstances should determine whether to conduct prayers once or twice a day and whether students should be required to attend religious services.

Neither state-supported colleges nor denominational colleges are adequate. Christian non-sectarian colleges are needed, and the best sponsors for them are Congregationalists because they do not recognize any superior body as having authority over either a local church or a college. The success of Congregationalism as the foundation of colleges is well-witnessed by the achievements of Yale, Williams, Amherst, Middlebury, and Bowdoin, which have served the people of New England well regardless of their students' denominational affiliations. Men of wealth should generously support such worthy institutions in all regions.

In a subsequent article Sturtevant presented a negative response to his question, "Shall Colleges Be Denominational?" Christianity is universal and the colleges must be protected from the conflicts engendered by sectarianism. Sturtevant added a new recommendation regarding governance, that alumni be given a voice in governing their alma mater. "Colleges ought to be controlled by the republic, and not by the aristocracy of letters."

In his essay on "Religion and the Public Schools" Sturtevant expressed his willingness to consider the secularists' position that the Bible should not be used in schools. However, he asserted, the notion that it should be excluded by law would shock "the most sacred convictions and sentiments of every man who accepts the Bible as a revelation from God." That would limit teachers' liberty and the circulation of the word of God. While it may not be important whether the Bible is read in school, the character of teachers is supremely important. By far the most significant function of schools is the formation of character and therefore all teachers ought to be evangelical Christians. Indeed, "the man who has no faith in Christ and no loving interest in the progress of his religion in the world, cannot be regarded as a fit educator of children of Christians." Even if it is agreed that the instruction "should be strictly secular it would not follow that Papists, Jews and unbelievers are better fitted to give such instruction, than devout Protestant believers." There is just as much danger that an unbeliever will influence his students as the believer. Moreover, to omit religion would be illiberal. Religion must be examined by "thoughtful study—study in a cool philosophic spirit" because it is an essential element in the study of history. It inevitably enters into science, which leads to the origin of things and to the question of an intelligent Creator. Whether the teacher champions theism or atheism will be very plain to the students.

The completion of the railroad from Jacksonville to Waverly in February 1871 was celebrated by a festival in the latter town. A special train from Jacksonville brought numerous civic and other leaders who gave speeches and toasts on behalf of various groups. President Sturtevant thanked the citizens of Waverly for their hospitality; likely he was recognized as having selected the town's site and for encouraging his mother's relatives to settle there. The great crowd assembled in "the large Congregational church" and was called to order by one of its members serving as chairman. Sturtevant had organized that church in 1836, one year after the town was founded; the building was constructed in 1851. Behind the church was the old seminary building which once housed an academy taught by John Brooks and now hosted a sumptuous feast. The train left Waverly about 10:30 in the evening and reached Jacksonville about midnight.[11]

Julian Sturtevant's prominence in Morgan County was acknowledged when he was invited to deliver the main address at the Old Settlers' Reunion on 17 August 1871. The early settlers, said Sturtevant, were determined to lay "the foundation of a Christian civilization among those crude beginnings...." (8) The great achievement of their generation was "the spread of civilization, education, social order, liberty, [and] Christianity," across the continent of North America. This growth was providential, demonstrating "that there is a God in history, and that He planned the settlement of North America; that He hid away that continent through all the struggles of the world's previous history, until he had prepared a people to take possession of it...." (10) Sturtevant compared the American people with the ancient Israelites but noted significant differences: the settlers from England opened their country to immigrants from every nation in Europe and sought to extend liberty and their institutions far beyond national borders. The success of the American effort in establishing civilized communities was dependent upon the exercise of the voluntary principle. Wherever they went Americans did not wait for government to act but took upon themselves the responsibility for the public good as well as their private needs. Underlying their great vision and achievement was the conviction that the church of Christ must be founded to bring the influence of Christian faith and worship to bear on the whole population.

The development of communities such as Jacksonville, Sturtevant noted, often involved sharp conflicts because each group had its own history, beliefs, social customs, educational purposes, and distinctive views of family life. Conflicts will continue but one principle undergirds the whole effort. "It is the principle of the largest liberty of thought and utterance. Every man has a right to think—so far as his fellowmen are concerned, to think erroneously, and to give his reasons for so thinking, provided that he concedes to every other man the same right.... In a free country like ours...that is to be esteemed a good citizen that loves truth, thinks freely and honestly, and sincerely defends the results of his thinking; and that however mistaken he may be; and no opinions have a right to live that cannot live by a fair argumentative appeal to the understanding of mankind." (16-17)

Sturtevant reminded his peers that their participation in preparing a good heritage for the coming generations would soon end. The churches, schools, and other public institutions they had established were far more important than any private wealth. The younger generation would receive a sacred trust to be preserved and transmitted to their posterity. Much work was yet to be done, for the country, for the church of God, and for posterity.

The *Atlas Map of Morgan County*, published in 1872, was a combination of maps and drawings with descriptions of the county and its institutions (including Illinois College) and biographies of its leading citizens (among them Sturtevant). On a map of the city of Jacksonville the initials "J.M.S." designated the small farm which Sturtevant owned on the west side of Lincoln Avenue and directly north of the Catholic Cemetery. (*Atlas Map*, 39, 42, 76) On the *Atlas Map* (80) a drawing of a tree designates the site of the College Cemetery. In 1870 the trustees had voted not to remove the graves from the College cemetery to a new location. City records, however, indicate that many graves, including those of the Sturtevant family, were removed to Diamond Grove Cemetery in 1873.

As President of Illinois College Sturtevant was invited to deliver a Fourth of July oration at Carthage in 1873. The people in that vicinity planned a grand celebration.

Defining the Faith; Christian Unity

The 1871 National Council of the Congregational Churches, meeting at Oberlin, had prepared a declaration of faith which Sturtevant reviewed in an article on "Our Doctrinal Basis." Although the statement was not precisely what he would have written, it was adequate. He heartily endorsed efforts to state the faith in terms meaningful to the living age. However, said Sturtevant, those at Oberlin had no thought of renouncing Calvinism and adopting Arminianism.[12] Sturtevant believed that the recent phenomenal expansion of Congregationalism could be attributed to its openness to God's continuing revelation through new insight into the Scriptures. Its power was in its ability to unite Christians on the basis of "simple evangelic faith" true to the system of doctrine taught by Jesus Christ and his disciples. Sturtevant anticipated "the millennial future of the church of God" when evangelical faith would unite all Christians.

Subsequently Sturtevant acknowledged the importance of holy living, but he rejected the claim that so long as a person lives rightly beliefs do not matter. The Bible contains a definite system of beliefs which can be derived by the same laws for interpreting language which are applied to any other work. "Orthodoxy" includes the biblical account of Christ. "His life, his character, his teachings, his works and pre-eminently his death, resurrection and ascension are the faith once delivered to the saints." "Savior" expresses the aim of Christ's mission, to save the lost through the shedding of his blood for the remission of sins. Those accepting these teachings are Christians; those rejecting them are not. "It is as easy to know what the faith once delivered to the saints is, as it is to know the astronomy which is taught by Copernicus, Newton, and La Plas."

Other denominations charged that Congregationalism was held together only by a rope of sand, but Sturtevant countered that "Our Bond of Union" is our "living, loving faith in Christ." The strength and power of a Congregational Church lies precisely in the strength of its people's faith; there is no ritual nor hierarchy to hold them together. The vitality of that simple faith is illustrated in the unsurpassed record of the Congregationalists in home and foreign missions and in establishing schools and higher institutions.

Sturtevant elaborated his interpretation of biblical prophecy and forcefully expressed his conviction that "The Kingdom of Heaven" will be over this world and also in it. It was part of the mission of Christ, he declared, "to establish a new social order in the world," ...an empire of righteousness, peace and love," displacing all despotic tyranny. Christ has been present among his people, already working to redeem human society from sin and evil although his kingdom has not yet been fully realized. Christ proposed "to reform society by a radical reformation of individual character" and "set in motion a train of moral forces," constantly accelerating, to achieve a social renovation.[13] Perhaps Sturtevant was seeking to reconcile the individualism of the revival movement with the growing awareness of the Gospel's social implications.

The divisions among Christians, fragmenting the body of Christ into many separate and often hostile sects, were a subject of continuing concern to Julian Sturtevant. Following his retirement in 1876 he had the leisure while in Connecticut to prepare three articles on sectarianism and its remedy. He noted that Jacksonville with twenty-one churches for twelve thousand people was a vivid illustration of the prodigality of Protestantism. In the struggle for funds "All the most improved machinery for raising money for churches is worked to its utmost capacity. Fairs, strawberry festivals, oyster suppers, public dinners, and the like devices, are resorted to by the ladies with a zeal and self-sacrificing public spirit which we greatly admire, while we regret the necessity which calls it into exercise." The congregations want bigger edifices, more elaborate organs, more costly music, and "more eloquent and attractive pastors." The result is that churches have almost nothing left to contribute to "the one common Christian enterprise of evangelizing the world."

Sturtevant did not, however, recommend withholding aid to a congregation despite the multiplicity of churches. That would leave it at the mercy of the "Darwinian principle of 'the survival of the fittest.'" The "waste" of church resources was due to the great diversity of the conceptions of the church. Now even in New England there were new churches representing "every form of religious organization existing in all the States and nations from which our immigrants come...." The situation in America had become like that of ancient Rome, which brought the gods of all the peoples who were conquered into the city. Happily, each group was zealous to reach out to others because Christianity still exhibited the spirit of propagandism which generally had died out in the other religions of the world. A good example of "The Remedy" favored by Sturtevant was demonstrated in a small community when a union church was formed on congregational principles. Congregationalists should be in the forefront in such churches because they need sacrifice neither faith nor polity.

In analyzing "Judicial Power in the Church" Sturtevant asserted that the church "is a theocracy of which God only is the Law-giver, Judge and Executive, with no visible or human representative in any department." He insisted that the procedure in Matt. 18:15-18 does not prescribe judicial action but is solely for restoring an erring person to fellowship. The right to the Lord's Supper is given directly by God to the person and the church can neither give it nor withdraw it. Respondents with contrary views quickly expressed their fears of relaxing or eliminating church discipline. Sturtevant's prompt rejoinder was that the proceedings of "ecclesiastical courts" are contrary to the spirit of Jesus Christ. He was familiar with church "trials" in Congregationalism from his boyhood, and in his early ministry he himself had experienced such an ordeal in a so-called court of Jesus Christ convened by the Presbyterian Church. Even if a church conducts the preliminary steps prescribed in Matthew in the spirit of reconciliation, the brother who is admonished is apt to conclude that "They are going to church me." If the effort were indeed made in a loving spirit few cases would result in a trial, but that attitude was often lacking. Many New Englanders changed to other denominations simply to escape the humiliation of a public trial. Sturtevant sympathized with such persons even though they were entering churches much more litigious and legalistic than Congregationalism. If church trials are necessary, "they ought to be provided for otherwise than by converting a popular assembly into a court of justice."

In a lengthy essay on "The Sect System" Sturtevant noted that Paul and the Apostles insisted on tolerating differences within the same church. Moreover, anyone who professes faith and leads a Christian life and is in good standing in any church is entitled to a seat at the Lord's table wherever it is spread. Only a year before, Sturtevant reminded his readers, there was a memorable union communion service at the Madison Square Presbyterian Church, when the Evangelical Alliance met in New York City. For a brief time it seemed that the church had reached the Promised Land. He added wistfully, with an allusion to Bunyan's *Pilgrim's Progress*, "It was only a glimpse of the 'gate of the celestial city' from the 'Delectable Mountains.'" (566) The spirit which pervaded that occasion ought to have become permanent, but regrettably the divisions are "likely to last till the millennium at least." (569)

A critic had accused Sturtevant of holding a "liberal" theory of church membership. Sturtevant denied that, declaring "we shall never belong to the self-styled liberal party in religion. Nothing can be liberal but the candid and loving reception of all the truth which God hath revealed." (570) The truth is liberal enough for him, he said, and he should not be charged with the sickly liberalism which would yield any part of Christian truth simply because someone objected to it. He refuted the charge that he had rejected all church government; although the divine government is invisible and spiritual, it is certainly real. Referring again to the issue of sectarianism, Sturtevant quoted a couplet from Alexander Pope. Sturtevant substituted for "Vice," the initial word, a word not altogether foreign to the original meaning: "Sect 'is a monster of so frightful mien, / As to be dreaded needs but to be seen.'" (572)

An even more dangerous tendency in the Christian Church is "Indifferentism." A person who earnestly and sincerely maintains his own position is neither a sectarian nor a bigot; he is an honest person although perhaps mistaken. A person unaware of the real differences among the various sects may think it unimportant which of the evangelical sects may prevail. But none of us, said Sturtevant, would say it is of no importance to our country or the world whether Protestantism or Catholicism, ritualism or evangelicalism, will prevail. The worst feature of indifferentism is the hypocrisy of people who acknowledge that there is no reason for adhering to a particular sect but nevertheless cling to it tenaciously. Sturtevant's advice was blunt: "Let us all be done with such dawdling." If people have good reasons for their views they should state them frankly and enter into a Christian discussion of their differences. Sadly, indifference is at its worst among Congregationalists—and to the detriment of the growth of their order.

Church and State, Religion and Culture

In 1876 Sturtevant reported to his Yale classmates that it had been his life-long desire to undertake "extended literary enterprises." In the past decade he had contributed more to periodical literature than in any previous time. He mentioned his tribute to Theron Baldwin and named the journals which had printed several of his lengthy articles, the *Congregational Quarterly* (Boston) and the *New Englander* (New Haven). Sturtevant's bibliography reflects his shift from the *New York Independent* to the *Chicago Advance* as his major vehicle for reaching the wider Congregational public. A new periodical, the *Advance* printed nearly a score of his articles in the years 1867-1874. Its staff described the newspaper as denominational but not narrowly sectarian and urged people to subscribe (at $2.50) because they published "able articles from the soundest thinkers and most noted writers of the time." Rev. Horace

Bushnell led the list of thirty-two. Rev. Thomas Beecher was third, and Rev. J. M. Sturtevant sixth. Leonard Bacon and Truman Post were among other prominent friends of Sturtevant who were named. (*Advance*, 1 Dec. 1870; 5 Dec. 1872)

Sturtevant reflected on the mutual influences of "Church and State" in a nation where the two are regarded as properly separate. He referred to Tocqueville's "profoundly philosophical treatise," *Democracy in America,* in which the author argued that church and state should be mutually independent and furthermore that religion should have no connection with political power. His first principle was widely accepted, said Sturtevant, but was the corollary true? *"What principles of church government are most favorable to the full development and permanent reign of republican liberty?"* (509) His answer was that despotism in religion tends toward despotism in the state, while freedom in the exercise of religion tends toward civil liberty. He declared his determination to analyze the political implications of the various kinds of church government even if he appeared to violate the truce presently existing "between the high contracting powers that assume to govern the religious world." (510)

History shows that religion is one of the strongest and most enduring forces in human life. Human beings, in awe of invisible powers, are influenced by their anticipation of immortality and retribution. Rulers have long known that religion is one of the chief elements in their exercise of power and consequently people have been compelled to adopt the form of religion imposed by the state. Liberty is impossible when people are subjected to the double penalty of secular and eternal punishments. An essential step toward achieving human freedom is the development of conscience which places allegiance to the God of heaven above loyalty to the state. Real freedom requires that secular government be confined to its own sphere, leaving religion as a matter between the individual and his God. In illustration Sturtevant cited numerous examples from the Bible and history.

In America all the major Protestant bodies except those which are congregational in organization have sprung from Europe's national churches. If human organization is to control the religious function in human life, the question arises whether it is to be centralized (as the Papal church) or manifold (as in Protestantism).

Sturtevant warned that if the Roman Catholic hierarchy ever gained ascendancy in the nation like it had achieved in New York City, "American Liberty, the American Republic, will be at an end." (517) The Papal system strives for power which it uses for its own ends. Sovereignty is divided, directed partly by a foreign "despot whose spirit and principles are more hostile to all free institutions …than those of the Czar of Russia…." (518) Sturtevant was well aware of historical precedents and also of recent pronouncements by the papacy. The Pope claimed to be successor to Peter but in reality, wrote Sturtevant, he was successor to the Caesars. Sturtevant noted that only three years before [in 1870] the Pope had been deprived of the sword but expected the armies of Catholic nations to restore his power.

James Madison's view in the *Federalist* (No. 51) was widely accepted, that just as civil rights can be protected in a free government only by a multiplicity of interests, so religious rights can be maintained only by a multiplicity of sects. Sturtevant acknowledged that it is the nature of power, individual and organized, secular and ecclesiastical, to seek its own aggrandizement. Indeed, because religious power is wielded in the name of God it has even greater force. The church's claim of authority over its members is analogous to the civil government's power over life, liberty, and property. Sturtevant maintained that no person or organization can be permitted power over religion without grave danger to civil liberty, and therefore true Christianity recognizes such power "IN GOD ALONE." (527) Christ came to found a kingdom but it is a kingdom not of this world, and God is its "only Legislator, Judge, and Executor." (527) The church must acknowledge that it has no power of its own and cannot of itself give or withhold the sacraments. Churches will no longer threaten human liberty when they cease claiming power over the political sphere or control over the treasury of God's grace. There will be no Papal power to terrorize kings nor Mormon claims to dignify concubinage as marriage. Sturtevant's conclusion was forceful: "the church of the Apostles [is] the only church that can ever solve the problem of Church and State." (535)

Unusual high praise was given to a book by Professor J. C. Shairp of Scotland, *Culture and Religion in Some of Their Relations.*

Sturtevant declared the work to be excellent in aim, admirable in spirit, and refreshingly clear and true. He was so much in agreement with Shairp that it is difficult and probably unnecessary to distinguish between the reviewer's thought and the author's. Sturtevant's essay is a cogent argument in favor of the thesis that culture (including science) and religion are compatible when both are properly understood. He himself was a devout Christian. He was also a cultured person, well-educated in theology, history, the classics, and English literature—and in mathematics, physics, and astronomy. Either at Yale or subsequently he had become familiar with the work of intellectual leaders of the recent past such as David Hume, Johann Goethe, and almost certainly Immanuel Kant, whose work in philosophy, science, and astronomy was very influential. The names of Blaise Pascal of the seventeenth century and Herbert Spencer, a younger contemporary of Sturtevant's, can be added.

A man with the highest level of culture is necessarily religious although not all who are religious are of high culture. "Culture implies the development of the social, esthetic, and intellectual, as well as of the moral nature...." (202) In the present age "many of the most highly cultivated minds have rejected the religion of Christ [thus giving the impression] that high culture is antagonistic to religious faith." (203) Some of these persons even hope that science will overcome religion. On the other hand, many narrow-minded religious men consider culture, and especially science, as favoring unbelief and fear that science will prevail over religion.

Religion is often partial and inadequate and to some extent untrue, and this is one reason why cultured men reject it. Sturtevant referred to Jesus' teaching about self-denial, which the Catholic Church corrupted to asceticism and self-inflicted punishment. The Puritans have not been blameless; they were not opposed to all pleasure, as some have said, but there is a partial truth in that claim. The peculiar creeds, ceremonies, and practices of much of contemporary Christianity have departed far from the original Founder and doubtless have contributed much to the antipathy toward religion. The antagonism of religion and culture cannot be overcome until the church of today is brought closer to the original church.

Religion seeks to bring man into the right relationship with God, while culture often is limited to the intellectual and esthetic

spheres. Goethe and Hume, both eminent men of culture, illustrated this limitation. Such men do not like religion because they
wish to ignore the rebuke it utters against them. Outstanding men
are presumed qualified to speak authoritatively and their claim to
be cultured leads the public to assume that culture and religion are
antagonistic. The greatest injustice to Christianity is its rejection
by men profoundly ignorant of it.

Religion and science differ in aim and method. Religion seeks a
personal God, while science is interested in the uniform laws of
nature. Using observation and experience for its data, science relies
on logical deduction to determine its conclusions. In contrast,
"religion soars higher, and listens for the voice of God himself...."
(210) Sturtevant believed Shairp had conceded too much in saying
that no telescope can enable us to see God; telescopes cannot discern
the law of gravitation either. "[T]he universe around us is full of
phenomena, open to universal experience and observation, of
which the existence of a designing Creator and righteous moral
Governor of all things is the one only [sic] adequate explanation.
Science as truly gives us God as it gives us gravitation." (211)
Probably Sturtevant was aware of Kant's view that *knowledge* is
restricted to the realm of science; "God" was for him a hypothe-
sis. Sturtevant clearly disagreed. He likely was familiar also with
Pascal's example of the wager, that we have all to gain and nothing
to lose by believing in God. He went far beyond Kant and Pascal
in his assurance of knowledge of God based on the truth of the
Scriptures and personal experience.

The dominance of exclusively scientific culture tends to prejudice
the mind against the kind of evidence upon which we necessarily
depend in most of our practical concerns of daily living. People
must and do rely upon probable evidence, in contrast to the rigid
demonstration and sensory data which physical science demands.
(On this point Sturtevant could have found support in both Hume
and Kant.) Some scientists, such as Herbert Spencer, decried the
reliance upon authority in the study of the classics, and it is true
that absolute certainty is nowhere to be found. Rather a man must
"balance opposing probabilities and believe doubtingly and yet act
as though [he] believed certainly...." Religion is a practical matter
and in religion as in every day life wisdom must be exercised, the

passions must be controlled, and the whole man subjected "to the governing power of reason and conscience." (215)

The humble spirit is crucial both for religion and culture and, as well, for happiness in the domestic situation and for order in the state. The greatest enemy to our nation is that education which arouses the human mind and makes knowledge available to it but which then fails to train it to humility and faith. The lamented antagonism between religion and culture is the result of the weaknesses of both. The remedy is to permeate practical religion with the spirit of the Master and to develop culture so that it is comprehensive not only of the intellectual and esthetic but also the moral [religious] nature of man. The foolish effort of the Roman Pope to impose the doctrine of infallibility and the Protestant multiplication of sects are examples of the lack of due humility. Religious men must give up such manmade accretions to Christianity; much progress has been made in the past three centuries, but much work remains.

Important Issues: Biblical Studies, Evolution

Two major intellectual fields of great significance for religion and higher education developed in the latter half of the nineteenth century, biblical criticism and biological evolution. Literary and historical analysis had been applied to the study of the Bible in Europe, especially Germany, and the increasing numbers of Americans who went abroad for advanced study brought that scholarship to the United States. Such studies became prominent in America in the later decades of the century, and Julian Sturtevant was aware of them and the controversies they aroused regarding biblical interpretation. None of his published articles was directed specifically to the subject, although fragmentary statements, some in manuscript and some typewritten, are among his papers. Sturtevant had great reverence for the Bible as the Word of God, and he also believed in the exercise of intelligence and the accepted principles of literary interpretation in understanding the Bible.

In an unpublished essay on German biblical criticism Sturtevant rejected the religious and moral skepticism which resulted from these studies. The first six pages of the nine-page typewritten statement are missing but his conclusions are presented in the final paragraphs. The future of the world appears hopeless, Sturtevant said, to those whose only "gospel" is that negation which cannot renovate individual character nor purify society. Among the ancient Greeks and Romans a cultivated class adopted skepticism as the only alternative to "the deepest darkest superstition." There may be in contemporary society a class which regards science and philosophy as leading to refined skepticism. For them, a real alternative is present: the Christian religion is "a widely prevalent, deeply-rooted faith in a personal God and Savior, and the rewards and punishments of the life to come." Adherents to this faith need have no fear of the outcome in the conflict between Christianity and infidelity. "To them 'German criticism' has not undermined and never can undermine those evidences of Christianity on which they rely."

Another tendency was "to undervalue or even to deny any vital connexion [sic]" between the Old Testament and the New. Sturtevant analyzed this relationship in a typewritten essay. He noted the remarkable and enthusiastic response of the multitudes to the preaching of John the Baptist and Jesus and the similar response to the present-day evangelism of "Mr. Moody and Mr. Pentecost." The long expectation of the Messiah and the Kingdom of God, kept alive by the people of the Old Testament, made people of the ancient world ready to listen to the Gospel. Divine Providence in far-off geologic periods stored up vital energy for the use of civilized man. Similarly, "in the history and the literature of ancient Israel He treasured up the moral force by which in the fullness of time the Messiah would introduce himself to the Jewish race, and through them to mankind for the healing and the saving of the nations."

An important review article by Sturtevant (1875) dealt with the truth of the Bible in relationship to culture. He examined the claim by Matthew Arnold, a foremost literary critic, that the Bible is literature and not dogma. Sturtevant agreed and sympathized with Arnold's purpose to make "religious re-adjustments, to meet the exigencies of the age and of coming ages...." (92) However, Arnold rejected miracle and prophecy, denied that Jesus claimed to be the Messiah, and redefined religion as morality. Sturtevant insisted that the readjustment was to be in the language and not in the substance of the faith. He maintained that the New

Testament portrayal of Jesus is literally true in the facts, the doctrines, and the morality it presents. Arnold's concept of "extra belief" to designate the accretions which had accumulated through the centuries was reasonable and Sturtevant agreed that the speculative thought and hierarchical church polity which had developed from Augustine onward must be eliminated. Only then can Christianity be presented "to the men of this age in the purity and simplicity of its original conception in the thought of its Founder." (93)

Arnold regarded religion as morality and declared that to be three-fourths of life. He was wrong on two counts, charged Sturtevant. Conduct is all of life, and religion is more than ethics heightened by emotion. For Sturtevant, "Religion is morality sustained, exalted, and enforced by the devout worship of the only living and true God as revealed in the Bible." (96)

Arnold's discussion of the word "God" was characterized by a certain animosity due to rejecting the biblical conception of God as personal. Sturtevant agreed that the Bible's language about God is that of poetry, not theological dogmatism. That did not, however, justify substituting for "Father" the phrase "an enduring power, not ourselves, that makes for righteousness." (98) According to Arnold the personal conception of God is unacceptable to science because it cannot be verified. Sturtevant, schooled in physics, pointed out that there are many concepts in science which cannot be verified by experiment and observation, such as the law of matter. He believed that we are compelled to conclude that the universe is the creation of a personal God. Moreover, to reject the personal concept of God is to reject moral science. Moral action assumes that men have freedom to act and are accountable. This is not verifiable; it is an original intuition of the human mind.

Making no distinction between the miracles of the New Testament and those reported by the Roman Catholic Church, Arnold denied the truth of all of them. Sturtevant countered that the great biblical miracles involved actual persons and known events and were attested by large numbers of witnesses. Arnold attributed the spread of Christianity to the popular appeal of Jesus' ethical teachings. Sturtevant rejoined that the sermons preached by the disciples said little of Jesus' ethics and much about his crucifixion and resurrection in fulfillment of biblical prophecy.

"Ethical lectures have never been a power in any age; they are not in our own…." (112) Sturtevant maintained that the remarkable spread of Christianity is explained by the fact that Jesus "was the Messiah of ancient prophecy." (513) Jesus had the foreknowledge and he had the power to escape the suffering which he anticipated, but he did not turn aside. The power of the narrative lies in Jesus' consciousness of his Messiahship and his crucifixion, followed by the testimony of his disciples that he had risen from the dead.

If Arnold's criticism were accepted, it would have a devastating effect on the Bible and the Christian religion. Worship would be eliminated because no one would worship an abstraction such as a power not ourselves. Prayer would be pointless if addressed to something like the law of gravitation. Without a personal God there would be no divine Saviour and no salvation and no church. The affirmation of the truth and power of the Bible, and the obliteration of the remnants of the dark and superstitious ages, will "prepare the Church for the mighty conflicts of the present and the immediate future." (122)

In the mid-nineteenth century the sciences of geology and biology made rapid advances which led to intense discussion of evolution. The concept had long been a philosophical notion, but now it became a fundamental scientific theory. The publication in 1859 of Charles Darwin's *Origin of Species* set off a debate which has not yet subsided about the origin of life and the place of human beings in the scheme of nature. The earliest reference at Illinois College to the general subject pre-dated Darwin's *Origin*. In 1854 Phi Alpha sponsored an address by Rev. Harvy [*sic*] Curtis of Chicago who asked, "Have men made real progress?" Curtis discarded the notion of development in nature from the simple to the complex and disclaimed monkeys as ancestors.[14]

Sturtevant on his trips to the East frequently visited New Haven and engaged in discussions with professors and ministers there and elsewhere, and it can be assumed that the subject of evolution was discussed. The newspapers Sturtevant read, such as the *Independent* and *Advance*, published reports and articles in the 1870s on evolution. James B. Dana, science professor at Yale, reviewed the Darwinian theory in a lengthy letter to the editor of the *Independent*.

He declared that evidence was lacking to support the thesis that species had been produced by natural selection; moreover, it had not been proved that man resulted from that process. Dana regarded the role of the Divine in the creation as outside the sphere of mere natural science. The man who is aware of the exalted role of humans in nature and who acknowledges allegiance to the Author "will see God in his works, [and] his faith will have no occasion to waver...."[15]

In 1873 Thomas K. Beecher published articles in the *Advance* in which he sought to reconcile conflicts between science and religion.[16] He asserted that "A good, old-fashioned, orthodox Calvinist and a modern thinker of the severely scientific school" will soon find themselves in basic agreement because both assert the dependence of human life. In pursuing his continuing interest in science, he corresponded with both Charles Darwin and Thomas Huxley. Beecher's generalizations were somewhat romanticized, and it does not seem likely that Sturtevant would have found them persuasive.

A lengthy article on "Darwinism"[17] by his long-time colleague, Dr. Samuel Adams, may provide insight into Sturtevant's probable views on evolution. Adams had come to Illinois College in 1838 to teach chemistry, mineralogy, and geology. He was a devout Christian whose orthodoxy was upheld, as was Sturtevant's, by an ecclesiastical inquiry in 1846. In 1877, following Adams' deeply lamented death, Sturtevant described him as a teacher and scientist who was thorough, hard-working, and impartial in considering evidence. Adams had prepared careful reviews of selected works of Charles Darwin, Auguste Comte, and Herbert Spencer, and was keenly interested in the import of these thinkers for religion.

In his article Adams examined what Darwin had actually said, the evidence relevant to his theory, and the implications for religion. Darwin was cautious and did not claim that the massive data proved the truth of his theory of the origin of species (or even varieties) by natural selection. Adams declared that the data do not contradict the doctrine of divine interposition in the origin of species. Moreover, the geological record lacked evidence of intermediate stages in the gradual development of one species from another. In the last third of his review, Adams dealt with the bearing of Darwinism and materialism on the question of a personal

Creator. He feared that Darwin's theory would lend support to the currently widespread skeptical philosophy and intensify the effort to utilize material forms to explain human life. However, no bridge between inorganic matter and living forms had been established but even if it were God would not be left out of the world. Indeed, there is an "almost universal recognition of an intelligent Creator, as the only adequate cause of the phenomena…." (353)

Adams and Sturtevant surely discussed the subject of the article while Adams was preparing it. It is reasonable to conclude that just as the two men were in essential agreement regarding religion and the church, Sturtevant found Adams' argument and conclusions on this subject to be congenial.

In 1875 Sturtevant refuted Herbert Spencer's thesis that we have "Two Religions." Spencer asserted that on the evolutionary scale humans had emerged just far enough beyond the stage of Thomas Hobbes' warfare of each against all to have a mixture of that antagonistic spirit with a philanthropic attitude. He maintained that at the present stage of development humans necessarily have two religions, the religion of enmity (defense of the self against others) and the religion of amity (concern for others). He speculated that in the remote future evolution would advance so that only amity would be practiced. In a sharp comment Sturtevant declared that Spencer, claiming to be a philosopher, clearly did not understand Christianity and was himself much in "need of further 'development' and 'evolution.'" Christianity teaches that the true aim of life is to serve all intelligent, moral beings. The Christian is required to care for himself and attain the highest perfection of body and mind so that he can serve God and humanity. The duty to self and to others constitutes not two religions but one, and that is what Christianity teaches. The recent great Rebellion was a prime illustration of the religion of amity stirring millions to rise on behalf of the oppressed slaves and to engage in a terrible, costly war on their behalf. "It was not enmity to the South, but love, love of liberty and social order and justice, of universal humanity, of the South herself, that impelled to the war." As soon as the oppressors were overcome, the victors sought to heal the wounds of the conquered. Christianity "is as ready, when the awful necessity comes, to strike down the enemies of righteousness and mercy, of peace and social order, as it is to lift up the lowly, comfort the sorrowing, deliver the oppressed, and forgive the penitent sinner."

In his 1863 article about the African race Sturtevant had demonstrated that the Negro, once freed, would be unable to compete with white labor and would eventually disappear. In his 1876 article deploring the excessive number of churches, he referred to the "Darwinian principle of 'the survival of the fittest.'" His text on *Economics* (1878) renewed his earlier argument that competition in a free marketplace eventually results in the elimination of a minority group because of its inability to provide for families and children. Sturtevant acknowledged the strong similarity between his explanation and the "*survival of the strongest*," which Mr. Darwin has shown to be very widely prevalent, both in the animal and vegetable kingdoms." (272) Without providing examples, he said he rejected Darwin's "extreme inferences." He also emphasized that he had expressed his view "years before we had any knowledge of Mr. Darwin's observations." (272)

A typewritten sheet with the title, "'The Missing Links,'" is fragmentary and unsigned but presumably was written by Sturtevant. He argued that there is no evidence of intermediate stages in the hypothetical evolutionary chain. If humans evolved from lower animal forms there should be a succession of gradations linking the two; if they once existed, why had they perished? The statement also refers to Herbert Spencer's studies in sociology which demonstrated not only evolution to higher types but also descent to lower types.

Sturtevant and Adams were by no means behind the times in refusing to accept Darwinist theory as sufficiently demonstrated and in holding steadfastly to their conviction that it did not supersede or destroy religion. Horace Bushnell, a religious liberal, regarded science very favorably but considered Darwinism and religion as incompatible. He believed that if the evolutionary theory were proved it might be necessary to abandon religion. Robert Edwards has noted that the professors of science at Harvard and Yale in that period were very conservative in their views of religion and evolutionary theory.[18]

The limited information indicates that at the time evolution was not accepted by the faculty of Illinois College as explaining human existence. Similarly, the record does not show that the views of William Jennings Bryan (Class of 1881) on this subject and on religion generally were the result of his collegiate education.[19] The faculty were strongly committed to the truth of the Christian faith but also keenly aware of the validity of scientific knowledge and discovery. In religion the future was left open to new insights and to revising the forms in which the enduring faith is expressed. They may well have accepted a broad extension of John Robinson's declaration: God has yet more light and truth to break forth not only from his holy word but also from his book of nature.

James Warren's Death; The Family

Death called frequently at the Sturtevant home in earlier years but avoided the family for nearly two decades before striking again. James Warren had secured employment as private secretary to the treasurer of the Hannibal and St. Joseph Rail Road and was living in Hannibal, Missouri. His painful illness was reported in a letter of 6 July 1872 from Libbie to Lucy, who was in Kansas. The parents were in the East and the two other brothers, having gone to see Warren, wrote to inform them of his sickness. The parents returned home and Hannah went to Hannibal to assist in caring for Warren, who was suffering from an abdominal abscess and had alternating chills and fever. By July 28th he was more comfortable and was taking hot tea, cream toast, and a toddy every three hours. Father also visited his son and in September Warren was brought home. Unfortunately there was no real improvement and he suffered greatly until his death on 1 May 1873. The funeral service was held at the family home and was conducted by the pastor of the Congregational Church, with the assistance of the Hannibal pastor. Julian Jr. and his family were present for the funeral and remained for some time.

Of Julian Sturtevant's six children who reached adulthood, Warren was the first to die and the only one to precede the father in death. In his report to his Yale classmates in 1876 Julian characterized his son as "a graduate of Illinois College, an excellent scholar, a man of cultivation and exquisite taste, both in English and in classical literature, and an earnest and exemplary Christian. Extreme distrust of himself had prevented his engaging in professional life…. [H]e was never married." Julian Sr. felt the loss severely, and he did not think it best "in view of recent afflictions, to hold the usual reception at his house on the evening of Commencement day." (FM, 15 May 1873)

The Sigma Pi Literary Society in a series of resolutions praised Warren for his Christ-like actions and refined culture and expressed grief for the loss of a brother who had done so much for the organization. Many letters of condolence were received by the family; often they expressed the thought that however deep their sorrow the family must remember that Warren's death was the will of God and they should rejoice in the knowledge that they will have a happy reunion with him.

Warren had named his father as executor of his estate,[20] esti-

Julian Sr.

Julian Jr.

Hannah Augusta

James Warren

Family Pictures
(undated; taken at different years)

mated at $7,000—an indication that Warren had been both in-
dustrious and thrifty. All expenses were to be paid and the sum of
$3,000 was bequeathed to "my friend, Georgiana Barde of Hanni-
bal, Missouri." The remainder was to be placed in a trust fund with
the income to go to his father during his lifetime and the principal then divided among his brothers and sisters.

Sturtevant himself suffered a lingering illness in early 1871, a
sickness sufficiently serious to be reported in a St. Louis newspaper. In mid-March he asked to be excused from the meetings of

Hannah

Elizabeth (Libbie)

Lucy

Alfred

Family Pictures
(undated; taken at different years)

The Club; he had now recovered but was not yet strong enough for an evening meeting. By late August he was well again.

The few reports about household affairs include mention of the excellent crop of strawberries in 1873 when Fred picked four to five quarts a day. Libbie told about making pie plant pies and pies of currants and raspberries mixed; she admitted to having trouble at first with the pie crusts. She and Aunt Jane made gooseberry jam and jelly and raspberry jam. The local newspaper took note of an unusual plant at the Sturtevant household, a night blooming cereus, with two large and beautiful flowers; the

Bust of Julian Sturtevant
Robert C. Smith, Sculptor

plant was really a tree, being some ten feet in height. Mary Jane Fayerweather had a reputation as a fine gardener and may have been responsible for the plant. Hannah expressed her familiar complaint, being "quite disgusted with the whole class of servant women. They are so faithless and unprincipled." (HRS to JMS, 12 June 1873)

Hannah accompanied her husband on some of his journeys and visited relatives in Greenwich and Hartford, meanwhile keeping in touch by letter with the family at home. In the summer of 1875 Julian and Hannah, accompanied by Libbie, had a very special trip—a family vacation—when they went to Colorado to visit son Julian, then minister of Denver's First Congregational Church. The family traveled in the mountains with a driver and handyman who had charge of the team and wagon and helped to set up the nightly camp. The family housekeeper came along to prepare meals and assist in other ways. The son reported his father's great enthusiasm about the scenery. Coming upon a panorama of peaks at Belle View, "Father simply shouted with delight." (JMSJR, 111) He was utterly delighted when they awakened one morning to see the mountains covered with snow. Though seventy and despite having recently broken his ankle, father had done much hiking.

The party, caught in a heavy rain, refused to go to a hotel because they were dressed for camping. The son's friend in Central City suggested that they stay in a church, but no one slept at all. The next night their camp was in a wild spot near a trout stream. Growling was heard on the rocks above and the horses came racing back to the camp. The son gave up fishing and that night the driver kept the flames of the camp fire high. They observed the Sabbath the next day with their family worship and read Psalms which referred to mountains. Father was in "one of those cheery moods when everything seemed beautiful and full of our Heavenly Father's love and care." (JMSJR, 112) Libbie and her brother sang "Oft in the Stilly Night," and father thought it was the sweetest music he had ever heard. He "often afterwards spoke of that Sabbath as among the brightest in his life." (A, 333)

In 1876 a local artist, Robert Campbell Smith, formerly a student in Illinois College, sculpted a life-size bust of President Sturtevant in marble. The bust was exhibited at the Jacksonville Art Association show in March 1876 and later that year was entered in the Illinois Department at the Centennial Exposition in Philadelphia, where it won a first prize.[21] Initially the sculptor proposed that the faculty purchase the work but the professors had no authority to expend funds. However, the College subsequently obtained the sculpture and it was formally presented at commencement in June 1881.

Presumably Julian and Hannah attended concerts and plays and saved as mementos the programs now among the family papers. A "Greate Concerte" of sacred hymns and tunes and "Worldly Songs of a secular sort" was presented at the Congregational Church in Springfield, 8 December 1873. The spelling and printing were in archaic style and the singers were given quaint names intended to suggest Pilgrim times. A concert in Jacksonville was performed by "The Teachers of Music and the Orchestra" of the Illinois Institution for the Blind and presented at the Illinois State Hospital. The teacher of the orchestra was Miss Alice Rhoads, a member of the Congregational Church. A concert in Philadelphia in 1876 was given for the benefit of the Exhibition of Women's Work at the Centennial Exposition; the printed program was *said* to be an exact copy of one used for a 1776 concert held in New Haven to aid the building fund of Yale College.

Perhaps when the Sturtevants were in the East that summer they represented Illinois College at the Centennial Exposition in Philadelphia and possibly Julian unveiled the Smith sculpture.

The eldest son and daughter in the family maintained their own households. While Julian Jr. was serving the Congregational Church in Ottawa, Illinois, he and his wife became parents of a daughter, Amy, born 24 March 1871. In 1873, when Colorado was still a territory, Julian Jr. accepted a call to the First Congregational Church of Denver, remaining there for about three years. He was a member of the Board of Trustees for Colorado College, a school founded by Congregationalists in Colorado Springs in 1874, and was chairman for a time. Daughter Hannah Palmer and her son were expected to come for a good visit in July 1872. Two more sons were born to the Palmers, Warren Sturtevant on 1 March 1873 and Willard Holbrook on 22 July 1874.

The younger Sturtevants remained at home. Lucy taught painting and drawing at the Jacksonville Female Academy in 1874-75. During the next two years Libbie was instructor in German at the Academy. In 1871 Lucy had become a life member of the American Congregational Association, headquartered in Boston, by paying the fee of $1.00. She received a certificate with two engravings depicting the Mayflower and the landing at Plymouth.

Fred, the youngest of the family, graduated from Illinois College in 1870 and that autumn began more than a decade of service as an instructor at the College. In March 1871 his father wrote to President Woolsey of Yale to introduce his son and request that he be allowed the privileges of the library and certain lecture courses during a proposed four-months' stay in New Haven. Alfred, he wrote, had "a very respectable standing as a scholar" and had a special interest in pursuing studies in German. Even before he completed his college studies Alfred was called on to meet Latin classes when Edward Tanner was ill. Later, when his father was away from the College in the summer, Alfred looked after some of the administrative duties. For example, in the summer of 1872 Fred was busy for a few days sending out catalogs at the rate of two hundred a day. He and Mr. Bailey, instructor in Greek, worked nearly every afternoon to prepare a catalog of the College's Library. Fred had planned a northern trip in 1873 but canceled the arrangement when he was called to Warren's bedside in Hannibal. He was there to meet Lucy at the train when she stopped en route to Jacksonville.

In 1873 Alfred was awarded the Master's degree and delivered the Master's oration at Commencement. On 11 June 1874 he married Harriet Morse, a graduate of the Jacksonville Female Academy in the Class of 1869. Harriet joined the Congregational Church in November 1874. Alfred, already a member, was elected clerk at the annual meeting in 1874 and was re-elected in subsequent years. In 1876 he was named Principal of Whipple Academy.

During his last years as president, Julian Sturtevant enjoyed the greatest financial security he ever knew. The President's Fund provided his salary, which for the year 1874-1875 amounted to $2,237.06. In September 1875 he was paid $312.95 for interest; he had loaned the College $1,000 in May 1874 for the new dormitory and must have made some other loans. The sketch in the 1872 *Atlas Map* noted that although he had "always served the College on a very moderate, often on a very scanty and insufficient, salary," he had a competency because of an inheritance and the rise of real estate. (42)

The incomplete file of tax receipts shows that the valuation of Sturtevant's property remained rather constant, as did his city taxes, until equalization was applied in 1873 and 1874. His city taxes then increased substantially. Complete tax receipts are extant for 1874, when Sturtevant paid $627 for real estate and personal property. The only other complete tax receipt is for 1877, when valuations were lower in all categories and the tax bill was much lower, $364.

Information about Julian's contact with his brothers during these years is almost non-existent. After Christopher moved to Minneapolis in 1873, Julian visited him there—probably soon after, but the date is unknown. Ephraim and Julian were together at Yale in 1876 for their fiftieth anniversary reunion. Ephraim's older son, Warren DeForest, had practiced medicine in Illinois until his death in 1873. Libbie mentioned in an 1872 letter to Lucy that Wheeler, Ephraim's second son, had come to call. Aunt Jane, she said, could hardly keep from laughing because he came to visit as soon as the folks had left; he had worn out his welcome some years before.

Julia Fayerweather Chamberlain, the oldest of the Fayerweather siblings, was widowed when her husband, Timothy, died at their home southeast of Jacksonville on 26 July 1873. Sturtevant returned to Jacksonville and conducted the funeral services at the Chamberlain home. Brother James Fayerweather kept the Jacksonville sisters informed about his family and also about the children of their brother Abraham in Hawaii. In writing to Hannah in March 1876 James told of the birth of another child to Julia Fayerweather Afong and her husband, bringing the total number of their children to thirteen daughters and one son. "Quite a family," wrote James. Others thought so, too. In 1961 the family was the subject of a Broadway musical, *Thirteen Daughters*. Jack London's "Chun Ah Chun" is a fictionalized account of the husband and his daughters and was published in a collection of short stories, *The House of Pride*.

Through the years the Blatchford family maintained contact with the Sturtevants by correspondence and through visiting them in Jacksonville and by entertaining them in their Chicago home. In January 1875 Sturtevant went to Chicago to participate in the funeral services for Blatchford's mother; he had known both parents even before their son came to Illinois College. Warm appreciation was expressed to Sturtevant for "coming to us in the hour of our affliction" and for the kind words he had spoken. Blatchford tactfully designated his check, a slight token of his appreciation, for Hannah's trip and for purchasing some books to remind them of his mother. Later, reading of Julian's resignation, Blatchford expressed his regret but said he realized that the action had not been taken hastily.

An old friend and neighbor in Connecticut, Burton Gilbert, recalled in a letter (27 July 1872) their dear mothers "who are now laid in the land of silence" and remembered that his mother had often given Julian a bit of bread and butter on his return from school. He mentioned the Sabbath when Julian, his brother, several cousins, and other boys had come to meeting barefoot. He recalled also the time they had met their old minister on his way to the mill. "We children turned front face & raised our hats & my sister Polly [made] a courtesy and then our old minister says, a beautiful sight to see." Gilbert remembered seeing the brothers leave Warren in a wagon covered over with a white cloth. Thinking of such men as Julian and Charles G. Finney, both of whom became college presidents, Gilbert remarked: "Many of our Warren people have made bright spots around the world."

Once the closest of friends, Julian Sturtevant and Elizur Wright were estranged in 1833 and agreed not to meet again. However, both men were present at the 1876 reunion of their class at Yale. Wright had accomplished important actuarial studies for life insurance.[22]

Retirement from the Presidency

In his 1876 report to his Yale classmates Julian Sturtevant summarized his career and mentioned his recent retirement. He was determined now to continue his writing and especially to present in extended form his views on two subjects of great interest to him, the church, and economics. Sturtevant believed, correctly, that this would be the last such report he would submit; his death occurred a few months before the sixtieth anniversary of his graduation from Yale. Stating the basic principles and purposes which had governed his life, he expressed his farewell to his classmates.

> In closing this last communication which I can ever hope to make to my classmates, I wish to express my unwavering conviction that nothing is worth living for, but to make our country and mankind more virtuous and more happy; and that the Christian religion, in its primitive purity and simplicity, is the only instrument by which this can be accomplished. In just so far as I have earnestly devoted my life to that end, in the diligent use of that only instrument of moral power that can save humanity from degradation, meanness and ruin, I am satisfied with my life. But I…often look back on the past with much sorrow. And yet I look to the future with cheerful hope for myself, and for my country and humanity. As the landscapes of earth are rendered sombre by the deepening shadows of fast oncoming evening, the Christian's unique hope of immortality becomes more precious than language can express.[23]

Sturtevant submitted his resignation from the Presidency of Illinois College at the meeting of the Board of Trustees on 31 May 1876. The Minutes report that "he desired to be relieved from the duties of the Presidency, and all care and responsibility connected with the discipline and government of the College, but would consent to continue his duties as instructor and to conduct the religious exercises of

Sunday afternoon upon a salary of $1500.00 per annum." These arrangements were approved and Professor Crampton was designated to act as executive officer.[24] Sturtevant, Crampton, and Rev. M. K. Whittlesey were named a committee to obtain information about "filling the Presidential Chair."

In a resolution the trustees gave deserved recognition to Sturtevant as one of the founders of Illinois College. They recorded their "Sense of the inestimable value of the services which he has rendered to our State and Country, and to the World of Letters, and to the Church of God, in his life-long devotion to the cause of learning in connection with this Institution." He was congratulated for the College's attainment of the "high degree of efficiency, honor and usefulness" it reached under his leadership and for the "assurance of an increased influence and prosperity." (TM, 31 May 1876) Sturtevant continued in the teaching post he had held since 1870 as Professor of Mental Science and Science of Government.

The editor of the *Congregationalist* was one of many who gave public praise to Sturtevant. He declared that Sturtevant had rendered "a noble, an indisputable service…. Meanwhile his clear head, firm convictions, and ready voice, have been powerfully felt in all good enterprises in Illinois and the West. We are glad to see that even now his eye is not dim, nor his natural force abated." (21 June 1876) With due allowance for the difference between leading a nation and leading a college, the allusion to Moses was not inappropriate. (Cf. Deut. 34:7) His long and arduous service in the presidency was viewed positively by Sturtevant himself. Near the end of his life he remarked that the presidency, despite its heavy burdens, had brought him "great happiness for many years." (A, 259)

Sturtevant could take pride in the College's very survival and in the improvement in its financial condition since 1844. The College had what was then an enormous debt of $30,000 which required interest payments at the rate of 10%. The net worth of the property was scarcely $25,000 and the large amount of land owned by the College was virtually unsalable. In 1876 the College's funds amounted to $100,000, most of it yielding a 10% return. The income for the preceding year was $17,000 and the number of students had greatly increased. The College was featured in the *Illinois Schoolmaster*[25]and described in positive terms. Located in a beautiful, half-rural city of twelve thousand, and the first college in the state, Illinois College was the nucleus of numerous educational and charitable institutions. The College's curriculum was composed of the traditional classical course and a scientific course. The seven men of the current faculty were highly qualified in their fields and sought to exert a strong moral and religious influence, free from sectarian bias. Students attended morning prayers and the Sabbath afternoon lectures by Dr. Sturtevant, "whose pungent and powerful discourses produce lasting impressions." The graduates and former students had become leaders in thought and action, in the church and civil life. Two examples were given, Richard Yates, Governor of Illinois and U.S. Senator, and Newton Bateman, for eight years Superintendent of Public Instruction and now president of Knox College. Although not on the plane of Yale and Harvard, Illinois College was comparable to most Eastern colleges.

The original building was now being used by the men's literary societies for their meetings and by the College for its Library, Cabinet of Natural History, and the classes in Greek. The College's collection totaled eight thousand books and the societies' libraries three thousand. The facilities provided in "College Hall" were the Chapel, six classrooms, and the apparatus room. The fine dormitory, recently completed, was well-equipped with steam heat and gas lights. Its twenty-eight suites could house fifty-six men; each study room had a large table and each bedroom a woven wire mattress bed. The well-managed Club House provided student dining at a cost of $2. to $2.25 per week. Total student expenses for a year, including tuition, board, room, fuel, gas, and text books, amounted to about $175.

The *College Annual for 1877* spoke of Sturtevant in the most positive terms: "He is well known throughout the country as a man of purest life, of vigorous and independent thought, and of eminent ability. To his unwearied efforts and self-sacrificing devotion the College owes very much of what it is and of what it may become in the future."[26] A few years earlier Sturtevant's role in the cause of education in the State of Illinois had been acknowledged with equal admiration. The Illinois State Teachers' Association bestowed a well-deserved accolade, hailing him as "the pioneer of all present teachers in the state."[27]

Charles Henry Rammelkamp, as president of Illinois College (1905-1932), had a unique vantage point for evaluating his predecessor. He characterized Sturtevant's tenure as "thirty-two years of notable service," saying that his "own life and that of the College were so closely interwoven that the institution became, in fact, an expression of his personality and character." (CH, 262, 264) Rammelkamp believed that Sturtevant's intellectual and moral leadership influenced the whole Middle West. He had sought for the College the highest educational standards and endeavored to inculcate in all those at the College respect for truth and perseverance in duty. Rammelkamp regarded Sturtevant as somewhat austere but possessed of a sense of humor and a kindly disposition. He concluded that Sturtevant was not the sort of teacher and administrator who would gain popularity but nevertheless "his students admired him and caught real inspiration in his classroom." (CH, 265)

A summary of the College's financial status at the time of Sturtevant's retirement was compiled by Rammelkamp. The Presidency Fund was over $22,000; income from it provided the president's salary, the amount varying according to the rate of interest. The Hitchcock Fund was over $26,000 and the General Fund was nearly $61,000. The total, including prize funds and cash, was $112,474. The actual income from these sources in 1876 was about $7,000. The relatively good financial condition had been achieved in part by the sale of most of the College's real estate, the original campus of over two hundred acres having been reduced to merely twelve.

A suitable commendation for Julian Sturtevant's mission on behalf of Illinois College can be adapted from the book he revered and lived by and from words spoken by the Lord he served so devotedly: "Well done, thou good and faithful servant: thou hast been faithful over...many things: enter thou into the joy of thy lord." (Cf. Matt. 25:21, KJV)

Chapter 10: 1876-1885

Crowning a Half Century of Achievement

Sturtevant's New Role

Julian Sturtevant's tenure as President of Illinois College ended with the 1876 Commencement exercises which closed the academic year. He had resigned because he no longer had the strength for such arduous duties. During his last years of service, as in his early years, he was a member of the faculty. He retained his appointment as Professor of Mental Science and the Science of Government and continued to assign Tocqueville's *American Democracy*. He also taught Political Economy (economics) and presented the Sabbath afternoon lectures on religion. His courses were taken by the seniors in both the classical and scientific programs. Sturtevant met regularly with the faculty and took his turn in offering the opening prayer. He was designated as the Senior Class Officer.

The task assigned to Sturtevant and others on the presidential search committee was accomplished easily. Although Professor Rufus Crampton declined the permanent title he agreed to be acting-president and served very ably for six years. In 1882 Rev. Edward A. Tanner became president but did not arrange a formal inauguration because of financial exigency. Tanner's statement of the College's mission was consistent with his cousin's: "to liberalize this region with Christian learning and leaven it with righteousness for the Salvation of men and the Glory of the King." (TM, 6 June 1883) Among his significant achievements were increased financial resources and the resulting improvements: an enlarged faculty, an enriched curriculum, and the re-purchase of the lots between the College buildings and Park Street. Whipple Academy was brought to the campus in 1876 and provided with a handsome new building in 1882.[1] A program in agricultural science was begun. Two professors were appointed: Harvey Milligan (in Rhetoric and English Literature, 1882) and Edward Clapp ('75) (Greek, 1883). Measures were taken to formalize alumni representation on the Board of Trustees, a policy Sturtevant had advocated but did not carry out systematically.

The Osage Orange hedge surrounding the campus was rooted out by teams of faculty and students on a "holiday" in May 1882. Sturtevant served as captain of the freshman class. A year later the event was commemorated by another holiday, with varied activities and a picnic. Thus began the traditional Osage Orange Picnic still enjoyed a century later.

The faculty suffered the first loss of a professor by death when Dr. Samuel Adams died on 27 April 1877 following a brief illness. Sturtevant had already gone East and for the first time was not available to deliver the eulogy for a major figure in the College community. Libbie Sturtevant played the organ for the funeral at the Congregational Church. (JJ, 20 Apr., 1 May 1877)

The first issue of the *Illinois College College Rambler*, in magazine format, appeared in January 1878. The lead article, "Salutatory," paid tribute to the "venerable Dr. Sturtevant" as the first teacher on the hilltop campus. The *Rambler* was a serious publication with thoughtful editorial comment, feature articles on current issues, student essays and orations, and frequent contributions by faculty and alumni. Some articles probably were written by students in Sturtevant's courses.

The *Rambler's* staff published an article by the former president in the first issue. Describing "The Growth of Our College," Sturtevant declared that a college grows from within by the intellectual and moral character of the men who imbue it with their own personality. This College, he wrote, had the guidance of a remarkable group—Beecher, Post, Turner, and Adams; he modestly omitted himself. Differing widely, these men "had one common characteristic"—a profound interest in "the great practical questions of this age, and of our country." They were "men of as much freedom of utterance as of thought. No one could associate with them without knowing that they were among the living forces of the age." Having engaged in the conflicts of the past, the College now was better fitted for "its great function in the future." Students at Illinois College were educated "for a real life in the active service of their country, the church of God, and humanity. [Educators are needed who] know the past and revere it, but live in the present and for the future—men that know the abstract, only to translate its lessons into the concrete." (7) Illinois College, no exotic hot-house plant, could endure "the winters and the summers, the pelting storms and scorching sunshine, that are yet to be encountered." (8)

Much of the available information about Sturtevant's College duties and personal life during these years is in the "locals," brief notices in the *Rambler*. The editors, upperclassmen, reported when the seniors reviewed a certain subject, when examinations were scheduled, and when a new subject commenced. Seniors wondered, when they saw the examination questions for the Mental Science examination, "Will I be able to 'floor' it?" (Dec. 1878, 119) After his week-long absence due to a "distressing illness," Sturtevant's recovery was happily reported. (Feb. 1879, 8) In turn Dr. Sturtevant used the campus newspaper to convey messages to his students. He requested the seniors to write their examinations legibly because he would be responsible not for what they meant "but only for what he may be able to make out." (Dec. 1879, 87) He praised the Class of '80 for having done far better in the examination on logic than the previous year's class. He announced "double time" for the class on Mental Science so that they would finish by Christmas in 1880.

When Professor Grosvenor retired in 1880, Sturtevant's title was expanded to include "Instructor in Political Economy, Moral Philosophy, and Evidences of Christianity."[2] Sturtevant was now relieved of responsibility for the course in logic. Sometimes students from Whipple Academy were in his classes. The *Rambler* noted that "the boys" did not object when their professor announced that he would conduct the Evidences class by lecture only; presumably there were no reading assignments. When he was away for a few days "the Seniors enjoyed a holiday." (22 Oct. 1881, 89) In the spring of 1882 Sturtevant devoted his Sunday afternoon religion discourses to "Evidences of Christianity," allowing under-

classmen as well to attend the required senior class. A large
number of students attended the last lecture.

The campus newspaper occasionally employed irony and even
levity in reporting about Sturtevant. Responding to a complaint
about required attendance, the editors recalled that Sturtevant
once remarked that the students were given so much freedom to
enable them to learn self-government. Some humor was pure jest,
such as the report that Sturtevant had energetically proposed to
"Ajax" that they take up saloon-keeping. Ajax, not identified, was
supposedly nonplused and his only objection was that there would
be too many in the business. Overall there was great respect for the
senior member of the faculty and deep appreciation for his teaching
ability. "The class in Mental Science have [sic] wandered so far in
the categories of the mind, that to advance or retreat seem alike to
be ruinous, but they have a good pilot, and will, no doubt, make
the trip." (ICCR, 19 Nov. 1881, 111) John Strong ('54) remembered
"with affectionate gratitude the hearty encouragement given a
poor green boy by President Sturtevant." He enrolled five weeks
late and Sturtevant met with him daily to enable him to catch up
with his class. (ICCR, 31 Oct. 1885, 76)

In November 1881 Sturtevant read "a very interesting lecture"
to the seniors on the "Ownership of Land." Many students assembled to hear Sturtevant speak on the relation of capital to labor—
and on a Saturday evening! The *Rambler* commented that "the
Professor was at home on this subject, and commanded the close
attention of his hearers." (4 Feb. 1882, 136) Sturtevant arranged
for the students in the economics class to debate various topics,
such as free trade. He was responsible for selecting the topics and
selecting the winner in the annual contest for the Milligan Prize in
Economics. In 1877 the subject was free trade; in 1880, "Causes
and Remedies of Pauperism"; in 1881, the true economic theory
of population; and in 1883, David Ricardo's theory of rent.
Sturtevant dealt with all these topics in his course. In 1877 he left
for the East before the papers were due and arranged to have them
forwarded to him in New Haven.

An intriguing question is the influence Sturtevant may have had
on William Jennings Bryan ('81), the most famous of the College's
alumni. Some of Bryan's orations, printed in the *Rambler*, were on

economic and governmental issues and may have been inspired by Sturtevant's classes and special lectures. Sturtevant had lectured on silver for the seniors on the Tuesday before Christmas vacation in 1879. Bryan, a sophomore, may have heard about the lecture from another student. Certainly some of his views were developed independently of the College's influence.[3] In a visit to the campus in the election year of 1896 Bryan remarked that Sturtevant's book on economics, which he had read as a student, emphasized the importance of a stable monetary system. He implied that Sturtevant would have supported his campaign for the free coinage of silver. Sturtevant's children objected strongly to this effort to associate their father with the "free silver heresy." However, no one would object to Bryan's claim that his love of free trade was learned from Professor Sturtevant. Nor would anyone protest Bryan's acknowledgment that it was Dr. Sturtevant who aroused his interest in current public issues. (CH, 413-16)

The handsome dormitory, largely the result of Crampton's efforts and later named for him, strengthened the College's appeal to students. Their concentration on the campus facilitated a marked development in student activities, duly reported in the *Rambler*. Phi Alpha invited Sigma Pi and the women's societies from the female seminaries to its open meeting in March 1884. The Sigs later entertained the Ellis Literary Society of the Jacksonville Female Academy and soon after Phi Alpha did likewise. Rivalry between College students and those in the commercial school found expression in a very physical manner in football. The College students disdained the other group because they were not studying Greek and Latin. In an allusion to a Biblical passage the *Rambler* (Mar. 1878, 114) remarked that "Dr. Sturtevant is now casting his lecture pearls before the Business College students," insinuating that they were swine. (Matt. 7:6) Improved rail transportation dramatically increased intercollegiate contacts. Contests between students from various colleges had begun with oratory, long an important part of college life. Now baseball became a popular sport both locally and on the intercollegiate level. Football, tennis, and cycling were added also.

In 1877 Sturtevant offered the opening prayer when Sigma Pi

Literary Society dedicated its newly remodeled hall in upper Beecher and spoke to the members on "Illinois College and her Literary Societies."4 A series of "Home Lectures" arranged by Sigma Pi in 1883-1884 featured "prominent professional, scientific and literary lecturers resident in the community." Sturtevant was on their list.

Sickness had caused Sturtevant inconvenience and sometimes real suffering, and during his last two years of teaching the periods of illness became quite lengthy. He missed several weeks in early 1884, and at the June Board meeting Tanner reported that he had been attending Dr. Sturtevant's lectures and recitations two hours a day. He was preparing himself for that department ultimately and, in the meantime, to fill in should Dr. Sturtevant's health again break down for months. In the fall of 1884 injuries prevented Sturtevant from beginning his classes. In early November he was able to conduct the class in government, but Tanner continued for a time to teach intellectual science (psychology). In one case at least interruption of studies demoralized the seniors.

An early issue of the *Rambler* outlined the College's religious routine, commenting that it was not so rigorous as elsewhere. Morning prayers extending about fifteen minutes were conducted five times a week. (Two years later prayers were resumed on Saturdays, along with Weekly Rhetorical Society exercises.) On the Sabbath students were required to attend services at a church of their choice in the morning and at the College in the afternoon. The students themselves conducted prayer meetings Friday evenings. For one hour, the *Rambler* proclaimed, all class distinctions and society spirit are laid aside, and "unity in its fullest sense is experienced." (Nov. 1879, 78) Sturtevant was present at one of their sessions and encouraged the students in their good work. No great revival occurred during these years but there were some conversions. In mid-March 1882 Sturtevant had the privilege of telling the students at morning prayers that Professor Tanner had been elected to the presidency; every student smiled his approval.

The Sunday afternoon lectures on biblical and theological topics were given only during the first two terms after Sturtevant retired. In early 1878 he lectured on Saturday evenings as well as Sunday afternoons. On one occasion he dealt with the doctrine of eternal punishment and "successfully refuted the 'advanced ideas' of some of our sensational divines."5 When Sturtevant left in the spring of 1878 to spend the summer in the East, the *Rambler* commented favorably about his presentations. "The learning and research displayed, and, above all, the spirit of candor and fairness, made them of great value to the students, and cause sincere regret at their discontinuance." (May 1878, 71)

At commencement time in 1877 Dr. Sturtevant was in New Haven and Rev. M. K. Whittlesey, a trustee, preached the baccalaureate sermon. Sturtevant was present to deliver that address in 1879. Another sermon was noted as the first installment of a reply to Ingersoll's "last lecture."6 "All who heard it unite in saying that it was one of the very ablest of the Doctor's always able efforts." (ICCR, Oct. 1880, 67) Sturtevant lectured on improving personal behavior, such as ceasing to use profanity. Another time he reminisced about his friend and classmate at Yale, Dr. Horace Bushnell. The *Rambler* assessed the value of Sturtevant's instruction. "Dr. Sturtevant…interests the students of the college as no other man has ever been able to do. All have perfect confidence in him as a man, and respect him as a Christian." (Feb. 1880, 8) His manner was direct and he preached with intense conviction. When the final presentation in the spring of 1882 was announced, the editors observed that some seniors gravely realized this might be the last lecture they would hear from Dr. Sturtevant. The Sunday afternoon services were praised for the variety of good music now heard in Chapel.

The College branch of the Young Men's Christian Association was organized in 1882. In November 1883 the College community was invited to celebrate "Luther Day" in a service at Grace Methodist Episcopal Church; November 10th was the 400th anniversary of the birth of Martin Luther. In the fall of 1884 the Sunday afternoon Chapel service was shortened to forty-five minutes to allow a half-hour afterwards for the student prayer meeting in the Y.M.C.A. room.

The typewritten texts of two Chapel talks by Sturtevant are extant. The one in March 1883 was about Christianity as a super-natural gift, given first to people in Palestine and then dispersed among the peoples of the world. The second (10 May 1885) compared those engaged in economic life to those who are saved: both have the duty to supply the needs of others—the one by growing rich, the other by sharing the benefits of the moral law. "The Christian law is, make yourself of as much value as possible as an instrument of human well-being."

At the Day of Prayer for Colleges in 1878 Sturtevant "delivered an impressive discourse."[7] In 1881 he led a morning prayer meeting in the College Chapel. That afternoon he was called on for remarks at a union service with students from the two women's academies[8] and the Business College. He conducted the 1882 meeting, an hour-long exercise of prayers, singing, and short speeches. In 1883 he discoursed on "the necessity for moral development in American Colleges." (ICCR, 27 Jan., 146)

The College's 50th Anniversary; Sturtevant's Address

In early 1879 the faculty and the Alumni Association planned a suitable celebration for the College's semi-centennial anniversary. On the Sunday preceding Commencement Rev. Edward Beecher delivered the sermon at the Congregational Church, and Rev. Dr. Julian Sturtevant assisted with the service. On Wednesday afternoon, 4 June, many alumni were joined by alumnae of the two women's academies "and a host of others" in the College Building. Newton Bateman was called to chair the meeting and Rev. Beecher offered prayer. A song was sung to the tune of "America" and Professor Rufus Crampton spoke about the two groups who combined efforts to establish Illinois College. He declared that "We regard the existence of Illinois College as dating from this formal union of these two systems of effort...." The specific date was 18 April 1829, when the Jacksonville stockholders voted to accept the proposal of the New Haven Association.[9] President Sturtevant presented a historical discourse, and the program concluded with more singing and a talk by Rev. Thomas Beecher. That evening a banquet was served at the Cramptons' home. At the exercises the following day thirteen candidates were awarded the baccalaureate degree.[10] An editor of the *Chicago Advance* remarked that the large audience was "exceedingly impressive evidence of the pervasive, elevating and refining influence of the college." (12 June 1879)

The text of the address delivered by Sturtevant was printed in the *Rambler*. (May-June 1879, 34-41). No one would have refused the pardon he requested for an old man's display of "a little egotism" as he reviewed the College's early history. (36) He called the roll of the seven original members of the New Haven Association, noting that five still survived. He spoke movingly of John Ellis and the early trustees, all having departed this life. "Men have their brief day, sometimes, thank God, of great and beneficent influence, and then pass away: but institutions live on, and still exert their power, when the very names, perhaps, of their founders have perished from human memory." (35)

The audience's attention was directed to rhetorical questions: "What is a College? What is the function which it is to perform for the nation, or rather for civilization?" (35) Sturtevant declared that civilization is not a collection of separate parts, like a cathedral, but an organism comprised of many parts in harmony. Humans are the highest form of individual organisms, but society is even higher. And just as thought is the highest function in the individual man, so there must be in the society "an undying, unsleeping thought function" which pervades and controls it. (35) The society must have seers, independent thinkers, who serve this need, and it is the purpose of a college to assist men to qualify for that high office. Higher education is intended for only "a few minds that are destined and naturally designated to perform a peculiar and most important service to mankind." (36) Character formation is an essential purpose of a college, if not indeed the primary one.

The slavery issue was among the serious obstacles confronting Illinois College. "The same power that ordered and obtained the martyrdom of Lovejoy was dogging the footsteps of the prominent teachers of this college by night and by day, and ever ready to let loose upon them the dogs of war." (37) An even greater hindrance to Illinois College's progress and one still affecting it has been the sectarian spirit among Christians. Sturtevant emphasized that "Christianity [is] the only possible basis of free and permanent society...." Thus "The Christian religion is an essential element of our national life." (38)

Compared with its condition in 1855, Illinois College in 1879 was vastly improved. Two fine buildings had been erected and the permanent fund had increased from about $25,000 to $94,000 and the income from about $5,000 to $12,000. The top faculty salary, then $750, was now $1,800. Sturtevant acknowledged that within the past fifteen years his expectations had been "very much modified, moderated, shall I speak the word?—sobered." (40) He no longer desired to make Illinois College like Harvard and Yale but only to achieve "a steady, vigorous growth." More income was essential to enlarge the faculty, enhance the library, and obtain scientific equipment for instruction and original research. Three buildings were needed, for a chapel, science instruction, and Whipple Academy.

A complete collegiate system was necessary for society as a whole and was "an indispensable necessity of Protestantism." (41) Illinois College, founded on the voluntary principle, supported by Christian people, and never sectarian, was the right kind of college. Its founders intended it to be "sacred to Christ and His church universal, sacred to religion, to humanity, to well regulated liberty, to *civilization*. We mean to make it a vital organ of a great, free, civilized, Christian people." (41) Others may have differing convictions, Sturtevant acknowledged, but he invited all to cooperate: "Give us your wisdom [and] do not withhold your active co-operation in a work so great and excellent." (41)

Sturtevant's 1879 address added another chapter to the ongoing historical record of the College. While still at Yale the men of the Illinois Association had recorded their plans and achievements. Subsequent accounts were prepared, among them the 1855 address by Sturtevant. In 1881 he was named chairman of a Historical Committee "to secure and put in permanent form such historical facts and memorials connected with the College as may in their opinion be of value." (TM, 1 June 1881)

A newspaper article denounced the claim someone had made that Illinois College was the oldest theological school in the state. Sturtevant, his indignation aroused, retorted that it never was a theological school, and he exulted that the writer had proved unintentionally that Illinois College is the oldest college in Illinois. Instruction began very soon after its establishment in

1829 and has never been suspended. In 1835 the College "graduated its first class, while the institutions at Lebanon [McKendree] and Alton [Shurtleff] were scarcely organized. It would not have been very difficult at that time, Sturtevant asserted, to know which was the oldest college in the State.[11] In 1830 or 1831 Rev. John M. Peck had written to him to ask whether the Baptists might appoint a professor to serve at Illinois College. Surely Dr. Peck would not have made such an inquiry if the Baptists already had a college at Upper Alton.

An essay on "Practical Education" was Sturtevant's response to the insistent claim that liberal education was not useful. (ICCR, 21 Jan. 1881, 124) Education designed only to enhance a man's occupational success represents a very low conception of a human life. A businessman should be able not only to conduct his affairs successfully but also to make his life "a blessing to the community in which he lives and to himself…." The professional man and especially the statesman should attain to the highest culture of the age, with eminence in literature, or philosophy, or classical learning. The reputation of America demanded that more attention be given to liberal education. Too often American diplomats were unable to speak the language of the nation to which they were sent—or even to speak a language which its officials could be expected to know. "[A] truly practical education…will truly qualify [a man] to serve the public in any trust which may be committed to him…." (126)

Sturtevant considered the cost and accessibility of higher education. The system of "Gratuitous Education" should provide at public expense those branches of knowledge which are essential to all. In the past fifty years publicly supported education had expanded greatly but, regrettably, not judiciously. Tocqueville discerned that democracy extends the notion of equality to intellect, and when applied to the educational system this idea leads to the erroneous conclusion that all intellects are equal. Some branches of education are beyond both the need and the capability of the great masses and should be provided for those who are capable by voluntary support. Free education at the higher level tempts youth to undertake studies they are incapable of mastering. The lack of free college education need not exclude talented youth from fulfilling their potential. New England sent her sons to college, including poor students who were given limited assistance. It is better for boys to demonstrate their worth by overcoming such difficulties. One who does so "does not need a palace car to take him up at his father's door." Colleges must and do provide help to the needy, but it is not a blessing for most families to relieve them of their children's educational expenses.

In an essay in 1880 Sturtevant argued vigorously that Christianity must be "an element in liberal education," in both character formation and academic studies. In all academies and colleges *character-building* is the most important function of the teacher. The history of the Christian nations—their governments, social life, art, and literature—cannot be taught without attention to Christianity. "No man can be made to understand the present or be enabled to forecast the future, except by the diligent study of the past. [Without] the spirit of a sound historical criticism, he is to a great extent an uneducated, uncultured man. The individual was not intended to grow, like the one lone tree on the otherwise treeless prairie, but as an individual branch on the historic stem. All our systems of social and political science grow from roots which run far back into the historic past." Religion is also essential in studying physical science because all science seeks to trace causation to the ultimate cause. A devout parent will want for his son's science teacher a man who advocates theism and the soul's immortality as opposed to a flippant skeptic.

In 1865 Sigma Pi Society had raised $250 for a portrait of President Sturtevant painted by the noted George P. A. Healy of Chicago.[12] In correspondence that year Baldwin relayed a request for a picture of Sturtevant, who said there was no photo of himself he would be willing for a publication to use because he always appeared so expressionless. However, he added, there was a full-sized bust portrait of himself in Chicago which soon would be brought to Jacksonville. An engraving could be made from that but no one, he said, would want to go to that expense. Phi Alpha also obtained a portrait of Sturtevant, painted by R. A. Clifford of Bloomington. On the occasion of the Society's banquet at Dunlap House, 4 June 1878, Dr. Nehemiah Wright, one of the founders,

Portrait of Julian Sturtevant
R. A. Clifford
(Phi Alpha Literary Society)

presented the portrait on behalf of the older members of the group. The *Rambler* remarked that there were several portraits of "this distinguished scholar" but this was regarded as the most correct and elaborate. (Nov. 1878, 108) Regrettably the portrait was vandalized in recent years; however, a good photograph of it had been printed in the local newspaper.[13]

In 1881 Phi Alpha held a banquet in Armory Hall and "adorned the walls of the banqueting room" with portraits of Dr.

Sturtevant and Dr. Adams as well as of founders of the Society. (ICCR, 4 June 1881, 75) In the series of toasts Sturtevant was called to respond to the question, "The 'Odium Theologicum,' Will it be revived over the new version of the New Testament?" The Latin phrase was an allusion to the fierce hatreds engendered in the past by theological disputes. The "new version" was the 1881 English Revision of the New Testament, a scholarly revision of the King James Version designed to correct errors and to improve understanding through cautious use of contemporary language. The reporter commented that this was a favorite topic of the professor's and that his former pupils had great pleasure in hearing him. Sturtevant most likely favored the new version.

In 1881 the seniors instituted "Class Day" and on Tuesday of commencement week a large crowd assembled despite the threat of rain. The background and future prospects of the graduates were reported and at that point a downpour forced adjournment to the Chapel. There the class poem was read and a spokesman "reviewed briefly what the seniors believed to be the lessons which their honored instructor had endeavored to instill in their minds." Appreciation was expressed for the encouragement Dr. Sturtevant had given them "to lead manly lives, to have regard for right and justice in all their undertakings, and most of all to seek for that higher reward, essential to true happiness." An album with pictures of the class was presented to their professor who, after thanking the students for their sympathy and respect, "invoked the blessing of God on their future life-work."

A very special feature of the 1881 commencement was the presentation to the College of the marble bust of Dr. Sturtevant made by Robert Campbell Smith.[14] The bust, and pictures which had been hung in the College Library, were later moved to the Chapel; the Beecher portrait was hung above the "statue" of Dr. Sturtevant. During that same commencement week Sturtevant presented "an elegantly framed and strikingly life-like portrait of Rev. Thomas Lippincott, one of the founders and early patrons of the college." The painting was the gift of Lippincott's son. Sturtevant's remarks were characterized as "an especially fitting address commemorative of the early founders of Illinois College and their efforts in behalf of the noble institution." (JJ, 3 June 1981) A portrait of Mason Grosvenor was given by his wife.

There were less formal and less permanent expressions of student esteem for the faculty. An example of the students' friendly feeling was the serenading of the faculty at their homes. Professor and Mrs. Sturtevant were of course included.

In the last decade of his life Sturtevant witnessed essentially a complete turnover in the membership of the Board of Trustees. In early 1878 Sturtevant went to Quincy for the funeral of Frederick Collins, one of the earliest Jacksonville trustees. In April 1884 another former trustee, C. G. Hammond, died and Sturtevant attended the funeral service in Chicago. By the end of 1886, the year of Sturtevant's death, the last member of the Illinois Association had retired from the Board.

Due to financial stringency in 1884 the salaries of President Tanner and the faculty were reduced. The harsh measure was applied to Sturtevant's salary, and this led to a strong protest from him in a very long letter dated 13 March 1885.[15] He believed that the trustees had no right to approve such a change, and the fact that he learned about it only indirectly did not help. In his letter he described in detail the establishment in 1866 of the "Sturtevant Foundation," the endowed fund to pay the president's salary. The Board had been deeply divided along denominational lines and no one was willing to make contributions. Sturtevant declared that he could not modestly explain why people would give to a fund to pay his salary when they would not give to the College; it was because he was then at the height of his reputation. "It is not every man that puts a little spare reputation he may have on hand to as good a use." (MS, 12) From 1866 until he resigned as president, Sturtevant's salary was the income from the Foundation, neither more nor less; the amount averaged $2,000.

When he retired from the presidency Sturtevant had agreed to a salary of $1,500, to be paid from the Presidency Fund; the balance of the income was for the College's use. Now the trustees had reduced his salary to an even greater degree than that of other faculty members. He submitted letters written by Hammond and Blatchford in 1881 in support of his claim that income from the

Sturtevant Foundation was to be his salary for life. When he resigned Col. Hammond asked whether he had taken sufficient steps to safeguard his interest in the Fund. Sturtevant believed there was no question about it and thought that raising the issue would impugn the good faith of the trustees. If his circumstances allowed, Sturtevant said, he would "gladly resign all work and all pay. But I cannot do that without subjecting myself to a degree of straitness from which I am sure it was the intention of the Founders of that fund to shield me. To avoid this I must work as long as any power to work remains." In consideration of the College's present state he proposed that as of 1 June 1885 he would be released from further class duties and paid a stipend of $750 per year, half the amount he was due. He was willing to be listed as Emeritus and to give occasional Sabbath lectures in the Chapel and to address classes on Mental, Moral, and Social Philosophy, when requested and as health permitted.

Members of the Board were sympathetic, but there was no written record of any agreement that an individual was to have a life interest in the income from the Presidency Fund. Due to the financial straits, the only alternative was to distribute the funds among those who did the work. The trustees therefore designated Sturtevant as "Instructor in Political Economy, Democracy in America, Evidences of Christianity and Logic," for a salary of $500. He was to have one recitation daily.

Family sickness and Sturtevant's own illness and death occurred about midway in the school year, and the actual financial loss was not great. Nevertheless, the hurt was deep. Sturtevant himself had been utterly unselfish in his strenuous service and his personal financial contributions. The conflict was a sad conclusion to a lifetime of loyal service.

Family, Friends, and Community

On 15 November 1879 family and neighbors gathered at Julian Sturtevant's home to commemorate the fiftieth anniversary of his arrival in Jacksonville. (JJ, 16 Nov. 1879) His leadership in education and religion and his service to numerous institutions and many good causes merited his recognition as one of the important early citizens of the town. A reporter took special note of his role at Illinois College, declaring that "the history of the two, man and college, are identical, and by far too well-known to require review at this time." Thirty to forty persons were present, among them all the children and grandchildren of "the venerable president." Following a 7:30 supper Professor Grosvenor offered prayer and Miss Libbie Sturtevant read a poem, "Fifty Years Ago." Mrs. Hannah Sturtevant read a letter written to friends in the East by her sister Elizabeth, the first Mrs. Sturtevant, on the second day after her arrival in Jacksonville. Dr. Sturtevant responded to the guests and spoke with feeling about the events and the changes he had witnessed during fifty years. Rev. Julian Sturtevant Jr., J.B. Turner, and Mason Grosvenor made appropriate remarks. The social evening closed with "the warmest congratulations [for] the honored president and his good wife."

Personal tribute was paid to Sturtevant by several families who named sons for him. Julian Sturtevant Wadsworth, born in 1860, graduated from Illinois College in 1881. Julian Sturtevant Goddard, a grandson of Sturtevant's brother Christopher, was born in 1871. Responding on 5 June 1883 to the news that Dr. and Mrs. H. A. Gilman had named their infant son for him, Sturtevant expressed the hope that the dear boy might have a long life and that his "manly and unflinching testimony to Christ" would be a comfort to them in their old age. Years later President and Mrs. C. H. Rammelkamp named one of their sons Julian Sturtevant; born in 1917, he graduated from Illinois College in 1939.

The first Methodist station charge in Illinois was established in Jacksonville in 1833, twelve years after the founding of the congregation later named Centenary United Methodist Church. In 1883 that church invited "the venerable Dr. Sturtevant, who had then lived in the city fifty-four years," to reminisce about the Methodist Society and the Presbyterian Church—the only churches in Jacksonville in 1829. He called Jacksonville "a sort of a Jerusalem where great things were to be done for the christian [sic] cause." He rejoiced that there was much more Christian spirit now than in the early days when some religious leaders spoke harshly about other churches.[16]

In December 1881 Sturtevant addressed the Temperance Society of Jacksonville. His remarks were characterized as "more than usually interesting." (ICCR, 10 Dec. 1881, 119) C. B. Barton ('36) recalled that soon after Sturtevant's arrival a man brought a package for him from Naples and, refusing payment, supposed that he would be "treated" to some liquor. Sturtevant expressed his willingness to pay the man for his time and effort but declared emphatically, "I do not treat." (ICCR, 13 Mar. 1886, 7)

A brief reference indicates that Sturtevant would never have joined the Masonic chapter established in Jacksonville in its early years. He declared his strong opposition to Freemasonry, saying that it is "an institution of evil tendency" which is opposed by both Papal and Protestant churches.[17]

The Club continued to provide serious intellectual discourse on a wide range of important topics. Sturtevant was present at more than half of the five hundred recorded meetings from its founding in 1861 until his death. He was frequently the host and more often leader of the evening's discussion. During his later years his son-in-law, James Palmer, was also a member. Guests invited from time to time included his son Alfred, Edward Beecher, and occasionally an outsider such as a missionary just returned from overseas. Several times the ladies were invited and twice, when the names of guests were listed, Mrs. Hannah Sturtevant was present. An especially important occasion was the joint meeting on 2 February 1883 of The Club, the Literary Union, Sorosis, and the Round-Table, to which Alfred belonged. Writing to his daughter, Lucy, Sturtevant expected that someone else would write in detail and his comment was disappointingly short: "It was a great affair. I presided." The joint meetings became annual events but The Club's records mention them only briefly.

Sturtevant's presentations often paralleled his activities and the articles he was preparing for publication. In March 1876 he shared an "inside view of the Brooklyn Council" which dealt with the alleged scandalous conduct of Henry Ward Beecher. That September he talked about the nation's Centennial Exposition in Philadelphia, which he probably had attended. In January 1878 he presented "a lengthy written essay on the moral teaching of Jesus compared with the ethical systems of the Ancients, slightly touching upon some modern systems." In March 1879 his topic was early church history; he was then preparing the text of his forthcoming book, *The Keys of Sect*. In February 1881 he discussed the International Sunday School lessons.

Sturtevant presented, in March 1877, "the scheme" of a book on political economy, to be entitled *Wealth*. Subsequently he led discussions on specific topics in economics: competition as the law of wages; taxation; "combinations" of capital and of labor; the ownership of land; the present financial depression; and the decline of the merchant marine of the United States. In February 1881 Sturtevant reported on notices published in England regarding his book on economics.

Other discussions led by Sturtevant focused on a variety of subjects, among them municipal reforms in Jacksonville, proposed reforms of spelling in the English language, public free education for the professions, and the scientific basis of monogamy. The last meeting for which Sturtevant was the leader was held on 26 January 1885, when he proposed changes in the Federal Constitution regarding the election of the president.[18]

Often discussions led by others greatly interested Sturtevant: the harmony of the Mosaic account of creation and modern science, the procession of the equinoxes, comets, Herbert Spencer's ethical views, Mormonism, a book on Preadamite man, polygamy in Utah, the survival of the fittest, the bearing of geology on the theory of evolution, and Christ's Creed. In April 1884 the Institution for the Deaf and Dumb invited The Club to see the new dynamo recently installed to provide electric lighting. Sturtevant last attended on 13 July 1885, when the topic was Emerson's poetry.

On 15 April 1881 the second anniversary memorial service in honor of President Lincoln was held at the National Lincoln Monument in Oak Ridge Cemetery in Springfield. Rev. J. M. Sturtevant, D.D., shared the platform with several other speakers. (SJ, 16 Apr. 1881) Lincoln's Gettysburg Address and portions of his other speeches were read, and the Y.M.C.A. Chorus sang several selections. Rev. Roswell Post of Springfield's First Congregational Church offered the concluding prayer and benediction; he was the nephew of Truman Post and later served the

Congregational Church of Jacksonville. Sturtevant began his address by recalling the shock of the awful news he heard that April 15th morning in 1865. "The Nation's friend, brother, father had fallen by a cruel and guilty hand." The sorrow spread over the whole of the country, from the Atlantic to the Pacific and from Lake Superior to the Gulf. The inclusion of the South was intentional because of the four million "grateful, emancipated slaves [who mourned] the cruel death of their liberator."

The great lessons of Lincoln's life would never be forgotten. He had shown that it is possible in our country for one to rise from obscurity to the loftiest position in the land. Moreover, his example demonstrated that "the surest way to lasting renown was by way of truth and righteousness." The primary motivation for Lincoln's life of public service was his love of country and righteousness. Sturtevant reminded his hearers of several incidents in the Lincoln-Douglas debates to show that Lincoln had a most "deliberately sensitive conscience." Within the limits of the Constitution he always chose universal liberty when the only alternative was universal slavery. Someone said that Mr. Lincoln was too honest to be a first-rate Supreme Court lawyer; that very honesty, said Sturtevant, was one of "the most fundamental and beautiful traits in his character." The trait which he most admired in Lincoln was his conservatism; the claim of his enemies that he was a radical was a slander. Lincoln revered the Constitution and the foundational principle of liberty which the founding fathers had embedded in it. Under his administration the Constitution was "defended and developed according to the true design of the instrument."

Mr. Lincoln was a truly devout man with "a sublime faith in truth, righteousness, and God...." When he stood on the platform of the Great Western Railway station on the eve of his departure for Washington in 1860, he asked people to pray for him. The people in the audience were not so devout that he had to feign a devotion he did not sincerely feel. Aware of the peril the country and he himself faced, Lincoln requested his hearers to join with him in looking to God as their only effective help. It was in that profound trust in God that his power lay. Sturtevant's concluding statement was reported thus by the newspaper: "The seed from which our Nation is to grow and flower and bear fruit for the healing of the nations is found in the moral virtue and the religious devoutness of a righteous man."

Scholar, Minister, Author

Despite his frequent illnesses and the infirmities of advancing age, compounded sometimes by injuries, Julian Sturtevant remained intellectually active throughout his later years. College duties and church responsibilities occupied much of his time but did not exhaust his mental energies. He not only continued his literary output, he increased it; in his last decade he published half a dozen major essays and nearly thirty brief articles. Even more impressive was the publication of a text on economics, a volume on sectarianism, and a monograph on sense perception. At the urging of his family he began dictating his life-story. Unfortunately the deaths of family members and of Sturtevant himself intervened and the *Autobiography* was never completed; his last chapter presented his reflections on the Civil War and his mission to England. Julian Jr. edited this work, added a concluding chapter, and arranged publication.[19]

His "wretched" handwriting was a source of embarrassment to Sturtevant—and of grief for friends and printers. Mercifully some of his letters and articles in the last years were typewritten. There is evidence that he himself was the typist at least some of the time. A curious note complains about the mistakes the machine made. The top line bears Sturtevant's name, typed twice, and then the admission, "I CANOT UNDERSTAND THIS MACHINE. I DO NOT KNOW WHAT MAKES IT SO CAPRICIOUS IN ITS WORKING. SOMETIMES IT WILL WORK WELL, AND YET AT OTER TIMES THE CARRIAGE WILL NOT STIR. IT HAS MADE ON FAILURE IN THIS LINE TO MOVE WHEN IT OUGHT." [The errors are in the original.] Portions of the extant chapters of the draft of the *Autobiography* were also typewritten, presumably by Julian Jr. or at his direction.

The College Archives include letters from persons who corresponded with Sturtevant about his articles and about subjects of mutual interest. English corespondents found in Sturtevant a kindred soul regarding the nature of the church. The files also include manuscripts of articles sent to Sturtevant, perhaps for his comment. President Noah Porter of Yale replied to some inquiries from Sturtevant about the writings of Herbert Spencer. Sturtevant doubtless agreed with Porter's judgment that Spencer's writings espoused an atheism "all sugared over with modern phraseology."[20]

Sturtevant's preaching in these years was generally restricted to the College Chapel and to local churches. The records of Morgan County do not list Sturtevant as officiating at any marriages during these years, but previously there were fifty-two marriages for which he was the clergyman of record.

After his retirement Sturtevant had much more freedom for personal travel and he made several trips to the East. In May 1877 he participated in Yale Seminary's Anniversary. Introduced as "President Sturtevant," he offered the prayer at the beginning of the commencement exercises. That afternoon, as one of the oldest living graduates, he was given the honor of presiding at the alumni meeting. The topic for discussion was the implications of revival preaching for present-day ministerial duties. Sturtevant gave "a vigorous ten minutes' speech." He said that the revivals had brought forth the great truth that the preacher is to seek diligently for power from on high and to look constantly to this source for aid. (*Advance*, 31 May 1877, 78)

Spending vacation time to read William Thackeray's *History of Henry Desmond*, Sturtevant in a review first seemed to compliment the author. However, he said, an uncritical reader would conclude that marriage legitimates the husband as a tyrant, fully supported by law and religion, while the wife is his helpless and hopeless slave "whose highest virtue lies in wearing the chains that bind her with a life-long, unresisting patience, meekness and submission." Such a view of marriage causes disgusting scenes in the divorce courts.

Corruption and even depravity occur in some marriages, but Christianity and law do not sanction that kind of marriage. Marriage requires a measure of true virtue and if there is none in the persons, no law, no religion, no ceremony, can uplift the relationship. Christian marriage does not require a wife to submit to "a domestic tyrant." Too many women bear in silence and sorrow wrongs which they ought to resist. Such women should refuse to live with their husbands and should receive from them an ample maintenance. However, the usual human faults are not sufficient reason to annul the marriage; marriage is for life, except for the offense of adultery. [Cf. Matt. 19:3-9] The wife's refusal to live with a tyrannical husband should not be grounds for allowing him a divorce.

Among Sturtevant's papers is an untitled, undated draft of a monograph on woman's nature and her role in American society. It is more than one hundred closely typed half-sheets. Sturtevant systematically developed the general principles he had enunciated in published articles. He asserted that the true well-being of a woman is in domestic life—ideally her own family, but if not, then as a helper in another's household. "Society is an organism," consisting of smaller organisms, families, which are "the true unit of society." (12, 14) Sturtevant discussed women's employment and wages and again he dismissed claims for women's rights as misguided. He linked men's right to vote with their duty to defend their country; if women were to have the ballot, they would also have to assume the duty to be soldiers. Such dreams of political equality are sickly dreams. In civilized society the relationship of the sexes is diversity, not equality. The education of women is the gravest of all these issues. Sturtevant cited two books by a Dr. Edward H. Clarke in support of his own view that men's education is not suitable for women and indeed dangerously interferes with the physical development of young women. Sturtevant also lamented the serious decline in childbearing among women of the original American stock.

Christ's Church . . . Congregationalism

Throughout his life Julian Sturtevant was steadfast in his faith in Jesus Christ. He was constant also in his devotion to the church; Timothy Dwight's hymn, "I Love Thy Kingdom, Lord," was always his favorite. Convinced that the scriptural church was the local congregation, he believed that the function of "congregationalism" was to unite men "in the Gospel which teaches repentance toward God and faith in our Lord Jesus Christ," and puts no other yoke upon them. (A, 209)

The Congregational Church of Jacksonville was the local expression of the New Testament church and exemplified much of what Sturtevant believed to be the spirit of true Christianity. The church was strongly committed to evangelism. Fifty of the eight hundred members listed on its rolls up to 1883 were (or became) ordained ministers. Not surprisingly, Jacksonville gained the reputation of being a Puritan stronghold; Sturtevant's presence and long tenure certainly added to that reputation. He described the church as having been "helpful to every good cause" despite its limited membership and scarce resources. That generosity included Illinois College, care for the poor, and a welcome to the handicapped. A dozen students from the "Deaf and Dumb Asylum" were members, beginning in the 1850s.

Members of Sturtevant's "great family" were active in the Jacksonville church. Alfred served several terms on the Board of Trustees. Libbie was one of the ladies assigned to inspect the interior of the parsonage and report on needed repairs. In due course Sturtevant's grandchildren living in Jacksonville were received into the fellowship.

The relationship of the Congregational Church and Westminster Presbyterian Church demonstrated the unity of spirit and practical cooperation which Sturtevant advocated. In 1879 they combined their summer services, with the Congregational pastor preaching to the joint congregations at the Westminster Church and the Presbyterian pastor then preaching to them at the Congregational Church. Westminster Church and First Presbyterian sent delegates to the Congregational Church when it called a council to dissolve a pastoral relationship in 1880.

A local paper, reporting on one of Sturtevant's last sermons, said that it was "very acceptable" and demonstrated that his nearly four-score years had not impaired his vigorous mind. There was similar praise when he preached at the Congregational Church in Cleveland where his son was now the pastor. His subject was the Messianic prophecies of the Old Testament and their fulfillment in the Savior. "The fire of youth broke afresh from those eloquent lips, and his whole frame...was aglow with the intensity of interest which he himself manifestly took in the great subject." (*Congregationalist*, 13 Aug. 1885)

Along with having various committee appointments in the church, Sturtevant taught a Sunday School class, for which Samuel Nichols and others expressed appreciation in a letter. Sturtevant's financial support for the church included a generous contribution for the huge new bell, ordered in 1882 to replace the original bell which had been cracked when rung too hard to celebrate the fall of Richmond. He also represented the congregation at other churches, as at Quincy and Waverly on such occasions as the installation of a new pastor. He was a delegate from the local church to area and state meetings and often delivered addresses on theology at those sessions. In 1880 he attended the National Council of Congregational Churches at the Pilgrim Church in St. Louis and was named a delegate to a corresponding body, the Presbyterian General Assembly. In 1881 he attended the St. Louis meeting of the American Board and spoke at the Home Missionary convention in Chicago. In 1882 he preached the sermon at the opening session of the state association. He continued to meet with colleagues from the Midwest at the Triennial State Conventions in Chicago.

Illinois Congregationalists had devised a method for dealing with controversial subjects which avoided the divisive voting previously required to adopt resolutions "on slavery, on temperance, on the Sabbath, on Free Masonry, and on everything else...." Now papers were presented on various aspects of an issue, and the ensuing discussion served sufficiently to influence churches and the public. Sturtevant proposed that this method should be adopted by "The National Council," especially in the forthcoming effort to revise the Congregational statement of faith. Any claim of authority by the National Council to decide this matter is not Congregational. Similarly, it is impertinent for the Council to seek to control the volunteer societies, which are independent, by adopting resolutions.

Requirements for church membership and participation in the Lord's Supper were in some ways even more exacting in Congregationalism. Sturtevant was determined to bring such matters into harmony with the practices in apostolic times. In his memorial address for Dr. Samuel Adams he explained his colleague's delay in joining the local church. Adams could not conscientiously give public assent to the congregation's statement of faith when he did not fully endorse its wording. Sturtevant now questioned requiring such assent for church membership. He had previously concluded that church membership is not required for participation in the Lord's Supper.

An early alumnus of Illinois College, Rev. C. B. Barton, told of a student (himself) who regarded Sturtevant as his spiritual counselor as well as his teacher. The student asked the privilege of going to the Lord's table, although he was not a church member. Refused, he asked Sturtevant for the reason and was told that it was not customary. Years later when the two met Sturtevant asked his former student whether he remembered the incident, and Barton replied that he had never forgotten it. Sturtevant acknowledged that he had been wrong. (ICCR, 13 Mar. 1886, 6-7)

Sturtevant rejoiced in his late years because after forty years of argument Dr. R. W. Patterson now agreed that a true Christian should not be required to give assent to the Westminster Confession for ordination to the Presbyterian ministry. Sturtevant believed that Patterson was even approaching the tenets of Congregationalism.

The Congregational connections of Illinois College were manifested in several ways. For a time the local church conducted a Sunday School for College students and it also sponsored "sociables" which students attended. One such event caused the *Rambler* to declare that both the quantity eaten and the manners of the students "gave them away badly." (Nov. 1879, 77) The faculty approved advertising in such Congregational publications as *Advance*, the *Congregationalist*, and the new *Christian News* of St. Louis. Ads were also placed in the *Independent*, the *Sunday School Times*, and *Youth's Companion*. College catalogs were mailed to Congregational ministers but apparently mass mailings were not made to Presbyterian clergy. Reports about the College's status were made to the state Congregational organization. The College awarded an honorary degree in 1883 to the secretary of the American Missionary Association, an important Congregational agency.

Brief articles dealt with a variety of issues, such as "Gospel Repentance." A murderer who repented an hour before his execution attracted public attention. Granted that only God can know whether such repentance is genuine, the Gospel proclaims that even the most degraded sinner can repent. Sturtevant queried, "Would you have God so vindictive that he will only forgive respectable sinners?" The victim was a good woman but an unbeliever. Did she reject the life, death, and teaching of Jesus? "Unbelief," said Sturtevant, "is a much graver indication of character than [the inquirer] seemed to suppose."

A Catholic Bishop had asserted that it would be impossible to find a Protestant theology. Sturtevant declared that if Harvard is excluded, because it is not representative of American Protestantism, the task can be accomplished. The basic theme is repentance, and next would be Jesus' teachings about the Kingdom of Heaven and how people's response to the Gospel determines their destiny. Other topics include the Last Supper, Gethsemane, the trial, the crucifixion, and certainly the resurrection of Jesus, and then Pentecost. "Protestant Theology" draws its life from "that conception of Jesus the Christ of God, which is set forth in the imperishable pages of the Divine Word," and no priestly authoritative church is needed to tell us what it means.

During his late years Sturtevant published nearly a dozen articles on the nature of the church and the problem of sectarianism. He frequently drew sharp contrasts between Congregationalism and Catholicism and expressly denied that "The Keys of the Kingdom of Heaven" given to Peter had been transferred to the Roman Church. Declaring that his interpretation was "sanctioned by the ripest and most devout scholarship of the nineteenth century," he asserted that Peter's "primacy was personal, moral, spiritual, not official, legislative or administrative." Moreover, there is no indication that any organization was to control access to the sacraments. Paul, in 1 Corinthians, gave no hint that the church could exclude anyone; rather, each was to determine his worthiness.

Pope Gregory VII's despotic claim to have control over the Lord's Supper filled Europe with desperate fear. Faith in God gave the Reformers courage to oppose the Papal church and they insisted on "the great fundamental truth of the forgiveness of sins through faith in Christ...." However, the Reformers also erred in claiming that the church controlled the sacraments. The New Testament's lack of an explicit statement of the constitution of the church resulted in the formation and multiplication of Protestant sects.

There are logically only two alternatives. All Christendom could accept one ecclesiastical authority, which would "establish over the human mind a rigorous spiritual despotism, under which all freedom of thought and even civilization itself must perish." The only escape is to acknowledge the church universal, a spiritual fraternity governed only by the Word and Spirit of God. ("The Keys of Sect")

In a spirited exchange with Rev. F. Alvord, a Protestant clergyman, Sturtevant denied that the church controls admission to the Lord's Supper. (*Advance*, May, June 1880) The only way to resolve this issue is "before the tribunal of a sound and just historical criticism applied to the extant apostolic records." Sturtevant drew upon the analogy with Judaism. The local churches founded by the apostles "stood related to the church universal, precisely as the Jewish synagogues were related to the institution of religion established by Moses." A synagogue could put a man out, but it could not deprive him of the right to celebrate the Passover or attend Temple worship. "The local churches of the apostles were the synagogue Christianized." The apostles were not founding a new religion but developing the religion of Moses according to its true intent and spirit. ("What Saith the Scripture?")

The theological argument intensified when Alvord shifted the focus of their debate. Without proof, Sturtevant asserted, Alvord wrongly accused him of going over to the "Socinians," "Unitarians," and "Liberals." Sturtevant steadfastly maintained his orthodoxy, saying that reliance upon "the authority of Scripture alone, is not infidelity and does not tend to infidelity." He acknowledged that evolution may be "the true law of church-government and history," but he insisted that the germ which has evolved into the church must be found in the Scripture. There is no record that Jesus at the Last Supper established any authority over admission to it. (*Advance*, 6 Jan. 1881)

Responding to a call for a "Congress of the Denominations," Sturtevant wished that all the Protestant denominations would convene in the cause of unity. He feared however that such a conference would be like a Congress of the Great Powers of Europe, with each Power so intent on preserving its own interests that the fundamental issue could not be resolved. Similarly, the Lord's people are devoted to "the idols of denominationalism." "In God's own good time [the obstacles to unity] will be overcome. The church of Christ will surely triumph."

In reviewing the demand for "Economy in Home Missions," Sturtevant objected to consolidating all the churches of a community simply for the sake of economy; one church is not as good as another. Fortunately, "There is in the Word of God a definite conception of the church...." (270) Suppose that earnest Christians from six rival Protestant churches were to unite by accepting no creed but the Word of God and by acknowledging no authority over them but "the one Shepherd and Bishop of their souls...." Such a church could well be called "Congregational" but that name is dispensable; let that church be called simply the "*Church of Christ.*"[21] That name is shorter, it sounds better, and it has "a far more evangelistic ring." (271)

The Congregational Church's 50th

When the Congregational Church of Jacksonville arranged to celebrate its fiftieth anniversary on 15 December 1883, Sturtevant was the obvious choice for the customary historical discourse. Explaining his reluctance to accept the assignment, he said it involved "peculiar difficulty and delicacy" even though few of those who were present when the church was founded were still alive. But their children and children's children were among the living and "it cannot be supposed that the antagonisms and the passions of that time are dead...." (8)

The significance of the Congregational churches organized in Illinois in the early 1830s, and especially the one in Jacksonville, is expressed in the title Sturtevant gave his address: "The Origin of 'Western Congregationalism.'" He proposed to answer three questions: Why was this church founded? What principles did it represent in the minds of the founders? What is its true place among the elements of our religious civilization? He repeated the basic convictions about the nature of the church which he had expressed previously.

Sturtevant recalled the severe criticism, locally and in the East, aroused by the founding of the Jacksonville church—an act regarded as violating the Plan of Union.[22] That Plan was intended to advance the Christian mission in the West through the cooperation of the two denominations. The actual result was the abandonment of their heritage by "the entire flood of the Congregational emigration to parts west of the Hudson," and laymen and ministers alike became Presbyterians. (10-11) Congregationalism declined from being the most numerous church body to fifth place. But why, Sturtevant queried, should it have seemed improper to form a Congregational church among Congregationalists from New England? "The case certainly was peculiar." (10) The wisdom of later experience demonstrated that sectarian divisions are "eminently beneficial, tending greatly to promote healthy religious activity and a spirit of free inquiry." (11) [This is a surprisingly positive statement about sectarianism.] The Presbyterians also suffered from the Plan because it introduced elements which led to schism.

The first Congregational churches in the interior were the four in Illinois.[23] The founding of the Jacksonville church, especially, "startled and shocked our fathers in New England." (15) It was unique in being located in a town which already had a Presbyterian church and thus it represented "an ecclesiastical revolution" (16) of great significance. Sturtevant reminded the audience that it was not ministers who agitated the founding; it had "originated wholly with the laity." (20) The primary factor was their desire to have the kind of church they had known in New England. That concern was amplified by the unpleasant conflicts within Presbyterianism and especially by the heresy trial of 1833. Together the four early churches were "the first practical expression of a change of opinion in large masses of our people" which eventually led to nationalizing Congregationalism. (16) By 1883 there were 1,481 Congregational churches in New England; west and south of New England, there were 2,455. Had it not been for the emergence of Congregationalism in the West, the churches of New England— already moving toward Presbyterianism—might well have become substantially if not in name Presbyterian.

The fundamental principle on which the local church was founded, Sturtevant declared, was expressed by the inscription[24] on the archway above the pulpit: "JESUS CHRIST THE SON

Congregational Church, Jacksonville
Observing 50th Anniversary, 1883

OF GOD, THE SAVIOR OF THE WORLD." (23) That was the
foundation of the Apostles' faith and it was the sufficient creed of
the newly organized church. The founders were "no sectarians"
and rejected any test of membership other than Christian character.
(24) The circumstances in central Illinois explained why the
church had always been small. The population of the region was
mainly Southern in origin and from 1835 to 1865 "this church
carried the stigma of being the anti-slavery church." Its members
encountered serious dangers as a consequence. Despite these difficulties the church was self-sustaining and had fine pastors although
it often provided only scanty support for them. Its evangelism
brought precious revivals and many were won to Christ. Many
were consecrated to the Christian ministry and foreign missions.
This church was always in the forefront of any united effort in this
community on behalf of the Kingdom of God.

The entire Christian Church must return, Sturtevant said, "to
the simpler organization of the churches of the apostles." (30)
Since the Reformation the stream of church history has constantly
flowed in that direction and indeed, "the Congregational conception of the church [is] *the Church of the Future*." (31) Unity among

Christians can be established on the basis of their common loyalty to Christ, manifested in "that one church of God which comprehends us all." (32) Sectarian divisions in the church are analogous to the loyalty which the Southerners in the recent rebellion directed to the states instead of to the nation. Sturtevant closed with the declaration, "I devoutly believe in the Holy Catholic Church," and he quoted the words of Timothy Dwight: "For her my tears shall fall / For her my prayers ascend. / To her my cares and toils be given, / Till cares and toils shall end." (32)

This address exhibits a broader perspective than a "Sketch" of the same subject which Sturtevant presented to the Southern Association of Illinois.[25] He noted in the Sketch that New England Congregationalists had experienced a controversy over the adoption of new measures such as conversion and revivalism and had resolved the problem peaceably. In the early years in Jacksonville Presbyterians confronted a similar problem. That and other factors led former Congregationalists to withdraw to found their own church. Even then efforts were made to bring the two groups together again. Because of the fundamental contradiction in their church orders, the effort failed. Sturtevant described the Jacksonville experiment as "really a decisive one for the whole continent west of the Hudson."

The next-to-last published article of record by Sturtevant (1885) was his final commentary on the factors hindering the full fellowship of the two denominations. He agreed with Dr. Leonard Bacon's analysis of the trouble with Congregationalism: to a large extent its clergy either had not understood it or had not believed in it. The Congregationalists had thought it very important to have a united mission in the West. Because the Presbyterians would not yield, Congregationalists decided "the best thing [they] could do was to give up the ghost for the public good." Even "The world-renowned Pres. Dwight, of Yale College, was one of the number." [This may explain why Sturtevant disliked the man.] Sturtevant insisted that despite the multitude of sects the existence of Congregationalism is justified because it "imposes no yoke but the Gospel on any [man]." He sharply distinguished between the two old rivals: "Given a perfect Christian, and you have all that is necessary to constitute a perfect Congregationalist. To make a good Presbyterian of him, you must make him [submit to all the church's judicatories and accept the Westminster Confession and Catechisms]." Denying that Congregationalism had a monopoly on God's grace, Sturtevant made a single far-reaching claim: "All which we assert for our polity is, that it is the true conception of the church of Christ." Had its clergy understood their polity, Congregationalism today would be strong everywhere, "from Plymouth Rock to the Golden-Gate."

A Major Work on Church and Sects

The summation of Sturtevant's lifelong study of the Christian Church, with regard to its biblical basis and historical development, was published in book form in 1880. The title is lengthy: *The Keys of Sect; or, The Church of the New Testament Compared with the Sects of Modern Christendom.* The first part of the four-hundred page book is an analysis of the New Testament church. The second part focuses on "the transition church," the long period of hierarchical church order from the second century to the Reformation and the origin of religious liberty. The latter half of the book reviews "modern Christendom" with its multiple sects and discusses the prospect for restoring the unity and purity of the New Testament church.

For Sturtevant the New Testament is *the only acceptable source* for determining the intentions Jesus had for the church and the nature of the churches established by the apostles. It must be interpreted "according to the received laws of literary and historical criticism...." (293) Such study reveals only two meanings of the word "church," the local church which is the only scripturally authentic *organization,* and the Holy Catholic [universal] Church. The latter embraces all true followers and is characterized by its fervent adherence to the crucified and risen Christ, its moral and spiritual nature, and the righteous lives of its people. It is a perpetual theocracy, an absolute "monarchy" in which every one of the faithful is directly responsible to God; there is no human intermediary and consequently believers have perfect spiritual freedom. The mission of Jesus Christ was to establish this theocratic principle as "the dominant element in the civilization of all Christian ages and lands." (25) The church is a "republic," with everyone sharing in the kingly, priestly, and prophetic functions. The Lord's Supper is not a priestly sacrament but a commemorative feast for rejoicing

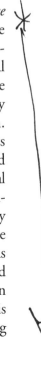

in the sacrifice which has brought salvation. Any Christian can conduct the rite, and all Christians are permitted to participate.[26]

The seeds of ecclesiastical corruption were sown in the second and third centuries when elaborate pagan ritualism and priestly control of the sacraments were adopted. Ultimate corruption was ensured when the church accepted as the model for its organization and power the erstwhile Roman Empire. Sturtevant, citing Tocqueville's observation that religion and political opinion exist in juxtaposition, observed that the decay of the church nearly over-whelmed its spiritual dimension.[27] The claim to absolute power made by Pope Gregory VII in the eleventh century was the assertion of a tyrant. "No despotism is so much to be dreaded as that which is to be exercised in the name of God and religion." (171) More recently that pretension to power was illustrated by the "daring and impious" decree of the Pope [Pius IX, in 1870] that he was "rendered by the grace of God infallible in all his official acts." (181)

The New Testament, "sacredly preserved," enables Christianity to maintain reforming power, in contrast to Buddhism which likely will become extinct along with "the decaying civilization" of which it is a part. (190, 191) The great men of the Reformation were motivat-ed to restore "the primitive gospel of Christ." (195) Luther's work, great as it was, constituted only a beginning; unfortunately most of the Reformers held fast to the notion that the church is to be gov-erned by clergy who control the sacraments and make dubious alliances with the state. Nevertheless, wherever it becomes domi-nant, Protestantism eventually brings religious freedom because of its conviction that every individual person owes allegiance directly to God. Freedom is not permission to ignore religion nor exemption from moral responsibility; however, the offender in such matters is responsible to God, not to the church or any human tribunal.

Protestantism has experienced divisions so extensive and conflicts so serious that they are painful to contemplate. Most such groups in America had their origin in Great Britain, "the hot-beds of sect," although the national Protestant churches of Europe were also represented among the immigrants. (242) America's unique contribution is the African Methodist Episcopal Church, separated not by religious opinion but by social aversions. Sturtevant wryly noted that this division originated in the desire for separate accommodations while members were still in the body, although presumably they all have the same destiny in a future life. The bitter quarrels of the various sects have led to a truce, with the unfortunate consequence that public examination of differences is impossible. Such silence prevents the application of "those unerring tests by which the human mind discriminates truth from falsehood." (255)

The root of sectarianism is the interposition of human authority between the individual and God as manifested in clerical control of baptism and the Lord's Supper. In contrast, our Lord's intention is demonstrated in the kind of polity which provides fraternal and loving cooperation among his followers. In practical organizational terms this requires reducing the proliferation of local churches, colleges, organizations, and publications to permit adequate support and improved quality.

The Roman Catholic Church is virtually the complete contradiction of the Scriptural church. Three major branches of Protestantism also fail to meet the New Testament norm. The Anglicans honor prelacy and emphasize liturgical forms which are human additions. The Presbyterians recognize the importance of doctrine but err in requiring ministers to subscribe to fixed statements; moreover, they impose hierarchical authority over the local church. The Methodists began in a genuine revival of religious faith but often provide only an itinerant ministry; because of their highly structured organization and their numbers they have become the most sectarian of all the Protestants.

Congregationalism, especially as seen in the churches of the early Pilgrim fathers, accords well with the New Testament church in spirit and organization. But it too has divisions, based merely on personal feelings and social class. "The spirit of the gospel pre-eminently requires that the high and the low, the rich and the poor, the learned and the ignorant should meet together in the worship of God...." (373) Congregationalists have even exercised the so-called power of the keys to try, convict, and punish those who have been considered guilty regarding faith or conduct. Some have even recognized a league of churches as having power over local congregations; the very lack of a written constitution may increase the exercise of such presumed authority. However, when

Congregationalism is refined to the New Testament model, it can "endure till the millennium." (393)

The notion that mankind will outgrow religion was rejected by Sturtevant. Enlightened men can believe in a personal God, the continued existence of human personality after death, and moral obligation and accountability. The Bible will never become obsolete because it is not of human origin but a revelation from a "divine, all-knowing mind." (357) Our knowledge of it, however, is progressive, as demonstrated in the important scholarship of the last two centuries. The language of Scripture is concrete, having been drawn from "the great, deep, permanent sources of human nature and human life." (358) The realization that language also changes makes it obvious that the creeds of earlier times are simply inadequate to express contemporary faith. "Living thought always grows, and requires…living, growing language…." (357) Sturtevant cited an unbeliever who quoted from the *New England Primer* to show that church people believe that the wicked are tormented in hell by literal fire. That, he said, was an earlier belief and is no longer current.

The future will witness the defeat of hierarchical religion and the triumph of the church of the New Testament.[28] The spirit of loving persuasion characteristic of the early church is manifest in the evangelical preaching of the present and at those meetings which bring together Christians of different denominations. Sturtevant was confident that the Lord will soon conduct his people into the promised land of the spiritual kingdom of God on earth. His final sentences were a joyful expression of his faith and his hope.

> The life, the moral character and teachings of Jesus of Nazareth, …combine with the resistless proof of his resurrection from the dead, to give him a perpetually increasing influence over human society in its most cultivated ages…. The multitudes who adopt [faith in that Christ] will become to a constantly increasing extent a world-wide fraternity, [impelled] to imitate him in a never-ceasing endeavor to save all that are lost. This, THIS, is to be THE CHURCH OF THE FUTURE. (413)

A College Text on Economics

A lecture by Joseph Cook on 1 October 1877 was reported in the

Congregationalist and inspired several articles by Sturtevant regarding wages and labor. These issues were current because of serious railroad strikes during the depression which began in 1873. Sturtevant endorsed the moral and religious truths expressed by Cook but judged his economic doctrines to be unsound. Cook's error was his assumption that competition is an unprincipled practice of "grinding the face of the poor." Sturtevant countered that true competition is actually "a beneficent force, impartially friendly to the buyer and the seller, to the laborer and the capitalist." Cook had asserted that the laborer supporting a wife and three children on one dollar a day is paid "starvation wages." Sturtevant agreed that such an amount is "an inconveniently small income" but denied it is necessarily starvation wages. The real issue is why labor is paid that amount; it is because many men are willing to work for that wage. The misconception that wages are determined by the arbitrary will of employers was "the volcanic element in the great strike of 1877" when laborers used violence against their employers. Wages are determined by "a great law of nature as quiet and impartial as sunlight, and in the long run as irresistible as gravitation."

Considering the effective "Remedy," Sturtevant rejected legislative attempts, or strikes, or differential wages for married men. Laws should protect workers against employers' oppression. Children must be protected from parents who would subject them to unsuitable labors. Factory owners must be prohibited from practices which are injurious to health and morals. But with regard to wages, "The only function of the legislator is to secure to all parties the full benefit of free, fair competition." Competition is a law of nature, "an irresistible force." All must learn to live on their income; a man whose wages cannot support a family must not marry. The alternative is to improve one's skills to qualify for better pay.

The United States officially had a bimetallic standard of money, with gold and silver supposedly interchangeable at a fixed rate. But, wrote Sturtevant, the system never existed in fact. No legislation can make silver equally desirable with gold.[29] When greenbacks were made legal tender in 1862 both gold and silver disappeared from circulation. To equalize silver with gold is harder than Charles V's attempt to make two timepieces run just alike; "The ex-king gave it up."

In his "Review of Prof. Perry's Political Economy," Sturtevant offered some praise and much criticism. He believed that precise definitions of terms, such as "wealth," are possible and that basic laws determine much economic activity. Just as physical astronomy rests on the law of gravitation, economic science is founded on the law of ownership. Wealth must be defined to include both labor and its products; these are exchangeable with each other, and value "is relative desirableness as ascertained by competition." (25) Sturtevant expanded Perry's definition of labor. "The economic system of the universe is that all are laborers, and as such must be rewarded according as they contribute to the supply of human want." This view explains "the place in the system of the teacher, the professional man, the inventor, the poet, the artist." (28) The mother is also a laborer and likewise the child in the cradle. The mother has "direct claim both upon the labor and capital of her husband to be supported in the enjoyment of the comforts and conveniences of life." (28)

Some say that the science of political economy is just a theory; so it is, until "time can be afforded for verification by experiment." (29) Human will introduces many contingencies in economic activity, making it unlike physical science. The ultimate purpose of economic science is to determine the conditions under which the human race can achieve "that permanent prosperity and happiness…destined by the Creator." (33)

Because of the loss of the family's farm in Connecticut, Sturtevant early experienced the problems of land ownership. Later he observed and participated in land transactions in Illinois. When in Great Britain he observed a system which for centuries had denied to thousands of tenant farmers possession of the land they tilled. In a lengthy essay on "The Private Ownership of Land" Sturtevant declared that probably the fundamental cause of the unrest which had been troubling Europe for a century was discontent with the systems of land tenure. It was the central issue of those agitating in the interest of communism and socialism. Americans should be profoundly grateful to God that their society is built on an "impregnable foundation," the private ownership of land. "[A]ll agrarians and social levellers" should learn that the remedy is not to abolish but to establish private ownership. (146)

Agreeing with what "Mr. Locke said long ago," Sturtevant asserted that people gain ownership of anything commonly available by the labor they exert to produce something from it. (126) For example, anything in nature, such as fruit or a metal, is available to many; it becomes the property of the person who collects it and either uses it or makes it usable by others. Ownership once gained can then be transferred in exchange for something of equivalent value. Sturtevant refuted Herbert Spencer's argument that labor does not grant ownership. He also refuted Ricardo's theory of rent, which was widely adopted by the British and by the American Henry George. Rent is in fact based on productivity, not on the amount of the initial investment. The lands of Illinois are among the easiest in the world to prepare for cultivation. This factor together with improvements in equipment and transportation provide America with a unique agricultural situation. New farming methods in Minnesota and the Dakota Territory give promise of more efficient production and greater profitability.

In an article in 1884 Sturtevant took issue with James G. Blaine, the Republican nominee for President. Blaine proposed high tariffs to protect American industry from cheaper goods imported from Spanish America. Exports to those countries should be increased, Sturtevant said, but there are only two ways to induce them to buy more from us. One is to make them love us so intensely that they will do so even though our prices are higher; those who know human nature would not be hopeful about that prospect. The other way is to invest capital and labor in goods which we can produce more cheaply than others. Protective tariffs not only increase the price of the products on which they are levied but raise prices on other items as well. Thus, "we must become a nation of free-traders." Sturtevant's comments sparked editorial response in the local newspapers, one rejecting his views, the other supporting him.[30]

Having failed to find an adequate text in political economy, Julian Sturtevant accomplished what many teachers aspire to do. He wrote a book to correct the errors and supply the deficiencies of other textbooks and entitled it, *Economics, or The Science of Wealth*.[31] He acknowledged Adam Smith as the father of economics and adopted certain of John Locke's views.[32] Citing the flaws of recent theorists, he provided alternative interpretations of their data. To support his arguments he drew upon his frontier experience, his observations in England, and current news.

The book was intended for students in a liberal arts college founded on Christian principles. Sturtevant wrote to some of his "companions in tribulation, Presidents of Western colleges," to tell them the publisher would send a copy.[33] He stated that he had "re-thought and re-stated the whole subject, and [had] developed the whole science logically from a single law of nature." He hoped that the book would not be thought the worse for being from a "Fresh-water College." The text, first listed in Illinois College's *Catalogue* for 1878-1879, was used until two years after Sturtevant's final retirement. Priced at $1.75, it was adopted by Oberlin and "many other colleges."[34]

Noah Porter, former president of Yale, had praised Sturtevant in a letter.[35] He wrote that "Rev. Prest. Sturtevant of Illinois college...is a bold literary thinker and writer and makes his mark whenever he takes up any subject." The *Chicago Times* complimented Sturtevant. Observing that preachers often do not fare well in discussing economics or politics, the editor was pleased that "now and then one succeeds well.... A D.D., Mr. J. M. Sturtevant, has produced the best of recent works on economics." The *Rambler's* first issue noted this praise of their professor's book.[36]

In his text Sturtevant maintained steadfastly that economics is a science, and although he took pains to distinguish the subject from moral issues, he frequently discussed them. He interjected Christian doctrines and quoted Scripture passages to demonstrate that economics is consistent with religion. A statement from Paul is quoted on the title page: "If any one will not work neither shall he eat." (2 Thess. 3:10) That quotation is in *Greek*, thus doubly distinguishing the book from texts published today. Sturtevant regarded the world and its economic laws as the creation of God and indeed identified the "law of nature" with "the will of God." His presentation of the subject is in three parts: a short treatment of production, a longer analysis of exchange, and a very extensive discussion of distribution. Sturtevant gave thorough consideration to such standard topics as money, credit, interest, and taxation. Of greater interest are his views of human nature and economic activity and the ideal society which, he believed, can be approximated if certain conditions are met.

According to Sturtevant, a fundamental intuition underlies the development of sciences relating to social and political phenomena: "*Every man owns himself, and all which he produces by the voluntary exertion of his own powers.*" (1) John Locke first stated this principle, saying that the elements of nature belong to everyone until an individual makes some of those elements his own property by the act of obtaining them and rendering them suitable for use. Sturtevant defined wealth as anything which can be owned and exchanged for equivalent value. Economics, the science of wealth, is concerned only with how wealth is produced, exchanged, and distributed. It is a law of human nature that in every transaction one will seek to gain as much as he can in exchange for the minimal amount of his own wealth. When this can be done without corruption or government interference, free trade can exist and people are able to buy cheap and sell dear. The moral aspects of how people ought to live and work belong to the province of ethics, a subject derived from the fundamental intuition of the individual's inviolability.

Work which has *direct* economic significance is accomplished by able-bodied, male adults. All men are, or ought to be, laborers: manual laborers, managers, traders, artists, scholars, those engaged in every useful occupation. The same law which makes a man the owner of all he produces places on him the responsibility to support not only himself but a family. The Creator intends the family to be the social unit, embracing all individuals: the mother, the children, the aged, and the infirm. All these are worthy of support, within the framework of the family. The father is responsible for providing his family with food, clothing, shelter, and education. The incapacity or failure of some men to marry and care for a family denies to some women the role of wife and mother, the task best suited to them.

A strong economic system requires workers who are "intelligent" [educated] and able to add to the accumulation of the world's wealth, beyond simply maintaining themselves and their families. Moral virtues—hard work, truthfulness, honesty, and fairness—are essential for the system to function. Sturtevant's model was the farming people of New England who prospered because they had the advantages of free trade in land, public education, and sound morals and religion. When circumstances necessitated changing occupation and residence, they emigrated in great numbers to the West where they sought to establish the same kind of high, Christian civilization.

The basic human appetites, hunger, thirst, and sex, motivate people to work. The divine law is that "By the sweat of thy face shalt thou eat thy bread." (317; Gen. 3:19) Hence, government efforts to remove the threat of unemployment are contrary to human nature. On the positive side there are noble impulses, such as *the love of social prosperity and well-being."* (334) The ability to make the world helpful to human welfare gratifies natural desires for satisfying basic needs, for producing beauty, and for striving toward that perfected civilization which is the common inheritance of mankind.

The divine purpose for human life is fulfilled to the extent that society and the economic system comply with the natural laws and moral standards which God established. The whole human family is to be united "into one great economic world." (77) As the Scripture says, "All ye are brethren." (118; Matt. 23:8) Hope, and peace, are essential that all may work to enjoy the Creator's bounties. Perfect freedom of international trade promotes the goal powerfully. There is every prospect for continuing progress toward a universal, high civilization. Probably there is some limit to the earth's ability to provide a full life for everyone, but that is so remote in the future as to be irrelevant to the present economic system.

Capitalists perform useful work in managing capital and employing men to utilize the tools and plants they finance. The ideal arrangement is for the workers to own a minority share of the stock because as part-owners they will work more efficiently. However, the management must always be retained by primary owners. Employer and employees are not natural enemies; both are bound by the law of competition, which is "absolute, universal and unrelenting over every economic question." (156) It is not, however, a blind force but acts through rational minds and free wills. Wages are actually set by competition, and if too low or too high, will be brought into balance in due time. Wages should provide not merely subsistence but a good standard of living, with adequate resources for the higher culture. With present communications and transportation, no laborers will continue to work for starvation wages, *"unless they have been reduced to utter despondency by generations of experience in hopeless poverty.*" (179) Indeed, labor is international; Americans can go anywhere to work because their labor is part of the wealth which belongs to the world.

Competition results in the division of labor, ensuring that workers are in the right occupation, or in the best location. This applies to industries and countries as well as individuals. Certain conditions are required. The "intelligence," that is, the knowledge and ability, of both employers and employees must be substantially equal; and there must be moral integrity, including truthfulness. There must be complete freedom of exchange, among nations as well as within a country. Protectionism is misguided even when retaliatory; revenge is sweet but it has no commercial value.

The "combinations" of either workers or employers in the effort to dominate the other interfere with the economic system and in the end must fail. This issue constitutes "one of the gravest questions of modern civilization." (159) If either side turns to violence the government should suppress it "with the utmost promptness and rigor" to avoid anarchy, revolution, and distress. (169) Government must protect the right of employees to accept or refuse work at the wage offered and the right of the employer to determine wages and whether to operate his plant.

Labor-saving machinery lowers the cost of products and brings them within range of more people; the consequent increase in demand results in more employment. Such machinery can provide not merely necessities but the comforts and conveniences of a truly civilized life to more people. Recent inventions have done much to improve the efficiency of production and exchange. However, agriculture is the one industry which would not benefit from increased use of machinery because rent and transportation, the main costs of production, are not affected by it.[37]

Profit is an essential element in the economic system, but there are strict limitations on the means to achieve it. Monopolies are in most cases contrary to economic well-being. Inventions and books and other intellectual property, however, must be given protection, and those who produce them are entitled to appropriate remuneration, which sometimes may be very great. The very high compensation paid to certain managers or to inventors is appropriate reward for their important work.

Substitutes for competition have been urged, particularly by certain enthusiasts in Europe. Socialism, rejecting private ownership in favor of community control of capital and wealth, is contrary to human nature. Proposals to abolish the private ownership of land are a *"wild scheme of iniquity and folly."* (292) Man "is formed for individual self-care, self-support, self-reliance, self-direction. The desire for individual possession and the sense of individual rights are in every man strong, clear and irrepressible." (282) Sturtevant acknowledged that "Nature herself has provided a modification of this law" of individualism in the family." (283)

Government must be "just, equitable and enlightened," declared Sturtevant. (18) Agreeing with John Locke, he viewed the purpose of government as defending the peace and protecting the rights of the people, including of course their property. However, when the survival of the society is at stake, government can claim the property and personal service of every citizen. Other proper governmental functions include enforcement of contracts and debts, providing a sound monetary system, maintaining postal service, and constructing thoroughfares between communities. The laws prohibiting usury are proper but beyond that government should not interfere with the rates of interest. Government should educate all citizens in language and arithmetic because such skills are necessary for the economic system to function. A government representing Christian people must provide care for the unfortunate —the deaf and dumb, the blind, the feeble-minded, and the insane—although families which are affluent should pay for care given their members.[38] The most important of all governmental functions is to protect its citizens against the tyranny and injustice of government itself. Taxes represent the "wages" of government but too often they are excessive, especially on the municipal level. Justice demands that only those who pay taxes should vote on whether they should be collected and how they should be expended.

In his *Economics* Sturtevant again expressed his conviction that woman's proper role is to be homemaker and mother. He also reiterated his view that the Indians had no title to the land because they did not labor to improve it. "A higher law" predestined the land of America to belong to a civilized humanity, and the Indians should have been encouraged to forsake their savage life and "accept the blessings of civilization." (198,199)

Malthus had indeed made economics a melancholy subject by advancing his thesis that population outstrips the capability for providing subsistence. What he did not realize is that the law of competition ensures that the soundest and healthiest people will produce the succeeding generations. Sturtevant acknowledged that his argument was similar to Darwin's concepts but pointed out that his views were published before he knew of Darwin. (272)

Christianity and humanitarian impulses agree that help is due those who are incapacitated, but the terrors of poverty must never be removed. It is better that some should perish of want than to allow a cancer like England's poor laws to be established in America. *"Still the ear of humanity cannot be entirely deaf to the cry of suffering, perishing poverty."* (316-17) Certain guidelines must be followed: aid should be provided only at designated places, never at the homes; and the able-bodied must work for their food, any products being sold at fair market prices. The claim that the government should provide work and wages to the unemployed is "the most radical and the most subversive of all social order of any of the wild schemes of the [socialist] sect." (294) Men obviously living in self-indulgence which will bring themselves and their families into a state of want are to be arrested and placed under reformatory influences. Such persons, among them inebriates and the indolent, are never to be regarded as mere victims. In instances in which government has tolerated the sale of harmful substances, the government must accept responsibility for the care of the widows and orphans.

Among the many institutions and public graces which cannot be supplied by government are libraries, colleges, universities, and monuments to the achievements of honored men. Of these, only the educational institutions make a contribution to a prosperous economy because an intelligent citizenry is essential to success. The resources for all these institutions must be provided by men of means, who are obligated to lead constructive lives and to contribute leadership as well as wealth to the society.

Sturtevant believed that it is God's purpose that all people should share in the good life. That does not mean equality; the differences among people in their natural capabilities, their moral fiber, and of course their circumstances preclude that. The human self is complex and includes not only physical but social, moral, aesthetic, and intellectual dimensions which need cultivation and expression. All persons should have more than a subsistence standard of living; to be fully human means the ability to have comforts and conveniences and to participate in the higher culture. God's beneficent design is intended to produce that result, and Sturtevant regarded society as capable of "limitless progress" although change should be made conservatively. (19) America more fully corresponds to the ideal society than any other country, offering unequaled opportunities for gaining wealth—and expending it. The world will be blessed by the spread of that [Protestant] Christian culture which has achieved so much in America and holds promise of greater success.

Sense-Perception and Knowledge

Deriving his basic understanding from John Locke's writings, Sturtevant prepared a monograph on sense-perception.[39] His purpose was to explain how knowledge is obtained with the aid of the senses. He believed that reliable knowledge of the soul [self] and of the external world can be attained—always subject to further inquiry.[40] The fundamental principle is that "every man consciously possesses the power to know, to feel and to choose. The human soul is that entity to which these powers belong.... It is equally unquestionable, that, at the beginning of human life, we are in the profoundest ignorance of everything." (1)

Certain intuited understandings spring up in each mind through experience, and other selves have similar experiences from which arise those same ideas. Consequently people can agree upon a word which will express that understanding. An example is *consciousness,* "the knowledge or the power of knowing one's own mental states and activities." (2) In the conscious experience of joy and sorrow, desire and gratification and purpose, we come to know our own individual existence. Perhaps the most important question is how the self makes the transition from self-knowledge to knowledge of the external universe. The senses are the link. Sturtevant provided sufficient detail about the eye and ear to demonstrate his familiarity with their structure and functioning. He gave briefer attention to taste and smell but did not consider touch as a special sense because it has no specific organ. Sex should also be ranked as a special sense but because it provides little knowledge of the external world and because of "the indelicacy of the subject," Sturtevant omitted it. (6,7)

Sight is the chief means for extending our knowledge of the external world, and Sturtevant drew upon his understanding of physics in analyzing the process by which light rays produce inverted images on the retina. Sight also provides us with "the power of reading at a glance the minds, hearts and characters of our fellow-men." (40) Hearing provides certain data which no other sense can and thus enlarges still more our knowledge of the external world. Sturtevant noted that early deafness makes it impossible for certain persons ever to acquire the power of speech; he was of course familiar with the state school for the deaf a few blocks from the Illinois College campus. The ear also gives "knowledge of the feelings, intentions and characters of our fellow-men by direct intimation." (46) Sensations have a double function, to provide the data for perception and "to impart to the soul a high and peculiar delight" (21) which encompasses both esthetic pleasure and intellectual enjoyment.

The senses of smell and taste rely on organs which are subject to severe limitations. They serve important functions with regard to the selection of food but also provide "superadded" and exquisite pleasures. All creatures participate in sensual enjoyment, which is closely connected with taste and smell and sex. Esthetic appreciation is a characteristic of the human mind and is enhanced by "the eye and the ear, as instruments of the culture and elevation of the human soul." (54) Man has a rational and moral nature, to which all the senses should be kept subject, and great ruin results when a man fails to control the lower senses and indulges them. (54-55) "[T]he rational nature of man separates him from all the irrational creatures that surround him...." (55) "Any account of the origin of man which does not recognize this broad distinction between human and brute life cannot be true." (57)

Sturtevant frequently referred to the esthetic dimensions of human life. He declared that "there is in the human soul a natural capability of discerning in the universe that mysterious, undefined and undefinable quality which we call beauty. It is undefinable just as color is undefinable. It can be known only by experience.... To discern this quality and to present it to the mind as one of the most fertile and elevating sources of human happiness is the esthetic function of sensation." (57-58) This quality is present in the infant but reaches its height when cultivated by the highest intellectual endeavor.

Sturtevant concluded that "no one sense is of itself adequate to any perception. Every possible case of sense-perception is a case of cooperation either of one sense with another, or of a sense with some form of muscular sensibility." (61) An important example is oral and written language, which depends upon the cooperation of sight and hearing with each other and with muscular sensibility. In a remarkable manner, language conveys meaning from one rational soul to another with great rapidity. The signs which the mind designs for these meanings can be preserved and transmitted to later generations. The mind is also capable of inventing instruments which can transmit those meanings over great distances. Sturtevant commented on the superiority of the English language which requires only a modest number of signs for writing in contrast to the huge number needed in Chinese. Another example of the relationship of the senses to each other and to muscular sensibility is seen in music. Music is independent of the sense of sight but highly dependent on muscular sensibility to produce and distinguish the varieties of pitch. The blind can participate in music and can read music written in raised letters. Here too Sturtevant could draw upon the presence in Jacksonville of a state institution, the school for the blind, for such insights.

The soul is active rather than passive in the experience of sense-perception, as seen in the frequent cases in which a person fails to be attentive and thus learns nothing from a sensation which has impinged upon one of his senses. "We perceive what we attend to and that which we do not attend to we do not perceive." (69) Sturtevant described two men who journey together. "[O]ne returns with a mind stored with a knowledge of innumerable objects of interest of which the other has learned nothing at all. To one mind the universe, nature, society, history—all things are full of lessons of wisdom. To another mind…the whole scene around him is a blank…." (70) Self-consciously or not, Sturtevant had described his own life-long curiosity in characterizing the person with the active mind.

Chapter 11: 1886

Celebrations, Memories, and the Close of Life

Reminiscences and Final Retirement

The summer heat in Jacksonville was debilitating for Sturtevant and during his late years he and Hannah spent most of the season in the more comfortable climate of New England. Residence in New Haven provided access to library resources, and with Hannah as his amanuensis he prepared his books on economics and the church, capping his life-long ambition for authorship. The elder son said that his father "never lost his early affection for Yale, and highly esteemed every opportunity of friendly intercourse with its president and professors. His eastern relatives and friends always gave him a cordial welcome, and his love for them was unabated to the end." (A, 333)

The Sturtevants' visits to Connecticut and Ohio continued as late as 1883 and 1884, with a final trip to Ohio in 1885. In 1883 Julian participated in the sesquicentennial observance of the Congregational Church of New Canaan; it was a congregation he loved deeply and, of course, it was Hannah's home church. In his "Address" Sturtevant recalled the building in use when he first attended services there. It was "plain and unpretending...and how dreary and uncomfortable in those cold winter days." (82) Yet the glory of God was displayed there in the worshipping congregation. The people of New England had developed "a closely woven network of just such institutions," constituting an "efficacious and adequate provision...for the religious instruction and edification of an entire population," eventually reaching over much of the earth. Many of those mother churches remained vigorous despite having sent two and three times their numbers as emigrants to the regions stretching to the Pacific.

Sturtevant emphasized that the permanency of the Christian Church depended upon the people's fidelity to Christ. He acknowledged that he was not the old church's son but he was her son-in-law, and he declared his faithfulness to her. He remembered the great revivals of 1826 and 1827 and the prayer meetings and the Sabbath gatherings. He remembered too that it was here where he first breathed "into woman's ear the sweet tale of love" and where he first received "the smile of woman's love in return." He was bound to this place by "all the holy and tender ties." (87)

In 1884 the Sturtevants visited Mrs. Theron Baldwin in Vermont and relatives and friends in Connecticut. Revisiting his childhood home at Warren, Sturtevant wrote about the changes which had occurred since the family left in 1817. Now all that remained of that cherished boyhood home was a chimney, and except for a row of currant bushes still bearing fruit, the old farm was barren. The desolation was everywhere; thousands of acres were forsaken by farmers who had moved to the cheaper lands of the West. Much of the present population was foreign born and Catholic in religion, but remarkably the social, educational, and religious institutions of the region had not been destroyed. Indeed, the schools of Warren were even better and provided education not only for the remaining descendants of the original settlers but also for the children of the foreigners. The Congregational Church was still thriving, its vitality unimpaired. The emigrant children of those New England fathers "have aided in founding Protestant Christian institutions across the whole continent to the shores of the Pacific." There was no reason to fear the presence of foreigners in New England.

Health-related problems afflicted Sturtevant in his last years. On 13 August 1884 Sturtevant fell on a rock while visiting in Connecticut and suffered a severe fracture of his hip. It was feared that he would never walk again. Delayed by his injury, the Sturtevants returned home in October and fortunately, after some weeks, Julian was able to walk with the aid of a cane. Both the *Rambler* and the *Jacksonville Journal* gave notice of his illnesses and absences from the classroom. The student newspaper expressed its regret in April 1883 that Dr. Sturtevant was confined to his room and noted that he had been in feeble health all winter.

The next February Sturtevant was severely ill and his elder son feared one night that his father would not survive. But his father was not ready to yield up his spirit and while on his sick-bed he insisted on discussing public issues. A few days later he dictated his article on private ownership of land. More than once Sturtevant had recovered from illnesses and injuries but they had weakened him, and he now made arrangements to resign from all College duties effective 1 June 1885. Although he stated that he severed all formal ties with the College, the trustees adopted a resolution to employ him for one recitation daily at a salary of $500. They may have felt it necessary to justify the allocation of scarce funds by keeping him on the faculty in a nominal role. The *Rambler* reported simply that "Dr. Sturtevant has retired from college duties." (17 Oct. 1885, 67)

The Sturtevants remained in Jacksonville in the early summer of 1885. On 26 July Julian matched the biblical maximum of four-score years. Friends arranged a surprise party and relatives and neighbors came to the home. (JJ, 28 July 1885) At the festive gathering he was presented with "a willow chair, roll style, with cushion on back and seat covered with silk plush." Professor Rufus Crampton gave a moving speech,[1] declaring that it was apparent to all that Sturtevant had borne the chief responsibility for Christian education at Illinois College. Moreover he had always been a leader in the discussion of public questions—political, economic, social, and moral. He had been in advance of his age in seeking greater religious liberty, and similarly he had been in the forefront of the cause of Christian unity, now professed by all Protestant denominations. High among the achievements to his credit was the graduation of fifty classes from the College he helped to found. As students those men had felt the influence of his "quickening thought, elevating character, [and] widening mental and moral vision...." They had gone out from the College and had become "leaders of society, Church and State in this great valley of the West."

More than any one else connected with Illinois College, Crampton declared, Sturtevant was the leading figure in establishing

Christian culture in Illinois. Crampton spoke also of the Christian home which Sturtevant had established with the aid and affection of a devoted wife, and he mentioned the children and grandchildren "whose younger lives have become a part of your own."

J. B. Turner spoke feelingly of the many years he had spent in the company of Dr. Sturtevant. Congratulatory messages from friends who could not be present were read aloud; among them was an overseas cable from E. W. Blatchford. Truman Post, in a lengthy and effusive letter, praised Sturtevant's great achievements as an educator and evangelist in "*the rising new world of the West.*" A frank reference to his friend's controversial temperament was softened by acknowledging that Sturtevant had mellowed in his later years. "If there seems less of the warrior armed for fight, less of the vehemence of the Iconoclast,...less of Pilgrim battling with Apolyons in the valley of the shadow of death, there is more of the Christian in the quiet shades and soft sweet airs of Beulah.... [I]f *such* is the order of change, we feel it is well; it is in the way of *nearer* approach to the city of light."

Sturtevant's wit was still keen. He said he felt like remaining silent lest he undo some of the favorable impressions that had been made. Parrying the thrust by Post he declared, "My life has been one of considerable conflict. No man can be faithful to his duty and true to his honest, intelligent convictions without numerous conflicts." Noting that most of those who had begun the journey with him were no longer living, he declared that all of them would "enjoy the sympathy of Him who came to seek and save that which was lost." Despite his many failures, "which my friends are too kind to see or too good to mention," he had a clear conscience and he expressed the wish that all those present might, in their closing years, "be surrounded with like sympathy and love."

Sturtevant wrote to Mrs. Baldwin informing her that "The contract into which I entered with my brethren of the 'Illinois Association' in February, 1829 was finally terminated on the 1st. [*sic*] of June, 1885, having controlled the greater part of the activity of my life through more than fifty-six years." He had depended very greatly on her husband's cooperation and praised his wisdom, his helpfulness in times of difficulty (which had been frequent), and his unselfish friendship. He assured Mrs. Baldwin that he himself was still vigorous both in mind and body and had some work yet to do for the Master. "The themes to which I have devoted my attention for so many years, religious, ecclesiastical and social, were never more interesting to me than to-day." Sturtevant expressed his regret that Congregationalism still had not become aware of its own strength and of the function which God intended it to fulfill. He believed it to be "God's own instrumentality for breaking all the bands of sect and fusing the whole Christian brotherhood into that spiritual kingdom which the Son of Man came to establish." Declaring that "God will be with you to the end," he signed the letter, "Yours very affectionately, J. M. Sturtevant." (A, 338-39)

After a few days of rest the Sturtevants journeyed to Cleveland to visit their elder son, who had recently begun his pastorate at the Jennings Avenue Congregational Church (later known as the Pilgrim Church). Father and son engaged in long conversations in which the senior Sturtevant told many stories of the past. They also spoke freely of the country which they loved so much and of the even dearer church of God. Julian Jr. thought that his father's continuing keen interest in all living questions and his conviction that all problems would ultimately be resolved seemed to be a promise of immortality.

Sturtevant now revisited another of his several homes, the place he had helped his father and older brother hew out of the Ohio wilderness. His son described the nostalgic visit.

> We went to Tallmadge, where he had such a welcome from old friends as warmed his heart. We visited the now deserted site of the first cabin and saw the chestnut rails "his feeble strokes" had helped to split in 181[7]. We followed the course of an old road where his parents were once lost. We worshiped in the ancient church....We stood by the graves of his parents while he gave orders for a simple headstone to mark the spot. Every memory seemed beautiful and precious. He was living his life over again, and every scene was touched with the glory of gratitude and the brightness of hope. (A, 340)

While in Cleveland Sturtevant preached several times, with all the vigor of his earlier years. His son preserved the outline his father had prepared for the last sermon. The texts from Luke 18:22 and 19:8,9 revealed that Jesus, like a true physician, treated each case individually. The young ruler was instructed to sell all he had and give his money to the poor, while Zacchaeus was praised for proposing to give half of his possessions to the poor and to restore fourfold anything he had obtained by fraud. In both instances the Lord expected total consecration, which indeed he expects of all. The final point noted "The blessedness which will follow now and forever from this consecration." (A, 341)

One Monday Julian Jr. invited about twenty Congregational ministers to meet with his father to discuss the problem of sectarianism and his view that Congregationalism represented the solution. The ensuing lively discussion was one of the factors which stimulated Julian Sr. to prepare his *Autobiography*.

The Sturtevants returned to Jacksonville in late September (1885) and on 9 October he began the first draft of his *Autobiography*, continuing after a very long interval a task he had begun years before. Now with the aid of his wife and his son-in-law, James Palmer, he worked steadily. He had seemed stronger than usual and dictated what proved to be his final chapter on 4 January 1886. His work was interrupted permanently by the illness of other members of the family, leaving the rest of the story to be told, all too briefly, by his elder son.

In these later years the house at 252 Park was home for three generations: Julian and Hannah; their three children, Elizabeth, Lucy, and Alfred; Alfred's wife Harriet; and the children of Alfred and Harriet. Mary Jane Fayerweather was still a part of the household. The 1880 census report listed a female servant, L. Talkemeyer[?], born in Westphalia and 21 years old, and recently employed in the household. A hired girl named Ellen was also present. Considering the numerous permanent residents and the prospect of additional grandchildren, it is not surprising that in the spring of 1884 "Dr. Sturtevant [added] several rooms to his residence on College Hill." (JJ, 15 Apr. 1984) By 1884 four youngsters had been born to Alfred and Harriet: Edgar in 1875; Helen, two years later; Charles in 1879; and Julian Monson in 1882. Their family would continue to increase: Bradford was born in 1885, and Alfred in 1891.

The house on Park Street had been the Sturtevants' home for more than thirty years. It was convenient to the College for the elder Sturtevant during the many years he trod his straight path to his office in the Chapel and also for Alfred as student and teacher. The house frequently provided hospitality for relatives and friends and was the site for College functions.

Amy, the surviving child of Julian Jr. and Katie, was joined by brother Hayward in 1878 and by sister Faith in 1883. Julian Jr., sometimes accompanied by his family, visited his parents. Whenever possible he scheduled his trips to coincide with commencement. At the "Fiftieth Commencement" in 1879 he was awarded the honorary D.D. degree.

Only Julian Jr. had permanently left Jacksonville. Hannah Sturtevant Palmer and her family lived next door (at 1042 Grove) for about ten years. The two unmarried daughters, Elizabeth and Lucy, lived with their parents during most of their lives. Lucy was with her parents one summer in Greenwich and was in Olathe, Kansas, perhaps for an extended period.[2] Her father in a typewritten letter to her in February 1883 admitted that there were typing errors but he believed she could make it all out. The weather, he wrote, was "the most remarkable storm of ice and sleet I ever saw." Melting snow, rain, and then freezing temperatures had covered the ground with several inches of almost solid ice. The boys had fine skating anywhere on the College grounds. No street cars or trains could run, and there was no mail service or telegraph. The family had only a limited supply of wood but had plenty of coal and coke if needed. The temperature was a minus 8 degrees that morning, and yet the sun was shining brightly. "[A]ll around is a scene of gorgeous magnificence never equaled in my former experience. Every twig on the trees is a diamond."

His own health was about as usual, Sturtevant informed Lucy, but he had suffered much from catarrh and did not intend to expose himself until mild weather returned. He had preached regularly at the College Chapel except for one Sabbath but had not dared to venture out to church for nearly two months because of the cold and the uncertain heating system. Like a student, Sturtevant measured the time until his next long vacation; it was only one or two days more than six weeks until he could be free. He would like to go to some quiet place for the summer, but "Mr. Palmer" was in financial difficulty. Sturtevant was paying two of his grandsons $1.50 per week for their work around the place. He thought perhaps he himself must stay home and save all he could. He asked Lucy whether she had received the book on political economy which the publisher was to send her. He enclosed a draft for $17, her "dividend" for last November.

Alfred had combined responsibilities at Illinois College and Whipple Academy for thirteen years. The student newspaper alluded to the birth of a son to Alfred and his wife when it reported that, in celebration of a happy event, he had marked "10" (the highest grade) for all the boys. (20 May 1882, 53) In 1883 Alfred resigned his position to engage in full-time farming.

Julian Sturtevant's cousin, Edward A. Tanner, Professor of Latin since 1865, assumed the office of president in 1882. Although he sometimes met Sturtevant's classes when illness required, Tanner was not named Professor of Intellectual and Moral Philosophy and of Natural Theology and Evidences of Christianity until 1886. Those titles had belonged to Sturtevant who continued, so long as he was able, to teach the courses generally expected of the College's president.

After being relieved of the heavy responsibilities of the presidency, Sturtevant had time to engage in business affairs. In 1877 he purchased Turner's interest in ten acres in the northwest quarter of Section 29, south of Morton and east of Lincoln. Two years later he made the highest bid at an auction and obtained seven and a half acres in the same area for the princely sum of $1,098 or approximately $140 per acre. In March of 1880 he purchased ninety-one acres in Section 30, south of Morton and east of Massey Lane, for $6,374 ($70 per acre). Two days later Sturtevant bought another tract to the south for $1,300; he was required to grant a perpetual right of way for horsemen, footmen, livestock, and vehicles of all kinds along a designated strip. In the fall of 1883 Sturtevant joined with Alfred in buying a plot west of Lincoln; a month later he bought Alfred's interest. The Sturtevants sold part of lot 31 in the city for $850 in 1879. They also sold the west half of lots 53 and 54 to William A. Kirby in 1882.

The task of tracing Sturtevant's land transactions is difficult because of the often vague descriptions of smaller plots in the area south of Morton Avenue. Joint ownership of some lots and acreage, fluctuations in land values, and inflation confound the effort to determine whether Sturtevant made or lost money in his real estate dealings. In the earlier years the Sturtevants suffered much economic hardship, but in their later years they were able to travel and even to reside in the East for extended periods. After the Sturtevants died, the family continued to own some of the lands for several years.

In April 1882 Julian Sturtevant sent a letter to Yale to report the death of his brother Ephraim on 12 December 1881.[3] Ephraim, after a decade in Florida, returned to Ohio in 1880 to live with his daughter in Cleveland. Julian noted that his brother died "a true patriot and an earnest Christian." His other brother, Christopher, and his family had lived in Minneapolis since 1873. After some years as Secretary of the Minneapolis Board of Trade and commercial editor for the *Minneapolis Tribune* and the *St. Paul Pioneer Press*, Christopher became Secretary of the Chamber of Commerce. He was pleased to tell Julian that his new position paid a much better salary. Christopher wrote nearly a dozen letters to Julian between January 1880 and January 1886. He described his own activities, reported on family health, and exclaimed about the amazing growth of Minneapolis and the Northwest. He commented at length about Plymouth Congregational Church in that city, with details not always flattering to the congregation or pastor. Upon learning of Ephraim's death, Christopher reminisced.

> Memories of the past Crowd on me…. The Trials and Sorrows of our Mother, her Self-Sacrificing Spirit the day when you two left us for College. The old horse & waggon [*sic*] that was to convey you far away and the anxiety of Mother all during those years you spent at Yale. [H]ow impatient at the delay of those mails only once a week and how hard it was sometimes to raise the 25c for postage. Stil [*sic*] I never heard our Mother complain. I shall never forget her joy when you graduate[d]…. (16 Dec. 1881)

In early January 1886 Christopher wrote promptly to reply to Julian's first message in a long time. He himself thought that because of Julian's long service to Illinois College his salary should be lifelong; "I look on it as base ingratitude that it is not." Julian, he knew, would be glad to learn that there were fifteen Congregational churches in Minneapolis, compared with three or four in 1873. He urged Julian to bring Hannah aboard a river boat at St. Louis or Quincy and travel to Minneapolis. His letter ended, "Enough. Good bye. All unite in love to yourself and family, Your aff. Brother, C. C. Sturtevant." Unhappily, it was indeed, "Good bye." Five weeks later Julian died.

James, the only Fayerweather brother to survive past 1850, died in Burlington, Iowa, in 1877. The Fayerweather sisters, other than Elizabeth, all lived to a ripe age. Mary Jane was a long-term member of the Sturtevant household and was noted as a gardener; she had brought the first "greenhouse plants" to Jacksonville and shared slips from them with many others. (Eames, 240) Her loan of $1,000 to Illinois College was repaid in 1882. Sister Julia, widowed, moved to her daughter's home in the city.

E. W. Blatchford kept in touch with his Jacksonville friends. When both Sturtevant and Tanner made appeals on behalf of the College in 1883, he subscribed $1,000. When traveling in Italy he wrote, "How well I remember the interest that attached to your letters when you made that journey [to England] of more import than perhaps you thought." Responding to a different kind of appeal from Sturtevant, he offered Mr. Palmer temporary employment in accounting for a salary of $75 to $100 per month and asked, "Would this be of aid to Mr. Palmer?" (26 Dec. 1885)

The Deaths of Hannah and Julian Sturtevant

James Palmer, gravely ill, had returned from Chicago in early January 1886, and both Hannah and Julian did all they could to assist in caring for him. Hannah herself became desperately ill from exposure as she went back and forth to the Palmers' house next door, and Julian despaired of her recovery. Having urged her daughters to look after their father, Hannah died on 17 January. Julian was devastated and did not think he could live without her. He had grieved deeply over the death of his first wife and was surprised to find that Hannah's loss affected him even more. She had been his devoted wife for nearly forty-five years and was the mother of their five children and step-mother to Elizabeth's children. She was her husband's adviser and aided him in his literary efforts. She sought constantly to guard him from the excessive demands of his College duties. Julian described Hannah's last days in a two-

page typewritten letter to his wife's cousin in the East. Hannah
had repeated verses from the 23rd Psalm, and when Julian asked
if she wanted him to say a prayer, she replied affirmatively. About
seven o'clock on Sunday morning her life ended and she was
released from her agony. Julian told Laura that "Hannah is sainted
now, and she joined the sainted Elizabeth." His letter ended,
"Your heart-broken cousin, J. M. Sturtevant." (to Laura Mead, 18
Jan. 1886)

The funeral was on 19 January at the family home, with Rev.
H. E. Butler, minister of the Congregational Church, officiating.
A quartet of two men from the College and two ladies provided
the music and some hymns were sung. As Julian stood beside his
wife's coffin, he remarked that "this dear hand has written almost
all that I have published about the Church." (A, 345) The procession of mourners left the home led by students from the College
who formed a double file of march until they reached Lincoln
Avenue. They then separated into two lines and the carriage with
Julian Sturtevant passed between them. Graveside rites at Diamond
Grove Cemetery were simple. (JJ, 20 Jan. 1886)

Julian Jr. characterized his step-mother as a woman of "sincerity, good judgment and self-control" who had managed a large
household with a limited income and moreover had taught the
children Latin and mathematics. "For forty-five years father and
my own mother's sister lived happily together" and indeed, he
declared, "few marriages are happier or more beneficent." (JMSJR,
15) Both Jacksonville newspapers printed long obituaries which
were full of praise for Hannah's sweet disposition, her devotion as
a wife and mother, her active role in the church and social and
charitable responsibilities, and her kindness to all. The *Rambler*
praised Mrs. Sturtevant and said that Dr. Sturtevant's grateful
acknowledgment of their presence at her funeral made them "the
more thankful that the tribute was paid."[4]

Only two members of her own family survived Hannah
Fayerweather Sturtevant. Mary Jane died on 3 April 1887 and
Julia, the last survivor of that generation of the Jacksonville
Fayerweathers and Sturtevants, died on 22 June 1888.

Julian sought diversion by writing on subjects other than his life
story. When entertaining visitors he was cheerful, and he enjoyed

listening when the family read to him from the *Life of Samuel Johnson*. He continued to conduct family prayers and on 28 January he presided at the Day of Prayer for Colleges. Julian Jr. recalled a conversation about the assaults of unbelief. "A strange light seemed to flash in father's still brilliant eyes and, speaking almost with his old ringing tones, he said: 'Do not be afraid, my son. They cannot take Jesus Christ away from us and nothing indispensable is lost while He remains.'" Father then quoted the words of Jesus: "'In my Father's house are many mansions.... I go to prepare a place for you...that where I am there ye may be also.'" (JMSJR, 114)

The Day of Prayer, an annual observance, was the occasion of Sturtevant's last appearance on the campus. The Y.M.C.A. room was crowded by "those who wished to listen once more to the kindly voice of Dr. Sturtevant. A suitable subject was chosen, and its lessons strongly impressed by the ringing words of the venerable doctor, whose words were given additional power by his evident proximity to the other shore." This comment in the *Rambler* for 6 February 1886 (125) was prophetic.

Unfortunately James Palmer died on 1 February, bringing further grief to all the family and another shock to Julian Sr. The funeral was at the Sturtevant home the next day. On Sunday, 7 February, the weather was cold but Julian attended church and delivered the meditation at the communion service. He seemed very frail and yet was bright and full of courage; his message was that the primary duty in life is to hold Christ up for men. But his strength was now ebbing and when he developed a cold he sensed that it was the beginning of the end. On Wednesday evening those who were at home were with him in his bedroom. Someone read the 23rd Psalm and Alfred offered a prayer. Julian repeated the phrase "Thy rod and thy staff" and declared, "O my son, you have no idea of the prostration of dying." About dawn on Thursday, 11 February, his appearance suddenly changed and he died. "It seems wonderful," wrote Julian Jr., "that a form so slight and a constitution seemingly so delicate could have endured eighty years of almost constant activity." (A, 346)

Eulogies and Memorials

A local paper announced Sturtevant's death with a simple testimony to his character: "A Good Man Gone." (JJ, 12 Feb. 1886) A confident subheading declared, "Rev. J. M. Sturtevant, D.D., Ends His Useful Life on Earth to Continue It in Heaven." Sturtevant's wise counsel in both ecclesiastical and civil affairs was mentioned, as well as his exemplary family life. His role in Illinois College was emphasized: "He was almost passionately devoted to the institution with which he was connected and gave to it, for small compensation, the services of a lifetime.... Though so eminent in his attainments he was peculiarly free from vanity and always exercised toward all he met the utmost kindness and consideration." The Jacksonville Ministers' Association adopted a resolution praising Sturtevant for his "rare ability and power as a preacher of the gospel," his scholarship and service to Christian education, "his fearless and patriotic course as a citizen," and "the tenderness, purity and nobility of his private life." (JJ, 13 Feb. 1886)

The trustees adopted a resolution gratefully acknowledging Sturtevant's "singular devotion to the interests of this institution for almost three score years.... His love of truth and his fidelity to his convictions, have always commanded our admiration." The faculty witnessed to "Dr. Sturtevant's wisdom in council, vigor in administration, power in the Class room, and eloquence in the pulpit." The two groups united in their "high appreciation of the intellectual endowments, the enthusiastic spirit and the inflexible Christian character of the departed. His beneficent career has gladdened liberal learning and the Redeemer's Kingdom." Their sympathy was extended to the mourning family. (TM, 13 Feb. 1886)

The funeral service was arranged for 2:00 P.M. Sunday at the Congregational Church. About 1:00 the faculty, students, and alumni of the College gathered at the Sturtevant residence and the solemn procession escorted the remains down College Avenue. The church bell tolled and the organist played a funeral march. Accompanying the casket were six clergymen who had a role in the service. They were followed by other clergy from the community, the faculty and trustees, the family and friends, and the alumni and students. A funeral chant, "Blessed are the Dead who die in the Lord," was sung by a quartet, and a portion of 1 Corinthians 15 was read. Following a prayer the choir sang Sturtevant's favorite hymn, "I love thy Kingdom, Lord." Rev. Butler in the principal discourse depicted Sturtevant as a scholar who was not a recluse but one who "took a lively interest in men and business all about him." He had sought to uplift his fellow men through his efforts and through proclaiming the great truth of Christ redeeming the lost. (JC, 15 Feb.; JJ, 16 Feb, 1886)

On behalf of his colleagues, Professor Rufus Crampton, the senior faculty member, gave the eulogy. (ICCR, 13 Mar. 1886, 3-5) He declared that "Illinois College mourns the loss of one who has been to her what no other man has been [or] ever can be...." No other member of the Yale association had borne so large a share of their great work as Sturtevant. Along with his duties as President and as Professor of Mental and Political Science, for many years he instructed the seniors in "Moral Science, Political Economy, Evidences of Christianity, History and Logic.... For fifty years 'his energy and enthusiasm were the nerve and heart-beat of the College enterprise'" and under his leadership the College survived a series of financial threats and other difficulties. Throughout "he lived with unflinching adherence to truth and freedom, with the same fidelity to his convictions of duty. We have long since come out into a larger liberty, and even before his departure he had his reward."

In his relations with the faculty, Crampton remarked, Sturtevant was kind, appreciative, and considerate, regarding himself as first among equals rather than as their superior. He described Sturtevant's leadership in the College in detail:

By the exalted standard he held up before us, he stimulated each instructor to excellence in his own department. By his comprehensive views of truth, by his high conception of what the College should be, of what it should do for Christian culture, he spurred on our sometimes lagging faith and zeal, and made us feel that it was a high privilege to work with such a leader. If disagreements arose, he always tried to meet them in a spirit of justice and Christian charity....

As instructor in the broad fields of Moral, Mental, Political and Economic Sciences, he had no superiors and few equals. His clear perception, keen logic, his vast appreciation of the common sense of things, his varied research and learning gave a mighty impulse to every Senior class that came to his room. Above all did his pupils feel the tremendous uplift of his *enthusiasm for truth*. Under his teaching they were led to loftier views of citizenship, of moral responsibility, of Christian manhood. Few ever closed a year under his instruction without at least saying: 'Almost thou persuadest me to be a Christian.'

Crampton noted that Sturtevant's "College work was never merely intellectual, but devoted to Christ" and that his religious fervor was evident in the Sabbath afternoon lectures, which faculty as well as students attended. Indeed, his presentation of the salvation of men through the Gospel was overpowering.

Crampton quoted the passage from Exodus 33:15 which was later inscribed on the tablet honoring Sturtevant: "If the Lord go not with us, carry us not up hence." That had been Sturtevant's constant prayer and indeed the Lord had been with him to uplift and save thousands. Crampton quoted also the final paragraph of Sturtevant's address at the semi-centennial anniversary in 1879, that the College was to be Christian, not sectarian, and dedicated to religion, humanity, liberty, and *civilization*. The intention was "to build on the foundation of the apostles and prophets, Jesus the Christ Himself being the chief corner stone." Crampton's final words were a benediction: "President Sturtevant has fallen asleep. His lifework is nobly done. God help us that each may do his whole duty in the cause he loved so well."

The eloquent Rev. Truman Post declared that "as long as the college exists he will be remembered. His works will live in the church he loved so much and served so faithfully." Other ministers also spoke in praise of the man who ranked among the very best, and then the choir sang "Nearer My God to Thee." After the benediction, the organist played the "Dead March" from Handel's *Saul* and the people left the church to accompany the hearse to Diamond Grove Cemetery. Sturtevant's body was interred in a grave adjacent to the one where Hannah had so recently been buried. The monument at Sturtevant's grave, erected in April 1889, was described as "a large massive block of finely polished Quincy granite in the sarcophagus form."5

Rev. Butler prepared a carefully-written report on Sturtevant's death and funeral and a commentary on the significance of his long service to education and religion in Illinois.[6] The *Rambler* also provided a detailed report. An editorial opined that if Washington is the father of his country, Julian M. Sturtevant, "in a fuller sense of the word," is the father of Illinois College. "The present undergraduates can only testify to his power and ability in the pulpit, but their frequent praises evince a respect and love for him that is hardly less than that of the Alumni, who were his pupils and who so frequently refer to his instruction as the most valuable and memorable part of their college course." Students representing the four College classes and the Academy prepared a resolution which the *Rambler* printed along with a detailed account of the students' participation in the final rites and their "final look on the face of the dead." (20 Feb., 129-30, 133-34, 136)

Words of praise came from many sources. The *Congregationalist* (25 Feb.) notified its readers of Sturtevant's death, declaring that "few men in our American Congregational history, from the first, have with finer prophetic vision apprehended the meaning and the emergencies of their own day and generation...." The 1887 *Congregational Year-Book* entered an official notice in the denomination's Necrology with the publication of an obituary outlining Sturtevant's career and listing nineteen articles and books which he had written. The *New York Times* noted that Sturtevant had joined "the famous 'Yale Band'" and that "he had a national reputation in ecclesiastical circles, and was frequently tendered positions of great honor at prominent gatherings."[7]

Rev. Joseph E. Roy, an early home missionary in Illinois, acknowledged Sturtevant's crucial role in the very existence of Illinois College: "Men die, but institutions live, and blessed is the man whose life abides in an institution."[8] George F. Magoun, first president of Iowa College and the biographer of Asa Turner, characterized Sturtevant as a man with a strong and analytical mind and as argumentative in discussion. He was a vigorous preacher and debater and a superior teacher. Sturtevant, he wrote, "in fifty-six years of self-denying toil built his own monument."[9]

Rev. C. B. Barton ('36) shared some of his memories in a letter to the *Rambler*. Recalling the disorderly and sometimes violent behavior common in the early days, he said that Sturtevant had applied his untiring energy to build up the good and "to expose, resist and destroy" all that would undermine good government, morality, and the rights and interests of all. Barton vividly remembered Sturtevant's role in informing the public of the facts regarding the "peace society" meeting in 1833 and his eloquent plea on behalf of freedom of speech. (ICCR, 27 Mar. 1886, 28)

President Tanner, one of several to compare Sturtevant with Moses, also likened his "convictions of truth and duty" to "the consuming zeal of an Elijah." He recalled that Dr. Bacon had characterized him as "an antagonist squared for the encounter." Tanner mentioned the tenderness which complemented the logical and argumentative elements of Sturtevant's personality.[10] C. H. Dummer, Class of 1876, said that in contrast to Professor Adams, Sturtevant was not "calm and meditative" in spirit but "was of a different type. Living in an age of controversy he was by nature a controversialist. He was logic incarnate. He was a man of the strongest conceivable convictions. He was bold to speak the truth as he saw it, and one who in an earlier age would have gone to the stake rather than give up his opinions or deny them. He was an intellectual athlete and would handle any theme in which he was interested with...skill, directness and power...." (ICCR, 14 Apr. 1888, 29-30)

Rev. Robert W. Patterson ('37) published a remarkably positive tribute. One of Sturtevant's earliest and most persistent critics, he now spoke with warm praise for his one-time mentor and long-term antagonist. From the very first Sturtevant was "habitually sympathetic and kindly in his treatment of his pupils" and had given him encouragement when he was in great need of it. Sturtevant's influence upon his student was "peculiarly stimulating. His mind was remarkably active, and his utterances were forceful alike in the class-room and in public...." Sturtevant not only taught his students to think for themselves but felt "real pleasure in freedom of thought on the part of [his] pupils...." Indeed, Patterson wrote, "Dr. Sturtevant enjoyed the respectful boldness of a student who dared to controvert his declared views, and gave plausible reasons for his dissent."

Patterson declared that Sturtevant's "general position and influence through life were on the side of conservative progress both in religion and moral reforms." Opposed to slavery and the evils of alcohol, he was firm and outspoken in regard to principles but conservative in the measures he advocated for reform. In religion he believed in "the progressive knowledge of divine truth.... He had no sympathy with that kind of conservation which teaches that progress in theology was possible before the Westminster Assembly [1643-1649] but has been impossible ever since." He also rejected those who ignored the thinking of the past. Sturtevant's personal conduct was unblemished, avoiding even the appearance of evil. The foundation of his strong faith was that "he heartily accepted the written Word as the only and the sufficient rule of faith and practice."[11]

Frederic Dan Huntington, now an Episcopalian Bishop, was another former antagonist who gave generous praise. Learning of Sturtevant's death, Huntington characterized him as "that stalwart defender of gospel truth, and intelligent lover and expounder of the polity of the Pilgrims. Clear-headed, large-hearted, laborious, self-sacrificing, prayerful, with a prophet's vision of the future, patriotic and fatherly, how many young men has he trained for eminent usefulness in his almost threescore years' work in Illinois College."[12]

The Congregational Church of Jacksonville adopted a memorial resolution honoring the many who had served it but naming only one, Julian Sturtevant. "His character, his life and his teaching have left an indelible impress upon this community and all who came in contact with him. Profound in his convictions, high in his aims, single in purpose and unswerving in fidelity to Jesus Christ & his Kingdom, he fought life's battle bravely and well. With force unabated, with eye undimmed, and with armor on he reached the end." (CCM, 17 Mar. 1886)

The members of The Club expressed their regard for Sturtevant and the quality of his intellectual life. Due to "his long connection with the college and his numerous writings [he was] doubtless more widely known throughout this country and Europe than any other of our Jacksonville citizens." His name led the list of charter members and for more than three decades he was an active and faithful member. "He was a leader in nearly all our discussions;

always positive in his views and convictions, and earnest in their
presentation, but respectful of the opinions of others, and courteous
in debate; as a Neighbor and Friend, he was kind and social,
warmhearted and true; as a Man, he was a Christian gentleman,
upright, conscientious and devout." (Minutes, 22 Mar.)

A month after Sturtevant's death Professor H. W. Milligan
addressed an open letter in the *Rambler* to the College community.
He proposed that a tablet of white Vermont marble be inscribed
in commemoration of Dr. Sturtevant[13] and placed on the wall of
the Chapel back of the rostrum. A committee of students, chaired
by a senior, was appointed to solicit funds and suggestions.[14] The
tablet was duly installed and years later it was removed to the
Chapel-Auditorium in Jones Hall. Subsequent to the demolition
of that building in 1980 it and other tablets were mounted at the
broad landing on the lower level of Rammelkamp Chapel. The
lintel with the name of "The Jones Memorial" and decorative tiles
from that building were mounted as a partial frame.

The trustees in 1888 accepted President Tanner's recommendation to name the buildings on the campus in honor of appropriate
persons. The "old building, the first erected in the history of the
College, and known as the Library building," was thereafter to be
called Beecher Hall. The Chapel building, erected during the presidency of Dr. Sturtevant, was to be named Sturtevant Hall "in
memory of his life-long devotion to the College." Because
Professor Crampton was chiefly responsible for the construction
of the "Dormitory Building," it was to be called Crampton Hall.
(TM, 2 June 1888)

The Alumni Association unanimously adopted resolutions in
grateful memory of Sturtevant at the triennial meeting held on 13
June 1889. The language of praise was effusive: no one else was for
so long a "a vital part of our alma mater as Dr. Sturtevant.... He
opened up the minds of the youth of Illinois to higher education
[and he] witnessed the upgrowing of the state and grander development of the republic, both of which Mr. Sturtevant helped to
advance and maintain."[15]

The preparation of his father's *Autobiography* for publication

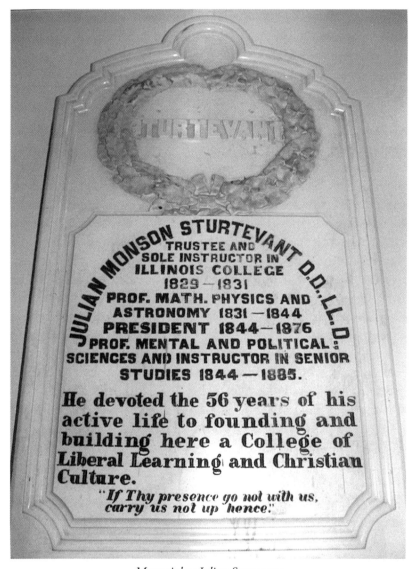

Memorial to Julian Sturtevant
First displayed in the College Chapel [Sturtevant Hall], then in Jones Chapel, it is now in
Rammelkamp Chapel.

represented a very special remembrance by Julian M. Sturtevant Jr.
The senior Sturtevant did not complete his life-story nor was he
able to revise the considerable amount which he had dictated. The
elder son carried out those tasks which, because of his meticulous
care in editing and his own poor health, took years to complete.

His procedure was to send sections of the work, as he completed them, to his sisters for their review and suggestions. The dictated material with which he worked has been preserved in the College's Archives along with some pages of corrected typescript.

The final chapter of the *Autobiography* is the summary which the son wrote to cover the last twenty-three years of his father's life. Although very condensed, the account includes anecdotes and comments with revealing insights into Sturtevant's inner character and his family life. The son reported that his father was very honest and feared both debt and the possibility that he would pay less than he should for some purchase. He was also absolutely fair; a man who had outraged Sturtevant's sense of justice was wrongly accused in a serious matter. Aware that the charge was unjust, he testified on behalf of the man.

Julian Sturtevant Jr., in his own autobiography, remarked about his father's "wonderful blue eyes" and declared that his "Father was naturally very intense." (42) He recalled vividly his father's remarkable earnestness arising from his deep Christian faith. "To me, in my childhood, that trait of his character seemed positively awful. I never knew anyone to whom duty seemed so sacred or the service of God so glorious and joyful a reality. He realized what so many of us try to feel that he and all that he had belonged to God." (A, 347)

* * * * * * *

Postscript

Sturtevant's Estate . . . The Next Generation

Julian Sturtevant planned early to provide for his family. He had signed his will on 18 January 1845, about four years after his marriage to Hannah. Each of his children living at the time of his death should receive five dollars when they attained the age of twenty-one or were married. His wife Hannah would have full power to sell or dispose of all real estate and personal property and to use the proceeds for her own support and for the education and support equally of all his children. If any property remained when she died it was to be divided equally among all his children.

Hannah was not to be required to make an inventory of his personal estate nor to give bond; however, if Hannah remarried her power of executrix would cease.

Julian Jr. as the elder son petitioned the court to appoint Alfred as the executor of their father's will. (Morgan County Will Book, File #2651) The required legal notices were published in the *Jacksonville Journal* and posted in six public places in Morgan County. At the time of his death Sturtevant possessed real and personal property, "all of said personal estate being estimated to be worth about four thousand Dollars." The 1870 census had reported the value of Sturtevant's real estate as $14,000 and his personal estate as $12,000; the 1880 census did not include comparable financial information. The tax receipts for 1877 indicated assessed valuations of real estate at $5,156 and personal property at $3,180; the total tax bill was for $364.32. The decrease in Sturtevant's assets may be explained in part by his reduced College income and the larger number in the household.

The most significant property was the house at 252 Park, the family's home for more than three decades. There were also several lots east of the campus, a large lot to the west, and some plots which the Sturtevants had owned jointly with the Fayerweathers. Various tracts were sold from time to time.

Following the deaths of the parents, Elizabeth, Lucy, and Alfred and his family continued to live at 252 Park. After James Palmer's death, his wife Hannah Augusta and the children also shared the family home. Hannah Augusta died five years later, on 13 May 1891, after suffering intensely from cancer. Respiratory difficulties led Alfred to seek a change of climate and about 1898 he and his family moved to Kushla, Alabama, about a dozen miles north of Mobile. There he and his sons developed a three-hundred-fifty acre farm with a hundred dairy cattle. Elizabeth apparently accompanied Alfred's family in the move to Alabama. The family home was sold in 1899; Lucy Sturtevant regained ownership in 1903 but a few years later it was sold again. Lucy, having remained in Jacksonville while Alfred's son Bradford attended Illinois College, joined the family in Alabama.

Julian Jr. died in Arlington, Massachusetts, on 9 October 1921 and was buried in the family plot at Jacksonville. His sisters died in Alabama, Elizabeth on 2 August 1922 and Lucy on 24 June 1930; both were buried at Jacksonville. Alfred suffered a stroke in 1927 and died in June 1930; he was buried in Alabama.

Twelve grandchildren survived Julian Sr. and one more was born a few years after his death. The first two daughters born to Julian Jr. and his wife, Katherine, died in infancy; three other children survived to adulthood: Amy, born 1871; Hayward, 1878; and Faith, 1883. All three married and had families. James and Hannah Augusta Palmer were parents of four children, all surviving to adulthood: James, born 1870; Warren, 1873; Willard, 1874; and Lucy, 1878. All three of the Palmer sons married and two had children. Alfred and his wife Harriet had five sons and one daughter: Edgar, 1875; Helen, 1877; Charles, 1879; Julian Monson, 1882; Bradford, 1885; and Alfred, 1891. Bradford died at age 18; his brothers and sisters all married, and four of them had children. The vital statistics for all these and subsequent generations are provided in Robert H. Sturtevant's family genealogy, *Descendants of Samuel Sturtevant* (1986).

After the Sturtevants left Jacksonville, the house at 252 S. Park was occupied by a succession of residents. It was the home of President and Mrs. C. H. Rammelkamp from 1907 to 1910. In 1929 Illinois College purchased the house from Mr. C. C. Capps, who owned it for many years. In 1933 it was made a women's dormitory and named "Fayerweather House" in honor of Elizabeth and Hannah.

The picture of the house in Sturtevant's *Autobiography* is reproduced in this volume (p. 202). A later photograph is the frontispiece of a book of poems by Elizabeth (Libbie) Sturtevant, *Songs of a Golden Age* (1916), in the Schewe Archives.

Epilogue

Reflections on the Life and Work of Julian Sturtevant

Committed and intelligent Christian, pioneer educator, fervent preacher of the Gospel, earnest patriot, champion of freedom of thought and speech, founder of institutions, master of literary skills and prolific author, beloved and respected head of family—these phrases highlight prominent dimensions of the life and work of Julian Monson Sturtevant. Arising from humble beginnings, possessed of a physique which was less than sturdy and susceptible to debilitating illnesses, he accomplished great things despite limiting situations and sustained opposition by able opponents.

Sturtevant was one of Yale's best, exemplifying the power of the disciplined mind well-furnished with knowledge. He was well-educated in the Christian religion, classical languages and literature, English history and literature, and American history and government. He gained mastery in diverse fields: the Bible and theology, mathematics and astronomy, economics and nascent psychology, and American government. He continued to learn throughout his life, reading much, conversing with friends, traveling to the eastern states frequently, and journeying once to England and Europe. He maintained strong ties with his alma mater and friends and relatives.

Possessed of a logical mind and honing his native facility for lucid expression, he could and did speak boldly. He preached persuasively and wrote vivid and graceful prose. He delivered numerous public addresses to important audiences and fulfilled his ambition to publish on a wide variety of subjects, not least among them religion and education. He was a serious teacher who challenged his students to think for themselves. He appreciated music and he wanted students to share in the enjoyment of beauty.

This was a man whose education and expertise were not limited to books and words. He knew how to plow and reap; how to care for gardens, orchards, and livestock; how to construct buildings; and how to organize and manage institutions so that they were faithful to their purpose.

Faithfulness to God is, according to Sturtevant, fundamental to happiness, to freedom, to truth, and to the fulfillment of life's potential. He believed that intelligent understanding of the Scriptures, studied with regard to historical and literary methods, would lead Christians to the simplicity of their faith and hence to unity with each other. He emphasized the personal nature of religion and developed a radical laicism, asserting that any man may fulfill the ministerial functions. Sturtevant opposed centralization of power, whether in church or society. He exemplified, even as he taught, the necessity of personal responsibility and the exercise of individual freedom. He also believed that society is organic and has a prior claim. He experienced the conflict which can occur between the social order and individual freedom in student protests at the College.

A powerful conviction that individual freedom cannot exist apart from an appropriate social structure guided Sturtevant's public philosophy. Declaring that governmental authority ought to be exercised at the lowest possible level, he also affirmed the necessity for a strong national union. Institutions, he said, are essential for perpetuating social values and providing individual nurture. Church, school (and college), and government must therefore be organized and maintained. Along with these enduring institutions a democratic society requires a host of voluntary organizations, individuals banding together for a commonly accepted purpose regardless of denominational and other differences. Networks of institutions, Sturtevant maintained, can enable individuals to live and work together effectively in bringing the good life and happiness to all.

His zeal to establish New England ways in Illinois subjected Sturtevant to criticism. Of course, he and his colleagues were not the only ones who sought to promote a particular way of life. The

Southern immigrants who preceded them preferred a more casual style, and Catholic clergy seemed intent on transferring the old European order to the New World. The Yale men insisted that the social order they promoted was more faithful to biblical Christianity and more democratic. They advocated an educated citizenry, the right and responsibility of private judgment both in religion and politics, and popular participation in government and in social-political institutions. They were instrumental in developing the social order which proved capable of incorporating large numbers of immigrants into a great nation.

Sturtevant faced many difficulties, some of them severe and long-lasting. The slavery issue and insufficient funds were the gravest threats confronting the College and the most likely to have caused its demise. For nearly four decades the denominational struggle for control of the College hampered its growth and frustrated Sturtevant. Although Illinois College was the first school in the state to function as a college, it was not long before competition from other private schools and eventually from state universities posed severe challenges. The multiplicity of higher institutions under diverse auspices ensured that no one institution would have sufficient resources. Sturtevant was so committed to having one really fine university in the state that he was willing to yield Illinois College to achieve it. He strongly supported public education for all children and helped secure the future of public higher education by insisting that funds be directed toward one university rather than divided among many competing colleges. He advocated public responsibility for caring for the disabled and helpless.

Certain personality traits compounded the difficulties Sturtevant encountered. He was in some ways rigid, and yet he presided over a college which was open to change, in curriculum and pedagogy and student amenities. He was controversial by nature, with a stubbornness often strengthened by the opposition he faced. He was seemingly forced into hard positions by opponents, especially in the field of theology. He had to assert his orthodoxy, not only to protect himself but to preserve the College. Particularly irksome to staunch Presbyterians was his outspoken advocacy of Congregationalism. Had he been less vociferous, he would have provoked less antagonism. Actually, most Presbyterians appreciated his educational leadership and respected the depth of his religious commitment—and most were generous in their toleration. Sturtevant maintained standing as an ordained Presbyterian minister for a quarter of a century, witnessing to the good faith on both sides.

Issues involving minorities inspired some of Sturtevant's noblest statements—and some of his worst. He could praise the heroism of the missionary wife on the frontier but be quite insensitive to the employed woman who preferred to struggle independently rather than live as a housemaid caring for another's family. Sturtevant could deplore, in moving language, the auctioning of female beauty under slavery but visualize no more than a bleak future for the freed Negro. He could proclaim the red man to be God's creation yet would grant him leave to continue his way of life only if he retreated to a remote region.

Sturtevant's life spanned most of the 19th century. He observed the remarkable growth of a weak, young nation into a powerful giant which he saw as capable of overtaking even Great Britain. He witnessed tremendous social, political, and technological change. He lived in an exciting period, and he was a keen observer and an active participant. Having avoided politics for decades, he came to realize the significance of political action for establishing the good society. He thus became an active supporter of Abraham Lincoln, and he transformed his anti-slavery attitude into active abolitionism.

The bold prediction that America would become a great power was not fulfilled until after Sturtevant's death, and he did not anticipate its role as peacemaker, food-supplier, and advocate for human rights for the world. Nor did he live long enough to confront the increasingly severe challenges to faith brought by science and by biblical scholarship. He did not foresee the revival of the great religions of Asia and the Middle East and their challenge to the supremacy of Christianity.

Great dismay would accompany Sturtevant's quick perception that America is lax in its faithfulness to God, and his realization that the God-given mission, to Christianize the world, will not be fulfilled by the year 2000. Yet he would likely discern that the mission is continuing in secularized form, devoted now to bringing health-care, education, democracy, and a modern economic system to other nations. He would perhaps realize the degree to which custom and prejudice are responsible for the disabilities society has attributed to its minorities. Surely he would acknowledge that education, modern medicine, welfare programs, and the Civil Rights movement have improved the lives of many of the less fortunate.

The two greatest achievements of Julian Sturtevant's long career of service were in the two realms to which he devoted his life. He fulfilled his covenant to serve Illinois College, and more than any other person, he guided and sustained it throughout half a century. He steadfastly supported liberal arts as the most practical education, and he was uncompromising in upholding freedom to think and to speak. Sturtevant was also an ardent churchman, a vigorous spokesman for the Christian faith and in the forefront of those who encouraged Christian unity. He was among the first to recognize the appropriateness and need for establishing Congregational Churches at "the West."

If Julian Sturtevant were to return to Jacksonville, after a slumber much longer than Rip Van Winkle's, his observations would surely overwhelm him. He would rejoice that his beloved College still stands on the Hilltop, now financially secure and thriving to a degree he could not have imagined. Buildings erected in his lifetime and exquisitely restored would delight him, and he would eagerly inspect the many new buildings on the enlarged campus. Houses where friends and colleagues once lived would bring pleasant memories, and he would set out on a walking tour to see a familiar public square and court house, churches with familiar names but different buildings and locations, and the jewel he himself helped to build, the Congregational Church.

It would be reassuring for Sturtevant to find that Illinois College has remained true to its long tradition of liberal education. He would recall that in his day also it had been necessary periodically to develop new programs to meet current needs. He would be happy to see that the school is still a Christian college, church-related but not controlled by any church. The lack of periodic "seasons of refreshment," intended to aid students in making their commitment to Christ, would be deeply troubling. The current acceptance of a demarcation between the churchly function of evangelism and the educational function of the College would perplex him. Yet he would find reassurance in the wide range of churches represented by the students and faculty, a demonstration of practical Christian unity and fellowship which was only beginning to emerge in his late years. The large number of Roman Catholics on the campus would spark his curiosity, and the changes wrought in the Catholic Church by the Second Vatican Council would amaze and gratify him. International students on the campus would strike him as a positive result, in part, of the mission work of his generation.

On campus, Sturtevant would be eager to learn about computers and the amazing improvements in communications. He would marvel at the convenience of the automobile and its conspicuous presence. He would observe immediately the presence of women on the campus, both faculty and students, and would be amazed by the incredible athletic achievements of women students. Upon examining personnel files and the roster of Phi Beta Kappa, he would be convinced of the equality of women in scholarship. The *Epsilon* chapter would, of course, salute him; he was that Society's first representative on the campus.

Illinois College is the unique and most obvious monument to Julian Sturtevant's long presence in this place. The College has fulfilled the prayer which, his elder son reported, his father often uttered in College Chapel: that it might become "a copious fountain of blessing to many generations." (*Autobiography*, 349) The Lord had indeed been with Julian Sturtevant, and not only in bringing him to this place. The Lord had sustained him and Illinois College through half a century. With such aid and the help of many people, Sturtevant had prepared an institution which not only has survived but has surpassed his fondest expectations.

If Julian Sturtevant were to visit the campus, I would like very much to meet him.

THE FAMILY OF JULIAN MONSON STURTEVANT

JULIAN M. STURTEVANT   26 July 1805   11 Feb. 1886
ELIZABETH MARIA FAYERWEATHER STURTEVANT
26 April 1806   12 Feb. 1840
HANNAH RICHARDS FAYERWEATHER STURTEVANT
19 Dec. 1816   17 Jan. 1886

Married ELIZABETH M. FAYERWEATHER, 11 August 1829
  1. JULIAN MONSON   7 June 1830   11? May 1831
  2. ELIZABETH MARIA   24 Feb. 1832   29? Nov. 1840
  3. JULIAN MONSON   2 Feb. 1834   9 Oct. 1921
  4. JAMES WARREN   27 Feb. 1836   1 May 1873
  5. HANNAH AUGUSTA   12 May 1838   13? May 1891
  6. EDGAR LEWIS   29 Jan. 1840   ? July 1840

Married HANNAH R. FAYERWEATHER, 3 March 1841
  7. ELIZABETH FAYERWEATHER
                           2 Dec. 1841   2 Aug. 1922
  8. CAROLINE WILDER   23? Sept. 1843   13 May 1845
  9. LUCY ELLA   15 July 1846   24? June 1930
 10. EDGAR HOWARD   1? Aug. 1848   11 Oct. 1855
 11. ALFRED HENRY   9 Dec. 1850   8 June 1930

All of the above children were born in Jacksonville; all, except Alfred, were buried in Diamond Grove Cemetery, Jacksonville, along with the parents.

J. M. Sturtevant Jr. married Katherine Hayward, 26 Nov. 1861
        Children: Elizabeth, Caroline, Amy, James H., Faith
Hannah A. Sturtevant married James H. Palmer, 29 May 1869
        Children: Warren, James, Willard, Lucy
Alfred H. Sturtevant married Harriet Morse, 11 June 1874
        Children: Edgar, Helen, Charles, Julian Monson,
                Bradford, Alfred Henry

Family Picture: Three Daughters and A Son
Standing: Elizabeth (Libbie)   Lucy (right)
Seated: Alfred   Hannah Augusta
(undated; perhaps 1870s)

(Courtesy Harriet Sturtevant Shapiro, granddaughter of Alfred Sturtevant)

MEMBERS OF THE ILLINOIS ASSOCIATION

Name	Dates Born in	Education	Arrived Illinois	Service to College

FIRST DIVISION

Name	Dates Born in	Education	Arrived Illinois	Service to College
BALDWIN, Theron	1801-70 Conn.	Yale 27 YCTD 27-29	1829	Trustee 1829-1870
BROOKS, John	1801-88 N.Y.	Hamilton 28 YCTD 31	1831	Trustee 1829-1886
GROSVENOR, Mason	1800-86 Conn.	Yale 27 YCTD 31	1852 1870	Trustee 1829-1833

(Instructor, Math, 12/52-53, 53-54?; Prof., Religion, 1870-1880)

Name	Dates Born in	Education	Arrived Illinois	Service to College
JENNEY, Elisha	1803-82 Mass.	Dartmouth 27 YCTD 31	1831? 1832?	Trustee 1829-1870
KIRBY, William	1805-51 Conn.	Yale 27 YCTD 31	1831	Trustee 1829-1851
STURTEVANT, Julian	1805-86 Conn.	Yale 26 YCTD 28-29	1829	Prof. 29-85 Pres. 44-76
TURNER, Asa	1799-1885 Mass.	Yale 27 YCTD 30	1830	Trustee 1829-44

SECOND DIVISION

Name	Dates Born in	Education	Arrived Illinois	Service to College
BARNES, Romulus	1800-46 Conn.	Yale 28 YCTD 31	1831	
BASCOM, Flavel	1804-90 Conn.	Yale 28 YCTD 32	1833	
BEECHER, Edward	1803-95 N.Y.	Yale 22 Andover	1830	President 1831-44
CARTER, William	1803-71 Conn.	Yale 28 YCTD 33	1833	Trustee 1833-71
FARNHAM, Lucian	1799-1874 Conn.	Amherst 27 Andover 30	1830	Instructor 1831
FOSTER, Lemuel	1799-1872 Conn.	Yale 28 YCTD 1831	1832? 1833?	
HALE, Albert	1799-1891 Conn.	Yale 27 YCTD 31	1831 49-85	Trustee
HERRICK, Henry	1803-95 Conn.	Yale 22 YCTD 28	1830	
MESSENGER, Benoni	1800-66 Mass.	(?) YCTD 30	1830	
WILCOX, Jairus	1802-61 Conn.	(?) YCTD 33	1838	

MEMBERS OF THE ILLINOIS ASSOCIATION
Professional Careers (in Illinois, unless noted)
(very condensed; incomplete)

FIRST DIVISION

BALDWIN. HM, Vandalia; AHMS; Principal, Monticello Female Academy (near Alton), 38-47; Secretary, College Society, New York 1843-70.

BROOKS. HM, 31; Teacher, Belleville, Waverly Academy, Springfield Academy, 1832-53.

GROSVENOR. M, Mass., Conn., Ohio.

JENNEY. M, Alton, 32-35; ABCFM, 36-37; M, Congregational Church, Waverly, 37-40; AHMS, 58-68.

KIRBY. Instructor, I.C., 31-33.; M, Mendon Congregational, 36-45; AHMS, 46-51 (resided in Jacksonville).

STURTEVANT. HM, 29-30; trustee, 29-31, 44-76; interim and occasional preacher, numerous churches; prominent in College Society.

TURNER. HM; M, Presby.-Congl. Church, Quincy, 30-38; M, Denmark, Iowa, 38-69; a founder, Davenport College (Grinnell).

SECOND DIVISION

BARNES. HM; M, Presby. and Congl. Churches, 31-46.

BASCOM. HM, 33-39; AHMS, 39-40; M, 1st Presby., Chicago; M, Galesburg, Princeton; AMA, 56-57; Trustee, Beloit, Knox, Colleges.

BEECHER. M, Park St. Congl.., Boston, 26-30; M, Boston, Galesburg; founder, editor, *Congregationalist*, 49-53.

CARTER. M, Congl., Jacksonville, 34-38; M, Pittsfield Congl., 39-66.

FARNHAM. HM; M, Jacksonville, 32-33; M, Princeton, Batavia, 33-57.

FOSTER. HM; M, Bloomington, Alton. (Prayed daily for IC, gave $1,000)

HALE. ATS, S. States, 30-31; HM, 31-39; M, 2nd Presby. Springfield, 39-67.

HERRICK. HM, Carrollton, 30-31. Sabbath schools, academies, and M, E. and So. States, 32-67.

MESSENGER. HM, 30-33; M, Mt. Sterling, 50; M, Conn., Ohio; ABS, Ohio, 58-66.

WILCOX. HM, Geneseo, 38-45; M, Chicago, 45-48; business, Chicago, 58-.

ABCFM, American Board of Commissioners for Foreign Missions; ABS, American Bible Society; AMA, American Missionary Association; ATS, American Tract Society. HM, Home Missionary; IC, Illinois College; M, Minister; YCTD, Yale College Theological Department.

Some men experienced serious illness requiring them to return to the East; some engaged for a time in secular (business) pursuits.

Illinois College Faculty and Curriculum, 1864-1865; Courses Taught by President Sturtevant

The *Catalogue of the Officers and Students of Illinois College for the Academical Year 1864-65* was the first catalog to provide a detailed description of the curriculum. The "Outline of the System of Instruction" was printed on pages 16-26. The curriculum was organized in ten departments. The students were not classified by year. These arrangements continued until 1868 when the College resumed the traditional classification of students and listed briefly the studies for each class each semester.

President Sturtevant probably taught all the courses listed in the Departments of Moral Philosophy and Social and Religious Philosophy. The following three pages were reproduced from the 1864-65 *Catalogue*.

The Members of the Faculty
Rev. Julian M. Sturtevant, D.D., President
Samuel Adams, A.M., M.D.,
      Professor of Chemistry and Natural Philosophy [Physics]
Rev. William D. Sanders, A.M.,
      Professor of Rhetoric and Elocution
Rev. Rufus Nutting, Jr., A.M.,
      Collins Professor of the Greek Language and Literature
Rufus C. Crampton, A.M.,
      Professor of Mathematics and Astronomy
_____ Professor of the Latin Language and Literature
William T. Masters, Tutor

The Departments of Instruction (in the order listed)
Moral Philosophy, Social and Religious Philosophy, History, Natural Philosophy and Chemistry, Greek Language, Latin Language, Rhetorical Department, English Language and Literature, Mathematics and Astronomy, and Modern Languages.

Outline of the System of Instruction.

THE Course of Instruction pursued in this Institution is comprehensively exhibited in the following outline:

DEPARTMENT OF MORAL PHILOSOPHY.

LOGIC.

Propositions analyzed and distinguished in respect to Substance, Quality and Quantity; Distribution of Terms; Analysis of Syllogism; Rules for testing the validity of all Syllogisms; Mood and Figure of Syllogisms; Rules for Hypothetical Reasoning; Enthymeme; Sorites; All valid arguments capable of being expressed in the Syllogistic form; Classification and detection of fallacies; Practice in Logical Analysis.

MENTAL PHILOSOPHY.

The Genesis of human Knowledge, Sensation, Perception; Reproduction of Sensations and perceptions, Memory, Imagination; Abstraction, Generalization, Reasoning; Intuition, Ideas of Space, Time and Power, Beauty and Sublimity, Right; The Sensibilities, the Emotions, the Desires, Instincts, Appetites, Propensities and Affections; the Will, its function and its freedom.

ETHICS, THEORETICAL.

The Elements of Authority; The Conditions of Moral Accountability; Twofold Function of Conscience; Moral Judgment, its Standard; Moral Enforcement; Relation of the Will of God to moral judgment; the Will of God, how made known, Intuition, Experience of Consequences, Natural Religion, Revelation.

PRACTICAL ETHICS.

Duties to God; Duties to Man; Love, the substance of both. Duties to God, Reverence, Obedience, Prayer, and the observance of the Sabbath. Duties to man, justice in respect to liberty, property, character and reputation; Veracity in respect to facts, promises, contracts and oaths. Civil Society, origin of obligation to it; Duties and rights of Individuals; of societies. Relations of the sexes; Marriage, Parents, Children.

TEXT BOOKS.

Whately's Logic.
Upham's and Haven's Mental Philosophy.
Wayland's Moral Science.

DEPARTMENT OF SOCIAL AND RELIGIOUS PHILOSOPHY.

EVIDENCES OF RELIGION—NATURAL RELIGION.

A future State; Rewards and Punishments; Moral Government; State of Probation as implying danger of failure, and formation of character preparatory to a future state; Objections urged by Fatalists answered; the vastness of the scheme of Providence showing our incapacity to judge of its wisdom and goodness.

REVEALED RELIGION.

Three branches of the argument, Miracles, Prophecy, and Influence on the Soul and on History; Presumption against miracles, how great and how removed; the objections that the knowledge of Revelation is partial, and that the historical evidence is less than might have been conceived; Objections against the doctrines of a Mediator considered; Direct historical evidence that miracles have been wrought; Prophecy, nature and outline of the argument; Influence of Revelation on the soul of man; Influence on History and on the present state of the world.

POLITICAL ECONOMY.

Cost; Value, intrinsic and exchangeable; Competition, its fundamental relation to the science; all production the result of labor; conditions of the greatest efficiency and productiveness of labor, freedom to create and enjoy wealth, the most perfect implements, the subjugation of natural agents to man's use, division of labor—first two-fold, mental and muscular, subdivisions of each, utility and limitations of divisions of labor; Exchange, its necessity, modes of facilitating it, Circulating medium, Banks, Paper money; Distribution of Wealth; law of wages, relation of wages to population, relation of capital to wages, interest, rent; Consumption of wealth, productive and unproductive, and why it should be as small as possible.

*2

18   SYSTEM OF INSTRUCTION.

PHILOSOPHY OF AMERICAN DEMOCRACY.

Origin of the American Republic; Township Organization; Local administration as distinguished from central; counties; State governments; Legislative and judicial departments; Powers of the Federal Government distinguished from those of the States; Federal courts and their jurisdiction; characteristic which distinguishes our Federal Government from those which have preceded it; advantages of the Federal system; influence of a Democratic constitution of society; Parties; freedom of the Press; Universal suffrage; the durability of the Union, and prospective destinies of the American people.

TEXT BOOKS.

Paley's Evidences of Christianity.
Butler's Analogy.
Wayland's Political Economy.
De Tocqueville's American Democracy.

DEPARTMENT OF HISTORY.
ANCIENT HISTORY.

The infancy of civilization; Age of Grecian greatness and glory; the decline and fall of Grecian liberty; the Macedonian Empire; the founding and early history of Rome; the subjugation of Italy; the Punic wars and the conquests of Greece and Carthage; the decline and fall of Roman liberty; the fall of the Empire of the West.

MODERN HISTORY.

Middle Ages; Triumph of Monarchy over the other social elements, Fifteenth century; the Reformation and wars of religious liberty, Sixteenth century; the English Revolution, Seventeenth century; the struggle of the great monarchies for universal empire, Eighteenth century; American and French Revolutions, Eighteenth century; career of Napoleon; Revolutions of the Nineteenth century.

TEXT BOOK.

Wilson's Outlines of History.

1836 Map of the Illinois College Campus
and "Plot of Lands" Offered for Sale

A small pamphlet of 12 pages, with cover, was published in 1836 to offer Illinois College lands for sale to prospective buyers in Philadelphia, Boston, and New York. The purpose was to raise funds needed for faculty salaries, buildings, and operating expenses. The lots were priced at various levels from $500 (for corner lots) to $100. A notation at the bottom of the map, enclosed in a pocket on the inside back cover, indicates that the College Farm of 112 acres was to the south.

The pamphlet was signed by E. Beecher, President. Nathaniel Coffin was designated as the agent for the Trustees and would be visiting eastern cities on behalf of the College.

Presumably the buildings numbered "1" and "2" represent the two College buildings, the "Chapel" [Beecher Hall] and the 4-story dormitory. Several buildings were mentioned by Theron Baldwin in his *Historical Sketch*, but there is no way to correlate them with the numbered diagrams on the map nor to determine whether the buildings were laid out with such regularity. Some of the streets which were planned were never opened.

The pamphlet's title was printed in several sizes of lettering:

DESCRIPTION
of
JACKSONVILLE
and of the
PLOT OF LANDS
Hereto Annexed,
and Now Offered for Sale in Behalf of
ILLINOIS COLLEGE.

77 78 79 80

81 82 83 84

85 86 87 88

89 90 91 92

93 94 95 96

221   Judge Lockwood

South Walnut   St.

97 98 99 100

101 102 103 104

105 106 107 108

109 110 111 112

113 114 115 116

117 118 119 120

121 122 123 124

Washington

South Middle

Grove

College Grove
and
Buildings

College   St.

South Elm.   St.

125 126 127 128

129 130 131 132

133 134 135 136

7   6

South Locust   St.

137 138 139 140

141 142 143 144

145 146 147 148

149 150 151 152

153 154 155 156

157 158 159 160

161 162 163 164

1
2

7   5

2   3   4

St.   St.   St.   St.

Park   St.

165 166 167 168

169 170 171 172

173 174 175 176

177 178 179 180

181 182 183 184

185 186 187 188

189 190 191 192

193 194 195 196   197 198 199 200

201 202   203 204

205 206   207 208

209 210   211 212

213 214   215 216

217 218   219 220

Chapel   St.

1872 Map of West Side of Jacksonville, Showing Location of Illinois College

The map shows the location of the Illinois College campus with reference to the Illinois "Deaf & Dumb Asylum" and the Illinois "State Insane Asylum." The street bordering the latter on the north is the present-day Morton Avenue.

The street running south from "Ills. College" is the county road, Lincoln Avenue. The grave marker on the east side of that street, just north of the Town Brook, designates the site of the College Cemetery, still in use at this time.

Further south, on the west side of the county road and just north of the Catholic Cemetery, is a plot marked "J.M.S." Presumably this was the family farm where Julian Sturtevant taught his sons how to plow.

The area shown is a portion of the map on page 76 of the *Atlas Map of Morgan County, Illinois*.

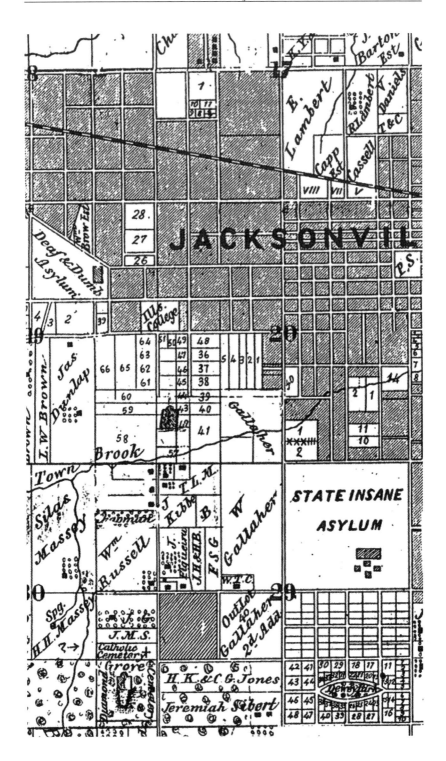

NOTES
Chapter 1: 1805-1829

(See Bibliographies for authors and works cited in notes. See also list of Abbreviations and Symbols.)

1. Sturtevant's implicit repudiation of "stage effect" and manipulation to produce "artificial results" is regarded by Hedrick (30 n) as an allusion to Charles G. Finney's evangelistic methods, known as "new measures." For other statements describing the kind of evangelism of which Sturtevant approved, see his *Autobiography*, 104-11, 114-16. Finney's new measures included referring to sinners by name in sermons and calling those who were wavering to the "anxious bench" for special prayers. See also, Ahlstrom, 459-61, and Mead, 204.

2. Hedrick, 30 n, 32 n.

3. Hedrick presents convincing evidence from church records and comparison of weather conditions to show that the year was not 1816, as Sturtevant stated in his *Autobiography* (40), but 1817. Sturtevant acknowledged uncertainty about the dates of the events of his early life. (A, 32)

4. Charles C. Bronson, "Historical Notebooks," Vol. 2A, 40. (Courtesy, Frank E. Lawrence, Tallmadge, Ohio)

5. Ibid., Vol. 2B, 26; based on notes by Cyrus Hard.

6. "First Congregational Church," Tallmadge, Ohio (n.d., n.p.).

7. Prayer and Bible study were also very acceptable means. While their use was characteristic of New England revivalism and distinguished it from "Old School" Presbyterianism, such methods were very restrained in comparison with Finney's.

8. Lucy Sturtevant to "Ever dear Children," Tallmadge [Ohio], 16 October 1822.

9. Phi Beta Kappa, *Alpha* Chapter, Yale College, Minutes, 19 July 1825. (Yale University MSS Collection; used by permission.)

10. For President Jefferson's views, see Stephen E. Ambrose, *Undaunted Courage: Meriwether Lewis, Thomas Jefferson, and the Opening of the American West* (New York: Simon & Schuster, 1996), 57.

11. Elizur Wright Jr. reported in detail regarding Julian's sickness and recovery: to "Dear Parents," Yale College, 10 Mar., 4 Apr. 1826. (Elizur Wright Papers, Courtesy of Library of Congress)

12. American Education Society, *Tenth Annual Report*, 29 May 1826 (Andover, Mass.: Flagg and Gould, 1826), 5, 19, 20.

13. George P. Fisher, *A Discourse, Commemorative of the History of the Church of Christ in Yale College....* (New Haven: Thomas H. Pease, 1858), 37. (Yale Divinity School, Misc. Personal Papers: George Park Fisher, Group No. 30, Box No. 114)

14. "Records of the Year, 1823: Records of the Church of Christ in Yale College," 21. See also "Chronological Catalogue of the Members of the Church of Christ in Yale College, 1820-1841, Book B." (Yale University MSS Collection; used by permission)

15. "Yale Moral Society, Book C, Constitution," and "Moral Society of Yale College, 1820-1841, Book B," Minutes: 2 Jan., 24 Aug., 24 Nov. 1823. (Yale University MSS Collection; used by permission)

16. K. Alan Snyder, "Foundations of Liberty: The Christian Republicanism of Timothy Dwight and Jedidiah Morse," *New England Quarterly* 56 (Sept. 1983): 382, 397.

17. Rev. Eleazar T. Fitch, D.D., *Sermons, Practical and Descriptive...* (New Haven: Judd and White, 1871), 15.

18. Six letters written by Julian, at New Canaan, to Elizur are in the Elizur Wright

Papers, Library of Congress. Five letters were dated 5 October, 9, 19, and 30 November, and 28 December, 1826; the letter dated 25 January 1826 was actually written in 1827. All six letters were written from New Canaan and addressed to Elizur at Groton.

19. *Canaan Parish, 1733-1933; Being the Story of the Congregational Church of New Canaan, Connecticut* (New Canaan: New Canaan Advertiser, 1935), 94, 98.

20. Among the Sturtevant family's possessions is a very small bound book, *Zion's Harp* (1824), with numerous tunes but without words. It is inscribed, "J. M. Sturtevant, Rockaway, Long Island, August l8 1827."

21. Hannah Moore, *Coelebs in Search of a Wife* (1809).

22. This is the title of ch. 29 of Ahlstrom's *History*.

23. See Mead, 158-59, 168; also Yale College, *Catalogue 1830/31*, 38-39.

24. Mead, 110-14. Taylor believed sin to be the consequence of a person's free agency, not the eternal decree of God. For reasons such as this, Sidney Mead subtitled his biography of Taylor, *A Connecticut Liberal.*

25. Noah Porter, "Dr. Taylor and His Theology," in Yale Divinity School, *Semi-Centennial Anniversary*, 97-98.

26. "Moral Society of Yale College, 1820-1841, Book B," Minutes: 23 Apr. 1829. (Yale University MSS Collection; used by permission.)

27. Theological Athenaeum, "Records," Jan. 1829. (Divinity School Papers, Yale University MSS Collection; used by permission)

28. Quoted by J. M. Sturtevant Jr., Sermon, Seventy-fifth Anniversary, Congregational Church, Jacksonville; in "Their Diamond Jubilee," JC, 21 Dec. 1908.

29. JMS, "Yale and Home Missions" (1872), 66.

30. Robert L. Edwards, *Of Singular Genius, Of Singular Grace: A Biography of Horace Bushnell* (Cleveland, Ohio: Pilgrim Press, 1992), 156-57. Bushnell served for some years on the Board of Directors for the Western College Society (SPCTEW). His views regarding theology and education led both Sturtevant and Baldwin to express negative opinions about him in their correspondence.

31. JMS, "Historical Discourse" (1855), 18.

32. "Constitution of the Society for Christian Research in the Theological Seminary, Yale College," Art. I, Sec. 2. (Divinity School Papers, Yale University MSS Collection; used by permission)

33. "Society for Christian Research, Record Book, 1825-1837," Minutes, 27 Nov. 1827. (Divinity School Papers, Yale University MSS Collection; used by permission)

34. Baldwin, *Historical Sketch*, 3.

35. See Bibliography of Manuscript and Document Collections.

36. Mason Grosvenor to Rev. J. M. Ellis, New Haven, Theological Seminary, 5 Dec. 1828. Two copies of the letter exist: the rough draft with a preliminary date of Nov. [n.d.]. 1828, written on loose sheets inserted in the volume of "Records," and the revised copy dated 5 Dec. 1828, which was actually sent.

37. JMS, Sketch (12 Mar. 1829), "Records of the Illinois Association, 1829," 1-2. (MS) Sturtevant wrote the account at the direction of the Association.

38. JMS, "Historical Discourse" (1855), 15.

39. "Society for Christian Research, Record Book, 1825-1837," Minutes, 30 Dec. 1828. (Divinity School Papers, Yale University MSS Collection; used by permission)

40. TB, Remarks, "The Social Re-Union," ICQCC, 44.

41. Thomas Lippincott, "A History of the First Rise and Establishment of Illinois College." (MS)

42. The original name of the Yale group, in their "Records," was "Howard Association." The only other known reference to that name is in John Brooks to Jane E. Bradley, Yale College, 4 Mar. 1829. (John Brooks Papers, MSS Collection, ISHL)

43. Sidney E. Mead, "means," in *An Encyclopedia of Religion*, ed. Vergilius Ferm (New York: Philosophical Library, 1945).

44. The original Compact is in the Archives of Illinois College. See CH, 24, and Yeager, *Church and College*, xii.

45. See the New York Statesman, 20 Oct. 1829.

46. Yeager, "The Good Names of Illinois College," ICAQ (Fall 1989): 7-13, discusses all members of the Illinois Association.

47. Cited by John R. Willis, *God's Frontiersmen: The Yale Band in Illinois* (Washington, D.C.: University Press of America, 1979), 29 n. 23. Willis listed his source as "Hall to Sturtevant, [AHMS] Letter Book C, Sept. 2, 1829, #128."

48. Professor Rufus Crampton, acting President of Illinois College from 1876 to 1882, believed 18 April 1829 should be regarded as the founding date. See "Explanatory Statement," delivered at the Semi-Centennial Observance of Illinois College. (JC, 5 June 1879)

49. A copy of the "Circular," with the subscription list, was preserved because John Brooks used it to write to Jane E. Bradley, 11 Aug. 1829. (John Brooks Papers, MSS Collection, ISHL) One side stated the great need of the West and described the proposed college at Jacksonville; the reverse side was ruled for entering subscribers' names, residences, and their pledges.

50. An unidentified clipping provides this information. (Archives, 378.773/Di)

Chapter 2: 1829-1833

1. JMS, A, 142. Other sources give the date as 26 or 27 August. See YDS *Catalogue*, 1922; Norton, 157; Hedrick, 87 n.

2. Sturtevant reported receiving the M.A. degree in 1829, but the date is given as "30" in the YDS *Catalogue*, 1922. He is listed with the Theological Department's Class of 1830.

3. TB, *Historical Sketch*, 7.

4. JMS to Lippincott, 22 Feb. 1844, 1.

5. For an account by another early visitor, see Edmund Flagg, *The Far West, 1836-1837* (New York: Harper, 1838), reprinted in Reuben Gold Thwaites, ed., *Early Western Travels, 1748-1846* (Cleveland: Arthur H. Clark, 1907), 26:304-14.

6. Sturtevant to Elizur Wright Jr., Jacksonville, Ill., Jan. 1 1830 (Elizur Wright Papers, Library of Congress). Wright's reply of Mar. 8 1830 is in the Eldridge Collection, Illinois College. Wright rejoiced in the success of Illinois College and commented about the positive signs of religious commitment among students at Western Reserve College, Hudson, Ohio, where he was a Professor. Wright also alluded to the "black & white" issue. Both these themes were prominent in the correspondence between Wright and Sturtevant.

7. JMS, "Historical Discourse" (1855), 22-23.

8. JMS to Absalom Peters, 5 Feb., 6 Sept. 1830.

9. See John Brooks to Jane E. Bradley, Yale Coll[ege], 11 Aug. 1829. (John Brooks Papers, MSS Collection, ISHL)

10. For John Ellis's plans see "Outline of a Plan for the Institution of a Seminary in the State of Illinois," January 1828, and a "Letter To the Friends of

Science and Religion, on the subject of the contemplated Seminary, etc." (Illinois College Archives)

11. An 1836 map of the campus shows seven numbered buildings, but the only ones which can be identified (by location) are "1," "Seminary Hall" (Beecher) and "2," the large dormitory of 1832-1833. See TB, *Historical Sketch*, 8-9, for list of buildings.

12. George P. Schmidt, *The Liberal Arts College: A Chapter in America's Cultural History* (New Brunswick, N.J.: Rutgers Univ. Press, 1957), 86-87.

13. Harold E. Gibson, "Old Illinois," ICAQ (Spring, 1989):18-19, quoting the *Jacksonville Western Observer*, 28 Aug. 1830.

14. *Jacksonville Western Observer*, 14 Aug. 1830.

15. Ibid.

16. See text of the Yale Report in Hofstadter, 1:275-91. The Report follows selections from Sturtevant's *Autobiography* (84-85, 90-91), in which he both praises and criticizes instruction at Yale.

17. Although some lists do not include Farnham as a member, Sturtevant did so in his "Historical Discourse" (1855) and "Yale and Home Missions" (1872).

18. The MS of Russell's speech is in the Office of the President of Illinois College; the other speeches are not extant.

19. Photocopy provided by the American Antiquarian Society, Worcester, Mass.

20. The "Order of Exercises of the Commencement of Illinois College" is in the Archives. See also JP, 12 Oct. 1833.

21. See the publications of the Jacksonville Female Academy, and Eames, 69-73.

22. Circular, Illinois State Lyceum (with letter from John Russell to JMS, 25 June 1832). See also *American Journal of Education*, 16 (Mar. 1866): 149; and Carl Bode, *The American Lyceum: Town Meeting of the Mind* (Carbondale, Ill.: Southern Illinois University Press, 1968), 96-98.

23. A brief account of the College appeared in the *Illinois Monthly Magazine* 2 (Dec. 1831): 102.

24. JMS to Lippincott, 26 Feb. 1844.

25. John M. Ellis to AHMS, Jacksonville, 15 Apr. 1830.

26. *First Annual Report* of the Directors of the Illinois Branch of the American Education Society, August 14 1832 (Jacksonville: James G. Edwards, 1832). (ISHL)

27. Frank J. Heinl, "Newspapers and Periodicals in the Lincoln-Douglas Country, 1831-1832," *Journal*, ISHS, 23 (Oct. 1930): 371-438.

28. Quoted in JP, 26 Jan. 1833, from SH, 12 Jan. 1833.

29. The models for "voluntary associations" were their British counterparts, especially the British and Foreign Bible Society, founded in 1804. Peace Societies, however, had their origin in America. See Smith, *American Christianity*, 2:10-19, 58-63.

30. Reprinted in JP, 2 Feb. 1833, from SH.

31. See JP, 2 Feb. 1833; SH, 12 Jan., 16 Feb. 1833; JMS to Lippincott, 26 Feb. 1844; Erastus Colton to JMS, Roscoe, Ill., 14 July 1883; ICCR, 27 Mar. 1886, 28.

32. Twelve letters exchanged by the two are known to be extant: 9 written by Sturtevant in 1826 (6), 1830 (1), and 1833 (2); and 3 by Wright in 1830 (1) and 1833 (2). Sturtevant's letters are in the Elizur Wright Papers, Library of Congress; Wright's are in the Illinois College Archives.

33. W. L. Garrison published the *Liberator*, a strident and powerful abolitionist periodical, from 1831 to 1865. Copies were delivered, some time in 1831 and 1832, to two subscribers, Charles E. Blood and Robert W. Patterson. Both were students in Illinois

College, and both subsequently graduated in 1837. Neither Beecher nor Sturtevant was identified as receiving the paper. See Frank J. Heinl, "Newspapers and Periodicals in the Lincoln-Douglas Country, 1831-1832," *Journal*, ISHS, 23 (Oct. 1930): 371-438.

34. Frances (Fanny) Wright, 1795-1852, was a wealthy English woman who lived in the United States for many years. She promoted a plan for the emancipation of slaves and was a severe critic of religion, education, and traditional marriage.

35. Jacksonville readers of the local *Patriot* were informed about the situation at Western Reserve and also about anti-slavery activities in New York. See JP, 5 Oct., 2 Nov. 1833.

36. Elizur was dismissed, along with two colleagues, in 1833. Elizur Wright (1804-1885) was a prominent abolitionist. In later years he revolutionized the life insurance industry by developing actuarial tables and promoting government regulation. Wright became an atheist; see Lawrence H. Goodheart, *Abolitionist, Actuary, Atheist: Elizur Wright and the Reform Impulse* (Kent, Ohio: Kent State University Press, 1990). There is no evidence in the extant correspondence with Sturtevant that this had occurred to cause the disruption of their friendship; presumably Wright's defection from his childhood faith was later in life.

37. In his letter of 3 July, Elizur acknowledged receiving two letters from Julian, one dated 12 April, the other 14 June; the latter is not available.

38. Thus far any letter sent by Sturtevant to Wright, subsequent to 3 July, has not been located.

39. The incident of 6 Feb. was reported in the first entry in the Faculty Minutes, 1 May 1833. See also SH, 16 Feb. 1833.

40. See A, 201-2; FM, 26 July 1833; JMS to Lippincott, 26 Feb. 1844; JP, 22 June, 20 July, 10, 17, 24 Aug. 1833.

41. JMS, "Western Congregationalism" (1883), 20.

42. See Spinka, 15, 328 n. 6.

43. JMS, "Letter" (1855).

44. See Wm. Irvine Blair, *The Presbyterian Synods of Illinois* (n.p.: Mattoon Presbytery, 1952), 43. Blair presents a strongly Presbyterian perspective on the denominational struggle to control Illinois College.

45. JMS to Lippincott, 26 Feb. 1844.

46. See JMS to Lippincott, 26 Feb. 1844, and A, 199-200.

47. The church at Naperville, organized in 1833 as a Presbyterian church, was reorganized as a Congregational church in 1834. (Spinka, 29, 30)

48. JMS to Professors Taylor and Goodrich (at Yale) and to Pastor Bacon of the Center Church (of New Haven), Illinois College, 1 Jan. 1834. (Bacon Family Papers, Yale University)

49. TB, *Historical Sketch*, 3.

50. Richard Lyle Power, *Planting Corn Belt Culture: The Impress of the Upland Southerner and Yankee in the Old Northwest* (Indianapolis: Indiana Historical Society, 1953), 174.

51. For Fayerweather family correspondence, see EC 5, 7, 17, 18. See also Erastus Colton to JMS, Roscoe, Ill., 14 July 1883. For Richard Fayerweather, see *Landmarks of New Canaan* (New Canaan, Conn.: New Canaan Historical Society, 1951), 404-5.

52. Julia Fayerweather to Elizabeth Sturtevant, New Canaan, Conn., 15 Aug. 1831, and Abraham Fayerweather to Jane Fayerweather, Honolulu, 7 May 1833.

53. See also Harriet Eliza [_____?] to HRF, Newport, 27 May 1833.

54. Abraham Fayerweather to R. Fayerweather, Honolulu, 7 May 1833.

55. See Harriet Eliza [_____?] to HRF, Mobile [Ala.], 12 Aug. 1834.

56. HRF, Text Book (MS), 19.

Chapter 3: 1834-1844

1. J. M. Peck, *A Gazetteer of Illinois* (Jacksonville: R. Goudy, 1834), 148-49, 264-65. (Connecticut State Library, Hartford)

2. Heinl, "Congregationalism," 448-49.

3. Ibid, 449.

4. JMS to faculty, New Canaan, 18 Jan. 1835.

5. The text of the Charter, with amendments, is in CH, 543-48.

6. JMS to Lippincott, 7 Mar. 1844.

7. See similar program for 1831: "Order of Exercises at the Annual Exhibition of Illinois College, August 17, 1831."

8. JMS to Lippincott, 13 Mar. 1844.

9. G. W. Horton Jr., "The Literary Society on the American College Campus," in Yeager, *Sesquicentennial Papers*, 307.

10. See Jack Nortrup, "Illinois Commentary: College Letters of Samuel Willard," *Journal*, ISHS, 66 (Summer 1974): 446-47. Reprinted in ICAQ (Summer, 1974): 9-10.

11. See FM, 8 Oct. 1840 to 24 June 1842. Lyman Beecher to JMS, Walnut Hills, 28 Aug. 1842. (typewritten copy)

12. JMS to Lippincott, 26 Feb. 1844.

13. JMS to Lippincott, 13 Mar. 1844.

14. TM, 16 Sept. 1839, 28 June 1842, 29 June 1843; JMS to faculty, Lewiston and Farmington, Ill., 18, 19 July 1843; S-B, 22 Nov. 1844 (cited in CH, 91); CH, 89-91, 141.

15. L. W. Bacon, 223-25.

16. Norton, ch. 2.

17. William Carter, "Commemorative Discourse," 10. In *A Memorial Discourse* (Quincy: Whig and Republican Press, 1863).

18. S-B, 12 May 1843. The letter, no longer extant, is quoted at length in CH, 123-24.

19. J. B. Turner, "Creeds" and "Articles of Belief," *Jacksonville Illinois Statesman*, 29 Apr. 1844.

20. R. W. Patterson to JMS, Chicago, 10 July 1843.

21. Ahlstrom, 399, 402, 598n., 600, 605. See Ethel Seybold, "Transcendentalism comes to Jacksonville," JC, 21 Oct. 1991.

22. Gibson, *Sigma Pi Society*, 32.

23. Willard, a skeptic as a student, was exceptionally moral. In later years he reaffirmed the traditional faith.

24. JMS, "A Memorial Sketch" (1877), 9-10.

25. TM, 27 Nov. 1844; MS, "Illinois College, Apr. 1845," with Norton to Judge Lockwood, 26 Oct. 1844, and faculty statements.

26. JMS to Leonard Bacon, Illinois College, 11 Dec. 1844. (Bacon Family Papers, Yale University MSS Collection; used by permission.)

27. JMS to J. B. Turner and faculty, Greenwich, Conn., 2 Oct. 1844. A small group of Congregationalists took a step toward abrogating the Plan of Union in 1846 when they organized the American Missionary Association, based on a strong anti-slavery platform. The Plan was formally declared at an end by a national convention of Congregationalists at Albany in 1852. See Atkins, 196-98, 400. Sturtevant argued that the Presbyterians' requirement in 1830 that Congregational ministers must answer the constitutional questions was the first act of abrogation.

28. Sturtevant also knew Lovejoy's brother, Owen, who had come to Jacksonville in 1838 seeking Episcopal ordination; he was a guest of the Sturtevants. Owen was

refused ordination because he would not pledge silence regarding his antislavery views. See Ch. 7 for JMS's memorial speech, 1864. See also Edward Magdol, *Owen Lovejoy: Abolitionist in Congress* (New Brunswick, N.J.: Rutgers University Press, 1967), 32-33.

29. See CH, ch. V, and Spinka, 69, 140-45.

30. A commemorative marker is just south of Sturtevant Hall.

31. A, 226-29; JMS to Lippincott, 13 Mar. 1844.

32. "Diary of Mrs. Joseph Duncan (Elizabeth Caldwell Smith)," ed. Elizabeth Duncan Putnam, *Journal*, ISHS 21 (Apr. 1928): 41.

For information about the Society, see Ahlstrom, 650. A long list of Jacksonville-area contributors to the Society does not include any of the College staff. The list was not dated but probably was compiled about 1848. The list is in the file on Governor Duncan's estate, Morgan Country Court House.

33. See CH, 114-15. The poster is in the Archives.

Samuel Willard's contemporary account, with an accompanying essay, is in Mark E. Steiner, "Abolitionists and Escaped Slaves in Jacksonville," *Illinois Historical Journal*, Illinois Historic Preservation Agency, 89, (Winter, 1996): 213-31.

34. Mrs. E. L. Reed to Rev. H. E. Butler, Berkeley, Calif., 4 Dec. 1883, in Congregational Church, *Fiftieth Anniversary*, 76.

35. W. Gaylord, *Life and Labors of Rev. Reuben Gaylord* (Omaha: Reco, 1889), 44.

36. J. C. Chandler, "Dr. Charles Chandler: His Place in the American Scene," *Journal*, ISHS 24 (1931-1932): 454-55.

37. *Jacksonville Illinoian*, 19 Jan. 1844; SJ, 25 Jan., 1844.

38. JMS, *Governor Duncan's Funeral* (1844).

39. Elizabeth Duncan Putnam, *The Life and Service of Joseph Duncan, Governor of Illinois.* Reprinted from *Transactions*, ISHL, (Springfield, Illinois, 1921), 177.

40. JMS to faculty, Lewiston and Farmington, 18, 19 July 1843.

41. "Illinois State Teachers' Association," *American Journal of Education* 16 (Mar. 1866): 151-52.

42. JMS, "Manual Labor Seminaries" (1837), 73-74.

43. M. W. Cleary, "History of the Illinois School for the Deaf," *Journal*, ISHS 35 (Dec. 1942): 368-69.

44. *The Constitution and By-Laws of the Jacksonville Mechanics' Union* (Jacksonville: Goudy, 1840). (ISHL) See Doyle, 156-93, passim, regarding voluntary associations in Jacksonville.

45. JMS, "World's Conversion" (1844), 194, 196, 207.

46. JMS, "Education of Indigent Young Men" (1843), and "American Colporteur System" (1844).

47. JMS, "Address" (1834), 84-85.

48. Nine letters, written by Sturtevant during this period, were reviewed by Pres. Rammelkamp but are no longer extant.

49. Elizabeth F. Sturtevant to "My dear Cousin Laura" [Mead], Illinois College, 2 Jan. 1838; HRF to "My dear Cousin Caroline," [3 Jany. 1838]. (Edited for punctuation and paragraphing.)

50. See *Morgan County Marriage Book B.*

51. Public Domain Land Tract Record Listing, State of Illinois, Archives Division (Microfiche, 04/26/84).

52. Sturtevant acquired lots 26, 27, 29, 30, 31, and 32. He also obtained lot (17) on State Street, north of the campus. The lots obtained in 1840 were renumbered 16 and 18 in the 1847 plan.

53. Hedrick (227 n. 27) incorrectly identifies James, Julia, and Mary Jane as the uncle and aunts of Sturtevant's wife; they were Elizabeth's (and Hannah's) siblings. (Carney, 73-74) James had come to Illinois in 1831.

The "Emily" mentioned by Hannah is not identified in the records. Possibly she was Emily Logan, whose freedom was secured by Elihu Wolcott. Or, perhaps she was the young girl who accompanied Richard Fayerweather and his two daughters to Illinois. Mary Jane Fayerweather, in a reminiscence decades later, stated that they had brought with them "a colored girl, about 12," who was bound to her sister Julia (Eames, 240). There is no evidence that she was a slave or that the Fayerweathers acquired her en route.

The New Canaan Census Reports for 1820 and 1830 show that numerous persons in that town had indentured servants who were "colored;" a few had "colored" slaves. Richard Fayerweather in 1820 and 1830 had a free Black female as an indentured servant, but she was beyond the age of 12. (Sharon L. Truro, New Canaan Historical Society, to Iver F. Yeager, June 20 1998; the Society has extensive documentation on free and slave Blacks in New Canaan during the early decades of the nineteenth century.) Presumably the Fayerweathers relied on such assistance with their boarders.

54. Theron Baldwin, *Historical Address, Delivered in Monticello, Illinois, June 27, 1855, at the Seventeenth Anniversary of Monticello Female Seminary* (New York: John F. Trow, n.d.), 24. See also Norton, 452-53.

55. J. B. Turner to Rhodolphia Kibbe, Jacksonville, 29 Aug. 1835; quoted in CH, 75.

56. The dates in family records sometimes differ from those in the Jacksonville cemetery records.

57. "J.H.S.," "Jacksonville, Its Institutions and Men," St. Louis Press, 29 July 1866. The identity of the author is problematic but likely it was J. B. Shaw, Class of 1846.

58. Two of Sturtevant's colleagues, Elisha Jenney and John Brooks, each married a sister of his deceased wife.

59. Ephraim and Julia Sturtevant, Tallmadge, 16 August 1841, to JMS and HRS.

60. C. C. Sturtevant to JMS, Rushville, 23 May, 3 June, 23 Aug., and 27 Dec. 1841.

61. The marriage of Warren Sturtevant and Harriet Beres on 27 April 1843 was recorded in Portage County, Ohio. (L.D.S. Microfiche, Ohio 718, U.S. 18, 41/75) Three letters from Warren Sturtevant to his son Julian in 1847 and 1857 refer to his wife but not by name.

Chapter 4: 1844-1850

1. L. Bacon to TB, New Haven, 15 Nov. 1844.

2. S-B, 2 Dec. 1844; quoted in CH, 138-39. The original letter is not extant.

3. See typewritten copy, prepared by Lucy Sturtevant, in the Archives.

4. JJ, 27 June 1845. Another local paper, the *Jacksonville Western Star*, 2 July 1845, stated attendance was poor because of rain. (Courtesy, The Chicago Historical Society.)

5. See also, Gibson, 59-60.

6. Sturtevant had referred to Tocqueville in his 1841 address on democracy. Tocqueville's completed work was published ten years after he visited the U.S. in 1830. He is regarded as one of the most astute observers of American society.

7. McConnell adapted to his own situation the words spoken in 312 by Constantine, who saw in a vision a cross of light with the inscription, "Conquer by this sign." Victorious in the battle, Constantine later became Emperor of Rome.

The booklet was given by B. F. Lane to Iver F. Yeager for Illinois College.

8. S-B, 24 Aug. 1846; in CH, 142. The letter is not extant.

9. JMS, "Collegiate Education" (1846).

10. See also, JMS, "Constructive Nature of Puritanism," *Home Missionary* 22 (Feb. 1850): 247-48.

11. Sturtevant presented these views vigorously in *American Colleges* (1845), "Collegiate Education" (1846), and his 1847 and 1849 SPC addresses.

12. An early student, Joseph Town, was a missionary to the Ojibway Indians; such work was then under the American Board.

13. S-B, 26 Nov. 1845. See the thirty manuscript pages Sturtevant wrote to Baldwin in 1843 (Archives, Box IA, 2).

14. B-S, 5 Oct. 1846, 19 Mar. 1847. The quotations from the Towne-Eddy Report are from a typewritten copy prepared from the original manuscript by Richard S. Taylor. See also Taylor's "Western Colleges as 'Securities of Intelligence & Virtue': The Towne-Eddy Report of 1846," *Old Northwest* 7 (Spring 1981): 41-65. Excerpts from the Report were printed in SPC-3; see 36, 37.

15. The denominational control of Illinois College was a frequent topic in the correspondence between Sturtevant and Baldwin; see, among others, S-B, 31 July 1845, 10 Nov., 22 Dec. 1847; B-S, 30 Nov. 1847. The denominational control of colleges in general was the subject of later articles by Sturtevant. For a strongly Presbyterian view of the denominational relationship of Illinois College, see William Irvine Blair, *The Presbyterian Synods of Illinois* (Mattoon Presbytery, 1952), 76-79, 115-16, etc.

16. Both articles were published under the pseudonym Sturtevant used for several years —Robinson, or John Robinson. John Robinson was pastor of the Pilgrims in Holland. The use of his name clearly identified Sturtevant with Congregationalism. See Atkins, 60, 65; von Rohr, 16-18, 20-21, 53-56.

17. JMS [Robinson, pseud.], "Letter from Illinois," 28 Sep. 1850.

18. Union Theological Seminary was founded by the two denominations in New York City in 1836.

19. *Jacksonville Illinois Statesman*, 12 Feb. 1844.

20. JMS, "Collegiate Education in the Western States." (1846) See S-B, 19 May 1846, for Sturtevant's vigorous protest.

21. The method of voting in early elections was to call out the name of the favored candidate.

22. A, 279; *World Book Encyclopedia* (Chicago: Field Enterprises, 1958).

23. Basler, Vol. 8, App. 2, 433.

24. JMS, "Historical Discourse" (1855), 28-29, 34, 36.

25. See the Minutes (MSS) of two meetings; also, Ensley Moore, "Jacksonville High School," JJ, 26 Sept. 1920; *Holland's Jacksonville City Directory for 1871-1872* (Chicago: Western Publishing Co., 1871).

26. S-B, 25 Apr. 1849; Miss Beecher to JMS, New Bedford, 30 July 1849. (Typewritten copy) William Slade was governor of Vermont, 1844-1846, and from 1846 to 1869 he was the agent for the Board of National Popular Education. In 1847 he visited Jacksonville as a guest of the Sturtevants. (S-B, 19 Feb. 1847)

27. In 1848 the name was changed to "Illinois Institution for the Education of the Deaf and Dumb."

28. D. L. Dix to JMS, Springfield, 9 Mar. 1847.

29. S-B, 15 Jan. 1849. See Walter B. Hendrickson, *From Shelter to Self-Reliance. A History of the Illinois Braille and Sight-Saving School* (Jacksonville: Illinois Braille and Sight Saving School, 1972), 5, 9. A copy of the printed "Memorial to the General Assembly of the State of Illinois," in support of providing education for

the blind, bears the name of J. M. Sturtevant and eight others. (Illinois State Archives)

30. In 1851 the first of several name changes was made when the school was designated as a college. The name was changed to "MacMurray College for Women" in 1939 and to "MacMurray College" in 1969. See especially Mary Watters, *The First Hundred Years of MacMurray College* ([Jacksonville]: MacMurray College for Women, 1947), 11-18, 49-50, 462-63.

31. See George R. Poage, "The Coming of the Portuguese," *Journal,* ISHS 18 (Apr. 1925): 101-35. Poage (125-26) includes the text of JMS to Rev. Herman Norton, 10 July 1849.

32. CCM, 10 Apr. 1848, 16 Apr. 1849, 15 Jan. 1850; B-S, 27 Mar. 1850.

33. S-B, New Haven, 13 Mar. 1845; Illinois College, 19 May 1846.

34. Hedrick, ch. 7, discusses these meetings and the issues central to them. See also Atkins, 303-04, and von Rohr, 278-80.

35. JMS, "Collegiate Education." (1846)

36. For example, S-B, 10 Dec. 1845, 3 Aug. 1846, 4 May 1848; B-S, 19 Mar. 1846, 30 Aug. 1848, 8 June 1849.

37. The *Christian Messenger* was published by the American Tract Society.

38. Sturtevant sought unsuccessfully to have the *Evangelist* and the *Observer* print notices of the College's *Catalogue.* He now asked Baldwin to request this of the *Evangelist.*

39. Later, the *Congregational Herald.* S-B, 25 Apr. 1849; B-S, 8 June 1849.

40. JMS, "Illinois College." (1850) See S-B, 27 Aug. 1850.

41. JMS [John Robinson, pseud.], "The Pilgrim Fathers." (1850)

42. S-B, 18 Sep. 1848. Ralph Havener to Iver F. Yeager, University of Missouri, 10 Dec. 1981, confirmed the degree.

43. The *Atlas Map* (1872) designated an area on the west side of Lincoln Avenue, directly north of the Catholic Cemetery, as "J.M.S." This likely was the field referred to. (Note: modern street names have been used.)

44. Charles C. Bronson, "Historical Notebooks," Vol. 4, 82.

45. For information about the Fayerweathers, see EC 4-6, 17, 18. See also John B. Carney, "In Search of Fayerweather: The Fayerweather Family of Boston," *New England Historical and Genealogical Register* 146 (Jan. 1992): 72-76.

46. See HRS to Rev. Ephm. W. Clark, 18 Feb. 1851 (photocopy from Robert Dye, Kailua, Hawaii); and E. W. Clark to HRS, Honolulu, 24 June 1851.

47. HRS to JMS, 5 Aug. 1852.

Chapter 5: 1851-1855

1. For an account of Beecher's mystical union with Christ and his controversial doctrine of the pre-existence of souls, see Rugoff, 88-90, 401-06. For another example of Sturtevant's own "practical" orientation, see S-B, 16 Nov. 1852.

2. Circulars: "ILLINOIS COLLEGE," New York, 13 May 1853; "Illinois College," Jacksonville, Ill., 26 Sept. 1854.

3. Rev. Wm. Carter to JMS, Pittsfield, 31 Dec. 1852.

4. A letter from Baldwin to Sturtevant, 29 Apr. 1852, reported information which purported to show that Gideon Blackburn had not actually designated Carlinville as the site for his seminary and, moreover, had not intended the bulk of his wealth from the lands to be inherited by his heirs. Such allegations, had they been proved, might have aided the cause of Illinois College. In any event, the court's decision was unfavorable.

The letter was found in 1998 among David A. Smith's papers, where it apparently remained since the case was in trial.

5. JMS, *The Memory of the Just* (1852). See Bibliography.

6. Hesperian [pseud.], "Burning of Illinois College," *Independent*, 20 Jan. 1853. The author was probably Rev. Edwin Johnson, Pastor, Congregational Church of Jacksonville, 1851-1858, and a trustee of Illinois College, 1852-1858. See also "College Building," *Independent*, 9 Nov. 1854.

7. Rev. E. Johnson to JMS, Jacksonville, 30 May 1853.

8. S-B, 1 Jan. 1853. Cf. Joseph Thompson, SPC-8 (Oct. 1851) and his letter in Paul Angle, ed., *Prairie State: Impressions of Illinois, 1673-1967, By Travelers and Other Observers* (Chicago: University of Chicago Press, [1968]), 269.

9. JMS to Rev. Julius Reed, 17 Feb. 1854. (Courtesy of Grinnell College)

10. Photocopy of program provided by the Presbyterian Historical Society. For Post's remarks see *Congregational Herald*, 2 Nov. 1854 (copied from the *Morgan Journal*). The hymn's author may have been Professor Adams, acknowledged by Sturtevant as a poet. A cornerstone box was found in May 1993; see Iver F. Yeager, "Treasure in the Tower," ICAQ (Summer 1993): 18-20.

11. Hesperian [pseud.], "Commencement at Illinois College," *Independent*, 22 July 1852.

12. JMS, "Revival" (1853).

13. B-S, 20 Aug., 4 Oct. 1855; Orange, N.J., 18 Oct. 1855; S-B, 30 Oct. 1855. Turner's "Creed," which differed significantly from the prevailing Protestant orthodoxy, had been published in his newspaper, *Illinois Statesman*, 29 Apr. 1844. See Carriel, 235-37, for a later statement of Turner's views.

14. SPC-8, 55-58; Thompson, in Angle, 268-69..

15. An earlier analysis of the detrimental effect of sectarian competition in founding colleges was presented in 1829 by Philip Lindsley, University of Nashville; quoted in Hofstadter, 1:233.

16. JMS to HRS, New York, 4 May 1853; S-B, New Haven, 4 June 1853; S-B, E. Cleveland, 2 July 1853; S-B, 30 July 1853.

17. Sturtevant warned against "that spirit of superficialism, mammonism, and materialism, which is the greatest danger that threatens our country." (SPC-9, 22) He believed the danger was especially great for the West because its institutions did not enjoy the support given to their counterparts in New England

18. S-B, 2 June; B-S, 11 June, 1851.

19. The Congregational Church building on the east side of the public square was also used as an auditorium. Sigma Pi paid $36 in 1853 for using it. CCM, 17 Jan., 15 Dec. 1853.

20. The building, extensively remodeled, is still in use by the First Congregational Church of Waverly.

21. T. A. Post, *Truman Marcellus Post, D.D., A Biography, Personal and Literary* (Boston and Chicago: Congregational Sunday-School and Publishing Society, 1891), 204, 206. Only after the church decided to become Congregational did Post become the champion of Congregationalism in Missouri.

22. "The Congregational Convention," *Congregational Year-Book*, 1854, 338-47.

23. Congregational ministers are members of local churches as well as Associations. Presbyterian ministers are members of Presbyteries but not of local churches.

24. JMS, "Who is the Hero?" (1853)

25. Someone stated this vividly, if in prosaic terms: "They have milked our

Congregational cows, but have made nothing but Presbyterian butter and cheese." Quoted by Power, 172.

26. P. 50. For comment by a contemporary, see "Congregationalism," *Boston Watchman and Reflector*, 23 Aug. 1855.

Congregational polity was affirmed and extended in 1957 when the Congregational Christian Churches merged with the Evangelical and Reformed Church to become the United Church of Christ. That historic action culminated a long series of negotiations and litigation. Among the Congregationalists, both the proponents and opponents of merger agreed that the autonomy of the local church was an absolute requirement. The courts ultimately ruled that the "Basis of Union" and the "Interpretations" sufficiently protected that polity. The large majority of Congregational Churches voted for inclusion in the United Church. Cf. von Rohr, 433-36.

Note examples of congregational independence in some Presbyterian churches; cf. John P. Burgess, "Conversation, conviction and the Presbyterian identity crisis," *Christian Century*, 24 Feb. 1993, 205. Note the increased participation by laity in the Roman Catholic Church, as presented in the media; cf. CBS, "Sixty Minutes" (22 Jan. 1995) and Richard Rodriguez, "Spiritual Roots," MacNeil-Lehrer News Hour, PBS, 28 Dec. 1994.

27. *Congregational Quarterly* 1 (1859): 60.

28. Baldwin to Messrs. Editors, *New-York Evangelist*, 6 Aug. 1855; *New-York Evangelist*, 16 Aug. 1855; B-S, 4 Oct. 1855.

29. For a Presbyterian view of "who killed Cock Robin" see "Cooperation with Presbyterians," *New-York Evangelist*, 26 July 1855.

30. JMS, "Letter" (1855). Sturtevant withdrew from Presbytery in 1855; see Roy, "History of Congregationalism in Illinois," 36.

31. See Heinl, "Congregationalism," 450-52, regarding the slavery issue in central Illinois and in Congregational churches.

Prof. James E. Davis of Illinois College emphasizes that even among those who regarded slavery as a great evil, diverse views were common. Moreover, opposition to abolitionism was deeply rooted. The resulting controversy was often bitter, and there was fear that it would result in violence and perhaps even dissolve the Union. For decades some northerners had strongly opposed actions of the national government, and some political leaders spoke of nullification and even secession. Some northern states adopted personal liberty legislation to thwart the Fugitive Slave law. All these actions were great irritants to people in various regions who held differing views of slavery. (Summarized from a memorandum, 2 June 1998)

32. Heinl, "Congregationalism," 456.

33. SJ, 20 Dec. 1851; 27 Feb., 11 Mar. 1854.

34. See Bibliographies for early accounts of Illinois College.

35. Sturtevant alluded to a seventeenth century movement in England directed toward equality for the less privileged classes.

36. *American Journal of Education* 1 (Jan. 1856): 225-30.

37. Pierson was an Illinois College alumnus, Class of 1848, and presumably was bound for Hawaii under the American Board.

38. See S-B, 1 Jan. 1853; B-S, 7 Jan. 1853.; JMS, "Revivals," 1853; and CCM, 23 Jan. 1853.

39. Julian Sr. returned a few days later. FM, 15 Oct. 1855.

Chapter 6: 1856-1860

1. Don Doyle, Lecture, "Work and Leisure on the American Frontier," Illinois College, 9 Dec. 1975.

2. The three-year program omitted Latin and Greek. Later, it was expanded to four years and included Latin but not Greek; (*Catalogues, 1852-'53, 1874-75*)

3. Quoted in the *Jacksonville Sentinel,* 8 May 1857.

4. Quoted in CH, 201.

5. Rammelkamp thoroughly discussed this issue, CH, 198-201.

6. *Catalogues, 1855-6, 1856-7.* Powell was admitted as a member of the Congregational Church on 2 Mar. 1855. See JMSJR, 96-97, for the opinion that Powell later became an extreme materialist.

7. *Congregational Herald,* 12 May 1859.

8. Sturtevant had prepared an article on this subject in 1846. (S-B, 3 Aug. 1846) He was persuaded not to publish it at that time lest, by declaring his own ecclesiastical views, he stir up denominational antagonisms. The long delay did not lessen the impact of publishing his own convictions and his critique of views held by some of his Presbyterian antagonists. (See Hedrick, 458-61.) Commentary on Sturtevant's article was published in the *Congregational Herald,* 14 Jan. 1858.

9. Among many references to the Beecher Professorship, see B-S, 4 Dec. 1855, 25 Mar. 1856, 21 June 1858; S-B, 4 Mar. 1856.

10. JMS to son Warren, Tallmadge, Ohio, 8 July 1858.

11. The trustee was identified as Smith in S-B, 1 June 1858.

12. S-B, 23 Nov. 1859, 2 Jan. 1860; B-S, 27 Jan. 1860.

13. See *The History of Presbyterianism In Morgan County, Illinois: 1827-1967* (Jacksonville: First Presbyterian Church, 1967); and *The First Presbyterian Church in Jacksonville, Illinois* (Jacksonville: First Presbyterian Church, 1977), 14.

14. B-S, 7 Aug. 1860. The church referred to was founded as the "Church of Christ in Tallmadge" in 1809, as part of a Christian community exemplifying "New England civilization." (*A Brief History: The First Congregational Church of Tallmadge, Ohio* [The Men's Fellowship, 1940, 1959], 4, 5) A staff member of the Church, Nancy Beken, stated that the Church had always been Congregationalist. (Telephone conversation, 2 Feb. 1999)

15. None of the three numbers published has been located.

16. S-B, 25 Mar., 3, 9 Apr. 1856; *Congregational Quarterly* 2 (1860): 189; *Chicago Theological Seminary: Quarter Centennial Historical Sketch* (Chicago: Jameson & Morse, 1879), 13, 48; A. C. McGiffert Jr., *No Ivory Tower: The Story of the Chicago Theological Seminary* (Chicago: Chicago Theological Seminary, 1965), 31; *Congregational Quarterly* 2 (1860): 189.

17. S-B, 3 April, 20 June, 26 Nov. 1856; FM, 13 Oct. 1856; JMS to son Warren, N.Y., 22 Aug. 1859 and I.C., 12 Mar. 1860; *Congregational Herald,* 12 May 1859.

18. JMS to son Warren, Tallmadge, Ohio, 9 July 1858. Beecher, now at Elmira, N.Y., was for forty-six years the innovative and much-loved pastor of its First Congregational Church.

19. JMS to son Warren, Tallmadge, 9 July 1858.

20. [15?] July 1859. (Rockford College Archives)

21. Sturtevant declared: "Our instruments of locomotion and communication are commensurate with the resources of our planet. While I am speaking, preparations are in progress for uniting Europe and America in marriage, by the telegraph wire. The iron track of the steam chariot will soon be continuous, from the Hudson to the Columbia,

and from the English Channel to the Yellow Sea." Such transportation will, he thought, enable Americans to expand "upon any unoccupied lands on the face of the whole earth." (*American Emigration,* 14)

22. See Heinl, *Epitome,* for pertinent entries, 1853-1856; and Heinl, "Congregationalism," 458.

23. A, 288. The biographical sketch in the *Atlas Map* stated that Sturtevant was never a partisan in politics, but also noted that "he entered with the greatest fervor" into the organization of the Republican Party in 1856. (42)

24. JMS to Hon. A. Lincoln, Illinois College, Sept. 16, 1856. (Courtesy of Library of Congress)

25. A copy of the letter, A. Lincoln to Rev. J. M. Sturtevant, Springfield, Sept. 27, 1856, is in the Illinois College Archives.

26. John M. Palmer was elected to the Illinois Senate in 1854. He supported Lincoln.

27. Sturtevant said the "first speech" in which he heard Lincoln speak about slavery was when he addressed two thousand people from Morgan County and the surrounding area. (A, 287) Heinl (*Epitome*) notes that on 27 Sept. 1858 "Abraham Lincoln spoke to monster Republican meeting in Public Square." Sturtevant (A, 291) heard Lincoln's famous "house-divided speech," delivered on 16 June 1858, and thus prior to the mass meeting. It does not seem possible to reconcile the dates of these occasions, unless Lincoln twice addressed large crowds in Jacksonville. The date when Sturtevant walked with Lincoln to the hotel has not been established.

28. See Wayne C. Temple, "Lincoln as a Lecturer on 'Discoveries, Inventions, and Improvements,'" JC, 23 May 1982.

29. A Jacksonville newspaper declared (Nov. 1860) that statements by Lincoln and Seward about abolition have "justly been regarded by the people of the south as a declaration of war against their constitutional rights." See JC, 5 Nov. 1980.

30. Ahlstrom, 394; Atkins, 130.

31. JMSJR to Libby [*sic*], Hartford, 20 Apr. 1857. Most letters from Julian Jr. during seminary were from Andover, Mass.

32. CCM, 24 Apr., 1 May, 25 June, 15 Sept. 1859; 21 Mar. and June [n.d.], 1860. JMS to son Warren, 12 Mar. 1860.

33. See Morgan County Marriage Register, 11 Jan. 1860.

34. Information about the Beardstown Sturtevants, the Beardstown Congregational Church, and the 1850 Cass County census, was provided by Mrs. G. H. Bell, Church Archivist.

35. Julia Afong to HRS, Honolulu, Oahu, 20 Feb. 1860. (For a recent biography of Julia Afong's husband, Chun Afong, see Bob Dye, *Merchant Prince of the Sandalwood Mountains* (Honolulu: University of Hawaii Press, 1997). Dye's wife is a great-great-granddaughter of Chun and Julia Afong.)

Chapter 7: 1861-1865

1. The lower part of the building still exists; it is incorporated in the remodeled structure on the south side of Central Park Plaza, on the west side of Main Street.

2. *Jacksonville Sentinel,* 20, 27 June, 4 July 1862; CH, 205-8.

3. See B-S, 15 July 1857, 15 Sept. 1861, 1 Oct. 1862; S-B, 29 Nov. 1862; B-S, 16 Dec. 1862; S-B, 5 Nov. 1863; B-S, 2 Mar. 1864.

4. JMS, "Foreign Intervention." (1862)

5. JMS, "Classes at the South." (1862)

6. Sturtevant paraphrased Paul, 2 Cor. 6:2.

7. JMS to Gov. Richard Yates, 20 Sept. 1862; quoted in A, 299-301, with Yates' letter of 18 Sept.

8. JMS, "The Destiny of the African Race." (1863) See JMS to Lucy, London, 4 May 1863, and *Economics*, 272, regarding his authorship.

9. See F. James Davis, *Who Is Black? One Nation's Definition* (University Park, Penn.: Pennsylvania State University Press, 1991); and, *Newsweek,* cover story, "What Color Is Black? Science, Politics and Racial Identity," 13 Feb. 1995.

10. In his *Economics* (272) Sturtevant acknowledged the similarity between his reasoning and Darwin's but denied any debt to Darwin because he had written the essay years before he learned about Darwin's observations.

11. For Blatchford's career, see his obituaries: *Chicago Tribune,* 26 Jan. 1914; *Chicago Record Herald,* 26 Jan. 1914; JJ, 28 Jan. 1914;

12. JMS, "Lord Palmerston on the Great Rebellion." (1862)

13. Daughter Hannah to JMS, 30 June 1863.

14. The flyer announcing an address at Writtle Chapel on 9 June is in the College Archives; also reproduced in CH, 212.

15. Sturtevant's letters were addressed to Mrs. Sturtevant unless otherwise noted.

16. JMS to HRS, Bristol 2 [June]; slightly edited.

17. The Congregational Church building on West College was built under Sturtevant's leadership (1859). See Ch. 6.

18. The surrender by the Confederates was on 4 July.

19. The *Soldier's Hymn Book* (Y.M.C.A.) was used in the service. (Congregational Church Archives)

20. See S-B, 10 Feb. 1864, and B-S, 2 Mar. 1864; *Independent,* 23, 30 July 1863, etc.; and Rugoff, 391-93.

21. Sturtevant seldom published in the *Independent* thereafter; see Bibliography, 1867, 1868. His articles appeared frequently in the *Congregationalist* and, from 1867, in the *Chicago Advance.*

22. See the *Evangelist* 18 Feb., 17 Mar. 1864; also JMS to Rev. Henry M. Field, 17 Mar. 1864; B-S, 2 Mar. 1864; S-B, 2, 15 Mar. 1864. Baldwin (2 Mar.) corrected the lines from *Hudibras.*

23. In Britain only a small percentage of white adult males had the vote; in the U.S., suffrage was nearly universal for that group.

24. Sturtevant's blanket condemnation of the British people is understandable, under the circumstances, but it was not justified. Regarding positive efforts on behalf of the Negroes in America, see W. Harrison Daniel, "British Congregationalists and the American Crisis of the 1860s," *Andover Newton Quarterly,* November 1978, 128-41.

25. Presumably the Mr. Mellor heard by Sturtevant at the Congregational Union in Great Britain in 1863.

26. See CH, 557-58; Gibson, *Sigma Pi Society,* 79n.; and James E. Davis, "Campus in Crisis," ICAQ (Fall 1989): 18-20.

27. Tusculum College (Tenn.) had the same arrangement.

28. S-B, 31 Dec. 1866 and 6, 9 Feb. 1867. See CH, 233-42.

29. President Lincoln, aware that many were urging him to act, utilized the narrow Union victory at Antietam as an opportune backdrop for issuing his Emancipation Proclamation on 22 September. The declaration freed, as of 1 January 1863, the slaves in

the territory controlled by the Confederates. The text of Lincoln's note is reproduced in Basler, 7:388.

30. Turner was believed by some to have Unitarian sympathies. See also Carriel, Ch. 8.

31. See Hermann R. Muelder, "Congregationalists and the Civil War," in Matthew Spinka, ed., *Illinois Congregational Churches*, 139-57. Muelder believed that the Congregationalists' unbending opposition to slavery made the Civil War inevitable.

32. *Debates*, 6, 7, 9, 10, 15, 29, 134, 135-47, 196, 245, 321-26, 486.

33. Quoted in Rev. E. Lyman Hood, *The National Council of Congregational Churches of the United States* (Boston: Pilgrim Press, n.d.), 56.

34. *Independent*, 22, 29 June, 6 July 1865; Sturtevant's "Sermon," 6 July.

35. See the Introduction regarding the post-millennialist character of Sturtevant's view.

36. See also William E. Barton, *Congregational Creeds and Covenants* (Chicago: Advance, 1917), 214.

37. JMS to Bacon, 10, 20 July and 7, 14 Aug. (Bacon Family Papers, Box 7, Folders 136, 137, Sterling Library, Yale University.)

38. *Congregationalist*, 18 Feb. 1886.

39. William Hanchett, "An Illinois Physician and the Civil War Draft, 1864-1865: Letters of Dr. Joshua Nichols Speed," *Journal*, ISHS, 59 (Summer 1966): 147.

40. See "C. C. Sturtevant," in *History of Minneapolis and Hennepin County, Minnesota*, ed. by Isaac Atwater and John H. Stevens (New York: Munsell Publishing Co., 1895), 1012-14.

41. Rugoff, 406-7, 412-13.

Chapter 8: 1866-1870

1. Cited in Joseph E. Roy, "What Home Missions Have Done for Illinois," *Congregational Review* 9 (Sept. 1869), 422.

2. The cover title of the *Illinois College Catalogue, 1869-70*, included the name of the Jacksonville Business College.

3. S-B, 13 Feb. 1868. Cf. 2 Cor. 4:8,9.

4. JMS, "To the Trustees of Illinois College," Illinois College, 5 June 1866. (MS. IB, #461) See Lucy Sturtevant to Pres. Rammelkamp, Kushla, Alabama, 26 Nov. 1906. Miss Sturtevant sent the MS with the comment that "it is probably the fullest and strongest expression which exists of his views on the question of sect as related to the college.... [H]e wanted [Illinois College] to be a Christian college.... In his mind this ideal for the college was not only in harmony with giving the highest intellectual training, it was a necessity of it." Miss Sturtevant added that the report would help others to understand the family's feeling regarding "the change in foundation" of the College. She alluded to the merger in 1903 of Illinois College with Jacksonville Female Academy, resulting in the College becoming Presbyterian. (See also CH, 448-49.)

See Baldwin's lengthy letter to Rev. Thomas Brainerd, New York, 9 May 1862, in which he states essentially the same position as Sturtevant. (Typewritten copy, Schewe Archives)

5. Cf. "Colleges of Special Interest to Congregationalists," *Congregational Quarterly*, 11 (July 1869), 420. Illinois College, Yale, and Harvard were listed as "Undenominational." Illinois College and other colleges co-sponsored by the two denominations were sometimes called "union colleges," a more accurate label.

6. HRS to JMS, 18 Apr. 1866. Presumably the table and five matching chairs shown

in an 1883 photograph of the Church's interior were the result of the women's endeavor. The furniture is still in use.

7. Cf. Dan. 2:31-45. The passage was written long before the Roman Empire was established, and scholars today identify the beast as the Greek (Alexandrian) Empire. A printer's error in the text attributed the vision to "David" rather than to Daniel.

8. JMS to Rev. Charles Peabody, 1 Apr. 1870.

9. JMS to Rev. Messrs Blanchard, Fowler, and Burroughs, 26 Oct. 1866, in *Chicago Tribune,* 31 Oct. 1866; JMS to the Editors of the *Chicago Tribune,* 3 Nov. 1866.

10. "Our Decennial," *Advance,* 6 Sept. 1877.

11. Sturtevant alluded to the forthcoming presidential contest. That fall, the Republican candidate, Gen. U. S. Grant, had a narrow margin in the popular vote over Democrat Horatio Seymour of New York.

12. "The Plains," "The Buffalo Hunt," and "The Western Problem." (1869)

13. Two years before Sturtevant went to Kansas, President Johnson had instructed the Indian Commissioner "to press upon these wild and roving people the importance and necessity of abandoning their present savage and unsettled mode of life, and applying themselves to industry and the habits of civilization." (JJ, 15 Aug. 1985) Many European-Americans regarded the Indians as "an alien presence" to be pushed back beyond the edge of civilization. See Winthrop S. Hudson, *Religion in America,* Third Ed. (New York: Scribner's, 1981), 22; and E. Gaustad, *Dissent in American Religion* (Chicago: University of Chicago Press, 1973), 87.

14. Haines, *A Biographical Sketch* (1866), 90-91. The information was supplied by Sturtevant but the sketch, written in the third person, was prepared by the editor.

15. Ephraim and his first wife, Helen Louisa Oviatt, were parents of a daughter who survived her mother's early death but died a year later. He and his second wife, Julia DeForest, were parents of two sons (Warren DeForest and Wheeler DeForest) and one daughter (Helen Louisa). The three children survived Julia, who died in 1845. Possibly Helen Louisa was the "Helen Sturtevant" who joined the Congregational Church of Beardstown in 1855; she died in 1856. The older son (Warren) died in 1873. Ephraim's third wife was Frances Pierce Leonard, and one daughter, named Julia, was born of this marriage. (See also Haines, *Biographical Sketches,* 1866, 1876.)

16. Ensley Moore, "Old Jacksonville: Wm. Francis F[a]yerweather," JJ, 14 Sept. 1921.

Chapter 9: 1871-1876

1. JMS, Wm. H. Savage, and R. C. Crampton, "To the Alumni and Former Students of Illinois College." [1871]

2. Many from Jacksonville did attend. Cf. JJ, 25 Aug. 1996: "You can't throw a stone in the streets nowadays without hitting a man who has been to the Centennial."

3. FM, 8 Dec. 1871; TM, 20 May, 4 June 1873, 26 May 1874. See also, "A Circular to the Alumni, the Former Students & the Friends of Illinois College," dated 10 June 1874.

4. Quoted by Parker G. Marden, "The Special Contributions, and Obligations, of Small Liberal Arts Colleges in a Challenging Future," in Yeager, *160th Anniversary Papers,* 78.

5. *Home Missionary* 45 (Apr. 1873), 291.

6. See V. Ferm, ed., *Encyclopedia of Religion* (New York: Philosophical Library, 1945).

7. The local *Journal* advertised Speer's wine "For the Communion Table and Family Use," for sale by Jacksonville firms. (19 Apr. 1866, 2, col. 7)

8. "Plymouth Church Letter Missive," *Advance,* 10 Feb. 1876.

9. JMS to Leonard Bacon, 5 Feb. 1876. (Bacon Family Papers, Yale University Library)

10. Information about the Beecher affair was derived from Rugoff, ch. 25, and

sources as noted. See also JMS to Leonard Bacon, 3 May 1876. (Yale University Library, Bacon Family Papers)

11. *Jacksonville Sentinel,* 10 Feb.; see also JC, 31 Jan. 1871.

12. Arminian theology arose in opposition to strict Calvinism and emphasized human freedom with regard to committing sin or rejecting God's grace. It stressed practical rather than speculative theology and became widespread in the 18th century when adopted by Methodism and similar movements.

13. Sturtevant shared the views of the post-millennialists, that after the Gospel had been brought to the whole world and made effective, Christ would begin a thousand year reign.

14. *Jacksonville Constitutionist,* 15 July 1854.

15. James D. Dana, "The Darwinian Theory," *Independent,* 23 Mar. 1871.

16. See Thomas K. Beecher, *Advance,* 1873: "The Gospel of Geology," 20 Mar.; "New Terms for Old Truths," 8 May; "About Instinct," 21 Aug.

17. Samuel Adams, "Darwinism," *Congregational Review* 59 (May, July, 1871): 233-53, 338-61.

18. Robert L. Edwards, *Of Singular Genius, of Singular Grace: A Biography of Horace Bushnell* (Cleveland: Pilgrim Press, 1992), 206-7.

19. See ICCR, Oct. 1879: W. J. Bryan, "Prize Composition," 59-60, and an unsigned essay, "The Evolution of Government," 60-61. Also, George R. Poage, "College Career of William Jennings Bryan," *Mississippi Valley Historical Review* 15 (Sept. 1928), esp. 168-69. For a later case regarding this issue, see CH, 325, 386.

20. Morgan County Will Book C, 249, File #2907.

21. Walter Hendrickson, "A Look at Jacksonville's 1870s Artists," JC, 29 Jan. 1978.

22. A, 219-22; *Supplement, Yale Class of 1826,* 38-39. For a recent biography, see L. B. Goodheart, *Abolitionist, Actuary, Atheist: Elizur Wright and the Reform Impulse* (Kent, Ohio: Kent State University Press, 1990).

23. Sturtevant had expressed the importance of contributing to the progress of virtue and happiness in human life in his junior oration at Yale. This later emphasis not only demonstrates the constancy of his life purpose but it reflects the enduring influence of Professor Taylor's ethic of benevolence. See Frank Hugh Foster, *A Genetic History of New England Theology* (New York: Russell and Russell, 1963), 468.

24. It was Crampton's decision to accept the appointment only as acting president with the consequence that despite his excellent leadership for six years his name is omitted from the official roster of the College's presidents. (CH, 267)

25. *Illinois College, Located at Jacksonville, Ill., 1876.* Reprinted from *Illinois Schoolmaster,* December 1876.

26. *The College Annual for 1877* (Jacksonville, Ills.[*sic*]: Illinois Courier, 1877), 22.

27. *Illinois Teacher* (July 1871): 291.

Chapter 10: 1876-1885

1. The drawings of the campus in the *Catalogues* and the *Rambler* depict the changes made in the decade after Sturtevant retired. One important change was the new Whipple Academy building (1882).

2. Class notes on Sturtevant's lectures on "Evidences," by a student, William Gardner (Class of 1884), are in the Archives.

3. See John S. Whitehead, "The Yale Band and the Collegiate Ideal," in Yeager, *160th Anniversary Papers,* 40. See also G. R. Poage, "College Career of William Jennings Bryan," *Mississippi Valley Historical Review* 15 (Sept. 1928), 165-82.

4. See Gibson, *Sigma Pi*, 83; ICCR, 2 Apr. 1881, 26.

5. ICCR, Feb. 1878, 32. The *Rambler* was not explicit, but Sturtevant likely referred to theologians who embraced aspects of biblical scholarship which he himself rejected.

6. Ingersoll may have visited Jacksonville; JJ, 3 Mar. 1997.

7. See FM, 18 Jan. 1877; ICCR, Mar. 1878, 46; 27 Jan. 1881, 104; 6 Feb. 1886, 125.

8. ICCR, Feb. 1880, 9. In February 1882 several boys brought "their lady friends" to the Chapel; ICCR, 18 Feb. 1882, 144.

9. "Fifty Years Old." [JJ], 5 June 1879.

10. The 1879 Commencement was noted as the "Fiftieth," counting the 1830 exercise as the first. The early "commencements" at the College represented the beginning of a new academic year. The first *Catalogue* (1832-33) stated that "the Annual Commencement will be holden on the third Wednesday in August in each year." Beginning in 1840 the exercise was held in early summer. The 1877 exercises were designated as the "Forty-Third Commencement," an enumeration based on counting 1835, when the first degrees were awarded, as the first. In recent years the commencement program simply acknowledged the year of the College's operation. Thus the ceremony on 17 May 1998 was the "Annual Commencement, One Hundred and Sixty-Ninth Year."

11. SJ, 20 Sept. 1879. See also "Our Oldest College, Jacksonville's Great Institution," *Chicago Herald*, 15 Feb. 1890.

12. JMS to TB, 12 May 1865. The Healy portrait hung in Sigma Pi Hall from 1865 to 1932, when it was moved to Tanner Hall. (Gibson, *Sigma Pi*, 77) The portrait was returned to Sigma Pi Hall after Beecher was remodeled in 1991.

13. JC, 22 Jan 1978. See JMSJR to Pres. Rammelkamp, Cleveland, 10 June 1919. Dr. Walter Hendrickson identified the artist as R. A. Clifford of Bloomington. See Hendrickson, "A Look at Jacksonville's 1870s Artists," JC, 29 Jan. 1978.

14. Smith was a member of the Sigma Pi committee which arranged for the Healy portrait. Smith painted several portraits of Illinois College faculty and alumni which are in Sigma Pi Hall. See Gibson, *Sigma Pi*, 76, 256. See also ICCR, 6 May 1882, 40; 17 Oct. 1885, 69; also 4 June 1881, 72, 76.

15. TM, 27 Mar., 5 June 1878; 6 June 1883; 13 Mar., 19 Mar., 3 June 1885.

16. *150th Anniversary of Centenary United Methodist Church, October 17, 1971*, 5. (Pamphlet; courtesy Bob Dalton)

17. "The Basis of Church Government" (1880). A Masonic Club was organized on the campus in 1923.

18. A 10-page typescript is in the Archives.

19. An apparently complete draft of the *Autobiography* was found in Tanner Vault in December 1995. The first 176 pages are in typescript, the remainder (284 pages) in manuscript.

20. Noah Porter to JMS, "U.C.," 12 Nov. 1881. For other correspondence, unpublished essays, and articles by others, see Box IA, esp. 12, 46, and EC, 21.

21. The First Congregational Church of Waverly was originally named the "Church of Christ."

22. The text of the Plan of Union of 1801 is included in the Congregational Church's *Fiftieth Anniversary*, 33-34.

23. Sturtevant named the four churches: Mendon, Quincy, Princeton, and Jacksonville. "The Mounds" Church was organized near Timewell in 1833 but became Presbyterian the following year. See Yeager, *Church and College*, 29.

24. An 1883 photograph of the chancel of the church is in the Archives of Illinois College.

25. See Archives, Congregational Church, for typescript.

26. The followers of Alexander Campbell believed only laymen can preside at the Supper. Sturtevant often took communion with them and was impressed by the reverence of their rite.

27. Sturtevant surmised that if "the Messiah himself were to come again" to a church dominated by priestly authority, "he would be silenced by the voice of an authority which would not tolerate him for a moment." (*The Keys of Sect,* 31) Cf. Dostoevsky's dramatic portrayal of the Grand Inquisitor.

28. In the late decades of the twentieth century there has been some movement toward "congregationalism" in some centrally organized churches. See John F. Burgess, "Conversation, conviction and the Presbyterian identity crisis," *Christian Century,* 24 Feb. 1993, 204-05; and, David Stagaman, "Democratizing the Catholic Church," *Christian Century,* 20 Oct. 1993, 1020-21. See Deborah A. Brown, "Christianity, politics, and social change in China," *Christian Century,* 19 Apr. 1995, 418-22, regarding possible political influences resulting from the emergence of Protestantism in China.

29. The U.S. adopted a single gold standard in 1873, but the issue of bimetallism was still very much alive in the West at the time of Bryan's 1896 campaign.

30. See also JC, 14 Aug. 1884; 18 Aug. 1884.

31. The Preface to *Economics* was dated 3 Sept. 1877. The copyright date was 1877 but the publication date was 1878. The *Catalogues* list the book in use from 1878-1879 through 1886-1887.

32. Locke's views on property and related topics are expressed in his *Second Treatise on Civil Government,* 1690, esp. in ch. 5 (on property) and in ch. 7 (on political society). For Locke's enormous influence on American political thought, see Wm. Ebenstein, *Great Political Thinkers,* Fourth Ed. (Hinsdale, Ill.: Dryden Press, 1969), 400; Ebenstein remarks that the Declaration of Independence is "pure Locke."

33. JMS to A. L. Chapin, 7 Sept. 1877. (Beloit College Archives)

34. Poage, 166.

35. Noah Porter to Mr. Armstrong, New Haven, 2 July 1877.

36. *Chicago Times,* 4 Dec. 1877, 6 (Chicago Historical Society microfilm); ICCR, Jan. 1878, 12. For the general attitude of clergymen regarding economic issues in this period, see Smith, vol. 2, 368-72; also Hudson, 305-12.

37. Sturtevant must not have seen the report in 1877 that "the Chicago and Alton Railroad transports 10,000,000 bushels of grain per year." (JC, 12 Feb. 1997)

38. All these services were provided in Jacksonville by the various State of Illinois institutions.

39. The monograph, *An Elementary Treatise on Sense-Perception,* was printed for the author's students and was "not published." Copies were sent to teachers and friends, whose comments were requested. (See note on copyright page.)

40. Sturtevant made it very clear that knowledge about God is possible, both from the divine revelation in the Scriptures and from the natural world. All three of his major works deal with the knowledge relevant to the given subject, the basis for it, how it is obtained, and its application to present-day life and institutions. The diversity of Sturtevant's interests and the care with which he pursued these subjects and wrote about them are convincing evidence that even in his last years he continued to have a keen interest in the world of human experience and in learning about it and sharing his learning with others in clear and cogent prose.

Chapter 11: 1886

1. A, 335-38. See JJ, 28 July 1885 for a more complete account.

2. Rev. George A. Gordon to Miss [Lucy] Sturtevant, Kennebunkport, Me., 27 Sept. 1926. JMS to Lucy, 3-5 Feb. 1883; Possibly Lucy, accomplished in art and music, was teaching.

3. JMS to Prof. Franklin Dexter, 22 Apr. 1882. (F. B. Dexter Papers, Yale University MSS Collection; used by permission.)

4. JC, 18 Jan.; JJ, 19, 20 Jan.; ICCR, 23 Jan., 113, 118. The New Canaan Historical Society has an undated clipping from the local paper.

5. JC, 10 Apr. 1989. Julian and Hannah Sturtevant are buried in Lot 53, south and west of the Mausoleum. The graves of other family members are nearby.

6. An unidentified clipping is in Lucy Sturtevant's scrapbook.

7. For other notices of Sturtevant's death, see: SJ, 12 Feb.; *Chicago Daily Inter-Ocean,* 12 Feb.; *New York Times,* 12 Feb.; ICCR, 20 Feb. 1886, [129]-130, 133, 134, 136, and 13 Mar., 3-5; *Jacksonville Female Academy Review,* Feb; also, unidentified clippings in Lucy Sturtevant's Scrapbook. The *New York Times* derived its information from a Chicago newspaper. The clipping from the *Times* is in a scrapbook at the New Canaan Historical Society, Conn. The original report from the unidentified Chicago paper was provided by the Chicago Historical Society (Scrapbook 46).

8. Roy, 60.

9. George F. Magoun, *Asa Turner, A Home Missionary Patriarch, and His Times* (Boston and Chicago: Congregational Sunday-School and Publishing Society, 1889), 82, 103.

10. Edward A. Tanner, "Ex-President J. M. Sturtevant," *Advance,* 18 Feb. 1886.

11. Rev. R. W. Patterson, "Dr. Julian M. Sturtevant," *Advance,* 18 Mar. 1886.

12. [Bishop Frederic Dan] Huntington, "Letter from New York," *Congregationalist,* 18 Feb. 1886.

13. The biblical quotation was adapted from Ex. 33:15. Crampton quoted it in his eulogy. See also S-B, 2 Dec. 1844, cited in CH,139.

14. ICCR, 13 Mar., 3; 27 Mar., 36; 10 Apr., 39.

15. Illinois College Archives, IL378.773/Fsti.

BIBLIOGRAPHIES

For many sources, symbols or brief titles (with date) are used in the text; brief titles are indicated below in brackets. Brief references are usually embedded in the text.

JULIAN MONSON STURTEVANT
CHRONOLOGICAL BIBLIOGRAPHY OF PUBLISHED WORKS
(Note: "John Robinson" and "Robinson" were Sturtevant's pseudonyms.)

BOOKS

1878
Economics: or, The Science of Wealth. New York: G. P. Putnam's Sons, 1878. [*Economics*]
1880
The Keys of Sect; or, The Church of the New Testament Compared with the Sects of Modern Christendom. Boston: Lee and Shepard, 1880; New York: Charles T. Dillingham, 1880. [*Keys of Sect*]
1883
An Elementary Treatise on Sense-Perception. Privately printed. New Haven: Tuttle, Morehouse and Taylor, 1883. [*Sense-Perception*]
1896 [Published posthumously]
Julian M. Sturtevant: An Autobiography. Ed. J. M. Sturtevant Jr. New York: Fleming H. Revell Co., 1896. [A]

ADDRESSES, ARTICLES, ESSAYS, SERMONS, AND LETTERS TO EDITORS

Most of Sturtevant's longer addresses and articles were printed in quarterly journals or pamphlets. Many are included in two bound volumes in the Schewe Archives. Fifty-nine briefer articles are in a scrapbook entitled "J. M. Sturtevant—Articles by and about, collected by Lucy Sturtevant."

Numerous additional articles have been obtained by Iver F. Yeager from bound-periodicals or microfilmed editions in various libraries; the major sources are named in the Preface. Also included are informal addresses and reports made by Sturtevant to a variety of organizations.

Most of Sturtevant's writings appeared in publications intended for readers with a serious interest in religion. He published numerous articles in the following: *The Advance* (Chicago), *The Congregationalist* (Boston); *The Independent* (New York), and *The New Englander* (New Haven).

1830
"From Rev. J. M. Sturtevant, Jacksonville, Ill. Feb. 5, 1830. His Appointment as Instructor in 'Illinois College.'" Excerpt, *Home Missionary* 2 (Apr. 1830): 194.

1831

(Sketch of Illinois College.) In J. M. Peck, *A Guide for Emigrants, Containing Sketches of Illinois...*, 249-54. Boston: Lincoln and Edmands, 1831.

1833

"Professor Sturtevant's Letter." To Mr. Brooks, *Springfield Illinois Herald,* Jacksonville, 17 Jan.; reprinted in *Jacksonville Illinois Patriot,* 2 Feb., from the *Springfield Illinois Herald.*

Letter to Mr. Brooks, Jacksonville, 2 Feb., *Springfield Illinois Herald,* 16 Feb.

Statements regarding H. A. Cyrus. *Springfield Illinois Herald,* 16 Feb.

1834

"Address." Delivered at the Eighth Anniversary, American Home Missionary Society. *Home Missionary* 7 (Sept. 1834): 83-85. ["Address," 1834]

1835

"Mr. Sturtevant's Remarks," 23 Sept. 1835. Ladies' Association for Educating Females, *Second Annual Report,* 17-22. Jacksonville: E. T. & C. Goudy, 1835. [LES-*2,* 1835]

1837

"Manual Labor Seminaries." (Summary) Delivered 19 Sept. 1837, during Education Week, Jacksonville, Ill., before Teachers' Association of Illinois. *Common School Advocate* 1 (Oct. 1837): 73-74.

1839

"Remarks: Rev. Mr. Sturtevant." Summary of remarks, 18 Sept. 1839. Ladies' Association for Educating Females, *Sixth Annual Report,* 19-20. Jacksonville: Goudy's, 1839. [LES-*6,* 1839]

1842

Democracy. An Address Delivered before the Jacksonville Mechanic's Union, Sept. 20, 1841. Jacksonville: J. M. Lucas, 1842. (Pamphlet)

"The Levitical Law of Incest." *American Biblical Repository,* 2d ser., 8 (Oct. 1842): 423-44.

1843

"Review of Mormonism in All Ages." Review of *Mormonism in All Ages, or the Rise, Progress, and Causes of Mormonism,* by J. B. Turner. *American Biblical Repository,* 2d ser., 9 (Jan. 1843): 109-27.

"The Education of Indigent Young Men for the Ministry." *American Biblical Repository,* 2d ser., 10 (Oct. 1843): 462-86. ["Education of Indigent Young Men"]

1844

A Discourse, Delivered at the Funeral of Hon. Joseph Duncan, Ex-Governor of the State of Illinois, January 16, 1844. Jacksonville: A. V. Putman, 1844. (Pamphlet) [*Gov. Duncan's Funeral*]

"Something Wanting to the World's Conversion." *New Englander* 2 (Apr. 1844): 194-208. ["World's Conversion"]

"The American Colporteur System." *American Biblical Repository,* 2d ser., 12 (July 1844): 214-43.

1845

American Colleges. An Address Delivered by J. M. Sturtevant, at His Inauguration as President of Illinois College, June 25th, 1845. Jacksonville: Wm. C. Swett, 1845. (Pamphlet)

1846

"Collegiate Education in the Western States." *New Englander* 4 (Apr. 1846): 274-88. ["Collegiate Education"]

1847

"President Sturtevant's Discourse." (Excerpts) In behalf of the Society for the Promotion of Collegiate and Theological Education at the West, *Fourth Report* (Oct., 1847): 45-48. [SPC-*4,* 1847]

1848

"Address." Annual Meeting, 11 July 1848, Ladies' Association for Educating Females, *Fifteenth Annual Report,* 14-16. Jacksonville: Wm. C. Swett, 1848. [LES-*15,* 1848]

"Illinois College." Society for the Promotion of Collegiate and Theological Education at the West, *Fifth Report.* 14-15, 34-36 (Oct. 1848). [SPC-5, 1848]

1849

John Robinson. "How It Strikes Us at the West." *Independent,* 5 April.

Robinson. "Congregationalism and Presbyterianism." *Independent,* 27 Sept.

"Illinois College." Society for the Promotion of Collegiate and Theological Education at the West, *Sixth Report* (Oct. 1849): 22-23. [SPC-6, 1849]

"Address of Rev. J. M. Sturtevant, D.D." Society for the Promotion of Collegiate and Theological Education at the West, Sixth Anniversary Meeting, *Sixth Report* (Oct. 1849): 47-51. ["Address," SPC-6, 1849]

1850

"Constructive Nature of Puritanism." *Home Missionary* 22 (Feb. 1850): 247-48.

John Robinson. "The Pilgrim Fathers." *Independent,* 25 Apr.

"Illinois College." *Independent,* 12 Sept.

Robinson. "Letter from Illinois." *Independent,* 24 Oct.

1851

[The following six articles were signed "Robinson."]

"Collegiate Education Society [—No. 1]." *Independent,* 22 May.

"Collegiate Education Society.—No. 2." *Independent,* 29 May.

"Collegiate Education Society.—No. 3." *Independent,* 5 June.

"Collegiate Education Society.—No. 4." *Independent,* 12 June.

"Collegiate Education Society.—No. 5." *Independent,* 26 June.

"Collegiate Education Society.—No. 6." *Independent,* 3 July.

"Letter from President Sturtevant." *New-York Evangelist,* 23 Aug.

1852

The Memory of the Just: A Sermon Commemorative of the Life and Labors of the Rev. William Kirby, Who Died, December 20, 1851. New York: Baker, Godwin, 1852. (Pamphlet)

Robinson. "Rev. William Kirby." *Independent,* 29 Jan.

"Rev. William Kirby." *Home Missionary* 24 (Mar. 1852): 265-67.
"Narrative" (of the State of Religion). *Independent,* 10 June. (with S. G. Wright as co-author)
"The Convention: Letter from Pres. Sturtevant." *Independent,* 30 Sept.
"Illinois College.—$50,000 effort." Society for the Promotion of Collegiate and Theological Education at the West, *Ninth Report* (Oct. 1852): 22-24. [SPC-9, 1852]

1853

"Revival in Illinois College." (Excerpt, letter to Theron Baldwin, 23 Dec. 1852.) *New-York Evangelist,* 13 Jan. [The original MS is not extant.]
An Address in Behalf of the Society for the Promotion of Collegiate and Theological Education at the West. Delivered in Boston, May 25, 1853. New York: John F. Trow, 1853. (Pamphlet) [*College Society*]
"Who Is the Hero?" *Home Missionary* 26 (Sept. 1853): 128-30.

1854

"The Baccalaureate." (Summary) *Jacksonville Weekly Constitutionist,* 15 July 1854.

1855

"Alton Locke." Review of *Alton Locke: Tailor and Poet.—An Autobiography* [by Charles Kingsley]. *New Englander* 13 (May 1855): 161-83.
"The Anti-Sectarian Tendency of Congregational Church Polity." In *Addresses of Rev. Drs. Sturtevant and Stearns, at the Anniversary of the American Congregational Union, May, 1855,* 5-50. Andover: Warren F. Draper, 1855. (Pamphlet) [*Congregational Polity*]
After-dinner Remarks. Festival of the Congregational Union. *Independent,* 17 May.
"Historical Discourse." By the President, Rev. J. M. Sturtevant,D.D." (11 July 1855) In *Quarter-Century Celebration at Illinois College,* 5-37. New York, John F. Trow, [1855]. Pamphlet. Excerpt in *History of Morgan County, Illinois.* Abridged in "A Sketch of the History of Illinois College," 1856.
"Letter from President Sturtevant." Jacksonville, Ill., 6 Aug. 1855. *New-York Evangelist,* 23 Aug. Reprinted in *Congregational Herald,* 6 Sept.

1856

"A Sketch of the History of Illinois College, Jacksonville, Ill." *American Journal of Education* 1 (Jan. 1856): 225-30. Abridged from "Historical Discourse," 1855.
"The West Still Needy." Letter from Pres. Sturtevant. *Independent,* 20 Nov.
"Consistency." *Independent,* 20 Nov.

1857

"The Edinburgh Review and Mrs. Stowe." *Independent,* 19 Feb.
"What Is Logic?" *American Journal of Education and College Review* (Feb. 1857): 122-30.
American Emigration. A Discourse in Behalf of the American Home Missionary Society. May, 1857. New York: American Home Missionary Society, 1857. (Pamphlet) Excerpt in *Home Missionary* 30 (Nov. 1857): 165-71.
"Protestantism in America." Review of *A Sketch of the Political, Social and*

Religious Character of the United States of North America..., by Philip Schaff.
   New Englander 15 (Nov. 1857): 537-52. ["Protestantism in America"]

                                   1859

"Rights of Women." *Rockford Illinois Register,* 14[?] July.
   [No author is indicated for some of the following articles; Sturtevant
   reported his authorship in his letter to Baldwin, 11 Oct. 1859.]
"The Basis of Church Fellowship." *Independent,* 11 Aug.
"What Is Sectarianism?" *Independent,* 11 Aug.
"Jesuitism." *Independent,* 25 Aug.
"Church-Extension and Home Missions" [1]. *Independent,* 25 Aug.
"Church-Extension and Home Missions" [2]. *Independent,* 1 Sept.
"Church-Extension and Home Missions" [3]. *Independent,* 8 Sept.
"Two Conceptions of the Church." *Independent,* 22 Sept.
"What Is Sectarianism?" *Independent,* 27 Oct.
"Elihu Wolcott." (Excerpt) *Congregational Quarterly* 1 (Oct. 1859): 414-15.

                                   1860

"Denominational Colleges." *New Englander* 18 (Feb. 1860), 68-89.

                                   1861

"Pulpit Drama." *Congregational Herald,* 11 Apr.
"Pulpit Eloquence." *Congregational Herald,* 25 Apr.
The Lessons of Our National Conflict. Address to the Alumni of Yale College, at
   Their Annual Meeting, July 24, 1861. New Haven: Thomas J. Stafford,
   1861. (Pamphlet) Reprinted with slight revisions in the *New Englander*
   19 (Oct. 1861): 894-912.

                                   1862

"The Claims of the Higher Seminaries of Learning on the Liberality of the
   Wealthy." *New Englander* 21 (Jan. 1862): 84-97. ["Claims on Wealthy"]
   Excerpts reprinted in SPC-*21*, 31.
"Foreign Intervention." *Independent,* 12 June.
"'Classes at the South.'" *Independent,* 21 Aug.
"Lord Palmerston on the Great Rebellion." *Independent,* 4 Sept.
"The Christian War Meeting: Address of President Sturtevant." *Chicago
   Tribune,* 9 Sept.

                                   1863

"Faith and Order of the Evangelical Churches, by Ministers of Each. No. I.—
   Congregational." *Independent,* 1 Jan.
"A Note from President Sturtevant: To the Editors of the Independent."
   Independent, 19 Feb.
"The Destiny of the African Race in the United States." *Continental Monthly*
   (May 1863): 600-10.
"English Opinion on the American War." *Independent,* 19 Nov.

                                   1864

"Letter from Rev. Dr. Sturtevant." Illinois College, 2 Mar. 1864. *New-York
   Evangelist,* 17 Mar.

"Speech of President Sturdevant." [*sic*] Owen Lovejoy Memorial Meeting, Princeton, Ill., 1 June 1864. *Bureau County Republican,* Princeton, Ill., 9 June 1864.

Three Months in Great Britain. A Lecture on the Present Attitude of England towards the United States. Chicago: John A. Norton, 1864. (Pamphlet) [*Three Months*]

English Institutions and the American Rebellion. Excerpts from *Three Months in Great Britain.* Manchester [England]: A. Ireland, 1864. (Pamphlet)

"Hannah Thurston." Review of *Hannah Thurston: A Story of American Life,* by Bayard Taylor. *New Englander* 23 (July 1864): 496-516.

1865

"The Home Reception to Gov. Yates: Address by President Sturtevant." *Springfield Daily Illinois State Journal,* 19 Jan. 1865.

"Sermon." Preached at Boston at the opening session of the National Council of Congregational Churches, 15 June, 1865. *Independent,* 6 July 1865. *Congregational Quarterly* 7 (July and Oct. 1865): 244-60. Also in *Debates and Proceedings,* 31-52. Re-published in England [auspices unknown].

Letters to the *Boston Daily Evening Traveller.* A series of letters in an exchange with Rev. Frederic Dan Huntington, usually printed under the heading "The Theological Controversy" or "The Theological Discussion." They are listed below by date of letter and by date of the *Traveller.* Except for the first six, the columns were date-lined from Illinois College.

> Hartford [Conn.], 7 July; *T,* 13 July.
> Greenwich, Conn., 29 July; *T,* 1 Aug.
> Greenwich, Conn., 1 Aug.; *T,* 4 Aug.
> Greenwich, Conn., 2 Aug.; *T,* 15 Aug.
> Canaan, Conn., 14 Aug.; *T,* 18 Aug.
> Canaan, Conn., 18 Aug.; *T,* 23 Aug.
> 8 Sept.; *T,* 27 Sept.
> [n.d.]; *T,* 6 Oct.
> 11 Sept.; *T,* 11 Oct.
> 15 Sept.; *T,* 18 Oct.
> 26 Sept.; *T,* 23 Oct.
> 29 Sept.; *T,* 9 Nov.
> 19 Oct.; *T,* 15 Nov.
> 3 Nov.; *T,* 22 Nov.
> 21 Nov.; *T,* 13 Dec.
> 24 Nov.; *T,* 28 Dec.

1866

"Julian Monson Sturtevant." [A biographical sketch with information from Sturtevant restated in the third person by the editor.] In Haines (1866), 90-91.

"President Sturtevant's Lecture: Characteristics of a Truly American System of Education." (Summary) *Springfield Daily Illinois State Journal,* 31 Jan.

"The Revival in Illinois College." *Congregationalist,* 1 June. Identical report in
    SPC-23, Nov. 1866.
"Remarks of President Sturtevant." Address to the State Teachers' Association,
    Jacksonville, Dec. 1866. *Jacksonville Daily Journal,* 31 Dec. 1866.

1867

"Sectarianism. Is the Division of Protestant Christians into Many Different
    Denominations, as It Now Exists, an Evil?" *Western Pulpit* 2 (Jan. 1867):
    1-14.
"Faith and the Church." *Advance,* 12 Sept.
"'The Enthusiasm of Humanity.'" *Advance,* 10 Oct.
"Women's Wages." *Congregationalist,* 10 Oct.
"Origin of 'The Enthusiasm of Humanity.'" *Advance,* 31 Oct.
"Home Missionaries at Large." *Advance,* 28 Nov.
"Woman's Independence." *Congregationalist,* 12 Dec.
"Religion and Theology." *Independent,* 19 Dec.

1868

"The New Year." *Independent,* 2 Jan.
"Sectarianism." *Advance,* 2 Jan.
"Dr. Thompson's Missionary Sermon." *Advance,* 30 Jan.
"Hard Times." *Advance,* 27 Feb.
"'A Plea for a Friend.'" *Independent,* 12 Mar.
"Woman's Employments." *Congregationalist,* 19 Mar.
"Wages of Men and Women." *Advance,* 2 Apr.
"Freedom of Speech." *Advance,* 7 May.
"Baccalaureate Address." *Daily Jacksonville Journal,* 2,3 June.
"The True Conception of the Christian Ministry." *New Englander* 27 (Oct.
    1868): 698-720.
*Proceedings at the Quarter-Century Anniversary of the Society for the Promotion of
    Collegiate and Theological Education at the West.* Marietta, Ohio, Nov. 7-
    10, 1868. New York: Trow & Smith, 1868.
        "Remarks of President Sturtevant," 5-7;
        "What Has Illinois College Done? President Sturtevant
        Answers," 58-60;
        "Remarks," 112-14.
"Unity vs. Division." *Advance,* 19 Nov.
"'True Conception of the Christian Ministry' Again." *Congregationalist,* 3 Dec.

1869

"'Among the Hills.'" *Advance,* 21 Jan.
"The Morality of Skepticism." *Congregationalist,* 21 Jan.
"The Plains." *Advance,* 24 June.
"The Buffalo Hunt." *Advance,* 15 July.
"The Western Problem." *Advance,* 12 Aug.
The Crisis of the Hour. A Sermon Preached Before the American Missionary
    Association, at its Twenty-Third Anniversary, Mount Vernon, Ohio,

October 27th, 1869. New York: American Missionary Association, 1870. (Pamphlet)

1870

"'Ruined Young Men.'" *Advance,* 20 Jan.

"The Basis of Suffrage." *Congregational Review* 10 (Mar. 1870): 138-57.

"The Trial Question." *Advance,* 28 Apr.

"Rev. Theron Baldwin, D.D." *Congregational Review* 10 (July 1870): 353-63.

1871

The Relation of the Congregational Churches of the Northwest to Collegiate Education. Reprinted from the *New Englander* 30 (Jan. 1871). (Pamphlet)

"Shall Colleges Be Denominational?" *Congregationalist,* 25 May.

"Who Are the Shylocks?" *Advance,* 22 June.

Address. Morgan County Old Settlers' Reunion, Jacksonville, Illinois, 17 Aug. 1871. Jacksonville: J. K. Long, [n.d.]. (Pamphlet)

"William Carter." *Congregational Quarterly,* 2d ser., 13 (Oct. 1871): 497-513.

1872

"Our Doctrinal Basis." *Advance,* 1 Feb.

"The Antagonism of Religion and Culture." Review of *Culture and Religion in Some of Their Relations,* by J. C. Shairp. *New Englander* 31 (Apr. 1872): 201-18.

"Yale Theological Seminary and Home Missions." In *Yale University, The Divinity School: The Semi-Centennial Anniversary of the Divinity School of Yale College,* 64-72. New Haven: Tuttle, Morehouse and Taylor, 1872. ["Yale and Home Missions"]

1873

"Colleges and State Universities." *New Englander* 32 (July 1873): 453-67.

"Church and State." *Congregational Quarterly,* 2d ser., 5 (Oct. 1873): 508-35.

1874

"Judicial Power in the Church." *Advance,* 12 Mar.

"Church Discipline." *Advance,* 26 Mar.

"Sectarianism." *Church Union,* 2 May.

"The Sect System." *New Englander* 33 (July 1874): 554-72.

1875

"Matthew Arnold's 'Literature and Dogma.'" Review of *Literature and Dogma: An Essay toward a Better Apprehension of the Bible,* by Matthew Arnold. *New Englander* 34 (Jan. 1875): 92-122.

Sketch of Theron Baldwin. Boston: Alfred Mudge, 1875. (Pamphlet) Reprinted from *Congregational Quarterly* 17 (April and July 1875). Excerpt, "Origin of the College Society," in *Home Missionary* 52 (May 1879): 18-19.

"Have We Two Religions?" *Congregationalist,* 16 Sept.

1876

"Our Bond of Union." *Christian News,* Jan.

"President Sturtevant's Address." In *Proceedings of the Advisory Council of Congregational Churches and Ministers,...February 15-20, 1876,* 336-39. New York: A. S. Barnes, 1876.

"The Advisory Council." *Christian News,* Apr.

"The Commission of Five." *Congregationalist,* 26 Apr.

"Julian Monson Sturtevant." In Haines (1876), 36-38.

"Orthodoxy." *Christian News,* July.

"Overburdened with Churches." *Congregationalist,* 12 July.

"Why Was This Waste Made?" *Congregationalist,* 26 July.

"The Remedy." *Congregationalist,* 30 Aug.

"Indifferentism." *Congregationalist,* 20 Sept.

"Religion and the Public Schools." *Christian News,* Nov.

"The Kingdom of Heaven." *Christian Union,* 29 Nov.

1877

"A Memorial Sketch of Samuel Adams, M.D." In *A Tribute to the Memory of Dr. Samuel Adams,* 1-16. (Pamphlet) [no place or publisher] 1877. [Memorial Sketch, 1877]

"Joseph Cook and the Labor Question." *Congregationalist,* 7 Nov.

1878

"The Growth of Our College." ICCR, Jan., 7-8.

"Commemorative Sketch." In *Memorial of Cleveland J. Salter,* 14-18. Denver: Rocky Mountain News, [1878]. (Pamphlet)

"What Is the Remedy?" *Congregationalist,* 3 Apr.

1879

Gospel Repentance. Dated 11 Jan. 1879 and reprinted from *Christian Union,* Jan. 1879. (Pamphlet)

"Review of Prof. Perry's Political Economy." Review of *Elements of Political Economy,* by Arthur Latham Perry, *New Englander* 38 (Jan. 1879): 19-33.

"The Bi-Metallic Standard of Money." *Advance,* 16 Jan.

"The Church of Christ." *Christian Union,* 28 May.

"Address at the Semi-Centennial Anniversary of the Founding of Illinois College." ICCR, May and June, 34-41.

"Battle of the Colleges: Which Is the Older—Illinois College or Shurtleff?" *Springfield Illinois State Journal,* 20 Sept. Reprinted from the *Jacksonville Illinois Courier.*

1880

"The Basis of Church Government." *Advance,* 22 Apr.

"Keys of the Kingdom of Heaven." *Advance,* 13 May.

"The Keys of Sect." *Advance,* 17 June.

"What Saith the Scripture?" *Advance,* 29 July.

"The National Council." *Christian Mirror,* 14 Aug.

"Thackeray's Pictures of Married Life." *Congregationalist,* 1 Sept.

"Christianity as an Element in Liberal Education." *Advance,* 9 Dec. Reprinted as tract: 8 pages, Boston: Beacon Press, Thomas Todd; n.d.

1881

"Ecclesiastical Evolution." *Advance,* 6 Jan.

"Practical Education." ICCR, 21 Jan., 124-26.

"The Martyr's Memorial: Dr. Sturtevant's Address." (Synopsis) Second Anniversary Service of Lincoln Guard of Honor, Springfield, 15 Apr. *Springfield Illinois State Journal,* 16 Apr. Reprinted from *Jacksonville Illinois Courier.*

1882

"The Private Ownership of Land." *Princeton Review* (Mar. 1882): 125-47.

"Gratuitous Education." *Congregationalist,* 23 Aug.

"A Congress of Denominations." *Advance,* 19 Oct.

1883

"What Is Protestant Theology?" *Advance,* 31 May.

"Address of Rev. Dr. Sturtevant." In *Historical Account of the Celebration of the One Hundred and Fiftieth Anniversary of the Organization of the Congregational Church of New Canaan, Conn., June 20, 1883,* 80-87. Stanford, Conn.: Gillespie Brothers, [n.d.]

"The Origin of 'Western Congregationalism.'" A Historical Discourse, Delivered December 15, 1883. In Congregational Church, *Fiftieth Anniversary,* 8-32. (Pamphlet) ["Western Congregationalism"]

1884

"Blaine's American Policy." *Jacksonville Illinois Courier,* 9 Aug.

"The Home of Childhood Revisited." *Congregationalist,* 28 Aug.

"Economy in Home Missions." *Home Missionary* 57 (Nov. 1884): 268-71.

1885

"Address of Dr. J. M. Sturtevant,...Upon the Subject of Political Economy." *Jacksonville College Record* 6 (Dec. 1885): 2.

"What Hath Hindered and Doth Still Hinder?" *Advance,* 25 June.

BIBLIOGRAPHY OF MANUSCRIPT SOURCES

ILLINOIS COLLEGE MANUSCRIPT AND DOCUMENT COLLECTIONS AND EARLY RECORDS RELEVANT TO JULIAN MONSON STURTEVANT

The early records of Illinois College, including manuscript and document collections, are in the College's Archives. Most source materials are in Schewe Library except for the Minutes of the Trustees and Faculty, which are in the Tanner Vault.

Papers of Julian Sturtevant (Box IA)

These papers include the Tisdale Collection and contain, among other items:

—manuscripts from Sturtevant's years at Yale College;

—personal financial records;

—correspondence, including some letters by Sturtevant and numerous letters by his wife and family;

—sermons and addresses (some in pamphlet form);

—lecture notes on physics;

—unpublished essays and articles.

Of particular note are four letters reporting the history of Illinois College from 1829 to 1844: JMS to Thomas Lippincott, Illinois College, 22, 26 Feb., 7, 13 Mar., 1844. (File 7)

The Sturtevant-Baldwin Correspondence
(Box IB: Files 1830, 1843, 1845-1870)

This collection contains more than 500 original letters exchanged between Sturtevant and his life-long friend, Theron Baldwin. Microfilmed copies of these letters are in the Schewe Archives of Illinois College and the Illinois State Historical Library, Springfield.

The Eldridge Collection—England

Dorothy Hope Tisdale Eldridge (Mrs. Carey DeWitt Eldridge), great-grand-daughter of Julian Sturtevant, contributed this collection of twenty-five letters written by Julian Sturtevant in 1863 while in Great Britain and Europe. The letters were sent, in 1983, to Iver F. Yeager for Illinois College.

The Eldridge Collection

This includes several hundred letters and documents by and about the Sturtevant family and (to a lesser extent) the Fayerweather family. Among the items are a few written by Sturtevant and numerous letters by Mrs. Hannah Sturtevant to her husband, including many while he was in Great Britain in 1863. This collection was obtained in 1992 from Mr. Carey DeWitt Eldridge by Iver F. Yeager on behalf of Illinois College.

Early History of Illinois College (Box IV)

Early manuscripts and printed documents regarding the founding and development of Illinois College are in Files 1-50. Other files include late 19th century records and some recent material.

Minutes of Illinois College Founders, Trustees, and Faculty

"Records" of the Illinois Association, 1829-1830, formerly the Howard Association and later known in Illinois as the "Yale Band." The bound volume includes a brief History, Minutes of Meetings, and some copied correspondence.

Minutes of The Trustees of Illinois College.

Minutes of the Faculty of Illinois College.

OTHER UNPUBLISHED SOURCES, FROM
RELATED ORGANIZATIONS AND INDIVIDUALS

Baldwin, Theron. "An address made by Theron Baldwin before the Young

Men's Christian Association, New York City." [1858] Typewritten copy. Yale University, Sterling Library, Miscellaneous MSS B, Theron Baldwin Collection.

The Club. Minutes, 1861-1886. The Club is a men's literary society in Jacksonville, Illinois, and was founded in 1861 with Sturtevant as a charter member. Microfilmed copies of the Minutes are in the Schewe Archives, the Jacksonville Public Library, and the Illinois State Historical Library, Springfield.

Congregational Church, Jacksonville. Minutes, Register of Members, and other records, 1833-1886. Microfilmed copies are at the Church, Schewe Archives, and the Jacksonville Public Library.

Sturtevant, Julian Monson, Jr. "Some Things Which Have Interested an Octogenarian." Typewritten. Cincinnati, Ohio: 1918. An autobiographical account, with much information about his parents and family life during his early years as well as his later career as a minister. Schewe Archives; copy sent by Mrs. Dorothy Hope Tisdale Eldridge, in 1982, to Iver F. Yeager, for Illinois College.

GENERAL BIBLIOGRAPHY OF PUBLISHED SOURCES

The following works provided information especially useful in preparing the biography. Other sources referred to only once or twice are usually presented in the endnotes only.

Brief titles used in the text and in the endnotes are indicated in brackets.

PUBLICATIONS BY ILLINOIS COLLEGE

Baldwin, Theron. *Historical Sketch of the Origin, Progress, and Wants, of Illinois College.* New York: John T. West, 1832. [Baldwin, *Historical Sketch*]

Beecher, Edward, and Theron Baldwin. *An Appeal in Behalf of the Illinois College, Recently Founded at Jacksonville, Illinois.* New York: D. Fanshaw, 1831. [Beecher-Baldwin]

Illinois College Catalogues, 1832—33 through 1887-'88. (Various printers)

Illinois College Alumni Quarterly. [ICAQ] (Various issues as noted in text or endnotes.)

Illinois College College Rambler. [ICCR]
1 January 1878 through 22 December 1888.

Illinois College. *Quarter Century Celebration at Illinois College. Historical Discourse by the President, Rev. J. M. Sturtevant, D.D., with the Social Reunion of the Founders, Patrons, Alumni and Friends of the College, at Jacksonville, Illinois. July 11, 1855.* New York: John F. Trow [1855]. [ICQCC]

Rammelkamp, Charles Henry. *Illinois College: A Centennial History, 1829-*

1929. [New Haven]: Published for Illinois College by Yale University Press, 1928. [CH]

Abridged by Charles E. Frank in *Pioneer's Progress: Illinois College, 1829-1979,* 8-148. [Carbondale]: Published for Illinois College by Southern Illinois University Press, 1979.

Yeager, Iver F. *Church and College on the Illinois Frontier: The Beginnings of Illinois College and the United Church of Christ in Central Illinois, 1829-1867.* Jacksonville: Illinois College, 1980. [Yeager, *Church and College*]

Yeager, Iver F., ed. *Illinois College: 160th Anniversary Papers.* Jacksonville, Ill.: Illinois College, 1990. [Yeager, *160th Anniversary*]

Yeager, Iver F., ed. *Sesquicentennial Papers: Illinois College.* [Carbondale]: Published for Illinois College by Southern Illinois University Press, 1982. [Yeager, *Sesquicentennial Papers*]

OTHER SOURCES

Ahlstrom, Sydney E. *A Religious History of the American People.* New Haven: Yale University Press, 1972. [Ahlstrom]

American Congregational Union. *American Congregational Union, Year-Book.* Boston: American Congregational Union. [*Year-Book*, 18__]

American Home Missionary Society. *American Home Missionary Society Papers, 1816-1894.* Ser. 1, *Incoming Correspondence, 1816-1893.* Glen Rock, N.J.: Microfilming Corp. of America. The Illinois Collection amounts to almost forty reels and is available in the Illinois State Historical Library, Springfield. Selected reels with letters from Sturtevant and others associated with Illinois College are in the Schewe Archives.

American Home Missionary Society. *The Home Missionary and American Pastor's Journal.* New York: American Home Missionary Society, 1828-. [*Home Missionary*]

Atkins, Gaius Glenn, and Frederick L. Fagley. *History of American Congregationalism.* Boston: Pilgrim Press, 1942. [Atkins]

Atlas Map of Morgan County, Illinois. Davenport, Iowa: Andreas, Lyter and Co., 1872. [*Atlas Map*]

Bacon, Leonard Woolsey. *The Story of the Churches: The Congregationalists.* New York: Baker and Taylor, 1904. [L. W. Bacon]

Baldwin, Theron. *Historical Address, Delivered in Monticello, Illinois, June 27, 1855, at the Seventeenth Anniversary of Monticello Female Seminary.* New York: John F. Trow, n.d.

Basler, Roy P., ed. *The Collected Works of Abraham Lincoln.* Vols. 2, 6, 7, 8. New Brunswick, N.J.: Rutgers University Press, 1953. [Basler]

Beard, Charles A., Mary R. Beard, and William Beard. *The Beards' New Basic History of the United States.* Garden City, N.Y.: Doubleday and Co., 1960. [Beard]

Blumenfeld, Edward Marvin. "The Plan of Union in Illinois." M.A. Thesis, Northwestern University, 1961.

The Cambridge Platform of 1648; A Platform of Church Discipline. Cambridge [Massachusetts Bay Colony], 1649. Facsimile edition printed by the General Council for the Congregational Christian Churches; New York, [1948].

Carney, John B. "In Search of Fayerweather: The Fayerweather Family of Boston [continued]." *New England Historical and Genealogical Register,* 146 (Jan. 1992): 59-76.

Carriel, Mary Turner. *The Life of Jonathan Baldwin Turner.* Urbana: University of Illinois Press, 1961.

Congregational Church, Jacksonville, Ill. *Celebration of the Fiftieth Anniversary of the Organization of the Congregational Church, Jacksonville, Ill., December 15th and 16th, 1883.* Jacksonville, Ill.: Daily Journal, 1884. [Congregational Church, *Fiftieth Anniversary*]

Debates. See National Council of Congregational Churches.

Doyle, Don Harrison. *The Social Order of a Frontier Community: Jacksonville, Illinois, 1825-70.* Urbana: University of Illinois Press, 1978. [Doyle]

Eames, Charles M., comp. *Historic Morgan and Classic Jacksonville.* Jacksonville: Daily Journal, 1885. [Eames]

Gibson, Harold E. *Sigma Pi Society of Illinois College, 1843-1971: A History of A Literary Society.* Jacksonville, Ill.: Sigma Pi Society, 1972. [Gibson]

Haines, Selden, comp. *A Biographical Sketch of the Class of 1826, Yale College.* Utica, N.Y.: Roberts, 1866. [Haines, 1866]

Haines, Selden, comp. *A Supplement to the Biographical Sketch of the Class of 1826, Yale College.* Rome, N.Y.: Sandford & Carr, 1876. [Haines, 1876]

Heinl, Frank J., comp. *An Epitome of Jacksonville History to 1875, Chronologically Arranged.* Jacksonville, Ill.: Centennial Commission, 1925. [Heinl, *Epitome*]

Heinl, Frank J. "Congregationalism in Jacksonville and Early Illinois." *Journal, Illinois State Historical Society,* 27 (Jan. 1935): 441-62. [Heinl, "Congregationalism"]

Hedrick, Travis Keene, Jr. *Julian Monson Sturtevant and the Moral Machinery of Society: The New England Struggle Against Pluralism in the Old Northwest, 1829-1877.* Ph.D. Dissertation, Brown University, 1974; University Microfilms International, Ann Arbor, Michigan, 1982.

Historical Encyclopedia of Illinois, Newton Bateman and Paul Selby, eds., and *History of Morgan County,* William F. Short, ed. Chicago: Munsell, 1906. [*Historical Encyclopedia*]

Hofstadter, Richard, and Wilson Smith, eds. *American Higher Education: A Documentary History.* Vol. 1. Chicago: University of Chicago Press, 1961. [Hofstadter]

Hudson, Winthrop S. *Religion in America.* 3rd ed. New York:Scribner's, 1981. [Hudson]

Johnson, Daniel Thomas. *Puritan Power in Illinois Higher Education Prior to 1870.* Ph.D. Dissertation, University of Wisconsin-Madison, 1974; University Microfilms.

Kofoid, Carrie Prudence. "Puritan Influences in the Formative Years of Illinois History." M.S. Thesis, University of Illinois, [1905?]. In *Transactions of the Illinois State Historical Society for the Year 1905; Publication No. 10 of the Illinois State Historical Society,* 261-338. Springfield: Illinois State Journal, 1905.

Ladies' Association for Educating Females. *The First Annual Report.* Jacksonville: Calvin Goudy, 1834. (Subsequent reports were printed by various publishers.) In 1853 the name of the Association was changed to Ladies' Education Society. [LES-]

Mead, Sidney Earl. *Nathaniel William Taylor, 1786-1858: A Connecticut Liberal.* Chicago: University of Chicago Press, 1942. [Mead]

National Council of Congregational Churches. *Debates and Proceedings of the National Council of Congregational Churches, held at Boston, Mass., June 14-24, 1865.* Boston: American Congregational Association, 1866. [*Debates*]

New Canaan [Connecticut] Historical Society. *Readings in New Canaan History.* New Canaan: New Canaan Historical Society, 1949.

Norton, A. T. *History of the Presbyterian Church, in the State of Illinois.* Vol. 1. St. Louis: W. S. Bryan, 1879. [Norton]

Power, Robert Lyle. *Planting Corn Belt Culture: The Impress of the Upland Southerner and Yankee in the Old Northwest.* Indianapolis: Indiana Historical Society, 1953. [Power]

Roy, Joseph E. "History of Congregationalism in Illinois." In *Congregational. Statement and Papers,* 24-66. Chicago: Illinois Society of Church History, 1895; printed by David Oliphant.

Rugoff, Milton. *The Beechers: An American Family in the Nineteenth Century.* New York: Harper and Row, 1981. [Rugoff]

Seybold, Ethel. "Transcendentalism Comes to Jacksonville: Hiram K. Jones and the Jacksonville Platonists." *Jacksonville Journal Courier,* 21 October 1981, Sec. B, 37-40.

Smith, H. Shelton, Robert T. Handy, and Lefferts A. Loetscher. *American Christianity: An Historical Interpretation with Representative Documents.* Vol. 1, 1607-1820. New York: Charles Scribner's Sons, 1960. [Smith]

Society for the Promotion of Collegiate and Theological Education at the West. *Reports, 1844-1874.* (*The First Report.* New-York: J. F. Trow and Co., 1844. Subsequent reports similarly titled and numbered and with various publishers.) [SPC-_]

Spinka, Matthew, ed., with Frederick Kuhns, Hermann R. Muelder, and Others. *A History of Illinois Congregational and Christian Churches.* Chicago: Congregational and Christian Conference of Illinois, 1944. [Spinka]

Sturtevant, Robert Hunter, comp. *Descendants of Samuel Sturtevant*. Waco, Texas: Texian Press, 1986.

Sweet, William Warren. *Religion on the American Frontier, 1783-1850*. Vol. 3, *The Congregationalists*. Chicago: University of Chicago Press, 1939. [Sweet]

von Rohr, John. *The Shaping of American Congregationalism, 1620-1957*. Cleveland: Pilgrim Press, 1992. [von Rohr]

Willard, Samuel. "Memorial of the Life and work of Rev. Dr. Julian M. Sturtevant." *In Sixteenth Biennial Report of the Superintendent of Public Instruction of the State of Illinois, July 1 1884-June 30, 1886*, XCVI-CIII. Springfield: H. W. Rokker, 1886. [Willard]

Willis, John Randolph. *God's Frontiersmen: The Yale Band in Illinois*. Washington, D.C.: University Press of America, 1979. Ph.D. Dissertation, Yale University, 1946.

Yale Divinity School. *Eighth General Catalogue of the Yale Divinity School: Centennial Issue, 1822-1922*. New Haven: Published by the University, 1922. [YDS 1922]

Yale Divinity School. *Semi-Centennial Anniversary of the Divinity School of Yale College*. New Haven: Tuttle, Morehouse and Taylor, 1872. [YDS 1872]

Yeager, Iver F. "Sturtevant, others tried to model early Jacksonville on New England." *Jacksonville Journal Courier,* 21 October 1981, Sec. A, 49.

INDEX

Most entries in this Index pertain to Julian M. Sturtevant, or Illinois College, or both; the nature of the entry will indicate which. Generally, references which are not explicit refer to Sturtevant or the College. The Index does not include every mention of a person or topic. Illustrations are indicated by italicized numerals in parentheses.

Iver F. Yeager

A native of Wyoming, Iver F. Yeager attended public schools in Denver, Colorado, and at Maurine and Newell, South Dakota. He is a graduate of Macalester College. During World War II he was the communications and tactical radar officer on a destroyer in the southwest Pacific. Subsequently he was granted the M.A. degree by Chicago Theological Seminary and the Ph.D. by the University of Chicago Divinity School.

Yeager taught at the College of Wooster and Missouri Valley College before coming to Illinois College as Dean, a position he held for twelve years. Subsequently he was appointed Scarborough Professor of Religion and Philosophy. He was the recipient of the Dunbaugh Distinguished Professor Award.

Yeager and his wife, Natalee, are the parents of two sons and a daughter and have three grandchildren. The Yeagers are active members of the Congregational Church of Jacksonville. An ordained minister of the United Church of Christ, Yeager is a member of The Club, a men's literary society, and of Rotary.